GIVE ME LIBERTY!

AN AMERICAN HISTORY

★

Brief Fourth Edition

GIVE ME LIBERTY!

AN AMERICAN HISTORY

Brief Fourth Edition

VOLUME 1: TO 1877

ERIC FONER

W · W · NORTON & COMPANY
NEW YORK · LONDON

For my mother, Liza Foner (1909–2005), an accomplished artist who lived through most of the twentieth century and into the twenty-first

W. W. Norton & Company has been independent since its founding in 1923, when William Warder Norton and Mary D. Herter Norton first published lectures delivered at the People's Institute, the adult education division of New York City's Cooper Union. The firm soon expanded its program beyond the Institute, publishing books by celebrated academics from America and abroad. By mid-century, the two major pillars of Norton's publishing program— trade books and college texts—were firmly established. In the 1950s, the Norton family transferred control of the company to its employees, and today—with a staff of 400 and a comparable number of trade, college, and professional titles published each year— W. W. Norton & Company stands as the largest and oldest publishing house owned wholly by its employees.

Editor: Steve Forman
Associate Editor: Justin Cahill
Editorial Assistant: Penelope Lin
Managing Editor, College: Marian Johnson
Managing Editor, College Digital Media: Kim Yi
Project Editor: Diane Cipollone
Copy Editor: Elizabeth Dubrulle
Marketing Manager: Sarah England
Media Editors: Steve Hoge, Tacy Quinn
Assistant Editor, Media: Stefani Wallace
Production Manager: Sean Mintus
Art Director: Rubina Yeh
Designer: Chin-Yee Lai
Photo Editor: Stephanie Romeo
Photo Research: Donna Ranieri
Permissions Manager: Megan Jackson
Permissions Clearing: Bethany Salminen
Composition and Layout: Jouve
Manufacturing: RR Donnelley

Library of Congress Cataloging-in-Publication Data has been applied for.

This edition:
ISBN 978-0-393-92033-8 (pbk.)

W. W. Norton & Company, Inc., 500 Fifth Avenue, New York, NY 10110-0017
wwnorton.com

W. W. Norton & Company Ltd., Castle House, 75/76 Wells Street, London W1T 3QT
5 6 7 8 9 0

ABOUT THE AUTHOR

ERIC FONER is DeWitt Clinton Professor of History at Columbia University, where he earned his B.A. and Ph.D. In his teaching and scholarship, he focuses on the Civil War and Reconstruction, slavery, and nineteenth-century America. Professor Foner's publications include *Free Soil, Free Labor, Free Men: The Ideology of the Republican Party before the Civil War*; *Tom Paine and Revolutionary America*; *Nothing but Freedom: Emancipation and Its Legacy*; *Reconstruction: America's Unfinished Revolution, 1863–1877*; *The Story of American Freedom*; and *Forever Free: The Story of Emancipation and Reconstruction*. His history of Reconstruction won the Los Angeles Times Book Award for History, the Bancroft Prize, and the Parkman Prize. He has served as president of the Organization of American Historians and the American Historical Association. In 2006 he received the Presidential Award for Outstanding Teaching from Columbia University. His most recent book is *The Fiery Trial: Abraham Lincoln and American Slavery*, winner of the Lincoln Prize, the Bancroft Prize, and the Pulitzer Prize.

★

CONTENTS

★

About the Author ... v

List of Maps, Tables, and Figures ... xviii

Preface ... xx

1. A NEW WORLD ... 1

THE FIRST AMERICANS ... 3

The Settling of the Americas ... 3 ★ Indian Societies of the Americas ... 3 ★ Mound Builders of the Mississippi River Valley ... 5 ★ Western Indians ... 6 ★ Indians of Eastern North America ... 6 ★ Native American Religion ... 7 ★ Land and Property ... 9 ★ Gender Relations ... 10 ★ European Views of the Indians ... 10

INDIAN FREEDOM, EUROPEAN FREEDOM ... 11

Indian Freedom ... 11 ★ Christian Liberty ... 12 ★ Freedom and Authority ... 12 ★ Liberty and Liberties ... 13

THE EXPANSION OF EUROPE ... 13

Chinese and Portuguese Navigation ... 14 ★ Freedom and Slavery in Africa ... 14 ★ The Voyages of Columbus ... 16

CONTACT ... 16

Columbus in the New World ... 16 ★ Exploration and Conquest ... 17 ★ The Demographic Disaster ... 19

THE SPANISH EMPIRE ... 20

Governing Spanish America ... 21 ★ Colonists and Indians in Spanish America ... 21 ★ Justifications for Conquest ... 22 ★ Piety and Profit ... 23 ★ Reforming the Empire ... 24 ★ Exploring North America ... 25 ★ Spanish in Florida and the Southwest ... 25 ★ The Pueblo Revolt ... 27

Voices of Freedom: *From* Bartolomé de las Casas, *History of the Indies* (1528), and *From* "Declaration of Josephe" (December 19, 1681) ... 28

THE FRENCH AND DUTCH EMPIRES ... 30

French Colonization ... 32 ★ New France and the Indians ... 32 ★ The Dutch Empire ... 34 ★ Dutch Freedom ... 34 ★ The Dutch and Religious Toleration ... 35 ★ Settling New Netherland ... 36 ★ Features of European Settlement ... 36

REVIEW ... 37

2. BEGINNINGS OF ENGLISH AMERICA, 1607-1660 ... 38

ENGLAND AND THE NEW WORLD ... 40

Unifying the English Nation ... 40 ★ England and Ireland ... 40 ★ England and North America ... 40 ★ Motives for Colonization ... 41 ★ The Social Crisis ... 42 ★ Masterless Men ... 43

THE COMING OF THE ENGLISH ... 43

English Emigrants ... 43 ★ Indentured Servants ... 44 ★ Land and
Liberty ... 44 ★ Englishmen and Indians ... 45 ★ The Transformation
of Indian Life ... 46

SETTLING THE CHESAPEAKE ... 47

The Jamestown Colony ... 47 ★ Powhatan and Pocahontas ... 48 ★ The
Uprising of 1622 ... 49 ★ A Tobacco Colony ... 50 ★ Women and the
Family ... 50 ★ The Maryland Experiment ... 52 ★ Religion in
Maryland ... 52

THE NEW ENGLAND WAY ... 53

The Rise of Puritanism ... 53 ★ Moral Liberty ... 53 ★ The Pilgrims at
Plymouth ... 54 ★ The Great Migration ... 55 ★ The Puritan Family ... 55 ★
Government and Society in Massachusetts ... 56 ★ Church and State in
Puritan Massachusetts ... 58

NEW ENGLANDERS DIVIDED ... 59

Roger Williams ... 60 ★ Rhode Island and Connecticut ... 60 ★ The Trials
of Anne Hutchinson ... 61 ★ Puritans and Indians ... 61

Voices of Freedom: *From* "The Trial of Anne Hutchinson" (1637),
and *From* John Winthrop, Speech to the Massachusetts General Court
(July 3, 1645) ... 62

The Pequot War ... 64 ★ The New England Economy ... 65 ★ A Growing
Commercial Society ... 66

RELIGION, POLITICS, AND FREEDOM ... 67

The Rights of Englishmen ... 67 ★ The English Civil War ... 68 ★
England's Debate over Freedom ... 68 ★ The Civil War and English
America ... 69 ★ Cromwell and the Empire ... 70

REVIEW ... 71

3. CREATING ANGLO-AMERICA, 1660-1750 ... 72

GLOBAL COMPETITION AND THE EXPANSION OF
ENGLAND'S EMPIRE ... 74

The Mercantilist System ... 74 ★ The Conquest of New Netherland ... 74 ★
New York and the Indians ... 75 ★ The Charter of Liberties ... 77 ★ The
Founding of Carolina ... 77 ★ The Holy Experiment ... 78 ★ Land in
Pennsylvania ... 79

ORIGINS OF AMERICAN SLAVERY ... 80

Englishmen and Africans ... 80 ★ Slavery in History ... 81 ★ Slavery
in the West Indies ... 81 ★ Slavery and the Law ... 82 ★ The Rise of
Chesapeake Slavery ... 83 ★ Bacon's Rebellion: Land and Labor in
Virginia ... 83 ★ A Slave Society ... 85

COLONIES IN CRISIS ... 86

The Glorious Revolution ... 86 ★ The Glorious Revolution in America ... 87 ★ The Salem Witch Trials ... 89

THE GROWTH OF COLONIAL AMERICA ... 90

A Diverse Population ... 90 ★ The German Migration ... 91

Voices of Freedom: *From* Memorial against Non-English Immigration (December 1727), and *From* Letter by a Swiss-German Immigrant to Pennsylvania (August 23, 1769) ... 92

Religious Diversity ... 95 ★ Indian Life in Transition ... 95 ★ Regional Diversity ... 96 ★ The Consumer Revolution ... 97 ★ Colonial Cities ... 97 ★ An Atlantic World ... 98

SOCIAL CLASSES IN THE COLONIES ... 99

The Colonial Elite ... 99 ★ Anglicization ... 100 ★ Poverty in the Colonies ... 100 ★ The Middle Ranks ... 101 ★ Women and the Household Economy ... 101 ★ North America at Mid-Century ... 102

REVIEW ... 103

4. SLAVERY, FREEDOM, AND THE STRUGGLE FOR EMPIRE, TO 1763 ... 104

SLAVERY AND EMPIRE ... 106

Atlantic Trade ... 106 ★ Africa and the Slave Trade ... 107 ★ The Middle Passage ... 109 ★ Chesapeake Slavery ... 109 ★ The Rice Kingdom ... 110 ★ The Georgia Experiment ... 111 ★ Slavery in the North ... 112

SLAVE CULTURES AND SLAVE RESISTANCE ... 113

Becoming African-American ... 113 ★ African Religion in Colonial America ... 113 ★ African-American Cultures ... 114 ★ Resistance to Slavery ... 115

AN EMPIRE OF FREEDOM ... 116

British Patriotism ... 116 ★ The British Constitution ... 117 ★ Republican Liberty ... 117 ★ Liberal Freedom ... 118

THE PUBLIC SPHERE ... 119

The Right to Vote ... 119 ★ Political Cultures ... 120 ★ The Rise of the Assemblies ... 121 ★ Politics in Public ... 121 ★ The Colonial Press ... 122 ★ Freedom of Expression and Its Limits ... 122 ★ The Trial of Zenger ... 123 ★ The American Enlightenment ... 124

THE GREAT AWAKENING ... 125

Religious Revivals ... 125 ★ The Preaching of Whitefield ... 126 ★ The Awakening's Impact ... 126

IMPERIAL RIVALRIES ... 127

Spanish North America ... 127 ★ The Spanish in California ... 127 ★ The French Empire ... 129

BATTLE FOR THE CONTINENT ... 130

The Middle Ground ... 130 ★ The Seven Years' War ... 130 ★ A World Transformed ... 131 ★ Pontiac's Rebellion ... 132 ★ The Proclamation Line ... 132

Voices of Freedom: *From* Pontiac, *Speeches* (1762 and 1763), and *From The Interesting Narrative of the Life of Olaudah Equiano, or Gustavus Vassa, the African* (1789) ... 134

Pennsylvania and the Indians ... 136 ★ Colonial Identities ... 137

REVIEW ... 138

5. THE AMERICAN REVOLUTION, 1763–1783 ... 139

THE CRISIS BEGINS ... 140

Consolidating the Empire ... 140 ★ Taxing the Colonies ... 142 ★ Taxation and Representation ... 143 ★ Liberty and Resistance ... 144 ★ The Regulators ... 145

THE ROAD TO REVOLUTION ... 145

The Townshend Crisis ... 145 ★ The Boston Massacre ... 146 ★ Wilkes and Liberty ... 147 ★ The Tea Act ... 148 ★ The Intolerable Acts ... 148

THE COMING OF INDEPENDENCE ... 149

The Continental Congress ... 149 ★ The Continental Association ... 150 ★ The Sweets of Liberty ... 150 ★ The Outbreak of War ... 151 ★ Independence? ... 151 ★ Paine's *Common Sense* ... 152 ★ The Declaration of Independence ... 153 ★ An Asylum for Mankind ... 154 ★ The Global Declaration of Independence ... 155

Voices of Freedom: *From* Thomas Paine, *Common Sense* (1776), and *From* Jonathan Boucher, *A View of the Causes and Consequences of the American Revolution* (1775) ... 156

SECURING INDEPENDENCE ... 158

The Balance of Power ... 158 ★ Blacks in the Revolution ... 158 ★ The First Years of the War ... 159 ★ The Battle of Saratoga ... 161 ★ The War in the South ... 162 ★ Victory at Last ... 162

REVIEW ... 166

6. THE REVOLUTION WITHIN ... 167

DEMOCRATIZING FREEDOM ... 169

The Dream of Equality ... 169 ★ Expanding the Political Nation ... 169 ★ The Revolution in Pennsylvania ... 170 ★ The New Constitutions ... 171 ★ The Right to Vote ... 171

TOWARD RELIGIOUS TOLERATION ... 172

Catholic Americans ... 173 ★ Separating Church and State ... 173 ★ Jefferson and Religious Liberty ... 174 ★ Christian Republicanism ... 175 ★ A Virtuous Citizenry ... 175

DEFINING ECONOMIC FREEDOM ... 176

Toward Free Labor ... 176 ★ The Soul of a Republic ... 176 ★ The Politics of Inflation ... 177 ★ The Debate over Free Trade ... 178

THE LIMITS OF LIBERTY ... 178

Colonial Loyalists ... 178 ★ The Loyalists' Plight ... 179 ★ The Indians' Revolution ... 181

SLAVERY AND THE REVOLUTION ... 182

The Language of Slavery and Freedom ... 182 ★ Obstacles to Abolition ... 183 ★ The Cause of General Liberty ... 183 ★ Petitions for Freedom ... 184 ★ British Emancipators ... 185 ★ Voluntary Emancipations ... 185

Voices of Freedom: From Abigail Adams to John Adams, Braintree, Mass. (March 31, 1776), and From Petitions of Slaves to the Massachusetts Legislature (1773 and 1777) ... 186

Abolition in the North ... 188 ★ Free Black Communities ... 188

DAUGHTERS OF LIBERTY ... 189

Revolutionary Women ... 189 ★ Republican Motherhood ... 190 ★ The Arduous Struggle for Liberty ... 190

REVIEW ... 192

7. FOUNDING A NATION, 1783-1791 ... 193

AMERICA UNDER THE CONFEDERATION ... 195

The Articles of Confederation ... 195 ★ Congress, Settlers, and the West ... 196 ★ The Land Ordinances ... 198 ★ The Confederation's Weaknesses ... 200 ★ Shays's Rebellion ... 200 ★ Nationalists of the 1780s ... 201

A NEW CONSTITUTION ... 202

The Structure of Government ... 202 ★ The Limits of Democracy ... 203 ★ The Division and Separation of Powers ... 204 ★ The Debate over Slavery ... 205 ★ Slavery in the Constitution ... 205 ★ The Final Document ... 207

THE RATIFICATION DEBATE AND THE ORIGIN OF THE BILL OF RIGHTS ... 208

The Federalist ... 208 ★ "Extend the Sphere" ... 208 ★ The Anti-Federalists ... 209

Voices of Freedom: From David Ramsay, The History of the American Revolution (1789), and From James Winthrop, Anti-Federalist Essay Signed "Agrippa" (1787) ... 210

The Bill of Rights ... 214

"WE THE PEOPLE" ... 215

National Identity ... 215 ★ Indians in the New Nation ... 215 ★ Blacks and the Republic ... 217 ★ Jefferson, Slavery, and Race ... 218 ★ Principles of Freedom ... 219

REVIEW ... 220

8. SECURING THE REPUBLIC, 1791–1815 ... 221

POLITICS IN AN AGE OF PASSION ... 222

Hamilton's Program ... 223 ★ The Emergence of Opposition ... 223 ★ The Jefferson-Hamilton Bargain ... 224 ★ The Impact of the French Revolution ... 225 ★ Political Parties ... 226 ★ The Whiskey Rebellion ... 226 ★ The Republican Party ... 226 ★ An Expanding Public Sphere ... 227

Voices of Freedom: *From* Judith Sargent Murray, "On the Equality of the Sexes" (1790), and *From* Address of the Democratic-Republican Society of Pennsylvania (December 18, 1794) ... 228

The Rights of Women ... 230

THE ADAMS PRESIDENCY ... 231

The Election of 1796 ... 231 ★ The "Reign of Witches" ... 232 ★ The Virginia and Kentucky Resolutions ... 233 ★ The "Revolution of 1800" ... 233 ★ Slavery and Politics ... 234 ★ The Haitian Revolution ... 235 ★ Gabriel's Rebellion ... 235

JEFFERSON IN POWER ... 236

Judicial Review ... 237 ★ The Louisiana Purchase ... 237 ★ Lewis and Clark ... 239 ★ Incorporating Louisiana ... 240 ★ The Barbary Wars ... 241 ★ The Embargo ... 241 ★ Madison and Pressure for War ... 242

THE "SECOND WAR OF INDEPENDENCE" ... 243

The Indian Response ... 243 ★ The War of 1812 ... 244 ★ The War's Aftermath ... 246 ★ The End of the Federalist Party ... 247

REVIEW ... 248

9. THE MARKET REVOLUTION, 1800–1840 ... 249

A NEW ECONOMY ... 251

Roads and Steamboats ... 251 ★ The Erie Canal ... 252 ★ Railroads and the Telegraph ... 254 ★ The Rise of the West ... 255 ★ The Cotton Kingdom ... 257

MARKET SOCIETY ... 259

Commercial Farmers ... 260 ★ The Growth of Cities ... 260 ★ The Factory System ... 261 ★ The "Mill Girls" ... 262 ★ The Growth of Immigration ... 263 ★ The Rise of Nativism ... 265 ★ The Transformation of Law ... 266

THE FREE INDIVIDUAL ... 267

The West and Freedom ... 267 ★ The Transcendentalists ... 267 ★ The Second Great Awakening ... 268 ★ The Awakening's Impact ... 269

Voices of Freedom: *From* Ralph Waldo Emerson, "The American Scholar" (1837), and *From* "Factory Life as It Is, by an Operative" (1845) ... 270

The Emergence of Mormonism ... 272

THE LIMITS OF PROSPERITY ... 273

Liberty and Prosperity ... 273 ★ Race and Opportunity ... 274 ★ The Cult of Domesticity ... 275 ★ Women and Work ... 276 ★ The Early Labor Movement ... 277 ★ The "Liberty of Living" ... 277

REVIEW ... 279

10. DEMOCRACY IN AMERICA, 1815–1840 ... 280

THE TRIUMPH OF DEMOCRACY ... 281

Property and Democracy ... 281 ★ The Dorr War ... 282 ★ Tocqueville on Democracy ... 282 ★ The Information Revolution ... 283 ★ The Limits of Democracy ... 284 ★ A Racial Democracy ... 284

NATIONALISM AND ITS DISCONTENTS ... 285

The American System ... 285 ★ Banks and Money ... 287 ★ The Panic of 1819 ... 287 ★ The Missouri Controversy ... 288

NATION, SECTION, AND PARTY ... 289

The United States and the Latin American Wars of Independence ... 289 ★ The Monroe Doctrine ... 290 ★ The Election of 1824 ... 291

Voices of Freedom: From President James Monroe, Annual Message to Congress (1823), and From John C. Calhoun, "A Disquisition on Government" (ca. 1845) ... 292

The Nationalism of John Quincy Adams ... 294 ★ "Liberty Is Power" ... 294 ★ Martin Van Buren and the Democratic Party ... 294 ★ The Election of 1828 ... 295

THE AGE OF JACKSON ... 296

The Party System ... 296 ★ Democrats and Whigs ... 297 ★ Public and Private Freedom ... 298 ★ South Carolina and Nullification ... 299 ★ Calhoun's Political Theory ... 299 ★ The Nullification Crisis ... 301 ★ Indian Removal ... 301 ★ The Supreme Court and the Indians ... 302

THE BANK WAR AND AFTER ... 304

Biddle's Bank ... 304 ★ Pet Banks, the Economy, and the Panic of 1837 ... 306 ★ Van Buren in Office ... 307 ★ The Election of 1840 ... 307

REVIEW ... 310

11. THE PECULIAR INSTITUTION ... 311

THE OLD SOUTH ... 312

Cotton Is King ... 313 ★ The Second Middle Passage ... 314 ★ Slavery and the Nation ... 314 ★ The Southern Economy ... 314 ★ Plain Folk of the Old South ... 316 ★ The Planter Class ... 317 ★ The Paternalist Ethos ... 318 ★ The Proslavery Argument ... 318 ★ Abolition in the Americas ... 320 ★ Slavery and Liberty ... 320

LIFE UNDER SLAVERY ... 321

Slaves and the Law ... 321 ★ Conditions of Slave Life ... 322 ★ Free
Blacks in the Old South ... 322 ★ Slave Labor ... 323 ★ Slavery in the
Cities ... 324 ★ Maintaining Order ... 325

SLAVE CULTURE ... 326

The Slave Family ... 326 ★ The Threat of Sale ... 327 ★ Gender Roles
among Slaves ... 327 ★ Slave Religion ... 328 ★ The Desire for Liberty ... 329

RESISTANCE TO SLAVERY ... 330

Forms of Resistance ... 330

Voices of Freedom: *From* Letter by Joseph Taper to Joseph Long
(1840), and *From* "Slavery and the Bible" (1850) ... 332
The *Amistad* ... 334 ★ Slave Revolts ... 335 ★ Nat Turner's Rebellion ... 336

REVIEW ... 338

12. AN AGE OF REFORM, 1820-1840 ... 339

THE REFORM IMPULSE ... 340

Utopian Communities ... 341 ★ The Shakers ... 343 ★ Oneida ... 343 ★
Worldly Communities ... 344 ★ Religion and Reform ... 345 ★ Critics of
Reform ... 346 ★ Reformers and Freedom ... 346 ★ The Invention of the
Asylum ... 347 ★ The Common School ... 347

THE CRUSADE AGAINST SLAVERY ... 348

Colonization ... 348 ★ Militant Abolitionism ... 349 ★ Spreading the
Abolitionist Message ... 350 ★ Slavery and Moral Suasion ... 351 ★ A
New Vision of America ... 352

BLACK AND WHITE ABOLITIONISM ... 353

Black Abolitionists ... 353 ★ Gentlemen of Property and Standing ... 354

THE ORIGINS OF FEMINISM ... 356

The Rise of the Public Woman ... 356 ★ Women and Free Speech ... 356 ★
Women's Rights ... 357 ★ Feminism and Freedom ... 358 ★ Women and
Work ... 358 ★ The Slavery of Sex ... 359

Voices of Freedom: *From* Angelina Grimké, Letter in *The Liberator*
(August 2, 1837), and *From* Frederick Douglass, Speech on July 5,
1852, Rochester, New York ... 360
"Social Freedom" ... 362 ★ The Abolitionist Schism ... 363

REVIEW ... 365

13. A HOUSE DIVIDED, 1840-1861 ... 366

FRUITS OF MANIFEST DESTINY ... 368

Continental Expansion ... 368 ★ The Mexican Frontier: New Mexico and
California ... 368 ★ The Texas Revolt ... 370 ★ The Election of 1844 ... 370
★ The Road to War ... 372 ★ The War and Its Critics ... 372 ★ Combat

in Mexico ... 373 ★ Race and Manifest Destiny ... 374 ★ Gold-Rush California ... 376 ★ Opening Japan ... 377

A DOSE OF ARSENIC ... 378

The Wilmot Proviso ... 378 ★ The Free Soil Appeal ... 379 ★ Crisis and Compromise ... 380 ★ The Great Debate ... 380 ★ The Fugitive Slave Issue ... 381 ★ Douglas and Popular Sovereignty ... 382 ★ The Kansas-Nebraska Act ... 382

THE RISE OF THE REPUBLICAN PARTY ... 383

The Northern Economy ... 383 ★ The Rise and Fall of the Know-Nothings ... 385 ★ The Free Labor Ideology ... 386 ★ "Bleeding Kansas" and the Election of 1856 ... 387

THE EMERGENCE OF LINCOLN ... 388

The Dred Scott Decision ... 389 ★ Lincoln and Slavery ... 390 ★ The Lincoln-Douglas Campaign ... 390 ★ John Brown at Harpers Ferry ... 391

Voices of Freedom: *From* The Lincoln-Douglas Debates (1858) ... 392

The Rise of Southern Nationalism ... 394 ★ The Election of 1860 ... 395

THE IMPENDING CRISIS ... 397

The Secession Movement ... 397 ★ The Secession Crisis ... 398 ★ And the War Came ... 399

REVIEW ... 401

14. A NEW BIRTH OF FREEDOM: THE CIVIL WAR, 1861-1865 ... 402

THE FIRST MODERN WAR ... 403

The Two Combatants ... 404 ★ The Technology of War ... 405 ★ The Public and the War ... 406 ★ Mobilizing Resources ... 407 ★ Military Strategies ... 407 ★ The War Begins ... 408 ★ The War in the East, 1862 ... 409 ★ The War in the West ... 410

THE COMING OF EMANCIPATION ... 410

Slavery and the War ... 410 ★ Steps toward Emancipation ... 413 ★ Lincoln's Decision ... 413 ★ The Emancipation Proclamation ... 414 ★ Enlisting Black Troops ... 416 ★ The Black Soldier ... 416

THE SECOND AMERICAN REVOLUTION ... 417

Liberty, Union, and Nation ... 418 ★ The War and American Religion ... 419

Voices of Freedom: *From* Letter of Thomas F. Drayton (April 17, 1861), and *From* Abraham Lincoln, Address at Sanitary Fair, Baltimore (April 18, 1864) ... 420

Liberty in Wartime ... 422 ★ The North's Transformation ... 422 ★ Government and the Economy ... 423 ★ The War and Native Americans ... 423 ★ A New Financial System ... 425 ★ Women and the War ... 425 ★ The Divided North ... 426

THE CONFEDERATE NATION ... 428

Leadership and Government ... 428 ★ The Inner Civil War ... 428 ★ Economic Problems ... 429 ★ Women and the Confederacy ... 430 ★ Black Soldiers for the Confederacy ... 431

TURNING POINTS ... 431

Gettysburg and Vicksburg ... 431 ★ 1864 ... 433

REHEARSALS FOR RECONSTRUCTION AND THE END OF THE WAR ... 434

The Sea Islands Experiment ... 434 ★ Wartime Reconstruction in the West ... 435 ★ The Politics of Wartime Reconstruction ... 435 ★ Victory at Last ... 436 ★ The War and the World ... 438 ★ The War in American History ... 438

REVIEW ... 440

15. "WHAT IS FREEDOM?": RECONSTRUCTION, 1865–1877 ... 441

THE MEANING OF FREEDOM ... 443

Families in Freedom ... 443 ★ Church and School ... 444 ★ Political Freedom ... 444 ★ Land, Labor, and Freedom ... 445 ★ Masters without Slaves ... 445 ★ The Free Labor Vision ... 447 ★ The Freedmen's Bureau ... 447 ★ The Failure of Land Reform ... 448 ★ The White Farmer ... 449

Voices of Freedom: From Petition of Committee in Behalf of the Freedmen to Andrew Johnson (1865), and From A Sharecropping Contract (1866) ... 450

Aftermath of Slavery ... 453

THE MAKING OF RADICAL RECONSTRUCTION ... 454

Andrew Johnson ... 454 ★ The Failure of Presidential Reconstruction ... 454 ★ The Black Codes ... 455 ★ The Radical Republicans ... 456 ★ The Origins of Civil Rights ... 456 ★ The Fourteenth Amendment ... 457 ★ The Reconstruction Act ... 458 ★ Impeachment and the Election of Grant ... 458 ★ The Fifteenth Amendment ... 460 ★ The "Great Constitutional Revolution" ... 461 ★ The Rights of Women ... 461

RADICAL RECONSTRUCTION IN THE SOUTH ... 462

"The Tocsin of Freedom" ... 462 ★ The Black Officeholder ... 464 ★ Carpetbaggers and Scalawags ... 464 ★ Southern Republicans in Power ... 465 ★ The Quest for Prosperity ... 465

THE OVERTHROW OF RECONSTRUCTION ... 466

Reconstruction's Opponents ... 466 ★ "A Reign of Terror" ... 467 ★ The Liberal Republicans ... 469 ★ The North's Retreat ... 470 ★ The Triumph of the Redeemers ... 471 ★ The Disputed Election and Bargain of 1877 ... 472 ★ The End of Reconstruction ... 473

REVIEW ... 474

EQUALITY OF RIGHTS
IS THE FIRST OF RIGHTS.
Charles Sumn

APPENDIX

DOCUMENTS

The Declaration of Independence (1776) ... A-2

The Constitution of The United States (1787) ... A-5

From George Washington's Farewell Address (1796) ... A-17

The Seneca Falls Declaration of Sentiments And Resolutions (1848) ... A-22

From Frederick Douglass's "What, To the Slave, Is The Fourth Of July?" Speech (1852) ... A-25

The Gettysburg Address (1863) ... A-29

Abraham Lincoln's Second Inaugural Address (1865) ... A-30

The Populist Platform of 1892 ... A-31

Franklin D. Roosevelt's First Inaugural Address (1933) ... A-34

From The Program For The March On Washington For Jobs And Freedom (1963) ... A-37

Ronald Reagan's First Inaugural Address (1981) ... A-38

Barack Obama's First Inaugural Address (2009) ... A-42

TABLES AND FIGURES

Presidential Elections ... A-46

Admission of States ... A-54

Population of the United States ... A-55

Historical Statistics of The United States:

Labor Force—Selected Characteristics Expressed As A Percentage of The Labor Force, 1800–2010 ... A-56

Immigration, By Origin ... A-56

Unemployment Rate, 1890–2013 ... A-57

Union Membership As A Percentage Of Nonagricultural Employment, 1880–2012 ... A-57

Voter Participation in Presidential Elections 1824–2012 ... A-57

Birthrate, 1820–2011 ... A-57

SUGGESTED READINGS ... A-59

GLOSSARY ... A-67

CREDITS ... A-95

INDEX ... A-99

MAPS

CHAPTER 1

The First Americans ... 4
Native Ways of Life, ca. 1500 ... 8
The Old World on the Eve of American
    Colonization, ca. 1500 ... 15
Voyages of Discovery ... 18
Early Spanish Conquests and Explorations in the
    New World ... 26
The New World—New France and New
    Netherland, ca. 1650 ... 31

CHAPTER 2

English Settlement in the Chesapeake,
    ca. 1650 ... 48
English Settlement in New England,
    ca. 1640 ... 59

CHAPTER 3

Eastern North America in the Seventeenth and
    Early Eighteenth Centuries ... 76
European Settlement and Ethnic Diversity on the
    Atlantic Coast of North America, 1760 ... 94

CHAPTER 4

Atlantic Trading Routes ... 107
The Slave Trade in the Atlantic World,
    1460–1770 ... 108
European Empires in North America,
    ca. 1750 ... 128
Eastern North America after the Peace of
    Paris, 1763 ... 133

CHAPTER 5

The Revolutionary War in the North,
    1775–1781 ... 160
The Revolutionary War in the South,
    1775–1781 ... 163
North America, 1783 ... 164

CHAPTER 6

Loyalism in the American Revolution ... 180

CHAPTER 7

Western Lands, 1782–1802 ... 197
Western Ordinances, 1785–1787 ... 199
Ratification of the Constitution ... 213

CHAPTER 8

The Presidential Election of 1800 ... 234
The Louisiana Purchase ... 239
The War of 1812 ... 245

CHAPTER 9

The Market Revolution: Roads and Canals,
    1840 ... 253
Travel Times from New York City in 1800
    and 1830 ... 256
The Market Revolution: The Spread of
    Cotton Cultivation, 1820–1840 ... 258
Cotton Mills, 1820s ... 263

CHAPTER 10

The Missouri Compromise, 1820 ... 289
The Presidential Election of 1824 ... 291
The Presidential Election of 1828 ... 296
Indian Removals, 1830–1840 ... 302
The Presidential Election of 1840 ... 308

CHAPTER 11

Slave Population, 1860 ... 315
Size of Slaveholdings, 1860 ... 319
Major Crops of the South, 1860 ... 325
Slave Resistance in the Nineteenth-Century
    Atlantic World ... 331

CHAPTER 12

Utopian Communities, Mid-Nineteenth
    Century ... 342

CHAPTER 13

The Trans-Mississippi West, 1830s–1840s ... 369
The Mexican War, 1846–1848 ... 374
Continental Expansion through 1853 ... 375
The Kansas-Nebraska Act, 1854 ... 383

The Railroad Network, 1850s ... 384
The Presidential Election of 1856 ... 389
The Presidential Election of 1860 ... 396

CHAPTER 14

The Secession of Southern States, 1860–1861 ...
    404
The Civil War in the East, 1861–1862 ... 409
The Civil War in the West, 1861–1862 ... 411
The Emancipation Proclamation ... 414
The Civil War, 1863 ... 432
The Civil War, Late 1864–1865 ... 437

CHAPTER 15

The Barrow Plantation ... 446
Sharecropping in the South,
    1880 ... 452
The Presidential Election of 1868 ... 460
Reconstruction in the South,
    1867–1877 ... 471
The Presidential Election of 1876 ... 472

TABLES AND FIGURES

CHAPTER 1

Table 1.1 Estimated Regional Populations:
    The Americas, ca. 1500 ... 24
Table 1.2 Estimated Regional Populations:
    The World, ca. 1500 ... 25

CHAPTER 3

Table 3.1 Origins and Status of Migrants
    to British North American Colonies,
    1700–1775 ... 91

CHAPTER 4

Table 4.1 Slave Population as Percentage of
    Total Population of Original Thirteen
    Colonies, 1770 ... 112

CHAPTER 7

Table 7.1 Total Population and Black Population
    of the United States, 1790 ... 217

CHAPTER 9

Table 9.1 Population Growth of Selected Western
    States, 1800–1850 (Excluding Indians)... 257
Table 9.2 Total Number of Immigrants by
    Five-Year Period ... 264
Figure 9.1 Sources of Immigration, 1850 ... 265

CHAPTER 11

Table 11.1 Growth of the Slave Population ... 314
Table 11.2 Slaveholding, 1850 (in Round
    Numbers) ... 318

CHAPTER 14

Figure 14.1 Resources for War: Union versus
    Confederacy ... 407

PREFACE

S ince it originally appeared late in 2004, *Give Me Liberty! An American History* has gone through three editions and been adopted for use in survey courses at close to one thousand two- and four-year colleges in the United States, as well as a good number overseas. Of course, I am extremely gratified by this response. The book offers students a clear narrative of American history from the earliest days of European exploration and conquest of the New World to the first decade of the twenty-first century. Its central theme is the changing contours of American freedom.

The comments I have received from instructors and students encourage me to think that *Give Me Liberty!* has worked well in the classroom. These comments have also included many valuable suggestions, ranging from corrections of typographical and factual errors to thoughts about subjects that need more extensive treatment. In preparing new editions of the book I have tried to take these suggestions into account, as well as incorporating the insights of recent historical scholarship.

Since the original edition was written, I have frequently been asked to produce a more succinct version of the textbook, which now runs to some 1,200 pages. This Brief Edition is a response to these requests. The text of the current volume is about one-third shorter than the full version. The result, I believe, is a book more suited to use in one-semester survey courses, classes where the instructor wishes to supplement the text with additional readings, and in other situations where a briefer volume is desirable.

Since some publishers have been known to assign the task of reduction in cases like this to editors rather than the actual author, I wish to emphasize that I did all the cutting and necessary rewriting for this Brief Edition myself. My guiding principle was to preserve the coverage, structure, and emphases of the regular edition and to compress the book by eliminating details of secondary importance, streamlining the narrative of events, and avoiding unnecessary repetition. While the book is significantly shorter, no subject treated in the full edition has been eliminated entirely and nothing essential, I believe, has been sacrificed. The sequence of chapters and subjects remains the same, and the freedom theme is present and operative throughout.

In abridging the textbook I have retained the original interpretive framework as well as the new emphases added when the second and third editions of the book were published. The second edition incorporated new material about the history of Native Americans, an area of American history that has been the subject of significant new scholarship in the past few years. It also devoted greater attention to the history of immigration and the controversies surrounding it—issues of considerable relevance to American social and political life today.

The most significant change in the third edition reflected my desire to place American history more fully in a global context. In the past few years, scholars writing about the American past have sought to delineate the influences of the United States on the rest of the world as well as the global developments that have helped to shape the course of events here at home. They have also devoted greater attention to transnational processes—the expansion of empires, international labor migrations, the rise and fall of slavery, the globalization of economic enterprise—that cannot be understood solely within the confines of one country's national boundaries. Without seeking in any way to homogenize the history of individual nations or neglect the domestic forces that have shaped American development, this edition retains this emphasis.

The most significant changes in this Fourth Edition reflect my desire to integrate more fully into the narrative the history of American religion. Today, this is a thriving subfield of American historical writing, partly because of the increased prominence in our own time of debates over the relations between government and religion and over the definition of religious liberty—issues that are deeply rooted in the American experience. The Brief Edition also employs a bright new design for the text and its various elements. The popular Voices of Freedom feature—a pair of excerpts from primary source documents in each chapter that illuminate divergent interpretations of freedom—is present here. So too are the useful chapter opening focus questions, which appear in the running heads of the relevant text pages as well. There are chapter opening chronologies and end-of-chapter review pages with questions and key terms. As a new feature in the Brief Edition there are marginal glosses in the text pages that are meant to highlight key points and indicate the chapter structure for students. They are also useful means for review. The Brief Edition features more than 400 illustrations and over 100 captioned maps in easy to read four-color renditions. The Further Readings sections appear in the Appendix along with the Glossary and the collection of key documents. The Brief Edition is fully supported by the same array of print and electronic supplements that support the other editions of *Give Me Liberty!* These materials have been revised to match the content of the Brief Edition.

Americans have always had a divided attitude toward history. On the one hand, they tend to be remarkably future-oriented, dismissing events of even the recent past as "ancient history" and sometimes seeing history as a burden to be overcome, a prison from which to escape. On the other hand, like many other peoples, Americans have always looked to history for a sense of personal or group identity and of national cohesiveness. This is why so many Americans devote time and energy to tracing their family trees and why they visit historical museums and National Park Service historical sites in ever-increasing numbers. My hope is that this book will help to convince readers with all degrees of interest that history does matter to them.

The novelist and essayist James Baldwin once observed that history "does not refer merely, or even principally, to the past. On the contrary, the great force of history comes from the fact that we carry it within us, . . . [that] history is literally present in all that we do." As Baldwin recognized, the power of history is evident in our own world. Especially in a political democracy like the United States, whose government is designed to rest on the consent of informed citizens, knowledge of the past is essential—not only for those of us whose profession is the teaching and writing of history, but for everyone. History, to be sure, does not offer simple lessons or immediate answers to current questions. Knowing the history of immigration to the United States, and all of the tensions, turmoil, and aspirations associated with it, for example, does not tell us what current immigration policy ought to be. But without that knowledge, we have no way of understanding which approaches have worked and which have not—essential information for the formulation of future public policy.

History, it has been said, is what the present chooses to remember about the past. Rather than a fixed collection of facts, or a group of interpretations that cannot be challenged, our understanding of history is constantly changing. There is nothing unusual in the fact that each generation rewrites history to meet its own needs, or that scholars disagree among themselves on basic questions like the causes of the Civil War or the reasons for the Great Depression. Precisely because each generation asks different questions of the past, each generation formulates different answers. The past thirty years have witnessed a remarkable expansion of the scope of historical study. The experiences of groups neglected by earlier scholars, including women, African-Americans, working people, and others, have received unprecedented attention from historians. New subfields—social history, cultural history, and family history among them—have taken their place alongside traditional political and diplomatic history.

Give Me Liberty! draws on this voluminous historical literature to present an up-to-date and inclusive account of the American past, paying due attention to the experience of diverse groups of Americans while in no way neglecting the events and processes Americans have experienced in common. It devotes serious attention to political, social, cultural, and economic history, and to their interconnections. The narrative brings together major events and prominent leaders with the many groups of ordinary people who make up American society. *Give Me Liberty!* has a rich cast of characters, from Thomas Jefferson to campaigners for woman suffrage, from Franklin D. Roosevelt to former slaves seeking to breathe meaning into emancipation during and after the Civil War.

The unifying theme of freedom that runs through the text gives shape to the narrative and integrates the numerous strands that make up the American experience. This approach builds on that of my earlier book, *The Story of American Freedom* (1998), although *Give Me Liberty!* places events and personalities in the foreground and is more geared to the structure of the introductory survey course.

Freedom, and battles to define its meaning, has long been central to my own scholarship and undergraduate teaching, which focuses on the nineteenth century and especially the era of Civil War and Reconstruction (1850–1877). This was a time when the future of slavery tore the nation apart and emancipation produced a national debate over what rights the former slaves, and all Americans, should enjoy as free citizens. I have found that attention to clashing definitions of freedom and the struggles of different groups to achieve freedom as they understood it offers a way of making sense of the bitter battles and vast transformations of that pivotal era. I believe that the same is true for American history as a whole.

No idea is more fundamental to Americans' sense of themselves as individuals and as a nation than freedom. The central term in our political language, freedom—or liberty, with which it is almost always used interchangeably—is deeply embedded in the record of our history and the language of everyday life. The Declaration of Independence lists liberty among mankind's inalienable rights; the Constitution announces its purpose as securing liberty's blessings. The United States fought the Civil War to bring about a new birth of freedom, World War II for the Four Freedoms, and the Cold War to defend the Free World. Americans' love of liberty has been represented by liberty poles, liberty caps, and statues of liberty, and acted out by burning stamps and burning draft cards, by running away from slavery, and by demonstrating for the right to vote. "Every man in the street, white, black, red or yellow," wrote the educator and statesman Ralph Bunche in 1940, "knows that this is 'the land of the free' . . . 'the cradle of liberty.'"

The very universality of the idea of freedom, however, can be misleading. Freedom is not a fixed, timeless category with a single unchanging definition. Indeed, the history of the United States is, in part, a story of debates, disagreements, and struggles over freedom. Crises like the American Revolution, the Civil War, and the Cold War have permanently transformed the idea of freedom. So too have demands by various groups of Americans to enjoy greater freedom. The meaning of freedom has been constructed not only in congressional debates and political treatises, but on plantations and picket lines, in parlors and even bedrooms.

Over the course of our history, American freedom has been both a reality and a mythic ideal—a living truth for millions of Americans, a cruel mockery for others. For some, freedom has been what some scholars call a "habit of the heart," an ideal so taken for granted that it is lived out but rarely analyzed. For others, freedom is not a birthright but a distant goal that has inspired great sacrifice.

Give Me Liberty! draws attention to three dimensions of freedom that have been critical in American history: (1) the meanings of freedom; (2) the social conditions that make freedom possible; and (3) the boundaries of freedom that determine who is entitled to enjoy freedom and who is not. All have changed over time.

In the era of the American Revolution, for example, freedom was primarily a set of rights enjoyed in public activity—including the right of a community to be governed by laws to which its representatives had consented and of individuals to engage in religious worship without governmental interference. In the nineteenth century, freedom came to be closely identified with each person's opportunity to develop to the fullest his or her innate talents. In the twentieth, the "ability to choose," in both public and private life, became perhaps the dominant understanding of freedom. This development was encouraged by the explosive growth of the consumer marketplace which offered Americans an unprecedented array of goods with which to satisfy their needs and desires. During the 1960s, a crucial chapter in the history of American freedom, the idea of personal freedom was extended into virtually every realm, from attire and "lifestyle" to relations between the sexes. Thus, over time, more and more areas of life have been drawn into Americans' debates about the meaning of freedom.

A second important dimension of freedom focuses on the social conditions necessary to allow freedom to flourish. What kinds of economic institutions and relationships best encourage individual freedom? In the colonial era and for more than a century after independence, the answer centered on economic autonomy, enshrined in the glorification of the independent small producer—the farmer, skilled craftsman, or shopkeeper—who did not have to depend on another person for his livelihood. As the industrial economy matured, new conceptions of economic freedom came to the fore: "liberty of contract" in the Gilded Age, "industrial freedom" (a say in corporate decision making) in the Progressive era, economic security during the New Deal, and, more recently, the ability to enjoy mass consumption within a market economy.

The boundaries of freedom, the third dimension of this theme, have inspired some of the most intense struggles in American history. Although founded on the premise that liberty is an entitlement of all humanity, the United States for much of its history deprived many of its own people of freedom. Non-whites have rarely enjoyed the same access to freedom as white Americans. The belief in equal opportunity as the birthright of all Americans has coexisted with persistent efforts to limit freedom by race, gender, class, and in other ways.

Less obvious, perhaps, is the fact that one person's freedom has frequently been linked to another's servitude. In the colonial era and nineteenth century, expanding freedom for many Americans rested on the lack of freedom—slavery, indentured servitude, the subordinate position of women—for others. By the same token, it has been through battles at the boundaries—the efforts of racial minorities, women, and others to secure greater freedom—that the meaning and experience of freedom have been deepened and the concept extended into new realms.

Time and again in American history, freedom has been transformed by the demands of excluded groups for inclusion. The idea of freedom as a universal birthright owes much to abolitionists who sought to extend the blessings of liberty to blacks and to immigrant groups who insisted on full recognition as American citizens. The principle of equal protection of the law without regard to race, which became a central element of American freedom, arose from the antislavery struggle and Civil War and was reinvigorated by the civil rights revolution of the 1960s, which called itself the "freedom movement." The battle for the right of free speech by labor radicals and birth control advocates in the first part of the twentieth century helped to make civil liberties an essential element of freedom for all Americans.

Freedom is the oldest of clichés and the most modern of aspirations. At various times in our history, it has served as the rallying cry of the powerless and as a justification of the status quo. Freedom helps to bind our culture together and exposes the contradictions between what America claims to be and what it sometimes has been. American history is not a narrative of continual progress toward greater and greater freedom. As the abolitionist Thomas Wentworth Higginson noted after the Civil War, "revolutions may go backward." While freedom can be achieved, it may also be taken away. This happened, for example, when the equal rights granted to former slaves immediately after the Civil War were essentially nullified during the era of segregation. As was said in the eighteenth century, the price of freedom is eternal vigilance.

In the early twenty-first century, freedom continues to play a central role in our political and social life and thought. It is invoked by individuals and groups of all kinds, from critics of economic globalization to those who seek to export American freedom overseas. As with the longer version of the book, I hope that this Brief Edition of *Give Me Liberty!* will offer beginning students a clear account of the course of American history, and of its central theme, freedom, which today remains as varied, contentious, and ever-changing as America itself.

ACKNOWLEDGMENTS

All works of history are, to a considerable extent, collaborative books, in that every writer builds on the research and writing of previous scholars. This is especially true of a textbook that covers the entire American experience, over more than five centuries. My greatest debt is to the innumerable historians on whose work I have drawn in preparing this volume. The Suggested Reading list in the Appendix offers only a brief introduction to the vast body of historical scholarship that has influenced and informed this book. More specifically, however, I wish to thank the following scholars, who generously read portions of this work and offered valuable comments, criticisms, and suggestions:

Wayne Ackerson, Salisbury University
Mary E. Adams, City College of San Francisco
Jeff Adler, University of Florida
David Anderson, Louisiana Tech University
John Barr, Lone Star College, Kingwood
Lauren Braun-Strumfels, Raritan Valley Community College
James Broussard, Lebanon Valley College
Michael Bryan, Greenville Technical College
Stephanie Cole, The University of Texas at Arlington
Ashley Cruseturner, McLennan Community College
Jim Dudlo, Brookhaven College
Beverly Gage, Yale University
Monica Gisolfi, University of North Carolina, Wilmington
Adam Goudsouzian, University of Memphis
Mike Green, Community College of Southern Nevada
Vanessa Gunther, California State University, Fullerton
David E. Hamilton, University of Kentucky
Brian Harding, Mott Community College
Sandra Harvey, Lone Star College–Cy Fair
April Holm, University of Mississippi
David Hsiung, Juniata College
James Karmel, Harford Community College
Kelly Knight, Penn State University
Marianne Leeper, Trinity Valley Community College
Jeffrey K. Lucas, University of North Carolina at Pembroke
Tina Margolis, Westchester Community College
Kent McGaughy, HCC Northwest College
James Mills, University of Texas, Brownsville
Gil Montemayor, McLennan Community College
Jonathan Noyalas, Lord Fairfax Community College
Robert M. O'Brien, Lone Star College–Cy Fair

Joseph Palermo, California State University, Sacramento
Ann Plane, University of California, Santa Barbara
Nancy Marie Robertson, Indiana University–Purdue University
    Indianapolis
Esther Robinson, Lone Star College–Cy Fair
Richard Samuelson, California State University, San Bernadino
Diane Sager, Maple Woods Community College
John Shaw, Portland Community College
Mark Spencer, Brock University
David Stebenne, Ohio State University
Judith Stein, City College, City University of New York
George Stevens, Duchess Community College
Robert Tinkler, California State University, Chico
Elaine Thompson, Louisiana Tech University
David Weiman, Barnard College
William Young, Maple Woods Community College

I am particularly grateful to my colleagues in the Columbia University Department of History: Pablo Piccato, for his advice on Latin American history; Evan Haefeli and Ellen Baker, who read and made many suggestions for improvements in their areas of expertise (colonial America and the history of the West, respectively); and Sarah Phillips, who offered advice on treating the history of the environment.

I am also deeply indebted to the graduate students at Columbia University's Department of History who helped with this project. Theresa Ventura offered invaluable assistance in gathering material for the new sections placing American history in a global context. April Holm provided similar assistance for new coverage in this edition of the history of American religion and debates over religious freedom. James Delbourgo conducted research for the chapters on the colonial era. Beverly Gage did the same for the twentieth century. Daniel Freund provided all-round research assistance. Victoria Cain did a superb job of locating images. I also want to thank my colleagues Elizabeth Blackmar and Alan Brinkley for offering advice and encouragement throughout the writing of this book.

Many thanks to Joshua Brown, director of the American Social History Project, whose website, History Matters, lists innumerable online resources for the study of American history. Nancy Robertson at IUIPUI did a superb job revising and enhancing the in-book pedagogy. Monica Gisolfi (University of North Carolina, Wilmington) and Robert Tinkler (California State University, Chico) did excellent work on the Instructor's Manual and Test Bank. Kathleen Thomas (University of Wisconsin, Stout) helped greatly in the revisions of the companion media packages.

At W. W. Norton & Company, Steve Forman was an ideal editor—patient, encouraging, and always ready to offer sage advice. I would also like to thank Steve's assistants, Justin Cahill and Penelope Lin, for their indispensable and always cheerful help on all aspects of the project; Ellen Lohman and Debbie Nichols for their careful copyediting and proof reading work. Stephanie Romeo and Donna Ranieri for their resourceful attention to the illustrations program; Hope Miller Goodell and Chin-Yee Lai for their refinements of the book design; Mike Fodera and Debra Morton-Hoyt for splendid work on the covers for the Fourth Edition; Kim Yi for keeping the many threads of the project aligned and then tying them together; Sean Mintus for his efficiency and care in book production; Steve Hoge for orchestrating the rich media package that accompanies the textbook; Jessica Brannon-Wranosky, Texas A&M University–Commerce, our digital media author for the terrific new web quizzes and outlines; Volker Janssen, California State University, Fullerton, for the helpful new online reading exercises; Nicole Netherton, Steve Dunn, and Mike Wright for their alert reads of the U.S. survey market and their hard work in helping establish *Give Me Liberty!* within it; and Drake McFeely, Roby Harrington, and Julia Reidhead for maintaining Norton as an independent, employee-owned publisher dedicated to excellence in its work.

Many students may have heard stories of how publishing companies alter the language and content of textbooks in an attempt to maximize sales and avoid alienating any potential reader. In this case, I can honestly say that W. W. Norton allowed me a free hand in writing the book and, apart from the usual editorial corrections, did not try to influence its content at all. For this I thank them, while I accept full responsibility for the interpretations presented and for any errors the book may contain. Since no book of this length can be entirely free of mistakes, I welcome readers to send me corrections at ef17@columbia.edu.

My greatest debt, as always, is to my family—my wife, Lynn Garafola, for her good-natured support while I was preoccupied by a project that consumed more than its fair share of my time and energy, and my daughter, Daria, who while a ninth and tenth grader read every chapter as it was written and offered invaluable suggestions about improving the book's clarity, logic, and grammar.

Eric Foner
New York City
July 2013

GIVE ME LIBERTY!

AN AMERICAN HISTORY

★

Brief Fourth Edition

CHAPTER 1

A
NEW WORLD

★

7000 BC	Agriculture developed in Mexico and Andes
900–1200 AD	Hopi and Zuni tribes build planned towns
1200	Cahokia city-empire along the Mississippi
1400s	Iroquois League established
1434	Portuguese explore sub-Saharan African Coast
1487	Bartolomeu Dias reaches the Cape of Good Hope
1492	*Reconquista* of Spain
	Columbus's first voyage to the Americas
1498	Vasco da Gama sails to the Indian Ocean
1500	Pedro Cabral claims Brazil for Portugal
1502	First African slaves transported to the Caribbean islands
1517	Martin Luther's *Ninety-Five Theses*
1519	Hernán Cortés arrives in Mexico
1528	Las Casas's *History of the Indies*
1530s	Pizarro's conquest of Peru
1542	Spain promulgates the New Laws
1608	Champlain establishes Quebec
1609	Hudson claims New Netherland
1610	Santa Fe established
1680	Pueblo Revolt

France Bringing the Faith to the Indians of New France. European nations justified colonization with the argument that they were bringing Christianity—without which freedom was impossible—to Native Americans. In this painting from the 1670s, an Indian kneels before a female representation of France. Both hold a painting of the Trinity.

FOCUS QUESTIONS

- *What were the major patterns of Native American life in North America before Europeans arrived?*

- *How did Indian and European ideas of freedom differ on the eve of contact?*

- *What impelled European explorers to look west across the Atlantic?*

- *What happened when the peoples of the Americas came in contact with Europeans?*

- *What were the chief features of the Spanish empire in America?*

- *What were the chief features of the French and Dutch empires in North America?*

"The discovery of America," the British writer Adam Smith announced in his celebrated work *The Wealth of Nations* (1776), was one of "the two greatest and most important events recorded in the history of mankind." Historians no longer use the word "discovery" to describe the European exploration, conquest, and colonization of a hemisphere already home to millions of people. But there can be no doubt that when Christopher Columbus made landfall in the West Indian islands in 1492, he set in motion some of the most pivotal developments in human history. Immense changes soon followed in both the Old and New Worlds; the consequences of these changes are still with us today.

The peoples of the American continents and Europe, previously unaware of each other's existence, were thrown into continuous interaction. Crops new to each hemisphere crossed the Atlantic, reshaping diets and transforming the natural environment. Because of their long isolation, the inhabitants of North and South America had developed no immunity to the germs that also accompanied the colonizers. As a result, they suffered a series of devastating epidemics, the greatest population catastrophe in human history. Within a decade of Columbus's voyage, a fourth continent—Africa—found itself drawn into the new Atlantic system of trade and population movement. In Africa, Europeans found a supply of unfree labor that enabled them to exploit the fertile lands of the Western Hemisphere. Indeed, of approximately 10 million men, women, and children who crossed from the Old World to the New between 1492 and 1820, the vast majority, about 7.7 million, were African slaves.

From the vantage point of 1776, the year the United States declared itself an independent nation, it seemed to Adam Smith that the "discovery" of America had produced both great "benefits" and great "misfortunes." To the nations of western Europe, the development of American colonies brought an era of "splendor and glory." Smith also noted, however, that to the "natives" of the Americas the years since 1492 had been ones of "dreadful misfortunes" and "every sort of injustice." And for millions of Africans, the settlement of America meant a descent into the abyss of slavery.

Long before Columbus sailed, Europeans had dreamed of a land of abundance, riches, and ease beyond the western horizon. Europeans envisioned America as a religious refuge, a society of equals, a source of power and glory. They searched the New World for golden cities and fountains of eternal youth. Some of these dreams would indeed be fulfilled. To many European settlers, America offered a far greater chance to own land and worship as they pleased than existed in Europe, with its rigid, unequal social order and official churches. Yet the New World also became the site of many forms of unfree labor, including indentured servitude, forced labor, and one of the most brutal and unjust systems, plantation slavery. The conquest and settlement of the Western Hemisphere opened new chapters in the long histories of both freedom and slavery.

THE FIRST AMERICANS

The Settling of the Americas

The residents of the Americas were no more a single group than Europeans or Africans. They spoke hundreds of different languages and lived in numerous kinds of societies. Most, however, were descended from bands of hunters and fishers who had crossed the Bering Strait via a land bridge at various times between 15,000 and 60,000 years ago—the exact dates are hotly debated by archaeologists.

The New World was new to Europeans but an ancient homeland to those who already lived there. The hemisphere had witnessed many changes during its human history. First, the early inhabitants and their descendants spread across the two continents, reaching the tip of South America perhaps 11,000 years ago. As the climate warmed, they faced a food crisis as the immense animals they hunted, including woolly mammoths and giant bison, became extinct. Around 9,000 years ago, at the same time that agriculture was being developed in the Near East, it also emerged in modern-day Mexico and the Andes, and then spread to other parts of the Americas, making settled civilizations possible.

Emergence of agriculture

Indian Societies of the Americas

North and South America were hardly an empty wilderness when Europeans arrived. The hemisphere contained cities, roads, irrigation systems, extensive trade networks, and large structures such as the pyramid-temples whose beauty still inspires wonder. With a population close to 250,000, **Tenochtitlán**, the capital of the Aztec empire in what is now Mexico, was one of the world's largest cities. Farther south lay the Inca kingdom, centered in modern-day Peru. Its population of perhaps 12 million was linked by a complex system of roads and bridges that extended 2,000 miles along the Andes mountain chain.

Roads, trade networks, and irrigation systems

Indian civilizations in North America had not developed the scale, grandeur, or centralized organization of the Aztec and Inca societies to their south.

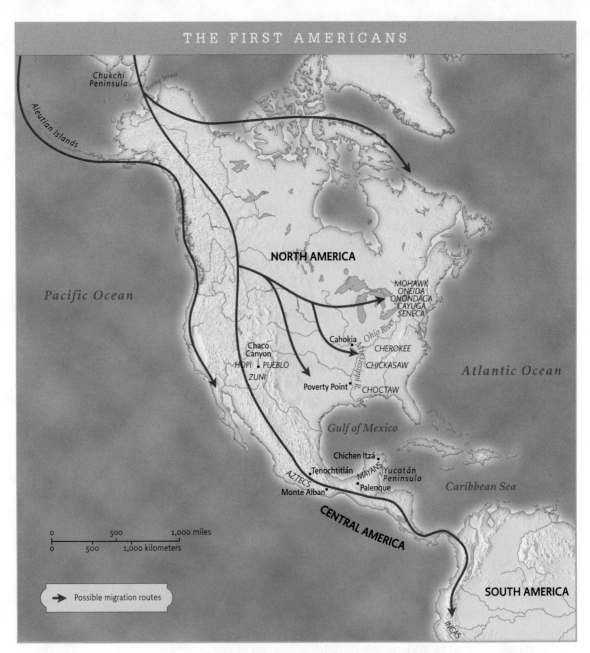

A map illustrating the probable routes by which the first Americans settled the Western Hemisphere at various times between 15,000 and 60,000 years ago.

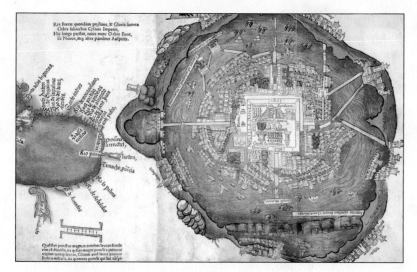

Map of the Aztec capital Tenochtitlán and the Gulf of Mexico, probably produced by a Spanish conquistador and published in 1524 in an edition of the letters of Hernán Cortés. The map shows the city's complex system of canals, bridges, and dams, with the Great Temple at the center. Gardens and a zoo are also visible.

North American Indians lacked the technologies Europeans had mastered, such as metal tools and machines, gunpowder, and the scientific knowledge necessary for long-distance navigation. No society north of Mexico had achieved literacy (although some made maps on bark and animal hides). Their "backwardness" became a central justification for European conquest. But, over time, Indian societies had perfected techniques of farming, hunting, and fishing, developed structures of political power and religious belief, and engaged in far-reaching networks of trade and communication.

Justification for conquest

Mound Builders of the Mississippi River Valley

Remarkable physical remains still exist from some of the early civilizations in North America. Around 3,500 years ago, before Egyptians built the pyramids, Native Americans constructed a large community centered on a series of giant semicircular mounds on a bluff overlooking the Mississippi River in present-day Louisiana. Known today as Poverty Point, it was a commercial and governmental center whose residents established trade routes throughout the Mississippi and Ohio River valleys.

More than a thousand years before Columbus sailed, Indians of the Ohio River valley, called "mound builders" by eighteenth-century settlers who encountered the large earthen burial mounds they created, had traded across half the continent. After their decline, another culture flourished in the Mississippi River valley, centered on the city of **Cahokia** near present-day St. Louis, a fortified community with between 10,000 and

"Mound builders"

30,000 inhabitants in the year 1200. It stood as the largest settled community in what is now the United States until surpassed in population by New York and Philadelphia around 1800.

Western Indians

Village life and trade

In the arid northeastern area of present-day Arizona, the Hopi and Zuni and their ancestors engaged in settled village life for over 3,000 years. During the peak of the region's culture, between the years 900 and 1200, these peoples built great planned towns with large multiple-family dwellings in local canyons, constructed dams and canals to gather and distribute water, and conducted trade with groups as far away as central Mexico and the Mississippi River valley. The largest of their structures, Pueblo Bonita, in Chaco Canyon, New Mexico, stood five stories high and had over 600 rooms. Not until the 1880s was a dwelling of comparable size constructed in the United States.

After the decline of these communities, probably because of drought, survivors moved to the south and east, where they established villages and perfected the techniques of desert farming. These were the people Spanish explorers called the Pueblo Indians (because they lived in small villages, or *pueblos*, when the Spanish first encountered them in the sixteenth century). On the Pacific coast, another densely populated region, hundreds of distinct groups resided in independent villages and lived primarily by fishing, hunting sea mammals, and gathering wild plants and nuts.

A modern aerial photograph of the ruins of Pueblo Bonita, in Chaco Canyon in present-day New Mexico. The rectangular structures are the foundations of dwellings, and the circular ones are *kivas,* or places of religious worship.

Indians of Eastern North America

In eastern North America, hundreds of tribes inhabited towns and villages scattered from the Gulf of Mexico to present-day Canada. They lived on corn, squash, and beans, supplemented by fishing and hunting deer, turkeys, and other animals. Indian trade routes crisscrossed the eastern part of the continent. Tribes frequently warred with one another to obtain goods, seize captives, or take revenge for the killing of relatives. They conducted diplomacy and made peace. Little in the way of centralized authority existed until, in the fifteenth century, various leagues or confederations emerged in an effort to bring order to local regions. In the Southeast, the Choctaw, Cherokee, and Chickasaw each united dozens of towns in loose alliances. In present-day New York and Pennsylvania, five **Iroquois** peoples—the Mohawk, Oneida, Cayuga, Seneca, and Onondaga—formed a Great League of Peace, bringing a period of stability to the area.

The most striking feature of Native American society at the time Europeans arrived was its sheer diversity. Each group had its own political system and set of religious beliefs, and North America was home to literally hundreds of mutually unintelligible languages. Indians did not think of themselves as a single unified people, an idea invented by Europeans and only many years later adopted by Indians themselves. Indian identity centered on the immediate social group—a tribe, village, chiefdom, or confederacy. When Europeans first arrived, many Indians saw them as simply one group among many. The sharp dichotomy between Indians and "white" persons did not emerge until later in the colonial era.

Diversity of Native American society

Native American Religion

Nonetheless, the diverse Indian societies of North America did share certain common characteristics. Their lives were steeped in religious ceremonies often directly related to farming and hunting. Spiritual power, they

The Village of Secoton, by John White, an English artist who spent a year on the Outer Banks of North Carolina in 1585–1586 as part of an expedition sponsored by Sir Walter Raleigh. A central street links houses surrounded by fields of corn. In the lower part, dancing Indians take part in a religious ceremony.

NATIVE WAYS OF LIFE, ca. 1500

TLINGIT
INUIT
Hudson Bay
INUIT
TSHIMSHIAN

thinly populated
CREE
MICMAC
PENOBSCOT
ABENAKI

KWAKIUTLS
NOOTKIN SHUSWAP
KOOTENAY
BLACKFEET
ASSINIBOINE CHIPPEWA
L. Superior
ALGONQUIAN

SKAGIT
WALLA
CHINOOK WALLA
NEZ
CAYUSE PERCE
FLATHEAD
CHEYENNE SIOUX
CHIPPEWA
WAMPANOAG
MENOMINEE OTTOWA HURON
NEUTRAL IROQUOIS
MOHEGAN
PEQUOT
NARRAGANSETT

TILLAMOOK
KLAMATH
POMO MODOC
MAIDU
COSTANO
HIDATSA
MANDAN SIOUX
KIOWA ARAPAHO
SHOSHONE PAWNEE
IOWA
WINNEBAGO
POTAWATOMI ERIE
SAUK MOSOPELEA
KICKAPOO
ILLINOIS SHAWNEE
KASKASKIA
SUSQUEHANNOCK

thinly populated

UTE
WICHITA
CHEROKEE
PAMLICO
TUSCARORA

CHEMEHUEVI SOUTHERN
CHUMASH PAIUTE
SERRANO
LUISENO
CAHUILLA
DIEGUENO
HOPI ZUNI TEWA
COMANCHE
CADDO
CHICKASAW
CREEK
YAMASEE
MESCALERO
CHOCTAW
TIMUCUA
APALACHEE
NATCHEZ

JUMANO
CONCHO
YACHI
LAGUERNO
KABANKAWA
CALUSA
COAHUILTEC

Pacific Ocean
Gulf of Mexico
ARAWAK

0   250   500 miles
0   250   500 kilometers

Ways of Life in North America, AD 1515

- Arctic hunter-gatherers
- Subarctic hunter-fisher-gatherers
- Northwest coast marine economy
- Plains hunter-gatherers
- Plains horticulturalists
- Non-horticultural rancherian peoples
- Rancherian peoples with low-intensity horticulture
- Rancherian peoples with intensive horticulture
- Pueblos with intensive horticulture
- Seacoast foragers
- Marginal horticultural hunters
- River-based horticultural chiefdoms
- Orchard-growing alligator hunters
- Tidewater horticulturalists
- Fishers and wild-rice gatherers

The native population of North America at the time of first contact with Europeans consisted of numerous tribes with their own languages, religious beliefs, and economic and social structures. This map suggests the numerous ways of life existing at the time.

believed, suffused the world, and sacred spirits could be found in all kinds of living and inanimate things—animals, plants, trees, water, and wind. Through religious ceremonies, they aimed to harness the aid of powerful supernatural forces to serve human interests. Indian villages also held elaborate religious rites, participation in which helped to define the boundaries of community membership. In all Indian societies, those who seemed to possess special abilities to invoke supernatural powers—shamans, medicine men, and other religious leaders—held positions of respect and authority.

Indian religious rituals

In some respects, Indian religion was not that different from popular spiritual beliefs in Europe. Most Indians held that a single Creator stood atop the spiritual hierarchy. Nonetheless, nearly all Europeans arriving in the New World quickly concluded that Indians were in dire need of being converted to a true, Christian faith.

Land and Property

Equally alien in European eyes were Indian attitudes toward property. Generally, village leaders assigned plots of land to individual families to use for a season or more, and tribes claimed specific areas for hunting. Unclaimed land remained free for anyone to use. Families "owned" the right to use land, but they did not own the land itself. Indians saw land as a common resource, not an economic commodity. There was no market in real estate before the coming of Europeans.

Land as a common resource

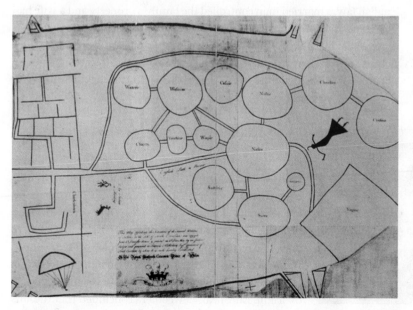

A Catawba map illustrates the differences between Indian and European conceptions of landed property. The map depicts not possession of a specific territory, but trade and diplomatic connections between various native groups and with the colony of Virginia, represented by the rectangle on the lower right. The map, inscribed on deerskin, was originally presented by Indian chiefs to Governor Francis Nicholson of South Carolina in 1721. This copy, the only version that survives, was made by the governor for the authorities in London. It added English labels that conveyed what the Indians had related orally with the gift.

Nor were Indians devoted to the accumulation of wealth and material goods. Especially east of the Mississippi River, where villages moved every few years when soil or game became depleted, acquiring numerous possessions made little sense. However, status certainly mattered in Indian societies. Tribal leaders tended to come from a small number of families, and chiefs lived more splendidly than average members of society. But their reputation often rested on their willingness to share goods with others rather than hoarding them for themselves.

Gift giving

Generosity was among the most valued social qualities, and gift giving was essential to Indian society. Trade, for example, meant more than a commercial transaction—it was accompanied by elaborate ceremonies of gift exchange that bound different groups in webs of mutual obligation. "There are no beggars among them," reported the English colonial leader Roger Williams of New England's Indians.

Gender Relations

Matrilineal societies

The system of gender relations in most Indian societies also differed markedly from that of Europe. Membership in a family defined women's lives, but they openly engaged in premarital sexual relations and could even choose to divorce their husbands. Most, although not all, Indian societies were matrilineal—that is, centered on clans or kinship groups in which children became members of the mother's family, not the father's. Under English law, a married man controlled the family's property and a wife had no independent legal identity. In contrast, Indian women owned dwellings and tools, and a husband generally moved to live with the family of his wife. Because men were frequently away on the hunt, women took responsibility not only for household duties but for most agricultural work as well.

Indian women planting crops while men break the sod. An engraving by Theodor de Bry, based on a painting by Jacques Le Moyne de Morgues. Morgues was part of an expedition of French Huguenots to Florida in 1564; he escaped when the Spanish destroyed the outpost in the following year.

European Views of the Indians

Europeans tended to view Indians in extreme terms. They were regarded either as "noble savages," gentle, friendly, and superior in some ways to Europeans, or as uncivilized and brutal savages. Over time, however, negative images of Indians came to overshadow positive ones. Early European descriptions of North American Indians as barbaric centered on three areas—religion, land use, and gender relations. Whatever their country of origin, European newcomers concluded that Indians lacked genuine religion, or in fact worshiped the devil. Whereas the Indians saw nature as a world of spirits and souls, the Europeans viewed it as a collection of potential commodities, a source of economic opportunity.

Europeans invoked the Indians' distinctive pattern of land use and ideas about property to answer the awkward question raised by a British minister at an early stage of England's colonization: "By what right or warrant can we enter into the land of these Savages, take away their rightful inheritance from them, and plant ourselves in their places?" While the Spanish claimed title to land in America by right of conquest and papal authority, the English, French, and Dutch came to rely on the idea that Indians had not actually "used" the land and thus had no claim to it. Despite the Indians' highly developed agriculture and well-established towns, Europeans frequently described them as nomads without settled communities.

In the Indians' gender division of labor and matrilineal family structures, Europeans saw weak men and mistreated women. Hunting and fishing, the primary occupations of Indian men, were considered leisure activities in much of Europe, not "real" work. Because Indian women worked in the fields, Europeans often described them as lacking freedom. Europeans insisted that by subduing the Indians, they were actually bringing them freedom—the freedom of true religion, private property, and the liberation of both men and women from uncivilized and unchristian gender roles.

A seventeenth-century engraving by a French Jesuit priest illustrates many Europeans' view of Indian religion. A demon hovers over an Iroquois longhouse, suggesting that Indians worship the devil.

INDIAN FREEDOM, EUROPEAN FREEDOM

Indian Freedom

Although many Europeans initially saw Indians as embodying freedom, most colonizers quickly concluded that the notion of "freedom" was alien to Indian societies. European settlers reached this conclusion in part because Indians did not appear to live under established governments or fixed laws, followed their own—not European—definitions of authority, and lacked the kind of order and discipline common in European society. Indians also did not define freedom as individual autonomy or tie it to the ownership of property—two attributes important to Europeans.

What were the Indians' ideas of freedom? The modern notion of freedom as personal independence had little meaning in most Indian societies, but individuals were expected to think for themselves and did not always have to go along with collective decision making. Far more important

Freedom in the group

than individual autonomy were kinship ties, the ability to follow one's spiritual values, and the well-being and security of one's community. In Indian culture, group autonomy and self-determination, and the mutual obligations that came with a sense of belonging and connectedness, took precedence over individual freedom. Ironically, the coming of Europeans, armed with their own language of liberty, would make freedom a preoccupation of American Indians, as part and parcel of the very process by which they were reduced to dependence on the colonizers.

Christian Liberty

On the eve of colonization, Europeans held numerous ideas of freedom. Some were as old as the city-states of ancient Greece, others arose during the political struggles of the early modern era. Some laid the foundations for modern conceptions of freedom, others are quite unfamiliar today. Freedom was not a single idea but a collection of distinct rights and privileges, many enjoyed by only a small portion of the population.

Freedom as a spiritual condition

One conception common throughout Europe understood freedom less as a political or social status than as a moral or spiritual condition. Freedom meant abandoning the life of sin to embrace the teachings of Christ. **"Christian Liberty,"** however, had no connection to later ideas of religious toleration, a notion that scarcely existed anywhere on the eve of colonization. Every nation in Europe had an established church that decreed what forms of religious worship and belief were acceptable. Dissenters faced persecution by the state as well as condemnation by church authorities. Religious uniformity was thought to be essential to public order; the modern idea that a person's religious beliefs and practices are a matter of private choice, not legal obligation, was almost unknown.

Freedom and Authority

In its secular form, the equating of liberty with obedience to a higher authority suggested that freedom meant not anarchy but obedience to law. The identification of freedom with the rule of law did not, though, mean that all subjects of the crown enjoyed the same degree of freedom. Early modern European societies were extremely hierarchical, with marked gradations of social status ranging from the king and hereditary aristocracy down to the urban and rural poor. Inequality was built into virtually every social relationship.

Hierarchy in the family

Within families, men exercised authority over their wives and children. According to the widespread legal doctrine known as "coverture," when a woman married she surrendered her legal identity, which became "covered" by that of her husband. She could not own property or sign contracts in her own name, control her wages if she worked, write a separate will, or, except in the rarest of circumstances, go to court seeking a divorce. The husband had the exclusive right to his wife's "company," including domestic labor and sexual relations.

Everywhere in Europe, family life depended on male dominance and female submission. Indeed, political writers of the sixteenth century explicitly compared the king's authority over his subjects with the husband's over his family. Both were ordained by God.

Liberty and Liberties

In this hierarchical society, liberty came from knowing one's social place and fulfilling the duties appropriate to one's rank. Most men lacked the freedom that came with economic independence. Property qualifications and other restrictions limited the electorate to a minuscule part of the adult male population. The law required strict obedience of employees, and breaches of labor contracts carried criminal penalties.

Hierarchy in society

European ideas of freedom still bore the imprint of the Middle Ages, when "liberties" meant formal, specific privileges such as self-government, exemption from taxation, or the right to practice a particular trade, granted to individuals or groups by contract, royal decree, or purchase. Only those who enjoyed the "freedom of the city," for example, could engage in certain economic activities. Numerous modern civil liberties did not exist. The law decreed acceptable forms of religious worship. The government regularly suppressed publications it did not like, and criticism of authority could lead to imprisonment. Nonetheless, every European country that colonized the New World claimed to be spreading freedom—for its own population and for Native Americans.

THE EXPANSION OF EUROPE

It is fitting that the second epochal event that Adam Smith linked to Columbus's voyage of 1492 was the discovery by Portuguese navigators of a sea route from Europe to Asia around the southern tip of Africa. The European conquest of America began as an offshoot of the quest for a sea route to India, China, and the islands of the East Indies, the source of the silk, tea, spices, porcelain, and other luxury goods on which international trade in the early modern era centered. For centuries, this commerce had been conducted across land, from China and South Asia to the Middle East

Sea route to the East

and the Mediterranean region. Profit and piety—the desire to eliminate Islamic middlemen and win control of the lucrative trade for Christian western Europe—combined to inspire the quest for a direct route to Asia.

Chinese and Portuguese Navigation

At the beginning of the fifteenth century, one might have predicted that China would establish the world's first global empire. Between 1405 and 1433, Admiral Zheng He led seven large naval expeditions in the Indian Ocean. The first convoy consisted of 62 ships that were larger than those of any European nation, along with 225 support vessels and more than 25,000 men. On his sixth voyage, Zheng explored the coast of East Africa. Had his ships continued westward, they could easily have reached North and South America. But as a wealthy land-based empire, China did not feel the need for overseas expansion, and after 1433 the government ended support for long-distance maritime expeditions.

Zheng He's voyages

It fell to Portugal, far removed from the overland route to Asia, to begin exploring the Atlantic. Taking advantage of new long-distance ships known as **caravels** and new navigational devices such as the compass and quadrant, the Portuguese showed that it was possible to sail down the coast of Africa and return to Portugal. No European sailor had seen the coast of Africa below the Sahara. But in that year, a Portuguese ship brought a sprig of rosemary from West Africa, proof that one could sail beyond the desert and return.

New techniques of sailing and navigation

Little by little, Portuguese ships moved farther down the coast. In 1485, they reached Benin, an imposing city whose craftsmen produced bronze sculptures that still inspire admiration for their artistic beauty and superb casting techniques. The Portuguese established fortified trading posts on the western coast of Africa. The profits reaped by these Portuguese "factories"—so named because merchants were known as "factors"—inspired other European powers to follow in their footsteps.

Portugal also began to colonize Madeira, the Azores, and the Canary and Cape Verde Islands, which lie in the Atlantic off the African coast. The Portuguese established plantations on the Atlantic islands, eventually replacing the native populations with thousands of slaves shipped from Africa—an ominous precedent for the New World.

Portuguese explorations

Freedom and Slavery in Africa

Slavery in Africa long predated the coming of Europeans. Traditionally, African slaves tended to be criminals, debtors, and captives in war. They worked within the households of their owners and had well-defined rights, such as possessing property and marrying free persons. It was not uncom-

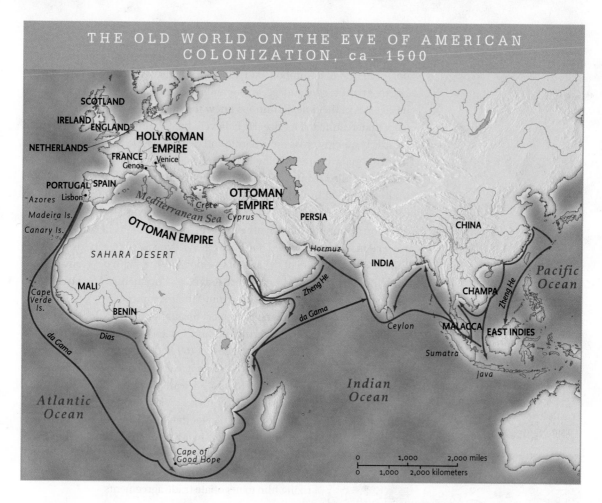

THE OLD WORLD ON THE EVE OF AMERICAN COLONIZATION, ca. 1500

mon for African slaves to acquire their freedom. Slavery was one of several forms of labor, not the basis of the economy as it would become in large parts of the New World. The coming of the Portuguese, soon followed by traders from other European nations, accelerated the buying and selling of slaves within Africa. At least 100,000 African slaves were transported to Spain and Portugal between 1450 and 1500.

Having reached West Africa, Portuguese mariners pushed their explorations ever southward along the coast. Bartholomeu Dias reached the Cape of Good Hope at the continent's southern tip in 1487. In 1498, Vasco da Gama sailed around it to India, demonstrating the feasibility of a sea route to the East. With a population of under 1 million, Portugal established a vast trading empire, with bases in India, southern China, and Indonesia. But six years before da Gama's voyage, Christopher Columbus had, he believed, discovered a new route to China and India by sailing west.

In the fifteenth century, the world known to Europeans was limited to Europe, parts of Africa, and Asia. Explorers from Portugal sought to find a sea route to the East in order to circumvent the Italian city-states and Middle Eastern rulers who controlled the overland trade.

THE EXPANSION OF EUROPE | 15

The Voyages of Columbus

A seasoned mariner and fearless explorer from Genoa, a major port in northern Italy, Columbus had for years sailed the Mediterranean and North Atlantic, studying ocean currents and wind patterns. Like nearly all navigators of the time, Columbus knew the earth was round. But he drastically underestimated its size. He believed that by sailing westward he could relatively quickly cross the Atlantic and reach Asia. No one in Europe knew that two giant continents lay 3,000 miles to the west. The Vikings, to be sure, had sailed from Greenland to Newfoundland around the year 1000 and established a settlement, Vinland. But this outpost was abandoned after a few years and had been forgotten, except in Norse legends.

Norse settlement

For Columbus, as for other figures of the time, religious and commercial motives reinforced one another. A devout Catholic, he drew on the Bible for his estimate of the size of the globe. Along with developing trade with the East, he hoped to convert Asians to Christianity and enlist them in a crusade to redeem Jerusalem from Muslim control.

Columbus sought financial support throughout Europe for the planned voyage. Eventually, King Ferdinand and Queen Isabella of Spain agreed to become sponsors. Their marriage in 1469 had united the warring kingdoms of Aragon and Castile. In 1492, they completed the *reconquista*—the "reconquest" of Spain from the Moors, African Muslims who had occupied part of the Iberian Peninsula for centuries. With Spain's territory united, Ferdinand and Isabella—like the rulers of the Italian city-states—were anxious to circumvent the Muslim stranglehold on eastern trade. It is not surprising, then, that Columbus set sail with royal letters of introduction to Asian rulers, authorizing him to negotiate trade agreements.

Columbus's Landfall, an engraving from *La lettera dell'isole* (Letter from the Islands). This 1493 pamphlet reproduced, in the form of a poem, Columbus's first letter describing his voyage of the previous year. Under the watchful eye of King Ferdinand of Spain, Columbus and his men land on a Caribbean island, while local Indians flee.

CONTACT

Columbus in the New World

On October 12, 1492, after only thirty-three days of sailing from the Canary Islands, where he had stopped to resupply his three ships, Columbus and his expedition arrived at the Bahamas. Soon afterward, he encountered the far larger islands of Hispaniola (today the site of Haiti and the Dominican Republic) and Cuba. When one of his ships ran aground, he abandoned it and left thirty-eight men behind on Hispaniola. But he found room to bring ten inhabitants of the island back to Spain for conversion to Christianity.

In the following year, 1493, Columbus returned with seventeen ships and more than 1,000 men to explore the area and establish a Spanish outpost. Columbus's settlement on the island of Hispaniola, which he named La Isabella, failed, but in 1502 another Spanish explorer, Nicolás de Ovando, arrived with 2,500 men and established a permanent base, the first center of the Spanish empire in America. Columbus went to his grave believing that he had discovered a westward route to Asia. The explorations of another Italian, Amerigo Vespucci, along the coast of South America between 1499 and 1502 made plain that a continent entirely unknown to Europeans had been encountered. The New World would come to bear not Columbus's name but one based on Vespucci's—America. Vespucci also realized that the native inhabitants were distinct peoples, not residents of the East Indies as Columbus had believed, although the name "Indians," applied to them by Columbus, has endured to this day.

Hispaniola settlement

Vespucci

Exploration and Conquest

Thanks to Johannes Gutenberg's invention of the printing press in the 1430s, news of Columbus's achievement traveled quickly, at least among the educated minority in Europe. Other explorers were inspired to follow in his wake. John Cabot, a Genoese merchant who had settled in England, reached Newfoundland in 1497. Soon, scores of fishing boats from France, Spain, and England were active in the region. Pedro Cabral claimed Brazil for Portugal in 1500.

But the Spanish took the lead in exploration and conquest. Inspired by a search for wealth, national glory, and the desire to spread Catholicism, Spanish conquistadores, often accompanied by religious missionaries and carrying flags emblazoned with the sign of the cross, radiated outward from Hispaniola. In 1513, Vasco Núñez de Balboa trekked across the isthmus of Panama and became the first European to gaze upon the Pacific Ocean. Between 1519 and 1522, Ferdinand Magellan led the first expedition to sail around the world, encountering Pacific islands and peoples previously unknown to Europe.

Spain takes the lead

The first explorer to encounter a major American civilization was Hernán Cortés, who in 1519 arrived at Tenochtitlán, the nerve center of the Aztec empire, whose wealth and power rested on domination of numerous subordinate peoples nearby. The Aztecs were violent warriors who engaged in the ritual sacrifice of captives and others, sometimes thousands at a time. This practice thoroughly alienated their neighbors.

Cortés

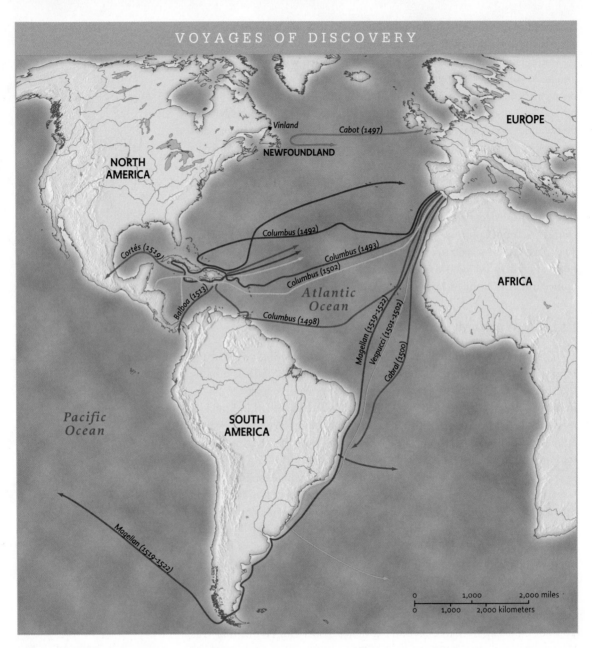

VOYAGES OF DISCOVERY

Vinland

Cabot (1497)

NEWFOUNDLAND

EUROPE

NORTH AMERICA

Columbus (1492)

Cortés (1519)

Columbus (1493)

Columbus (1502)

Balboa (1513)

Atlantic Ocean

Columbus (1498)

AFRICA

Magellan (1519–1522)

Vespucci (1501–1502)

Cabral (1500)

Pacific Ocean

SOUTH AMERICA

Magellan (1519–1522)

| 0 | 1,000 | 2,000 miles |
| 0 | 1,000 | 2,000 kilometers |

Christopher Columbus's first Atlantic crossing, in 1492, was soon followed by voyages of discovery by English, Portuguese, Spanish, and Italian explorers.

With only a few hundred European men, Cortés conquered the Aztec city, relying on superior military technology such as iron weapons and gunpowder, as well as shrewdness in enlisting the aid of some of the Aztecs' subject peoples, who supplied him with thousands of warriors. His most powerful ally, however, was disease—a smallpox epidemic that devastated Aztec society. A few years later, Francisco Pizarro conquered the great Inca kingdom centered in modern-day Peru. Pizarro's tactics were typical of the conquistadores. He captured the Incan king, demanded and received a ransom, and then killed the king anyway. Soon, treasure fleets carrying cargoes of gold and silver from the mines of Mexico and Peru were traversing the Atlantic to enrich the Spanish crown.

Engravings, from the *Florentine Codex*, of the forces of Cortés marching on Tenochtitlán and assaulting the city with cannon fire. The difference in military technology between the Spanish and Aztecs is evident. Indians who allied with Cortés had helped him build vessels and carry them in pieces over mountains to the city. The codex (a volume formed by stitching together manuscript pages) was prepared under the supervision of a Spanish missionary in sixteenth-century Mexico.

The Demographic Disaster

The transatlantic flow of goods and people is sometimes called the **Columbian Exchange**. Plants, animals, and cultures that had evolved independently on separate continents were now thrown together. Products introduced to Europe from the Americas included corn, tomatoes, potatoes, peanuts, and tobacco, while people from the Old World brought wheat, rice, sugarcane, horses, cattle, pigs, and sheep to the New. But Europeans also carried germs previously unknown in the Americas.

No one knows exactly how many people lived in the Americas at the time of Columbus's voyages—current estimates range between 50 and 90 million, most of whom lived in Central and South America. In 1492, the Indian population within what are now the borders of the United States was between 2 and 5 million. The Indian populations of the Americas suffered a catastrophic decline because of contact with Europeans and their wars, enslavement, and especially diseases like smallpox, influenza, and measles. Never having encountered these diseases, Indians had not developed antibodies to fight them. The result was devastating. The population of Mexico would fall by more than 90 percent in the sixteenth century, from perhaps 20 million to under 2 million. As for the area that now forms the United States, its Native American population fell continuously. It reached its lowest point around 1900, at only 250,000.

Decline of Indian populations

Overall, the death of perhaps 80 million people—close to one-fifth of humankind—in the first century and a half after contact with Europeans represents the greatest loss of life in human history. It was disease as much as military prowess and more advanced technology that enabled Europeans to conquer the Americas.

THE SPANISH EMPIRE

By the middle of the sixteenth century, Spain had established an immense empire that reached from Europe to the Americas and Asia. The Atlantic and Pacific oceans, once barriers separating different parts of the world, now became highways for the exchange of goods and the movement of people. Spanish galleons carried gold and silver from Mexico and Peru eastward to Spain and westward to Manila in the Philippines and on to China.

Extent of the empire

Stretching from the Andes Mountains of South America through present-day Mexico and the Caribbean and eventually into Florida and the southwestern United States, Spain's empire exceeded in size the Roman empire of the ancient world. Its center was Mexico City, a magnificent capital built on the ruins of the Aztec city of Tenochtitlán that boasted churches, hospitals, monasteries, government buildings, and the New World's first university. Unlike the English and French New World empires, Spanish

A late-seventeenth-century painting of the Plaza Mayor (main square) of Mexico City. The image includes a parade of over 1,000 persons, of different ethnic groups and occupations, dressed in their characteristic attire.

America was essentially an urban civilization. For centuries, its great cities, notably Mexico City, Quito, and Lima, far outshone any urban centers in North America and most of those in Europe.

Governing Spanish America

At least in theory, the government of Spanish America reflected the absolutism of the newly unified nation at home. Authority originated with the king and flowed downward through the Council of the Indies—the main body in Spain for colonial administration—and then to viceroys in Mexico and Peru and other local officials in America. The Catholic Church also played a significant role in the administration of Spanish colonies, frequently exerting its authority on matters of faith, morals, and treatment of the Indians.

Authority in Spanish America

Successive kings kept elected assemblies out of Spain's New World empire. Royal officials were generally appointees from Spain, rather than *criollos*, as persons born in the colonies of European ancestry were called. But as Spain's power declined in Europe beginning in the seventeenth century, the local elite came to enjoy more and more effective authority over colonial affairs.

Colonists and Indians in Spanish America

Despite the decline in the native population, Spanish America remained populous enough that, with the exception of the West Indies and a few cities, large-scale importations of African slaves were unnecessary. Instead, the Spanish forced tens of thousands of Indians to work in gold and silver mines, which supplied the empire's wealth, and on large-scale farms, or *haciendas*, controlled by Spanish landlords. In Spanish America, unlike other New World empires, Indians performed most of the labor.

Labor in Spanish America

The opportunity for social advancement drew numerous colonists from Spain—225,000 in the sixteenth century and a total of 750,000 in the three centuries of Spain's colonial rule. Eventually, a significant number came in families, but at first the large majority were young, single men, many of them laborers, craftsmen, and soldiers. Many also came as government officials, priests, professionals, and minor aristocrats, all ready to direct the manual work of Indians, since living without having to labor was a sign of noble status. The most successful of these colonists enjoyed lives of luxury similar to those of the upper classes at home.

Unlike in the later British empire, Indian inhabitants always outnumbered European colonists and their descendants in Spanish America, and large areas remained effectively under Indian control for many years.

Spanish authorities granted Indians certain rights within colonial society and looked forward to their eventual assimilation. Indeed, the success of the Spanish empire depended on the nature of the native societies on which it could build. In Florida, the Amazon, and Caribbean islands like Jamaica, which lacked major Indian cities and large native populations, Spanish rule remained tenuous.

The Spanish crown ordered wives of colonists to join them in America and demanded that single men marry. But with the population of Spanish women remaining low, the intermixing of the colonial and Indian peoples soon began. As early as 1514, the Spanish government formally approved of such marriages, partly as a way of bringing Christianity to the native population. By 1600, **mestizos** (persons of mixed origin) made up a large part of the urban population of Spanish America. Over time, Spanish

A hybrid culture

America evolved into a hybrid culture, part Spanish, part Indian, and in some areas part African, but with a single official faith, language, and governmental system.

Justifications for Conquest

The Europeans who crossed the Atlantic in the wake of Columbus's voyage had immense confidence in the superiority of their own cultures to those they encountered in America. They expected these societies to abandon their own beliefs and traditions and embrace those of the newcomers. Failure to do so reinforced the conviction that these people were uncivilized "heathens" (non-Christians). In addition, Europeans brought with them a long history of using violence to subdue their foes and a missionary zeal to spread the benefits of their own civilization to others, while reaping the benefits of empire. Spain was no exception.

The Virgin of Guadalupe, a symbol of Mexican culture, in an image from 1770. She is portrayed as the protector of the Indians.

To further legitimize Spain's claim to rule the New World, a year after Columbus's first voyage Pope Alexander VI divided the non-Christian world between Spain and Portugal. The line was subsequently adjusted to give Portugal control of Brazil, with the remainder of the Western Hemisphere falling under Spanish authority. Its missionary purpose in colonization was already familiar because of the long holy war against Islam within Spain itself and Spain's 1492 order that all Muslims and Jews had to convert to Catholicism or leave the country. But missionary zeal was powerfully reinforced in the sixteenth century, when the Protestant Reformation divided the Catholic Church. In 1517, Martin Luther, a German priest, posted his Ninety-Five Theses, which accused the Church of worldliness and corruption. Luther wanted to cleanse the Church of abuses such as the sale of indulgences (official dispensations forgiving sins). He insisted that all

Spanish conquistadores murdering Indians at Cuzco, in Peru. The Dutch-born engraver Theodor de Bry and his sons illustrated ten volumes about New World exploration published between 1590 and 1618. A Protestant, de Bry created vivid images that helped to spread the Black Legend of Spain as a uniquely cruel colonizer.

believers should read the Bible for themselves, rather than relying on priests to interpret it for them. His call for reform led to the rise of new Protestant churches independent of Rome and plunged Europe into more than a century of religious and political strife.

Spain, the most powerful bastion of orthodox Catholicism, redoubled its efforts to convert the Indians to the "true faith." Spain insisted that the primary goal of colonization was to save the Indians from heathenism and prevent them from falling under the sway of Protestantism.

Converting Indians

Piety and Profit

To the Spanish colonizers, the large native populations of the Americas were not only souls to be saved but also a labor force to be organized to extract gold and silver for the mother country. The tension between these two outlooks would mark Spanish rule in America for three centuries. On the one hand, religious orders established missions throughout the empire, and over time millions of Indians were converted to Catholicism. On the other hand, Spanish rule, especially in its initial period, decimated the Indian population and subjected Indians to brutal labor conditions. The conquistadores and subsequent governors, who required conquered peoples to acknowledge the Catholic Church and provide gold and silver,

Tensions in the empire

THE SPANISH EMPIRE | 23

saw no contradiction between serving God and enriching themselves. Others, however, did.

As early as 1537, Pope Paul III, who hoped to see Indians become devout subjects of Catholic monarchs, outlawed Indians' enslavement (an edict never extended to apply to Africans). Fifteen years later, the Dominican priest Bartolomé de Las Casas published an account of the decimation of the Indian population with the compelling title *A Very Brief Account of the Destruction of the Indies*.

Las Casas

Las Casas's writings denounced Spain for causing the death of millions of innocent people and for denying Indians their freedom. He narrated in shocking detail the "strange cruelties" carried out by "the Christians," including the burning alive of men, women, and children and the imposition of forced labor. "The entire human race is one," he proclaimed, and while he continued to believe that Spain had a right to rule in America, largely on religious grounds, he called for Indians to enjoy "all guarantees of liberty and justice" from the moment they became subjects of Spain. Las Casas also suggested, however, that importing slaves from Africa would help to protect the Indians from exploitation.

Reforming the Empire

Largely because of Las Casas's efforts, Spain in 1542 promulgated the New Laws, commanding that Indians no longer be enslaved. In 1550, Spain abolished the *encomienda* system, under which the first settlers had been granted authority over conquered Indian lands with the right to extract forced labor from the native inhabitants. In its place, the government established the *repartimiento* **system**, whereby residents of Indian villages remained legally free and entitled to wages, but were still required to perform a fixed amount of labor each year. The Indians were not slaves—they had access to land, were paid wages, and could not be bought and sold. But since the requirement that they work for the Spanish remained the essence of the system, it still allowed for many abuses by Spanish landlords and by priests who required Indians to toil on mission lands as part of the conversion process.

Over time, Spain's brutal treatment of Indians improved somewhat. But Las Casas's writings, translated almost immediately into several European languages, contributed to the spread of the **Black**

TABLE 1.1 Estimated Regional Populations: The Americas, ca. 1500	
North America	3,800,000
Mexico	17,200,000
Central America	5,625,000
Hispaniola	1,000,000
The Caribbean	3,000,000
The Andes	15,700,000
South America	8,620,000
Total	54,945,000

Legend—the image of Spain as a uniquely brutal and exploitative colonizer. This image would provide a potent justification for other European powers to challenge Spain's predominance in the New World.

Exploring North America

While the Spanish empire centered on Mexico, Peru, and the West Indies, the hope of finding a new kingdom of gold soon led Spanish explorers into territory that now forms part of the United States. Juan Ponce de León, who had conquered Puerto Rico, entered Florida in 1513 in search of slaves, wealth, and a fabled fountain of youth, only to be repelled by local Indians. In the late 1530s and 1540s, Juan Rodriguez Cabrillo explored the Pacific coast as far north as present-day Oregon, and expeditions led by Hernando de Soto, Cabeza de Vaca, Francisco Vásquez de Coronado, and others marched through the Gulf region and the Southwest, fruitlessly searching for another Mexico or Peru. These expeditions, really mobile communities with hundreds of adventurers, priests, potential settlers, slaves, and livestock, spread disease and devastation among Indian communities. De Soto's was particularly brutal. His men tortured, raped, and enslaved countless Indians and transmitted deadly diseases. When Europeans in the seventeenth century returned to colonize the area traversed by de Soto's party, little remained of the societies he had encountered.

De Soto

Spain in Florida and the Southwest

Nonetheless, these explorations established Spain's claim to a large part of what is now the American South and Southwest. The first region to be colonized within the present-day United States was Florida. Spain hoped to establish a military base there to combat pirates who threatened the treasure fleet that each year sailed from Havana for Europe loaded with gold and silver from Mexico and Peru. Spain also wanted to forestall French incursions in the area. In 1565, Philip II of Spain authorized the nobleman Pedro Menéndez de Avilés to lead a colonizing expedition to Florida. Menéndez destroyed a small outpost at Fort Caroline, which a group of Huguenots (French Protestants) had established in 1562 near present-day

Florida as military base

TABLE 1.2 Estimated Regional Populations: The World, ca. 1500	
India	110,000,000
China	103,000,000
Other Asia	55,400,000
Western Europe	57,200,000
The Americas	55,000,000
Russia and Eastern Europe	34,000,000
Sub-Saharan Africa	38,300,000
Japan	15,400,000
World Total	467,300,000

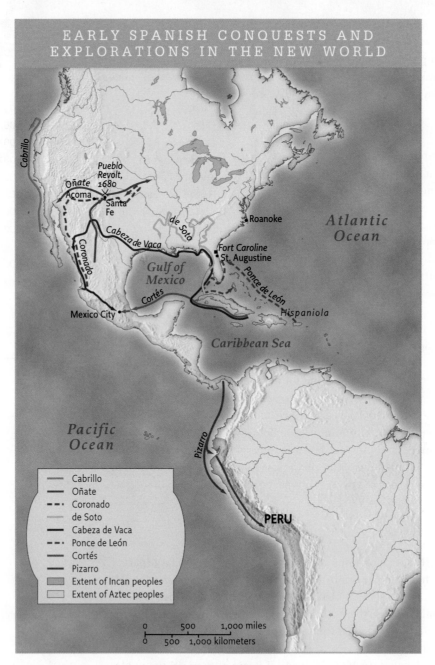

EARLY SPANISH CONQUESTS AND EXPLORATIONS IN THE NEW WORLD

Cabrillo

Oñate
Pueblo Revolt, 1680
Acoma
Santa Fe
de Soto
Roanoke
Atlantic Ocean
Coronado
Cabeza de Vaca
Gulf of Mexico
Fort Caroline
St. Augustine
Cortés
Ponce de León
Mexico City
Hispaniola
Caribbean Sea

Pacific Ocean

Pizarro

PERU

— Cabrillo
— Oñate
--- Coronado
— de Soto
— Cabeza de Vaca
--- Ponce de León
— Cortés
— Pizarro
Extent of Incan peoples
Extent of Aztec peoples

0   500   1,000 miles
0   500   1,000 kilometers

By around 1600, New Spain had become a vast empire stretching from the modern-day American Southwest through Mexico, Central America, and into the former Inca kingdom in South America. This map shows early Spanish exploration, especially in the present-day United States, Mexico, and Peru.

Jacksonville. Menéndez and his men went on to establish Spanish forts on St. Simons Island, Georgia, and at St. Augustine, Florida. The latter remains the oldest site in the United States continuously inhabited by European settlers and their descendants. In general, though, Florida failed to attract settlers, remaining an isolated military settlement, in effect a fortified outpost of Cuba. As late as 1763, Spanish Florida had only 4,000 inhabitants of European descent.

Spain took even longer to begin the colonization of the American Southwest. It was not until 1598 that Juan de Oñate led a group of 400 soldiers, colonists, and missionaries north from Mexico to establish a permanent settlement. While searching for fabled deposits of precious metals, Oñate's nephew and fourteen soldiers were killed by inhabitants of Acoma, the "sky city" located on a high bluff in present-day New Mexico.

Juan de Oñate in New Mexico

Oñate decided to teach the local Indians a lesson. After a two-day siege, his forces scaled the seemingly impregnable heights and destroyed Acoma, killing more than 800 of its 1,500 or so inhabitants, including 300 women. Of the 600 Indians captured, the women and children were consigned to servitude in Spanish families, while adult men were punished by the cutting off of one foot. Oñate's message was plain—any Indians who resisted Spanish authority would be crushed. In 1606, however, Oñate was ordered home and punished for his treatment of New Mexico's Indians. In 1610, Spain established the capital of New Mexico at Santa Fe, the first permanent European settlement in the Southwest.

The Pueblo Revolt

In 1680, New Mexico's small and vulnerable colonist population numbered less than 3,000. Relations between the Pueblo Indians and colonial authorities had deteriorated throughout the seventeenth century, as governors, settlers, and missionaries sought to exploit the labor of an Indian population that declined from about 60,000 in 1600 to some 17,000 eighty years later. Franciscan friars worked relentlessly to convert Indians to Catholicism, often using intimidation and violence. As the Inquisition—the persecution of non-Catholics—became more and more intense in Spain, so did the friars' efforts to stamp out traditional religious ceremonies in New Mexico. At the same time, the Spanish assumed that the Indians could never unite against the colonizers. In August 1680, they were proven wrong.

Religious tensions

Little is known about the life of Popé, who became the main organizer of an uprising that aimed to drive the Spanish from the colony and restore the Indians' traditional autonomy. Under Popé's leadership, New Mexico's Indians joined in a coordinated uprising. Ironically, because

Popé

VOICES OF FREEDOM

From Bartolomé de Las Casas,
History of the Indies (1528)

Las Casas was the Dominican priest who condemned the treatment of Indians in the Spanish empire. His widely disseminated *History of the Indies* helped to establish the Black Legend of Spanish cruelty.

The Indians [of Hispaniola] were totally deprived of their freedom and were put in the harshest, fiercest, most horrible servitude and captivity which no one who has not seen it can understand. Even beasts enjoy more freedom when they are allowed to graze in the fields. But our Spaniards gave no such opportunity to Indians and truly considered them perpetual slaves, since the Indians had not the free will to dispose of their persons but instead were disposed of according to Spanish greed and cruelty, not as men in captivity but as beasts tied to a rope to prevent free movement. When they were allowed to go home, they often found it deserted and had no other recourse than to go out into the woods to find food and to die. When they fell ill, which was very frequently because they are a delicate people unaccustomed to such work, the Spaniards did not believe them and pitilessly called them lazy dogs and kicked and beat them; and when illness was apparent they sent them home as useless. . . . They would go then, falling into the first stream and dying there in desperation; others would hold on longer but very few ever made it home. I sometimes came upon dead bodies on my way, and upon others who were gasping and moaning in their death agony, repeating "Hungry, hungry." And this was the freedom, the good treatment and the Christianity the Indians received.

About eight years passed under [Spanish rule] and this disorder had time to grow; no one gave it a thought and the multitude of people who originally lived on the island . . . was consumed at such a rate that in these eight years 90 per cent had perished. From here this sweeping plague went to San Juan, Jamaica, Cuba and the continent, spreading destruction over the whole hemisphere.

Josephe was a Spanish-speaking Indian questioned by a royal attorney in Mexico City investigating the Pueblo Revolt. The revolt of the Indian population, in 1680, temporarily drove Spanish settlers from present-day New Mexico.

Asked what causes or motives the said Indian rebels had for renouncing the law of God and obedience to his Majesty, and for committing so many of crimes, [he answered] the causes they have were alleged ill treatment and injuries received from [Spanish authorities], because they beat them, took away what they had, and made them work without pay. Thus he replies.

Asked if he has learned if it has come to his notice during the time that he has been here the reason why the apostates burned the images, churches, and things pertaining to divine worship, making a mockery and a trophy of them, killing the priests and doing the other things they did, he said that he knows and had heard it generally stated that while they were besieging the villa the rebellious traitors burned the church and shouted in loud voices, "Now the God of the Spaniards, who was their father, is dead, and Santa Maria, who was their mother, and the saints, who were pieces of rotten wood," saying that only their own god lived. Thus they ordered all the temples and images, crosses and rosaries burned, and their function being over, they all went to bathe in the rivers, saying that they thereby washed away the water of baptism. For their churches, they placed on the four sides and in the center of the plaza some small circular enclosures of stone where they went to offer flour, feathers, and the seed of maguey [a local plant], maize, and tobacco, and performed other superstitious rites, giving the children to understand that they must all do this in the future. The captains and the chiefs ordered that the names of Jesus and Mary should nowhere be uttered. . . . He has seen many houses of idolatry which they have built, dancing the dance of the cachina [part of a traditional Indian religious ceremony], which this declarant has also danced. Thus he replies to the question.

> **QUESTIONS**
>
> 1. *Why does Las Casas, after describing the ill treatment of Indians, write, "And this was the freedom, the good treatment and the Christianity the Indians received"?*
>
> 2. *What role did religion play in the Pueblo Revolt?*
>
> 3. *What ideas of freedom are apparent in the two documents?*

St. Anthony and the Infant Jesus, painted on a tanned buffalo hide by a Franciscan priest in New Mexico in the early eighteenth century. This was not long after the Spanish reconquered the area, from which they had been driven by the Pueblo Revolt.

the Pueblos spoke six different languages, Spanish became the revolt's "lingua franca" (a common means of communication among persons of different linguistic backgrounds). Some 2,000 warriors destroyed isolated farms and missions, killing 400 colonists, including 21 Franciscan missionaries. Most of the Spanish survivors, accompanied by several hundred Christian Indians, made their way south out of New Mexico. Within a few weeks, a century of colonization in the area had been destroyed.

The **Pueblo Revolt** was the most complete victory for Native Americans over Europeans and the only wholesale expulsion of settlers in the history of North America. Cooperation among the Pueblo peoples, however, soon evaporated. By the end of the 1680s, warfare had broken out among several villages, even as Apache and Navajo raids continued. Popé died around 1690. In 1692, the Spanish launched an invasion that reconquered New Mexico. Some communities welcomed them back as a source of military protection. But Spain had learned a lesson. In the eighteenth century, colonial authorities adopted a more tolerant attitude toward traditional religious practices and made fewer demands on Indian labor.

THE FRENCH AND DUTCH EMPIRES

If the Black Legend inspired a sense of superiority among Spain's European rivals, the precious metals that poured from the New World into the Spanish treasury aroused the desire to match Spain's success. The establishment of Spain's American empire transformed the balance of power in the world economy. The Atlantic replaced the overland route to Asia as the major axis of global trade. During the seventeenth century, the French, Dutch, and English established colonies in North America. England's mainland colonies, to be discussed in the next chapter, consisted of agricultural settlements with growing populations whose hunger for land produced incessant conflict with native peoples. New France and

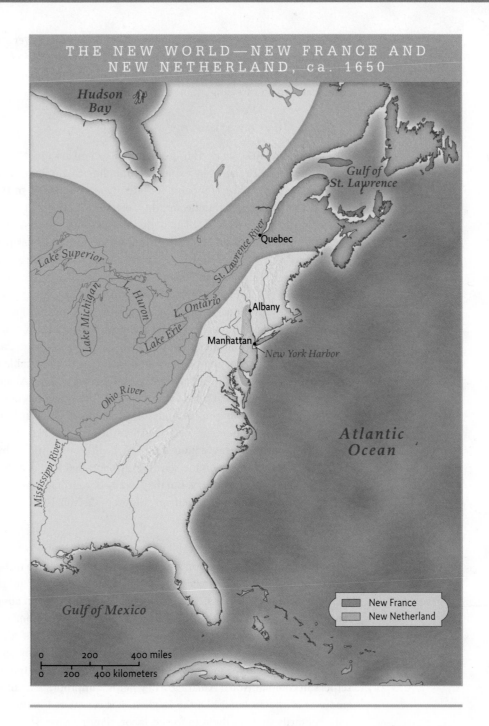

THE NEW WORLD—NEW FRANCE AND
NEW NETHERLAND, ca. 1650

Hudson
Bay

Gulf of
St. Lawrence

Lake Superior

Lake Michigan

L. Huron

L. Ontario

Lake Erie

St. Lawrence River

Quebec

Albany

Manhattan

New York Harbor

Ohio River

Mississippi River

Atlantic
Ocean

Gulf of Mexico

New France
New Netherland

| 0 | 200 | 400 miles |
| 0 | 200 | 400 kilometers |

New Netherland were primarily commercial ventures that never attracted large numbers of colonists. More dependent on Indians as trading partners and military allies, these French and Dutch settlements allowed Native Americans greater freedom than the English.

French Colonization

The first of Spain's major European rivals to embark on New World explorations was France. The explorer Samuel de Champlain, sponsored by a French fur-trading company, founded Quebec in 1608. In 1673, the Jesuit priest Jacques Marquette and the fur trader Louis Joliet located the Mississippi River, and by 1681 René-Robert Cavelier, Sieur de La Salle, had descended to the Gulf of Mexico, claiming the entire Mississippi River valley for France. New France eventually formed a giant arc along the St. Lawrence, Mississippi, and Ohio rivers.

Settlement in New France

By 1700, the number of white inhabitants of New France had risen to only 19,000. With a far larger population than England, France sent many fewer emigrants to the Western Hemisphere. The government at home feared that significant emigration would undermine France's role as a European great power and might compromise its effort to establish trade and good relations with the Indians. Unfavorable reports about America circulated widely in France. Canada was widely depicted as an icebox, a land of savage Indians, a dumping ground for criminals. Most French who left their homes during these years preferred to settle in the Netherlands, Spain, or the West Indies. The revocation in 1685 of the Edict of Nantes, which had extended religious toleration to French Protestants, led well over 100,000 Huguenots to flee their country. But they were not welcome in New France, which the crown desired to remain an outpost of Catholicism.

New France and the Indians

With its small white population and emphasis on the fur trade rather than agricultural settlement, the viability of New France depended on friendly relations with local Indians. The French prided themselves on adopting a more humane policy than their imperial rivals. "Only our nation," declared one French writer, "knows the secret of winning the Indians' affection." The French worked out a complex series of military, commercial, and diplomatic connections, the most enduring alliances between Indians and settlers in colonial North America. They neither appropriated substantial amounts of Indian land, like the English, nor conquered native inhabitants militarily and set them to forced labor, like the Spanish. Samuel de Champlain, the intrepid explorer who dominated the early history of New

Alliances with Indians

This engraving, which appears in Samuel de Champlain's 1613 account of his voyages, is the only likeness of the explorer from his own time. Champlain, wearing European armor and brandishing an arquebus (an advanced weapon of the period), stands at the center of this pitched battle between his Indian allies and the hostile Iroquois.

France, denied that Native Americans were intellectually or culturally inferior to Europeans. Although he occasionally engaged in wars with local Indians, he dreamed of creating a colony based on mutual respect between diverse peoples. The Jesuits, a missionary religious order, did seek, with some success, to convert Indians to Catholicism. But unlike Spanish missionaries in early New Mexico, they allowed Christian Indians to retain a high degree of independence and much of their traditional social structure, and they did not seek to suppress all traditional religious practices.

Jesuits

Like other colonists throughout North America, however, the French brought striking changes in Indian life. Contact with Europeans was inevitably followed by the spread of disease. Participation in the fur trade drew natives into the burgeoning Atlantic economy, introducing new goods and transforming hunting from a search for food into a quest for marketable commodities. Indians were soon swept into the rivalries among European empires.

As in the Spanish empire, New France witnessed considerable cultural exchange and intermixing between colonial and native populations. On the "middle ground" of the upper Great Lakes region in French America, Indians and whites encountered each other for many years on a basis of relative equality. And *métis*, or children of marriages between Indian women and French traders and officials, became guides, traders, and interpreters. Like the Spanish, the French seemed willing to accept Indians as part of colonial society. Indians who converted to Catholicism were promised full citizenship. In fact, however, it was far rarer for natives to adopt French ways than for French settlers to become attracted to the "free" life of the Indians. "It happens more commonly," one official complained, "that a Frenchman becomes savage than a savage becomes a Frenchman."

The middle ground

Movement between societies

The Dutch Empire

In 1609, Henry Hudson, an Englishman employed by the Dutch East India Company, sailed into New York Harbor searching for a northwest passage to Asia. Hudson and his crew became the first Europeans to sail up the river that now bears his name. Hudson did not find a route to Asia, but he did encounter abundant fur-bearing animals and Native Americans more than willing to trade furs for European goods. He claimed the area for the Netherlands, and his voyage planted the seeds of what would eventually become a great metropolis, New York City. In 1624, the Dutch West India Company, which had been awarded a monopoly of Dutch trade with America, settled colonists on Manhattan Island.

Henry Hudson

These ventures formed one small part in the rise of the Dutch overseas empire. In the early seventeenth century, the Netherlands dominated international commerce, and Amsterdam was Europe's foremost shipping and banking center. The small nation had entered a golden age of rapidly accumulating wealth and stunning achievements in painting, philosophy, and the sciences. With a population of only 2 million, the Netherlands established a far-flung empire that reached from Indonesia to South Africa and the Caribbean and temporarily wrested control of Brazil from Portugal.

Dutch trade

Dutch Freedom

The Dutch prided themselves on their devotion to liberty. Indeed, in the early seventeenth century they enjoyed two freedoms not recognized elsewhere in Europe—freedom of the press and of private religious practice. Amsterdam became a haven for persecuted Protestants from all over Europe and for Jews as well.

New Netherland

Despite the Dutch reputation for cherishing freedom, New Netherland was hardly governed democratically. New Amsterdam, the main population center, was essentially a fortified military outpost controlled by appointees of the West India Company. Although the governor called on prominent citizens for advice from time to time, neither an elected assembly nor a town council, the basic unit of government at home, was established.

In other ways, however, the colonists enjoyed more liberty than their counterparts elsewhere in North America. Even their slaves possessed rights. Some enjoyed "half-freedom"—they were required to pay an annual fee to the company and work for it when called upon, but they were given land to support their families. Settlers employed slaves on family farms or for household or craft labor, not on large plantations as in the West Indies.

Women in the Dutch settlement enjoyed far more independence than in other colonies. According to Dutch law, married women retained their

NIEUW AMSTERDAM
op t Eylant Manhattans.

A view of New Amsterdam from 1651 illustrates the tiny size of the outpost.

separate legal identity. They could go to court, borrow money, and own property. Men were used to sharing property with their wives.

New Netherland attracted a remarkably diverse population. As early as the 1630s, at least eighteen languages were said to be spoken in New Amsterdam, whose residents included not only Dutch settlers but also Africans, Belgians, English, French, Germans, Irish, and Scandinavians.

The Dutch and Religious Toleration

The Dutch long prided themselves on being uniquely tolerant in religious matters compared to other European nations and their empires. It would be wrong, however, to attribute modern ideas of religious freedom to either the Dutch government and company at home or the rulers of New Netherland. Both Holland and New Netherland had an official religion, the Dutch Reformed Church, one of the Protestant national churches to emerge from the Reformation. The Dutch commitment to freedom of conscience extended to religious devotion exercised in private, not public worship in nonestablished churches.

When Jews, Quakers, Lutherans, and others demanded the right to practice their religion openly, Governor Petrus Stuyvesant adamantly refused, seeing such diversity as a threat to a godly, prosperous order. Twenty-three Jews arrived in New Amsterdam in 1654 from Brazil and the Caribbean. Referring to them as "members of a deceitful race," Stuyvesant ordered the newcomers to leave. But the company overruled him, noting that Jews at home had invested "a large amount of capital" in its shares.

Denial of religious freedom

Nonetheless, it is true that the Dutch dealt with religious pluralism in ways quite different from the practices common in other New World empires. Religious dissent was tolerated as long as it did not involve open and public worship. No one in New Netherland was forced to attend the official church, nor was anyone executed for holding the wrong religious beliefs (as would happen in Puritan New England).

Religious pluralism

Settling New Netherland

Sparse European settlement in New Netherland

During the seventeenth century, the Netherlands sent 1 million people overseas (many of them recent immigrants who were not in fact Dutch) to populate and govern their far-flung colonies. Very few, however, made North America their destination. By the mid-1660s, the European population of New Netherland numbered only 9,000. New Netherland remained a tiny backwater in the Dutch empire. So did an even smaller outpost near present-day Wilmington, Delaware, established in 1638 by a group of Dutch merchants. To circumvent the West India Company's trade monopoly, they claimed to be operating under the Swedish flag and called their settlement New Sweden. Only 300 settlers were living there when New Netherland seized the colony in 1655.

Features of European Settlement

The Dutch came to North America to trade, not to conquer. Mindful of the Black Legend of Spanish cruelty, the Dutch determined to treat the native inhabitants more humanely than the Spanish. Having won their own independence from Spain after the longest and bloodiest war of sixteenth-century Europe, many Dutch identified with American Indians as fellow victims of Spanish oppression.

The seal of New Netherland, adopted by the Dutch West India Company in 1630, suggests the centrality of the fur trade to the colony's prospects. Surrounding the beaver is *wampum*, a string of beads used by Indians in religious rituals and as currency.

From the beginning, Dutch authorities recognized Indian sovereignty over the land and forbade settlement in any area until it had been purchased. But they also required tribes to make payments to colonial authorities. Near the coast, where most newcomers settled, New Netherland was hardly free of conflict with the Indians. With the powerful Iroquois Confederacy of the upper Hudson Valley, however, the Dutch established friendly commercial and diplomatic relations.

Thus, before the planting of English colonies in North America, other European nations had established various kinds of settlements in the New World. Despite their differences, the Spanish, French, and Dutch empires shared certain features. All brought Christianity, new forms of technology and learning, new legal systems and family relations, and new forms of economic enterprise and wealth creation. They also brought savage warfare and widespread disease. These empires were aware of one another's existence. They studied and borrowed from one another, each lauding itself as superior to the others.

From the outset, dreams of freedom—for Indians, for settlers, for the entire world through the spread of Christianity—inspired and justified colonization. It would be no different when, at the beginning of the seventeenth century, England entered the struggle for empire in North America.

CHAPTER REVIEW AND ONLINE RESOURCES

REVIEW QUESTIONS

1. Describe why the "discovery" of America was one of the "most important events recorded in the history of mankind," according to Adam Smith.

2. Describe the different global economies that Europeans participated in or created during the European age of expansion.

3. One of the most striking features of Indian societies at the time of the encounter with Europeans was their diversity. Support this statement with several examples.

4. Compare and contrast European values and ways of life with those of the Indians. Consider addressing religion, views about ownership of land, gender relations, and notions of freedom.

5. What were the main factors fueling the European age of expansion?

6. Compare the different economic and political systems of Spain, Portugal, the Netherlands, and France in the age of expansion.

7. Compare the political, economic, and religious motivations behind the French and Dutch empires with those of New Spain.

8. How would European settlers explain their superiority to Native Americans and justify both the conquest of Native lands and terminating their freedom?

KEY TERMS

Tenochtitlán (p. 3)

Cahokia (p. 5)

Iroquois (p. 7)

"Christian Liberty" (p. 12)

caravels (p. 14)

reconquista (p. 16)

Columbian Exchange (p. 19)

mestizos (p. 22)

repartimiento system (p. 24)

Black Legend (p. 24)

Pueblo Revolt (p. 30)

métis (p. 33)

wwnorton.com
/studyspace

VISIT STUDYSPACE FOR THESE
RESOURCES AND MORE

- A chapter outline
- A diagnostic chapter quiz
- Interactive maps
- Map worksheets
- Multimedia documents

1215	Magna Carta
1584	Hakluyt's *A Discourse Concerning Western Planting*
1585	Roanoke Island settlement
1607	Jamestown established
1619	First Africans arrive in Virginia
1619	House of Burgesses convenes
1620	Pilgrims found Plymouth
1622	Uprising led by Opechancanough against Virginia
1624	Virginia becomes first royal colony
1630s	Great Migration to New England
1630	Massachusetts Bay Colony founded
1632	Maryland founded
1636	Roger Williams banished from Massachusetts to Rhode Island
1637	Anne Hutchinson placed on trial in Massachusetts
1637–1638	Pequot War
1639	Fundamental Orders of Connecticut
1641	Body of Liberties
1642–1651	English Civil War
1649	Maryland adopts an Act Concerning Religion
1662	Puritans' Half-Way Covenant
1691	Virginia outlaws English-Indian marriages

CHAPTER 2

BEGINNINGS OF ENGLISH AMERICA

★

1607-1660

The Armada Portrait of Queen Elizabeth I, by the artist George Gower, commemorates the defeat of the Spanish Armada in 1588 and appears to link it with English colonization of the New World. England's victorious navy is visible through the window, while the queen's hand rests on a globe, with her fingers pointing to the coast of North America.

On April 26, 1607, three small ships carrying colonists from England sailed into the mouth of Chesapeake Bay. After exploring the area for a little over two weeks, they chose a site sixty miles inland on the James River for their settlement, hoping to protect themselves from marauding Spanish warships. Here they established Jamestown (named for the king of England) as the capital of the colony of Virginia (named for his predecessor, Elizabeth I, the "virgin queen"). But despite these bows to royal authority, the voyage was sponsored not by the English government, which in 1607 was hard-pressed for funds, but by the **Virginia Company**, a private business organization whose shareholders included merchants, aristocrats, and members of Parliament, and to which the queen had given her blessing before her death in 1603.

When the three ships returned home, 104 settlers remained in Virginia. All were men, for the Virginia Company had more interest in searching for gold and in other ways exploiting the area's natural resources than in establishing a functioning society. Nevertheless, Jamestown became the first permanent English settlement in the area that is now the United States. The settlers were the first of tens of thousands of Europeans who crossed the Atlantic during the seventeenth century to live and work in North America. They led the way for new empires that mobilized labor and economic resources, reshaped societies throughout the Atlantic world, and shifted the balance of power at home from Spain and Portugal to the nations of northwestern Europe.

English North America in the seventeenth century was a place where entrepreneurs sought to make fortunes, religious minorities hoped to worship without governmental interference and to create societies based on biblical teachings, and aristocrats dreamed of re-creating a vanished world of feudalism. For ordinary men and women, emigration offered an escape from lives of deprivation and inequality. "No man," wrote John Smith, an early leader of Jamestown, "will go from [England] to have less freedom" in America. The settlers of English America came to enjoy greater rights than colonists of other empires, including the power to choose members of elected assemblies, protections of the common law such as the right to trial by jury, and access to land, the key to economic independence. In some colonies, though by no means all, colonists enjoyed considerably more religious freedom than existed in Europe.

Many degrees of freedom coexisted in seventeenth-century North America, from the slave, stripped completely of liberty, to the independent landowner, who enjoyed a full range of rights. The settlers' success, however, rested on depriving Native Americans of their land and, in some colonies, on importing large numbers of African slaves as laborers. Freedom and lack of freedom expanded together in seventeenth-century America.

FOCUS QUESTIONS

- *What were the main contours of English colonization in the seventeenth century?*

- *What challenges did the early English settlers face?*

- *How did Virginia and Maryland develop in their early years?*

- *What made the English settlement of New England distinctive?*

- *What were the main sources of discord in early New England?*

- *How did the English Civil War affect the colonies in America?*

ENGLAND AND THE NEW WORLD

Unifying the English Nation

As the case of Spain suggests, early empire building was, in large part, an extension of the consolidation of national power in Europe. But during the sixteenth century, England was a second-rate power racked by internal disunity. Henry VIII, crowned in 1509, launched the Reformation in England. When the Pope refused to annul his marriage to Catherine of Aragon, Henry severed the nation from the Catholic Church. In its place he established the Church of England, or Anglican Church, with himself

Religious strife in England

at the head. Decades of religious strife followed, as did considerable persecution of Catholics under Henry's successor, Edward VI. In 1553, Edward's half sister Mary became queen. She temporarily restored Catholicism as the state religion and executed a number of Protestants. Mary's successor, Elizabeth I (reigned 1558–1603), restored the Anglican ascendancy and executed more than 100 Catholic priests.

England and Ireland

England's long struggle to conquer and pacify Ireland, which lasted well into the seventeenth century, absorbed money and energy that might have been directed toward the New World. In subduing Ireland, whose Catholic population was deemed a threat to the stability of Protestant rule in England, the government employed a variety of approaches, including military conquest, the slaughter of civilians, the seizure of

Subduing Ireland

land and introduction of English economic practices, and the dispatch of large numbers of settlers. Rather than seeking to absorb the Irish into English society, the English excluded the native population from a territory of settlement known as the Pale, where the colonists created their own social order.

The methods used in Ireland anticipated policies England would undertake in America. Some sixteenth-century English writers directly compared the allegedly barbaric "wild Irish" with American Indians.

England and North America

Not until the reign of Elizabeth I did the English turn their attention to North America, although sailors and adventurers still showed more interest in raiding Spanish cities and treasure fleets in the Caribbean than establishing settlements. The government granted charters (grants of exclusive rights and privileges) to Sir Humphrey Gilbert and Sir Walter Raleigh, authorizing them to establish colonies in North America at their own expense.

With little or no support from the crown, both ventures failed. Gilbert, who had earned a reputation for brutality in the Irish wars by murdering civilians and burning their crops, established a short-lived settlement on Newfoundland in 1582. Three years later, Raleigh dispatched a fleet of five ships with some 100 colonists to set up a base on **Roanoke** Island, off the North Carolina coast. But the colonists, mostly young men under military leadership, abandoned the venture in 1586 and returned to England. A second group of 100 settlers, composed of families who hoped to establish a permanent colony, was dispatched that year. Their fate remains a mystery. When a ship bearing supplies arrived in 1590, the sailors found the colony abandoned. Raleigh, by now nearly bankrupt, lost his enthusiasm for colonization. To establish a successful colony, it seemed clear, would require more planning and economic resources than any individual could provide.

The failed Roanoke settlement

Motives for Colonization

As in the case of Spain, national glory, profit, and religious mission merged in early English thinking about the New World. The Reformation heightened the English government's sense of Catholic Spain as its mortal enemy (a belief reinforced in 1588 when a Spanish naval armada unsuccessfully attempted to invade the British Isles). By the late sixteenth century, anti-Catholicism had become deeply ingrained in English popular culture. Reports of the atrocities of Spanish rule were widely circulated. English translations of Bartolomé de Las Casas's writings appeared during Elizabeth's reign.

Religion and imperial purpose

Although atrocities were hardly confined to any one nation—as England's own conduct in Ireland demonstrated—the idea that the empire of Catholic Spain was uniquely murderous and tyrannical enabled the English to describe their own imperial ambitions in the language of freedom. In *A Discourse Concerning Western Planting*, written in 1584, the Protestant minister and scholar Richard Hakluyt listed twenty-three reasons that Queen Elizabeth I should support the establishment of colonies. Among them was the idea that English settlements would strike a blow against Spain's empire and therefore form part of a divine mission to rescue the New World and its inhabitants from the influence of Catholicism and tyranny.

Richard Hakluyt

An engraving by Theodor de Bry depicts colonists hunting and fishing in Virginia. Promotional images such as this emphasized the abundance of the New World and suggested that colonists could live familiar lives there.

But bringing freedom to Indians was hardly the only motivation Hakluyt and other writers advanced. National power and glory, they argued, could be achieved through colonization. England, a relatively minor power at the end of the sixteenth century, could come to rival great nations like Spain and France.

Yet another motivation was that colonists could enrich the mother country and themselves by providing English consumers with goods now supplied by foreigners and opening a new market for English products. Unlike early adventurers such as Raleigh, who thought of wealth in terms of deposits of gold, Hakluyt insisted that trade would be the basis of England's empire.

The Social Crisis

Equally important, America could be a refuge for England's "surplus" population, benefiting mother country and emigrants alike. The late sixteenth century was a time of social crisis in England, with economic growth unable to keep pace with the needs of a population that grew from 3 million in 1550 to about 4 million in 1600. In the sixteenth and seventeenth centuries, landlords sought profits by raising sheep for the expanding trade in wool and introducing more modern farming practices such as crop rotation. They evicted small farmers and fenced in "commons" previously open to all.

While many landlords, farmers, and town merchants benefited from the **enclosure movement**, as this process was called, thousands of persons were uprooted from the land. Many flooded into England's cities. Others, denounced by authorities as rogues, vagabonds, and vagrants, wandered the roads in search of work. "All our towns," wrote the Puritan leader John Winthrop in 1629, shortly before leaving England for Massachusetts, "complain of the burden of poor people and strive by all means to rid any such as they have." England, he added somberly, "grows weary of her inhabitants."

From poverty to emigration

For years, the government struggled to deal with this social crisis, sometimes resorting to extreme measures, such as whipping or hanging the unemployed or forcing them to accept any job offered to them. Another solution was to encourage the unruly poor to leave for the New World. As colonists, they could become productive citizens, contributing to the nation's wealth.

Masterless Men

Although authorities saw wandering or unemployed "masterless men" as a danger to society, working for wages was itself widely associated with servility and loss of liberty. Only those who controlled their own labor could be regarded as truly free. Indeed, popular tales and ballads romanticized the very vagabonds, highwaymen, and even beggars denounced by the propertied and powerful, since despite their poverty they at least enjoyed freedom from wage work.

The image of the New World as a unique place of opportunity, where the English laboring classes could regain economic independence by acquiring land and where even criminals would enjoy a second chance, was deeply rooted from the earliest days of settlement. John Smith had scarcely landed in Virginia in 1607 when he wrote that in America "every man may be the master and owner of his own labor and land." The main lure for emigrants from England to the New World was not so much riches in gold and silver as the promise of independence that followed from owning land. Economic freedom and the possibility of passing it on to one's children attracted the largest number of English colonists.

The New World as a land of opportunity

THE COMING OF THE ENGLISH

English Emigrants

Seventeenth-century North America was an unstable and dangerous environment. Diseases decimated Indian and settler populations alike. Without sustained immigration, most settlements would have collapsed. With a population of between 4 million and 5 million, about half that of Spain and a quarter of that of France, England produced a far larger number of men, women, and children willing to brave the dangers of emigration to the New World. In large part, this was because economic conditions in England were so bad.

Between 1607 and 1700, more than half a million people left England. North America was not the destination of the majority of these emigrants. Approximately 180,000 settled in Ireland, and about the same number migrated to the West Indies, where the introduction of sugar cultivation promised riches for those who could obtain land. Nonetheless, the population of England's mainland colonies quickly outstripped that of their rivals. The Chesapeake area, where the tobacco-producing colonies of Virginia

A pamphlet published in 1609 promoting emigration to Virginia.

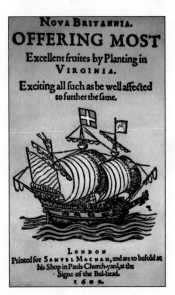

and Maryland developed a constant demand for cheap labor, received about 120,000 settlers. New England attracted 21,000 emigrants, nearly all of them arriving before 1640. In the second part of the seventeenth century, the Middle Colonies (New York, New Jersey, and Pennsylvania) attracted about 23,000 settlers. Although the arrivals to New England and the Middle Colonies included many families, the majority of newcomers were young, single men from the bottom rungs of English society, who had little to lose by emigrating.

Demographics of colonists

Indentured Servants

Settlers who could pay for their own passage—government officials, clergymen, merchants, artisans, landowning farmers, and members of the lesser nobility—arrived in America as free persons. Most quickly acquired land. In the seventeenth century, however, nearly two-thirds of English settlers came as **indentured servants**, who voluntarily surrendered their freedom for a specified time (usually five to seven years) in exchange for passage to America.

Like slaves, servants could be bought and sold, could not marry without the permission of their owner, were subject to physical punishment, and saw their obligation to labor enforced by the courts. But, unlike slaves, servants could look forward to a release from bondage. Assuming they survived their period of labor, servants would receive a payment known as "freedom dues" and become free members of society.

Slavery and indentured servitude

Given the high death rate, many servants did not live to the end of their terms. Freedom dues were sometimes so meager that they did not enable recipients to acquire land. Many servants found the reality of life in the New World less appealing than they had anticipated. Employers constantly complained of servants running away, not working diligently, or being unruly, all manifestations of what one commentator called their "fondness for freedom."

Land and Liberty

Access to land played many roles in seventeenth-century America. Land, English settlers believed, was the basis of liberty. Owning land gave men control over their own labor and, in most colonies, the right to vote. The promise of immediate access to land lured free settlers, and freedom dues that included land persuaded potential immigrants to sign contracts as indentured servants. Land in America also became a way for the king to

Landownership as the basis of liberty

reward relatives and allies. Each colony was launched with a huge grant of land from the crown, either to a company or to a private individual known as a proprietor. Some grants, if taken literally, stretched from the Atlantic Ocean to the Pacific.

Without labor, however, land would have little value. Since emigrants did not come to America intending to work the land of others (except temporarily in the case of indentured servants), the very abundance of "free" land eventually led many property owners to turn to slaves as a workforce.

Englishmen and Indians

Land in North America, of course, was already occupied. And the arrival of English settlers presented the native inhabitants of eastern North America with the greatest crisis in their history. Unlike the Spanish, English colonists were chiefly interested in displacing the Indians and settling on their land, not intermarrying with them, organizing their labor, or making them subjects of the crown. The English exchanged goods with the native population, and Indians often traveled through colonial settlements. Fur traders on the frontiers of settlement sometimes married Indian women, partly as a way of gaining access to native societies and the kin networks essential to economic relationships. Most English settlers, however, remained obstinately separate from their Indian neighbors. Moreover, the aim of converting Indians to Christianity foundered on Indian indifference to the religious disputes that racked Europe and the unavoidable reality that churches transplanted to English America had their hands full providing religious services for European colonists.

The English and Indian land

Failure of converting Indians

Despite their insistence that Indians had no real claim to the land since they did not cultivate or improve it, most colonial authorities acquired land by purchase, often in treaties forced upon Indians after they had suffered military defeat. To keep the peace, some colonial governments tried to prevent the private seizure or purchase of Indian lands, or they declared certain areas off-limits to settlers. But these measures were rarely enforced and ultimately proved ineffective. New settlers and freed servants sought land for themselves, and those who established families in America needed land for their children.

The seventeenth century was marked by recurrent warfare between colonists and Indians. These conflicts generated a strong feeling of superiority among the colonists and left them intent on maintaining the real and imagined boundaries separating the two peoples. Over time the English displaced the original inhabitants more thoroughly than any other European empire.

Recurrent warfare between colonists and Indians

The Transformation of Indian Life

Many eastern Indians initially welcomed the newcomers, or at least their goods, which they appreciated for their practical advantages. Items like woven cloth, metal kettles, iron axes, fishhooks, hoes, and guns were quickly integrated into Indian life. Indians also displayed a great desire for goods like colorful glass beads and copper ornaments that could be incorporated into their religious ceremonies.

Changes in Indian farming, hunting, and cooking practices

As Indians became integrated into the Atlantic economy, subtle changes took place in Indian life. European metal goods changed their farming, hunting, and cooking practices. Men devoted more time to hunting beaver for fur trading. Later observers would describe this trade as one in which Indians exchanged valuable commodities like furs and animal skins for worthless European trinkets. In fact, both Europeans and Indians gave up goods they had in abundance in exchange for items in short supply in their own society. But as the colonists achieved military superiority over the Indians, the profits of trade mostly flowed to colonial and European merchants. Growing connections with Europeans stimulated warfare among Indian tribes, and the overhunting of beaver and deer forced some groups to encroach on territory claimed by others. And newcomers from Europe brought epidemics that decimated Indian populations.

A drawing by the artist John White shows ten male and seven female Native Americans dancing around a circle of posts in a religious ritual. White was a careful observer of their clothing, body markings, and objects used in the ceremony.

As settlers fenced in more and more land and introduced new crops and livestock, the natural environment changed in ways that undermined traditional Indian agriculture and hunting. Pigs and cattle roamed freely, trampling Indian corn-fields and gardens. The need for wood to build and heat homes and export to England depleted forests on which Indians relied for hunting. The rapid expansion of the fur trade diminished the population of beaver and other animals. In short, Indians' lives were powerfully altered by the changes set in motion in 1607 when English colonists landed at Jamestown.

SETTLING THE CHESAPEAKE

The Jamestown Colony

The only known contemporary portrait of a New England Indian, this 1681 painting by an unnamed artist was long thought to represent Ninigret II, a leader of the Narragansetts of Rhode Island. It has been more recently identified as David, an Indian who saved the life of John Winthrop II, a governor of colonial Connecticut. Apart from the wampum beads around his neck, everything the Indian wears is of English manufacture.

The early history of Jamestown was, to say the least, not promising. The colony's leadership changed repeatedly, its inhabitants suffered an extraordinarily high death rate, and, with the Virginia Company seeking a quick profit, supplies from England proved inadequate. The first settlers were "a quarrelsome band of gentlemen and servants." They included few farmers and laborers and numerous sons of English gentry who preferred to prospect for gold rather than farm.

Disease and lack of food took a heavy toll. By the end of the first year, the original population of 104 had fallen by half. New arrivals (including the first two women, who landed in 1608) brought the numbers up to 400 in 1609, but by 1610, after a winter long remembered as the "starving time," only 65 settlers remained alive. At one point, the survivors abandoned Jamestown and sailed for England, only to be intercepted and persuaded to return to Virginia by ships carrying a new governor, 250 colonists, and supplies.

Only rigorous military discipline held the colony together. **John Smith** imposed a regime of forced labor on company lands. "He that will not work, shall not eat," Smith declared. Smith's autocratic mode of governing alienated many of the colonists. After being injured in an accidental

John Smith's iron rule

gunpowder explosion in 1609, he was forced to return to England. But his immediate successors continued his iron rule.

The Virginia Company slowly realized that for the colony to survive it would have to abandon the search for gold, grow its own food, and find a marketable commodity. It would also have to attract more settlers. With this end in view, it announced new policies in 1618. Instead of retaining all the land for itself, the company introduced the **headright system**, awarding fifty acres of land to any colonist who paid for his own or another's passage. Thus, anyone who brought in a sizable number of servants would immediately acquire a large estate. In place of the governor's militaristic regime, a "charter of grants and liberties" was issued, including the establishment of a **House of Burgesses**. When it convened in 1619, this became the first elected assembly in colonial America. Also in 1619, the first twenty blacks arrived in Virginia on a Dutch vessel. These events laid the foundation for a society that would one day be dominated economically and politically by slaveowning planters.

Powhatan and Pocahontas

When the English arrived at Jamestown, they landed in an area inhabited by some 15,000 to 25,000 Indians living in numerous small agricultural villages. Most acknowledged the rule of Wahunsonacock, a shrewd and forceful leader who had recently consolidated his authority over the region and collected tribute from some thirty subordinate tribes. Called Powhatan by the settlers after the Indian word for both his tribe and his title of paramount chief, he quickly realized the advantages of trade with the newcomers.

In the first two years of Jamestown's existence, relations with Indians were mostly peaceful and based on a fairly equal give-and-take. At one point, Smith was

By 1650, English settlement in the Chesapeake had spread well beyond the initial colony at Jamestown, as tobacco planters sought fertile land near navigable waterways.

ENGLISH SETTLEMENT IN THE CHESAPEAKE, ca. 1650

0   25   50 miles
0   25   50 kilometers

MARYLAND (1632)

NANTAUGHTACUND   ONAWMANIENT
MATTAPONI   CHICACOAN
RAPPAHANNOCK
CHICKAHOMINY   WICOCOMOCO
CUTTATOWOMEN
PAMUNKEY
VIRGINIA (1607)   CHISKIAK
APPOMATTOC
Jamestown
WEYANOCK
NANSEMOND

Chesapeake Bay

MARYLAND (1632)

ACCOHANNOCK
ACCOMAC

York R.
James R.

Roanoke R.

Roanoke Island

(1607)   Date of settlement
English settlement, ca. 1650

captured by the Indians and threatened with execution by Powhatan, only to be rescued by Pocahontas, reputedly the favorite among his many children by dozens of wives. The incident has come down in legend as an example of a rebellious, love-struck teenager defying her father. In fact, it was probably part of an elaborate ceremony designed by Powhatan to demonstrate his power over the colonists and incorporate them into his realm. Pocahontas subsequently became an intermediary between the two peoples, bringing food and messages to Jamestown. In 1614, she married the English colonist John Rolfe. Two years later, she accompanied her husband to England, where she caused a sensation in the court of James I as a symbol of Anglo-Indian harmony and missionary success. But she succumbed to disease in 1617. Her father died the following year.

The Uprising of 1622

Once it became clear that the English were interested in establishing a permanent and constantly expanding colony, not a trading post, conflict with local Indians was inevitable. In 1622, Powhatan's brother and successor, Opechancanough, led a brilliantly planned surprise attack that in a single day wiped out one-quarter of Virginia's settler population of 1,200. The surviving 900 colonists organized themselves into military bands, which then massacred scores of Indians and devastated their villages. By going to war, declared Governor Francis Wyatt, the Indians had forfeited any claim to the land. Virginia's policy, he continued, must now be nothing less than the "expulsion of the savages to gain the free range of the country."

The unsuccessful uprising of 1622 fundamentally shifted the balance of power in the colony. The settlers' supremacy was reinforced in 1644 when a last desperate rebellion led by Opechancanough, now said to be 100 years old, was crushed after causing the deaths of some 500 colonists. Virginia forced a treaty on the surviving coastal Indians, who now numbered less than 2,000, that acknowledged their subordination to the government at Jamestown and required them to move to tribal reservations to the west and not enter areas of European settlement without permission. Settlers spreading inland into the Virginia countryside continued to seize Indian lands.

The destruction caused by the **Uprising of 1622** was the last in a series of blows suffered by the Virginia Company. Two years later, it surrendered its charter and Virginia became the first royal colony, its governor now appointed by the crown. Investors had not turned a profit, and although the company had sent 6,000 settlers to Virginia, its white population

Powhatan, the most prominent Indian leader in the original area of English settlement in Virginia. This image, showing Powhatan and his court, was engraved on John Smith's map of Virginia and included in Smith's *General History of Virginia*, published in 1624.

The only portrait of Pocahontas made during her lifetime was engraved by Simon van de Passe in England in 1616. After converting to Christianity, Pocahontas took the name Rebecca.

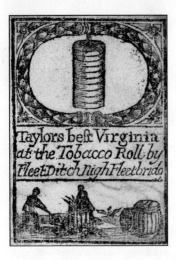

An advertisement for tobacco includes images of slaves handling barrels and tobacco plants.

Tobacco and social change in Virginia

numbered only 1,200 when the king assumed control. The government in London for years paid little attention to Virginia. Henceforth, the local elite, not a faraway company, controlled the colony's development. And that elite was growing rapidly in wealth and power thanks to the cultivation of a crop introduced from the West Indies by John Rolfe—tobacco.

A Tobacco Colony

King James I considered **tobacco** "harmful to the brain and dangerous to the lungs" and issued a spirited warning against its use. But increasing numbers of Europeans enjoyed smoking and believed the tobacco plant had medicinal benefits. Tobacco became Virginia's substitute for gold. It enriched an emerging class of tobacco planters, as well as members of the colonial government who assigned good land to themselves. The crown profited from customs duties (taxes on tobacco that entered or left the kingdom). The spread of tobacco farming produced a dispersed society with few towns and inspired a frenzied scramble for land. By the middle of the seventeenth century, a new influx of immigrants with ample financial resources—sons of merchants and English gentlemen—had taken advantage of the headright system and governmental connections to acquire large estates along navigable rivers. They established themselves as the colony's social and political elite.

The expansion of tobacco cultivation also led to an increased demand for field labor, met for most of the seventeenth century by young, male indentured servants. Despite harsh conditions of work in the tobacco fields, a persistently high death rate, and laws mandating punishments from whipping to an extension of service for those who ran away or were unruly, the abundance of land continued to attract migrants. Of the 120,000 English immigrants who entered the Chesapeake region during the seventeenth century, three-quarters came as servants. Virginia's white society increasingly came to resemble that of England, with a wealthy landed gentry at the top; a group of small farmers, mostly former indentured servants who had managed to acquire land, in the middle; and an army of poor laborers—servants and landless former indentured servants—at the bottom.

Women and the Family

Virginia, however, lacked one essential element of English society— stable family life. Given the demand for male servants to work in the tobacco fields, men in the Chesapeake outnumbered women for most

Processing tobacco was as labor intensive as caring for the plant in the fields. Here slaves and female indentured servants work with the crop after it has been harvested.

of the seventeenth century by four or five to one. The vast majority of women who emigrated to the region came as indentured servants. Since they usually had to complete their terms of service before marrying, they did not begin to form families until their mid-twenties. The high death rate, unequal ratio between the sexes, and late age of marriage retarded population growth and resulted in large numbers of single men, widows, and orphans.

In the colonies as in England, a married woman possessed certain rights before the law, including a claim to "**dower rights**" of one-third of her husband's property in the event that he died before she did. When the widow died, however, the property passed to the husband's male heirs. (English law was far less generous than in Spain, where a woman could hold independently any property inherited from her parents, and a man and wife owned jointly all the wealth accumulated during a marriage.)

Women's lives

Social conditions in the colonies, however, opened the door to roles women rarely assumed in England. A widow or one of the few women who never married could sometimes take advantage of her legal status as a femme sole (a woman alone, who enjoyed an independent legal identity denied to married women) to make contracts and conduct business. Margaret Brent, who emigrated to the Chesapeake in 1638, acquired land, managed her own plantation, and acted as a lawyer in court. But because most women came to Virginia as indentured servants, they could look forward only to a life of hard labor in the tobacco fields and early death.

The Maryland Experiment

The second Chesapeake colony, Maryland, followed a similar course of development. As in Virginia, tobacco came to dominate the economy and tobacco planters the society. But in other ways, Maryland's history was strikingly different.

Proprietary colony

Maryland was established in 1632 as a proprietary colony, that is, a grant of land and governmental authority to a single individual. This was Cecilius Calvert, the son of a recently deceased favorite of King Charles I. The charter granted him "full, free, and absolute power," including control of trade and the right to initiate all legislation, with an elected assembly confined to approving or disapproving his proposals. Although Calvert disliked representative institutions, the charter guaranteed to colonists "all privileges, franchises, and liberties" of Englishmen. While these were not spelled out, they undoubtedly included the idea of a government limited by the law. Here was a recipe for conflict, and Maryland had more than its share during the seventeenth century.

Religion in Maryland

Further aggravating instability in the colony was the fact that Calvert, a Catholic, envisioned Maryland as a refuge for his persecuted coreligionists in England, especially the younger sons of Catholic gentry who had few economic or political prospects in England. In Maryland, he hoped, Protestants and Catholics could live in a harmony unknown in Europe.

Maryland as a refuge for persecuted Catholics

Most appointed officials were Catholic, including relatives of the proprietor. But Protestants always formed a majority of the settlers. Most, as in Virginia, came as indentured servants.

As in Virginia, the death rate remained very high. Almost 70 percent of male settlers in Maryland died before reaching the age of fifty, and half the children born in the colony did not live to adulthood. But at least initially, Maryland seems to have offered servants greater opportunity for landownership than Virginia. Unlike in the older colony, freedom dues in Maryland included fifty acres of land. As tobacco planters engrossed the best land later in the century, however, the prospects for landless men diminished.

THE NEW ENGLAND WAY

The Rise of Puritanism

As Virginia and Maryland evolved toward societies dominated by a small aristocracy ruling over numerous bound laborers, a very different social order emerged in seventeenth-century New England. The early history of that region is intimately connected to the religious movement known as **"Puritanism,"** which arose in England late in the sixteenth century. The term was initially coined by opponents to ridicule those not satisfied with the progress of the Protestant Reformation in England. Puritans differed among themselves on many issues. But all shared the conviction that the Church of England retained too many elements of Catholicism in its religious rituals and doctrines. Puritans saw elaborate church ceremonies, the rule that priests could not marry, and ornate church decorations as vestiges of "popery." Many rejected the Catholic structure of religious authority descending from a pope or king to archbishops, bishops, and priests. Only independent local congregations, they believed, should choose clergymen and determine modes of worship. These Puritans were called "Congregationalists." They believed that neither the church nor the nation was living up to its ideals.

Puritanism and the Protestant Reformation in England

Puritans considered religious belief a complex and demanding matter and urged believers to seek the truth by reading the Bible and listening to sermons by educated ministers, rather than devoting themselves to sacraments administered by priests and to what Puritans considered formulaic prayers. The sermon was the central rite of Puritan practice. In the course of a lifetime, according to one estimate, the average Puritan listened to some 7,000 sermons. In their religious beliefs, Puritans followed the ideas of the French-born Swiss theologian John Calvin. The world, Calvin taught, was divided between the elect and the damned, but no one knew who was destined to be saved, which had already been determined by God. Nevertheless, leading a good life and prospering economically might be indications of God's grace, whereas idleness and immoral behavior were sure signs of damnation.

The Bible and the sermon

John Calvin

Moral Liberty

Puritanism was characterized by a zeal that alienated many who held differing religious views. A minority of Puritans (such as those who settled in Plymouth Colony) became separatists, abandoning the Church of England entirely to form their own independent churches. Most,

A portrait of John Winthrop, first governor of the Massachusetts Bay Colony, painted in the 1640s.

however, hoped to purify the church from within. But in the 1620s and 1630s, as Charles I seemed to be moving toward a restoration of Catholic ceremonies and the Church of England dismissed Puritan ministers and censored their writings, many Puritans decided to emigrate. When Puritans emigrated to New England, they hoped to escape what they believed to be the religious and worldly corruptions of English society. They would establish a "city set upon a hill," a Bible Commonwealth whose influence would flow back across the Atlantic and rescue England from godlessness and social decay.

Like so many other emigrants to America, Puritans came in search of liberty, especially the right to worship and govern themselves in what they deemed a truly Christian manner. Freedom certainly did not mean unrestrained action, improper religious practices, or sinful behavior, of which, Puritans thought, there were far too many examples in England. In a 1645 speech to the Massachusetts legislature explaining the Puritan conception of freedom, **John Winthrop**, the colony's governor, distinguished sharply between two kinds of liberty. "Natural" liberty, or acting without restraint, suggested "a liberty to do evil." This was the false idea of freedom supposedly adopted by the Irish, Indians, and bad Christians generally. Genuine **"moral" liberty** meant "a liberty to that only which is good." It was quite compatible with severe restraints on speech, religion, and personal behavior. True freedom, Winthrop insisted, depended on "subjection to authority," both religious and secular; otherwise, anarchy was sure to follow. To Puritans, liberty meant that the elect had a right to establish churches and govern society, not that others could challenge their beliefs or authority.

Freedom and subjection to authority

The Pilgrims at Plymouth

The first Puritans to emigrate to America were a group of separatists known as the **Pilgrims**. They had already fled to the Netherlands in 1608. A decade later, fearing that their children were being corrupted by the surrounding culture, they decided to emigrate to Virginia. In September 1620, the *Mayflower*, carrying 150 settlers and crew (among them many non-Puritans), embarked from England. Blown off course, they landed not in Virginia but hundreds of miles to the north, on Cape Cod. Here the 102 who survived the journey established the colony of Plymouth. Before landing, the Pilgrim leaders drew up the **Mayflower Compact**, in which the adult men going ashore agreed to obey "just and equal laws" enacted by representatives of their own choosing. This was the first written frame of government in what is now the United States.

Plymouth colony

The Pilgrims arrived in an area whose native population had recently been decimated by smallpox. They established Plymouth on the site of an abandoned Indian village whose fields had been cleared before the epidemic and were ready for cultivation. Nonetheless, the settlers arrived six weeks before winter without food or farm animals. Half died during the first winter, and the remaining colonists survived only through the help of local Indians. In the autumn of 1621, the Pilgrims invited their Indian allies to a harvest feast celebrating their survival, the first Thanksgiving.

The Pilgrims hoped to establish a society based on the lives of the early Christian saints. Their government rested on the principle of consent, and voting was not restricted to church members. All land was held in common until 1627, when it was divided among the settlers. Plymouth survived as an independent colony until 1691, but it was soon overshadowed by Massachusetts Bay to its north.

Seal of the Massachusetts Bay Colony. The Indian's scanty attire suggests a lack of civilization. His statement "Come Over and Help Us," based on an incident in the Bible, illustrates the English conviction that they were liberating the native population, rather than exploiting them as other empires had.

The Great Migration

Chartered in 1629, the Massachusetts Bay Company was founded by a group of London merchants who hoped to further the Puritan cause and turn a profit through trade with the Indians. The first five ships sailed from England in 1629, and by 1642 some 21,000 Puritans had emigrated to Massachusetts, a flow of population long remembered as the **Great Migration**. After 1640, migration to New England virtually ceased, and in some years more colonists left the region than arrived. Nonetheless, the Great Migration established the basis for a stable and thriving society.

In many ways, the settling of New England was unique. Although servants represented about one-quarter of the Great Migration, most settlers arrived in Massachusetts in families. Compared with colonists in Virginia and Maryland, they were older and more prosperous, and the number of men and women more equally balanced. Because of the even sex ratio and New England's healthier climate, the population grew rapidly, doubling every twenty-seven years. By 1700 New England's white population of 91,000 outnumbered that of both the Chesapeake and the West Indies.

A migration of families

The Puritan Family

Whatever their differences with other Englishmen on religious matters, Puritans shared with the larger society a belief in male authority within the household as well as an adherence to the common-law tradition that severely limited married women's legal and economic rights. Male authority was especially vital in America because in a farming society

Male authority in the household

The Savage Family, a 1779 painting by the New England artist Edward Savage, depicts several generations of a typically numerous Puritan family.

without large numbers of slaves or servants, control over the labor of one's family was essential to a man's economic success.

Women and Puritan religion

To be sure, Puritans deemed women to be the spiritual equals of men, and women were allowed to become full church members. Although all ministers were men, the Puritan belief in the ability of believers to interpret the Bible opened the door for some women to claim positions of religious leadership. The ideal Puritan marriage was based on reciprocal affection and companionship, and divorce was legal. Yet within the household, the husband's authority was virtually absolute.

Family and society

The family was the foundation of strong communities, and unmarried adults seemed a danger to the social fabric. The typical New England woman married at twenty-two, a younger age than her English counterpart, and gave birth seven times. Because New England was a far healthier environment than the Chesapeake, more children survived infancy. Thus, much of a woman's adult life was devoted to bearing and rearing children.

Government and Society in Massachusetts

Since Puritans feared excessive individualism and lack of social unity, the leaders of Massachusetts organized the colony in self-governing towns. Groups of settlers received a land grant from the colony's government and then subdivided it, with residents awarded house lots in a central area and land on the outskirts for farming. Much land remained in commons, either for collective use or to be divided among later settlers or the sons of the town's founders. Each town had its own Congregational Church. Each, according to a law of 1647, was required to establish a school, since the ability to read the Bible was central to Puritan belief. To train an educated ministry, Harvard College was established in 1636 (nearly a century after the Royal University of Mexico, founded in 1551), and two years later the first printing press in English America was established in Cambridge.

The New England town

Wishing to rule the colony without outside interference and to prevent non-Puritans from influencing decision making, the eight shareholders of the Massachusetts Bay Company emigrated to America, taking the charter with them and transforming a commercial document into a form of government. In 1634, a group of deputies elected by freemen (landowning church members) was added to form a single ruling body, the General Court. Ten years later, company officers and elected deputies were divided into two legislative houses. Unlike Virginia, whose governors were appointed first by a faraway company and, after 1624, by the crown, or Maryland, where authority rested with a single proprietor, the freemen of Massachusetts elected their governor.

The Massachusetts Bay Charter

The principle of consent was central to Puritanism. Churches were formed by voluntary agreement among members, who elected the

An embroidered banner depicting the main building at Harvard, the first college established in the English colonies. It was probably made by a Massachusetts woman for a husband or son who attended Harvard.

minister. No important church decision was made without the agreement of the male members. Towns governed themselves, and local officials, delegates to the General Court, and the colonial governor were all elected. Puritans, however, were hardly believers in equality. Church membership, a status that carried great prestige and power, was a restrictive category. Anyone could worship at a church, but to be a full member required demonstrating that one had experienced divine grace and could be considered a "visible saint," usually by testifying about a conversion experience. Voting in colony-wide elections was limited to men who had been accepted as full church members. Puritan democracy was for those within the circle of church membership; those outside the boundary occupied a secondary place in the Bible Commonwealth.

Church membership

Church and State in Puritan Massachusetts

Seventeenth-century New England was a hierarchical society in which socially prominent families were assigned the best land and the most desirable seats in church. Ordinary settlers were addressed as "goodman" and "goodwife," while the better sort were called "gentleman" and "lady" or "master" and "mistress." When the General Court in 1641 issued a Body of Liberties outlining the rights and responsibilities of Massachusetts colonists, it adopted the traditional understanding of liberties as privileges that derived from one's place in the social order. Inequality was considered an expression of God's will, and while some liberties, such as freedom of speech and assembly, applied to all inhabitants, there were separate lists of rights for freemen, women, children, and servants. The Body of Liberties also allowed for slavery. The first African slave appears in the records of Massachusetts Bay in 1640.

The Body of Liberties

Massachusetts forbade ministers to hold office so as not to interfere with their spiritual responsibilities. But church and state were closely interconnected. The law required each town to establish a church and to levy a tax to support the minister. Massachusetts prescribed the death penalty for, among other things, worshiping "any god, but the lord god," practicing witchcraft, or committing blasphemy.

Like many others in the seventeenth century, Puritans believed that religious uniformity was essential to social order. Thus, the church and civil government were intimately interconnected. Puritans did not believe in religious toleration—there was one truth, and their faith embodied it. Religious liberty meant the liberty to practice this truth. But the desire to give autonomy to local congregations soon clashed with the desire for religious uniformity.

Religious uniformity

NEW ENGLANDERS DIVIDED

Modern ideas of individualism, privacy, and personal freedom would have struck Puritans as quite strange. They considered too much emphasis on the "self" dangerous to social harmony and community stability. In the closely knit towns of New England, residents carefully monitored one another's behavior and chastised or expelled those who violated communal norms. Towns banished individuals for such offenses as criticizing the church or government, complaining about the colony in letters home to England, or, in the case of one individual, Abigail Gifford, for being "a very burdensome woman." Tolerance of difference was not high on the list of Puritan values.

By the mid-seventeenth century, English settlement in New England had spread well inland and up and down the Atlantic coast.

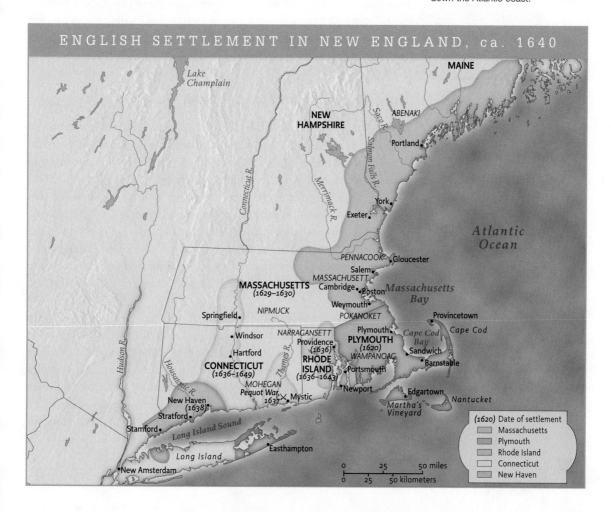

ENGLISH SETTLEMENT IN NEW ENGLAND, ca. 1640

Roger Williams

Roger Williams, New England's most prominent advocate of religious toleration.

Differences of opinion about how to organize a Bible Commonwealth, however, emerged almost from the founding of Massachusetts. With its emphasis on individual interpretation of the Bible, Puritanism contained the seeds of its own fragmentation. The first sustained criticism of the existing order came from the young minister Roger Williams, who arrived in Massachusetts in 1631 and soon began to insist that its congregations withdraw from the Church of England and that church and state be separated. Williams believed that any law-abiding citizen should be allowed to practice whatever form of religion he chose.

Williams aimed to strengthen religion, not weaken it. The embrace of government, he insisted, corrupted the purity of Christian faith and drew believers into endless religious wars like those that racked Europe. Furthermore, Williams rejected the conviction that Puritans were an elect people on a divine mission to spread the true faith. Williams denied that God had singled out any group as special favorites.

Rhode Island and Connecticut

Religious freedom in Rhode Island

Banished from Massachusetts in 1636, Williams and his followers moved south, where they established the colony of Rhode Island, which eventually received a charter from London. Rhode Island became a beacon of religious freedom. It had no established church, no religious qualifications for voting until the eighteenth century, and no requirement that citizens attend church. It became a haven for Dissenters (Protestants who belonged to denominations other than the established church) and Jews persecuted in other colonies. Rhode Island's frame of government was also more democratic. The assembly was elected twice a year, the governor annually, and town meetings were held more frequently than elsewhere in New England.

Connecticut

Religious disagreements in Massachusetts generated other colonies as well. In 1636, the minister Thomas Hooker established a settlement at Hartford. Its system of government, embodied in the Fundamental Orders of 1639, was modeled on that of Massachusetts—with the significant exception that men did not have to be church members to vote. Quite different was the colony of New Haven, founded in 1638 by emigrants who wanted an even closer connection between church and state. In 1662, Hartford and New Haven received a royal charter that united them as the colony of Connecticut.

The Trials of Anne Hutchinson

Another threat to the Puritan establishment both because of her gender and influential following was Anne Hutchinson. A midwife and the daughter of a clergyman, Hutchinson, wrote John Winthrop, was "a woman of a ready wit and bold spirit." Hutchinson began holding meetings in her home, where she led discussions of religious issues among men and women, including a number of prominent merchants and public officials. In Hutchinson's view, salvation was God's direct gift to the elect and could not be earned by good works, devotional practices, or other human effort. Most Puritans shared this belief. What set Hutchinson apart was her charge that nearly all the ministers in Massachusetts were guilty of faulty preaching for distinguishing "saints" from the damned on the basis of activities such as church attendance and moral behavior rather than an inner state of grace.

Hutchinson's criticisms of Puritan leaders

Critics denounced Hutchinson for Antinomianism (a term for putting one's own judgment or faith above both human law and the teachings of the church). In 1637, she was tried in civil court for sedition (expressing opinions dangerous to authority). An articulate woman, Hutchinson ably debated her university-educated accusers during her trial. But when she said God spoke to her directly rather than through ministers or the Bible, she violated Puritan doctrine and sealed her own fate. Such a claim, the colony's leaders felt, posed a threat to organized churches—and, indeed, to all authority. Hutchinson and a number of her followers were banished.

Hutchinson's trial

Anne Hutchinson lived in New England for only eight years, but she left her mark on the region's religious culture. As in the case of Roger Williams, her career showed how the Puritan belief in individual interpretation of the Bible could easily lead to criticism of the religious and political establishment. It would take many years before religious toleration—which violated the Puritans' understanding of "moral liberty" and social harmony—came to Massachusetts.

Significance of Anne Hutchinson

Puritans and Indians

Along with disruptive religious controversies, New England, like other colonies, had to deal with the difficult problem of relations with Indians. The native population of New England numbered perhaps 100,000 when the Puritans arrived. But because of recent epidemics, the migrants encountered fewer Indians near the coast than in other

VOICES OF FREEDOM

From "The Trial of Anne Hutchinson" (1637)

Anne Hutchinson began holding religious meetings in her home in Massachusetts in 1634. She attracted followers who believed that most ministers were not adhering strictly to Puritan theology. In 1637, she was placed on trial for sedition. In her defense, she claimed to be inspired by a revelation from God, a violation of Puritan beliefs. The examination of Hutchinson is a classic example of the clash between established power and individual conscience.

GOV. JOHN WINTHROP: Mrs. Hutchinson, you are called here as one of those that have troubled the peace of the commonwealth and the churches here; you are known to be a woman that hath had a great share in the promoting and divulging of those opinions that are the cause of this trouble, . . . and you have maintained a meeting and an assembly in your house that hath been condemned by the general assembly as a thing not tolerable nor comely on the sight of God nor fitting for your sex . . .

MRS. ANNE HUTCHINSON: That's matter of conscience, Sir.

GOV. JOHN WINTHROP: Your conscience you must keep, or it must be kept for you. . . . Your course is not to be suffered for. Besides we find such a course as this to be greatly prejudicial to the state. . . . And besides that it will not well stand with the commonwealth that families should be neglected for so many neighbors and dames and so much time spent. We see no rule of God for this. We see not that any should have authority to set up any other exercises besides what authority hath already set up . . .

MRS. ANNE HUTCHINSON: I bless the Lord, he hath let me see which was the clear ministry and which the wrong. . . . Now if you do condemn me for speaking what in my conscience I know to be truth I must commit myself unto the Lord.

MR. NOWEL (ASSISTANT TO THE COURT): How do you know that was the spirit?

MRS. ANNE HUTCHINSON: By an immediate revelation.

DEP. GOV. THOMAS DUDLEY: How! An immediate revelation. . . .

GOV. JOHN WINTHROP: Mrs. Hutchinson, the sentence of the court you hear is that you are banished from out of our jurisdiction as being a woman not fit for our society, and are to be imprisoned till the court shall send you away.

From John Winthrop,
Speech to the Massachusetts General Court
(July 3, 1645)

John Winthrop, governor of the Massachusetts Bay Colony, describes two very different definitions of liberty in this speech.

The great questions that have troubled the country, are about the authority of the magistrates and the liberty of the people. . . . Concerning liberty, I observe a great mistake in the country about that. There is a twofold liberty, natural (I mean as our nature is now corrupt) and civil or federal. The first is common to man with beasts and other creatures. By this, man, as he stands in relation to man simply, hath liberty to do what he lists; it is a liberty to do evil as well as to [do] good. This liberty is incompatible and inconsistent with authority, and cannot endure the least restraint of the most just authority. The exercise and maintaining of this liberty makes men grow more evil, and in time to be worse than brute beasts. . . . This is that great enemy of truth and peace, that wild beast, which all the ordinances of God are bent against, to restrain and subdue it.

The other kind of liberty I call civil or federal, it may also be termed moral. . . . This liberty is the proper end and object of authority, and cannot subsist without it; and it is a liberty to that only which is good, just, and honest. . . . This liberty is maintained and exercised in a way of subjection to authority; it is of the same kind of liberty wherewith Christ hath made us free. The woman's own choice makes . . . a man her husband; yet being so chosen, he is her lord, and she is to be subject to him, yet in a way of liberty, not of bondage; and a true wife accounts her subjection her honor and freedom, and would not think her condition safe and free, but in her subjection to her husband's authority. Such is the liberty of the church under the authority of Christ.

QUESTIONS

1. *To what extent does Hutchinson's being a woman play a part in the accusations against her?*

2. *Why does Winthrop consider "natural" liberty dangerous?*

3. *How do Hutchinson and Winthrop differ in their understanding of religious liberty?*

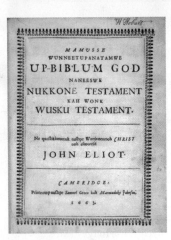

The title page of a translation of the Bible into the Massachusett language, published by John Eliot in 1663.

parts of eastern North America. In areas of European settlement, colonists quickly outnumbered the native population. Some settlers, notably Roger Williams, sought to treat the Indians with justice. Williams insisted that the king had no right to grant land already belonging to someone else. No town, said Williams, should be established before its site had been purchased. John Winthrop, on the other hand, believed uncultivated land could legitimately be taken. Although he recognized the benefits of buying land rather than simply seizing it, he insisted that such purchases require Indians to submit to English authority and pay tribute to the colonists.

To New England's leaders, the Indians represented both savagery and temptation. They enjoyed freedom but of the wrong kind—what Winthrop condemned as undisciplined "natural liberty." Puritans feared that Indian society might attract colonists who lacked the proper moral fiber. In 1642, the Connecticut General Court set a penalty of three years at hard labor for any colonist who abandoned "godly society" to live with the Indians. To counteract the attraction of Indian life, the leaders of New England also encouraged the publication of **"captivity" narratives** by those captured by Indians. The most popular was *The Sovereignty and Goodness of God* by Mary Rowlandson, who was seized with other settlers and held for three months until ransomed during an Indian war in the 1670s. Rowlandson acknowledged that she had been well treated and suffered "not the least abuse or unchastity," but her book's overriding theme was her determination to return to Christian society.

Puritans announced that they intended to bring Christian faith to the Indians, but they did nothing in the first two decades of settlement to accomplish this. They generally saw Indians as an obstacle to be pushed aside, rather than as potential converts.

The Pequot War

Conflict between Indians and New England colonists

Indians in New England lacked a paramount chief like Powhatan in Virginia. Coastal Indian tribes, their numbers severely reduced by disease, initially sought to forge alliances with the newcomers to enhance their own position against inland rivals. But as the white population expanded and new towns proliferated, conflict with the region's Indians became unavoidable. The turning point came in 1637 when a fur trader was killed by Pequots—a powerful tribe who controlled southern New England's fur trade and exacted tribute from other Indians. A force of Connecticut and Massachusetts soldiers, augmented by Narragansett allies, surrounded the main Pequot fortified village at Mystic and set it ablaze, killing those

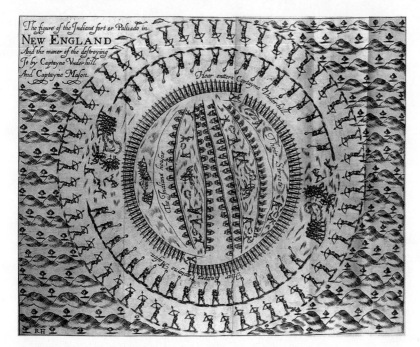

An engraving from John Underhill's *News from America*, published in London in 1638, shows the destruction of the Pequot village on the Mystic River in 1637. The colonial forces, firing guns, are aided by Indian allies with bows and arrows.

who tried to escape. Over 500 men, women, and children lost their lives in the massacre. By the end of the war a few months later, most of the Pequot had been exterminated or sold into Caribbean slavery. The treaty that restored peace decreed that their name be wiped from the historical record.

Massacre at Mystic

The colonists' ferocity shocked their Indian allies, who considered European military practices barbaric. Pilgrim leader William Bradford agreed: "It was a fearful sight to see them frying in the fire," he wrote of the raid on Mystic. But to most Puritans, the defeat of a "barbarous nation" by "the sword of the Lord" offered further proof that Indians were unworthy of sharing New England with the visible saints of the church.

The New England Economy

The leaders of the New England colonies prided themselves on the idea that religion was the primary motivation for emigration. But economic motives were hardly unimportant. One promotional pamphlet of the 1620s spoke of New England as a place "where religion and profit jump together."

Economic motivation for emigrants

Most Puritans came from the middle ranks of society and paid for their family's passage rather than indenturing themselves to labor. They sought in New England not only religious liberty but also economic advancement—if not riches, then at least a "competency," the economic independence that came with secure landownership or craft status.

Fish and timber exports

Lacking a marketable staple like sugar or tobacco, New Englanders turned to fishing and timber for exports. With very few slaves in seventeenth-century New England, most households relied on the labor of their own members, including women in the home and children in the fields. Sons remained unmarried into their mid-twenties, when they could expect to receive land from their fathers, from local authorities, or by moving to a new town.

A Growing Commercial Society

Per capita wealth in New England lagged far behind that of the Chesapeake, but it was much more equally distributed. A majority of New England families owned their own land, the foundation for a comfortable independence. Nonetheless, as in the Chesapeake, economic development produced some social inequalities. For example, on completing their terms, indentured servants rarely achieved full church membership or received grants of land. Most became disenfranchised wage earners.

New England gradually assumed a growing role within the British empire based on trade. As early as the 1640s, New England merchants shipped and marketed the staples of other colonies to markets in Europe and Africa. They engaged in a particularly profitable trade with the West Indies, whose growing slave plantations they supplied with fish, timber, and agricultural produce gathered at home. Especially in Boston, a powerful class of merchants arose who challenged some key Puritan policies, including the subordination of economic activity to the common good. As early as the 1630s, when the General Court established limits on prices and wages and gave a small group of merchants a monopoly on imports from Europe, others protested. Some left Boston to establish a new town at Portsmouth, in the region eventually chartered as the royal colony of New Hampshire. Others remained to fight, with increasing success, for the right to conduct business as they pleased. By the 1640s, Massachusetts had repealed many of its early economic regulations. Eventually, the Puritan experiment would evolve into a merchant-dominated colonial government.

Some Puritan leaders were understandably worried about their society's growing commercialization. By 1650, less than half the population of Boston had become full church members, which forced Puritan leaders to deal with the religious status of the third generation. Should they uphold the rigorous admission standards of the Congregational Church, thus limiting its size? Or should they make admission easier and remain con-

Mrs. Elizabeth Freake and Baby Mary. Painted by an anonymous artist in the 1670s, this portrait depicts the wife and daughter of John Freake, a prominent Boston merchant and lawyer. To illustrate the family's wealth, Mrs. Freake wears a triple strand of pearls, a garnet bracelet, and a gold ring, and her child wears a yellow silk dress.

nected to more people? The **Half-Way Covenant** of 1662 tried to address this problem by allowing for the baptism of and a kind of "half-way" membership for grandchildren of those who emigrated during the Great Migration. But church membership continued to stagnate.

By the 1660s and 1670s, ministers were regularly castigating the people for selfishness and a "great backsliding" from the colony's original purposes. These warnings, called "jeremiads" after the ancient Hebrew prophet Jeremiah, interpreted crop failures and disease as signs of divine disapproval and warned of further punishment to come if New Englanders did not mend their ways. Yet hard work and commercial success had always been central Puritan values. In this sense, the commercialization of New England was as much a fulfillment of the Puritan mission in America as a betrayal.

Jeremiads

RELIGION, POLITICS, AND FREEDOM

The Rights of Englishmen

Even as English emigrants began the settlement of colonies in North America, England itself became enmeshed in political and religious conflict, in which ideas of liberty played a central role. By 1600, the traditional definition of "liberties" as a set of privileges confined to one or another social group still persisted, but alongside it had arisen the idea that certain "rights of Englishmen" applied to all within the kingdom. This tradition rested on the Magna Carta (or Great Charter) of 1215. An agreement between King John and a group of barons, the Magna Carta listed a series of "liberties" granted by the king to "all the free men of our realm," a restricted group at the time, since many residents of England were serfs. The liberties mentioned in the Magna Carta included protection against arbitrary imprisonment and the seizure of one's property without due process of law.

The Magna Carta

Over time, the document came to be seen as embodying the idea of **"English freedom"**—that the king was subject to the rule of law, and that all persons should enjoy security of person and property. These rights were embodied in the common law, whose provisions, such as habeas corpus (a protection against being imprisoned without a legal charge), the right to face one's accuser, and trial by jury came to apply to all free subjects of the English crown. As serfdom slowly disappeared, the number of Englishmen considered "freeborn," and therefore entitled to these rights, expanded enormously.

Rights of "free borns"

The execution of Charles I in 1649, a central event of the English Civil War.

The English Civil War

At the beginning of the seventeenth century, when English emigrants began arriving in the New World, "freedom" still played only a minor role in England's political debates. But the political upheavals of that century elevated the notion of "English freedom" to a central place. The struggle for political supremacy between Parliament and the Stuart monarchs James I and Charles I culminated in the English Civil War of the 1640s.

The struggles of monarchy and Parliament

The leaders of the House of Commons (the elective body that, along with the hereditary aristocrats of the House of Lords, makes up the English Parliament) accused the Stuart kings of endangering liberty by imposing taxes without parliamentary consent, imprisoning political foes, and leading the nation back toward Catholicism. Civil war broke out in 1642, resulting in a victory for the forces of Parliament. In 1649, Charles I was beheaded, the monarchy abolished, and England declared "a Commonwealth and Free State"—a nation governed by the will of the people. Oliver Cromwell, the head of the victorious Parliamentary army, ruled for almost a decade after the execution of the king. In 1660, the monarchy was restored and Charles II assumed the throne. But by then, the breakdown of authority had stimulated intense discussions of liberty, authority, and what it meant to be a "freeborn Englishman."

England's Debate over Freedom

The Levellers and the Diggers

The idea of freedom suddenly took on new and expanded meanings between 1640 and 1660. The writer John Milton called for freedom of speech and of the press. New religious sects sprang up, demanding religious toleration for all Protestants as well as the end of public financing and special privileges for the Anglican Church. The Levellers, history's first democratic political movement, proposed a written constitution, the Agreement of the People, which began by proclaiming "at how high a rate we value our just freedom." Although "democracy" was still widely equated with anarchy, the document proposed to abolish the monarchy and House of Lords and to greatly expand the right to vote.

The Levellers offered a glimpse of the modern definition of freedom as a universal entitlement in a society based on equal rights, not a function of social class. Another new group, the Diggers, went even further, hoping to give freedom an economic underpinning through the common ownership of land. Previous discussion of freedom, declared Gerard Winstanley, the Diggers' leader, said that true freedom applied equally "to the poor as well as the rich"; all were entitled to "a comfortable livelihood in this their own land." Some of the ideas of liberty that flourished during the 1640s and 1650s would be carried to America by English emigrants.

Meeting of the General Council of the Army at Putney, scene of the debate in 1647 over liberty and democracy between Levellers and more-conservative army officers.

The Civil War and English America

The Civil War, accompanied by vigorous discussions of the rights of free-born Englishmen, inevitably reverberated in England's colonies, dividing them from one another and internally. Most New Englanders sided with Parliament in the Civil War of the 1640s. Some returned to England to join the Parliamentary army or take up pulpits to help create a godly common-wealth at home. But Puritan leaders were increasingly uncomfortable as the idea of religious toleration for Protestants gained favor in England.

Meanwhile, a number of followers of Anne Hutchinson became Quakers, one of the sects that sprang up in England during the Civil War. Quakers held that the spirit of God dwelled within every individual, not just the elect, and that this "inner light," rather than the Bible or teach-ings of the clergy, offered the surest guidance in spiritual matters. When Quakers appeared in Massachusetts, colonial officials had them whipped, fined, and banished. In 1659 and 1660, four Quakers who returned from exile were hanged. When Charles II, after the restoration of the monarchy in 1660, reaffirmed the Massachusetts charter, he ordered the colony to recognize the "liberty of conscience" of all Protestants.

The Quakers

In Maryland, the combination of the religious and political battles of the Civil War, homegrown conflict between Catholic and Protestant settlers, and anti-proprietary feeling produced a violent civil war within the colony, later recalled as the "plundering time." Indeed, Maryland in the 1640s verged on total anarchy, with a pro-Parliament force assaulting those loyal to Charles I.

Religious freedom in Maryland

After years of struggle between the Protestant planter class and the Catholic elite, Maryland in 1649 adopted an **Act Concerning Religion**, which institutionalized the principle of toleration that had prevailed from the colony's beginning. All Christians were guaranteed the "free exercise" of religion. Although the Act did not grant this right to non-Christians, it did, over time, bring some political stability to Maryland. The law was also a milestone in the history of religious freedom in colonial America.

Cromwell and the Empire

Oliver Cromwell, who ruled England from 1649 until his death in 1658, undertook an aggressive policy of colonial expansion, the promotion of Protestantism, and commercial empowerment in the British Isles and the Western Hemisphere. His army forcibly extended English control over Ireland, massacring civilians, banning the public practice of Catholicism, and seizing land owned by Catholics. In the Caribbean, England seized Jamaica, a valuable sugar island, from Spain.

England's colonial expansion

By the middle of the seventeenth century, several English colonies existed along the Atlantic coast of North America. Established as part of an ad hoc process rather than arising under any coherent national plan, they differed enormously in economic, political, and social structure. The seeds had been planted, in the Chesapeake, for the development of plantation societies based on unfree labor, and in New England, for settlements centered on small towns and family farms. Throughout the colonies, many residents enjoyed freedoms they had not possessed at home, especially access to land and the right to worship as they desired. Others found themselves confined to unfree labor for many years or an entire lifetime.

The next century would be a time of crisis and consolidation as the population expanded, social conflicts intensified, and Britain moved to exert greater control over its flourishing North American colonies.

CHAPTER REVIEW AND ONLINE RESOURCES

REVIEW QUESTIONS

1. *Compare and contrast settlement patterns, treatment of Indians, and religion of the Spanish and English in the Americas.*

2. *For English settlers, land was the basis of independence and liberty. Explain the reasoning behind that concept and how it differed from the Indians' conception of land.*

3. *Describe the factors promoting and limiting religious freedom in the New England and Chesapeake colonies.*

4. *Describe who chose to emigrate to North America from England in the seventeenth century and explain their reasons.*

5. *In what ways did the economy, government, and household structure differ in New England and the Chesapeake colonies?*

6. *The English believed that, unlike the Spanish, their motives for colonization were pure, and that the growth of empire and freedom would always go hand-in-hand. How did the expansion of the British empire affect the freedoms of Native Americans, the Irish, and even many English citizens?*

7. *Considering politics, social tensions, and debates over the meaning of liberty, how do the events and aftermath of the English Civil War demonstrate that the English colonies in North America were part of a larger Atlantic community?*

8. *How did the tobacco economy draw the Chesapeake colonies into the greater Atlantic World?*

KEY TERMS

Virginia Company (p. 39)

Roanoke (p. 41)

A Discourse Concerning Western Planting (p. 41)

enclosure movement (p. 42)

indentured servant (p. 44)

John Smith (p. 47)

headright system (p. 48)

House of Burgesses (p. 48)

Uprising of 1622 (p. 49)

tobacco (p. 50)

dower rights (p. 51)

Puritanism (p. 53)

John Winthrop (p. 54)

Moral liberty (p. 54)

Pilgrims (p. 54)

Mayflower Compact (p. 54)

Great Migration (p. 55)

captivity narratives (p. 64)

The Sovereignty and Goodness of God (p. 64)

Pequot War (p. 64)

Half-Way Covenant (p. 67)

English freedom (p. 67)

Act Concerning Religion (p. 70)

wwnorton.com
/studyspace

VISIT STUDYSPACE FOR THESE RESOURCES AND MORE

- A chapter outline
- A diagnostic chapter quiz
- Interactive maps
- Map worksheets
- Multimedia documents

1651	First Navigation Act issued by Parliament
1664	English seize New Netherland, which becomes New York
1670	First English settlers arrive in Carolina
1675	Lords of Trade established
1675–1676	King Philip's War
1676	Bacon's Rebellion
1677	Covenant Chain alliance
1681	William Penn granted Pennsylvania
1682	Charter of Liberty drafted by Penn
1683	Charter of Liberties and Privileges drafted by New York assembly
1686–1689	Dominion of New England
1688	Glorious Revolution in England
1689	Parliament enacts a Bill of Rights
	Maryland Protestant Association revolts
	Leisler's Rebellion
	Parliament passes Toleration Act
1691	Plymouth colony absorbed into Massachusetts
1692	Salem witch trials
1705	Virginia passes Slave Code
1715–1717	Yamasee uprising
1737	Walking Purchase

The Residence of David Twining, a painting of a Pennsylvania farm as it appeared in the eighteenth century. Edward Hicks, who had lived there as a youth, painted the scene from memory in the 1840s. Hicks depicts a prosperous farm, largely self-sufficient but also producing for the market, typical of colonial eastern Pennsylvania. One of the farm workers is a slave.

CHAPTER 3

CREATING ANGLO-AMERICA

1660–1750

In the last quarter of the seventeenth century, a series of crises rocked the European colonies of North America. Social and political tensions boiled over in sometimes ruthless conflicts between rich and poor, free and slave, settler and Indian, and members of different religious groups. At the same time, struggles within and between European empires echoed in the colonies.

The bloodiest and most bitter conflict occurred in southern New England, where in 1675 an Indian alliance launched attacks on farms and settlements that were encroaching on Indian lands. It was the most dramatic and violent warfare in the region in the entire seventeenth century.

New Englanders described the Wampanoag leader **Metacom** (known to the colonists as King Philip) as the uprising's mastermind, although in fact most tribes fought under their own leaders. By 1676, Indian forces had attacked nearly half of New England's ninety towns. Twelve in Massachusetts were destroyed. As refugees fled eastward, the line of settlement was pushed back almost to the Atlantic coast. Some 1,000 settlers, out of a population of 52,000, and 3,000 of New England's 20,000 Indians, perished in the fighting.

In mid-1676, the tide of battle turned and a ferocious counterattack broke the Indians' power once and for all. Although the uprising united numerous tribes, others remained loyal to the colonists. The role of the Iroquois in providing essential military aid to the colonists helped to solidify their developing alliance with the government of New York. Together, colonial and Indian forces inflicted devastating punishment on the rebels. Metacom was executed, Indian villages were destroyed, and captives were killed or sold into slavery in the West Indies. Both sides committed atrocities in this merciless conflict, but in its aftermath the image of Indians as bloodthirsty savages became firmly entrenched in the New England mind.

In the long run, **King Philip's War** produced a broadening of freedom for white New Englanders by expanding their access to land. But this freedom rested on the final dispossession of the region's Indians.

FOCUS QUESTIONS

- *How did the English empire in America expand in the mid-seventeenth century?*

- *How was slavery established in the Western Atlantic world?*

- *What major social and political crises rocked the colonies in the late seventeenth century?*

- *What were the directions of social and economic change in the eighteenth-century colonies?*

- *How did patterns of class and gender roles change in eighteenth-century America?*

GLOBAL COMPETITION AND THE EXPANSION OF ENGLAND'S EMPIRE

The Mercantilist System

By the middle of the seventeenth century, it was apparent that the colonies could be an important source of wealth for England. According to the prevailing theory known as "**mercantilism**," governments should regulate economic activity so as to promote national power. They should encourage manufacturing and commerce by special bounties, monopolies, and other measures. Above all, trade should be controlled so that more gold and silver flowed into countries than left them. That is, exports of goods, which generated revenue from abroad, should exceed imports, which required paying foreigners for their products. In the mercantilist outlook, the role *The role of colonies* of colonies was to serve the interests of the mother country by producing marketable raw materials and importing manufactured goods from home. "Foreign trade," declared an influential work written in 1664 by a London merchant, formed the basis of "England's treasure." Commerce, not territorial plunder, was the foundation of empire.

Parliament in 1651 passed the first **Navigation Act**, which aimed to wrest control of world trade from the Dutch, whose merchants profited from free trade with all parts of the world and all existing empires. Additional measures followed in 1660 and 1663. According to the Navigation laws, *Enumerated goods* certain "enumerated" goods—essentially the most valuable colonial products, such as tobacco and sugar—had to be transported in English ships and sold initially in English ports, although they could then be re-exported to foreign markets. Similarly, most European goods imported into the colonies had to be shipped through England, where customs duties were paid. This enabled English merchants, manufacturers, shipbuilders, and sailors to reap the benefits of colonial trade, and the government to enjoy added income from taxes. As members of the empire, American colonies would profit as well, since their ships were considered English. Indeed, the Navigation Acts stimulated the rise of New England's shipbuilding industry.

The Conquest of New Netherland

The restoration of the English monarchy when Charles II assumed the throne in 1660 sparked a new period of colonial expansion. The government chartered new trading ventures, notably the Royal African Company, which was given a monopoly of the slave trade. Within a generation, the number of English colonies in North America doubled.

First to come under English control was New Netherland, seized in 1664 during an Anglo-Dutch war that also saw England gain control of Dutch trading posts in Africa. King Charles II awarded the colony to his younger brother James, the duke of York, with "full and absolute power" to govern as he pleased. (Hence the colony's name became New York.) English rule transformed this minor military base into an important imperial outpost, a seaport trading with the Caribbean and Europe, and a launching pad for military operations against the French. New York's European population, around 9,000 when the English assumed control, rose to 20,000 by 1685.

English rule in New York

English rule expanded the freedom of some New Yorkers, while reducing that of others. The terms of surrender guaranteed that the English would respect the religious beliefs and property holdings of the colony's many ethnic communities. But English law ended the Dutch tradition by which married women conducted business in their own name and inherited some of the property acquired during marriage. There had been many female traders in New Amsterdam, but few remained by the end of the seventeenth century.

The English also introduced more restrictive attitudes toward blacks. In colonial New York City, as in New Amsterdam, those residents who enjoyed the status of "freeman," obtained by birth in the city or by an act of local authorities, enjoyed special privileges, including the right to work in various trades. But the English, in a reversal of Dutch practice, expelled free blacks from many skilled jobs.

English rule and blacks

Others benefited enormously from English rule. The duke of York and his appointed governors continued the Dutch practice of awarding immense land grants to favorites. By 1700, nearly 2 million acres of land were owned by only five New York families who intermarried regularly, exerted considerable political influence, and formed one of colonial America's most tightly knit landed elites.

New York and the Indians

Initially, English rule also strengthened the position of the Iroquois Confederacy of upstate New York. Sir Edmund Andros, who had been appointed governor of New York after fighting the French in the Caribbean, formed an alliance known as the **Covenant Chain**, in which the imperial ambitions of the English and Indians reinforced one another. The Five (later Six) Iroquois Nations assisted Andros in clearing parts of New York of rival tribes and helped the British in attacks on the French and

The Iroquois Nations

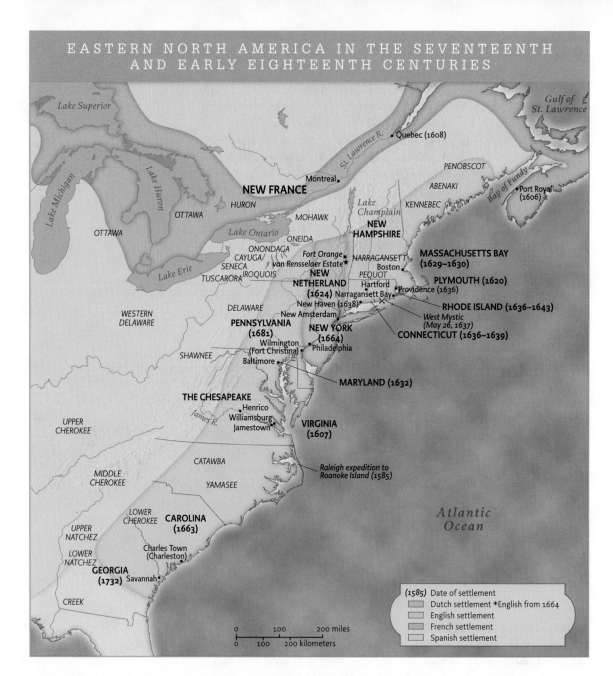

EASTERN NORTH AMERICA IN THE SEVENTEENTH AND EARLY EIGHTEENTH CENTURIES

Gulf of St. Lawrence

Lake Superior

Lake Michigan

Lake Huron

NEW FRANCE

Quebec (1608)

St. Lawrence R.

Montreal

PENOBSCOT

ABENAKI

Bay of Fundy

Port Royal (1606)

OTTAWA

HURON

MOHAWK

KENNEBEC

Lake Ontario

OTTAWA

ONONDAGA

ONEIDA

Lake Champlain

NEW HAMPSHIRE

CAYUGA

Fort Orange

NARRAGANSETT

MASSACHUSETTS BAY (1629–1630)

SENECA

van Rensselaer Estate★

Boston

Lake Erie

IROQUOIS

NEW NETHERLAND (1624)

Hartford

PLYMOUTH (1620)

TUSCARORA

New Haven (1638)

Narragansett Bay

Providence (1636)

RHODE ISLAND (1636–1643)

WESTERN DELAWARE

DELAWARE

New Amsterdam

NEW YORK (1664)

West Mystic (May 26, 1637)

CONNECTICUT (1636–1639)

PENNSYLVANIA (1681)

Wilmington (Fort Christina)

Philadelphia

SHAWNEE

Baltimore

MARYLAND (1632)

THE CHESAPEAKE

UPPER CHEROKEE

Henrico

James R.

Williamsburg

Jamestown

VIRGINIA (1607)

CATAWBA

Raleigh expedition to Roanoke Island (1585)

MIDDLE CHEROKEE

YAMASEE

Atlantic Ocean

LOWER CHEROKEE

CAROLINA (1663)

UPPER NATCHEZ

LOWER NATCHEZ

Charles Town (Charleston)

GEORGIA (1732)

Savannah

CREEK

(1585) Date of settlement
Dutch settlement *English from 1664
English settlement
French settlement
Spanish settlement

0   100   200 miles
0   100   200 kilometers

By the early eighteenth century, numerous English colonies populated eastern North America, while the French had established their own presence to the north and west.

their Indian allies. Andros, for his part, recognized the Iroquois claim to authority over Indian communities in the vast area stretching to the Ohio River. But beginning in the 1680s, Indians around the Great Lakes and Ohio Valley regrouped and with French aid attacked the Iroquois, pushing them to the east. By the end of the century, the Iroquois Nations adopted a policy of careful neutrality, seeking to play the European empires off one another while continuing to profit from the fur trade.

The Charter of Liberties

Many New York colonists, meanwhile, began to complain that they were being denied the "liberties of Englishmen," especially the right to consent to taxation. In 1683, the duke of York agreed to call an elected assembly, whose first act was to draft a Charter of Liberties and Privileges. The Charter required that elections be held every three years among male property owners and the freemen of New York City; it also reaffirmed traditional English rights such as trial by jury and security of property, as well as religious toleration for all Protestants.

English rights

The Founding of Carolina

For more than three decades after the establishment of Maryland in 1634, no new English settlement was planted in North America. Then, in 1663, Charles II awarded to eight proprietors the right to establish a colony

An engraving representing the Grand Council of the Iroquois Nations of the area of present-day upstate New York. From a book about American Indians published in Paris by a Jesuit missionary, who depicts the Indians in the attire of ancient Romans. Note the prevalence of wampum belts in the image, in the foreground and in the hand and at the feet of the central figure. Wampum was used to certify treaties and other transactions.

Carolina as a barrier to Spanish expansion

to the north of Florida, as a barrier to Spanish expansion. Not until 1670 did the first settlers arrive to found Carolina. In its early years, Carolina was the "colony of a colony," an offshoot of the tiny island of Barbados. In the mid-seventeenth century, Barbados was the Caribbean's richest plantation economy, but a shortage of available land led wealthy planters to seek opportunities in Carolina for their sons. At first, Carolinians armed friendly Indians, employing them on raids into Spanish Florida, and enslaved others, shipping them to other mainland colonies and the West Indies. Between 1670 and 1720, the number of Indian slaves exported from Charleston was larger than the number of African slaves imported. In 1715, the Yamasee and Creek rebelled, but the uprising was crushed, and most of the remaining Indians were enslaved or driven out of the colony into Spanish Florida.

The Fundamental Constitutions of Carolina

The Fundamental Constitutions of Carolina, issued by the proprietors in 1669, proposed to establish a feudal society with a hereditary nobility, serfs, and slaves. Needing to attract settlers quickly, however, the proprietors also provided for an elected assembly and religious toleration—by now recognized as essential to enticing migrants to North America. They also instituted a generous headright system, offering 150 acres for each member of an arriving family (in the case of indentured servants, of course, the land went to the employer) and 100 acres to male servants who completed their terms.

The proprietors instituted a rigorous legal code that promised slave-owners "absolute power and authority" over their human property and included imported slaves in the headright system. This allowed any persons who settled in Carolina and brought with them slaves instantly to acquire large new landholdings. In its early days, however, the economy centered on cattle raising and trade with local Indians. Carolina grew slowly until planters discovered the staple—rice—that would make them the wealthiest elite in English North America and their colony an epicenter of mainland slavery.

The Holy Experiment

The last English colony to be established in the seventeenth century was Pennsylvania in 1681. The proprietor, William Penn, envisioned it as a place where those facing religious persecution in Europe could enjoy spiritual freedom, and colonists and Indians would coexist in harmony.

William Penn

A devout member of the **Society of Friends, or Quakers**, Penn was particularly concerned with establishing a refuge for his coreligionists, who faced increasing persecution in England. He had already assisted a group of English Quakers in purchasing half of what became the colony of New Jersey from Lord John Berkeley, who had received a land grant from the duke of York. Penn was largely responsible for the frame of government announced in 1677, the West Jersey Concessions, which created an elected assembly with a broad suffrage and established religious liberty.

Like the Puritans, Penn considered his colony a "holy experiment," but of a different kind—"a free colony for all mankind that should go hither." He hoped that Pennsylvania could be governed according to Quaker principles, among them the equality of all persons (including women, blacks, and Indians) before God and the primacy of the individual conscience. To Quakers, liberty was a universal entitlement, not the possession of any single people—a position that would eventually make them the first group of whites to repudiate slavery. Penn also treated Indians with a consideration almost unique in the colonial experience, arranging to purchase land before reselling it to colonists and offering refuge to tribes driven out of other colonies by warfare. Since Quakers were pacifists who came to America unarmed and did not even organize a militia until the 1740s, peace with the native population was essential.

A Quaker Meeting, a painting by an unidentified British artist, dating from the late eighteenth or early nineteenth century. It illustrates the prominent place of women in Quaker gatherings.

Religious freedom was Penn's most fundamental principle. His Charter of Liberty, approved by the assembly in 1682, offered "Christian liberty" to all who affirmed a belief in God and did not use their freedom to promote "licentiousness." There was no established church in Pennsylvania, and attendance at religious services was entirely voluntary, although Jews were barred from office by a required oath affirming belief in the divinity of Jesus Christ. At the same time, the Quakers upheld a strict code of personal morality. Penn's Frame of Government prohibited swearing, drunkenness, and adultery. Not religious uniformity but a virtuous citizenry would be the foundation of Penn's social order.

Penn and religious liberty

Land in Pennsylvania

Given the power to determine the colony's form of government, Penn established an appointed council to originate legislation and an assembly elected by male taxpayers and "freemen" (owners of 100 acres of land for free immigrants and 50 acres for former indentured servants). These rules made a majority of the male population eligible to vote. Penn owned all the colony's land and sold it to settlers at low prices, which helped the colony prosper. Pennsylvania's religious toleration, healthy climate, and inexpensive land, along with Penn's aggressive efforts to publicize the colony's advantages, soon attracted immigrants from all over western Europe.

Freedoms in Pennsylvania

Ironically, the freedoms Pennsylvania offered to European immigrants contributed to the deterioration of freedom for others. The colony's successful efforts to attract settlers would eventually come into conflict with Penn's benevolent Indian policy. And the opening of Pennsylvania caused fewer indentured servants to choose Virginia and Maryland, a development that did much to shift those colonies toward reliance on slave labor.

ORIGINS OF AMERICAN SLAVERY

The turn to slavery

The incessant demand for workers spurred by the spread of tobacco cultivation eventually led Chesapeake planters to turn to the transatlantic trade in slaves. Compared with indentured servants, slaves offered planters many advantages. As Africans, they could not claim the protections of English common law. Slaves' terms of service never expired, and they therefore did not become a population of unruly landless men. Their children were slaves, and their skin color made it more difficult for them to escape into the surrounding society. African men, moreover, unlike their Native American counterparts, were accustomed to intensive agricultural labor, and they had encountered many diseases known in Europe and developed resistance to them, so were less likely to succumb to epidemics.

Englishmen and Africans

English views of alien peoples

The English had long viewed alien peoples with disdain, including the Irish, Native Americans, and Africans. They described these strangers in remarkably similar language as savage, pagan, and uncivilized, often comparing them to animals. "Race"—the idea that humanity is divided into well-defined groups associated with skin color—is a modern concept that had not fully developed in the seventeenth century. Nor had "racism"—an ideology based on the belief that some races are inherently superior to others and entitled to rule over them.

Nonetheless, anti-black stereotypes flourished in seventeenth-century England. Africans were seen as so alien—in color, religion, and social practices—that they were "enslavable" in a way that poor Englishmen were not. Most English also deemed Indians to be uncivilized. But the Indian population declined so rapidly, and it was so easy for Indians, familiar with the countryside, to run away, that Indian slavery never became viable in the Atlantic colonies.

Slavery in History

Slavery has existed for nearly the entire span of human history. It was central to the societies of ancient Greece and Rome. In the Mediterranean world, a slave trade in Slavic peoples survived into the fifteenth century. (The English word "slavery" derives from "Slav.") In West Africa, as noted in Chapter 1, slavery and a slave trade predated the coming of Europeans, and small-scale slavery existed among Native Americans. But slavery in nearly all these instances differed greatly from the institution that developed in the New World.

In the Americas, slavery was based on the plantation, an agricultural enterprise that brought together large numbers of workers under the control of a single owner. This imbalance magnified the possibility of slave resistance and made it necessary to police the system rigidly. Labor on slave plantations was far more demanding than the household slavery common in Africa, and the death rate among slaves much higher. In the New World, slavery would come to be associated with race, a concept that drew a permanent line between whites and blacks.

Plantation slavery

Slavery in the West Indies

A sense of Africans as alien and inferior made their enslavement by the English possible. But prejudice by itself did not create North American slavery. For this institution to take root, planters and government authorities had to be convinced that importing African slaves was the best way to solve their persistent shortage of labor. During the seventeenth century, the shipping of slaves from Africa to the New World became a major international business. By 1600, huge sugar plantations worked by slaves from Africa had made their appearance in Brazil, a colony of Portugal. In the seventeenth century, England, Holland, Denmark, and France joined Spain as owners of West Indian islands.

Sugar and slavery

With the Indian population having been wiped out by disease, and with the white indentured servants unwilling to do the back-breaking, monotonous work of sugar cultivation, the massive importation of slaves from Africa

Cutting Sugar Cane, an engraving from *Ten Views in Antigua*, published in 1823. Male and female slaves harvest and load the sugar crop while an overseer on horseback addresses a slave. During the eighteenth century, sugar was the chief crop produced by Western Hemisphere slaves.

began. On Barbados, for example, the slave population increased from 20,000 to more than 80,000 between 1660 and 1670. By the end of the seventeenth century, huge sugar plantations manned by hundreds of slaves dominated the West Indian economy, and on most of the islands the African population far outnumbered that of European origin.

Sugar was the first crop to be mass-marketed to consumers in Europe. Before its emergence, international trade consisted largely of precious metals like gold and silver, and luxury goods aimed at an elite market, like the spices and silks imported from Asia. Sugar was by far the most important product of the British, French, and Portuguese empires, and New World sugar plantations produced immense profits. Saint Domingue, today's Haiti, was the jewel of the French empire. In 1660, Barbados generated more trade than all the other English colonies combined.

Compared with its rapid introduction in Brazil and the West Indies, slavery developed slowly in North America. Slaves cost more than indentured servants, and the high death rate among tobacco workers made it economically unappealing to pay for a lifetime of labor. As late as 1680, there were only 4,500 blacks in the Chesapeake, a little over 5 percent of the region's population. The most important social distinction in the seventeenth-century Chesapeake was not between black and white but between the white plantation owners who dominated politics and society and everybody else—small farmers, indentured servants, and slaves.

Slavery and the Law

English and Spanish empires on slavery

Centuries before the voyages of Columbus, Spain had enacted a series of laws granting slaves certain rights relating to marriage, the holding of property, and access to freedom. These laws were transferred to Spain's American empire. They were often violated but nonetheless gave slaves opportunities to claim rights under the law. The law of slavery in English North America would become far more repressive than in the Spanish empire, especially on the all-important question of whether avenues existed by which slaves could obtain freedom.

For much of the seventeenth century, however, the legal status of Chesapeake blacks remained ambiguous and the line between slavery and freedom more permeable than it would later become. The first Africans, twenty in all, arrived in Virginia in 1619. Although the first black arrivals were almost certainly treated as slaves, it appears that at least some managed to become free after serving a term of years. To be sure, racial distinctions were enacted into law from the outset. As early as the 1620s, the law barred blacks from serving in the Virginia militia. In 1643, a poll tax (a tax levied on individuals) was imposed on African but not white women. In both Virginia and Maryland, however, free blacks could sue and testify in court, and some even managed to acquire land and purchase white servants or African slaves. Blacks and whites labored side by side in the tobacco fields, sometimes ran away together, and established intimate relationships.

Rights of the free blacks

The Rise of Chesapeake Slavery

Not until the 1660s did the laws of Virginia and Maryland refer explicitly to slavery. As tobacco planting spread and the demand for labor increased, the condition of black and white servants diverged sharply. Authorities sought to improve the status of white servants, hoping to counteract the widespread impression in England that Virginia was a death trap. At the same time, access to freedom for blacks receded.

A Virginia law of 1662 provided that in the case of a child one of whose parents was free and one slave, the status of the offspring followed that of the mother. (This provision not only reversed the European practice of defining a child's status through the father but also made the sexual abuse of slave women profitable for slaveholders, since any children that resulted remained the owner's property.) In 1667, the Virginia House of Burgesses decreed that religious conversion did not release a slave from bondage. Thus, Christians could own other Christians as slaves. Authorities also defined all offspring of interracial relationships as illegitimate. By 1680, even though the black population was still small, notions of racial difference were well entrenched in the law. In British North America, unlike the Spanish empire, no distinctive mulatto, or mixed-race, class existed; the law treated everyone with African ancestry as black.

Legal changes in the 1660s

Black slavery

Bacon's Rebellion: Land and Labor in Virginia

Virginia's shift from white indentured servants to African slaves as the main plantation labor force was accelerated by one of the most dramatic confrontations of this era, **Bacon's Rebellion** of 1676. Governor William

Berkeley had for thirty years run a corrupt regime in alliance with an inner circle of the colony's wealthiest tobacco planters. He rewarded his followers with land grants and lucrative offices. But as tobacco farming spread inland, planters connected with the governor engrossed the best lands, leaving freed servants (a growing population, since Virginia's death rate was finally falling) with no options but to work as tenants or to move to the frontier. By the 1670s, poverty among whites had reached levels reminiscent of England. In addition, the right to vote, previously enjoyed by all adult men, was confined to landowners in 1670. Governor Berkeley maintained peaceful relations with Virginia's remaining native population. His refusal to allow white settlement in areas reserved for Indians angered many land-hungry colonists.

Social tension in Virginia

Long-simmering social tensions coupled with widespread resentment against the injustices of the Berkeley regime erupted in Bacon's Rebellion. In 1676, after a minor confrontation between Indians and colonists on Virginia's western frontier, settlers demanded that the governor authorize the extermination or removal of the colony's Indians, to open more land for whites. When Berkeley refused, a series of Indian massacres quickly grew into a full-fledged rebellion against Berkeley and his system of rule.

Sir William Berkeley, governor of colonial Virginia, 1641–1652 and 1660–1677, in a portrait by Sir Peter Lely. Berkeley's authoritarian rule helped to spark Bacon's Rebellion.

To some extent, Bacon's Rebellion was a conflict within the Virginia elite—between Berkeley's men and the backers of Nathaniel Bacon, a wealthy and ambitious planter who disdained Berkeley's cronies. But Bacon's call for the removal of all Indians from the colony, a reduction of taxes at a time of economic recession, and an end to rule by "grandees" rapidly gained support from small farmers, landless men, indentured servants, and even some Africans. The bulk of his army consisted of discontented men who had recently been servants.

Bacon promised freedom (including access to Indian lands) to all who joined his ranks. In 1676, Bacon gathered an armed force for an unauthorized and indiscriminate campaign against those he called the governor's "protected and darling Indians." He refused Berkeley's order to disband and marched on Jamestown, burning it to the ground. The governor fled, and Bacon became the ruler of Virginia. Only the arrival of a squadron of warships from England restored order.

The specter of a civil war among whites greatly frightened Virginia's ruling elite, who took dramatic steps to consolidate their power and improve their image after Bacon's death in October 1676. They restored property qualifications for voting, which Bacon had rescinded, and reduced taxes. They also adopted a more aggressive Indian policy, opening western areas to small farmers, many of whom prospered from a rise in tobacco prices after 1680. To avert the further rise of a rebellious population of landless former indentured servants, Virginia's authorities accelerated the shift to slaves (who would never become free) on the tobacco plantations.

Effects of Bacon's Rebellion

A Slave Society

Between 1680 and 1700, slave labor began to supplant indentured servitude on Chesapeake plantations. Bacon's Rebellion contributed to this development, but so did other factors. As the death rate began to fall, it became more economical to purchase a laborer for life. Moreover, the Royal Africa Company's monopoly on the English slave trade ended, thus opening the door to other traders and reducing the price of imported African slaves.

By 1700, blacks constituted more than 10 percent of Virginia's population. Fifty years later, they made up nearly half. Recognizing the growing importance of slavery, the House of Burgesses in 1705 enacted a new **slave code**. Slaves were property, completely subject to the will of their masters and, more generally, of the white community. They could be bought and sold, leased, fought over in court, and passed on to one's descendants. Henceforth, blacks and whites were tried in separate courts. No black, free or slave, could own arms, strike a white man, or employ a white servant. Virginia had changed from a "society with slaves," in which slavery was one system of labor among others, to a "slave society," where slavery stood at the center of the economic process.

Slave code of 1705

One sentiment shared by Europeans, Native Americans, and Africans was fear of enslavement. Throughout history, slaves have run away and in other ways resisted bondage. They did the same in the colonial Chesapeake. Colonial newspapers were filled with advertisements for runaway slaves. These notices described the appearance and skills of the fugitive and included such comments as "he has great notions of freedom." After the suppression of a slave conspiracy in 1709, Alexander Spotswood, the governor of Virginia, warned planters to be vigilant. The desire for freedom, he reminded them, can "call together all those who long to shake off the fetters of slavery."

Runaway slaves

COLONIES IN CRISIS

King Philip's War of 1675 and Bacon's Rebellion the following year coincided with disturbances in other colonies. In Maryland, where the proprietor, Lord Baltimore, in 1670 had suddenly restricted the right to vote to owners of fifty acres of land or a certain amount of personal property, a Protestant uprising unsuccessfully sought to oust his government and restore the suffrage for all freemen. In several colonies, increasing settlement on the frontier led to resistance by alarmed Indians. The Pueblo Revolt of 1680 (discussed in Chapter 1) indicated that the crisis of colonial authority was not confined to the British empire.

Uprisings

The Glorious Revolution

Turmoil in England also reverberated in the colonies. In 1688, the long struggle for domination of English government between Parliament and the crown reached its culmination in the **Glorious Revolution**, which established parliamentary supremacy once and for all and secured the

Parliamentary supremacy

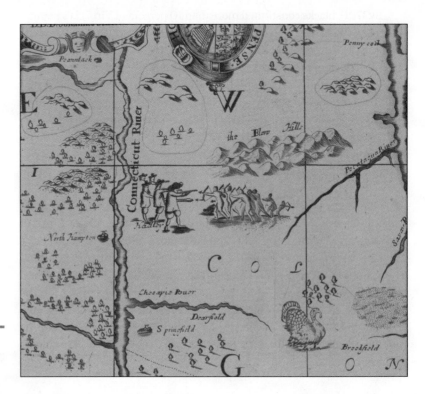

A scene from King Philip's War, included on a 1675 map of New England.

Protestant succession to the throne. Under Charles II, Parliament had asserted its authority in the formation of national policy. When Charles died in 1685, he was succeeded by his brother James II (formerly the duke of York), a practicing Catholic and a believer that kings ruled by divine right. In 1687, James decreed religious toleration for both Protestant Dissenters and Catholics. The following year, the birth of James's son raised the alarming prospect of a Catholic succession. A group of English aristocrats invited the Dutch nobleman William of Orange, the husband of James's Protestant daughter Mary, to assume the throne in the name of English liberties. As the landed elite and leaders of the Anglican Church rallied to William's cause, James II fled and the revolution was complete.

Unlike the broad social upheaval that marked the English Civil War of the 1640s, the Glorious Revolution was in effect a coup engineered by a small group of aristocrats in alliance with an ambitious Dutch prince. But the overthrow of James II entrenched more firmly than ever the notion that liberty was the birthright of all Englishmen and that the king was subject to the rule of law. To justify the ouster of James II, Parliament in 1689 enacted a **Bill of Rights**, which listed parliamentary powers such as control over taxation as well as rights of individuals, including trial by jury. In the following year, the Toleration Act allowed Protestant Dissenters (but not Catholics) to worship freely, although only Anglicans could hold public office.

Liberty as the birthright of all Englishmen

As always, British politics were mirrored in the American colonies. After the Glorious Revolution, Protestant domination was secured in most of the colonies, with the established churches of England (Anglican) and Scotland (Presbyterian) growing the fastest, while Catholics and Dissenters suffered various forms of discrimination. Throughout English America the Glorious Revolution powerfully reinforced among the colonists the sense of sharing a proud legacy of freedom and Protestantism with the mother country.

The Glorious Revolution in America

The Glorious Revolution exposed fault lines in colonial society and offered local elites an opportunity to regain authority that had recently been challenged. Until the mid-1670s, the North American colonies had essentially governed themselves, with little interference from England. Governor Berkeley ran Virginia as he saw fit; proprietors in New York, Maryland, and Carolina governed in any fashion they could persuade colonists to accept; and New England colonies elected their own officials and openly flouted trade regulations. In 1675, however, England established the

English authority and colonial autonomy

Lords of Trade to oversee colonial affairs. Three years later, the Lords questioned the Massachusetts government about its compliance with the Navigation Acts. They received the surprising reply that since the colony had no representatives in Parliament, the Acts did not apply to it unless the Massachusetts General Court approved.

In the 1680s, England moved to reduce colonial autonomy. Shortly before his death, Charles II revoked the Massachusetts charter, citing wholesale violations of the Navigation Acts. James II between 1686 and 1688 combined Connecticut, Plymouth, Massachusetts, New Hampshire, Rhode Island, New York, and East and West Jersey into a single super-colony, the **Dominion of New England**. It was ruled by the former New York governor Sir Edmund Andros, who did not have to answer to an elected assembly. These events reinforced the impression that James II was an enemy of freedom.

Rebellions in American colonies

In 1689, news of the overthrow of James II triggered rebellions in several American colonies. In April, the Boston militia seized and jailed Edmund Andros and other officials, whereupon the New England colonies reestablished the governments abolished when the Dominion of New England was created. In May, a rebel militia headed by Captain Jacob Leisler established a Committee of Safety and took control of New York. Two months later, Maryland's Protestant Association overthrew the government of the colony's Catholic proprietor, Lord Baltimore.

All of these new regimes claimed to have acted in the name of English liberties and looked to London for approval. But the degrees of success of these coups varied markedly. Concluding that Lord Baltimore had mismanaged the Maryland colony, William revoked his charter (although the proprietor retained his land and rents) and established a new, Protestant-dominated government. In 1715, after the Baltimore family had converted to Anglicanism, proprietary power was restored. But the events of 1689 transformed the ruling group in Maryland and put an end to the colony's unique history of religious toleration.

Turmoil in New York

The outcome in New York was far different. Although it was not his intention, Jacob Leisler's regime divided the colony along ethnic and economic lines. Members of the Dutch majority reclaimed local power after more than two decades of English rule, while bands of rebels ransacked the homes of wealthy New Yorkers. William refused to recognize Leisler's authority and dispatched a new governor, backed by troops. Many of Leisler's followers were imprisoned, and he himself was executed, a reflection of the hatred the rebellion had inspired. For generations, the rivalry between Leisler and anti-Leisler parties polarized New York politics.

The New England colonies, after deposing Edmund Andros, lobbied hard in London for the restoration of their original charters. Most were successful, but Massachusetts was not. In 1691, the crown issued a new charter that absorbed Plymouth into Massachusetts and transformed the political structure of the Bible Commonwealth. Town government remained intact, but henceforth property ownership, not church membership, would be the requirement to vote in elections for the General Court. The governor was now appointed in London rather than elected. Massachusetts became a royal colony, the majority of whose voters were no longer Puritan "saints." Moreover, it was required to abide by the **English Toleration Act** of 1690—that is, to allow all Protestants to worship freely.

Political change in Massachusetts

These events produced an atmosphere of considerable tension in Massachusetts, exacerbated by raids by French troops and their Indian allies on the northern New England frontier. The advent of religious toleration heightened anxieties among the Puritan clergy, who considered other Protestant denominations a form of heresy. Indeed, not a few Puritans thought they saw the hand of Satan in the events of 1690 and 1691.

The Salem Witch Trials

Belief in magic, astrology, and witchcraft was widespread in seventeenth-century Europe and America, existing alongside the religious beliefs sanctioned by the clergy and churches. Witches were individuals, usually women, who were accused of having entered into a pact with the devil to obtain supernatural powers, which they used to harm others or to interfere with natural processes. When a child was stillborn or crops failed, many believed that witchcraft was at work.

In Europe and the colonies, witchcraft was punishable by execution. It is estimated that between the years 1400 and 1800, more than 50,000 people were executed in Europe after being convicted of witchcraft. Witches were, from time to time, hanged in seventeenth-century New England. Most were women beyond childbearing age who were outspoken, economically independent, or estranged from their husbands, or who in other ways violated traditional gender norms.

Until 1692, the prosecution of witches had been sporadic. But in that year, a series of trials and executions took place in Salem that made its name to this day a byword for fanaticism and persecution. The crisis began when several young girls began to

An engraving from Ralph Gardiner's *England's Grievance Discovered*, published in 1655, depicts women hanged as witches in England. The letters identify local officials: A is the hangman, B the town crier, C the sheriff, and D a magistrate.

suffer fits and nightmares, attributed by their elders to witchcraft. Soon, three witches had been named, including Tituba, an Indian from the Caribbean who was a slave in the home of one of the girls. Since the only way to avoid prosecution was to confess and name others, accusations of witchcraft began to snowball. By the middle of 1692, hundreds of residents of Salem had come forward to accuse their neighbors. Although many of the accused confessed to save their lives, fourteen women and five men were hanged, protesting their innocence to the end.

Executions in Salem

As accusations and executions multiplied, it became clear that something was seriously wrong with the colony's system of justice. The governor of Massachusetts dissolved the Salem court and ordered the remaining prisoners released. The events in Salem discredited the tradition of prosecuting witches and encouraged prominent colonists to seek scientific explanations for natural events such as comets and illnesses, rather than attribute them to magic.

THE GROWTH OF COLONIAL AMERICA

As stability returned after the crises of the late seventeenth century, English North America experienced an era of remarkable growth. Between 1700 and 1770, crude backwoods settlements became bustling provincial capitals. The hazards of disease among colonists diminished, agricultural settlement pressed westward, and hundreds of thousands of newcomers arrived from the Old World. Thanks to a high birthrate and continuing immigration, the population of England's mainland colonies, 265,000 in 1700, grew nearly tenfold, to over 2.3 million seventy years later. (It is worth noting, however, that because of the decline suffered by the Indians, the North American population was considerably lower in 1770 than it had been in 1492.)

Population increase

A Diverse Population

Probably the most striking characteristic of colonial American society in the eighteenth century was its sheer diversity. In 1700, the colonies were essentially English outposts. In the eighteenth century, African and non-English European arrivals skyrocketed, while the number emigrating from England declined.

Surge in African and non-English arrivals

About 30 percent of European immigrants to the colonies during the eighteenth century continued to arrive as bound laborers who had

TABLE 3.1 Origins and Status of Migrants to British North American Colonies, 1700–1775

	TOTAL	SLAVES	INDENTURED SERVANTS	CONVICTS	FREE
Africa	278,400	278,400	—	—	—
Ireland	108,600	—	39,000	17,500	52,100
Germany	84,500	—	30,000	—	54,500
England/Wales	73,100	—	27,200	32,500	13,400
Scotland	35,300	—	7,400	2,200	25,700
Other	5,900	—	—	—	5,900
Total	585,800	278,400	103,600	52,200	151,600

temporarily sacrificed their freedom to make the voyage to the New World. But as the colonial economy prospered, poor indentured migrants were increasingly joined by professionals and skilled craftsmen—teachers, ministers, weavers, carpenters—whom England could ill afford to lose. This brought to an end official efforts to promote English emigration.

End of official English emigration efforts

Nevertheless, the government in London remained convinced that colonial development enhanced the nation's power and wealth. To bolster the Chesapeake labor force, nearly 50,000 convicts (a group not desired in Britain) were sent to work in the tobacco fields. Officials also actively encouraged Protestant immigration from the non-English (and less prosperous) parts of the British Isles and from the European continent, promising newcomers easy access to land and the right to worship freely.

Among eighteenth-century migrants from the British Isles, the 70,000 English newcomers were considerably outnumbered by 145,000 from Scotland and Ulster, the northern part of Ireland, where many Scots had settled as part of England's effort to subdue the island. Mostly Presbyterians, they added significantly to religious diversity in North America.

The German Migration

Germans the largest group of newcomers from Europe

Germans, 85,000 in all, formed the largest group of newcomers from the European continent. In the eighteenth century, Germany was divided into numerous small states, each with a ruling prince who determined the

VOICES OF FREEDOM

From Memorial against Non-English Immigration (December 1727)

Only a minority of emigrants from Europe to British North America in the eighteenth century came from the British Isles. Some English settlers, such as the authors of this petition from Pennsylvania to the authorities in London, found the growing diversity of the colonial population quite disturbing.

How careful every European state, that has Colonies in America, has been of preserving the advantages arising from them wholly to their own Nation and People, is obvious to all who will consider the policy & conduct of the Spanish, French & others in relation to theirs. . . .

About the year 1710 a Company of religious People called Menists [Mennonites] from the Palatinate of the Rhine, transported themselves into the Province of Pennsylvania from Holland in British shipping, and purchased Lands at low rates towards the River Susquehanna. The Terms & Reception they met with proved so encouraging, that they invited diverse of their relations and friends to follow them. In the succeeding years . . . several thousands were settled in that Province. . . . We are now assured by the same people that five or six thousand more are to follow them this next ensuing year. . . .

All these men young & old who arrived since the first, come generally very well armed. Many of them are Papists, & most of them appear inured to War & other hardships. They retire commonly back into the woods amongst or behind the remoter inhabitants, sometimes purchase land, but often sit down on any piece they find vacant that they judge convenient for them without asking questions. . . . Few of them apply now to be Naturalized, [and] they . . . generally . . . adhere to their own customs. The part of the country they principally settle in is that towards the French of Canada, whose interest, it may be apprehended, . . . (since several of them speak their language) [they] would as willingly favor as the English. . . . It is hoped therefore that nothing need be added to shew the present necessity of putting a stop to that augmentation of their strength. . . . A general provision against all Foreigners may be necessary.

From Letter by a Swiss-German Immigrant to Pennsylvania
(August 23, 1769)

Germans were among the most numerous immigrants to the eighteenth-century colonies. Many wrote letters to family members at home, relating their experiences and impressions.

Dearest Father, Brother, and Sister and Brother-in-law,

I have told you quite fully about the trip, and I will tell you what will not surprise you—that we have a free country. Of the sundry craftsmen, one may do whatever one wants. Nor does the land require payment of tithes [taxes to support a local landlord, typical in Europe]. . . . The land is very big from Canada to the east of us to Carolina in the south and to the Spanish border in the west. . . . One can settle wherever one wants without asking anyone when he buys or leases something. . . .

I have always enough to do and we have no shortage of food. Bread is plentiful. If I work for two days I earn more bread than in eight days [at home]. . . . Also I can buy many things so reasonably [for example] a pair of shoes for [roughly] seven Pennsylvania shillings. . . . I think that with God's help I will obtain land. I am not pushing for it until I am in a better position.

I would like for my brother to come . . . and it will then be even nicer in the country. . . . I assume that the land has been described to you sufficiently by various people and it is not surprising that the immigrant agents [demand payment]. For the journey is long and it costs much to stay away for one year. . . .

Johannes Hänner

QUESTIONS

1. *What do the petitioners find objectionable about non-English migrants to Pennsylvania?*

2. *What does Johannes Hänner have in mind when he calls America a "free country"?*

3. *How do these documents reflect different views of who should be entitled to the benefits of freedom in the American colonies?*

Among the most striking features of eighteenth-century colonial society was the racial and ethnic diversity of the population (except in New England). This resulted from increased immigration from the non-English parts of the British Isles and from mainland Europe, as well as the rapid expansion of the slave trade from Africa.

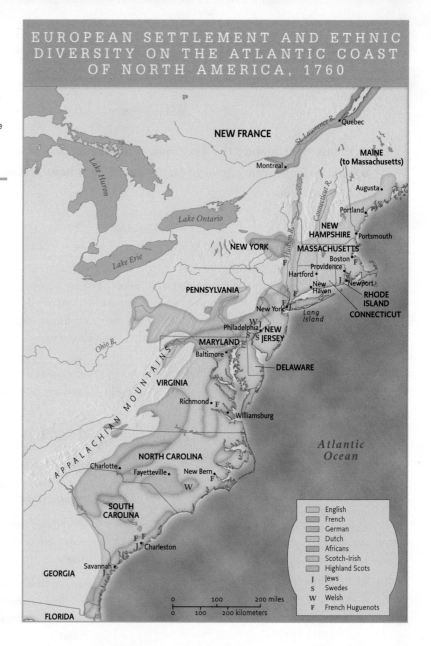

EUROPEAN SETTLEMENT AND ETHNIC DIVERSITY ON THE ATLANTIC COAST OF NORTH AMERICA, 1760

NEW FRANCE

Quebec

MAINE (to Massachusetts)

Montreal

Augusta

Portland

NEW HAMPSHIRE — Portsmouth

NEW YORK

MASSACHUSETTS

Boston

Providence

Hartford

New Haven — Newport

RHODE ISLAND

CONNECTICUT

PENNSYLVANIA

New York

Long Island

Philadelphia — NEW JERSEY

MARYLAND

Baltimore

DELAWARE

VIRGINIA

Richmond

Williamsburg

Atlantic Ocean

NORTH CAROLINA

Charlotte

Fayetteville

New Bern

SOUTH CAROLINA

Charleston

GEORGIA

Savannah

FLORIDA

Lake Huron

Lake Ontario

Lake Erie

Ohio R.

APPALACHIAN MOUNTAINS

St. Lawrence R.

Connecticut R.

Hudson R.

English
French
German
Dutch
Africans
Scotch-Irish
Highland Scots
J Jews
S Swedes
W Welsh
F French Huguenots

0   100   200 miles
0 100 200 kilometers

official religion. Those who found themselves worshiping the "wrong" religion—Lutherans in Catholic areas, Catholics in Lutheran areas, and everywhere, followers of small Protestant sects such as Mennonites, Moravians, and Dunkers—faced persecution. Many decided to emigrate.

Other migrants were motivated by persistent agricultural crises and the difficulty of acquiring land.

English and Dutch merchants created a well-organized system whereby "**redemptioners**" (as indentured families were called) received passage in exchange for a promise to work off their debt in America. Most settled in frontier areas—rural New York, western Pennsylvania, and the southern backcountry—where they formed tightly knit farming communities in which German for many years remained the dominant language.

German settlements

Religious Diversity

Eighteenth-century British America was not a "melting pot" of cultures. Ethnic groups tended to live and worship in relatively homogeneous communities. But outside of New England, which received few immigrants and retained its overwhelmingly English ethnic character, American society had a far more diverse population than Britain. Nowhere was this more evident than in the practice of religion.

Apart from New Jersey (formed from East and West Jersey in 1702), Rhode Island, and Pennsylvania, the colonies did not adhere to a modern separation of church and state. Nearly every colony levied taxes to pay the salaries of ministers of an established church, and most barred Catholics and Jews from voting and holding public office. But increasingly, de facto toleration among Protestant denominations flourished. By the mid-eighteenth century, dissenting Protestants in most colonies had gained the right to worship as they pleased and own their churches, although many places still barred them from holding public office and taxed them to support the official church. A visitor to Pennsylvania in 1750 described the colony's religious diversity: "We find there Lutherans, Reformed, Catholics, Quakers, Menonists or Anabaptists, Herrnhuters or Moravian Brethren, Pietists, Seventh Day Baptists, Dunkers, Presbyterians, . . . Jews, Mohammedans, Pagans."

William Penn's Treaty with the Indians. Penn's grandson, Thomas, the proprietor of Pennsylvania, commissioned this romanticized painting from the artist Benjamin West in 1771, by which time harmony between Indians and colonists had long since turned to hostility. In the nineteenth century, many reproductions of this image circulated, reminding Americans that Indians had once been central figures in their history.

Indian Life in Transition

The tide of newcomers, who equated liberty with secure possession of land, threatened to engulf the surviving Indian populations. By the eighteenth century, Indian societies that had existed for centuries had disappeared, the victims of disease and warfare, and the communities that remained were well integrated into the British imperial system. Indeed, Indian warriors did much of the fighting in the century's imperial wars. Few Indians chose to live among whites rather than in their own communities. But they had become well accustomed to using European products like knives, hatchets, needles, kettles, and firearms. Alcohol introduced by traders created social chaos in many Indian communities. One Cherokee told the governor of South Carolina in 1753, "The clothes we wear, we cannot make ourselves. . . . We use their ammunition with which we kill deer. . . . Every necessary thing we must have from the white people."

Indians and settlers

While traders saw in Indian villages potential profits and British officials saw allies against France and Spain, farmers and planters viewed Indians as little more than an obstruction to their desire for land. They expected Indians to give way to white settlers. In Pennsylvania, for example, the flood of German and Scotch-Irish settlers into the backcountry upset the relatively peaceful Indian-white relations constructed by William Penn. The infamous **Walking Purchase** of 1737 brought the fraudulent dealing so common in other colonies to Pennsylvania. The Lenni Lanape Indians agreed to cede a tract of land bounded by the distance a man could walk in thirty-six hours. To their amazement, Governor James Logan hired a team of swift runners, who marked out an area far in excess of what the Indians had anticipated. By 1760, when Pennsylvania's population, a mere 20,000 in 1700, had grown to 220,000, Indian-colonist relations, initially the most harmonious in British North America, had become poisoned by suspicion and hostility.

Regional Diversity

By the mid-eighteenth century, the different regions of the British colonies had developed distinct economic and social orders. Small farms tilled by family labor and geared primarily to production for local consumption predominated in New England and the new settlements of the **backcountry** (the area stretching from central Pennsylvania southward through the Shenandoah Valley of Virginia and into upland North and South

The backcountry

Carolina). The backcountry was the most rapidly growing region in North America. By the eve of the American Revolution, the region contained one-quarter of Virginia's population and half of South Carolina's. Most were farm families raising grain and livestock.

In the older portions of the Middle Colonies of New York, New Jersey, and Pennsylvania, farmers were more oriented to commerce than on the frontier. They grew grain both for their own use and for sale abroad and supplemented the work of family members by employing wage laborers, tenants, and in some instances slaves. With its fertile soil, favorable climate, initially peaceful Indian relations, generous governmental land distribution policy, and rivers that facilitated long-distance trading, Pennsylvania came to be known as "the best poor man's country." Ordinary colonists there enjoyed a standard of living unimaginable in Europe.

"The best poor man's country"

The Consumer Revolution

During the eighteenth century, Great Britain eclipsed the Dutch as the leading producer and trader of inexpensive consumer goods, including colonial products like coffee and tea, and such manufactured goods as linen, metalware, pins, ribbons, glassware, ceramics, and clothing. Trade integrated the British empire. As the American colonies were drawn more and more fully into the system of Atlantic commerce, they shared in the era's consumer revolution. In port cities and small inland towns, shops proliferated and American newspapers were filled with advertisements for British goods.

Inexpensive consumer goods

Consumerism in a modern sense—the mass production, advertising, and sale of consumer goods—did not exist in colonial America. Nonetheless, even modest farmers and artisans owned books, ceramic plates, metal cutlery, and items made of imported silk and cotton. Tea, once a luxury enjoyed only by the wealthy, became virtually a necessity of life.

This piece of china made in England and exported to New England celebrates the coronation of James II in 1685. It is an example of the growing colonial demand for English consumer goods.

Colonial Cities

Colonial cities like Boston, New York, Philadelphia, and Charleston were quite small by the standards of Europe or Spanish America. In 1700, when the population of Mexico City stood at 100,000, Boston had 6,000 residents and New York 4,500.

British North American cities were mainly gathering places for agricultural goods and for imported items to be distributed to the countryside. Nonetheless, the expansion of trade encouraged the rise of port cities, home to a growing population of colonial merchants and **artisans** (skilled craftsmen) as well as an increasing number of poor. In 1770, with some 30,000 inhabitants, Philadelphia was "the capital of the New World," at least its British component, and, after London and Liverpool, the empire's third busiest port. The financial, commercial, and cultural center of British America, Philadelphia founded its growth on economic integration with the rich agricultural region nearby. Philadelphia merchants organized the collection of farm goods, supplied rural storekeepers, and extended credit to consumers. They exported flour, bread, and meat to the West Indies and Europe.

The city was also home to a large population of furniture makers, jewelers, and silversmiths serving wealthier citizens, and hundreds of lesser artisans like weavers, blacksmiths, coopers, and construction workers. The typical artisan owned his own tools and labored in a small workshop, often his home, assisted by family members and young journeymen and apprentices learning the trade. The artisan's skill gave him a far greater degree of economic freedom than those dependent on others for a livelihood.

American craftsmen and the expanding consumer market

Despite the influx of British goods, American craftsmen benefited from the expanding consumer market. Most journeymen enjoyed a reasonable chance of rising to the status of master and establishing workshops of their own.

An Atlantic World

People, ideas, and goods flowed back and forth across the Atlantic, knitting together the empire and its diverse populations—British merchants and consumers, American colonists, African slaves, and surviving Indians—and creating webs of interdependence among the European empires. As trade expanded, the North American and West Indian colonies became the major overseas market for British manufactured goods. Although most colonial output was consumed at home, North Americans shipped

Trade in the Atlantic world

farm products to Britain, the West Indies, and with the exception of goods like tobacco "enumerated" under the Navigation Acts, outside the empire. Virtually the entire Chesapeake tobacco crop was marketed in Britain, with most of it then re-exported to Europe by British merchants. Most of the bread and flour exported from the colonies was destined for the West Indies. African slaves there grew sugar that could be distilled into rum, a product increasingly popular among both North American colonists and Indians, who obtained it by trading furs and deerskins that were then shipped to Europe. The mainland colonies carried on a flourishing trade in fish and grains with southern Europe. Ships built in New England made up one-third of the British empire's trading fleet.

Advantages of British empire

Membership in the empire had many advantages for the colonists. Most Americans did not complain about British regulation of their trade because commerce enriched the colonies as well as the mother country and lax enforcement of the Navigation Acts allowed smuggling to flourish. In a dangerous world, moreover, the Royal Navy protected American shipping.

And despite the many differences between life in England and its colonies, eighteenth-century English America drew closer to, and in some ways became more similar to, the mother country across the Atlantic.

SOCIAL CLASSES IN THE COLONIES

The Colonial Elite

Most free Americans benefited from economic growth, but as colonial society matured an elite emerged that, while neither as powerful or wealthy as the aristocracy of England, increasingly dominated politics and society. In New England and the Middle Colonies, expanding trade made possible the emergence of a powerful upper class of merchants, often linked by family or commercial ties to great trading firms in London. By 1750, the colonies of the Chesapeake and Lower South were dominated by slave plantations producing staple crops, especially tobacco and rice, for the world market. Here great planters accumulated enormous wealth. The colonial elite also included the rulers of proprietary colonies like Pennsylvania and Maryland.

Merchants, gentry, and planters

America had no titled aristocracy as in Britain. But throughout British America, men of prominence controlled colonial government. In Virginia, the upper class was so tightly knit and intermarried so often that the colony was said to be governed by a "**cousinocracy.**" Nearly every Virginian of note achieved prominence through family connections. Thomas Jefferson's grandfather was a justice of the peace (an important local official), militia captain, and sheriff, and his father was a member of the House of Burgesses. George Washington's father, grandfather, and great-grandfather had been justices of the peace. The Virginia gentry used its control of provincial government to gain possession of large tracts of land as western areas opened for settlement.

The richest group of mainland colonists were South Carolina planters. Like their Virginia counterparts, South Carolina grandees lived a lavish lifestyle amid imported furniture, fine wines, silk clothing, and other items from England. Their wealth enabled them to spend much of their

A 1732 portrait of Daniel, Peter, and Andrew Oliver, sons of a wealthy Boston merchant. The prominent display of their delicate hands tells the viewer that they have never had to do manual labor.

time enjoying the social life of Charleston, the only real urban center south of Philadelphia and the richest city in British North America.

Anglicization

For much of the eighteenth century, the American colonies had more regular trade and communications with Britain than among themselves. Rather than thinking of themselves as distinctively American, they became more and more English—a process historians call "Anglicization."

Wealthy Americans tried to model their lives on British etiquette and behavior. Somewhat resentful at living in provincial isolation—"at the end of the world," as one Virginia aristocrat put it—they sought to demonstrate their status and legitimacy by importing the latest London fashions and literature, sending their sons to Britain for education, and building homes equipped with fashionable furnishings modeled on the country estates and town houses of the English gentry.

Colonial elites and English identity

Throughout the colonies, elites emulated what they saw as England's balanced, stable social order. Liberty, in their eyes, meant, in part, the power to rule—the right of those blessed with wealth and prominence to dominate others. They viewed society as a hierarchical structure in which some men were endowed with greater talents than others and were destined to rule. Each place in the hierarchy carried with it different responsibilities, and one's status was revealed in dress, manners, and the splendor of one's home. On both sides of the Atlantic, elites viewed work as something reserved for common folk and slaves. Freedom from labor was the mark of the gentleman.

Poverty in the Colonies

At the other end of the social scale, poverty emerged as a visible feature of eighteenth-century colonial life. Although not considered by most colonists part of their society, the growing number of slaves lived in impoverished conditions. Among free Americans, poverty was hardly as widespread as in Britain, where in the early part of the century between one-quarter and one-half of the people regularly required public assistance. But as the colonial population expanded, access to land diminished rapidly, especially in long-settled areas, forcing many propertyless males to seek work in their region's cities or in other colonies.

Increase in poverty in eighteenth-century colonies

In colonial cities, the number of propertyless wage earners subsisting at the poverty line steadily increased. In Boston, one-third of the population in 1771 owned no property at all. In rural Augusta County, carved out of Virginia's Shenandoah River valley in 1738, land was quickly engrossed by planters and speculators. By the 1760s, two-thirds of the county's white men owned no land and had little prospect of obtaining it unless they migrated farther west. Taking the colonies as a whole, half of the wealth at mid-century was concentrated in the hands of the richest 10 percent of the population.

The richest 10 percent

Attitudes and policies toward poverty in colonial America mirrored British precedents. The better-off colonists generally viewed the poor as lazy, shiftless, and responsible for their own plight. To minimize the burden on taxpayers, poor persons were frequently set to labor in workhouses, where they produced goods that reimbursed authorities for part of their upkeep.

The Middle Ranks

The large majority of free Americans lived between the extremes of wealth and poverty. Along with racial and ethnic diversity, what distinguished the mainland colonies from Europe was the wide distribution of land and the economic autonomy of most ordinary free families. Altogether, perhaps two-thirds of the free male population were farmers who owned their own land.

Landownership and freedom

By the eighteenth century, colonial farm families viewed landownership almost as a right, the social precondition of freedom. They strongly resented efforts, whether by Native Americans, great landlords, or colonial governments, to limit their access to land. A dislike of personal dependence and an understanding of freedom as not relying on others for a livelihood sank deep roots in British North America.

This portrait of the Cheney family by an unknown late-eighteenth-century artist illustrates the high birthrate in colonial America and suggests how many years of a woman's life were spent bearing and raising children.

Women and the Household Economy

In the household economy of eighteenth-century America, the family was the center of economic life. The independence of the small farmer depended in considerable measure on the labor of dependent women and children. "He that hath an industrious family shall soon be rich," declared one colonial saying, and the high birthrate in part reflected the need for as many hands as possible on colonial farms.

As the population grew and the death rate declined, family life stabilized and more marriages became lifetime commitments. Free women were expected to devote their lives to being good wives and mothers. As colonial society became more structured, opportunities that had existed for women in the early period receded. In Connecticut, for example, the courts were informal and unorganized in the seventeenth century, and women often represented themselves. In the eighteenth century, it became necessary to hire a lawyer as one's spokesman in court. Women, barred from practicing as attorneys, disappeared from judicial proceedings. Because of the desperate need for labor in the seventeenth century, men and women both did various kinds of work. In the eighteenth century, the division of labor along gender lines solidified. Women's work was clearly defined, including cooking, cleaning, sewing, making butter, and assisting with agricultural chores. Even as the consumer revolution reduced the demands on many women by making available store-bought goods previously produced at home, women's work seemed to increase. Lower infant mortality meant more time spent in child care and domestic chores.

Division of labor along gender lines

North America at Mid-Century

By the mid-eighteenth century, the area that would become the United States was home to a remarkable diversity of peoples and different kinds of social organization, from Pueblo villages of the Southwest to tobacco plantations of the Chesapeake, towns and small farms of New England, and fur-trading outposts of the northern and western frontier. Elites tied to imperial centers of power dominated the political and economic life of nearly every colony. But large numbers of colonists enjoyed far greater opportunities for freedom—access to the vote, prospects of acquiring land, the right to worship as they pleased, and an escape from oppressive government—than existed in Europe. The colonies' economic growth contributed to a high birthrate, long life expectancy, and expanding demand for consumer goods.

Opportunities for freedom

Yet many others found themselves confined to the partial freedom of indentured servitude or to the complete absence of freedom in slavery. Both timeless longings for freedom and new and unprecedented forms of unfreedom had been essential to the North American colonies' remarkable development.

Freedom and unfreedom

CHAPTER REVIEW AND ONLINE RESOURCES

REVIEW QUESTIONS

1. Both the Puritans and William Penn viewed their colonies as "holy experiments." How did they differ?

2. The textbook states "Prejudice by itself did not create American slavery." Examine the economic forces, events, and laws that shaped the experiences of enslaved people.

3. How did English leaders understand the place and role of the American colonies in England's empire?

4. How did King Philip's War, Bacon's Rebellion, and the Salem witch trials illustrate a widespread crisis in British North America in the late seventeenth century?

5. The social structure of the eighteenth-century colonies was growing more open for some but not for others. Consider the statement with respect to: men and women; whites and blacks; and rich and poor.

6. By the end of the seventeenth century, commerce was the foundation of empire and the leading cause of competition between European empires. Explain how the North American colonies were directly linked to Atlantic commerce by laws and trade.

7. If you traveled from New England to the South, how would you describe the diversity you saw between the different colonies?

8. What impact did the family's being the center of economic life have on gender relations and the roles of women?

KEY TERMS

Metacom (p. 73)

King Philip's War (p. 73)

mercantilism (p. 74)

Navigation Acts (p. 74)

Covenant Chain (p. 75)

Society of Friends (Quakers) (p. 78)

sugar (p. 82)

Bacon's Rebellion (p. 83)

slave code of 1705 (p. 85)

Glorious Revolution (p. 86)

English Bill of Rights (p. 87)

Lords of Trade (p. 88)

Dominion of New England (p. 88)

English Toleration Act (p. 89)

Salem witch trials (p. 89)

redemptioners (p. 95)

Walking Purchase (p. 96)

backcountry (p. 96)

artisans (p. 97)

"cousinocracy" (p. 99)

wwnorton.com /studyspace

VISIT STUDYSPACE FOR THESE RESOURCES AND MORE

- A chapter outline
- A diagnostic chapter quiz
- Interactive maps
- Map worksheets
- Multimedia documents

1689	Locke's *Two Treatises of Government* published
1707	Act of Union creating Great Britain
1712	Slave uprising in New York City
1718	French establish New Orleans
1728	*Pennsylvania Gazette* established
1730s	Beginnings of the Great Awakening
1733	Georgia colony founded
1735	John Peter Zenger tried for libel
1739	Stono Rebellion
1791	Rumors of slave revolt in New York
1749	Virginia awards land to the Ohio Company
1754–1763	Seven Years' War
1754	Albany Plan of Union proposed
1763	Pontiac's Rebellion
	Proclamation of 1763
1764	Paxton Boys march on Philadelphia
1769	Father Serra establishes first mission in California
1789	*The Interesting Narrative of the Life of Olaudah Equiano* published

CHAPTER 4

SLAVERY, FREEDOM, AND THE STRUGGLE FOR EMPIRE

TO 1763

The Old Plantation, a late-eighteenth-century watercolor, depicts slaves dancing in a plantation's slave quarters, perhaps at a wedding. The musical instruments and pottery are African in origin while much of the clothing is of European manufacture, indicating the mixing of African and white cultures among the era's slaves. The artist has recently been identified as John Rose, owner of a rice plantation near Beaufort, South Carolina.

Sometime in the mid-1750s, Olaudah Equiano, the eleven-year-old son of a West African village chief, was kidnapped by slave traders. He soon found himself on a ship headed for Barbados. Equiano was sold to a plantation owner in Virginia and then purchased by a British sea captain, who renamed him Gustavus Vassa. While still a slave, he enrolled in a school in England where he learned to read and write, and then enlisted in the Royal Navy. In 1763, however, Equiano was sold once again and returned to the Caribbean. Three years later, he was able to purchase his freedom and went on to experience shipwrecks, a colonizing venture in Central America, and even an expedition to the Arctic Circle.

Equiano eventually settled in London, and in 1789 he published *The Interesting Narrative of the Life of Olaudah Equiano, or Gustavus Vassa, the African*, which he described as a "history of neither a saint, a hero, nor a tyrant," but of a victim of slavery who through luck or fate ended up more fortunate than most of his people. He condemned the idea that Africans were inferior to Europeans and therefore deserved to be slaves. The book became the era's most widely read account by a slave of his own experiences. Equiano died in 1797.

Recent scholars have suggested that Equiano may have been born in the New World rather than Africa. In either case, while his life was no doubt unusual, it illuminates broad patterns of eighteenth-century American history. As noted in the previous chapter, this was a period of sustained development for British North America. Compared with England and Scotland—united to create Great Britain by the Act of Union of 1707—the colonies were growing much more rapidly.

Ideas, people, and goods flowed back and forth across the ocean. Even as the colonies' populations became more diverse, they were increasingly integrated into the British empire. Their laws and political institutions were extensions of those of Britain, their ideas about society and culture reflected British values, their economies were geared to serving the empire's needs.

Equiano's life also underscores the greatest irony in the history of the eighteenth century—the simultaneous expansion of freedom and slavery. This was the era when the idea of the "freeborn Englishman" became powerfully entrenched in the outlook of both colonists and Britons. More than any other principle, liberty was seen as what made the British empire distinct. Yet the eighteenth century was also the height of the Atlantic slave trade, a commerce increasingly dominated by British merchants and ships. Although concentrated in the Chesapeake

FOCUS QUESTIONS

- *How did African slavery differ regionally in eighteenth-century North America?*

- *What factors led to distinct African-American cultures in the eighteenth century?*

- *What were the meanings of British liberty in the eighteenth century?*

- *What concepts and institutions dominated colonial politics in the eighteenth century?*

- *How did the Great Awakening challenge the religious and social structure of British North America?*

- *How did the Spanish and French empires in America develop in the eighteenth century?*

- *What was the impact of the Seven Years' War on imperial and Indian–white relations?*

The frontispiece of Olaudah Equiano's account of his life, the best-known narrative by an eighteenth-century slave. The portrait of Equiano in European dress and holding a Bible challenges stereotypes of blacks as "savages" incapable of becoming civilized.

Triangular trade routes

and areas farther south, slavery existed in every colony of British North America. And unlike Equiano, very few slaves were fortunate enough to gain their freedom.

SLAVERY AND EMPIRE

Of the estimated 7.7 million Africans transported to the New World between 1492 and 1820, more than half arrived between 1700 and 1800. The **Atlantic slave trade** would later be condemned by statesmen and general opinion as a crime against humanity. But in the eighteenth century, it was a regularized business in which European merchants, African traders, and American planters engaged in complex bargaining over human lives, all with the expectation of securing a profit. The slave trade was a vital part of world commerce.

In the British empire of the eighteenth century, free laborers working for wages were atypical and slavery was the norm. The first mass consumer goods in international trade were produced by slaves—sugar, rice, coffee, and tobacco. The rising demand for these products fueled the rapid growth of the Atlantic slave trade.

Atlantic Trade

In the eighteenth century, the Caribbean remained the commercial focus of the British empire and the major producer of revenue for the crown. A series of triangular trading routes crisscrossed the Atlantic, carrying British manufactured goods to Africa and the colonies, colonial products including tobacco, indigo, sugar, and rice to Europe, and slaves from Africa to the New World. Most colonial vessels, however, went back and forth between cities like New York, Charleston, and Savannah, and to ports in the Caribbean. Merchants in New York, Massachusetts, and Rhode Island participated actively in the slave trade, shipping slaves from Africa to the Caribbean or southern colonies. The slave economies of the West Indies were the largest market for fish, grain, livestock, and lumber exported from New England and the Middle Colonies. In Britain itself, the profits from slavery and the slave trade stimulated the rise of ports like Liverpool and Bristol and the growth of banking, shipbuilding, and insurance. They also helped to finance the early industrial revolution.

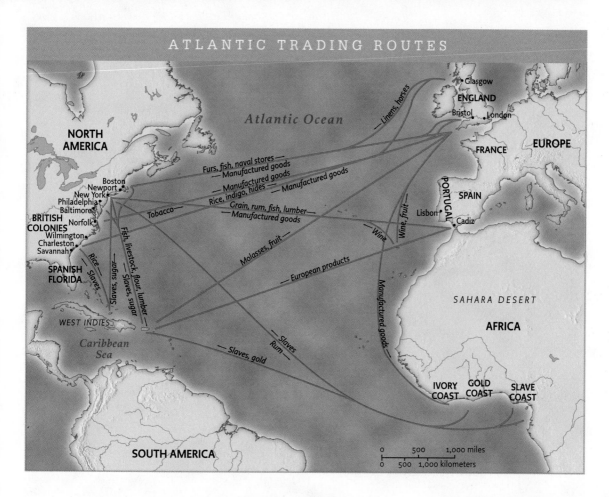

ATLANTIC TRADING ROUTES

Atlantic Ocean

- Glasgow
- **ENGLAND**
- Bristol • London

Linens, horses

NORTH AMERICA

FRANCE **EUROPE**

Furs, fish, naval stores —
— Manufactured goods
— Manufactured goods
Rice, indigo, hides — Manufactured goods
— Grain, rum, fish, lumber —
— Manufactured goods

Boston
Newport •
New York •
Philadelphia •
Baltimore •
BRITISH COLONIES Norfolk •
Wilmington •
Charleston •
Savannah •

Tobacco

SPAIN

PORTUGAL
Lisbon •
• Cadiz

Wine, fruit

Wine

Molasses, fruit

European products

Manufactured goods

SAHARA DESERT

AFRICA

SPANISH FLORIDA

Rice
Slaves
Fish, livestock, flour, lumber
Slaves, sugar

WEST INDIES

Slaves, gold

Slaves
Rum

Caribbean Sea

IVORY COAST **GOLD COAST** **SLAVE COAST**

SOUTH AMERICA

| 0 | 500 | 1,000 miles |
| 0 | 500 | 1,000 kilometers |

A series of trading routes crisscrossed the Atlantic, bringing manufactured goods to Africa and Britain's American colonies, slaves to the New World, and colonial products to Europe.

With slavery so central to Atlantic commerce, it should not be surprising that for large numbers of free colonists and Europeans, freedom meant in part the power and right to enslave others. And as slavery became more and more entrenched, so too, as the Quaker abolitionist John Woolman commented in 1762, did "the idea of slavery being connected with the black color, and liberty with the white."

Africa and the Slave Trade

A few African societies, like Benin for a time, opted out of the Atlantic slave trade, hoping to avoid the disruptions it inevitably caused. But most African rulers took part, and they proved quite adept at playing

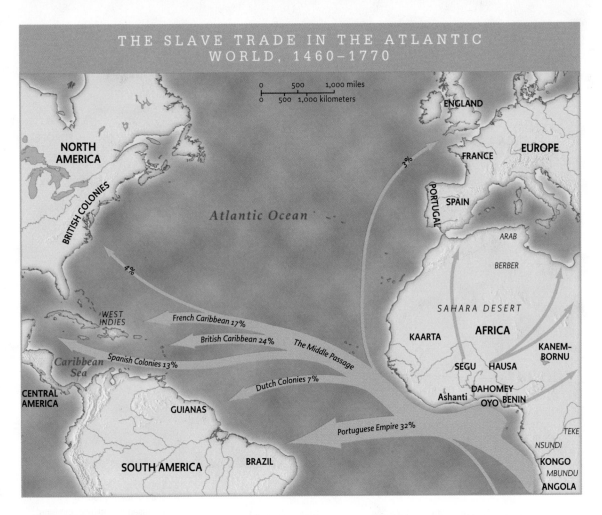

THE SLAVE TRADE IN THE ATLANTIC WORLD, 1460–1770

ENGLAND

NORTH AMERICA

FRANCE

EUROPE

BRITISH COLONIES

Atlantic Ocean

3%

PORTUGAL

SPAIN

ARAB

BERBER

SAHARA DESERT

4%

WEST INDIES

French Caribbean 17%

British Caribbean 24%

The Middle Passage

KAARTA

AFRICA

KANEM-BORNU

Spanish Colonies 13%

Caribbean Sea

SEGU   HAUSA

CENTRAL AMERICA

Dutch Colonies 7%

Ashanti   DAHOMEY   BENIN
                    OYO

GUIANAS

Portuguese Empire 32%

TEKE

NSUNDI

SOUTH AMERICA   BRAZIL

KONGO
MBUNDU
ANGOLA

The Atlantic slave trade expanded rapidly in the eighteenth century. The mainland colonies received only a tiny proportion of the Africans brought to the New World, most of whom were transported to Brazil and the West Indies.

Slavery's impact in West Africa

the Europeans off against one another, collecting taxes from foreign merchants, and keeping the capture and sale of slaves under their own control. Few Europeans ventured inland from the coast. Traders remained in their "factories" and purchased slaves brought to them by African rulers and dealers.

From a minor institution, slavery grew to become more and more central to West African society, a source of wealth for African merchants and of power for newly emerging African kingdoms. The loss every year of tens of thousands of men and women in the prime of their lives to the slave trade weakened and distorted West Africa's society and economy.

The Middle Passage

For slaves, the voyage across the Atlantic—known as the **Middle Passage** because it was the second, or middle, leg in the triangular trading routes linking Europe, Africa, and America—was a harrowing experience. Men, women, and children were crammed aboard vessels as tightly as possible to maximize profits. Equiano, who later described "the shrieks of the women and the groans of the dying," survived the Middle Passage, but many Africans did not. Diseases such as measles and smallpox spread rapidly, and about one slave in five perished before reaching the New World. Ship captains were known to throw the sick overboard in order to prevent the spread of epidemics.

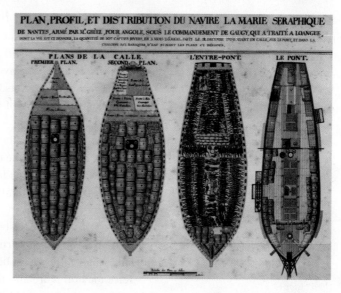

This image, made by a sailor in 1769 for the ship's owner, a merchant in Nantes, France, depicts the interior of a slave-trading vessel, the *Marie-Séraphique*. The cargo carried in barrels, generally guns, cloth, and metal goods, were to be traded for slaves. The third image from the left depicts the conditions under which slaves endured the Middle Passage across the Atlantic. The ship carried over 300 slaves. The broadside also included a calculation of the profit of the voyage.

Only a small proportion (less than 5 percent) of slaves carried to the New World were destined for mainland North America. The vast majority landed in Brazil or the West Indies, where the high death rate on the sugar plantations led to a constant demand for new slave imports. Overall, the area that was to become the United States imported between 400,000 and 600,000 slaves. By 1770, due to the natural reproduction of the slave population, around one-fifth of the estimated 2.3 million persons (not including Indians) living in the English colonies of North America were Africans and their descendants.

Chesapeake Slavery

By the mid-eighteenth century, three distinct slave systems were well entrenched in Britain's mainland colonies: tobacco-based plantation slavery in the Chesapeake, rice-based plantation slavery in South Carolina and Georgia, and nonplantation slavery in New England and the Middle Colonies. The largest and oldest of these was the plantation system of the Chesapeake, where more than 270,000 slaves resided in 1770, nearly half of the region's population. Virginia and Maryland were as closely tied to Britain as any other colonies and their economies were models of mercantilist policy (described in Chapter 3).

Tobacco-based plantation slavery

As Virginia expanded westward, so did slavery. By the eve of the American Revolution, the center of gravity of slavery in the colony had shifted from the Tidewater (the region along the coast) to the Piedmont farther inland. Most Chesapeake slaves, male and female, worked in the tobacco fields, but thousands labored as teamsters, as boatmen, and in skilled crafts. Numerous slave women became cooks, seamstresses, dairy maids, and personal servants. Slavery was common on small farms as well as plantations; nearly half of Virginia's white families owned at least one slave in 1770.

Hierarchy of Chesapeake society

Slavery transformed Chesapeake society into an elaborate hierarchy of degrees of freedom. At the top stood large planters, below them numerous lesser planters and landowning yeomen, and at the bottom a large population of convicts, indentured servants, tenant farmers (who made up half the white households in 1770), and, of course, the slaves. Violence lay at the heart of the slave system. Even a planter like Landon Carter, who prided himself on his concern for the well-being of his slaves, noted casually in his diary, "they have been severely whipped day by day."

Race as a line of social division

Race took on more and more importance as a line of social division. Whites increasingly considered free blacks dangerous and undesirable. Free blacks lost the right to employ white servants and to bear arms, were subjected to special taxes, and could be punished for striking a white person, regardless of the cause. In 1723, Virginia revoked the voting privileges of property-owning free blacks. Because Virginia law required that freed slaves be sent out of the colony, free blacks remained only a tiny part of the population—less than 4 percent in 1750.

The Rice Kingdom

As in early Virginia, frontier conditions allowed leeway to South Carolina's small population of African-born slaves, who farmed, tended livestock, and were initially allowed to serve in the militia to fight the Spanish and Indians. And as in Virginia, the introduction of a marketable staple crop, in this case rice, led directly to economic development, the large-scale importation of slaves, and a growing divide between white and black. In the 1740s, another staple, indigo (a crop used in producing blue dye), was developed. Like rice, indigo required large-scale cultivation and was grown by slaves.

Large-scale rice plantations

Since rice production requires considerable capital investment to drain swamps and create irrigation systems, it is economically advantageous for rice plantations to be as large as possible. Thus, South Carolina planters owned far more land and slaves than their counterparts in Virginia. Moreover, since mosquitoes bearing malaria (a disease to which

Benjamin Latrobe's watercolor, *An Overseer Doing His Duty*, was sketched near Fredericksburg, Virginia, in 1798. The title is meant to be ironic: the well-dressed overseer relaxes while two female slaves work in the fields.

Africans had developed partial immunity) flourished in the watery rice fields, planters tended to leave plantations under the control of overseers and the slaves themselves.

In the Chesapeake, field slaves worked in groups under constant supervision. Under the "task" system that developed in eighteenth-century South Carolina, individual slaves were assigned daily jobs, the completion of which allowed them time for leisure or to cultivate crops of their own. In 1762, one rice district had a population of only 76 white males among 1,000 slaves. By 1770, the number of South Carolina slaves had reached 100,000, well over half the colony's population.

The task system

The Georgia Experiment

Rice cultivation also spread into Georgia. The colony was founded in 1733 by a group of philanthropists led by James Oglethorpe, a wealthy reformer who sought to improve conditions for imprisoned debtors and abolish slavery. Oglethorpe hoped to establish a haven where the "worthy poor" of England could enjoy economic opportunity. The government in London supported the creation of Georgia to protect South Carolina against the Spanish and their Indian allies in Florida.

James Oglethorpe

Initially, the proprietors banned liquor and slaves, leading to continual battles with settlers, who desired both. By the 1740s, Georgia offered the spectacle of colonists pleading for the "English liberty" of self-government so that they could enact laws introducing slavery. In 1751, the proprietors surrendered the colony to the crown. The colonists quickly won the right to an elected assembly, which met in Savannah. It repealed the ban on slavery (and liquor), as well as an early measure that had limited landholdings to 500 acres. Georgia became a miniature version of South Carolina. By 1770, as many as 15,000 slaves labored on its coastal rice plantations.

Social and political change in Georgia

Slavery in the North

Small farms in northern colonies

Unlike in the plantation regions, slavery was far less central to the economies of New England and the Middle Colonies, where small farms predominated. Slaves made up only a small percentage of these colonies' populations, and it was unusual for even rich families to own more than one slave. Nonetheless, slavery was not entirely marginal to northern colonial life. Slaves worked as farm hands, in artisan shops, as stevedores loading and unloading ships, and as personal servants. But with slaves so small a part of the population that they seemed to pose no threat to the white majority, laws were less harsh than in the South. In New England, where in 1770 the 17,000 slaves represented less than 3 percent of the region's population, slave marriages were recognized in law; the severe physical punishment of slaves was prohibited; and slaves could bring suits in court, testify against whites, and own property and pass it on to their children—rights unknown in the South.

Slavery had been present in New York from the earliest days of Dutch settlement. As New York City's role in the slave trade expanded, so did slavery in the city. In 1746, its 2,440 slaves amounted to one-fifth of New York City's total population. Most were domestic workers, but slaves worked in all sectors of the economy. In 1770, about 27,000 slaves lived in New York and New Jersey, 10 percent

TABLE 4.1 Slave Population as Percentage of Total Population of Original Thirteen Colonies, 1770

COLONY	SLAVE POPULATION	PERCENTAGE
New Hampshire	654	1%
Massachusetts	4,754	2
Connecticut	5,698	3
Rhode Island	3,761	6
New York	19,062	12
New Jersey	8,220	7
Pennsylvania	5,561	2
Delaware	1,836	5
Maryland	63,818	32
Virginia	187,600	42
North Carolina	69,600	35
South Carolina	75,168	61
Georgia	15,000	45

of their total population. Slavery was also a significant presence in Philadelphia, although the institution stagnated after 1750 as artisans and merchants relied increasingly on wage laborers, whose numbers were augmented by population growth and the completion of the terms of indentured servants.

SLAVE CULTURES AND SLAVE RESISTANCE

Becoming African-American

The nearly 300,000 Africans brought to the mainland colonies during the eighteenth century were not a single people. They came from different cultures, spoke different languages, and practiced many religions. Slavery threw together individuals who would never otherwise have encountered one another and who had never considered their color or residence on a single continent a source of identity or unity. Their bond was not kinship, language, or even "race," but slavery itself. The process of creating a cohesive culture took many years. But by the nineteenth century, slaves no longer identified themselves as Ibo, Ashanti, Yoruba, and so on, but as African-Americans. In music, art, folklore, language, and religion, their cultural expressions emerged as a synthesis of African traditions, European elements, and new conditions in America.

Diverse origins

African-American culture

For most of the eighteenth century, the majority of American slaves were African by birth. Advertisements seeking information about runaways often described them by African origin ("young Gambia Negro," "new Banbara Negro fellow") and spoke of their bearing on their bodies "country marks"—visible signs of ethnic identity in Africa. Indeed, during the eighteenth century, black life in the colonies was "re-Africanized" as the earlier Creoles (slaves born in the New World) came to be outnumbered by large-scale importations from Africa.

African Religion in Colonial America

No experience was more wrenching for African slaves in the colonies than the transition from traditional religions to Christianity. Although African religions varied as much as those on other continents, they shared some elements, especially belief in the presence of spiritual forces in nature and a close relationship between the sacred and secular worlds. In the religions of West Africa, the region from which most slaves brought to British North America originated, there was no hard and fast distinction between the secular and spiritual worlds. Nature was suffused with spirits and the dead could influence the living. It was customary, Equiano wrote, before eating, to set aside some food for the spirits of departed ancestors.

Although some slaves came to the colonies familiar with Christianity or Islam, the majority of North American slaves practiced traditional African religions (which many Europeans deemed superstition or even witchcraft) well into the eighteenth century. When they did adopt Christian practices, many slaves merged them with traditional beliefs, adding the Christian God to their own pantheon of lesser spirits, whom they continued to worship.

African-American Cultures

Distinctive cultures

By the mid-eighteenth century, the three slave systems in British North America had produced distinct African-American cultures. In the Chesapeake, because of a more healthful climate, the slave population began to reproduce itself by 1740. Because of the small size of most plantations and the large number of white yeoman farmers, slaves here were continuously exposed to white culture. They soon learned English, and many were swept up in the religious revivals known as the Great Awakening, discussed later in this chapter.

In South Carolina and Georgia, two very different black societies emerged. On the rice plantations, slaves lived in extremely harsh conditions and had a low birthrate throughout the eighteenth century, making

An advertisement seeking the return of a runaway slave from Port Royal, in the Sea Islands of South Carolina. "Mustee" was a term for a person of mixed European and African ancestry. From the *South Carolina Gazette*, June 11, 1747.

Run away on the 13th of *March* laſt, a Muſtee Fellow named *Cyrus*, who lately belonged to Meſſrs. *Mulryne* and *Williams* of *Port-Royal*. Whoever ſecures, or brings the ſaid Fellow to me, or to Mr. *David Brown* of *Charles-Town* Shipwright, ſhall have Twenty Pounds Reward, and the Charges allow'd by Law. And whoever gives me Information of his being employed by any Perſon, ſo that he may be convicted thereof, ſhall, upon ſuch Conviction, have Thirty Pounds current Money paid him, by   *David Linn.*
A bay ſtray Horſe, about 13 Hands and an half

rice production dependent on continued slave imports from Africa. The slaves seldom came into contact with whites. They constructed African-style houses, chose African names for their children, and spoke Gullah, a language that mixed various African roots and was unintelligible to most whites. In Charleston and Savannah, however, the experience of slaves who labored as servants or skilled workers was quite different. They assimilated more quickly into Euro-American culture, and sexual liaisons between white owners and slave women produced the beginning of a class of free mulattos.

Regional differences

In the northern colonies, where slaves represented a smaller part of the population, dispersed in small holdings among the white population, a distinctive African-American culture developed more slowly. Living in close proximity to whites, they enjoyed more mobility and access to the mainstream of life than their counterparts farther south. But they had fewer opportunities to create stable family life or a cohesive community.

Resistance to Slavery

The common threads that linked these regional African-American cultures were the experience of slavery and the desire for freedom. Throughout the eighteenth century, blacks risked their lives in efforts to resist enslavement. Colonial newspapers, especially in the southern colonies, were filled with advertisements for runaway slaves. In South Carolina and Georgia, they fled to Florida, to uninhabited coastal and river swamps, or to Charleston and Savannah, where they could pass for free. In the Chesapeake and Middle Colonies, fugitive slaves tended to be familiar with white culture and therefore, as one advertisement put it, could "pretend to be free."

Slaves' desire for freedom

What Edward Trelawny, the colonial governor of Jamaica, called "a dangerous spirit of liberty" was widespread among the New World's slaves. The eighteenth century's first slave uprising occurred in New York City in 1712, when a group of slaves set fire to houses on the outskirts of the city and killed the first nine whites who arrived on the scene. During the 1730s and 1740s, continuous warfare involving European empires and Indians opened the door to slave resistance. In 1731, a slave rebellion in Louisiana, where the French and the Natchez Indians were at war, temporarily halted efforts to introduce the plantation system in that region.

Slave rebellions

Slaves seized the opportunity for rebellion offered by the War of Jenkins' Ear, which pitted England against Spain. In September 1739, a group of South Carolina slaves, most of them recently arrived from Kongo where some, it appears, had been soldiers, seized a store containing numerous weapons at the town of Stono. Beating drums to attract followers, the armed band marched southward toward Florida, burning houses and barns, killing whites they encountered, and shouting "Liberty." The **Stono Rebellion** took the lives of more than two dozen whites and as many as 200 slaves. Some slaves managed to reach Florida, where in 1740 they were armed by the Spanish to help repel an attack on St. Augustine by a force from Georgia.

Panic in New York

In 1741, a panic (which some observers compared to the fear of witches in Salem in the 1690s) swept New York City. Rumors spread that slaves, with some white allies, planned to burn part of the city, seize weapons, and either turn New York over to Spain or murder the white population. More than 150 blacks and 20 whites were arrested, and 34 alleged conspirators, including 4 white persons, were executed. Historians still disagree as to how extensive the plot was or whether it existed at all. In eighteenth-century America, dreams of freedom knew no racial boundary.

AN EMPIRE OF FREEDOM

British Patriotism

Despite the centrality of slavery to its empire, eighteenth-century Great Britain prided itself on being the world's most advanced and freest nation.

British power

It was not only the era's greatest naval and commercial power but also the home of a complex governmental system, with a powerful Parliament representing the interests of a self-confident landed aristocracy and merchant class. For much of the eighteenth century, Britain found itself at war with France, which had replaced Spain as its major continental rival. This situation led to a large military, high taxes, and the creation of the Bank of England to help finance the conflicts. For both Britons and colonists, war helped to sharpen a sense of national identity against foreign foes.

British identity

British patriotic sentiment became more assertive as the eighteenth century progressed. Symbols of British identity proliferated: the songs "God Save the King" and "Rule Britannia," and even the modern rules of cricket, the national sport. Writers hailed commerce as a progressive, civilizing force, a way for different peoples to interact for mutual benefit without domination or military conflict. Especially in contrast to France, Britain saw itself as a realm of widespread prosperity, individual liberty, the rule of law, and the Protestant faith. Wealth, religion, and freedom went together.

The British Constitution

Central to this sense of British identity was the concept of liberty. Eighteenth-century Britons believed power and liberty to be natural antagonists. To mediate between them, advocates of British freedom celebrated the rule of law, the right to live under legislation to which one's representatives had consented, restraints on the arbitrary exercise of political authority, and rights such as trial by jury enshrined in the common law. In its "balanced constitution" and the principle that no man, even the king, is above the law, Britons claimed to have devised the best means of preventing political tyranny. Until the 1770s, most colonists believed themselves to be part of the freest political system mankind had ever known.

A 1770 engraving from the *Boston Gazette* by Paul Revere illustrates the association of British patriotism and liberty. Britannia sits with a liberty cap and her national shield, and releases a bird from a cage.

These ideas sank deep roots not only within the "political nation"—those who voted, held office, and engaged in structured political debate—but also far more broadly in British and colonial society. Increasingly, the idea of liberty lost its traditional association with privileges derived from membership in a distinct social class and became more and more identified with a general right to resist arbitrary government. Ordinary persons thought nothing of taking to the streets to protest efforts by merchants to raise the cost of bread above the traditional "just price" or the Royal Navy's practice of "impressment"—kidnapping poor men on the streets for maritime service.

Power, liberty, and law

Republican Liberty

Liberty was central to two sets of political ideas that flourished in the Anglo-American world. One is termed by scholars "**republicanism**," which celebrated active participation in public life by economically independent citizens as the essence of liberty. Republicans assumed that only property-owning citizens possessed "**virtue**"—defined in the eighteenth century not simply as a personal moral quality but as the willingness to subordinate self-interest to the pursuit of the public good.

Moral and economic ideas of liberty

In eighteenth-century Britain, this body of thought about freedom was most closely associated with a group of critics known as the "Country

Party" because much of their support arose from the landed gentry. They called for the election of men of "independence" who could not be controlled by the ministry, and they criticized the expanding national debt and the growing wealth of financial speculators. Britain, they claimed, was succumbing to luxury and political manipulation—in other words, a loss of virtue—thereby endangering the careful balance of its system of government and, indeed, liberty itself. In Britain, Country Party writings had little impact, but they were eagerly devoured in the American colonies, whose elites were attracted to the emphasis on the political role of the independent landowner and their warnings against the constant tendency of political power to infringe on liberty.

Liberal Freedom

The second set of eighteenth-century political ideas celebrating freedom came to be known as **"liberalism"** (although its meaning was quite different from what the word suggests today). Whereas republican liberty had a public and social quality, liberalism was essentially individual and private. The leading philosopher of liberalism was John Locke, whose *Two Treatises of Government*, written around 1680, had limited influence in his own lifetime but became extremely well known in the next century. Government, he wrote, was formed by a mutual agreement among equals (the parties being male heads of households, not all persons). In this "social contract," men surrendered a part of their right to govern themselves in order to enjoy the benefits of the rule of law. They retained, however, their natural rights, whose existence predated the establishment of political authority. Protecting the security of life, liberty, and property required shielding a realm of private life and personal concerns—including family relations, religious preferences, and economic activity—from interference by the state. During the eighteenth century, Lockean ideas—individual rights, the consent of the governed, the right of rebellion against unjust or oppressive government—would become familiar on both sides of the Atlantic.

Like other Britons, Locke spoke of liberty as a universal right yet seemed to exclude many persons from its full benefits. The free individual in liberal thought was essentially the propertied white man. Slaves, he wrote, "cannot be considered as any part of civil society." Nonetheless, by proclaiming that all individuals possess natural rights that no government may violate, Lockean liberalism opened the door to the poor, women, and even slaves to challenge limitations on their own freedom.

The title page of John Locke's *Two Treatises of Government*, which traced the origins of government to an original state of nature and insisted that political authorities must not abridge mankind's natural rights.

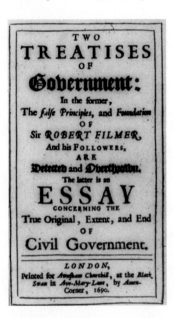

TWO
TREATISES
OF
Government:
In the former,
The *false Principles*, and *Foundation*
OF
Sir *ROBERT FILMER*,
And his FOLLOWERS,
ARE
Detected and **Overthrown.**
The latter is an
ESSAY
CONCERNING THE
True Original, Extent, and End
OF
Civil Government.

LONDON,
Printed for *Awnsham Churchill*, at the Black
Swan in *Ave-Mary-Lane*, by *Amen-*
Corner, 1690.

In the eighteenth century, republicanism and liberalism often rein-forced each other. Both political outlooks could inspire a commitment to constitutional government and restraints on despotic power. Both empha-sized the security of property as a foundation of freedom. Both traditions were transported to eighteenth-century America and would eventually help to divide the empire.

Relationship between
republicanism and liberalism

THE PUBLIC SPHERE

Colonial politics for most of the eighteenth century was considerably less tempestuous than in the seventeenth, with its bitter struggles for power and frequent armed uprisings. Political stability in Britain coupled with the maturation of local elites in America made for more tranquil government.

The Right to Vote

In many respects, politics in eighteenth-century America had a more democratic quality than in Great Britain. Suffrage requirements varied from colony to colony, but as in Britain the linchpin of voting laws was the property qualification. Its purpose was to ensure that men who possessed an economic stake in society and the independence of judgment that went with it determined the policies of the government. Slaves, servants, ten-ants, adult sons living in the homes of their parents, the poor, and women all lacked a "will of their own" and were therefore ineligible to vote. The wide distribution of property in the colonies, however, meant that a far higher percentage of the population enjoyed voting rights than in the Old World. It is estimated that between 50 and 80 percent of adult white men could vote in eighteenth-century colonial America, as opposed to fewer than 5 percent in Britain at the time.

Property and the vote

Colonial politics, however, was hardly democratic in a modern sense. Voting was almost everywhere considered a male prerogative. In some colonies, Jews, Catholics, and Protestant Dissenters like Baptists and Quakers could not vote. Propertied free blacks, who enjoyed the franchise in Virginia, North Carolina, South Carolina, and Georgia in the early days of settlement, lost that right during the eighteenth century (although North Carolina restored it in the 1730s). In the northern colonies, although the law did not bar blacks from voting, local custom did. Native Americans were generally prohibited from voting.

Limits on voting

Political Cultures

Despite the broad electorate among white men, "the people" existed only on election day. Between elections, members of colonial assemblies remained out of touch with their constituents. Strongly competitive elections were the norm only in the Middle Colonies. Considerable power in colonial politics rested with those who held appointive, not elective, office. Governors and councils were appointed by the crown in the nine royal colonies and by the proprietors of Pennsylvania and Maryland. Moreover, laws passed by colonial assemblies could be vetoed by governors or in London. In New England, most town officers were elected, but local officials in other colonies were appointed by the governor or by powerful officials in London.

Appointive office

Property qualifications for officeholding were far higher than for voting. In South Carolina, for example, nearly every adult white male could meet the voting qualification of fifty acres of land or payment of twenty shillings in taxes, but to sit in the assembly one had to own 500 acres of land and ten slaves or town property worth £1,000. As a result, throughout the eighteenth century nearly all of South Carolina's legislators were planters or wealthy merchants.

Qualifications for voting and office

In some colonies, an ingrained tradition of "deference"—the assumption among ordinary people that wealth, education, and social prominence carried a right to public office—sharply limited effective choice in elections. Virginia politics, for example, combined political democracy for white men with the tradition that voters should choose among candidates from the gentry. Aspirants for public office actively sought to ingratiate themselves with ordinary voters, distributing food and liquor freely at the courthouse where balloting took place. In Thomas Jefferson's first campaign for the House of Burgesses in 1768, his expenses included hiring two men "for

Democracy and deference

This 1765 engraving depicting an election in Pennsylvania suggests the intensity of political debate in the Middle Colonies, as well as the social composition of the electorate. Those shown arguing outside the Old Court House in Philadelphia include physicians (with wigs and gold-topped canes), ministers, and lawyers. A line of men wait on the steps to vote.

bringing up rum" to the polling place. Even in New England, with its larger number of elective positions, town leaders were generally the largest property holders, and offices frequently passed down from generation to generation in the same family.

The Rise of the Assemblies

In the seventeenth century, the governor was the focal point of political authority, and colonial assemblies were weak bodies that met infrequently. But in the eighteenth, as economic development enhanced the power of American elites, the assemblies they dominated became more and more assertive. Their leaders insisted that assemblies possessed the same rights and powers in local affairs as the House of Commons enjoyed in Britain. The most successful governors were those who accommodated the rising power of the assemblies and used their appointive powers and control of land grants to win allies among assembly members.

Colonial governors

Many of the conflicts between governors and elected assemblies stemmed from the colonies' economic growth. To deal with the scarcity of gold and silver coins, the only legal form of currency, some colonies printed paper money, although this was strongly opposed by the governors, authorities in London, and British merchants who did not wish to be paid in what they considered worthless paper. Numerous battles also took place over land policy (sometimes involving divergent attitudes toward the remaining Indian population) and the level of rents charged to farmers on land owned by the crown or proprietors.

Conflicts between governors and assemblies

In their negotiations and conflicts with royal governors, leaders of the assemblies drew on the writings of the English Country Party, whose emphasis on the constant tension between liberty and political power and the dangers of executive influence over the legislature made sense of their own experience. Of the European settlements in North America, only the British colonies possessed any considerable degree of popular participation in government. This fact reinforced the assemblies' claim to embody the rights of Englishmen and the principle of popular consent to government.

Popular participation in British colonial government

Politics in Public

The language of liberty reverberated outside the relatively narrow world of elective and legislative politics. The "political nation" was dominated by the American gentry, whose members addressed each other in letters, speeches, newspaper articles, and pamphlets filled with Latin expressions and references to classical learning. But especially in colonial towns and cities, the eighteenth century witnessed a considerable expansion of the "public sphere"—the world of political organization and debate independent of the government, where an informed citizenry openly discussed questions that had previously been the preserve of officials.

In Boston, New York, and Philadelphia, clubs proliferated where literary, philosophical, scientific, and political issues were debated. Such groups were generally composed of men of property and commerce, but some drew ordinary citizens into discussions of public affairs. Colonial taverns and coffeehouses also became important sites not only for social conviviality but also for political debates. In Philadelphia, one clergyman commented, "the poorest laborer thinks himself entitled to deliver his sentiments in matters of religion or politics with as much freedom as the gentleman or scholar."

The Colonial Press

Neither the Spanish possessions of Florida and New Mexico nor New France possessed a printing press, although missionaries had established one in Mexico City in the 1530s. In British North America, however, the press expanded rapidly during the eighteenth century. So did the number of political broadsides and pamphlets published, especially at election time. By the eve of the American Revolution, some three-quarters of the free adult male population in the colonies (and more than one-third of the women) could read and write, and a majority of American families owned at least one book. Circulating libraries appeared in many colonial cities and towns, making possible a wider dissemination of knowledge at a time when books were still expensive. The first, the Library Company of Philadelphia, was established by Benjamin Franklin in 1731.

The first continuously published colonial newspaper, the *Boston News-Letter*, appeared in 1704. There were thirteen colonial newspapers by 1740 and twenty-five in 1765, mostly weeklies with small circulations—an average of 600 sales per issue. Probably the best-edited newspaper was the *Pennsylvania Gazette*, established in 1728 in Philadelphia and purchased the following year by Benjamin Franklin. At its peak, the *Gazette* attracted 2,000 subscribers. By the 1730s, political commentary was widespread in the American press.

Freedom of Expression and Its Limits

The public sphere thrived on the free exchange of ideas. But freedom of expression was not generally considered one of the ancient rights of

Englishmen. The phrase "freedom of speech" originated in Britain during the sixteenth century. A right of legislators, not ordinary citizens, it referred to the ability of members of Parliament to express their views without fear of reprisal, on the grounds that only in this way could they effectively represent the people. Outside of Parliament, free speech had no legal protection. A subject could be beheaded for accusing the king of failing to hold "true" religious beliefs, and language from swearing to criticism of the government exposed a person to criminal penalties.

As for **freedom of the press**, governments on both sides of the Atlantic viewed this as extremely dangerous. Until 1695, when a British law requiring the licensing of printed works before publication lapsed, no newspaper, book, or pamphlet could legally be printed without a government license. After 1695, the government could not censor newspapers, books, and pamphlets before they appeared in print, although it continued to try to manage the press by direct payments to publishers and individual journalists. Authors and publishers could still be prosecuted for "seditious libel"—a crime that included defaming government officials—or punished for contempt.

Elected assemblies, not governors, most frequently discouraged freedom of the press in colonial America. Dozens of publishers were hauled before assemblies and forced to apologize for comments regarding one or another member. Colonial newspapers vigorously defended freedom of the press as a central component of liberty, insisting that the citizenry had a right to monitor the workings of government and subject public officials to criticism. But since government printing contracts were crucial for economic success, few newspapers attacked colonial governments unless financially supported by an opposition faction.

The Trial of Zenger

The most famous colonial court case involving freedom of the press demonstrated that popular sentiment opposed prosecutions for criticism of public officials. This was the 1735 trial of John Peter Zenger, a German-born printer who had emigrated to New York as a youth. Financed by wealthy opponents of Governor William Cosby, Zenger's newspaper, the *Weekly Journal*, lambasted the governor for corruption, influence peddling, and "tyranny." New York's council ordered four issues burned and had Zenger himself arrested and tried for

Freedom of speech

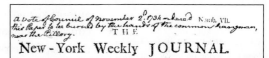

The first page of the *New York Weekly Journal*, edited by John Peter Zenger, one of four issues ordered to be burned by local authorities.

seditious libel. Zenger's attorney, Andrew Hamilton, urged the jury to judge not the publisher but the governor. If they decided that Zenger's charges were correct, they must acquit him, and, Hamilton proclaimed, "every man who prefers freedom to a life of slavery will bless you."

Zenger was found not guilty. The case sent a warning to prosecutors that libel cases might be very difficult to win, especially in the superheated atmosphere of New York partisan politics. The outcome helped to promote the idea that the publication of truth should always be permitted, and it demonstrated that the idea of free expression was becoming ingrained in the popular imagination.

Freedom of expression

The American Enlightenment

During the eighteenth century, many educated Americans began to be influenced by the outlook of the European Enlightenment. This philosophical movement, which originated among French thinkers and soon spread to Britain, sought to apply the scientific method of careful investigation based on research and experiment to political and social life. Enlightenment ideas crisscrossed the Atlantic along with goods and people. Enlightenment thinkers insisted that every human institution, authority, and tradition be judged before the bar of reason. The self-educated Benjamin Franklin's wide range of activities—establishing a newspaper, debating club, and library; publishing the widely circulated *Poor Richard's Almanack*; and conducting experiments to demonstrate that lightning is a form of electricity—exemplified the Enlightenment spirit and made him probably the best-known American in the eighteenth-century world.

Enlightenment thinkers hoped that "reason," not religious enthusiasm, could govern human life. During the eighteenth century, many prominent Americans moved toward the position called Arminianism, which taught that reason alone was capable of establishing the essentials of religion. Others adopted Deism, a belief that God essentially withdrew after creating the world, leaving it to function according to scientific laws without divine intervention. Belief in miracles, in the revealed truth of the Bible, and in the innate sinfulness of mankind were viewed by Arminians, Deists, and others as outdated superstitions that should be abandoned in the modern age.

In the seventeenth century, the English scientist Isaac Newton had revealed the natural laws that governed the physical universe. Here, Deists believed, was the purest evidence of God's handiwork. Deists concluded that the best form of religious devotion was to study the workings

A 1762 portrait of Benjamin Franklin, done in London by the English artist Mason Chamberlain while Franklin was in the city as agent for the Pennsylvania Assembly. Franklin is depicted as a scientist making notes on his experiments, rather than a politician.

of nature, rather than to worship in organized churches or appeal to divine grace for salvation. By the late colonial era, a small but influential group of leading Americans, including Benjamin Franklin and Thomas Jefferson, could be classified as Deists.

Deists

THE GREAT AWAKENING

Like freedom of the press, religion was another realm where the actual experience of liberty outstripped its legal recognition. Religion remained central to eighteenth-century American life. Sermons, theological treatises, and copies of the Bible were by far the largest category of material produced by colonial printers.

Religious Revivals

Many ministers were concerned that westward expansion, commercial development, the growth of Enlightenment rationalism, and lack of individual engagement in church services were undermining religious devotion. These fears helped to inspire the revivals that swept through the colonies beginning in the 1730s. Known collectively as the **Great Awakening**, the revivals were less a coordinated movement than a series of local events united by a commitment to a "religion of the heart," a more emotional and personal Christianity than that offered by existing churches.

A more emotional and personal Christianity

The eighteenth century witnessed a revival of religious fundamentalism in many parts of the world, in part a response to the rationalism of the Enlightenment and a desire for greater religious purity. In the Middle East and Central Asia, where Islam was widespread, followers of a form of the religion known as Wahabbism called for a return to the practices of the religion's early days. Methodism and other forms of enthusiastic religion were flourishing in Europe. Like other intellectual currents of the time, the Great Awakening was a transatlantic movement.

During the 1720s and 1730s, the New Jersey Dutch Reformed clergyman Theodore Frelinghuysen, his Presbyterian neighbors William and Gilbert Tennent, and the Massachusetts Congregationalist minister Jonathan Edwards pioneered an intensely emotional style of preaching. Edwards's famous sermon *Sinners in the Hands of an Angry God* portrayed sinful man as a "loathsome insect" suspended over a bottomless pit of eternal fire by a

Jonathan Edwards

George Whitefield, the English evangelist who helped to spark the Great Awakening in the colonies. Painted around 1742 by John Wollaston, who had emigrated from England to the colonies, the work depicts Whitefield's powerful effect on male and female listeners. It also illustrates Whitefield's eye problem, which led critics to dub him "Dr. Squintum."

slender thread that might break at any moment. Only a "new birth"—immediately acknowledging one's sins and pleading for divine grace—could save men from eternal damnation.

The Preaching of Whitefield

More than any other individual, the English minister George Whitefield, who declared "the whole world his parish," sparked the Great Awakening. For two years after his arrival in America in 1739, Whitefield brought his highly emotional brand of preaching to colonies from Georgia to New England. God, Whitefield proclaimed, was merciful. Rather than being predestined for damnation, men and women could save themselves by repenting of their sins. Whitefield appealed to the passions of his listeners, powerfully sketching the boundless joy of salvation and the horrors of damnation.

Tens of thousands of colonists flocked to Whitefield's sermons, which were widely reported in the American press, making him a celebrity and helping to establish the revivals as the first major intercolonial event in North American history. In Whitefield's footsteps, a host of traveling preachers or "evangelists" (meaning, literally, bearers of good news) held revivalist meetings, often to the alarm of established ministers.

The Awakening's Impact

By the time they subsided in the 1760s, the revivals had changed the religious configuration of the colonies and enlarged the boundaries of liberty. Whitefield had inspired the emergence of numerous Dissenting churches. Congregations split into factions headed by Old Lights (traditionalists) and New Lights (revivalists), and new churches proliferated—Baptist, Methodist, Presbyterian, and others. Many of these new churches began to criticize the colonial practice of levying taxes to support an established church; they defended religious freedom as one of the natural rights government must not restrict.

Although the revivals were primarily a spiritual matter, the Great Awakening threw into question many forms of authority, and inspired criticism of aspects of colonial society. Revivalist preachers frequently criticized commercial society, insisting that believers should make salvation, not profit, "the one business of their lives." Preaching to the small farmers of the southern backcountry, Baptist and Methodist revivalists criticized the worldliness of wealthy planters and attacked as sinful activities such

Critique of commercial society

as gambling, horse racing, and lavish entertainments on the Sabbath. A few preachers explicitly condemned slavery. Especially in the Chesapeake, the revivals brought numerous slaves into the Christian fold, an important step in their acculturation as African-Americans.

The revivals encouraged many colonists to trust their own views rather than those of established elites. In listening to the sermons of self-educated preachers, forming Bible study groups, and engaging in intense religious discussions, ordinary colonists asserted the right to independent judgment. Although the revivalists' aim was spiritual salvation, the independent frame of mind they encouraged would have significant political consequences.

Independent judgement

IMPERIAL RIVALRIES

Spanish North America

The rapid growth of Britain's North American colonies took place at a time of increased jockeying for power among European empires. But the colonies of England's rivals, although covering immense territories, remained thinly populated and far weaker economically. The Spanish empire encompassed an area that stretched from the Pacific coast and New Mexico into the Great Plains and eastward through Texas and Florida. After 1763, it also included Louisiana, which Spain obtained from France. On paper a vast territorial empire, Spanish North America actually consisted of a few small and isolated urban clusters, most prominently St. Augustine in Florida, San Antonio in Texas, and Santa Fe and Albuquerque in New Mexico.

Extent of Spanish empire

New Mexico's population in 1765 was only 20,000, equally divided between Spanish settlers and Pueblo Indians. Spain began the colonization of Texas at the beginning of the eighteenth century, partly as a buffer to prevent French commercial influence, then spreading in the Mississippi Valley, from intruding into New Mexico. The Spanish established complexes consisting of religious missions and *presidios* (military outposts) at Los Adaes, La Bahía, and San Antonio. But the region attracted few settlers. Texas had only 1,200 Spanish colonists in 1760. Florida stagnated as well.

Colonization of Texas

The Spanish in California

On the Pacific coast, Russian fur traders in the eighteenth century established a series of forts and trading posts in Alaska. Spain, alarmed by

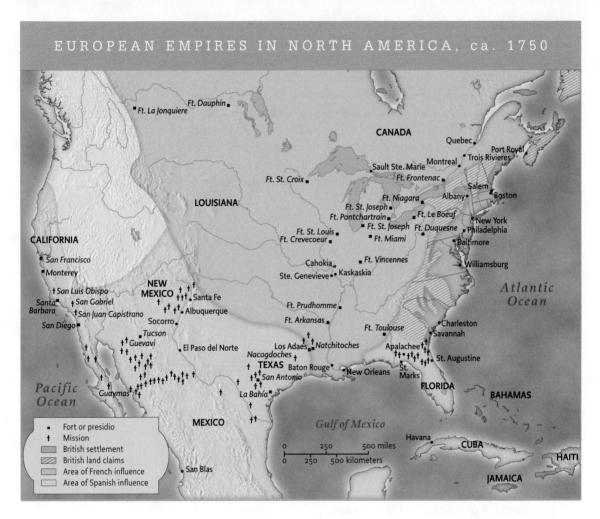

EUROPEAN EMPIRES IN NORTH AMERICA, ca. 1750

Three great empires—the British, French, and Spanish—competed for influence in North America for much of the eighteenth century.

what it saw as a danger to its American empire, ordered the colonization of California. A string of Spanish missions and *presidios* soon dotted the California coastline, from San Diego to Los Angeles, Santa Barbara, Monterey, San Francisco, and Sonoma. Born on the Spanish Mediterranean island of Mallorca, **Father Junípero Serra** became one of the most controversial figures in California's early history. He founded the first California mission, in San Diego, in 1769 and administered the mission network until his death in 1784. Serra was widely praised in Spain for converting thousands of Indians to Christianity. But forced labor and disease took a heavy toll among Indians who lived at the missions Serra directed.

Present-day California was a densely populated area, with a native population of perhaps 250,000 when Spanish settlement began. But as in other regions, the coming of soldiers and missionaries proved a disaster for the Indians. More than any other Spanish colony, California was a mission frontier. These outposts served simultaneously as religious institutions and centers of government and labor. Father Serra and other missionaries hoped to convert the natives to Christianity and settled farming. The missions also relied on forced Indian labor to grow grain, work in orchards and vineyards, and tend cattle. By 1821, when Mexico won its independence from Spain, California's native population had declined by more than one-third. But the area had not attracted Spanish settlers. When Spanish rule came to an end in 1821, *Californios* (California residents of Spanish descent) numbered only 3,200.

Spanish missions

The French Empire

A greater rival to British power in North America—as well as in Europe and the Caribbean—was France. During the eighteenth century, the population and economy of Canada expanded. At the same time, French traders pushed into the Mississippi River valley southward from the Great Lakes and northward from Mobile, founded in 1702, and New Orleans, established in 1718. In the St. Lawrence River valley of French Canada, prosperous farming communities developed. By 1750, the area had a population of about 55,000 colonists. Another 10,000 (about half Europeans, half African-American slaves) resided in Louisiana.

French expansion

Despite these gains, the population of French North America continued to be dwarfed by the British colonies. Prejudice against emigration to North America remained widespread in France because many there viewed the French colony as a place of cruel exile for criminals and social outcasts. Nonetheless, by claiming control of a large arc of territory and by establishing close trading and military relations with many Indian tribes, the French empire posed a real challenge to the British. French

French ties to Indian tribes

A sketch of New Orleans as it appeared in 1720.

forts and trading posts ringed the British colonies. The French were a presence on the New England and New York frontiers and in western Pennsylvania.

BATTLE FOR THE CONTINENT

The Middle Ground

The Ohio Valley

For much of the eighteenth century, the western frontier of British North America was the flashpoint of imperial rivalries. The Ohio Valley became caught up in a complex struggle for power involving the French, British, rival Indian communities, and settlers and land companies pursuing their own interests. On this **"middle ground"** between European empires and Indian sovereignty, villages sprang up where members of numerous tribes lived side by side, along with European traders and the occasional missionary.

By the mid-eighteenth century, Indians had learned that direct military confrontation with Europeans meant suicide, and that an alliance with a single European power exposed them to danger from others. The Indians of the Ohio Valley sought (with some success) to play the British and French empires off one another and to control the lucrative commerce with whites. The Iroquois were masters of balance-of-power diplomacy.

The Ohio Company

In 1750, few white settlers inhabited the Ohio Valley. But already, Scotch-Irish and German immigrants, Virginia planters, and land speculators were eyeing the region's fertile soil. In 1749, the government of Virginia awarded an immense land grant—half a million acres—to the Ohio Company. The company's members included the colony's royal governor, Robert Dinwiddie, and the cream of Virginia society—Lees, Carters, and the young George Washington. The land grant sparked the French to bolster their presence in the region. It was the Ohio Company's demand for French recognition of its land claims that inaugurated the Seven Years' War (known in the colonies as the French and Indian War), the first of the century's imperial wars to begin in the colonies and the first to result in a decisive victory for one combatant. It permanently altered the global balance of power.

The Seven Years' War

The world's leading empire

Only in the eighteenth century, after numerous wars against its great rivals France and Spain, did Britain emerge as the world's leading empire and its center of trade and banking. By the 1750s, British possessions and trade reached around the globe. The existence of global empires implied that warfare among them would also be global.

What became a worldwide struggle for imperial domination, which eventually spread to Europe, West Africa, and Asia, began in 1754 with British efforts to dislodge the French from forts they had constructed in western Pennsylvania. In the previous year, George Washington, then only twenty-one years old, had been dispatched by the colony's governor on an unsuccessful mission to persuade French soldiers to abandon a fort they were building on lands claimed by the Ohio Company. In 1754, Washington returned to the area with two companies of soldiers. After an ill-considered attempt against a larger French and Indian force, resulting in the loss of one-third of his men, Washington was forced to surrender. Soon afterward, an expedition led by General Edward Braddock against Fort Duquesne (today's Pittsburgh) was ambushed by French and Indian forces, leaving Braddock and two-thirds of his 3,000 soldiers dead or wounded.

Benjamin Franklin produced this famous cartoon in 1754, calling on Britain's North American colonies to unite against the French.

For two years, the war went against the British. The southern backcountry was ablaze with fighting among British forces, colonists, and Indians. Inhumanity flourished on all sides. Indians killed hundreds of colonists in western Pennsylvania and pushed the line of settlement all the way back to Carlisle, only 100 miles west of Philadelphia. In Nova Scotia, the British rounded up around 5,000 local French residents, called **Acadians**, confiscated their land, and expelled them from the region, selling their farms to settlers from New England. Some of those expelled eventually returned to France; others ended up as far away as Louisiana, where their descendants came to be known as Cajuns.

As the British government under Secretary of State William Pitt, who took office in 1757, raised huge sums of money and poured men and naval forces into the war, the tide of battle turned. By 1759, Britain—with colonial and Indian soldiers playing a major role—had captured the pivotal French outposts Forts Duquesne, Ticonderoga (north of Albany), and Louisbourg on Cape Breton Island, which guarded the mouth of the St. Lawrence River. In September of that year, a French army was defeated on the Plains of Abraham near Quebec. British forces also seized nearly all the islands in the French Caribbean and established control of India.

William Pitt

A World Transformed

Britain's victory fundamentally reshaped the world balance of power. In the Peace of Paris in 1763, France ceded Canada to Britain, receiving back in return the sugar islands of Guadeloupe and Martinique (far more lucrative colonies from the point of view of French authorities). Spain ceded

The global balance of power

Florida to Britain in exchange for the return of the Philippines and Cuba (seized by the British during the war). Spain also acquired from France the vast Louisiana colony. France's 200-year-old North American empire had come to an end. The entire continent east of the Mississippi River was now in British hands.

The costs of war

Eighteenth-century warfare, conducted on land and sea across the globe, was enormously expensive. The Seven Years' War put strains on all the participants. The war's cost produced a financial crisis in France that almost three decades later would help to spark the French Revolution. The British would try to recoup part of the cost of war by increasing taxes on their American colonies.

Pontiac's Rebellion

Throughout eastern North America, the abrupt departure of the French in the aftermath of the Seven Years' War eliminated the balance-of-power diplomacy that had enabled groups like the Iroquois to maintain a significant degree of autonomy. Domination by any outside power, Indians feared, meant the loss of freedom. Without consulting them, the French had ceded land Indians claimed as their own to British control. The Treaty of Paris left Indians more dependent than ever on the British and ushered in a period of confusion over land claims, control of the fur trade, and tribal relations in general.

Effect on Indians

In 1763, in the wake of the French defeat, Indians of the Ohio Valley and Great Lakes launched a revolt against British rule. Although known as **Pontiac's Rebellion** after an Ottawa war leader, the rebellion owed at least as much to the teachings of Neolin, a Delaware religious prophet. During a religious vision, the Master of Life instructed Neolin that his people must reject European technology, free themselves from commercial ties with whites and dependence on alcohol, clothe themselves in the garb of their ancestors, and drive the British from their territory (although friendly French inhabitants could remain). Neolin combined this message with the relatively new idea of pan-Indian identity. All Indians, he preached, were a single people, and only through cooperation could they regain their lost independence.

Neolin's message

The Proclamation Line

In the spring and summer of 1763, Ottawas, Hurons, and other Indians besieged Detroit, then a major British military outpost, seized nine other forts, and killed hundreds of white settlers who had intruded onto Indian

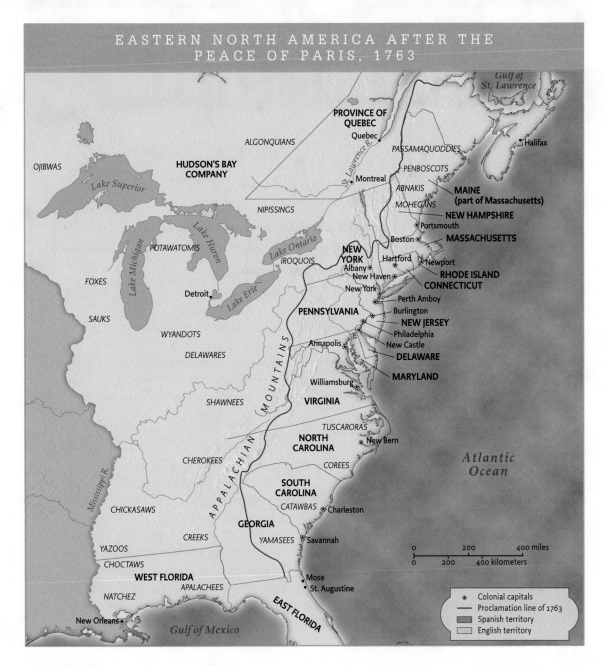

EASTERN NORTH AMERICA AFTER THE PEACE OF PARIS, 1763

The Peace of Paris, which ended the Seven Years' War, left all of North America east of the Mississippi in British hands, ending the French presence on the continent.

VOICES OF FREEDOM

From Pontiac, Speeches (1762 and 1763)

Pontiac was a leader of the pan-Indian resistance to English rule known as Pontiac's Rebellion, which followed the end of the Seven Years' War. Neolin was a Delaware religious prophet who helped to inspire the rebellion.

Englishmen, although you have conquered the French, you have not yet conquered us! We are not your slaves. These lakes, these woods, and mountains were left to us by our ancestors. They are our inheritance; and we will part with them to none. Your nation supposes that we, like the white people, cannot live without bread and pork and beef! But you ought to know that He, the Great Spirit and Master of Life, has provided food for us in these spacious lakes, and on these woody mountains.

[The Master of Life has said to Neolin:]

I am the Maker of heaven and earth, the trees, lakes, rivers, and all else. I am the Maker of all mankind; and because I love you, you must do my will. The land on which you live I have made for you and not for others. Why do you suffer the white man to dwell among you? My children, you have forgotten the customs and traditions of your forefathers. Why do you not clothe yourselves in skins, as they did, use bows and arrows and the stone-pointed lances, which they used? You have bought guns, knives, kettles and blankets from the white man until you can no longer do without them; and what is worse, you have drunk the poison firewater, which turns you into fools. Fling all these things away; live as your wise forefathers did before you. And as for these English—these dogs dressed in red, who have come to rob you of your hunting-grounds, and drive away the game—you must lift the hatchet against them. Wipe them from the face of the earth, and then you will win my favor back again, and once more be happy and prosperous.

From The Interesting Narrative of the Life of Olaudah Equiano, or Gustavus Vassa, the African (1789)

Olaudah Equiano's autobiography, published in London, was the most prominent account of the slave experience written in the eighteenth century. In this passage, which comes after Equiano's description of a slave auction in the Caribbean, he calls on white persons to live up to their professed belief in liberty.

———

We were not many days in the merchant's custody before we were sold after their usual manner, which is this: On a signal given (as the beat of a drum), the buyers rush in at once into the yard where the slaves are confined, and make choice of that parcel they like best. . . . In this manner, without scruple, are relations and friends separated, most of them never to see each other again. I remember in the vessel in which I was brought over, . . . there were several brothers, who, in the sale, were sold in different lots; and it was very moving on this occasion to see and hear their cries at parting.

O, ye nominal Christians! Might not an African ask you, learned you this from your God? Who says unto you, Do unto all men as you would men should do unto you? Is it not enough that we are torn from our country and friends to toil for your luxury and lust of gain? Must every tender feeling be sacrificed to your avarice? Are the dearest friends and relations, now rendered more dear by their separation from their kindred, still to be parted from each other, and thus prevented from cheering the gloom of slavery with the small comfort of being together and mingling their sufferings and sorrows? Why are parents to lose their children, brothers their sisters, or husbands their wives? Surely this is a new refinement in cruelty.

QUESTIONS

1. *What elements of Indian life does Neolin criticize most strongly?*

2. *What aspect of slavery does Equiano emphasize in his account, and why do you think he does so?*

3. *How do Pontiac and Equiano differ in the ways they address white audiences?*

lands. British forces soon launched a counterattack, and over the next few years the tribes one by one made peace. But the uprising inspired the government in London to issue the Proclamation of 1763, prohibiting further colonial settlement west of the Appalachian Mountains. These lands were reserved exclusively for Indians. Moreover, the Proclamation banned the sale of Indian lands to private individuals.

The British aim was less to protect the Indians than to stabilize the situation on the colonial frontier and to avoid being dragged into an endless series of border conflicts. But the Proclamation enraged both settlers and speculators hoping to take advantage of the expulsion of the French to consolidate their claims to western lands. They ignored the new policy. George Washington himself ordered his agents to buy up as much Indian land as possible, while keeping the transactions "a profound secret" because of their illegality. Failing to offer a viable solution to the question of westward expansion, the Proclamation of 1763 ended up further exacerbating settler-Indian relations.

Pennsylvania and the Indians

The Seven Years' War not only redrew the map of the world but produced dramatic changes within the American colonies as well. In Pennsylvania, the conflict shattered the decades-old rule of the Quaker elite and dealt the final blow to the colony's policy of accommodation with the Indians.

During the war, with the frontier ablaze with battles between settlers and French and Indian warriors, western Pennsylvanians demanded that colonial authorities adopt a more aggressive stance. When the governor declared war on hostile Delawares, raised a militia, and offered a bounty for Indian scalps, many of the assembly's pacifist Quakers resigned their seats, effectively ending their control of Pennsylvania politics.

In December 1763, while Pontiac's Rebellion still raged, a party of fifty armed men, mostly Scotch-Irish farmers from the vicinity of the Pennsylvania town of Paxton, destroyed the Indian village of Conestoga, massacring half a dozen men, women, and children who lived there

under the protection of Pennsylvania's governor. When the Paxton Boys marched on Philadelphia in February 1764, intending to attack Moravian Indians who resided near the city, the governor ordered the expulsion of much of the Indian population. By the 1760s, Pennsylvania's Holy Experiment was at an end and with it William Penn's promise of "true friendship and amity" between colonists and the native population.

Colonial Identities

Before the war, the colonies had been largely isolated from one another. Outside of New England, more Americans probably traveled to England than from one colony to another. The **Albany Plan of Union** of 1754, drafted by Benjamin Franklin at the outbreak of the Seven Years' War, envisioned the creation of a Grand Council composed of delegates from each colony, with the power to levy taxes and deal with Indian relations and the common defense. Rejected by the colonial assemblies, whose powers Franklin's proposal would curtail, the plan was never sent to London for approval.

Participation in the Seven Years' War created greater bonds among the colonies. But the war also strengthened colonists' pride in being members of the British empire. It has been said that Americans were never more British than in 1763. British victory in the Seven Years' War seemed a triumph of liberty over tyranny. The defeat of the Catholic French reinforced the equation of British nationality, Protestantism, and freedom.

The war and American identity

But soon, the American colonists would come to believe that membership in the empire jeopardized their liberty. When they did, they set out on a road that led to independence.

CHAPTER REVIEW AND ONLINE RESOURCES

REVIEW QUESTIONS

1. How did Great Britain's position in North America change relative to the other European powers during the first three-quarters of the eighteenth century?

2. How did the ideas of republicanism and liberalism differ in eighteenth-century British North America?

3. Three distinct slave systems were well entrenched in Britain's mainland colonies. Describe the main characteristics of each system.

4. How and why did the colonists' sense of a collective British identity change during the years before 1764?

5. What ideas generated by the American Enlightenment and the Great Awakening prompted challenges to religious, social, and political authorities in the British colonies?

6. How were colonial merchants in British America involved in the Atlantic economy, and what was the role of the slave trade in that economy?

7. We often consider the impact of the slave trade only on the United States, but its impact extended much further. How did it affect West African nations and society, other regions of the New World, and the nations of Europe?

8. How was an African-American collective identity created in these years and what role did slave rebellions play in that process?

KEY TERMS

Atlantic slave trade (p. 106)
Middle Passage (p. 109)
Stono Rebellion (p. 116)
republicanism (p. 117)
virtue (p. 117)
liberalism (p. 118)
freedom of the press (p. 123)
American Enlightenment (p. 124)
Great Awakening (p. 125)
Father Junípero Serra (p. 128)
"middle ground" (p. 130)
Acadians (p. 131)
Pontiac's Rebellion (p. 132)
Albany Plan of Union (p. 137)

wwnorton.com
/studyspace

VISIT STUDYSPACE FOR THESE RESOURCES AND MORE

- A chapter outline
- A diagnostic chapter quiz
- Interactive maps
- Map worksheets
- Multimedia documents

CHAPTER 5

THE AMERICAN REVOLUTION

★

1763-1783

1760	George III assumes the British throne
1764	Sugar Act
1765	Stamp Act
	Sons of Liberty organized
	Stamp Act Congress
1767	Townshend Acts
1767–1768	*Letters from a Farmer in Pennsylvania*
	British troops stationed in Boston
1770	Boston Massacre
1773	Tea Act
	Boston Tea Party
1774	Intolerable Acts
	First Continental Congress convenes
1775	Battles at Lexington and Concord
	Lord Dunmore's proclamation
1776	Thomas Paine's *Common Sense*
	Declaration of Independence
	Battle of Trenton
1777	Battle of Saratoga
1778	Treaty of Amity and Commerce with France
1781	Cornwallis surrenders at Yorktown
1783	Treaty of Paris

A rare print from 1776 depicts George Washington as commander of the American armies, "the supporter of liberty," and "benefactor of mankind." It illustrates the linkage of liberty and American independence, and Americans' conviction that their struggle was of worldwide significance.

FOCUS QUESTIONS

- *What were the roots and significance of the Stamp Act controversy?*

- *What key events sharpened the divisions between Britain and the colonists in the late 1760s and early 1770s?*

- *What key events marked the move toward American independence?*

- *How were American forces able to prevail in the Revolutionary War?*

On the night of August 26, 1765, a violent crowd of Bostonians assaulted the elegant home of Thomas Hutchinson, chief justice and lieutenant governor of Massachusetts. Hutchinson and his family barely had time to escape before the crowd broke down the front door and proceeded to destroy or carry off most of their possessions, including paintings, furniture, silverware, and notes for a history of Massachusetts Hutchinson was writing. By the time the crowd departed, only the outer walls of the home remained standing.

The immediate cause of the riot was the Stamp Act, a recently enacted British tax that many colonists felt violated their liberty. Only a few days earlier, Hutchinson had helped to disperse a crowd attacking a building owned by his relative Andrew Oliver, a merchant who had been appointed to help administer the new law. Both crowds were led by Ebenezer Mackintosh, a shoemaker who enjoyed a wide following among Boston's working people.

The riot of August 26 was one small episode in a series of events that launched a half-century of popular protest and political upheaval throughout the Western world. The momentous era that came to be called the Age of Revolution began in British North America, spread to Europe and the Caribbean, and culminated in the Latin American wars for independence. In all these struggles, liberty emerged as the foremost rallying cry for popular discontent. Rarely has the idea played so central a role in political debate and social upheaval.

If the attack on Hutchinson's home demonstrated the depths of feeling aroused by Britain's efforts to impose greater control over its empire, it also revealed that revolution is a dynamic process whose consequences no one can anticipate. The crowd's fury expressed resentments against the rich and powerful quite different from colonial leaders' objections to Parliament's attempt to tax the colonies. The Stamp Act crisis inaugurated not only a struggle for colonial liberty in relation to Great Britain but also a multisided battle to define and extend liberty within America.

THE CRISIS BEGINS

Consolidating the Empire

When George III assumed the throne of Great Britain in 1760, no one on either side of the Atlantic imagined that within two decades Britain's American colonies would separate from the empire. Having treated the colonists as allies during the war, Britain reverted in the mid-1760s to seeing them as subordinates whose main role was to enrich the mother country. During this period, the government in London concerned itself with the colonies in unprecedented ways, hoping to make British rule more efficient and systematic and to raise funds to help pay for the war and to finance the empire. Nearly all British political leaders supported the new laws that so enraged the colonists. Americans, Britons felt, should be grateful to the empire. To fight the Seven Years' War, Britain had borrowed from banks and individual investors more than £150 million (the equivalent of tens of trillions of dollars in today's money). It seemed only reasonable that the colonies should help pay this national debt, foot part of the bill for continued British protection, and stop cheating the treasury by violating the Navigation Acts.

According to the doctrine of "virtual representation," the House of Commons represented all residents of the British empire, whether or not they could vote for members. In this 1775 cartoon criticizing the idea, a blinded Britannia, on the far right, stumbles into a pit. Next to her, two colonists complain of being robbed by British taxation. In the background, according to an accompanying explanation of the cartoon, stand the "Catholic" city of Quebec and the "Protestant town of Boston," the latter in flames.

Nearly all Britons, moreover, believed that Parliament represented the entire empire and had a right to legislate for it. Millions of Britons, including the residents of major cities like Manchester and Birmingham, had no representatives in Parliament. But according to the widely accepted theory of **"virtual representation"**—which held that each member represented the entire empire, not just his own district—the interests of all who lived under the British crown were supposedly taken into account. When Americans began to insist that because they were unrepresented in Parliament, the British government could not tax the colonies, they won little support in the mother country.

The British government had already alarmed many colonists by issuing **writs of assistance** to combat smuggling. These were general search warrants that allowed customs officials to search anywhere they chose for smuggled goods. In a celebrated court case in Boston in 1761, the lawyer James Otis insisted that the writs were "an instrument of arbitrary power, destructive to English liberty, and the fundamental principles of the Constitution," and that Parliament therefore had no right to authorize them. ("American independence was then and there born," the Boston lawyer John Adams later remarked—a considerable exaggeration.) Many colonists were also outraged by the Proclamation of 1763 (mentioned in the previous chapter), which barred further settlement on lands west of the Appalachian Mountains.

Outrage in the colonies

Taxing the Colonies

The Sugar Act of 1764

In 1764, the **Sugar Act**, introduced by Prime Minister George Grenville, reduced the existing tax on molasses imported into North America from the French West Indies from six pence to three pence per gallon. But the act also established a new machinery to end widespread smuggling by colonial merchants. And to counteract the tendency of colonial juries to acquit merchants charged with violating trade regulations, it strengthened the admiralty courts, where accused smugglers could be judged without benefit of a jury trial. Thus, colonists saw the measure not as a welcome reduction in taxation but as an attempt to get them to pay a levy they would otherwise have evaded. At the same time, the Currency Act reaffirmed the earlier ban on colonial assemblies' issuing paper as "legal tender"—that is, money that individuals are required to accept in payment of debts.

The Stamp Act of 1765

The Sugar Act was an effort to strengthen the long-established (and long-evaded) Navigation Acts. The Stamp Act of 1765 was a new departure in imperial policy. For the first time, Parliament attempted to raise money from direct taxes in the colonies rather than through the regulation of trade. The act required that all sorts of printed material produced in the colonies—such as newspapers, books, court documents, commercial papers, land deeds, almanacs—carry a stamp purchased from authorities. Its purpose was to help finance the operations of the empire, including the cost of stationing British troops in North America, without seeking revenue from colonial assemblies.

Whereas the Sugar Act had mainly affected residents of colonial ports, the Stamp Act managed to offend virtually every free colonist—rich and poor, farmers, artisans, and merchants. It was especially resented by members of the public sphere who wrote, published, and read books and newspapers and followed political affairs. The prospect of a British army permanently stationed on American soil also alarmed many colonists. And by imposing the stamp tax without colonial consent, Parliament directly challenged the authority of local elites who, through the assemblies they controlled, had established their power over the raising and spending of money. They were ready to defend this authority in the name of liberty.

Opposition to the Stamp Act

Opposition to the Stamp Act was the first great drama of the revolutionary era and the first major split between colonists and Great Britain over the meaning of freedom. Nearly all colonial political leaders opposed the act. In voicing their grievances, they invoked the rights of the freeborn Englishman, which, they insisted, colonists should also enjoy. Opponents of the act occasionally referred to the natural rights of all mankind. More frequently, however, they drew on time-honored British principles such as a community's right not to be taxed except by its elected representatives. Liberty, they insisted, could not be secure where property was "taken away without consent."

Taxation and Representation

At stake were clashing ideas of the British empire itself. American leaders viewed the empire as an association of equals in which free settlers overseas enjoyed the same rights as Britons at home. Colonists in other outposts of the empire, such as India, the West Indies, and Canada, echoed this outlook. All, in the name of liberty, claimed the right to govern their own affairs. The British government and its appointed representatives in America, by contrast, saw the empire as a system of unequal parts in which different principles governed different areas, and all were subject to the authority of Parliament. To surrender the right to tax the colonies would set a dangerous precedent for the empire as a whole.

Views of the British empire

Some opponents of the Stamp Act distinguished between "internal" taxes like the stamp duty, which they claimed Parliament had no right to impose, and revenue legitimately raised through the regulation of trade. But more and more colonists insisted that Britain had no right to tax them at all, since Americans were unrepresented in the House of Commons. "No taxation without representation" became their rallying cry. Virginia's House of Burgesses approved four resolutions offered by the fiery orator Patrick Henry. They insisted that the colonists enjoyed the same "liberties, privileges, franchises, and immunities" as residents of the mother country and that the right to consent to taxation was a cornerstone of "British freedom." (The House of Burgesses rejected as too radical three other resolutions, including Henry's call for outright resistance to unlawful taxation, but these were also reprinted in colonial newspapers.)

"No taxation without representation"

In October 1765, the Stamp Act Congress, with twenty-seven delegates from nine colonies, including some of the most prominent men in America, met in New York and endorsed Virginia's position. Its resolutions began by affirming the "allegiance" of all colonists to the "Crown of Great Britain" and their "due subordination" to Parliament. But they went on to insist that the right to consent to taxation was "essential to the freedom of a people." Soon, merchants throughout the colonies agreed to boycott British goods until Parliament repealed the Stamp Act. This was the first major cooperative action among Britain's mainland colonies. In a sense, by seeking to impose uniformity on the colonies rather than dealing with them individually as in the past, Parliament had inadvertently united America.

This teapot protesting the Stamp Act was produced in England and marketed in colonial America, illustrating the close political and economic connections between the two.

Liberty and Resistance

No word was more frequently invoked by critics of the Stamp Act than "liberty." Throughout the colonies, opponents of the new tax staged mock funerals in which liberty's coffin was carried to a burial ground, only to have the occupant miraculously revived at the last moment, whereupon the assembled crowd repaired to a tavern to celebrate. As the crisis continued, symbols of liberty proliferated. The large elm tree in Boston on which protesters had hanged an effigy of the stamp distributor Andrew Oliver to persuade him to resign his post came to be known as the Liberty Tree. Its image soon appeared in prints and pamphlets throughout the colonies.

The Liberty Tree

Colonial leaders resolved to prevent the new law's implementation, and by and large they succeeded. Even before the passage of the Stamp Act, a **Committee of Correspondence** in Boston communicated with other colonies to encourage opposition to the Sugar and Currency Acts. Now, such committees sprang up in other colonies, exchanging ideas and information about resistance. Initiated by colonial elites, the movement against the Stamp Act quickly drew in a far broader range of Americans. The act, wrote John Adams, who drafted a set of widely reprinted resolutions against the measure, had inspired "the people, even to the lowest ranks," to become "more attentive to their liberties, more inquisitive about them, and more determined to defend them, than they were ever before known."

Organized resistance

Opponents of the Stamp Act, however, did not rely solely on debate. Even before the law went into effect, crowds forced those chosen to administer it to resign and destroyed shipments of stamps. In 1765, New York City residents were organized by the newly created **Sons of Liberty**, who led them in protest processions, posted notices reading "Liberty, Property, and No Stamps," and took the lead in enforcing the boycott of British imports.

A warning by the Sons of Liberty against using the stamps required by the Stamp Act, which are shown on the left.

Stunned by the ferocity of American resistance and pressured by London merchants and manufacturers who did not wish to lose their American markets, the British government retreated. In 1766, Parliament repealed the Stamp Act. But this concession was accompanied by the Declaratory Act, which rejected Americans' claims that only their elected representatives could levy taxes. Parliament, proclaimed this measure, possessed the power to pass laws for "the colonies and people of America . . . in all cases whatsoever." Since the debt-ridden British government continued to need money raised in the colonies, passage of the Declaratory Act promised further conflict.

The Regulators

The Stamp Act crisis was not the only example of violent social turmoil during the 1760s. Many colonies experienced contentious internal divisions as well. As population moved westward, the conflicting land claims of settlers, speculators, colonial governments, and Indians sparked fierce disputes. As in the Stamp Act crisis, "liberty" was the rallying cry, but in this case liberty had less to do with imperial policy than secure possession of land.

Beginning in the mid-1760s, a group of wealthy residents of the South Carolina backcountry calling themselves **Regulators** protested the underrepresentation of western settlements in the colony's assembly and the legislators' failure to establish local governments that could regularize land titles and suppress bands of outlaws.

A parallel movement in North Carolina mobilized small farmers, who refused to pay taxes, kidnapped local officials, assaulted the homes of land speculators, merchants, and lawyers, and disrupted court proceedings. Here, the complaint was not a lack of government, but corrupt county authorities. Demanding the democratization of local government, the Regulators condemned the "rich and powerful" (the colony's elite) who used their political authority to prosper at the expense of "poor industrious" farmers. At their peak, the Regulators numbered around 8,000 armed farmers. The region remained in turmoil until 1771, when, in the "battle of Alamance," the farmers were suppressed by the colony's militia.

Backcountry tensions

The emerging rift between Britain and America eventually superimposed itself on conflicts within the colonies. But the social divisions revealed in the Stamp Act riots and backcountry uprisings made some members of the colonial elite fear that opposition to British measures might unleash turmoil at home. As a result, they were more reluctant to challenge British authority when the next imperial crisis arose.

Social divisions and politics

THE ROAD TO REVOLUTION

The Townshend Crisis

In 1767, the government in London decided to impose a new set of taxes on Americans. They were devised by the chancellor of the Exchequer (the cabinet's chief financial minister), Charles Townshend. In opposing the Stamp Act, some colonists had seemed to suggest that they would not object if Britain raised revenue by regulating trade. Taking them at their word, Townshend persuaded Parliament to impose new taxes on goods imported into the colonies and to create a new board of customs commissioners to collect them and suppress smuggling. Although many merchants objected to the new enforcement procedures, opposition to the Townshend duties developed more slowly than in the case of the Stamp Act. Leaders in several colonies nonetheless decided in 1768 to reimpose the ban on importing British goods.

Homespun clothing, a symbol of American resistance

The boycott began in Boston and soon spread to the southern colonies. Reliance on American rather than British goods, on homespun clothing rather than imported finery, became a symbol of American resistance. It also reflected, as the colonists saw it, a virtuous spirit of self-sacrifice as compared with the self-indulgence and luxury many Americans were coming to associate with Britain. Women who spun and wove at home so as not to purchase British goods were hailed as **Daughters of Liberty**.

Nonimportation

The idea of using homemade rather than imported goods especially appealed to Chesapeake planters, who found themselves owing increasing amounts of money to British merchants. Nonimportation, wrote George Washington, gave "the extravagant man" an opportunity to "retrench his expenses" by reducing the purchase of British luxuries, without having to advertise to his neighbors that he might be in financial distress.

Urban artisans, who welcomed an end to competition from imported British manufactured goods, strongly supported the boycott. Philadelphia and New York merchants at first were reluctant to take part, although they eventually agreed to go along. Nonimportation threatened their livelihoods and raised the prospect of unleashing further lower-class turmoil. As had happened during the Stamp Act crisis, the streets of American cities filled with popular protests against the duties imposed by Parliament. Extralegal local committees attempted to enforce the boycott of British goods.

The Boston Massacre

Royal troops in Boston

Boston once again became the focal point of conflict. Royal troops had been stationed in the city in 1768 after rioting that followed the British seizure of the ship *Liberty* for violating trade regulations. The soldiers, who competed for jobs on Boston's waterfront with the city's laborers, became more and more unpopular. On March 5, 1770, a fight between a snowball-throwing crowd of Bostonians and British troops escalated into an armed confrontation that left five Bostonians dead. One of those who fell in what came to be called the **Boston Massacre** was Crispus Attucks, a sailor of mixed Indian-African-white ancestry. The commanding officer and eight soldiers were put on trial in Massachusetts. Ably defended by John Adams, who viewed lower-class crowd actions as a dangerous method of opposing British policies, seven were found not guilty, while two were convicted of manslaughter. But Paul Revere, a member of the Boston Sons of Liberty and a silversmith and engraver, helped to stir up indignation against the British army by producing a widely circulated (and quite inaccurate) print of the Boston Massacre depicting a line of British soldiers firing into an unarmed crowd.

By 1770, as merchants' profits shriveled and many members of the colonial elite found they could not do without British goods, the non-importation movement was collapsing. British merchants, who wished to remove a possible source of future interruption of trade, pressed for repeal of the Townshend duties. When the British ministry agreed, leaving in place only a tax on tea, and agreed to remove troops from Boston, American merchants quickly abandoned the boycott.

The Boston Massacre. Less than a month after the Boston Massacre of 1770, in which five colonists died, Paul Revere produced this engraving of the event. Although it inaccurately depicts what was actually a disorganized brawl between residents of Boston and British soldiers, this image became one of the most influential pieces of political propaganda of the revolutionary era.

Wilkes and Liberty

Once again, an immediate crisis had been resolved. Nonetheless, many Americans concluded that Britain was succumbing to the same pattern of political corruption and decline of liberty that afflicted other countries. The overlap of the Townshend crisis with a controversy in Britain over the treatment of John Wilkes reinforced this sentiment. A radical journalist known for scandalous writings about the king and ministry, Wilkes had been elected to Parliament from London but was expelled from his seat. "Wilkes and Liberty" became a popular rallying cry on both sides of the Atlantic. In addition, rumors circulated in the colonies that the Anglican Church in England planned to send bishops

William Hogarth's depiction of John Wilkes holding a liberty cap. Wilkes's publication, *North Briton*, bitterly attacked the king and prime minister, for which Wilkes was arrested, tried, and acquitted by a London jury. He became a popular symbol of freedom on both sides of the Atlantic.

to America. Among members of other Protestant denominations, the rumors—strongly denied in London—sparked fears that bishops would establish religious courts like those that had once persecuted Dissenters.

The Tea Act

The next crisis underscored how powerfully events in other parts of Britain's global empire affected the American colonies. The East India Company, a giant trading monopoly, effectively governed recently acquired British possessions in India. Numerous British merchants, bankers, and other individuals had invested heavily in its stock. A classic speculative bubble ensued, with the price of stock in the company rising sharply and then collapsing. To rescue the company and its investors, the British government decided to help it market its enormous holdings of Chinese tea in North America.

To further stimulate its sales and bail out the East India Company, the British government, now headed by Frederick Lord North, offered the company a series of rebates and tax exemptions. These enabled it to dump low-priced tea on the American market, undercutting both established merchants and smugglers.

The tax on tea was not new. But many colonists insisted that to pay it on this large new body of imports would acknowledge Britain's right to tax the colonies. As tea shipments arrived, resistance developed in the major ports. On December 16, 1773, a group of colonists disguised as Indians boarded three ships at anchor in Boston Harbor and threw more than 300 chests of tea into the water. The event became known as the **Boston Tea Party**. The loss to the East India Company was around £10,000 (the equivalent of more than $4 million today).

The Intolerable Acts

British response to the Tea Party

The British government, declared Lord North, must now demonstrate "whether we have, or have not, any authority in that country." Its response to the Boston Tea Party was swift and decisive. Parliament closed the port of Boston to all trade until the tea was paid for. It radically altered the Massachusetts Charter of 1691 by curtailing town meetings and authorizing the governor to appoint members to the council—positions previously filled by election. Parliament also empowered military commanders to lodge soldiers in private homes. These measures, called the Coercive or Intolerable Acts by Americans, united the colonies in opposition to what was widely seen as a direct threat to their political freedom.

At almost the same time, Parliament passed the Quebec Act. This extended the southern boundary of that Canadian province to the Ohio River and granted legal toleration to the Roman Catholic Church in Canada. The act not only threw into question land claims in the Ohio country but persuaded many colonists that the government in London was conspiring to strengthen Catholicism—dreaded by most Protestants—in its American empire.

The Mitred Minuet, a British cartoon from 1774, shows four Roman Catholic bishops dancing around a copy of the Quebec Act. On the left, British officials Lord Bute, Lord North, and Lord Mansfield look on, while the devil oversees the proceedings.

THE COMING OF INDEPENDENCE

The Continental Congress

Opposition to the Intolerable Acts now spread to small towns and rural areas that had not participated actively in previous resistance. In September 1774, in the town of Worcester, Massachusetts, 4,600 militiamen from thirty-seven towns (half the adult male population of the entire county) lined both sides of Main Street as the British-appointed officials walked the gauntlet between them. In the same month, a convention of delegates from Massachusetts towns approved a series of resolutions (called the Suffolk Resolves for the county in which Boston is located) that urged Americans to refuse obedience to the new laws, withhold taxes, and prepare for war.

Suffolk Resolves

To coordinate resistance to the Intolerable Acts, a Continental Congress convened in Philadelphia that month, bringing together the most prominent political leaders of twelve mainland colonies (Georgia did not take part). From Massachusetts came the "brace of Adamses"—John and his more radical cousin Samuel. Virginia's seven delegates included George Washington, Richard Henry Lee, and the renowned orator Patrick Henry. "The distinctions between Virginians, Pennsylvanians, New Yorkers, and New Englanders," Henry declared, "are no more. I am not a Virginian, but an American." In March 1775, Henry concluded a speech urging a Virginia convention to begin military preparations with a legendary credo: "Give me liberty, or give me death!"

Leaders of the Congress

The Continental Association

Before it adjourned at the end of October 1774, the Congress endorsed the Suffolk Resolves and adopted the Continental Association, which called for an almost complete halt to trade with Great Britain and the West Indies (at South Carolina's insistence, exports of rice to Europe were exempted). Congress authorized local Committees of Safety to oversee its mandates and to take action against "enemies of American liberty," including businessmen who tried to profit from the sudden scarcity of goods.

The Committees of Safety

The Committees of Safety began the process of transferring effective political power from established governments whose authority derived from Great Britain to extralegal grassroots bodies reflecting the will of the people. By early 1775, some 7,000 men were serving on local committees throughout the colonies, a vast expansion of the "political nation." The committees became training grounds where small farmers, city artisans, propertyless laborers, and others who had heretofore had little role in government discussed political issues and exercised political power. When the New York assembly refused to endorse the association, local committees continued to enforce it anyway.

The Sweets of Liberty

By 1775, talk of liberty pervaded the colonies. The past few years had witnessed an endless parade of pamphlets with titles like *A Chariot of Liberty* and *Oration on the Beauties of Liberty*. (The latter, a sermon delivered in Boston by Joseph Allen in 1772, became the most popular public address of the years before independence.) Sober men spoke longingly of the "sweets of liberty." One anonymous essayist reported a "night vision" of the word written in the sun's rays. Commented a British emigrant who arrived in Maryland early in 1775: "They are all liberty mad."

Natural rights

As the crisis deepened, Americans increasingly based their claims not simply on the historical rights of Englishmen but on the more abstract language of natural rights and universal freedom. The First Continental Congress defended its actions by appealing to the "principles of the English constitution," the "liberties of free and natural-born subjects within the realm of England," and the "immutable law of nature." John Locke's theory of natural rights offered a powerful justification for colonial resistance, as did Thomas Jefferson in *A Summary View of the Rights of British America*, written in 1774. Americans, Jefferson declared, were "a free people claiming their rights, as derived from the laws of nature, and not as the gift of their chief magistrate."

The Outbreak of War

By the time the Second Continental Congress convened in May 1775, war had broken out between British soldiers and armed citizens of Massachusetts. On April 19, a force of British soldiers marched from Boston toward the nearby town of Concord seeking to seize arms being stockpiled there. Riders from Boston, among them Paul Revere,

In March 1776, James Pike, a soldier in the Massachusetts militia, carved this scene on his powder horn to commemorate the battles of Lexington and Concord. At the center stands the Liberty Tree.

warned local leaders of the troops' approach. Militiamen took up arms and tried to resist the British advance. Skirmishes between Americans and British soldiers took place at Lexington and again at Concord. By the time the British retreated to the safety of Boston, some forty-nine Americans and seventy-three members of the Royal Army lay dead.

What the philosopher Ralph Waldo Emerson would later call "the shot heard 'round the world" began the American War of Independence. In May 1775, Ethan Allen and the Green Mountain Boys from Vermont, together with militiamen from Connecticut led by Benedict Arnold, surrounded Fort Ticonderoga in New York and forced it to surrender. The following winter, Henry Knox, George Washington's commander of artillery, arranged for some of the Ticonderoga cannon to be dragged hundreds of miles to the east to reinforce the siege of Boston, where British forces were ensconced. On June 17, 1775, two months after Lexington and Concord, the British had dislodged colonial militiamen from Breed's Hill, although only at a heavy cost in casualties. (The battle came to be named after the nearby Bunker Hill.) But the arrival of American cannon in March 1776 and their entrenchment above the city made the British position in Boston untenable. The British army under the command of Sir William Howe was forced to abandon the city. Before leaving, Howe's forces cut down the original Liberty Tree.

Conflict in Boston

Meanwhile, the Second Continental Congress authorized the raising of an army, printed money to pay for it, and appointed George Washington its commander. In response, Britain declared the colonies in a state of rebellion, dispatched thousands of troops, and ordered the closing of all colonial ports.

The Second Continental Congress

Independence?

By the end of 1775, the breach with Britain seemed irreparable. But many colonists shied away from the idea of independence. Pride in membership in the British empire was still strong, and many political leaders, especially in colonies that had experienced internal turmoil, feared that a complete break with the mother country might unleash further conflict.

Such fears affected how colonial leaders responded to the idea of independence. The elites of Massachusetts and Virginia, who felt supremely confident of their ability to retain authority at home, tended to support a break with Britain. Southern leaders not only were highly protective of their political liberty but also were outraged by a proclamation issued in November 1775 by **Lord Dunmore**, the British governor and military commander in Virginia, offering freedom to any slave who escaped to his lines and bore arms for the king.

In New York and Pennsylvania, however, the diversity of the population made it difficult to work out a consensus on how far to go in resisting British measures. Many established leaders drew back from further resistance. Joseph Galloway, a Pennsylvania leader and delegate to the Second Continental Congress who worked to devise a compromise between British and colonial positions, warned that independence would be accompanied by constant disputes within America. He even predicted a war between the northern and southern colonies.

Paine's *Common Sense*

As 1776 dawned, America presented the unusual spectacle of colonists at war against the British empire but still pleading for their rights within it. Ironically, it was a recent emigrant from England, not a colonist from a family long-established on American soil, who grasped the inner logic of the situation and offered a vision of the broad significance of American independence. Thomas Paine had emigrated to Philadelphia late in 1774. He quickly became associated with a group of advocates of the American cause, including John Adams and Dr. Benjamin Rush, a leading Philadelphia physician. It was Rush who suggested to Paine that he write a pamphlet supporting American independence.

Common Sense appeared in January 1776. The pamphlet began not with a recital of colonial grievances but with an attack on the "so much boasted Constitution of England" and the principles of hereditary rule and monarchical government. Rather than being the most perfect system of government in the world, Paine wrote, the English monarchy was headed by "the royal brute of England," and the English constitution was composed in large part of "the base remains of two ancient tyrannies . . . monarchical tyranny in the person of the king [and] aristocratical tyranny in the persons of the peers."

Turning to independence, Paine drew on the colonists' experiences to make his case. "There is something absurd," he wrote, "in supposing a

Continent to be perpetually governed by an island." With independence, moreover, the colonies could for the first time trade freely with the entire world and insulate themselves from involvement in the endless imperial wars of Europe. Membership in the British empire, Paine insisted, was a burden to the colonies, not a benefit.

Toward the close of the pamphlet, Paine moved beyond practical considerations to outline a breathtaking vision of the historical importance of the American Revolution. "The cause of America," he proclaimed in stirring language, "is in great measure, the cause of all mankind." The new nation would become the home of freedom, "an asylum for mankind."

Most of Paine's ideas were not original. What made *Common Sense* unique was his mode of expressing them and the audience he addressed. Previous political writings had generally been directed toward the educated elite. Paine, however, pioneered a new style of political writing, one designed to expand dramatically the public sphere where political discussion took place. He wrote clearly and directly, and he avoided the complex language and Latin phrases common in pamphlets aimed at educated readers. *Common Sense* quickly became one of the most successful and influential pamphlets in the history of political writing, selling, by Paine's estimate, some 150,000 copies. Paine directed that his share of the profits be used to buy supplies for the Continental army.

In the spring of 1776, scores of American communities adopted resolutions calling for a separation from Britain. Only six months elapsed between the appearance of *Common Sense* and the decision by the Second Continental Congress to sever the colonies' ties with Great Britain.

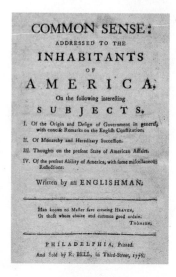

The cover of *Common Sense*, Thomas Paine's influential pamphlet denouncing the idea of hereditary rule and calling for American independence.

The Declaration of Independence

On July 2, 1776, the Congress formally declared the United States an independent nation. Two days later, it approved the **Declaration of Independence**, written by Thomas Jefferson and revised by the Congress before approval. (See the Appendix for the full text.) Most of the Declaration consists of a lengthy list of grievances directed against King George III, ranging from quartering troops in colonial homes to imposing taxes without the colonists' consent. One clause in Jefferson's draft, which condemned the inhumanity of the slave trade and criticized the king for overturning colonial laws that sought to restrict the importation of slaves, was deleted by the Congress at the insistence of Georgia and South Carolina.

Colonial grievances

The Declaration's enduring impact came not from the complaints against George III but from Jefferson's preamble, especially the second paragraph, which begins, "We hold these truths to be self-evident, that all

Jefferson's preamble

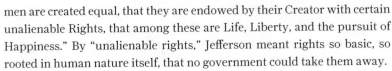

"Unalienable rights"

men are created equal, that they are endowed by their Creator with certain unalienable Rights, that among these are Life, Liberty, and the pursuit of Happiness." By "unalienable rights," Jefferson meant rights so basic, so rooted in human nature itself, that no government could take them away.

Jefferson then went on to justify the breach with Britain. Government, he wrote, derives its powers from "the consent of the governed." When a government threatens its subjects' natural rights, the people have the authority "to alter or to abolish it." The Declaration of Independence is ultimately an assertion of the right of revolution.

The Declaration and American freedom

The Declaration also changed forever the meaning of American freedom. It completed the shift from the rights of Englishmen to the rights of mankind as the object of American independence. No longer a set of specific rights, no longer a privilege to be enjoyed by a corporate body or people in certain social circumstances, liberty had become a universal entitlement.

When Jefferson substituted the "pursuit of happiness" for property in the familiar triad that opens the Declaration, he tied the new nation's star to an open-ended, democratic process whereby individuals develop their own potential and seek to realize their own life goals. Individual self-fulfillment, unimpeded by government, would become a central element of American freedom. Tradition would no longer rule the present, and Americans could shape their society as they saw fit.

An Asylum for Mankind

A distinctive definition of nationality resting on American freedom was born in the Revolution. From the beginning, the idea of "American exceptionalism"—the belief that the United States has a special mission to be a refuge from tyranny, a symbol of freedom, and a model for the rest of the world—has occupied a central place in American nationalism. The new nation declared itself, in the words of Virginia leader James Madison, the "workshop of liberty to the Civilized World." Countless sermons, political tracts, and newspaper articles of the time repeated this idea. Unburdened by the institutions—monarchy, aristocracy, hereditary privilege—that oppressed the peoples of the Old World, America and America alone was the place where the

America as a Symbol of Liberty, a 1775 engraving from the cover of the *Pennsylvania Magazine*, edited by Thomas Paine soon after his arrival in America. The shield displays the colony's coat of arms. The female figure holding a liberty cap is surrounded by weaponry of the patriotic struggle, including a cartridge box marked "liberty," hanging from a tree (*right*).

principle of universal freedom could take root. This was why Jefferson addressed the Declaration to "the opinions of mankind," not just the colonists themselves or Great Britain.

First to add his name to the Declaration of Independence was the Massachusetts merchant John Hancock, president of the Second Continental Congress, with a signature so large, he declared, according to legend, that King George III could read it without his spectacles.

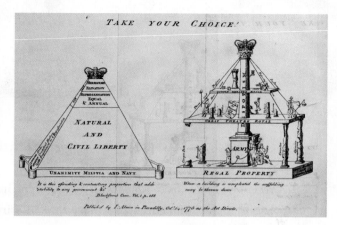

Inspired by the American Revolution, the British reformer John Cartwright published an appeal for the annual election of Parliament as essential to liberty in Britain. He included an engraving contrasting the principles of reform, on the left, with despotism, on the right.

The Global Declaration of Independence

The American colonists were less concerned with securing human rights for all mankind than with winning international recognition in their struggle for independence from Britain. But Jefferson hoped that this rebellion would become "the signal of arousing men to burst the chains . . . and to assume the blessings and security of self-government." And for more than two centuries, the Declaration has remained an inspiration not only to generations of Americans denied the enjoyment of their natural rights but to colonial peoples around the world seeking independence. The Declaration quickly appeared in French and German translations, although not, at first, in Spanish, since the government feared it would inspire dangerous ideas among the peoples of Spain's American empire.

In the years since 1776, numerous anti-colonial movements have modeled their own declarations of independence on America's, often echoing Jefferson's own words. Today more than half the countries in the world, in places as far-flung as China (issued after the revolution of 1911) and Vietnam (1945), have such declarations, though few of them include a list, like Jefferson's, of the rights of citizens that their governments cannot abridge.

Legacy of the Declaration

But even more than the specific language of the Declaration, the principle that legitimate political authority rests on the will of "the people" has been adopted around the world. The idea that "the people" possess rights was quickly internationalized. Slaves in the Caribbean, colonial subjects in India, and indigenous inhabitants of Latin America could all speak this language, to the dismay of those who exercised power over them.

The will of "the people"

VOICES OF FREEDOM

From Thomas Paine, *Common Sense* (1776)

A recent emigrant from England, Thomas Paine in January 1776 published *Common Sense*, **a highly influential pamphlet that in stirring language made the case for American independence.**

In the following pages I offer nothing more than simple facts, plain arguments, and common sense. . . .

Male and female are the distinctions of nature, good and bad the distinctions of heaven; but how a race of men came into the world so exalted above the rest, and distinguished like some new species, is worth enquiring into, and whether they are the means of happiness or of misery to mankind. . . . One of the strongest *natural* proofs of the folly of hereditary right in kings, is, that nature disapproves it, otherwise she would not so frequently turn it into ridicule, by giving mankind an *ass for a lion.* . . .

The sun never shined on a cause of greater worth. 'Tis not the affair of a city, a country, a province, or a kingdom, but of a continent—of at least one eighth part of the habitable globe. 'Tis not the concern of a day, a year, or an age; posterity are virtually involved in the context, and will be more or less affected, even to the end of time, by the proceedings now. Now is the seed time of continental union, faith and honor. . . .

I challenge the warmest advocate for reconciliation to show a single advantage that this continent can reap by being connected with Great Britain. . . . But the injuries and disadvantages which we sustain by that connection, are without number. . . . Any submission to, or dependence on, Great Britain, tends directly to involve this Continent in European wars and quarrels, and set us at variance with nations who would otherwise seek our friendship, and against whom we have neither anger nor complaint.

O ye that love mankind! Ye that dare oppose, not only the tyranny, but the tyrant, stand forth! Every spot of the old world is overrun with oppression. Freedom hath been hunted round the globe. Asia, and Africa, have long expelled her. Europe regards her like a stranger, and England hath given her warning to depart. O! Receive the fugitive, and prepare in time an asylum for mankind.

From Jonathan Boucher, *A View of the Causes and Consequences of the American Revolution* (1775)

An English-born Episcopal minister, Jonathan Boucher preached in Virginia from 1759 to 1775, when he returned to England after receiving threats on his life because of his loyalty to the crown. In 1797 he published in London a series of sermons he had delivered in 1775 explaining his opposition to the revolutionary movement.

Obedience to government is every man's duty, because it is every man's interest; but it is particularly incumbent on Christians, because . . . it is enjoined by the positive commands of God; and, therefore, when Christians are disobedient to human ordinances, they are also disobedient to God. If the form of government . . . be mild and free, it is our duty to enjoy it with gratitude and with thankfulness and, in particular, to be careful not to abuse it by licentiousness. If it be less indulgent and less liberal than in reason it ought to be, still it is our duty not to disturb and destroy the peace of the community by becoming refractory and rebellious subjects. . . . However humiliating such acquiescence may seem to men of warm and eager minds, the wisdom of God in having made it our duty is manifest. For, as it is the natural temper and bias of the human mind to be impatient under restraint, it was wise and merciful in the blessed Author of our religion . . . with the whole weight of his authority, altogether to discountenance every tendency to disobedience. . . .

Liberty is not the setting at nought and despising established laws—much less the making our own wills the rule of our own actions, or the actions of others . . . but it is the being governed by law and by law only. The Greeks described Eleutheria, or Liberty, as the daughter of Jupiter, the supreme fountain of power and law. . . . Their idea, no doubt, was that liberty was the fair fruit of just authority and that it consisted in men's being subjected to law. The more carefully well-devised restraints of law are enacted, and the more rigorously they are executed in any country, the greater degree of civil liberty does that country enjoy. To pursue liberty, then, in a manner not warranted by law, whatever the pretense may be, is clearly to be hostile to liberty; and those persons who thus *promise you liberty* are themselves *the servants of corruption.*

QUESTIONS

1. *What does Paine see as the global significance of the American struggle for independence?*

2. *Why does Boucher believe that obedience to government is particularly important for Christians?*

3. *How do the two writers differ in their understanding of freedom?*

SECURING INDEPENDENCE

The Balance of Power

Britain's advantages

Declaring Americans independent was one thing; winning independence another. The newly created American army confronted the greatest military power on earth. Viewing the Americans as traitors, Britain resolved to crush the rebellion. On the surface, the balance of power seemed heavily weighted in Britain's favor. It had a well-trained army (supplemented by hired soldiers from German states like Hesse), the world's most powerful navy, and experienced military commanders. The Americans had to rely on local militias and an inadequately equipped Continental army.

American advantages

On the other hand, American soldiers were fighting on their own soil for a cause that inspired devotion and sacrifice. During the eight years of war from 1775 to 1783, some 200,000 men bore arms in the American army (whose soldiers were volunteers) and militias (where service was required of every able-bodied man unless he provided a substitute). The patriots suffered dearly for the cause. Of the colonies' free white male population aged sixteen to forty-five, one in twenty died in the War of Independence, the equivalent of nearly 3 million deaths in today's population. But so long as the Americans maintained an army in the field, the idea of independence remained alive no matter how much territory the British occupied.

The role of France

Despite British power, to conquer the thirteen colonies would be an enormous and expensive task, and it was not at all certain that the public at home wished to pay the additional taxes that a lengthy war would require. Moreover, European rivals, notably France, welcomed the prospect of a British defeat. If the Americans could forge an alliance with France, a world power second only to Britain, it would go a long way toward equalizing the balance of forces.

Blacks in the Revolution

At the war's outset, George Washington refused to accept black recruits. But he changed his mind after Lord Dunmore's 1775 proclamation, which offered freedom to slaves who joined the British cause. Some 5,000 blacks enlisted in state militias and the Continental army and navy. Since individuals drafted into the militia were allowed to provide a substitute, slaves suddenly gained considerable bargaining power. Not a few acquired their freedom by agreeing to serve in place of an owner or his son. In 1778, Rhode Island, with a higher proportion of slaves in its population than any other New England state, formed a black regiment and promised freedom to slaves who enlisted,

Trading military service for freedom

while compensating the owners for their loss of property. Blacks who fought under George Washington and in other state militias did so in racially integrated companies (although invariably under white officers). They were the last black American soldiers to do so officially until the Korean War.

Except for South Carolina and Georgia, the southern colonies also enrolled free blacks and slaves to fight. They were not explicitly promised freedom, but many received it individually after the war ended.

American Foot Soldiers, Yorktown Campaign, a 1781 watercolor by a French officer, includes a black soldier from the First Rhode Island Regiment, an all-black unit of 250 men.

Fighting on the side of the British also offered opportunities for freedom. Before his forces were expelled from Virginia, 800 or more slaves had escaped from their owners to join Lord Dunmore's Ethiopian Regiment, wearing uniforms that bore the motto "Liberty to Slaves." Other escaped slaves served the Royal Army as spies, guided their troops through swamps, and worked as military cooks, laundresses, and construction workers. George Washington himself saw seventeen of his slaves flee to the British, some of whom signed up to fight the colonists. "There is not a man of them, but would leave us, if they believed they could make their escape," his cousin Lund Washington reported. "Liberty is sweet."

The First Years of the War

Had the British commander, Sir William Howe, prosecuted the war more vigorously at the outset, he might have nipped the rebellion in the bud by destroying Washington's army. But although Washington suffered numerous defeats in the first years of the war, he generally avoided direct confrontations with the British and managed to keep his army intact. Having abandoned Boston, Howe attacked New York City in the summer of 1776. Washington's army had likewise moved from Massachusetts to Brooklyn to defend the city. Howe pushed American forces back and almost cut off Washington's retreat across the East River.

Early setbacks

Howe pursued the American army but never managed to inflict a decisive defeat. Demoralized by successive failures, however, many American soldiers simply went home. Once 28,000 men, Washington's army dwindled to fewer than 3,000. To restore morale and regain the initiative, he launched successful surprise attacks on Hessian soldiers

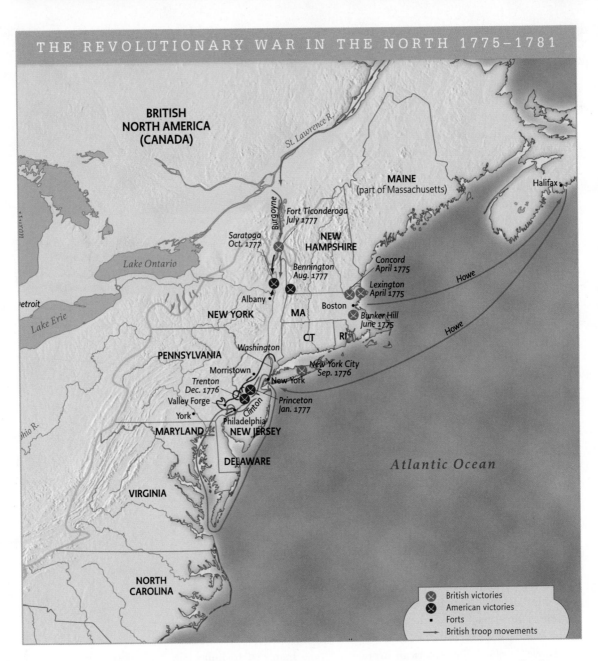

THE REVOLUTIONARY WAR IN THE NORTH 1775–1781

BRITISH NORTH AMERICA (CANADA)

St. Lawrence R.

MAINE (part of Massachusetts)

Halifax

Fort Ticonderoga July 1777

Burgoyne

Saratoga Oct. 1777

NEW HAMPSHIRE

Bennington Aug. 1777

Lake Ontario

Albany

NEW YORK

MA

Concord April 1775

Howe

Lexington April 1775

Boston

Bunker Hill June 1775

Detroit

Lake Erie

CT **RI**

Howe

Washington

PENNSYLVANIA

Morristown

New York City Sep. 1776

Trenton Dec. 1776

New York

Valley Forge

Clinton

Princeton Jan. 1777

York

Philadelphia

MARYLAND

NEW JERSEY

Ohio R.

DELAWARE

Atlantic Ocean

VIRGINIA

NORTH CAROLINA

⊗ British victories
⊗ American victories
■ Forts
→ British troop movements

Key battles in the North during the War of Independence included Lexington and Concord, which began the armed conflict; the campaign in New York and New Jersey; and Saratoga, sometimes called the turning point of the war.

at Trenton, New Jersey, on December 26, 1776, and on a British force at Princeton on January 3, 1777. Shortly before crossing the Delaware River to attack the Hessians, Washington had Thomas Paine's inspiring essay *The American Crisis* read to his troops. "These are the times that try men's souls," Paine wrote. "The summer soldier and the sunshine patriot will, in this crisis, shrink from the service of their country; but he that stands it *now*, deserves the love and thanks of man and woman."

The Battle of Saratoga

In the summer of 1777, a second British army, led by General John Burgoyne, advanced south from Canada, hoping to link up with Howe and isolate New England. But in July, Howe instead moved his forces from New York City to attack Philadelphia. In September, the Continental Congress fled to Lancaster in central Pennsylvania, and Howe occupied the City of Brotherly Love. Not having been informed of Burgoyne's plans, Howe had unintentionally abandoned him. American forces blocked Burgoyne's way, surrounded his army, and on October 17, 1777, forced him to surrender at Saratoga. The victory provided a significant boost to American morale.

Howe and Burgoyne

During the winter of 1777–1778, the British army, now commanded by Sir Henry Clinton, was quartered in Philadelphia. (In the Revolution, as in most eighteenth-century wars, fighting came to a halt during the winter.) Meanwhile, Washington's army remained encamped at Valley Forge, where they suffered terribly from the frigid weather. Men who had other options simply went home. By the end of that difficult winter, recent immigrants and African-Americans made up half the soldiers at Valley Forge, and most of the rest were landless or unskilled laborers.

Valley Forge

But Saratoga helped to persuade the French that American victory was possible. In 1778, American diplomats led by Benjamin Franklin concluded a Treaty of Amity and Commerce in which France recognized the United States and agreed to supply military assistance. Soon afterward, Spain also joined the war on the American side. French assistance would play a decisive part in the war's end. At the outset, however, the French fleet showed more interest in attacking British outposts in the West Indies than directly aiding the Americans. Nonetheless, French and Spanish entry transformed the War of Independence into a global conflict. By putting the British on the defensive in places ranging from Gibraltar to the West Indies, it greatly complicated their military prospects.

Alliance with France

The War in the South

In 1778, the focus of the war shifted to the South. Here the British hoped to exploit the social tensions between backcountry farmers and wealthy planters that had surfaced in the Regulator movements, to enlist the support of the numerous colonists in the region who remained loyal to the crown, and to disrupt the economy by encouraging slaves to escape. In December 1778, British forces occupied Savannah, Georgia. In May 1780, Clinton captured Charleston, South Carolina, and with it an American army of 5,000 men.

Setbacks in 1780

The year 1780 was arguably the low point of the struggle for independence. Congress was essentially bankrupt, and the army went months without being paid. The British seemed successful in playing on social conflicts within the colonies, as thousands of southern Loyalists joined up with British forces (fourteen regiments from Savannah alone) and tens of thousands of slaves sought freedom by fleeing to British lines. In August, Lord Charles Cornwallis routed an American army at Camden, South Carolina. The following month one of Washington's ablest commanders, Benedict Arnold, defected and almost succeeded in turning over to the British the important fort at West Point on the Hudson River.

Militia attacks

But the British failed to turn these advantages into victory. British commanders were unable to consolidate their hold on the South. Wherever their forces went, American militias harassed them. Hit-and-run attacks by militiamen under Francis Marion, called the "swamp fox" because his men emerged from hiding places in swamps to strike swiftly and then disappear, eroded the British position in South Carolina. A bloody civil war engulfed North and South Carolina and Georgia, with patriot and Loyalist militias inflicting retribution on each other and plundering the farms of their opponents' supporters. The brutal treatment of civilians by British forces under Colonel Banastre Tarleton persuaded many Americans to join the patriot cause.

Victory at Last

In January 1781, American forces under Daniel Morgan dealt a crushing defeat to Tarleton at Cowpens, South Carolina. Two months later, at Guilford Courthouse, North Carolina, General Nathanael Greene, while conducting a campaign of strategic retreats, inflicted heavy losses on Lord Charles Cornwallis, the British commander in the South. Cornwallis

Yorktown

moved into Virginia and encamped at Yorktown, located on a peninsula

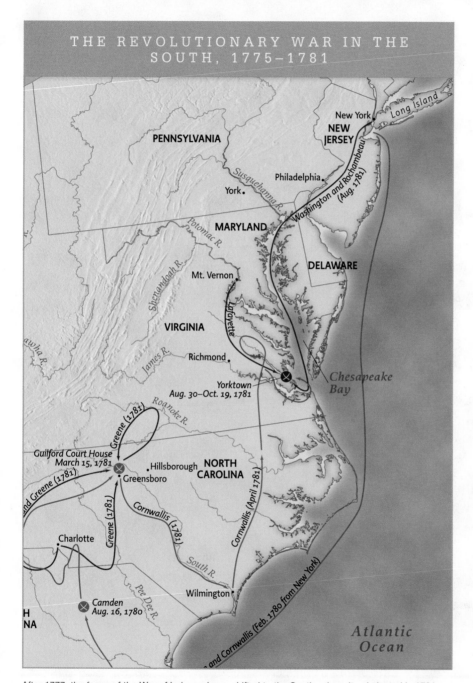

THE REVOLUTIONARY WAR IN THE SOUTH, 1775–1781

PENNSYLVANIA

New York

NEW JERSEY

Long Island

Philadelphia

York

Susquehanna R.

Washington and Rochambeau (Aug. 1781)

Potomac R.

MARYLAND

DELAWARE

Shenandoah R.

Mt. Vernon

Lafayette

VIRGINIA

James R.

Richmond

Kanawha R.

Yorktown
Aug. 30–Oct. 19, 1781

Chesapeake Bay

Greene (1781)

Roanoke R.

Guilford Court House
March 15, 1781

Hillsborough

NORTH CAROLINA

and Greene (1781)

Greensboro

Cornwallis (April 1781)

Greene (1781)

Cornwallis (1781)

Charlotte

South R.

Pee Dee R.

Wilmington

Camden
Aug. 16, 1780

H
NA

and Cornwallis (Feb. 1780 from New York)

Atlantic Ocean

After 1777, the focus of the War of Independence shifted to the South, where it culminated in 1781 with the British defeat at Yorktown.

NORTH AMERICA, 1783

UNEXPLORED

RUSSIA

UNEXPLORED

Hudson Bay

BRITISH NORTH AMERICA

Disputed by England and United States

Disputed by England and United States

HUDSON'S BAY COMPANY

NOVA SCOTIA

NEW BRUNSWICK

Disputed by Russia, Spain, and England

UNITED STATES

Atlantic Ocean

Pacific Ocean

LOUISIANA

Disputed by Spain and United States

SPANISH FLORIDA

Bahamas (British)

Cuba

Hispaniola

Gulf of Mexico

MEXICO

Saint Domingue

Jamaica (British)

BRITISH HONDURAS

Caribbean Sea

CENTRAL AMERICA

SOUTH AMERICA

England
Spain
Russia
France
United States

0   250   500 miles
0   250   500 kilometers

The newly independent United States occupied only a small part of the North American continent in 1783.

that juts into Chesapeake Bay. Brilliantly recognizing the opportunity to surround Cornwallis, Washington rushed his forces, augmented by French troops under the Marquis de Lafayette, to block a British escape by land. Meanwhile, a French fleet controlled the mouth of the Chesapeake, preventing supplies and reinforcements from reaching Cornwallis's army.

Imperial rivalries had helped to create the American colonies. Now, the rivalry of European empires helped to secure American independence. Taking land and sea forces together, more Frenchmen than Americans participated in the decisive Yorktown campaign. On October 19, 1781, Cornwallis surrendered his army of 8,000 men. When the news reached London, public support for the war evaporated and peace negotiations soon began.

Two years later, in September 1783, American and British negotiators concluded the **Treaty of Paris**. The American delegation—John Adams, Benjamin Franklin, and John Jay—achieved one of the greatest diplomatic triumphs in the country's history. They not only won recognition of American independence but also gained control of the entire region between Canada and Florida east of the Mississippi River and the right of Americans to fish in Atlantic waters off of Canada (a matter of considerable importance to New Englanders). At British insistence, the Americans agreed that colonists who had remained loyal to the mother country would not suffer persecution and that Loyalists' property that had been seized by local and state governments would be restored.

Until independence, the thirteen colonies had formed part of Britain's American empire, along with Canada and the West Indies. But Canada rebuffed repeated calls to join the War of Independence, and leaders of the West Indies, fearful of slave uprisings, also remained loyal to the crown. With the Treaty of Paris, the United States of America became the Western Hemisphere's first independent nation. Its boundaries reflected not so much the long-standing unity of a geographical region, but the circumstances of its birth.

A French engraving depicts New Yorkers tearing down the statue of King George III in July 1776, after the approval of the Declaration of Independence. Slaves are doing the work, while whites look on. The statue was later melted down to make bullets for the Continental army.

Territorial gains

CHAPTER REVIEW AND ONLINE RESOURCES

REVIEW QUESTIONS

1. *Patrick Henry proclaimed that he was not a Virginian, but rather an American. What unified the colonists and what divided them at the time of the Revolution?*

2. *Discuss the ramifications of using slaves in the British and Continental armies. Why did the British authorize the use of slaves? Why did the Americans? How did the slaves benefit?*

3. *Why did the colonists reach the conclusion that membership in the empire threatened their freedoms, rather than guaranteed them?*

4. *How did new ideas of liberty contribute to tensions between the social classes in the American colonies?*

5. *Why did people in other countries believe that the American Revolution (or the Declaration of Independence) was important to them or their own countries?*

6. *Summarize the difference of opinion between British officials and colonial leaders over the issues of taxation and representation.*

7. *How did the actions of the British authorities help to unite the American colonists during the 1760s and 1770s?*

KEY TERMS

virtual representation (p. 141)

writs of assistance (p. 141)

Sugar Act (p. 142)

Committee of Correspondence (p. 144)

Sons of Liberty (p. 144)

Regulators (p. 145)

Daughters of Liberty (p. 146)

Boston Massacre (p. 147)

Boston Tea Party (p. 148)

Lord Dunmore (p. 152)

Common Sense (p. 152)

Declaration of Independence (p. 153)

Treaty of Paris (p. 165)

wwnorton.com /studyspace

VISIT STUDYSPACE FOR THESE RESOURCES AND MORE

- A chapter outline
- A diagnostic chapter quiz
- Interactive maps
- Map worksheets
- Multimedia documents

CHAPTER 6

THE REVOLUTION WITHIN

★

1700   Samuel Sewall's *The Selling of Joseph*, first antislavery tract in America

1770s   Freedom petitions presented by slaves to New England courts and legislatures

1776   Adam Smith's *The Wealth of Nations*

John Adams's *Thoughts on Government*

1777   Vermont state constitution bans slavery

1779   Thomas Jefferson writes Bill for Establishing Religious Freedom

Phillipsburgh Proclamation

1780   Ladies' Association of Philadelphia founded

1782   Deborah Sampson enlists in Continental army

Liberty Displaying the Arts and Sciences. This 1792 painting by Samuel Jennings is one of the few visual images of the early republic explicitly linking slavery with tyranny and liberty with abolition. The female figure offers books to newly freed slaves. Other forms of knowledge depicted include a globe and an artist's palette. Beneath her left foot lies a broken chain. In the background, free slaves enjoy some leisure time.

FOCUS QUESTIONS

- How did equality become a stronger component of American freedom after the Revolution?

- How did the expansion of religious liberty after the Revolution reflect the new American ideal of freedom?

- How did the definition of economic freedom change after the Revolution, and who benefited from the changes?

- How did the Revolution diminish the freedoms of both Loyalists and Native Americans?

- What was the impact of the Revolution on slavery?

- How did the Revolution affect the status of women?

Born in Massachusetts in 1744, Abigail Adams became one of the revolutionary era's most articulate and influential women. At a time when educational opportunities for girls were extremely limited, she taught herself by reading books in the library of her father, a Congregational minister. In 1764, she married John Adams. During the War of Independence, with her husband away in Philadelphia and Europe serving the American cause, she stayed behind at their Massachusetts home, raising their four children and managing the family's farm. The letters they exchanged form one of the most remarkable correspondences in American history. A keen observer of public affairs, she kept her husband informed of events in Massachusetts and offered opinions on political matters. Later, when Adams served as president, he relied on her for advice more than on members of his cabinet.

In March 1776, a few months before the Second Continental Congress declared American independence, Abigail Adams wrote her best-known letter to her husband. She began by commenting indirectly on the evils of slavery. How strong, she wondered, could the "passion for Liberty" be among those "accustomed to deprive their fellow citizens of theirs." She went on to urge Congress, when it drew up a "Code of Laws" for the new republic, to "remember the ladies." All men, she warned, "would be tyrants if they could."

It was the leaders of colonial society who initiated resistance to British taxation. But as Abigail Adams's letter illustrates, the struggle for American liberty emboldened other colonists to demand more liberty for themselves. At a time when so many Americans—slaves, indentured servants, women, Indians, apprentices, propertyless men—were denied full freedom, the struggle against Britain threw into question many forms of authority and inequality.

Abigail Adams accepted the prevailing belief that a woman's primary responsibility was to her family. But she resented the "absolute power" husbands exercised over their wives. Her letter is widely remembered today. Less familiar is John Adams's response, which illuminated how the Revolution had unleashed challenges to all sorts of inherited ideas of deference and authority: "We have been told that our struggle has loosened the bands of government everywhere; that children and apprentices were disobedient; that schools and colleges were grown turbulent; that Indians slighted their guardians, and negroes grew insolent to their masters." To John Adams, this upheaval, including his wife's claim to greater freedom, was an affront to the natural order of things. To others, it formed the essence of the American Revolution.

DEMOCRATIZING FREEDOM

The Dream of Equality

The American Revolution took place at three levels simultaneously. It was a struggle for national independence, a phase in a century-long global battle among European empires, and a conflict over what kind of nation an independent America should be.

The Revolution unleashed public debates and political and social struggles that enlarged the scope of freedom and challenged inherited structures of power within America. In rejecting the crown and the principle of hereditary aristocracy, many Americans also rejected the society of privilege, patronage, and fixed status that these institutions embodied. The idea of liberty became a revolutionary rallying cry, a standard by which to judge and challenge homegrown institutions as well as imperial ones.

Jefferson's seemingly straightforward assertion in the Declaration of Independence that "all men are created equal" announced a radical principle whose full implications no one could anticipate. In both Britain and its colonies, a well-ordered society was widely thought to depend on obedience to authority—the power of rulers over their subjects, husbands over wives, parents over children, employers over servants and apprentices, slaveholders over slaves. Inequality had been fundamental to the colonial social order; the Revolution challenged it in many ways. Henceforth, American freedom would be forever linked with the idea of equality—equality before the law, equality in political rights, equality of economic opportunity, and, for some, equality of condition. "Whenever I use the words *freedom* or *rights*," wrote Thomas Paine, "I desire to be understood to mean a perfect equality of them. . . . The floor of Freedom is as level as water."

Expanding the Political Nation

In political, social, and religious life, previously marginalized groups challenged the domination by a privileged few. In the end, the Revolution did not undo the obedience to which male heads of household were entitled from their wives and children, and, at least in the southern states, their slaves. For free men, however, the democratization of freedom was dramatic. Nowhere was this more evident than in challenges to the traditional limitation of political participation to those who owned property.

Abigail Adams, a portrait by Gilbert Stuart, painted over several years beginning in 1800. Stuart told a friend that, as a young woman, Adams must have been a "perfect Venus."

The Revolution and equality

Political participation

In the political thought of the eighteenth century, "democracy" had several meanings. One, derived from the writings of Aristotle, defined democracy as a system in which the entire people governed directly. However, this was thought to mean mob rule. British thinkers sometimes used the word when referring to the House of Commons, the "democratic" branch of a mixed government. In the wake of the American Revolution, the term came into wider use to express the popular aspirations for greater equality inspired by the struggle for independence.

Throughout the colonies, election campaigns became freewheeling debates on the fundamentals of government. Universal male suffrage, religious toleration, and even the abolition of slavery were discussed not only by the educated elite but also by artisans, small farmers, and laborers, now emerging as a self-conscious element in politics. In many colonies-turned-states, members of the militia demanded the right to elect all their officers and to vote for public officials whether or not they met age and property qualifications. They thereby established the tradition that service in the army enabled excluded groups to stake a claim to full citizenship.

The Revolution in Pennsylvania

The Revolution's radical potential was more evident in Pennsylvania than in any other state. Nearly the entire prewar elite opposed independence, fearing that severing the tie with Britain would lead to rule by the "rabble" and to attacks on property. The vacuum of political leadership opened the door for the rise of a new pro-independence grouping, based on the artisan and lower-class communities of Philadelphia, and organized in extralegal committees and the local militia.

Staunch advocates of equality, Pennsylvania's radical leaders particularly attacked property qualifications for voting. "God gave mankind freedom by nature," declared the anonymous author of the pamphlet *The People the Best Governors*, "and made every man equal to his neighbors." The people, therefore, were "the best guardians of their own liberties," and every free man should be eligible to vote and hold office. Three months after independence, Pennsylvania adopted a new state constitution that sought to institutionalize democracy by concentrating power in a one-house legislature elected annually by all men over age twenty-one who paid taxes. It abolished the office of governor, dispensed with property qualifications for officeholding, and provided that schools with low fees be established in every county. It also included clauses guaranteeing "freedom of speech, and of writing," and religious liberty.

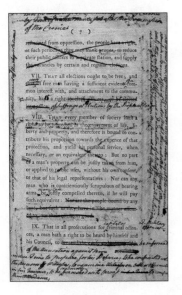

John Dickinson's copy of the Pennsylvania constitution of 1776, with handwritten proposals for changes. Dickinson, one of the more conservative advocates of independence, felt the new state constitution was far too democratic. He crossed out a provision that all "free men" should be eligible to hold office, and another declaring the people not bound by laws that did not promote "the common good."

The New Constitutions

Like Pennsylvania, every state adopted a new constitution in the aftermath of independence. Nearly all Americans now agreed that their governments must be **republics**, meaning that their authority rested on the consent of the governed, and that there would be no king or hereditary aristocracy.

New state constitutions

In part to counteract what he saw as Pennsylvania's excessive radicalism, John Adams in 1776 published ***Thoughts on Government***, which insisted that the new constitutions should create "**balanced governments**" whose structure would reflect the division of society between the wealthy (represented in the upper house) and ordinary men (who would control the lower). A powerful governor and judiciary would ensure that neither class infringed on the liberty of the other. Adams's call for two-house legislatures was followed by every state except Pennsylvania, Georgia, and Vermont. But only his own state, Massachusetts, gave the governor an effective veto over laws passed by the legislature. Americans had come to believe that excessive royal authority had undermined British liberty. They had long resented efforts by appointed governors to challenge the power of colonial assemblies. They preferred power to rest with the legislature.

Power in legislature

The Right to Vote

The issue of requirements for voting and officeholding proved far more contentious. To John Adams, as conservative on the internal affairs of America as he had been radical on independence, freedom and equality were opposites. Men without property, he believed, had no "judgment of their own," and the removal of property qualifications, therefore, would "confound and destroy all distinctions, and prostrate all ranks to one common level." Eliminating traditional social ranks, however, was precisely the aim of the era's radical democrats.

The property qualification for suffrage

Democracy gained the least ground in the southern states, whose highly deferential political traditions enabled the landed gentry to retain their control of political affairs. In Virginia and South Carolina, the new constitutions retained property qualifications for voting and authorized the gentry-dominated legislature to choose the governor.

The most democratic new constitutions moved much of the way toward the idea of voting as an entitlement rather than a privilege, but they generally stopped short of universal **suffrage**, even for free men. Pennsylvania's constitution no longer required ownership of property, but it retained the taxpaying qualification. As a result, it enfranchised nearly all of the state's free male population but still barred a small number, mainly paupers and domestic servants, from voting. Nonetheless, even with the taxpaying requirement, it was a dramatic departure from the colonial practice of restricting the suffrage to those who could claim to be economically independent. It elevated "personal liberty," in the words of one essayist, to a position more important than property ownership in defining the boundaries of the political nation.

Freedom and the right to vote

By the 1780s, except in Virginia, Maryland, and New York, a large majority of the adult white male population could meet voting requirements. New Jersey's new state constitution of 1776 granted the suffrage to all "inhabitants" who met a property qualification. Until the state added the word "male" (along with "white") in 1807, property-owning women, mostly widows, did cast ballots. In the popular language of politics if not in law, freedom and an individual's right to vote had become interchangeable.

TOWARD RELIGIOUS TOLERATION

As remarkable as the expansion of political freedom was the Revolution's impact on American religion. Religious toleration, declared one Virginia patriot, was part of "the common cause of Freedom." We have already seen that some colonies, like Rhode Island and Pennsylvania, had long made a practice of toleration. But freedom of worship before the Revolution arose

Religious pluralism

more from the reality of religious pluralism than from a well-developed theory of religious liberty. Most colonies supported religious institutions with public funds and discriminated in voting and officeholding against

A 1771 image of New York City lists some of the numerous churches visible from the New Jersey shore, illustrating the diversity of religions practiced in the city.

Catholics, Jews, and even dissenting Protestants. On the very eve of independence, Baptists who refused to pay taxes to support local Congregational ministers were still being jailed in Massachusetts. "While our country are pleading so high for liberty," the victims complained, "yet they are denying of it to their neighbors."

Catholic Americans

The War of Independence weakened the deep tradition of American anti-Catholicism. When the Second Continental Congress decided on an ill-fated invasion of Canada, it invited the inhabitants of predominantly Catholic Quebec to join in the struggle against Britain, assuring them that Protestants and Catholics could readily cooperate. In 1778, the United States formed an alliance with France, a Catholic nation. The indispensable assistance provided by France to American victory strengthened the idea that Catholics had a role to play in the newly independent nation. In fact, this was a marked departure from the traditional notion that the full rights of Englishmen applied only to Protestants. When America's first Roman Catholic bishop, John Carroll of Maryland, visited Boston in 1791, he received a cordial welcome.

Anti-Catholicism weakened

In *Side of the Old Lutheran Church in 1800, York, Pa.* A watercolor by a local artist depicts the interior of one of the numerous churches that flourished after independence. While the choir sings, a man chases a dog out of the building and another man stokes the stove. The institutionalization of religious liberty was one of the most important results of the American Revolution.

Separating Church and State

Many of the leaders of the Revolution considered it essential for the new nation to shield itself from the unruly passions and violent conflicts that religious differences had inspired during the past three centuries. Men like Thomas Jefferson, John Adams, James Madison, and Alexander Hamilton viewed religious doctrines through the Enlightenment lens of rationalism and skepticism. They believed in a benevolent Creator but not in supernatural interventions into the affairs of men.

The drive to separate church and state brought together Deists like Jefferson, who hoped to erect a **"wall of separation"** that would free politics and the exercise of the intellect from religious control, with

members of evangelical sects, who sought to protect religion from the corrupting embrace of government.

The movement toward religious freedom received a major impetus during the revolutionary era. Throughout the new nation, states disestablished their established churches—that is, deprived them of public funding and special legal privileges—although in some cases they appropriated money for the general support of Protestant denominations. The seven state constitutions that began with declarations of rights all declared a commitment to "the free exercise of religion."

To be sure, every state but New York—whose constitution of 1777 established complete religious liberty—kept intact colonial provisions barring Jews from voting and holding public office. Massachusetts retained its Congregationalist establishment well into the nineteenth century. It would not end public financial support for religious institutions until 1833. Throughout the country, however, Catholics gained the right to worship without persecution.

Jefferson and Religious Liberty

In Virginia, Thomas Jefferson drew up a **Bill for Establishing Religious Freedom**, which was introduced in the House of Burgesses in 1779 and adopted, after considerable controversy, in 1786. Jefferson's bill, whose preamble declared that God "hath created the mind free," eliminated religious requirements for voting and officeholding and government financial support for churches, and barred the state from "forcing" individuals to adopt one or another religious outlook. Late in life, Jefferson would list this measure, along with the Declaration of Independence and the founding of the University of Virginia, as the three accomplishments (leaving out his two terms as president) for which he wished to be remembered.

Religious liberty became the model for the revolutionary generation's definition of "rights" as private matters that must be protected from governmental interference. In an overwhelmingly Christian (though not necessarily churchgoing) nation, the separation of church and state drew a sharp line between public authority and a realm defined as "private," reinforcing the idea that rights exist as restraints on the power of government. It also offered a new justification for the idea of the United States as a beacon of liberty. In successfully opposing a Virginia tax for the general support of Christian churches, James Madison insisted that one reason for the complete separation of church and state was to reinforce the principle that the new nation offered "asylum to the persecuted and oppressed of every nation and religion."

The Revolution did not end the influence of religion on American society—quite the reverse. Thanks to religious freedom, the early republic witnessed an amazing proliferation of religious denominations. The most well-established churches—Anglican, Presbyterian, and Congregationalist—found themselves constantly challenged by upstarts like Free-Will Baptists and Universalists. Today, even as debate continues over the proper relationship between spiritual and political authority, more than 1,300 religions are practiced in the United States.

Christian Republicanism

Despite the separation of church and state, colonial leaders were not hostile to religion. Indeed, religious and secular language merged in the struggle for independence, producing an outlook scholars have called **Christian Republicanism**. Proponents of evangelical religion and of republican government both believed that in the absence of some kind of moral restraint (provided by religion and government), human nature was likely to succumb to corruption and vice. Samuel Adams, for example, believed the new nation would become a "Christian Sparta," in which Christianity and personal self-discipline underpinned both personal and national progress. American religious leaders interpreted the American Revolution as a divinely sanctioned event, part of God's plan to promote the development of a good society. Rather than being so sinful that it would have to be destroyed before Christ returned, as many ministers had previously preached, the world, the Revolution demonstrated, could be perfected.

Circle of the Social and Benevolent Affections, an engraving in The Columbian Magazine, 1789, illustrates various admirable qualities radiating outward from the virtuous citizen, including love for one's family, community, nation, and all humanity. Affection only for those of the same religion or "colour" is labeled "imperfect."

A Virtuous Citizenry

Patriot leaders worried about the character of future citizens, especially how to encourage the quality of "virtue," the ability to sacrifice self-interest for the public good. Some, like Jefferson, John Adams, and Benjamin Rush, put forward plans for the establishment of free, state-supported public schools. These would instruct future citizens in what Adams called "the principles of freedom," equipping them for participation in the now-expanded public sphere and for the wise election of representatives. A broad diffusion of

Plans for public schools

TOWARD RELIGIOUS TOLERATION | 175

knowledge was essential for a government based on the will of the people to survive and for America to avoid the fixed class structure of Europe. No nation, Jefferson wrote, could "expect to be ignorant and free."

DEFINING ECONOMIC FREEDOM

Toward Free Labor

In economic as well as political and religious affairs, the Revolution rewrote the definition of freedom. In colonial America, slavery was one part of a broad spectrum of kinds of unfree labor. In the generation after independence, with the rapid decline of indentured servitude and apprenticeship and the transformation of paid domestic service into an occupation for blacks and white females, the halfway houses between slavery and freedom disappeared, at least for white men.

Unfree labor

The democratization of freedom contributed to these changes. The lack of freedom inherent in apprenticeship and servitude increasingly came to be seen as incompatible with republican citizenship. In 1784, a group of "respectable" New Yorkers released a newly arrived shipload of indentured servants on the grounds that their status was "contrary to . . . the idea of liberty this country has so happily established." By 1800, indentured servitude had all but disappeared from the United States. This development sharpened the distinction between freedom and slavery and between a northern economy relying on what would come to be called **"free labor"** (that is, working for wages or owning a farm or shop) and a southern economy ever more heavily dependent on the labor of slaves.

Decline in indentured servitude

The Soul of a Republic

Americans of the revolutionary generation were preoccupied with the social conditions of freedom. Could a republic survive with a sizable dependent class of citizens? "A general and tolerably equal distribution of landed property," proclaimed the educator and newspaper editor Noah Webster, "is the whole basis of national freedom." "Equality," he added, was "the very soul of a republic." At the Revolution's radical edge, some patriots believed that government had a responsibility to limit accumulations of property in the name of equality. To most free Americans, however, "equality" meant equal opportunity, rather than equality of

Equal opportunity rather than equality of condition

View from Bushongo Tavern, an engraving from *The Columbian Magazine*, 1788, depicts the landscape of York County, Pennsylvania, exemplifying the kind of rural independence many Americans thought essential to freedom.

condition. Many leaders of the Revolution nevertheless assumed that in the exceptional circumstances of the New World, with its vast areas of available land and large population of independent farmers and artisans, the natural workings of society would produce justice, liberty, and equality.

Like many other Americans of his generation, Thomas Jefferson believed that to lack economic resources was to lack freedom. Among his achievements included laws passed by Virginia abolishing entail (the limitation of inheritance to a specified line of heirs to keep an estate within a family) and primogeniture (the practice of passing a family's land entirely to the eldest son). These measures, he believed, would help to prevent the rise of a "future aristocracy."

Abolishing entail and primogeniture

The Politics of Inflation

The Revolution thrust to the forefront of politics debates over whether local or national authorities should take steps to bolster household independence and protect Americans' livelihoods by limiting price increases. To finance the war, Congress issued hundreds of millions of dollars in paper money. Coupled with wartime disruption of agriculture and trade and the hoarding of goods by some Americans hoping to profit from shortages, this produced an enormous increase in prices.

Between 1776 and 1779, more than thirty incidents took place in which crowds confronted merchants accused of holding scarce goods off the market. Often, they seized stocks of food and sold them at the traditional "just price," a form of protest common in eighteenth-century England. In one such incident, a crowd of 100 Massachusetts women accused an "eminent, wealthy, stingy merchant" of hoarding coffee, opened his warehouse, and

Responses to wartime inflation

A cartoon from 1777 illustrates discontent with rising prices. One soldier identifies "extortioners" as "the worst enemies of the country." Another complains about serving "my country for sixteen pence per day."

Two visions of economic freedom

carted off the goods. "A large concourse of men," wrote Abigail Adams, "stood amazed, silent spectators of the whole transaction."

The Debate over Free Trade

In 1779, with inflation totally out of control (in one month, prices in Philadelphia jumped 45 percent), Congress urged states to adopt measures to fix wages and prices. This request reflected the belief that the task of republican government was to promote the public good, not individuals' self-interest. But when a Committee of Safety tried to enforce price controls, it met spirited opposition from merchants and other advocates of a free market.

In opposition to the traditional view that men should sacrifice for the public good, believers in **free trade** argued that economic development arose from economic self-interest. Adam Smith's great treatise on economics, *The Wealth of Nations*, published in England in 1776, was beginning to become known in the United States. Smith's argument that the "invisible hand" of the free market directed economic life more effectively and fairly than governmental intervention offered intellectual justification for those who believed that the economy should be left to regulate itself.

Advocates of independence had envisioned America, released from the British Navigation Acts, trading freely with all the world. Opponents of price controls advocated free trade at home as well. "Natural liberty" would regulate prices. Here were two competing conceptions of economic freedom—one based on the traditional view that the interests of the community took precedence over the property rights of individuals, the other that unregulated economic freedom would produce social harmony and public gain. After 1779, state and federal efforts to regulate prices ceased. But the clash between these two visions of economic freedom would continue long after independence had been achieved.

THE LIMITS OF LIBERTY

Colonial Loyalists

Not all Americans shared in the democratization of freedom brought on by the American Revolution. **Loyalists**—those who retained their allegiance to the crown—experienced the conflict and its aftermath as a loss of liberty. Many leading Loyalists had supported American resistance in the 1760s but drew back at the prospect of independence and war. Altogether, an estimated 20 to 25 percent of free Americans remained loyal to the British, and nearly 20,000 fought on their side.

A sizable Loyalist population

There were Loyalists in every colony, but they were most numerous in New York, Pennsylvania, and the backcountry of the Carolinas and Georgia. Some were wealthy men whose livelihoods depended on close working relationships with Britain—lawyers, merchants, Anglican ministers, and imperial officials. Many feared anarchy in the event of an American victory.

The struggle for independence heightened existing tensions between ethnic groups and social classes within the colonies. Some Loyalist ethnic minorities, like Highland Scots in North Carolina, feared that local majorities would infringe on their cultural autonomy. In the South, many backcountry farmers who had long resented the domination of public affairs by wealthy planters sided with the British, as did numerous slaves, who hoped an American defeat would bring them freedom.

Social bases of loyalism

The Loyalists' Plight

The War of Independence was in some respects a civil war among Americans. The new state governments, or in other instances crowds of patriots, suppressed newspapers thought to be loyal to Britain. Pennsylvania arrested and seized the property of Quakers, Mennonites, and Moravians—pacifist denominations who refused to bear arms because of their religious beliefs. With the approval of Congress, many states required residents to take oaths of allegiance to the new nation. Those who refused were denied the right to vote and in many cases forced into exile. Some wealthy Loyalists saw their land confiscated and sold at auction.

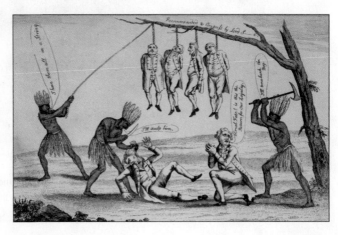

A 1780 British cartoon commenting on the "cruel fate" of American Loyalists. Pro-independence colonists are likened to savage Indians.

When the war ended, as many as 60,000 Loyalists (including 10,000 slaves) were banished from the United States or emigrated voluntarily—mostly to Britain, Canada, or the West Indies—rather than live in an independent United States. But for those who remained, hostility proved to be short-lived. In the Treaty of Paris of 1783, as noted in Chapter 5, Americans pledged to end the persecution of Loyalists by state and local governments and to restore property seized during the war. Loyalists who did not leave the country were quickly reintegrated

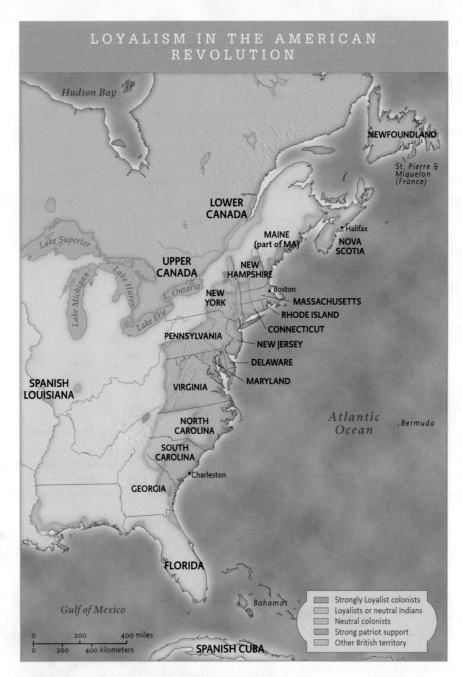

LOYALISM IN THE AMERICAN REVOLUTION

Hudson Bay

NEWFOUNDLAND

St. Pierre & Miquelon (France)

LOWER CANADA

MAINE (part of MA)

• Halifax

NOVA SCOTIA

Lake Superior

UPPER CANADA

NEW HAMPSHIRE

Lake Michigan

Lake Huron

L. Ontario

NEW YORK

• Boston

MASSACHUSETTS

Lake Erie

RHODE ISLAND

PENNSYLVANIA

CONNECTICUT

NEW JERSEY

DELAWARE

MARYLAND

SPANISH LOUISIANA

VIRGINIA

Atlantic Ocean

• Bermuda

NORTH CAROLINA

SOUTH CAROLINA

• Charleston

GEORGIA

FLORIDA

Bahamas

Gulf of Mexico

0   200   400 miles
0   200   400 kilometers

SPANISH CUBA

Legend:
- Strongly Loyalist colonists
- Loyalists or neutral Indians
- Neutral colonists
- Strong patriot support
- Other British territory

The Revolutionary War was, in some ways, a civil war within the colonies. There were Loyalists in every colony; they were most numerous in New York and North and South Carolina.

into American society, although confiscated Loyalist property was not returned.

The Indians' Revolution

Another group for whom American independence spelled a loss of freedom—the Indians—was less fortunate. About 200,000 Native Americans lived east of the Mississippi River in 1790. Like white Americans, Indians divided in allegiance during the War of Independence. Some, like the Stockbridge tribe in Massachusetts, suffered heavy losses fighting the British. Many tribes tried to maintain neutrality, only to see themselves break into pro-American and pro-British factions. Most of the Iroquois nations sided with the British, but the Oneida joined the Americans. Despite strenuous efforts to avoid conflict, members of the Iroquois Confederacy for the first time faced each other in battle. (After the war, the Oneida submitted to Congress claims for losses suffered during the war, including sheep, hogs, kettles, frying pans, plows, and pewter plates—evidence of how fully they had been integrated into the market economy.) In the South, younger Cherokee leaders joined the British while older chiefs tended to favor the Americans. Other southern tribes like the Choctaw and Creek remained loyal to the crown.

Indians' allegiances during the War of Independence

Among the grievances Jefferson listed in the Declaration of Independence was Britain's enlisting "savages" to fight on its side. But in the war that raged throughout the western frontier, savagery was not confined to either combatant. In the Ohio country, the British encouraged Indian allies to burn frontier farms and settlements. For their part, otherwise humane patriot leaders ignored the traditional rules of warfare when it came to Indians. Washington dispatched an expedition, led by **General John Sullivan**, against hostile Iroquois, with the aim of "the total destruction and devastation of their settlements and the capture of as many prisoners of every age and sex as possible." After his campaign ended, Sullivan reported that he had burned forty Indian towns, destroyed thousands of bushels of corn, and uprooted a vast number of fruit trees and vegetable gardens.

Savage warfare

Independence created governments democratically accountable to voters who coveted Indian land. But liberty for whites meant loss of liberty for Indians. Independence offered the opportunity to complete the process of dispossessing Indians of their rich lands in upstate New York, the Ohio Valley, and the southern backcountry. The only hope for the Indians, Jefferson wrote, lay in their "removal beyond the Mississippi."

Dispossession of Indian lands

American independence, a group of visiting Indians told the Spanish governor of St. Louis, was "the greatest blow that could have been dealt us." The Treaty of Paris marked the culmination of a century in which the balance of power in eastern North America shifted away from the Indians and toward white Americans. In the treaty, the British abandoned their Indian allies, agreeing to recognize American sovereignty over the entire region east of the Mississippi River, completely ignoring the Indian presence. In the end there seemed to be no permanent place for the descendants of the continent's native population in a new nation bent on creating an empire in the West.

SLAVERY AND THE REVOLUTION

Although Indians experienced American independence as a real threat to their own liberty, African-Americans saw in the ideals of the Revolution and the reality of war an opportunity to claim freedom. When the United States declared its independence in 1776, the slave population had grown to 500,000, about one-fifth of the new nation's inhabitants.

The Language of Slavery and Freedom

Slavery played a central part in the language of revolution. Apart from "liberty," it was the word most frequently invoked in the era's legal and political literature. In the era's debates over British rule, slavery was primarily a political category, shorthand for the denial of one's personal and political rights by arbitrary government. Those who lacked a voice in public affairs, declared a 1769 petition demanding an expansion of the right to vote in Britain, were "enslaved."

The presence of hundreds of thousands of slaves powerfully affected the meaning of freedom for the leaders of the American Revolution. In a famous speech to Parliament warning against attempts to intimidate the colonies, the British statesman Edmund Burke suggested that familiarity with slavery made colonial leaders unusually sensitive to threats to their own liberties. Where freedom was a privilege, not a common right, he observed, "those who are free are by far the most proud and jealous of their freedom." On the other hand, many British observers

Advertisement for newly arrived slaves, in a Savannah newspaper, 1774. Even as colonists defended their own liberty against the British, the buying and selling of slaves continued.

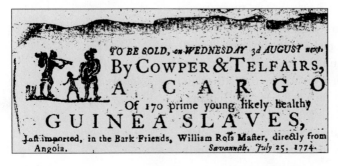

TO BE SOLD, on WEDNESDAY 3d AUGUST next,
By COWPER & TELFAIRS,
A CARGO
Of 170 prime young likely healthy
GUINEA SLAVES,
Juft imported, in the Bark Friends, William Rofs Mafter, directly from Angola.
Savannah, July 25, 1774.

could not resist pointing out the colonists' apparent hypocrisy. "How is it," asked Dr. Samuel Johnson, "that we hear the loudest yelps for liberty from the drivers of negroes?"

Obstacles to Abolition

The contradiction between freedom and slavery seems so self-evident that it is difficult today to appreciate the power of the obstacles to **abolition**. At the time of the Revolution, slavery was already an old institution in America. It existed in every colony and formed the basis of the economy and social structure from Maryland southward. Virtually every founding father owned slaves at one point in his life, including not only southern planters but northern merchants, lawyers, and farmers. (John Adams and Tom Paine were notable exceptions.) Thomas Jefferson owned more than 100 slaves when he wrote of mankind's unalienable right to liberty, and everything he cherished in his own manner of life, from lavish entertainments to the leisure that made possible the pursuit of arts and sciences, ultimately rested on slave labor.

Slavery entrenched

Some patriots, in fact, argued that slavery for blacks made freedom possible for whites. Eliminating the great bulk of the dependent poor from the political nation left the public arena to men of propertied independence. Owning slaves offered a route to the economic autonomy widely deemed necessary for genuine freedom, a point driven home by a 1780 Virginia law that rewarded veterans of the War of Independence with 300 acres of land—and a slave.

Slavery amidst freedom

The Cause of General Liberty

Nonetheless, by imparting so absolute a value to liberty and defining freedom as a universal entitlement rather than a set of rights specific to a particular place or people, the Revolution inevitably raised questions about the status of slavery in the new nation. Before independence, there had been little public discussion of the institution, even though enlightened opinion in the Atlantic world had come to view slavery as morally wrong and economically inefficient, a relic of a barbarous past.

Freedom as universal

Samuel Sewall, a Boston merchant, published *The Selling of Joseph* in 1700, the first antislavery tract printed in America. All "the sons of Adam," Sewall insisted, were entitled to "have equal right unto liberty." During the course of the eighteenth century, antislavery sentiments had spread among Pennsylvania's Quakers, whose belief that all persons possessed the divine "inner light" made them particularly receptive.

But it was during the revolutionary era that slavery for the first time became a focus of public debate. The Pennsylvania patriot Benjamin Rush in 1773 called on "advocates for American liberty" to "espouse the cause of . . . general liberty" and warned that slavery was one of those "national crimes" that one day would bring "national punishment."

Petitions for Freedom

The Revolution inspired widespread hopes that slavery could be removed from American life. Most dramatically, slaves themselves appreciated that by defining freedom as a universal right, the leaders of the Revolution had devised a weapon that could be used against their own bondage. The language of liberty echoed in slave communities, North and South. The most insistent advocates of freedom as a universal entitlement were African-Americans, who demanded that the leaders of the struggle for independence live up to their self-proclaimed creed.

African-Americans advocates for freedom

The first concrete steps toward emancipation in revolutionary America were "**freedom petitions**"—arguments for liberty presented to New England's courts and legislatures in the early 1770s by enslaved African-Americans. How, one such petition asked, could America "seek release from English tyranny and not seek the same for disadvantaged Africans in her midst?" The turmoil of war offered other avenues to freedom. Many slaves ran away from their masters and tried to pass as freeborn. The number of fugitive-slave advertisements in colonial newspapers rose dramatically in the 1770s and 1780s. As one owner put it in accounting for his slave Jim's escape, "I believe he has nothing in view but freedom."

A tray painted by an unknown artist in the early nineteenth century portrays Lemuel Haynes, a celebrated black preacher and critic of slavery.

In 1776, the year of American independence, **Lemuel Haynes**, a black member of the Massachusetts militia and later a celebrated minister, urged Americans to "extend" their conception of freedom. If liberty were truly "an innate principle" for all mankind, Haynes insisted, "even an African [had] as equally good a right to his liberty in common with Englishmen." Like Haynes, many black writers and leaders sought to make white Americans understand slavery as a concrete reality—the denial of all the essential elements of freedom—not a metaphor for lack of political representation, as many whites used the word.

Most slaves of the revolutionary era were only one or two generations removed from Africa. They did not need the ideology of the Revolution to persuade them that freedom was a birthright—the experience of their parents and grandparents suggested as much. "My love of freedom," wrote the black poet Phillis Wheatley in 1783, arose from the "cruel fate" of being "snatch'd from Afric's" shore. Yet when blacks invoked the Revolution's ideology of liberty to demand their own rights and defined freedom as a universal entitlement, they demonstrated how American they had become.

British Emancipators

As noted in the previous chapter, some 5,000 slaves fought for American independence, and many thereby gained their freedom. Yet far more slaves obtained liberty from the British. Lord Dunmore's proclamation of 1775, and the Phillipsburgh Proclamation of General Henry Clinton issued four years later, offered sanctuary to slaves who escaped to British lines. All told, nearly 100,000 slaves, including one-quarter of all the slaves in South Carolina and one-third of those in Georgia, deserted their owners and fled to British lines. This was by far the largest exodus from the plantations until the outbreak of the Civil War.

Some of these escaped slaves were recaptured as the tide of battle turned in the patriots' favor. But at the war's end, more than 15,000 black men, women, and children accompanied the British out of the country. They ended up in Nova Scotia, England, and Sierra Leone, a settlement for former slaves from the United States established by the British on the coast of West Africa. Some were re-enslaved in the West Indies.

The issue of compensation for the slaves who departed with the British poisoned relations between Britain and the new United States for decades to come. Finally, in 1827, Britain agreed to make payments to 1,100 Americans who claimed they had been improperly deprived of their slave property.

Voluntary Emancipations

For a brief moment, the revolutionary upheaval appeared to threaten the continued existence of slavery. During the War of Independence, nearly every state prohibited or discouraged the further importation of slaves from Africa. The war left much of the plantation South in ruins. During the 1780s and 1790s, a considerable number of slaveholders, especially in Virginia and Maryland, voluntarily emancipated their slaves. In 1796, for example, Richard Randolph, a member of a prominent Virginia family, drafted a will

A portrait of the poet Phillis Wheatley (1753–1784).

Freedom through the British

Voluntary emancipations in the South

VOICES OF FREEDOM

From Abigail Adams to John Adams, Braintree, Mass. (March 31, 1776)

From their home in Massachusetts, Abigail Adams maintained a lively correspondence with her husband while he was in Philadelphia serving in the Continental Congress. In this letter, she suggests some of the limits of the patriots' commitment to liberty.

I wish you would write me a letter half as long as I write you, and tell me if you may where your fleet have gone? What sort of defense Virginia can make against our common enemy? Whether it is so situated as to make an able defense? . . . I have sometimes been ready to think that the passion for Liberty cannot be equally strong in the breasts of those who have been accustomed to deprive their fellow creatures of theirs. Of this I am certain, that it is not founded upon that generous and Christian principle of doing to others as we would that others should do unto us. . . .

I long to hear that you have declared an independency, and by the way in the new Code of Laws which I suppose it will be necessary for you to make I desire you would Remember the Ladies, and be more generous and favorable to them than your ancestors. Do not put such unlimited power into the hands of the husbands. Remember all men would be tyrants if they could. If particular care and attention is not paid to the Ladies we are determined to foment a Rebellion, and will not hold ourselves bound by any such laws in which we have no voice, or representation.

That your sex are naturally tyrannical is a truth so thoroughly established as to admit of no dispute, but such of you as wish to be happy willingly give up the harsh title of Master for the more tender and endearing one of Friend. Why then, not put it out of the power of the vicious and the lawless to use us with cruelty and indignity with impunity? Men of sense in all ages abhor those customs which treat us only as the vassals of your sex. Regard us then as beings placed by providence under your protection and in imitation of the Supreme Being make use of that power only for our happiness.

From Petitions of Slaves to the Massachusetts Legislature (1773 and 1777)

Many slaves saw the struggle for independence as an opportunity to assert their own claims to freedom. Among the first efforts toward abolition were petitions by Massachusetts slaves to their legislature.

The efforts made by the legislative of this province in their last sessions to free themselves from slavery, gave us, who are in that deplorable state, a high degree of satisfaction. We expect great things from men who have made such a noble stand against the designs of their *fellow-men* to enslave them. We cannot but wish and hope Sir, that you will have the same grand object, we mean civil and religious liberty, in view in your next session. The divine spirit of *freedom*, seems to fire every breast on this continent. . . .

* * *

Your petitioners apprehend that they have in common with all other men a natural and unalienable right to that freedom which the great parent of the universe hath bestowed equally on all mankind and which they have never forfeited by any compact or agreement whatever but [they] were unjustly dragged by the hand of cruel power from their dearest friends and . . . from a populous, pleasant, and plentiful country and in violation of laws of nature and of nations and in defiance of all the tender feelings of humanity brought here . . . to be sold like beast[s] of burden . . . among a people professing the mild religion of Jesus. . . .

In imitation of the laudable example of the good people of these states your petitioners have long and patiently waited the event of petition after petition by them presented to the legislative body. . . . They cannot but express their astonishment that it has never been considered that every principle from which America has acted in the course of their unhappy difficulties with Great Britain pleads stronger than a thousand arguments in favor of your petitioners [and their desire] to be restored to the enjoyment of that which is the natural right of all men.

QUESTIONS

1. *What does Abigail Adams have in mind when she refers to the "unlimited power" husbands exercise over their wives?*

2. *How do the slaves employ the principles of the Revolution for their own aims?*

3. *What do these documents suggest about the boundaries of freedom in the era of the American Revolution?*

that condemned slavery as an "infamous practice," provided for the freedom of about 90 slaves, and set aside part of his land for them to own. Farther south, however, voluntary emancipation never got under way. Even during the war, when South Carolina needed more troops, the colony's leaders rejected the idea of emancipating some blacks to aid in the fight against the British. They would rather lose the war than lose their slaves.

Abolition in the North

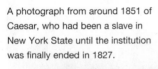

Legislation against slavery

Between 1777 (when Vermont drew up a constitution that banned slavery) and 1804 (when New Jersey acted), every state north of Maryland took steps toward emancipation, the first time in recorded history that legislative power had been invoked to eradicate slavery. But even here, where slavery was peripheral to the economy, the method of abolition reflected how property rights impeded emancipation. Generally, abolition laws did not free living slaves. Instead, they provided for the liberty of any child born in the future to a slave mother, but only after he or she had served the mother's master until adulthood as compensation for the owner's future economic loss.

Because of these legal provisions, abolition in the North was a slow, drawn-out process. The first national census, in 1790, recorded 21,000 slaves still living in New York and 11,000 in New Jersey. The New Yorker John Jay, chief justice of the United States, owned five slaves in 1800. As late as 1830, the census revealed that there were still 3,500 slaves in the North.

A photograph from around 1851 of Caesar, who had been a slave in New York State until the institution was finally ended in 1827.

Free Black Communities

All in all, the Revolution had a contradictory impact on American slavery and, therefore, on American freedom. Gradual as it was, the abolition of slavery in the North drew a line across the new nation, creating the dangerous division between free and slave states. Abolition in the North, voluntary emancipation in the Upper South, and the escape of thousands from bondage created, for the first time in American history, a sizable population of **free blacks** (many of whose members took new family names like Freeman or Freeland).

On the eve of independence, virtually every black person in America had been a slave. Now, free communities, with their own churches, schools, and leaders, came into existence. They formed a standing challenge to the logic of slavery, a haven for fugitives, and a springboard for further efforts at abolition. From 1776 to 1810, the number of free blacks residing in the United States grew from 10,000 to nearly 200,000, and many free black men, especially in the North, enjoyed the right to vote under new state constitutions.

Nonetheless, the stark fact is that slavery survived the War of Independence and, thanks to the natural increase of the slave population, continued to grow. The national census of 1790 revealed that despite all those who had become free through state laws, voluntary emancipation, and escape, the number of slaves in the United States had grown to 700,000—200,000 more than in 1776.

Growth in slave population

DAUGHTERS OF LIBERTY

Revolutionary Women

The revolutionary generation included numerous women who contributed to the struggle for independence. Deborah Sampson, the daughter of a poor Massachusetts farmer, disguised herself as a man and in 1782, at age twenty-one, enlisted in the Continental army. Ultimately, her commanding officer discovered her secret but kept it to himself, and she was honorably discharged at the end of the war. Years later, Congress awarded her a soldier's pension. Other patriotic women participated in crowd actions against unscrupulous merchants, raised funds to assist soldiers, contributed homespun goods to the army, and passed along information about British army movements.

Within American households, women participated in the political discussions unleashed by independence. "Was not every fireside," John Adams later recalled, "a theater of politics?" Gender, nonetheless, formed a boundary limiting those entitled to the full blessings of American freedom. The principle of "**coverture**" (described in Chapter 1) remained intact in the new nation. The husband still held legal authority over the person, property, and choices of his wife. Despite the expansion of democracy, politics remained overwhelmingly a male realm.

For men, political freedom meant the right to self-government, the power to consent to the individuals and political arrangements that ruled over them. For

The 1781 cipher book (a notebook for mathematics exercises) of Martha Ryan, a North Carolina girl, contains images of ships and a port town and the patriotic slogan "Liberty or Death," illustrating how women shared in the political culture of the revolutionary era.

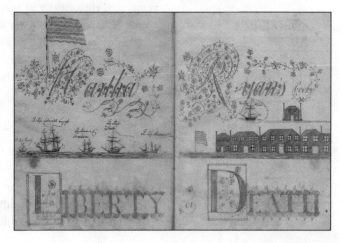

Portrait of John and Elizabeth Lloyd Cadwalader and Their Daughter Anne. This 1772 portrait of a prominent Philadelphia businessman and his family by the American artist Charles Willson Peale illustrates the emerging ideal of the "companionate" marriage, which is based on affection rather than male authority.

women, however, the marriage contract superseded the social contract. A woman's relationship to the larger society was mediated through her relationship with her husband. In both law and social reality, women lacked the essential qualification of political participation—the opportunity for autonomy based on ownership of property or control of one's own person. Overall, the republican citizen was, by definition, male.

Republican Motherhood

The Revolution nonetheless did produce an improvement in status for many women. According to the ideology of "**republican motherhood**" that emerged as a result of independence, women played an indispensable role by training future citizens. Even though republican motherhood ruled out direct female involvement in politics, it encouraged the expansion of educational opportunities for women, so that they could impart political wisdom to their children. Women, wrote Benjamin Rush, needed to have a "suitable education," to enable them to "instruct their sons in the principles of liberty and government."

The idea of republican motherhood reinforced the trend, already evident in the eighteenth century, toward the idea of "companionate" marriage, a voluntary union held together by affection and mutual dependency rather than male authority. In her letter to John Adams quoted above, Abigail Adams recommended that men should willingly give up "the harsh title of Master for the more tender and endearing one of Friend."

A more modern household

The structure of family life itself was altered by the Revolution. In colonial America, those living within the household often included indentured servants, apprentices, and slaves. After independence, southern slaves remained, rhetorically at least, members of the owner's "family." In the North, however, with the rapid decline of various forms of indentured servitude and apprenticeship, a more modern definition of the household as consisting of parents and their children took hold. Hired workers, whether domestic servants or farm laborers, were not considered part of the family.

The Arduous Struggle for Liberty

Significance of the Revolution

The Revolution changed the life of virtually every American. As a result of the long struggle against British rule, the public sphere, and with it the right to vote, expanded markedly. Bound labor among whites declined dramatically, religious groups enjoyed greater liberty, blacks mounted a challenge to slavery in which many won their freedom, and women in

America Triumphant and Britannia in Distress. An elaborate allegory representing American independence as a triumph of liberty, from an almanac published in Boston in 1781. An accompanying key explains the symbolism: (1) America [on the right] holds an olive branch of peace and invites all nations to trade with her. (2) News of America's triumph is broadcast around the world. (3) Britain, seated next to the devil, laments the loss of trade with America. (4) The British flag falls from a fortress. (5) European ships in American waters. (6) Benedict Arnold, the traitor, hangs himself in New York City [in fact, Arnold died of natural causes in London in 1801].

some ways enjoyed a higher status. On the other hand, for Indians, many Loyalists, and the majority of slaves, American independence meant a deprivation of freedom.

The winds of change were sweeping across the Atlantic world. The year 1776 saw not only Paine's *Common Sense* and Jefferson's Declaration but also the publication in England of Adam Smith's *Wealth of Nations*, which attacked the British policy of closely regulating trade, and Jeremy Bentham's *Fragment on Government*, which criticized the nature of British government. Moreover, the ideals of the American Revolution helped to inspire countless subsequent struggles for social equality and national independence, from the French Revolution, which exploded in 1789, to the uprising that overthrew the slave system in Haiti in the 1790s, to the Latin American wars for independence in the early nineteenth century, and numerous struggles of colonial peoples for nationhood in the twentieth. But within the new republic, the debate over who should enjoy the blessings of liberty would continue long after independence had been achieved.

The Revolution's legacy

CHAPTER REVIEW AND ONLINE RESOURCES

REVIEW QUESTIONS

1. *For the lower classes, colonial society had been based on inequality, deference, and obedience. How did the American Revolution challenge that social order?*

2. *Why did the Revolution cause more radical changes in Pennsylvania than elsewhere, and how was this radicalism demonstrated in the new state constitution?*

3. *How did ideas of political freedom affect people's ideas about economic rights and relationships?*

4. *What role did the founders foresee for religion in American government and society?*

5. *What was the impact of the American Revolution on Native Americans?*

6. *What were the most important features of the new state constitutions?*

7. *How did popular views of property rights prevent slaves from enjoying all the freedoms of the social contract?*

8. *How did revolutionary America see both improvements and limitations in women's roles and rights?*

KEY TERMS

republics (p. 171)
Thoughts on Government (p. 171)
balanced government (p. 171)
suffrage (p. 171)
wall of separation (p. 173)
Bill for Establishing Religious Freedom (p. 174)
Christian Republicanism (p. 175)
free labor (p. 176)
inflation (p. 177)
free trade (p. 178)
The Wealth of Nations (p. 178)
Loyalists (p. 178)
General John Sullivan (p. 181)
abolition (p. 183)
freedom petitions (p. 184)
Lemuel Haynes (p. 184)
free blacks (p. 188)
coverture (p. 189)
republican motherhood (p. 190)

wwnorton.com
/studyspace

VISIT STUDYSPACE FOR THESE RESOURCES AND MORE
- A chapter outline
- A diagnostic chapter quiz
- Interactive maps
- Map worksheets
- Multimedia documents

CHAPTER 7

FOUNDING A NATION

★

1783-1791

1777	Articles of Confederation drafted
1781	Articles of Confederation ratified
1782	*Letters from an American Farmer*
1783	Treaty of Paris
1784–1785	Land Ordinances approved
1785	Jefferson's *Notes on the State of Virginia*
1786–1787	Shays's Rebellion
1787	Constitutional Convention
	Northwest Ordinance of 1787
1788	*The Federalist*
	Constitution ratified
1790	Naturalization Act
	First national census
1791	Little Turtle defeats Arthur St. Clair's forces
	Bill of Rights ratified
1794	Little Turtle defeated at Battle of Fallen Timbers
1795	Treaty of Greenville
1808	Congress prohibits the slave trade

Banner of the Society of Pewterers. A banner carried by one of the many artisan groups that took part in New York City's Grand Federal Procession of 1788 celebrating the ratification of the Constitution. The banner depicts artisans at work in their shop and some of their products. The words "Solid and Pure," and the inscription at the upper right, link the quality of their pewter to their opinion of the new frame of government and hopes for the future. The inscription reads:

The Federal Plan Most Solid and Secure
Americans Their Freedom Will Endure
All Arts Shall Flourish in Columbia's Land
And All Her Sons Join as One Social Band

During June and July of 1788, civic leaders in cities up and down the Atlantic coast organized colorful pageants to celebrate the ratification of the U.S. Constitution. For one day, Benjamin Rush commented of Philadelphia's parade, social class "forgot its claims," as thousands of marchers—rich and poor, businessman and apprentice—joined in a common public ceremony. The parades testified to the strong popular support for the Constitution in the nation's cities. Elaborate banners and floats gave voice to the hopes inspired by the new structure of government. "May commerce flourish and industry be rewarded," declared Philadelphia's mariners and shipbuilders.

Throughout the era of the Revolution, Americans spoke of their nation as a "rising empire," destined to populate and control the entire North American continent. Whereas Europe's empires were governed by force, America's would be different. In Jefferson's phrase, it would be "an empire of liberty," bound together by a common devotion to the principles of the Declaration of Independence. Already, the United States exceeded in size Great Britain, Spain, and France combined. As a new nation, it possessed many advantages, including physical isolation from the Old World (a significant asset between 1789 and 1815, when European powers were almost constantly at war), a youthful population certain to grow much larger, and a broad distribution of property ownership and literacy among white citizens.

On the other hand, the nation's prospects at the time of independence were not entirely promising. Control of its vast territory was by no means secure. Nearly all of the 3.9 million Americans recorded in the first national census of 1790 lived near the Atlantic coast. Large areas west of the Appalachian Mountains remained in Indian hands. The British retained military posts on American territory near the Great Lakes, and there were fears that Spain might close the port of New Orleans to American commerce on the Mississippi River.

Away from navigable waterways, communication and transportation were primitive. The country was overwhelmingly rural—fewer than one American in thirty lived in a place with 8,000 inhabitants or more. The population consisted of numerous ethnic and religious groups and some 700,000 slaves, making unity difficult to achieve. No republican government had ever been established over so vast a territory or with so diverse a population. "We have no Americans in America," commented John Adams. It would take time for consciousness of a common nationality to sink deep roots.

Profound questions needed to be answered. What course of development should the United States follow? How could the competing claims of local self-government, sectional interests, and national authority be balanced? Who should be considered full-fledged members of the American people, entitled to the blessings of liberty? These issues became the focus of heated debate as the first generation of Americans sought to consolidate their new republic.

AMERICA UNDER THE CONFEDERATION

The Articles of Confederation

The first written constitution of the United States was the Articles of Confederation, drafted by Congress in 1777 and ratified by the states four years later. The Articles sought to balance the need for national coordination of the War of Independence with widespread fear that centralized political power posed a danger to liberty. It explicitly declared the new national government to be a "perpetual union." But it resembled less a blueprint for a common government than a treaty for mutual defense—in its own words, a "firm league of friendship" among the states. Under the Articles, the thirteen states retained their individual "sovereignty, freedom, and independence." The national government consisted of a one-house Congress, in which each state, no matter how large or populous, cast a single vote. There was no president to enforce the laws and no judiciary to interpret them. Major decisions required the approval of nine states rather than a simple majority.

Limitations of the Articles

The only powers specifically granted to the national government by the Articles of Confederation were those essential to the struggle for independence—declaring war, conducting foreign affairs, and making treaties with other governments. Congress had no real financial resources. It could coin money but lacked the power to levy taxes or regulate commerce. Its revenue came mainly from contributions by the individual states. To amend the Articles required the unanimous consent of the states, a formidable obstacle to change.

But Congress in the 1780s did not lack for accomplishments. The most important was establishing national control over land to the west of the thirteen states and devising rules for its settlement. Citing their original royal charters, which granted territory running all the way to the "South Sea" (the Pacific Ocean), states such as Virginia, the Carolinas, and Connecticut claimed immense tracts of western land. Land speculators, politicians, and prospective settlers from states with clearly

Accomplishments under the Articles

defined boundaries insisted that such land must belong to the nation at large. Only after the land-rich states, in the interest of national unity, ceded their western claims to the central government did the Articles win ratification.

Congress, Settlers, and the West

Establishing rules for the settlement of this national domain—the area controlled by the federal government, stretching from the western boundaries of existing states to the Mississippi River—was critical. Although some Americans spoke of it as if it were empty, some 100,000 Indians inhabited the region. Congress took the position that by aiding the British, Indians had forfeited the right to their lands. But little distinction was made among tribes that had sided with the enemy, aided the patriots, or played no part in the war at all. At peace conferences at Fort Stanwix, New York, in 1784 and Fort McIntosh near Pittsburgh the following year, American representatives demanded and received large surrenders of Indian land north of the Ohio River. Similar treaties soon followed with the Cherokee, Choctaw, and Chickasaw tribes in the South. The treaties secured national control of a large part of the country's western territory.

Treaties to secure Indian land

When it came to disposing of western land and regulating its settlement, the Confederation government faced conflicting pressures. Many leaders believed that the economic health of the new republic required that farmers have access to land in the West. But they also saw land sales as a potential source of revenue.

Rapid settlement in frontier areas

The arrival of peace meanwhile triggered a large population movement from settled parts of the original states into frontier areas like upstate New York and across the Appalachian Mountains into Kentucky and Tennessee. To settlers, the right to take possession of western lands and use them as they saw fit was an essential element of American freedom. When a group of Ohioans petitioned Congress in 1785, assailing landlords and speculators who monopolized available acreage and asking that preference in land ownership be given to "actual settlements," their motto was "Grant us Liberty."

Frontier fears

At the same time, however, like British colonial officials before them, many leaders of the new nation feared that an unregulated flow of population across the Appalachian Mountains would provoke constant warfare with Indians. Moreover, they viewed frontier settlers as disorderly and lacking in proper respect for authority.

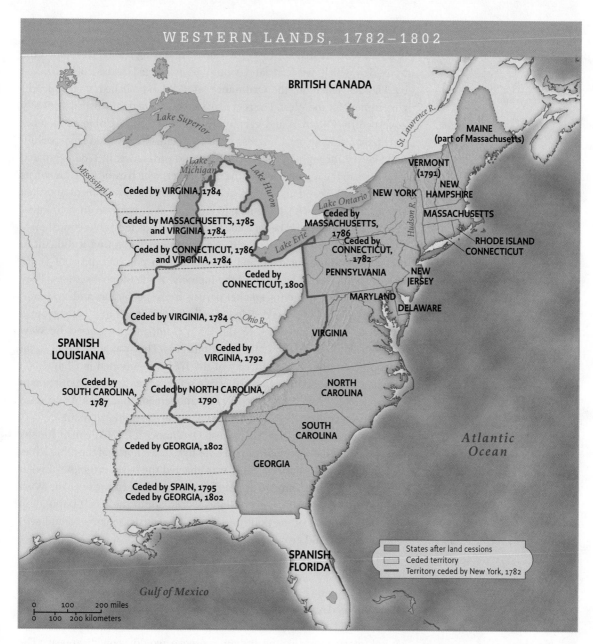

WESTERN LANDS, 1782–1802

BRITISH CANADA

Lake Superior

Mississippi R.

Lake Michigan

Lake Huron

St. Lawrence R.

MAINE
(part of Massachusetts)

VERMONT
(1791)

NEW
HAMPSHIRE

Lake Ontario

NEW YORK

Ceded by VIRGINIA, 1784

Ceded by MASSACHUSETTS, 1785
and VIRGINIA, 1784

Ceded by CONNECTICUT, 1786
and VIRGINIA, 1784

Lake Erie

Ceded by
MASSACHUSETTS,
1786

Ceded by
CONNECTICUT,
1782

MASSACHUSETTS

RHODE ISLAND
CONNECTICUT

Ceded by
CONNECTICUT, 1800

PENNSYLVANIA

Hudson R.

NEW
JERSEY

Ceded by VIRGINIA, 1784

Ohio R.

MARYLAND

DELAWARE

Ceded by
VIRGINIA, 1792

VIRGINIA

SPANISH
LOUISIANA

Ceded by
SOUTH CAROLINA,
1787

Ceded by NORTH CAROLINA,
1790

NORTH
CAROLINA

Ceded by GEORGIA, 1802

SOUTH
CAROLINA

GEORGIA

*Atlantic
Ocean*

Ceded by SPAIN, 1795
Ceded by GEORGIA, 1802

SPANISH
FLORIDA

States after land cessions
Ceded territory
Territory ceded by New York, 1782

Gulf of Mexico

0   100   200 miles
0   100   200 kilometers

The creation of a nationally controlled public domain from western land ceded by the states was one of the main achievements of the federal government under the Articles of Confederation.

The Land Ordinances

Western settlement and self-government

A series of measures approved by Congress during the 1780s defined the terms by which western land would be marketed and settled. Drafted by Thomas Jefferson, the **Ordinance of 1784** established stages of self-government for the West. The region would be divided into districts initially governed by Congress and eventually admitted to the Union as member states. By a single vote, Congress rejected a clause that would have prohibited slavery throughout the West. A second ordinance, in 1785, regulated land sales in the region north of the Ohio River, which came to be known as the Old Northwest. Land would be surveyed by the government and then sold in "sections" of a square mile (640 acres) at $1 per acre. In each township, one section would be set aside to provide funds for public education.

Price of land

Like the British before them, American officials found it difficult to regulate the thirst for new land. The minimum purchase price of $640, however, put public land out of the financial reach of most settlers. They generally ended up buying smaller parcels from speculators and land companies. In 1787, Congress decided to sell off large tracts to private groups, including 1.5 million acres to the Ohio Company, organized by New England land speculators and army officers. (This was a different organization from the Ohio Company of the 1750s, mentioned in Chapter 4.) For many years, actual and prospective settlers pressed for a reduction in the price of government-owned land, a movement that did not end until the Homestead Act of 1862 offered free land on the public domain.

A final measure, the **Northwest Ordinance of 1787**, called for the eventual establishment of from three to five states north of the Ohio River and east of the Mississippi. Thus was enacted the basic principle of what Jefferson called the **"empire of liberty"**—rather than ruling over the West as a colonial power, the United States would admit the area's population as equal members of the political system. Territorial expansion and self-government would grow together.

Territorial expansion and self-government

The Northwest Ordinance pledged that "the utmost good faith" would be observed toward local Indians and that their land would not be taken without consent. "It will cost much less," one congressman noted, "to conciliate the good opinion of the Indians than to pay men for destroying them." But national land policy assumed that whether through purchase, treaties, or voluntary removal, the Indian presence would soon disappear. The ordinance also prohibited slavery in the Old Northwest, a provision that would have far-reaching consequences when the sectional conflict between North and South developed. But for years, owners brought slaves into the area, claiming that they had voluntarily signed long-term labor contracts.

Slavery prohibited

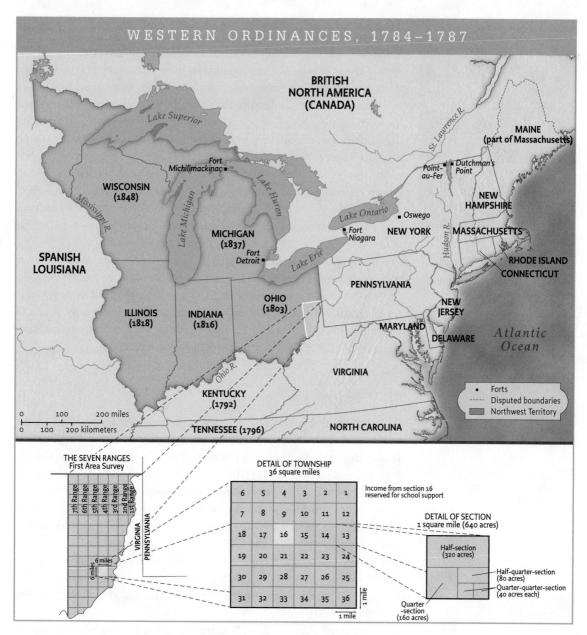

WESTERN ORDINANCES, 1784–1787

BRITISH
NORTH AMERICA
(CANADA)

Lake Superior

St. Lawrence R.

MAINE
(part of Massachusetts)

Point-au-Fer ■ Dutchman's Point

Fort Michilimackinac ■

WISCONSIN
(1848)

Mississippi R.

Lake Michigan

Lake Huron

NEW HAMPSHIRE

Oswego

MICHIGAN
(1837)

Fort Niagara ■

Lake Ontario

NEW YORK

MASSACHUSETTS

Hudson R.

SPANISH
LOUISIANA

Fort Detroit ■

Lake Erie

PENNSYLVANIA

RHODE ISLAND
CONNECTICUT

NEW JERSEY

ILLINOIS
(1818)

INDIANA
(1816)

OHIO
(1803)

MARYLAND

DELAWARE

Atlantic
Ocean

Ohio R.

VIRGINIA

KENTUCKY
(1792)

	Forts
---	Disputed boundaries
▨	Northwest Territory

0   100   200 miles

0   100   200 kilometers

TENNESSEE (1796)

NORTH CAROLINA

THE SEVEN RANGES
First Area Survey

7th Range
6th Range
5th Range
4th Range
3rd Range
2nd Range
1st Range

VIRGINIA
PENNSYLVANIA

6 miles
6 miles

DETAIL OF TOWNSHIP
36 square miles

6	5	4	3	2	1
7	8	9	10	11	12
18	17	16	15	14	13
19	20	21	22	23	24
30	29	28	27	26	25
31	32	33	34	35	36

1 mile

1 mile

Income from section 16
reserved for school support

DETAIL OF SECTION
1 square mile (640 acres)

Half-section
(320 acres)

Half-quarter-section
(80 acres)

Quarter-quarter-section
(40 acres each)

Quarter
-section
(160 acres)

A series of ordinances in the 1780s provided for both the surveying and sale of lands in the public domain north of the Ohio River and the eventual admission of states carved from the area as equal members of the Union.

The Confederation's Weaknesses

Whatever the achievements of the Confederation government, in the eyes of many influential Americans they were outweighed by its failings. Both the national government and the country at large faced worsening economic problems. To finance the War of Independence, Congress had borrowed large sums of money by selling interest-bearing bonds and paying soldiers and suppliers in notes to be redeemed in the future. Lacking a secure source of revenue, it found itself unable to pay either interest or the debts themselves. With the United States now outside the British empire, American ships were barred from trading with the West Indies. Imported goods, however, flooded the market, undercutting the business of many craftsmen, driving down wages, and draining money out of the country.

With Congress unable to act, the states adopted their own economic policies. Several imposed tariff duties on goods imported from abroad. In order to increase the amount of currency in circulation and make it easier for individuals to pay their debts, several states printed large sums of paper money. Others enacted laws postponing debt collection. Creditors considered such measures attacks on their property rights.

A Bankruptcy Scene. Creditors repossess the belongings of a family unable to pay its debts, while a woman weeps in the background. Popular fears of bankruptcy led several states during the 1780s to pass laws postponing the collection of debts.

Shays's Rebellion

In late 1786 and early 1787, crowds of debt-ridden farmers closed the courts in western Massachusetts to prevent the seizure of their land for failure to pay taxes. They called themselves "regulators"—a term already used by protesters in the Carolina backcountry in the 1760s. The uprising came to be known as **Shays's Rebellion**, a name affixed to it by its opponents, after Daniel Shays, one of the leaders and a veteran of the War of Independence. The participants in Shays's Rebellion modeled their tactics on the crowd activities of the 1760s and 1770s and employed liberty trees and liberty poles as symbols of their cause. They received no sympathy from Governor James Bowdoin, who dispatched an army headed by the former revolutionary war general Benjamin Lincoln. The rebels were dispersed in January 1787.

Uprising in Massachusetts

Observing Shays's Rebellion from Paris where he was serving as ambassador, Thomas Jefferson refused to be alarmed. "A little rebellion now and then is a good thing," he wrote to a friend. "The tree of liberty must be refreshed from time to time with the blood of patriots and tyrants." But the uprising was the culmination of a series of events in the 1780s that persuaded an influential group of Americans that the national government must be strengthened so that it could develop uniform economic policies and protect property owners from infringements on their rights by local majorities.

Among proponents of stronger national authority, liberty had lost some of its luster. The danger to individual rights, they came to believe, now arose not from a tyrannical central government, but from the people themselves. "Liberty," declared James Madison, "may be endangered by the abuses of liberty as well as the abuses of power." To put it another way, private liberty, especially the secure enjoyment of property rights, could be endangered by public liberty—unchecked power in the hands of the people.

Nationalists of the 1780s

Madison, a diminutive Virginian and the lifelong disciple and ally of Thomas Jefferson, thought deeply and creatively about the nature of political freedom. He was among the group of talented and well-organized men who spearheaded the movement for a stronger national government. Another was Alexander Hamilton, who had come to North America from the West Indies as a youth. Hamilton was perhaps the most vigorous proponent of an "energetic" government that would enable the new nation to become a powerful commercial and diplomatic presence in world affairs. Men like Madison and Hamilton were nation builders. They came to believe during the 1780s that Americans were squandering the fruits of independence and that the country's future greatness depended on enhancing national authority.

The concerns voiced by critics of the Articles found a sympathetic hearing among men who had developed a national consciousness during the Revolution. Nationalists included army officers, members of Congress accustomed to working with individuals from different states, and diplomats who represented the country abroad. Influential economic interests also desired a stronger national government. Among these were bondholders who despaired of being paid so long as Congress lacked a source of revenue, urban artisans seeking tariff protection from foreign imports, merchants desiring access to British markets, and all those who feared that the states were seriously interfering with property rights.

In September 1786, delegates from six states met at Annapolis, Maryland, to consider ways for better regulating interstate and international commerce. The delegates proposed another gathering, in Philadelphia, to amend the Articles of Confederation. Every state except Rhode Island, which had gone the furthest in developing its own debtor relief

James Madison, "father of the Constitution," in a miniature portrait painted by Charles Willson Peale in 1783. Madison was only thirty-six years old when the Constitutional Convention met.

Alexander Hamilton, another youthful leader of the nationalists of the 1780s, was born in the West Indies in 1755. This portrait was painted by Charles Willson Peale in the early 1790s.

The Philadelphia State House (now called Independence Hall), where the Declaration of Independence was signed in 1776 and the Constitutional Convention took place in 1787.

and trade policies, decided to send delegates to the Philadelphia convention. When they assembled in May 1787, they decided to scrap the Articles of Confederation entirely and draft a new constitution for the United States.

A NEW CONSTITUTION

The fifty-five men who gathered for the Constitutional Convention included some of the most prominent Americans. Thomas Jefferson and John Adams, serving as diplomats in Europe, did not take part. But among the delegates were George Washington (whose willingness to lend his prestige to the gathering and to serve as presiding officer was an enormous asset) and Benjamin Franklin (who had returned to Philadelphia after helping to negotiate the Treaty of Paris of 1783, and was now eighty-one years old). John Adams described the convention as a gathering of men of "ability, weight, and experience." He might have added, "and wealth." They earned their livings as lawyers, merchants, planters, and large farmers. Nearly all were quite prosperous by the standards of the day.

Elite convention delegates

At a time when fewer than one-tenth of 1 percent of Americans attended college, more than half the delegates had college educations. Their shared social status and political experiences bolstered their common belief in the need to strengthen national authority and curb what one called "the excesses of democracy." To ensure free and candid debate, the deliberations took place in private. Madison, who believed the outcome would have great consequences for "the cause of liberty throughout the world," took careful notes. They were not published, however, until 1840, four years after he became the last delegate to pass away.

The Structure of Government

Legislature, executive, and national judiciary

It quickly became apparent that the delegates agreed on many points. The new constitution would create a legislature, an executive, and a national judiciary. Congress would have the power to raise money without relying on the states. States would be prohibited from infringing on the rights of property. And the government would represent the people. Most delegates hoped to find a middle ground between the despotism of monarchy and aristocracy and what they considered the excesses of popular self-government. "We had been too democratic," observed George Mason of Virginia, but he warned against the danger of going to "the opposite extreme." The key to stable, effective republican government was finding a way to balance the competing claims of liberty and power.

Differences quickly emerged over the proper balance between the federal and state governments and between the interests of large and small states. Early in the proceedings, Madison presented what came to be called the Virginia Plan. It proposed the creation of a two-house legislature with a state's population determining its representation in each. Smaller states, fearing that populous Virginia, Massachusetts, and Pennsylvania would dominate the new government, rallied behind the New Jersey Plan. This called for a single-house Congress in which each state cast one vote, as under the Articles of Confederation. In the end, a compromise was reached—a two-house Congress consisting of a Senate in which each state had two members, and a House of Representatives apportioned according to population. Senators would be chosen by state legislatures for six-year terms. They were thus insulated from sudden shifts in public opinion. Representatives were to be elected every two years directly by the people.

Large vs. small states

Compromise on a two-house Congress

The Limits of Democracy

Under the Articles of Confederation, no national official had been chosen by popular vote. Thus, the mode of choosing the House of Representatives signaled an expansion of democracy. The Constitution, moreover, imposed neither property nor religious qualifications for voting, leaving it to the states to set voting rules.

Overall, however, the new structure of government was less than democratic. The delegates sought to shield the national government from the popular enthusiasms that had alarmed them during the 1780s and to ensure that the right kind of men held office. The delegates assumed that the Senate would be composed of each state's most distinguished citizens. They made the House of Representatives quite small (initially 65 members, at a time when the Massachusetts assembly had 200), on the assumption that only prominent individuals could win election in large districts.

Less than democratic structure

Nor did the delegates provide for direct election of either federal judges or the president. Members of the Supreme Court would be appointed by the president for life terms. The president would be chosen either by members of an electoral college or by the House of Representatives. A state's electors would be chosen either by its legislature or by popular vote.

Indirect elections

The actual system of election seemed a recipe for confusion. Each elector was to cast votes for two candidates for president, with the second-place finisher becoming vice president. If no candidate received a majority of the electoral ballots—as the delegates seem to have assumed would normally be the case—the president would be chosen from among the top three finishers by the House of Representatives, with each state casting one vote. The Senate would then elect the vice president. The delegates devised this extremely cumbersome system of indirect election because they did not trust ordinary voters to choose the president and vice president directly.

The Division and Separation of Powers

Hammered out in four months of discussion and compromise, the Constitution is a spare document of only 4,000 words that provides only the briefest outline of the new structure of government. (See the Appendix for the full text.) It embodies two basic political principles—**federalism**, sometimes called the "division of powers," and the system of "**checks and balances**" between the different branches of the national government, also known as the "**separation of powers.**"

Federalism

"Federalism" refers to the relationship between the national government and the states. Compared with the Articles of Confederation, the Constitution significantly strengthened national authority. It charged the president with enforcing the law and commanding the military. It empowered Congress to levy taxes, borrow money, regulate commerce, declare war, deal with foreign nations and Indians, and promote the "general welfare." The Constitution also included strong provisions to prevent the states from infringing on property rights. They were barred from issuing paper money, impairing contracts, interfering with interstate commerce, and levying their own import or export duties. On the other hand, most day-to-day affairs of government, from education to law enforcement, remained in the hands of the states. This principle of divided sovereignty was a recipe for debate, which continues to this day, over the balance of power between the national government and the states.

Checks and balances

The "separation of powers," or the system of "checks and balances," refers to the way the Constitution seeks to prevent any branch of the national government from dominating the other two. To prevent an accumulation of power dangerous to liberty, authority within the government is diffused and balanced against itself. Congress enacts laws, but the president can veto them, and a two-thirds majority is required to pass legislation over his objection. Federal judges are nominated by the president and approved by Congress, but to ensure their independence, the judges then serve for life. The president can be impeached by the House and removed from office by the Senate for "high crimes and misdemeanors."

This advertisement for the sale of 100 slaves from Virginia to states farther south appeared in a Richmond newspaper only a few months after the signing of the Constitution. Slavery was a major subject of debate at the Constitutional Convention.

The Debate over Slavery

The structure of government was not the only source of debate at the Constitutional Convention. As Madison recorded, "the institution of slavery and its implications" divided the delegates at many sessions. Those who gathered in Philadelphia included numerous slaveholders, as well as some dedicated advocates of abolition.

The words "slave" and "slavery" did not appear in the Constitution—a concession to the sensibilities of delegates who feared they would "contaminate the glorious fabric of American liberty." Nonetheless, the document contained strong protections for slavery. It prohibited Congress from abolishing the African slave trade for twenty years. It required states to return to their owners fugitives from bondage. And it provided that three-fifths of the slave population would be counted in determining each state's representation in the House of Representatives and its electoral votes for president.

South Carolina's delegates had come to Philadelphia determined to defend slavery, and they had a powerful impact on the final document. They originated the fugitive slave clause and the electoral college. They insisted on strict limits on the power of Congress to levy taxes within the states, fearing future efforts to raise revenue by taxing slave property. Gouverneur Morris, one of Pennsylvania's delegates, declared that he was being forced to decide between offending the southern states or doing injustice to "human nature." For the sake of national unity, he said, he would choose the latter.

South Carolina's influence

Slavery in the Constitution

The Constitution's slavery clauses were compromises, efforts to find a middle ground between the institution's critics and defenders. Taken together, however, they embedded slavery more deeply than ever in American life and politics. The slave trade clause allowed a commerce condemned by civilized society—one that had been suspended during

The slave trade clause

the War of Independence—to continue until 1808. On January 1, 1808, the first day that Congress was allowed under the Constitution, it prohibited the further importation of slaves. But in the interim, partly to replace slaves who had escaped to the British and partly to provide labor for the expansion of slavery to fertile land away from the coast, some 170,000 Africans were brought to the new nation as slaves. South Carolina and Georgia imported 100,000. This number accounted for more than one-quarter of all the slaves brought to mainland North America after 1700.

Fugitive slave clause

The fugitive slave clause accorded slave laws "extraterritoriality"—that is, the condition of bondage remained attached to a person even if he or she escaped to a state where slavery had been abolished. The Constitution gave the national government no power to interfere with slavery in the states. And the **three-fifths clause** allowed the white South to exercise far greater power in national affairs than the size of its free population warranted. The clause greatly enhanced the number of southern votes in the House of Representatives and therefore in the electoral college (where the number of electors for each state was determined by adding together its number of senators and representatives). Of the first sixteen presidential elections, between 1788 and 1848, all but four placed a southern slaveholder in the White House.

Nevertheless, some slaveholders detected a potential threat buried in the Constitution. Patrick Henry, who condemned slavery but feared abolition, warned that, in time of war, the new government might take steps to

The Signing of the Constitution, by mid-nineteenth-century American artist Thomas Pritchard Rossiter, depicts the conclusion of the Constitutional Convention of 1787. Among the founding fathers depicted are James Wilson, signing the document at the table in the center, and George Washington, presiding from the dais with an image of the sun behind him.

arm and liberate the slaves. "May Congress not say," he asked, "that every black man must fight?" What Henry could not anticipate was that the war that eventually destroyed slavery would be launched by the South itself to protect the institution.

The Final Document

Gouverneur Morris put the finishing touches on the final draft of the new Constitution, trying to make it, he explained, "as clear as our language would permit." For the original preamble, which began, "We the people of the States of New Hampshire, Massachusetts," etc., he substituted the far more powerful, "We the people of the United States." He added a statement of the Constitution's purposes, including to "establish justice," promote "the general welfare," and "secure the blessings of liberty"—things the Articles of Confederation, in the eyes of most of the delegates, had failed to accomplish.

The Preamble

The last session of the Constitutional Convention took place on September 17, 1787. Benjamin Franklin urged the delegates to put aside individual objections and approve the document, whatever its imperfections. Of the forty-five delegates who remained in Philadelphia, thirty-nine signed the Constitution. It was then sent to the states for ratification.

This satirical engraving by Amos Doolittle depicts some of the issues in the debate over the ratification of the Constitution. The wagon in the center is carrying Connecticut and sinking into the mud under the weight of debts and paper money as "Federals" and "Antifederals" try to pull it out. Federals call for the state to "comply with Congress" (that is, to pay money requisitioned by the national government); the Antifederals reply "tax luxury" and "success to Shays," a reference to Shays's Rebellion. The Connecticut shoreline and the buildings of Manhattan are on the right. Underneath the three merchant ships is a phrase criticizing the tariffs that states were imposing on imports from one another (which the Constitution prohibited). At the bottom is the biblical motto, "A house divided against itself cannot stand," later made famous by Abraham Lincoln.

The Constitution created a new framework for American development. It made possible a national economic market. It created national political institutions, reduced the powers of the states, and sought to place limits on popular democracy. The ratification process, however, unleashed a nationwide debate over the best means of preserving American freedom.

THE RATIFICATION DEBATE AND THE ORIGIN OF THE BILL OF RIGHTS

The Federalist

Even though the Constitution provided that it would go into effect when nine states, not all thirteen as required by the Articles of Confederation, had given their approval, ratification was by no means certain. Each state held an election for delegates to a special ratifying convention. A fierce public battle ensued, producing hundreds of pamphlets and newspaper articles and spirited campaigns to elect delegates. To generate support, Hamilton, Madison, and Jay composed a series of eighty-five essays that appeared in newspapers under the pen name Publius and were gathered as a book, ***The Federalist***, in 1788. Today, the essays are regarded as among the most important American contributions to political thought. At the time, however, they were only one part of a much larger national debate over ratification.

For ratification: Alexander Hamilton, James Madison, John Jay

Again and again, Hamilton and Madison repeated that rather than posing a danger to Americans' liberties, the Constitution in fact protected them. Any government, Hamilton insisted, could become oppressive, but with its checks and balances and division of power, the Constitution made political tyranny almost impossible. At the New York ratifying convention, Hamilton assured the delegates that the Constitution had created "the perfect balance between liberty and power."

"Extend the Sphere"

Madison, too, emphasized how the Constitution was structured to prevent abuses of authority. But in several essays, especially *Federalist* nos. 10 and 51, he moved beyond such assurances to develop a strikingly new vision of the relationship between government and society in the United States. Madison identified the essential dilemma, as he saw it, of the new republic—government must be based on the will of the people, yet the people had shown themselves susceptible to dangerous enthusiasms. The problem of balancing democracy and respect for property would only grow in the years ahead because, he warned, economic development would inevitably increase the numbers of poor. What was to prevent them from using their political power to secure "a more equal distribution" of wealth?

The answer, Madison explained, lay not simply in the way power balanced power in the structure of government, but in the nation's size and diversity. Previous republics had existed only in small territories—the Dutch republic or the Italian city-states of the Renaissance. But, argued Madison, the very size of the United States was a source of stability, not, as many feared, weakness. "Extend the sphere," he wrote. The multiplicity of religious denominations, he argued, offered the best security for religious liberty. Likewise, in a nation as large as the United States, so many distinct interests—economic, regional, and political—would arise, that no single one would ever be able to take over the government and oppress the rest.

Madison's writings did much to shape the early nation's understanding of its new political institutions. In arguing that the size of the republic helped to secure Americans' rights, they reinforced the tradition that saw continuous westward expansion as essential to freedom.

In this late-eighteenth-century engraving, Americans celebrate the signing of the Constitution beneath a temple of liberty.

America's size and diversity

The Anti-Federalists

Opponents of ratification, called **Anti-Federalists**, insisted that the Constitution shifted the balance between liberty and power too far in the direction of the latter. Anti-Federalists lacked the coherent leadership of the Constitution's defenders. They included state politicians fearful of seeing their influence diminish, among them such revolutionary heroes as Samuel Adams, John Hancock, and Patrick Henry. Small farmers, many of whom supported the state debtor-relief measures of the 1780s that

Against ratification: Samuel Adams, John Hancock, Patrick Henry

VOICES OF FREEDOM

From David Ramsay, The History of the American Revolution (1789)

A member of the Continental Congress from South Carolina, David Ramsay published his history of the Revolution the year after the Constitution was ratified. In this excerpt, he lauds the principles of representative government and the right of future amendment, embodied in the state constitutions and adopted in the national one, as unique American political principles and the best ways of securing liberty.

The world has not hitherto exhibited so fair an opportunity for promoting social happiness. It is hoped for the honor of human nature, that the result will prove the fallacy of those theories that mankind are incapable of self government. The ancients, not knowing the doctrine of representation, were apt in their public meetings to run into confusion, but in America this mode of taking the sense of the people, is so well understood, and so completely reduced to system, that its most populous states are often peaceably convened in an assembly of deputies, not too large for orderly deliberation, and yet representing the whole in equal proportion. These popular branches of legislature are miniature pictures of the community, and from their mode of election are likely to be influenced by the same interests and feelings with the people whom they represent. . . .

In no age before, and in no other country, did man ever possess an election of the kind of government, under which he would choose to live. The constituent parts of the ancient free governments were thrown together by accident. The freedom of modern European governments was, for the most part, obtained by concessions, or liberality of monarchs, or military leaders. In America alone, reason and liberty concurred in the formation of constitutions . . . In one thing they were all perfect. They left the people in the power of altering and amending them, whenever they pleased. In this happy peculiarity they placed the science of politics on a footing with the other sciences, by opening it to improvements from experience, and the discoveries of future ages. By means of this power of amending American constitutions, the friends of mankind have fondly hoped that oppression will one day be no more.

From James Winthrop, Anti-Federalist Essay Signed "Agrippa" (1787)

A local official in Middlesex, Massachusetts, James Winthrop published sixteen public letters between November 1787 and February 1788 opposing ratification of the Constitution.

It is the opinion of the ablest writers on the subject, that no extensive empire can be governed upon republican principles, and that such a government will degenerate into a despotism, unless it be made up of a confederacy of smaller states, each having the full powers of internal regulation. This is precisely the principle which has hitherto preserved our freedom. No instance can be found of any free government of considerable extent which has been supported upon any other plan. Large and consolidated empires may indeed dazzle the eyes of a distant spectator with their splendor, but if examined more nearly are always found to be full of misery. . . . It is under such tyranny that the Spanish provinces languish, and such would be our misfortune and degradation, if we should submit to have the concerns of the whole empire managed by one empire. To promote the happiness of the people it is necessary that there should be local laws; and it is necessary that those laws should be made by the representatives of those who are immediately subject to [them]. . . .

It is impossible for one code of laws to suit Georgia and Massachusetts. They must, therefore, legislate for themselves. Yet there is, I believe, not one point of legislation that is not surrendered in the proposed plan. Questions of every kind respecting property are determinable in a continental court, and so are all kinds of criminal causes. The continental legislature has, therefore, a right to make rules in all cases. . . . No rights are reserved to the citizens. . . . This new system is, therefore, a consolidation of all the states into one large mass, however diverse the parts may be of which it is composed. . . .

A bill of rights . . . serves to secure the minority against the usurpation and tyranny of the majority. . . . The experience of all mankind has proved the prevalence of a disposition to use power wantonly. It is therefore as necessary to defend an individual against the majority in a republic as against the king in a monarchy.

QUESTIONS

1. *Why does Ramsay feel that the power to amend the Constitution is so important a political innovation?*

2. *Why does Winthrop believe that a Bill of Rights is essential in the Constitution?*

3. *How do Ramsay and Winthrop differ concerning how the principle of representation operates in the United States?*

the Constitution's supporters deplored, also saw no need for a stronger central government. Some opponents of the Constitution denounced the document's protections for slavery; others warned that the powers of Congress were so broad that it might enact a law for abolition.

Anti-Federalists repeatedly predicted that the new government would fall under the sway of merchants, creditors, and others hostile to the interests of ordinary Americans. Popular self-government, they claimed, flourished best in small communities, where rulers and ruled interacted daily. The result of the Constitution, warned Melancton Smith of New York, a member of Congress under the Articles of Confederation, would be domination of the "common people" by the "well-born."

Rule by the "well-born"

"Liberty" was the Anti-Federalists' watchword. America's happiness, they insisted, "arises from the freedom of our institutions and the limited nature of our government," both threatened by the new Constitution. To the vision of the United States as an energetic great power, Anti-Federalists counterposed a way of life grounded in local, democratic institutions. Anti-Federalists also pointed to the Constitution's lack of a Bill of Rights, which left unprotected rights such as trial by jury and freedom of speech and the press.

Social bases of support and opposition

In general, pro-Constitution sentiment flourished in the nation's cities and in rural areas closely tied to the commercial marketplace. The Constitution's most energetic supporters were men of substantial property. But what George Bryan of Pennsylvania, a supporter of ratification, called the "golden phantom" of prosperity also swung urban artisans, laborers, and sailors behind the movement for a government that would use its "energy and power" to revive the depressed economy. Anti-Federalism drew its support from small farmers in more isolated rural areas such as the Hudson Valley of New York, western Massachusetts, and the southern backcountry.

Ratification

In the end, the supporters' energy and organization, coupled with their domination of the colonial press, carried the day. Ninety-two newspapers and magazines existed in the United States in 1787. Of these, only twelve published a significant number of Anti-Federalist pieces. Madison also won support for the new Constitution by promising that the first Congress would enact a Bill of Rights. By mid-1788, the required nine states had ratified. Only Rhode Island and North Carolina voted against ratification, and they subsequently had little choice but to join the new government. Anti-Federalism died. But as with other movements in American history that did not immediately achieve their goals—for example, the Populists of the late nineteenth century—some of the Anti-Federalists' ideas eventually entered the political mainstream. To this day, their belief that a too-powerful central government is a threat to liberty continues to influence American political culture.

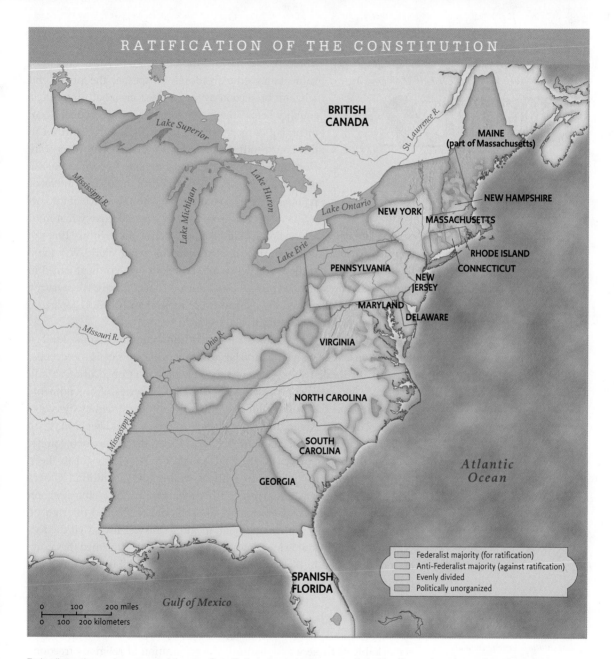

RATIFICATION OF THE CONSTITUTION

BRITISH CANADA

Lake Superior

MAINE
(part of Massachusetts)

St. Lawrence R.

Mississippi R.

Lake Michigan

Lake Huron

Lake Ontario

NEW HAMPSHIRE

NEW YORK

MASSACHUSETTS

Lake Erie

RHODE ISLAND

PENNSYLVANIA

CONNECTICUT

NEW JERSEY

Missouri R.

Ohio R.

MARYLAND

DELAWARE

VIRGINIA

NORTH CAROLINA

Mississippi R.

SOUTH CAROLINA

Atlantic Ocean

GEORGIA

SPANISH FLORIDA

Gulf of Mexico

Federalist majority (for ratification)
Anti-Federalist majority (against ratification)
Evenly divided
Politically unorganized

| 0 | 100 | 200 miles |
| 0 | 100 | 200 kilometers |

Federalists—those who supported the new Constitution—tended to be concentrated in cities and nearby rural areas, whereas backcountry farmers were more likely to oppose the new frame of government.

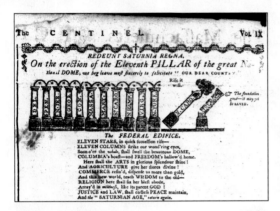

The CENTINEL Vol. IX

REDEUNT SATURNIA REGNA.
On the erection of the Eleventh PILLAR of the great National DOME, we beg leave most sincerely to felicitate " OUR DEAR COUNTRY."

The FEDERAL EDIFICE.

ELEVEN STARS, in quick succession rise—
ELEVEN COLUMNS strike our wond'ring eyes,
Soon o'er the whole, shall swell the beauteous DOME,
COLUMBIA's boast—and FREEDOM's hallow'd home.
Here shall the ARTS in glorious splendour shine !
And AGRICULTURE give her stores divine !
COMMERCE refin'd, dispense us more than gold,
And this new world, teach WISDOM to the old—
RELIGION here shall fix her blest abode,
Array'd in mildness, like its parent GOD !
JUSTICE and LAW, shall codless PEACE maintain,
And the " SATURNIAN AGE," return again.

An engraving and poem, published in 1788 in an American newspaper, after New York became the eleventh state to ratify the new Constitution. North Carolina would ratify in 1789 and Rhode Island in 1790.

First Amendment rights

Constitutional recognition of religious freedom

The Bill of Rights

Ironically, the parts of the Constitution Americans most value today—the freedoms of speech, the press, and religion; protection against unjust criminal procedures; equality before the law—were not in the original document. All of these but the last (which was enshrined in the Fourteenth Amendment after the Civil War) were contained in the first ten amendments, known as the **Bill of Rights**. Madison believed a Bill of Rights "redundant or pointless." "Parchment barriers" to the abuse of authority, he observed, would prove least effective when most needed. Madison's prediction would be amply borne out at future times of popular hysteria, such as during the Red Scare following World War I and the McCarthy era of the 1950s, when all branches of government joined in trampling on freedom of expression, and during World War II, when hatred of a foreign enemy led to the internment of more than 100,000 Japanese-Americans, most of them citizens of the United States.

Nevertheless, every new state constitution contained some kind of declaration of citizens' rights, and large numbers of Americans—Federalist and Anti-Federalist alike—believed the new national Constitution should also have one. Madison presented to Congress a series of amendments that became the basis of the Bill of Rights, which was ratified by the states in 1791. The First Amendment prohibited Congress from legislating with regard to religion or infringing on freedom of speech, freedom of the press, or the right of assembly. The Second upheld the people's right to "keep and bear arms" in conjunction with "a well-regulated militia." Others prohibited abuses such as arrests without warrants and forcing a person accused of a crime to testify against himself, and reaffirmed the right to trial by jury. The Tenth Amendment, meant to answer fears that the federal government would ride roughshod over the states, affirmed that powers not delegated to the national government or prohibited to the states continued to reside with the states.

Although the roots and even the specific language of some parts of the Bill of Rights lay far back in English history, other provisions reflected the changes in American life brought about by the Revolution. The most remarkable of these was constitutional recognition of religious freedom. Unlike the Declaration of Independence, which invokes the blessing of divine providence, the Constitution is a purely secular document that contains no reference to God and bars religious tests for federal officeholders. The First Amendment prohibits the federal government from legislating on the subject of religion—a complete departure from British and colonial precedent. Under the Constitution it was and remains possible, as one critic complained, for "a papist, a Mohomatan, a deist, yea an atheist" to become president of the United States. Madison was so adamant about separating church and state that he even opposed the appointment of chaplains to serve Congress and the military.

The Bill of Rights aroused little enthusiasm on ratification and for decades was all but ignored. Not until the twentieth century would it come to be revered as an indispensable expression of American freedom. Nonetheless, the Bill of Rights subtly affected the language of liberty. Applying only to the federal government, not the states, it reinforced the idea that concentrated national power posed the greatest threat to freedom. And it contributed to the long process whereby freedom came to be discussed in the vocabulary of rights.

Legacy of the Bill of Rights

Among the most important rights were freedom of speech and the press, vital building blocks of a democratic public sphere. Once an entitlement of members of Parliament and colonial assemblies, free speech came to be seen as a basic right of citizenship.

"WE THE PEOPLE"

National Identity

The Constitution opens with the words, "We the People." Although one might assume that the "people" of the United States included all those living within the nation's borders, the text made clear that this was not the case. The Constitution identifies three populations inhabiting the United States: Indians, treated as members of independent tribes and not part of the American body politic; "other persons"—that is, slaves; and the "people." Only the third were entitled to American freedom.

Exclusion of Indians and slaves

Indians in the New Nation

The early republic's policies toward Indians and African-Americans illustrate the conflicting principles that shaped American nationality. American leaders agreed that the West should not be left in Indian hands, but they disagreed about the Indians' ultimate fate. The government hoped to encourage the westward expansion of white settlement, which implied one of three things: the removal of the Indian population to lands even farther west, their total disappearance, or their incorporation into white "civilization" with the expectation that they might one day become part of American society.

Political status of Indian tribes

Indian tribes had no representation in the new government, and the Constitution excluded Indians "not taxed" from being counted in determining each state's number of congressmen. The treaty system gave them a unique status within the American political system. But despite this recognition of their sovereignty, treaties were essentially ways of transferring land from Indians to the federal government or the states.

Continuing warfare

Open warfare continued in the Ohio Valley after ratification. In 1791, Little Turtle, leader of the **Miami Confederacy**, inflicted a humiliating defeat on American forces led by Arthur St. Clair, the American governor of the Northwest Territory. With 630 dead, this was the costliest loss ever suffered by the U.S. Army at the hands of Indians. In 1794, 3,000 American troops under Anthony Wayne defeated Little Turtle's forces at the **Battle of Fallen Timbers**. This led directly to the **Treaty of Greenville** of 1795, in which twelve Indian tribes ceded most of Ohio and Indiana to the federal government. The treaty also established the **"annuity" system**—yearly grants of federal money to Indian tribes that institutionalized continuing government influence in tribal affairs and gave outsiders considerable control over Indian life.

Many prominent figures, however, rejected the idea that Indians were innately inferior to white Americans. Thomas Jefferson believed that Indians merely lived at a less advanced stage of civilization. Indians could become full-fledged members of the republic by abandoning communal landholding and hunting in favor of small-scale farming.

To pursue the goal of assimilation, Congress in the 1790s authorized President Washington to distribute agricultural tools and livestock to Indian men and spinning wheels and looms to Indian women. To whites, the adoption of American gender norms, with men working the land and women tending to their homes, would be a crucial sign that the Indians were becoming "civilized." But the American notion of civilization required so great a transformation of Indian life that most tribes rejected it. One missionary was told, "If we want to work, we know how to do it according to our own way and as it pleases us."

The signing of the Treaty of Greenville of 1795, painted by an unknown member of General Anthony Wayne's staff. In the treaty, a group of tribes ceded most of the area of the current state of Ohio, along with the site that became the city of Chicago, to the United States.

To Indians, freedom meant retaining tribal autonomy and identity, including the ability to travel widely in search of game. "Since our acquaintance with our brother white people," declared a Mohawk speaker at a 1796 treaty council, "that which we call freedom and liberty, becomes an entire stranger to us." There was no room for Indians who desired to retain their traditional way of life in the American empire of liberty.

Blacks and the Republic

By 1790, the number of African-Americans far exceeded the Indian population within the United States. The status of free blacks was somewhat indeterminate. Nowhere does the original Constitution define who in fact are citizens of the United States. The individual states were left free to determine the boundaries of liberty. The North's **gradual emancipation** acts assumed that former slaves would remain in the country, not be colonized abroad. During the era of the Revolution, free blacks enjoyed at least some of the legal rights accorded to whites, including, in most states, the right to vote. The large majority of blacks, of course, were slaves, and slavery rendered them all but invisible to those imagining the American community.

One of the era's most widely read books, ***Letters from an American Farmer***, published in France in 1782 by Hector St. John de Crèvecoeur, strikingly illustrated this process of exclusion. Born in France, Crèvecoeur eventually married the daughter of a prominent New York landowner and lived with his own family on a farm in Orange County. In this book, Crèvecoeur popularized the idea, which would become so common in the twentieth century, of the United States as a melting pot. "Here," he wrote, "individuals of all nations are melted

TABLE 7.1 Total Population and Black Population of the United States, 1790

STATE	TOTAL POPULATION	SLAVES	FREE BLACKS
New England:			
New Hampshire	141,899	158	630
Vermont*	85,341	0	271
Massachusetts	378,556	0	5,369
Connecticut	237,655	2,764	2,771
Rhode Island	69,112	948	3,484
Maine**	96,643	0	536
Middle States:			
New York	340,241	21,324	4,682
New Jersey	184,139	11,423	2,762
Pennsylvania	433,611	3,737	6,531
South:			
Delaware	59,096	8,887	3,899
Maryland	319,728	103,036	8,043
Virginia	747,610	292,627	12,866
North Carolina	395,005	100,572	5,041
South Carolina	249,073	107,094	1,801
Georgia	82,548	29,264	398
Kentucky*	73,677	12,430	114
Tennessee*	35,691	3,417	361
Total	3,929,625	697,624	59,557

*Vermont, Kentucky, and Tennessee were territories that had not yet been admitted as states.

**Maine was part of Massachusetts in 1790.

into a new one." When he posed the famous question, "What then is the American, this new man?" he answered, "a mixture of English, Scotch, Irish, French, Dutch, Germans, and Swedes. . . . He is either a European, or the descendant of a European." This at a time when fully one-fifth of the population (the highest proportion in U.S. history) consisted of Africans and their descendants.

Like Crèvecoeur, many white Americans excluded blacks from their conception of the American people. The Constitution empowered Congress to create a uniform system by which immigrants became citizens, and the Naturalization Act of 1790 offered the first legislative definition of American nationality. With no debate, Congress restricted the process of becoming a citizen from abroad to "free white persons." The word "white" in this act excluded a large majority of the world's population from emigrating to the "asylum for mankind" and partaking in the blessings of American freedom. For eighty years, no non-white immigrant could become a naturalized citizen. Africans were allowed to do so in 1870, but not until the 1940s did persons of Asian origin become eligible. (Native Americans were granted American citizenship in 1924.)

Jefferson, Slavery, and Race

The artist John Singleton Copley, best known for his portraits of prominent Americans and Britons, painted this young African-American in the late 1770s. The subject probably worked on a New England fishing boat. This is one of the era's very few portraits of a black person.

Man's liberty, John Locke had written, flowed from "his having reason." To deny liberty to those who were not considered rational beings did not seem to be a contradiction. White Americans increasingly viewed blacks as permanently deficient in the qualities that made freedom possible—the capacity for self-control, reason, and devotion to the larger community. These were the characteristics that Jefferson, in a famous comparison of the races in his book ***Notes on the State of Virginia***, published in 1785, claimed blacks lacked, partly due to natural incapacity and partly because the bitter experience of slavery had (quite understandably, he felt) rendered them disloyal to the nation.

Jefferson was obsessed with the connection between heredity and environment, race and intelligence. His belief that individuals' abilities and achievements are shaped by social conditions inclined him to hope that no group was fixed permanently in a status of inferiority. In the case of blacks, however, he could not avoid the "suspicion" that nature had permanently deprived them of the qualities that made republican citizenship possible. Benjamin Banneker, a free African-American from Maryland who had taught himself the principles of mathematics, sent Jefferson a copy of an astronomical almanac he had published, along with a plea for the abolition of slavery. Jefferson replied, "Nobody wishes more than I do to see such proofs as you exhibit, that nature has given to our black brethren, talents equal to the other colors of men." To his friend Joel Barlow, however, Jefferson suggested that a white person must have helped Banneker with his calculations.

"Nothing is more certainly written in the book of fate," wrote Jefferson, "than that these people are to be free." Yet he felt that America should have a homogeneous citizenry with common experiences, values, and inborn abilities. These contradictions in Jefferson reflected the divided mind of his generation. Some prominent Virginians assumed that blacks could become part of the American nation. Edward Coles, an early governor of Illinois, brought his slaves from Virginia, freed them, and settled them on farms. Washington, who died in 1799, provided in his will that his 277 slaves would become free after the death of his wife, Martha. Believing the slave trade immoral, Jefferson tried to avoid selling slaves to pay off his mounting debts. But his will provided for the freedom of only five, all relatives of his slave Sally Hemings, with whom he appears to have had fathered one or more children.

RUN away from the subscriber in *Albemarle*, a Mulatto slave called *Sandy*, about 35 years of age, his stature is rather low, inclining to corpulence, and his complexion light; he is a shoemaker by trade, in which he uses his left hand principally, can do coarse carpenters work, and is something of a horse jockey; he is greatly addicted to drink, and when drunk is insolent and disorderly, in his conversation he swears much, and in his behaviour is artful and knavish. He took with him a white horse, much scarred with traces, of which it is expected he will endeavour to dispose; he also carried his shoemakers tools, and will probably endeavour to get employment that way. Whoever conveys the said slave to me, in *Albemarle*, shall have 40 s. reward, if taken up within the county, 4 l. if elsewhere within the colony, and 10 l. if in any other colony, from

THOMAS JEFFERSON.

Thomas Jefferson, future author of the Declaration of Independence and in private a sharp critic of slavery, placed this advertisement in a Virginia newspaper in 1769, seeking the return of a runaway slave. Sandy was in fact recaptured, and Jefferson sold him in 1773.

Principles of Freedom

Even as the decline of apprenticeship and indentured servitude narrowed the gradations of freedom among the white population, the Revolution widened the divide between free Americans and those who remained in slavery. Race, one among many kinds of legal and social inequality in colonial America, now emerged as a convenient justification for the existence of slavery in a land that claimed to be committed to freedom. Blacks' "natural faculties," Alexander Hamilton noted in 1779, were "probably as good as ours." But the existence of slavery, he added, "makes us fancy many things that are founded neither in reason or experience."

Emergence of racial distinctions

"We the people" increasingly meant only white Americans. "Principles of freedom, which embrace only half mankind, are only half systems," declared the anonymous author of a Fourth of July speech in Hartford, Connecticut, in 1800. "Declaration of Independence," he wondered, "where art thou now?" The answer came from a Richmond newspaper: "Tell us not of principles. Those principles have been annihilated by the existence of slavery among us."

CHAPTER REVIEW AND ONLINE RESOURCES

REVIEW QUESTIONS

1. *How did the limited central government created by the Articles of Confederation reflect the issues behind the Revolution and fears for individual liberties?*

2. *What were the ideas and motivations that pushed Americans to expand west?*

3. *What events and ideas led to the belief in 1786 and 1787 that the Articles of Confederation were not working well?*

4. *The Constitution has been described as a "bundle of compromises." Which compromises were the most significant in shaping the direction of the new nation and why?*

5. *What were the major arguments in support of the Constitution given by the Federalists?*

6. *What were the major arguments against the Constitution put forth by the Anti-Federalists?*

7. *How accurate was Hector St. John de Crèvecoeur's description of America as a melting pot?*

KEY TERMS

Land Ordinances of 1784 and 1785 (p. 198)

Northwest Ordinance of 1787 (p. 198)

"empire of liberty" (p. 198)

Shays's Rebellion (p. 200)

federalism (p. 204)

checks and balances (p. 204)

separation of powers (p. 204)

three-fifths clause (p. 206)

The Federalist (p. 208)

Anti-Federalists (p. 209)

Bill of Rights (p. 214)

Miami Confederation (p. 216)

Battle of Fallen Timbers (p. 216)

Treaty of Greenville (p. 216)

"annuity" system (p. 216)

gradual emancipation (p. 217)

Letters from an American Farmer (p. 217)

Notes on the State of Virginia (p. 218)

wwnorton.com
/studyspace

VISIT STUDYSPACE FOR THESE RESOURCES AND MORE

- A chapter outline
- A diagnostic chapter quiz
- Interactive maps
- Map worksheets
- Multimedia documents

CHAPTER 8

SECURING THE REPUBLIC

★

1791–1815

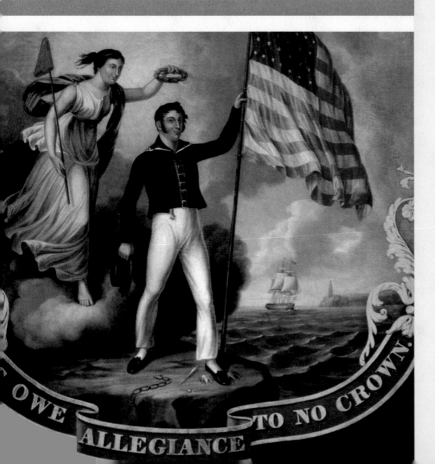

OWE ALLEGIANCE TO NO CROWN.

1789	Inauguration of George Washington
	French Revolution begins
1791	First Bank of the United States
	Hamilton's Report on Manufactures
1791–1804	Haitian Revolution
1791	Thomas Paine's *The Rights of Man*
1792	Mary Wollstonecraft's *A Vindication of the Rights of Woman*
1793	First federal fugitive slave law
1794	Whiskey Rebellion
	Jay's Treaty
1797	Inauguration of John Adams
1798	XYZ affair
	Alien and Sedition Acts
1800	Gabriel's Rebellion
1801	Inauguration of Thomas Jefferson
1801–1805	First Barbary War
1803	Louisiana Purchase
1804–1806	Lewis and Clark expedition
1809	Inauguration of James Madison
1812–1814	War of 1812
1814	Treaty of Ghent
	Hartford Convention

This colorful painting by the artist John Archibald Woodside from around the time of the War of 1812 contains numerous symbols of freedom, among them the goddess of liberty with her liberty cap, a broken chain at the sailor's feet, the fallen crown (under his left foot), a broken royal scepter, and the sailor himself, because English interference with American shipping was one of the war's causes.

On April 30, 1789, in New York City, the nation's temporary capital, George Washington became the first president under the new Constitution. All sixty-nine electors had awarded him their votes. Dressed in a plain suit of "superfine American broad cloth" rather than European finery, Washington took the oath of office on the balcony of Federal Hall before a large crowd that reacted with "loud and repeated shouts" of approval. He then retreated inside to deliver his inaugural address before members of Congress and other dignitaries.

Washington's speech expressed the revolutionary generation's conviction that it had embarked on an experiment of enormous historical importance, whose outcome was by no means certain. "The preservation of the sacred fire of liberty and the destiny of the republican model of government," Washington proclaimed, depended on the success of the American experiment in self-government.

American leaders believed that maintaining political harmony was crucial to this success. They were especially anxious to avoid the emergence of organized political parties, which had already appeared in several states. Parties were considered divisive and disloyal. "They serve to organize faction," Washington would later declare, and to substitute the aims of "a small but artful" minority for the "will of the nation." The Constitution makes no mention of political parties, and the original method of electing the president assumes that candidates would run as individuals, not on a party ticket (otherwise, the second-place finisher would not have become vice president). Nonetheless, national political parties quickly arose. Originating in Congress, they soon spread to the general populace. Instead of harmony, the 1790s became, in the words of one historian, an "age of passion." Political rhetoric became inflamed because the stakes seemed so high—nothing less than the legacy of the Revolution, the new nation's future, and the survival of American freedom.

POLITICS IN AN AGE OF PASSION

Washington's first administration

President Washington provided a much-needed symbol of national unity. He brought into his cabinet some of the new nation's most prominent political leaders, including Thomas Jefferson as secretary of state and Alexander Hamilton to head the Treasury Department. He also appointed a Supreme Court of six members, headed by John Jay of New York. But harmonious government proved short lived.

Hamilton's Program

Political divisions first surfaced over the financial plan developed by Secretary of the Treasury Hamilton in 1790 and 1791. Hamilton's immediate aims were to establish the nation's financial stability, bring to the government's support the country's most powerful financial interests, and encourage economic development. His long-term purpose was to make the United States a major commercial and military power. The goal of national greatness, he believed, could never be realized if the government suffered from the same weaknesses as under the Articles of Confederation.

Hamilton's program had five parts. The first step was to establish the new nation's credit-worthiness—that is, to create conditions under which persons would loan money to the government by purchasing its bonds, confident that they would be repaid. Hamilton proposed that the federal government assume responsibility for paying off at its full face value the national debt inherited from the War of Independence, as well as outstanding debts of the states. Second, he called for the creation of a new national debt. The old debts would be replaced by new interest-bearing bonds issued to the government's creditors. This would give men of economic substance a stake in promoting the new nation's stability, because the stronger and more economically secure the federal government, the more likely it would be to pay its debts.

The third part of Hamilton's program called for the creation of a **Bank of the United States**, modeled on the Bank of England, to serve as the nation's main financial agent. A private corporation rather than a branch of the government, it would hold public funds, issue bank notes that would serve as currency, and make loans to the government when necessary, all the while returning a tidy profit to its stockholders. Fourth, to raise revenue, Hamilton proposed a tax on producers of whiskey. Finally, in a **Report on Manufactures** delivered to Congress in December 1791, Hamilton called for the imposition of a tariff (a tax on imported foreign goods) and government subsidies to encourage the development of factories that could manufacture products currently purchased from abroad.

Liberty and Washington, painted by an unknown artist around 1800, depicts a female figure of liberty placing a wreath on a bust of the first president. She carries an American flag and stands on a royal crown, which has been thrown to the ground. In the background is a liberty cap. Washington had died in 1799 and was now immortalized as a symbol of freedom, independence, and national pride.

The Emergence of Opposition

Hamilton's vision of a powerful commercial republic won strong support from American financiers, manufacturers, and merchants. But it alarmed those who believed the new nation's destiny lay in charting a different path of development. Hamilton's plans hinged on close ties with Britain, America's main trading partner. To James Madison and Thomas Jefferson,

Support for Hamilton's plan

Venerate the Plough, a medal of the Philadelphia Society for the Promotion of Agriculture, 1786. Americans such as Jefferson and Madison believed that farmers were the most virtuous citizens and therefore agriculture must remain the foundation of American life.

the future lay in westward expansion, not connections with Europe. Their goal was a republic of independent farmers marketing grain, tobacco, and other products freely to the entire world. Jefferson and Madison quickly concluded that the greatest threat to American freedom lay in the alliance of a powerful central government with an emerging class of commercial capitalists, such as Hamilton appeared to envision.

To Jefferson, Hamilton's system "flowed from principles adverse to liberty, and was calculated to undermine and demolish the republic." Hamilton's plans for a standing army seemed to his critics a bold threat to freedom. The national bank and assumption of state debts, they feared, would introduce into American politics the same corruption that had undermined British liberty, and enrich those already wealthy at the expense of ordinary Americans. During the 1780s, speculators had bought up at great discounts (often only a few cents on the dollar) government bonds and paper notes that had been used to pay those who fought in the Revolution or supplied the army. Under Hamilton's plan, speculators would reap a windfall by being paid at face value while the original holders received nothing. Because transportation was so poor, moreover, many backcountry farmers were used to distilling their grain harvest into whiskey, which could then be carried more easily to market. Hamilton's whiskey tax seemed to single them out unfairly in order to enrich bondholders.

The Jefferson-Hamilton Bargain

Opposition to Hamilton's plan

At first, opposition to Hamilton's program arose almost entirely from the South, the region that had the least interest in manufacturing development and the least diversified economy. It also had fewer holders of federal bonds than the Middle States and New England. Because Hamilton insisted that all his plans were authorized by the Constitution's broad "general welfare" clause, many southerners who had supported the new Constitution now became "**strict constructionists**," who insisted that the federal government could exercise only powers specifically listed in the document. Jefferson, for example, believed the new national bank unconstitutional, because the right of Congress to create a bank was not mentioned in the Constitution.

A bargain struck

Opposition in Congress threatened the enactment of Hamilton's plans. Behind-the-scenes negotiations followed. They culminated at a famous dinner in 1790 at which Jefferson brokered an agreement whereby southerners accepted Hamilton's fiscal program (with the exception of subsidies to manufacturers) in exchange for the establishment of the permanent national capital on the Potomac River between Maryland and Virginia. Major Pierre-Charles L'Enfant, a French-born veteran of the War of Independence, designed a grandiose plan for the "federal city" modeled on the great urban centers of Europe, with wide boulevards, parks, and fountains. When it came to constructing public buildings in the nation's new capital, most of the labor was performed by slaves.

The national capital

The Impact of the French Revolution

Political divisions began over Hamilton's fiscal program, but they deepened in response to events in Europe. When it began in 1789, nearly all Americans welcomed the French Revolution, inspired in part by the example of their own rebellion. But in 1793, the revolution took a more radical turn with the execution of King Louis XVI along with numerous aristocrats and other foes of the new government, and war broke out between France and Great Britain.

Events in France became a source of bitter conflict in America. Jefferson and his followers believed that despite its excesses the revolution marked a historic victory for the idea of popular self-government, which must be defended at all costs. Enthusiasm for France inspired a rebirth of symbols of liberty. Liberty poles and caps reappeared on the streets of American towns and cities. To Washington, Hamilton, and their supporters, however, the revolution raised the specter of anarchy.

The rivalry between Britain and France did much to shape early American politics. The "permanent" alliance between France and the United States, which dated to 1778, complicated the situation. No one advocated that the United States should become involved in the European war, and Washington in April 1793 issued a proclamation of American neutrality. Meanwhile, the British seized hundreds of American ships trading with the French West Indies and resumed the hated practice of **impressment**—kidnapping sailors, including American citizens of British origin, to serve in their navy. Sent to London to present objections, while still serving as chief justice, John Jay negotiated an agreement in 1794 that produced the greatest public controversy of Washington's presidency. **Jay's Treaty** contained no British concessions on impressment or the rights of American shipping. Britain did agree to abandon outposts on the western frontier, which it was supposed to have done in 1783. In return, the United States guaranteed favored treatment to British imported goods. Critics of the administration charged that it aligned the United States with

The rivalry of Britain and France

Favored treatment to British imports

monarchical Britain in its conflict with republican France. Ultimately, Jay's Treaty sharpened political divisions in the United States and led directly to the formation of an organized opposition party.

Political Parties

By the mid-1790s, two increasingly coherent parties had appeared in Congress, calling themselves **Federalists and Republicans**. (The latter had no connection with today's Republican Party, which was founded in the 1850s.) Both parties laid claim to the language of liberty, and each accused its opponent of engaging in a conspiracy to destroy it.

Federalists supported Washington and favored Hamilton's economic program

The Federalists, supporters of the Washington administration, favored Hamilton's economic program and close ties with Britain. Prosperous merchants, farmers, lawyers, and established political leaders (especially outside the South) tended to support the Federalists. Their outlook was generally elitist, reflecting the traditional eighteenth-century view of society as a fixed hierarchy and of public office as reserved for men of economic substance—the "rich, the able, and the well-born," as Hamilton put it. Freedom, Federalists insisted, rested on deference to authority. Federalists feared that the "spirit of liberty" unleashed by the American Revolution was degenerating into anarchy and "licentiousness."

The Whiskey Rebellion

Opposition to the tax on distilled spirits

The Federalists may have been the only major party in American history forthrightly to proclaim democracy and freedom dangerous in the hands of ordinary citizens. The **Whiskey Rebellion** of 1794, which broke out when backcountry Pennsylvania farmers sought to block collection of the new tax on distilled spirits, reinforced this conviction. The "rebels" invoked the symbols of 1776, displaying liberty poles and banners reading "Liberty or Death." But Washington dispatched 13,000 militiamen to western Pennsylvania (a larger force than he had commanded during the Revolution). He accompanied them part of the way to the scene of the disturbances, the only time in American history that a president has actually commanded an army in the field. The "rebels" offered no resistance.

The Republican Party

Republicans favored self-government

Republicans, led by Madison and Jefferson, were more sympathetic to France than the Federalists and had more faith in democratic self-government. They drew their support from an unusual alliance of wealthy southern planters and ordinary farmers throughout the country. Enthusiasm for the French Revolution increasingly drew urban artisans into Republican ranks as well. Republicans were far more critical than the Federalists of social and economic inequality, and more accepting of broad democratic participation as essential to freedom.

Political language became more and more heated. Federalists denounced Republicans as French agents, anarchists, and traitors. Republicans called their opponents monarchists intent on transforming the new national government into a corrupt, British-style aristocracy. Each charged the other with betraying the principles of the War of Independence and of American freedom. Washington himself received mounting abuse. When he left office, a Republican newspaper declared that his name had become synonymous with "political iniquity" and "legalized corruption."

A 1794 painting by the Baltimore artist and sign painter Frederick Kemmelmayer depicting President George Washington as commander-in-chief of the army dispatched to put down the Whiskey Rebellion.

An Expanding Public Sphere

The debates of the 1790s produced not only one of the most intense periods of partisan warfare in American history but also an enduring expansion of the public sphere and with it the democratic content of American freedom. More and more citizens attended political meetings and became avid readers of pamphlets and newspapers. The establishment of nearly 1,000 post offices made possible the wider circulation of personal letters and printed materials. The era witnessed the rapid growth of the American press—the number of newspapers rose from around 100 to 260 during the 1790s, and reached nearly 400 by 1810.

Growth in American press

Inspired by the Jacobin clubs of Paris, supporters of the French Revolution and critics of the Washington administration in 1793 and 1794 formed nearly fifty Democratic-Republican societies. The Republican press publicized their meetings, replete with toasts to French and American liberty. Federalists saw the societies as another example of how liberty was getting out of hand. The government, not "self-created societies," declared the president, was the authentic voice of the American people. Forced to justify their existence, the societies developed a defense of the right of the people to debate political issues and organize to affect public policy. To the societies, political liberty

Democratic-Republican societies

VOICES OF FREEDOM

From Judith Sargent Murray, "On the Equality of the Sexes" (1790)

A prominent writer of plays, novels, and poetry, Judith Sargent Murray of Massachusetts was one of the first women to demand equal educational opportunities for women.

Is it upon mature consideration we adopt the idea, that nature is thus partial in her distributions? Is it indeed a fact, that she hath yielded to one half of the human species so unquestionable a mental superiority? I know that to both sexes elevated understandings, and the reverse, are common. But, suffer me to ask, in what the minds of females are so notoriously deficient, or unequal. . . .

Are we deficient in reason? We can only reason from what we know, and if an opportunity of acquiring knowledge hath been denied us, the inferiority of our sex cannot fairly be deduced from thence. . . . Will it be said that the judgment of a male of two years old, is more sage than that of a female's of the same age? I believe the reverse is generally observed to be true. But from that period what partiality! How is the one exalted, and the other depressed, by the contrary modes of education which are adopted! The one is taught to aspire, and the other is early confined and limited. As their years increase, the sister must be wholly domesticated, while the brother is led by the hand through all the flowery paths of science. Grant that their minds are by nature equal, yet who shall wonder at the *apparent* superiority. . . . At length arrived at womanhood, the uncultivated fair one feels a void, which the employments allotted her are by no means capable of filling. . . . She herself is most unhappy; she feels the want of a cultivated mind. . . . Should it . . . be vociferated, 'Your domestic employments are sufficient'—I would calmly ask, is it reasonable, that a candidate for immortality, for the joys of heaven, an intelligent being, who is to spend an eternity in contemplating the works of Deity, should at present be so degraded, as to be allowed no other ideas, than those which are suggested by the mechanism of a pudding, or the sewing the seams of a garment? . . .

Yes, ye lordly, ye haughty sex, our souls are by nature *equal* to yours.

From Address of the Democratic-Republican Society of Pennsylvania (December 18, 1794)

The creation of around fifty Democratic-Republican societies in 1793 and 1794 reflected the expansion of the public sphere. The Pennsylvania society issued an address defending itself against critics who questioned its right to criticize the administration of George Washington.

The principles and proceedings of our Association have lately been caluminated [tarred by malicious falsehoods]. We should think ourselves unworthy to be ranked as Freemen, if awed by the name of any man, however he may command the public gratitude for past services, we could suffer in silence so sacred a right, so important a principle, as the freedom of opinion to be infringed, by attack on Societies which stand on that constitutional basis.

Freedom of thought, and a free communication of opinions by speech through the medium of the press, are the safeguards of our Liberties. . . . By the freedom of opinion, cannot be meant the right of thinking merely; for of this right the greatest Tyrant cannot deprive his meanest slave; but, it is freedom in the communication of sentiments [by] speech or through the press. This liberty is an imprescriptable [unlimitable] right, independent of any Constitution or social compact; it is as complete a right as that which any man has to the enjoyment of his life. These principles are eternal—they are recognized by our Constitution; and that nation is already enslaved that does not acknowledge their truth. . . .

If freedom of opinion, in the sense we understand it, is the right of every Citizen, by what mode of reasoning can that right be denied to an assemblage of Citizens? . . . The Society are free to declare that they never were more strongly impressed with . . . the importance of associations . . . than at the present time. The germ of an odious Aristocracy is planted among us—it has taken root. . . . Let us remain firm in attachment to principles. . . . Let us be particularly watchful to preserve inviolate the freedom of opinion, assured that it is the most effectual weapon for the protection of our liberty.

QUESTIONS

1. *How does Murray answer the argument that offering education to women will lead them to neglect their "domestic employments"?*

2. *Why does the Democratic-Republican society insist on the centrality of "free communication of opinions" in preserving American liberty?*

3. *How do these documents reflect expanding ideas about who should enjoy the freedom to express one's ideas in the early republic?*

A print shop in the early republic. The increasing number of newspapers played a major role in the expansion of the public sphere.

meant not simply voting in elections but constant involvement in public affairs. It included the right to "exercise watchfulness and inspection, upon the conduct of public officers." Blamed by Federalists for helping to inspire the Whiskey Rebellion, the societies disappeared by the end of 1795. But much of their organization and outlook was absorbed into the emerging Republican Party. They helped to legitimize the right of "any portion of the people," regardless of station in life, to express political opinions and take an active role in public life.

The Rights of Women

The democratic ferment of the 1790s inspired renewed discussion about women's rights. In 1792, Mary Wollstonecraft published in England her extraordinary pamphlet *A Vindication of the Rights of Woman*. Wollstonecraft did not directly challenge traditional gender roles. Her call for greater access to education and to paid employment for women rested on the idea that this would enable single women to support themselves and married women to perform more capably as wives and mothers. But she did "drop a hint," as she put it, that women "ought to have representation" in government. Within two years, American editions of Wollstonecraft's work had appeared, signaling new opportunities for women in the public sphere. Increasing numbers began expressing their thoughts in print. **Judith Sargent Murray**, one of the era's most accomplished American women, wrote essays for the *Massachusetts Magazine* under the pen name "The Gleaner." In her essay "On the Equality of the Sexes," written in 1779 and published in 1790, Murray insisted that women had as much right as men to exercise all their talents and should be allowed equal educational opportunities to enable them to do so.

Women were contributing new ideas, but were they part of the new body politic? There was nothing explicitly limiting the rights in the Constitution to men. The Constitution's use of the word "he" to describe officeholders, however, reflected the widespread assumption that politics was a realm for men. The time had not yet come for a broad assault on gender inequality.

The men who wrote the Constitution did not envision the active and continuing involvement of ordinary citizens in affairs of state. But the rise

Mary Wollstonecraft

"On the Equality of the Sexes"

of political parties seeking to mobilize voters in hotly contested elections, the emergence of the "self-created societies," the stirrings of women's political consciousness, and even armed uprisings such as the Whiskey Rebellion broadened and deepened the democratization of public life set in motion by the American Revolution.

THE ADAMS PRESIDENCY

In 1792, Washington won unanimous reelection. Four years later, he decided to retire from public life, in part to establish the precedent that the presidency is not a life office. In his Farewell Address (mostly drafted by Hamilton and published in the newspapers rather than delivered orally; see the Appendix for excerpts from the speech), Washington defended his administration against criticism, warned against the party spirit, and advised his countrymen to steer clear of international power politics by avoiding "permanent alliances with any portion of the foreign world."

The Election of 1796

George Washington's departure unleashed fierce party competition over the choice of his successor. In this, the first contested presidential election, two tickets presented themselves: John Adams, with Thomas Pinckney of South Carolina for vice president, representing the Federalists, and Thomas Jefferson, with Aaron Burr of New York, for the Republicans. Adams received seventy-one electoral votes to Jefferson's sixty-eight. Because of factionalism among the Federalists, Pinckney received only fifty-nine votes, so Jefferson, the leader of the opposition party, became vice president. Voting fell almost entirely along sectional lines: Adams carried New England, New York, and New Jersey, while Jefferson swept the South, along with Pennsylvania.

In 1797, John Adams assumed leadership of a divided nation. His presidency was beset by crises. On the international front, the country was nearly dragged into the ongoing European war. As a neutral nation, the United States claimed the right to trade nonmilitary goods with both Britain and France, but both countries seized American ships with impunity. In 1797, American diplomats were sent to Paris to negotiate a treaty to replace the old alliance of 1778. French officials presented them with a demand for bribes before negotiations could proceed. When Adams made public the envoys' dispatches, the French officials were

An engraving from *The Lady's Magazine and Repository of Entertaining Knowledge*, published in Philadelphia in 1792. A woman identified as the "Genius of the Ladies Magazine" kneels before Liberty, presenting a petition for the "Rights of Women." In the foreground are symbols of the arts, science, and literature—knowledge that should be available to women as well as men.

Adams's presidency beset by crises

A New Display of the United States, an 1803 engraving by Amos Doolittle, depicts President John Adams surrounded by shields of sixteen states (the original thirteen plus Kentucky, Tennessee, and Vermont), with the population and number of senators and representatives of each. At the top, an eagle holds an arrow, an olive branch, and a banner reading "Millions for our Defence not a Cent for Tribute," a motto that originated during the XYZ affair of 1798 when French officials demanded bribes before entering into negotiations to avoid war with the United States.

Matthew Lyon

designated by the last three letters of the alphabet. This "**XYZ affair**" poisoned America's relations with its former ally. By 1798, the United States and France were engaged in a "quasi-war" at sea. Despite pressure from Hamilton, who desired a declaration of war, Adams in 1800 negotiated peace with France.

Adams was less cautious in domestic affairs. Unrest continued in many rural areas. In 1799, farmers in southeastern Pennsylvania obstructed the assessment of a tax on land and houses that Congress had imposed to help fund an expanded army and navy. A crowd led by John Fries, a local militia leader and auctioneer, released arrested men from prison. The army arrested Fries for treason and proceeded to terrorize his supporters, tear down liberty poles, and whip Republican newspaper editors.

The "Reign of Witches"

But the greatest crisis of the Adams administration arose over the **Alien and Sedition Acts of 1798**. Confronted with mounting opposition, some of it voiced by immigrant pamphleteers and editors, Federalists moved to silence their critics. A new Naturalization Act extended from five to fourteen years the residency requirement for immigrants seeking American citizenship. The Alien Act allowed the deportation of persons from abroad deemed "dangerous" by federal authorities. The Sedition Act (which was set to expire in 1801, by which time Adams hoped to have been reelected) authorized the prosecution of virtually any public assembly or publication critical of the government. The new law meant that opposition editors could be prosecuted for almost any political comment they printed. The main target was the Republican press.

The passage of these measures launched what Jefferson—recalling events in Salem, Massachusetts, a century earlier—termed a "reign of witches." Eighteen individuals, including several Republican newspaper editors, were charged under the Sedition Act. Ten were convicted of spreading "false, scandalous, and malicious" information about the government. Matthew Lyon, a member of Congress from Vermont and editor of a Republican newspaper, *The Scourge of Aristocracy*, received a sentence of four months in prison and a fine of $1,000. In Massachusetts, authorities indicted several men for erecting a liberty pole bearing the inscription, "No Stamp Act, no Sedition, no Alien Bill, no Land Tax; Downfall to the Tyrants of America."

The Virginia and Kentucky Resolutions

The Sedition Act thrust freedom of expression to the center of discussions of American liberty. Madison and Jefferson mobilized opposition, drafting resolutions adopted by the Virginia and Kentucky legislatures. Both resolutions attacked the Sedition Act as an unconstitutional violation of the First Amendment. Virginia's, written by Madison, called on the federal courts to protect free speech. The original version of Jefferson's Kentucky resolution went further, asserting that states could nullify laws of Congress that violated the Constitution—that is, states could unilaterally prevent the enforcement of such laws within their borders. The legislature prudently deleted this passage.

> *Opposition to the Sedition Act*

No other state endorsed the **Virginia and Kentucky resolutions**. Many Americans, including many Republicans, were horrified by the idea of state action that might endanger the Union. But the "crisis of freedom" of the late 1790s strongly reinforced the idea that "freedom of discussion" was an indispensable attribute of American liberty and of democratic government. Free speech, as the Massachusetts Federalist Harrison Gray Otis noted, had become the people's "darling privilege."

> *"Freedom of discussion"*

The "Revolution of 1800"

"Jefferson and Liberty" became the watchword of the Republican campaign of 1800. By this time, Republicans had developed effective techniques for mobilizing voters, such as printing pamphlets, handbills, and newspapers and holding mass meetings to promote their cause. The Federalists, who viewed politics as an activity for a small group of elite men, found it difficult to match their opponents' mobilization. Nonetheless, they still dominated New England and enjoyed considerable support in the Middle Atlantic states. Jefferson triumphed, with seventy-three electoral votes to Adams's sixty-five.

An 1800 campaign banner, with a portrait of Thomas Jefferson and the words, "John Adams is no more."

Before assuming office, Jefferson was forced to weather an unusual constitutional crisis. Each party arranged to have an elector throw away one of his two votes for president, so that its presidential candidate would come out a vote ahead of the vice presidential. But the designated Republican elector failed to do so. As a result, both Jefferson and his running mate, Aaron Burr, received seventy-three electoral votes. With no candidate having a majority, the election was thrown into the House of Representatives that had been elected in 1798, where the Federalists enjoyed a slight majority. For thirty-five ballots, neither man received a majority of the votes. Finally, Hamilton intervened. He disliked Jefferson

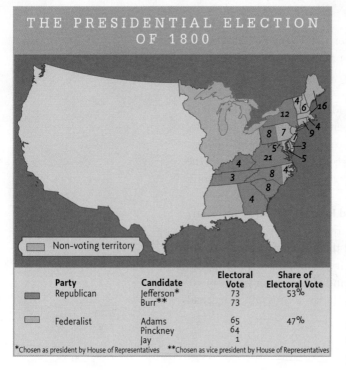

THE PRESIDENTIAL ELECTION OF 1800

- 16
- 6
- 4
- 12
- 8 7 7 9
- 4
- 5 3
- 4 21 5
- 3 8 4
- 8
- 4

Non-voting territory

Party	Candidate	Electoral Vote	Share of Electoral Vote
Republican	Jefferson*	73	53%
	Burr**	73	
Federalist	Adams	65	47%
	Pinckney	64	
	Jay	1	

*Chosen as president by House of Representatives **Chosen as vice president by House of Representatives

but believed him enough of a statesman to recognize that the Federalist financial system could not be dismantled.

Hamilton's support for Jefferson tipped the balance. To avoid a repetition of the crisis, Congress and the states soon adopted the Twelfth Amendment to the Constitution, requiring electors to cast separate votes for president and vice president. The election of 1800 also set in motion a chain of events that culminated four years later when Burr killed Hamilton in a duel.

The events of the 1790s demonstrated that a majority of Americans believed ordinary people had a right to play an active role in politics, express their opinions freely, and contest the policies of their government. To their credit, Federalists never considered resistance to the election result. Adams's acceptance of defeat established the vital precedent of a peaceful transfer of power from a defeated party to its successor.

Slavery and Politics

Lurking behind the political battles of the 1790s lay the potentially divisive issue of slavery. Jefferson, after all, received every one of the South's forty-one electoral votes. The triumph of "Jefferson and Liberty" would not have been possible without slavery. Had three-fifths of the slaves not been counted in apportionment, John Adams would have been reelected in 1800.

Franklin and abolition

The issue of slavery would not disappear. The very first Congress under the new Constitution received petitions calling for emancipation. One bore the weighty signature of Benjamin Franklin, who in 1787 had agreed to serve as president of the Pennsylvania Abolition Society. The blessings of liberty, Franklin's petition insisted, should be available "without distinction of color to all descriptions of people." Despite heated debate on both sides of the slavery question, Congress avoided the issue of emancipation. In 1793, to implement the Constitution's fugitive slave clause, Congress enacted a law providing for federal and state judges and local officials to facilitate the return of escaped slaves.

The Haitian Revolution

Events during the 1790s underscored how powerfully slavery defined and distorted American freedom. The same Jeffersonians who hailed the French Revolution as a step in the universal progress of liberty reacted in horror at the slave revolution that began in 1791 in Saint Domingue, the jewel of the French overseas empire situated not far from the southern coast of the United States. Toussaint L'Ouverture, an educated slave on a sugar plantation, forged the rebellious slaves into an army able to defeat British forces seeking to seize the island and then an expedition hoping to reestablish French authority. The slave uprising led to the establishment of Haiti as an independent nation in 1804.

Toussaint L'Ouverture

Although much of the country was left in ruins by years of warfare, the **Haitian Revolution** affirmed the universality of the revolutionary era's creed of liberty. It inspired hopes for freedom among slaves in the United States. Throughout the nineteenth century, black Americans would celebrate the winning of Haitian independence.

Among white Americans, the response to the Haitian Revolution was different. Thousands of refugees from Haiti poured into the United States, fleeing the upheaval. Many spread tales of the massacres of slaveowners and the burning of their plantations, which reinforced white Americans' fears of slave insurrection at home. When Jefferson became president, he sought to quarantine and destroy the hemisphere's second independent republic.

Toussaint L'Overture, leader of the slave revolution in Saint Domingue (modern-day Haiti). Painted in 1800 as part of a series of portraits of French military leaders, it depicts him as a courageous general.

Gabriel's Rebellion

The momentous year of 1800 witnessed not only the "revolution" of Jefferson's election but an attempted real one, a plot by slaves in Virginia itself to gain their freedom. It was organized by a Richmond blacksmith, Gabriel, and his brothers Solomon, also a blacksmith, and Martin, a slave preacher. The conspirators planned to march on the city, which had recently become the state capital, from surrounding plantations. They would kill some white inhabitants and hold the rest, including Governor James Monroe, hostage until their demand for the abolition of slavery was met. The plot was soon discovered and the leaders arrested. Twenty-six slaves, including Gabriel, were hanged and dozens more transported out of the state.

Blacks in 1800 made up half of Richmond's population. One-fifth were free. A black community had emerged in the 1780s and 1790s, and the conspiracy was rooted in its institutions. In cities like Richmond, many skilled slave craftsmen, including Gabriel himself, could read and write and enjoyed the privilege of hiring themselves out to employers—that is, negotiating their own labor arrangements, with their owner receiving their "wages." Their relative autonomy helps account for slave artisans' prominent role in the conspiracy.

Like other Virginians, the participants in the conspiracy spoke the language of liberty forged in the American Revolution and reinvigorated during the 1790s. "We have as much right," one conspirator declared, "to fight for our liberty as any men." After the rebellion, however, the Virginia legislature tightened controls over the black population—making it illegal for them to congregate on Sundays without white supervision—and severely restricted the possibility that masters could voluntarily free their slaves. Any slave freed after 1806 was required to leave Virginia or be sold back into slavery. The door to emancipation, thrown open during the American Revolution, had been slammed shut.

Tightening control over blacks in Virginia

JEFFERSON IN POWER

The first president to begin his term in Washington, D.C., Jefferson assumed office on March 4, 1801. The city, with its unpaved streets, impoverished residents, and unfinished public buildings, scarcely resembled L'Enfant's grand plan. At one point, part of the roof of the Capitol collapsed, narrowly missing the vice president.

Jefferson's inaugural address was conciliatory toward his opponents. "Every difference of opinion," he declared, "is not a difference of principle.... We are all Republicans, we are all Federalists." He went on to expound the policies his administration would follow—economy in government, unrestricted trade, freedom of religion and the press, friendship to all nations but "entangling alliances" with none. America, "the world's best hope," would flourish if a limited government allowed its citizens to be "free to regulate their own pursuits."

Jefferson's inauguration

Jefferson hoped to dismantle as much of the Federalist system as possible. Among his first acts as president was to pardon all those imprisoned under the Sedition Act. During his eight years as president, he reduced the number of government employees and slashed the army and navy. He abolished all taxes except the tariff, including the hated tax on whiskey, and paid off part of the national debt. He aimed to minimize federal power and eliminate government oversight of the economy. His policies ensured that the United States would not become a centralized state on a European model, as Hamilton had envisioned.

Dismantling the Federalist system

Judicial Review

Nonetheless, as Hamilton predicted, it proved impossible to uproot national authority entirely. Jefferson distrusted the unelected judiciary. But during his presidency, and for many years thereafter, the Federalist John Marshall headed the Supreme Court. A strong believer in national supremacy, Marshall established the Court's power to review laws of Congress and the states.

The Marshall court

The first landmark decision of the Marshall Court came in 1803, in the case of **Marbury v. Madison**. On the eve of leaving office, Adams had appointed a number of justices of the peace for the District of Columbia. Madison, Jefferson's secretary of state, refused to issue commissions (the official documents entitling them to assume their posts) to these "midnight judges." Four, including William Marbury, sued for their offices. Marshall's decision declared unconstitutional the section of the Judiciary Act of 1789 that allowed the courts to order executive officials to deliver judges' commissions. It exceeded the power of Congress as outlined in the Constitution and was therefore void. Marbury, in other words, may have been entitled to his commission, but the Court had no power under the Constitution to order Madison to deliver it. The Supreme Court had assumed the right to determine whether an act of Congress violates the Constitution—a power known as "judicial review."

Seven years later, in *Fletcher v. Peck*, the Court extended judicial review to state laws. In 1794, four land companies had paid nearly every member of the state legislature, Georgia's two U.S. senators, and a number of federal judges to secure their right to purchase land in present-day Alabama and Mississippi claimed by Georgia. Two years later, many of the corrupt lawmakers were defeated for reelection, and the new legislature rescinded the land grant and subsequent sales. Whatever the circumstances of the legislature's initial action, Marshall declared, the Constitution prohibited Georgia from taking any action that impaired a contract. Therefore, the individual purchasers could keep their land, and the legislature could not repeal the original grant.

Fletcher v. Peck

The Louisiana Purchase

But the greatest irony of Jefferson's presidency involved his greatest achievement, the **Louisiana Purchase** of 1803. This resulted not from astute American diplomacy but because the rebellious slaves of Saint Domingue defeated forces sent by the ruler of France, Napoleon Bonaparte, to reconquer the island. Moreover, to take advantage of the sudden opportunity to purchase Louisiana, Jefferson had to abandon his conviction that the federal government was limited to powers specifically mentioned in the Constitution, because the document said nothing about buying territory from a foreign power.

This vast Louisiana Territory, which stretched from the Gulf of Mexico to Canada and from the Mississippi River to the Rocky Mountains, had been ceded by France to Spain in 1762 as part of the reshuffling of colonial possessions at the end of the Seven Years' War. France secretly reacquired it in 1800. Soon after taking office, Jefferson learned of the arrangement. He had long been concerned about American access to the port of New Orleans, which lay within Louisiana at the mouth of the Mississippi River. The right to trade through New Orleans, essential to western farmers, had been acknowledged in the Treaty of San Lorenzo (also known as Pinckney's Treaty) of 1795 between the United States and Spain. But Jefferson feared that the far more powerful French might try to interfere with American commerce. Needing money for military campaigns in Europe and with his dreams of American empire in ruins because of his inability to reestablish control over Saint Domingue, Napoleon offered to sell the entire Louisiana Territory. The cost, $15 million (the equivalent of perhaps $250 million in today's money), made the Louisiana Purchase one of history's greatest real estate bargains.

Reasons for the Louisiana Purchase

In a stroke, Jefferson had doubled the size of the United States and ended the French presence in North America. Jefferson admitted that he had "done an act beyond the Constitution." But he believed the benefits justified his transgression. Farmers, Jefferson had written, were "the chosen

Effects of the Purchase

White Hall Plantation, painted around 1800, depicts a Louisiana plantation and the dynamism of the region's economy on the eve of its acquisition by the United States. Black oarsmen man a boat carrying bales of cotton for sale in New Orleans.

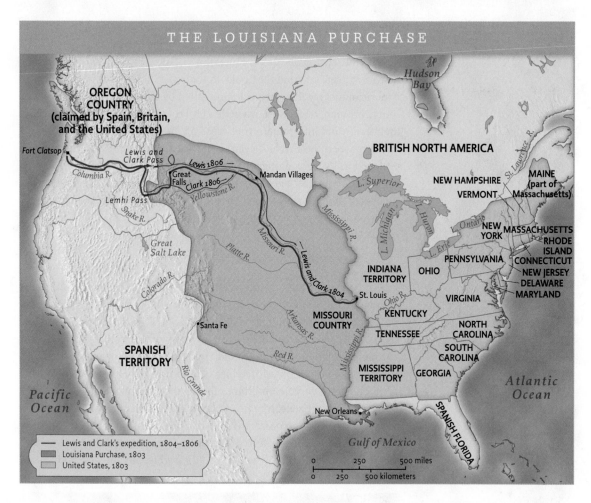

THE LOUISIANA PURCHASE

The Louisiana Purchase of 1803 doubled the land area of the United States.

people of God," and the country would remain "virtuous" as long as it was "chiefly agricultural." Now, Jefferson believed, he had ensured the agrarian character of the United States and its political stability for centuries to come.

Lewis and Clark

Within a year of the purchase, Jefferson dispatched an expedition led by Meriwether Lewis and William Clark, two Virginia-born veterans of Indian wars in the Ohio Valley, to explore the new territory. Their objects were both scientific and commercial—to study the area's plants, animal life, and geography, and to discover how the region could be exploited economically.

Scientific and commercial objectives

A page from William Clark's journal of the Lewis and Clark expedition, depicting a salmon. Among their tasks was to record information about the West's plants, animal life, and geography.

Jefferson hoped the explorers would establish trading relations with western Indians and locate a water route to the Pacific Ocean.

In the spring of 1804, Lewis and Clark's fifty-member "corps of discovery" set out from St. Louis on the most famous exploring party in American history. They were accompanied by a fifteen-year-old Shoshone Indian woman, Sacajawea, the wife of a French fur trader, who served as their guide and interpreter. After crossing the Rocky Mountains, the expedition reached the Pacific Ocean in the area of present-day Oregon. They returned in 1806, bringing with them an immense amount of information about the region as well as numerous plant and animal specimens. The success of their journey helped to strengthen the idea that American territory was destined to reach all the way to the Pacific.

Incorporating Louisiana

The only part of the Louisiana Purchase with a significant non-Indian population in 1803 was the region around New Orleans. When the United States took control, the city had around 8,000 inhabitants, including nearly 3,000 slaves and 1,300 free persons of color. Incorporating this diverse population into the United States was by no means easy. French and Spanish law accorded free blacks, many of whom were the offspring of unions between white military officers and slave women, nearly all the rights of white citizens. Moreover, Spain made it easy for slaves to obtain their freedom through purchase or voluntary emancipation by the owners.

The treaty that transferred Louisiana to the United States promised that all free inhabitants would enjoy "the rights, advantages, and immu-

New Orleans in 1803, at the time of the Louisiana Purchase. The painting shows a view of the city from a nearby plantation. The town houses of merchants and plantation owners line the broad promenade along the waterfront. At the lower center, a slave goes about his work. An eagle holds aloft a banner that suggests the heady optimism of the young republic: Under My Wings Every Thing Prospers.

UNDER MY WINGS EVERY THING PROSPERS

nities of citizens." Spanish and French civil codes, unlike British and American law, recognized women as co-owners of family property. Under American rule, Louisiana retained this principle of "community property" within marriage. But free blacks suffered a steady decline in status. And the local legislature soon adopted one of the most sweeping slave codes in the South. Louisiana's slaves had enjoyed far more freedom under the rule of tyrannical Spain than as part of the liberty-loving United States.

Louisiana slavery

The Barbary Wars

Jefferson hoped to avoid foreign entanglements, but he found it impossible as president to avoid being drawn into the continuing wars of Europe. Even as he sought to limit the power of the national government, foreign relations compelled him to expand it. The first war fought by the United States was to protect American commerce in a dangerous world.

The Barbary states on the northern coast of Africa had long preyed on shipping in the Mediterranean and Atlantic, receiving tribute from several countries, including the United States, to protect their vessels. In 1801, Jefferson refused demands for increased payments, and the pasha of Tripoli declared war on the United States. The naval conflict lasted until 1804, when an American squadron won a victory at Tripoli harbor (a victory commemorated in the official hymn of the Marine Corps, which mentions fighting on "the shores of Tripoli").

Protecting American commerce

The **Barbary Wars** were the new nation's first encounter with the Islamic world. In the 1790s, as part of an attempt to establish peaceful relations, the federal government declared that the United States was "not, in any sense, founded on the Christian religion." But the conflicts helped to establish a long-lasting pattern in which Americans viewed Muslims as an exotic people whose way of life did not adhere to Western standards.

The Embargo

Far more serious in its impact on the United States was warfare between Britain and France, which resumed in 1803 after a brief lull. By 1806, each combatant had declared the other under blockade, seeking to deny trade with America to its rival. The Royal Navy resumed the practice of impressment. By the end of 1807, it had seized more than 6,000 American sailors (claiming they were British citizens and deserters).

Blockades by Britain and France

To Jefferson, the economic health of the United States required freedom of trade with which no foreign government had a right to interfere. American farmers needed access to markets in Europe and the Caribbean.

Deciding to use trade as a weapon, in December 1807 he persuaded Congress to enact the **Embargo**, a ban on all American vessels sailing for foreign ports. For a believer in limited government, this was an amazing exercise of federal power.

In 1808, American exports plummeted by 80 percent. Unfortunately, neither Britain nor France, locked in a death struggle, took much notice. But the Embargo devastated the economies of American port cities. Just before his term ended, in March 1809, Jefferson signed the Non-Intercourse Act, banning trade only with Britain and France but providing that if either side rescinded its edicts against American shipping, commerce with that country would resume.

Effects of the Embargo

Madison and Pressure for War

Jefferson left office at the lowest point of his career. He had won a sweeping reelection in 1804, receiving 162 electoral votes to only 14 for the Federalist candidate, Charles C. Pinckney. With the exception of Connecticut, he even carried the Federalist stronghold of New England. Four years later, his handpicked successor, James Madison, also won an easy victory. The Embargo, however, had failed to achieve its diplomatic aims and was increasingly violated by American shippers. In 1810, Madison adopted a new policy. Congress enacted a measure known as Macon's Bill No. 2, which allowed trade to resume but provided that if either France or Britain ceased interfering with American rights, the president could reimpose an embargo on the other. With little to lose, since Britain controlled the seas, the French emperor Napoleon announced that he had repealed his decrees against neutral shipping. But the British continued to attack American vessels. In the spring of 1812, Madison reimposed the embargo on trade with Britain.

Macon's Bill No. 2

Meanwhile, a group of younger congressmen, mostly from the West, were calling for war with Britain. Known as the War Hawks, this new generation of political leaders had come of age after the winning of independence and were ardent nationalists. Their leaders included Henry Clay of Kentucky, elected Speaker of the House of Representatives in 1810, and John C. Calhoun of South Carolina. The War Hawks spoke passionately of defending the national honor against British insults, but they also had more practical goals in mind, notably the annexation of Canada and the conquest of Florida, a haven for fugitive slaves owned by Britain's ally Spain. Members of Congress also spoke of the necessity of upholding the principle of free trade and liberating the United States once and for all from European infringements on its independence.

War Hawks

THE "SECOND WAR OF INDEPENDENCE"

The growing crisis between the United States and Britain took place against the background of deteriorating Indian relations in the West, which also helped propel the United States down the road to war. Jefferson had long favored the removal beyond the Mississippi River of Indian tribes that refused to cooperate in "civilizing" themselves. He encouraged traders to lend money to Indians, in the hope that accumulating debt would force them to sell some of their holdings west of the Appalachian Mountains, thus freeing up more land for "our increasing numbers." On the other hand, the government continued President Washington's policy of promoting settled farming among the Indians.

Indian relations in the West

The Indian Response

By 1800, nearly 400,000 American settlers lived west of the Appalachian Mountains. They far outnumbered the remaining Indians, whose seemingly irreversible decline in power led some Indians to rethink their opposition to assimilation. Among the Creek and Cherokee, a group led by men of mixed Indian-white ancestry like Major Ridge and John Ross enthusiastically endorsed the federal policy of promoting "civilization." Many had established businesses as traders and slaveowning farmers with the help of their white fathers. Their views, in turn, infuriated "nativists," who strongly opposed assimilation.

Changing attitudes toward assimilation

The period from 1800 to 1812 was an "age of prophecy" among the Indians, as many tribal leaders sought to revitalize Indian life. A militant message was expounded by two Shawnee brothers—**Tecumseh**, a chief who had refused to sign the Treaty of Greenville in 1795, and **Tenskwatawa**, a religious prophet who called for complete separation from whites, the revival of traditional Indian culture, and resistance to federal policies. White people, Tenskwatawa preached, were the source of all evil in the world, and Indians should abandon American alcohol, clothing, food, and manufactured goods. His followers gathered at Prophetstown, located on the Wabash River in Indiana.

Tecumseh meanwhile traversed the Mississippi Valley, pressing the argument that the alternative to Indian resistance was extermination. He repudiated chiefs who had sold land to the federal government: "Sell a country! Why not sell the air, the great sea, as well as the earth? Did not the Great Spirit make them all for the use of his children?" In 1810, Tecumseh called for attacks on American frontier settlements. In November 1811,

Tenskwatawa (the Prophet), in a portrait by the American artist Charles Bird King, who painted numerous Indian leaders.

while he was absent, American forces under William Henry Harrison destroyed Prophetstown in the Battle of Tippecanoe.

The War of 1812

In 1795, James Madison had written that war is the greatest enemy of "true liberty." Nonetheless, Madison became a war president. Reports that the British were encouraging Tecumseh's efforts contributed to the coming of the War of 1812. In June 1812, with assaults on American shipping continuing, Madison asked Congress for a declaration of war. American nationality, the president declared, was at stake—would Americans remain "an independent people" or become "colonists and vassals" of Great Britain? The vote revealed a deeply divided country. Both Federalists and Republicans representing the states from New Jersey northward, where most of the mercantile and financial resources of the country were concentrated, voted against war. The South and West were strongly in favor. The bill passed the House by a vote of 79–49 and the Senate by 19–13. It was the first time the United States declared war on another country, and it was approved by the smallest margin of any declaration of war in American history.

America's first war declared

In retrospect, it seems remarkably foolhardy for a disunited and militarily unprepared nation to go to war with one of the world's two major powers. Fortunately for the United States, Great Britain at the outset was preoccupied with the struggle in Europe. But it easily repelled two feeble American invasions of Canada and imposed a blockade that all but destroyed American commerce. In 1814, having finally defeated Napoleon, Britain invaded the United States. Its forces seized Washington, D.C., and burned the White House, while the government fled for safety.

Americans did enjoy a few military successes. In August 1812, the American frigate *Constitution* defeated the British warship *Guerriere*. Commodore Oliver H. Perry defeated a British naval force in September 1813 on Lake Erie. In the following year, a British assault on Baltimore was repulsed when Fort McHenry at the entrance to the harbor withstood a British bombardment. This was the occasion when Francis Scott Key composed "The Star-Spangled Banner," an ode to the "land of the free and home of the brave" that became the national anthem during the 1930s.

Fighting the British and the Indians

Like the War of Independence, the War of 1812 was a two-front struggle—against the British and against the Indians. The war produced significant victories over western Indians who sided with the British. In 1813, pan-Indian forces led by Tecumseh (who had been commissioned a general in the British army) were defeated, and he himself was killed, at the Battle of the Thames, near Detroit, by an American force led by William Henry Harrison. In March 1814, an army of Americans and pro-assimilation

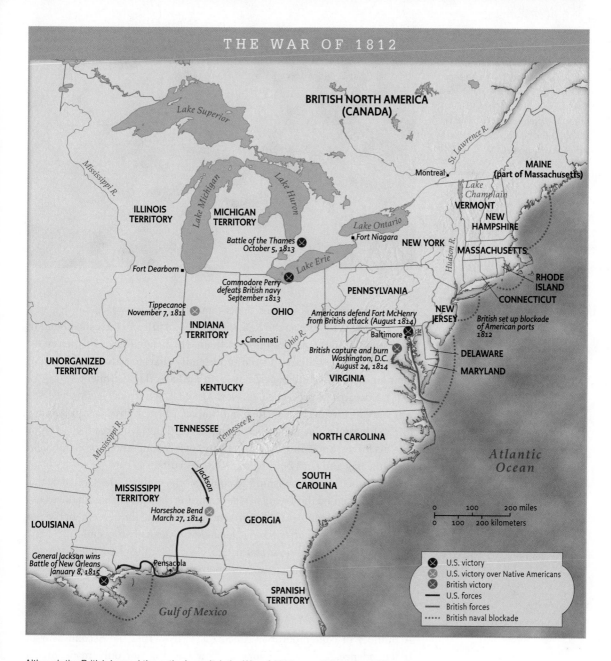

THE WAR OF 1812

BRITISH NORTH AMERICA (CANADA)

Lake Superior

Montreal

St. Lawrence R.

MAINE (part of Massachusetts)

Lake Champlain

VERMONT

NEW HAMPSHIRE

ILLINOIS TERRITORY

Lake Michigan

MICHIGAN TERRITORY

Lake Huron

Battle of the Thames October 5, 1813

Lake Ontario

Fort Niagara

NEW YORK

Hudson R.

MASSACHUSETTS

RHODE ISLAND

CONNECTICUT

Fort Dearborn

Commodore Perry defeats British navy September 1813

Lake Erie

PENNSYLVANIA

NEW JERSEY

British set up blockade of American ports 1812

Tippecanoe November 7, 1811

OHIO

Americans defend Fort McHenry from British attack (August 1814)

Baltimore

Ohio R.

Cincinnati

INDIANA TERRITORY

British capture and burn Washington, D.C. August 24, 1814

DELAWARE

MARYLAND

UNORGANIZED TERRITORY

Mississippi R.

KENTUCKY

VIRGINIA

TENNESSEE

Tennessee R.

NORTH CAROLINA

Atlantic Ocean

Mississippi R.

MISSISSIPPI TERRITORY

Jackson

SOUTH CAROLINA

Horseshoe Bend March 27, 1814

GEORGIA

LOUISIANA

General Jackson wins Battle of New Orleans January 8, 1815

Pensacola

SPANISH TERRITORY

Gulf of Mexico

| | 0 | 100 | 200 miles |
| 0 | 100 | 200 kilometers |

Legend:
- ⊗ U.S. victory
- ⊗ U.S. victory over Native Americans
- ⊗ British victory
- — U.S. forces
- — British forces
- ⋯ British naval blockade

Although the British burned the nation's capital, the War of 1812 essentially was a military draw.

The Hornet and Peacock, Or, John Bull in Distress, a watercolor by Amos B. Doolittle from 1813, celebrates a victory by the American warship *Hornet* over the British vessel *Peacock* during the War of 1812. Britain is represented as a half-bull, half-peacock creature being stung in the neck by a hornet.

Cherokees and Creeks under the command of Andrew Jackson defeated hostile Creeks known as the Red Sticks at the Battle of Horseshoe Bend in Alabama, killing more than 800 of them. He dictated terms of surrender that required the Indians, hostile and friendly alike, to cede more than half their land, over 23 million acres in all, to the federal government.

Battle of New Orleans

Jackson then proceeded to New Orleans, where he engineered the war's greatest American victory, fighting off a British invasion in January 1815. Although a slaveholder, Jackson recruited the city's free men of color into his forces, appealing to them as "sons of freedom" and promising them the same pay and land bounties as white recruits.

Treaty of Ghent

With neither side wishing to continue the conflict, the United States and Britain signed the Treaty of Ghent, ending the war. Although the treaty was signed in December 1814, ships carrying news of the agreement did not reach America until after the Battle of New Orleans had been fought. The treaty restored the previous status quo. No territory exchanged hands, nor did any provisions relate to impressment or neutral shipping rights.

The War's Aftermath

A number of contemporaries called the War of 1812 the Second War of Independence. Jackson's victory at New Orleans not only made him a national hero but also became a celebrated example of the ability of virtuous citizens of a republic to defeat the forces of despotic Europe.

American control east of the Mississippi

Moreover, the war completed the conquest of the area east of the Mississippi River, which had begun during the Revolution. Never again would the British or Indians pose a threat to American control of this vast region. In its aftermath, white settlers poured into Indiana, Michigan, Alabama, and Mississippi, bringing with them their distinctive forms of social organization.

Britain's defeat of Napoleon inaugurated a long period of peace in Europe. With diplomatic affairs playing less and less of a role in American public life, Americans' sense of separateness from the Old World grew ever stronger.

The End of the Federalist Party

War Party at Fort Douglas, a watercolor by the Swiss-born Canadian artist Peter Rindisbacher. Painted in 1823, it depicts an incident during the War of 1812 when Indian allies of Great Britain fired rifles into the air to greet their commander, Captain Andrew Bulger, pictured on the far right.

Jefferson and Madison succeeded in one major political aim—the elimination of the Federalist Party. At first, the war led to a revival of Federalist fortunes. With antiwar sentiment at its peak in 1812, Madison had been reelected by the relatively narrow margin of 128 electoral votes to 89 over his Federalist opponent, DeWitt Clinton of New York. But then came a self-inflicted blow. In December 1814, a group of New England Federalists gathered at Hartford, Connecticut, to give voice to their party's long-standing grievances, especially the domination of the federal government by Virginia presidents and their own region's declining influence as new western states entered the Union. Contrary to later myth, the **Hartford Convention** did not call for secession or disunion. But it affirmed the right of a state to "interpose" its authority if the federal government violated the Constitution.

The Hartford Convention had barely adjourned before Jackson electrified the nation with his victory at New Orleans. In speeches and sermons, political and religious leaders alike proclaimed that Jackson's triumph revealed, once again, that a divine hand oversaw America's destiny. The Federalists could not free themselves from the charge of lacking patriotism. Within a few years, their party no longer existed. Yet in their dying moments Federalists had raised an issue—southern domination of the national government—that would long outlive their political party. And the country stood on the verge of a profound economic and social transformation that strengthened the very forces of commercial development that Federalists had welcomed and many Republicans feared.

Legacy of Federalist Party

CHAPTER REVIEW AND ONLINE RESOURCES

REVIEW QUESTIONS

1. *Identify the major parts of Hamilton's financial plan, who supported these proposals, and why they aroused such passionate opposition.*

2. *How did the French Revolution and the ensuing global struggle between Great Britain and France shape early American politics?*

3. *How did the United States become involved in foreign affairs in this period?*

4. *How did the expansion of the public sphere and a new language of rights offer opportunities to women?*

5. *What caused the demise of the Federalists?*

6. *What impact did the Haitian Revolution have on the United States?*

7. *How did the Louisiana Purchase affect the situation of Native Americans in that region?*

8. *Whose status was changed the most by the War of 1812— Great Britain, the United States, or Native Americans?*

KEY TERMS

Bank of the United States (p. 223)
Report on Manufactures (p. 223)
strict constructionists (p. 224)
impressment (p. 225)
Jay's Treaty (p. 225)
Federalists and Republicans (p. 226)
Whiskey Rebellion (p. 226)
A Vindication of the Rights of Woman (p. 230)
Judith Sargent Murray (p. 230)
XYZ affair (p. 232)
Alien and Sedition Acts (p. 232)
Virginia and Kentucky resolutions (p. 233)
Haitian Revolution (p. 235)
Gabriel's Rebellion (p. 235)
Marbury v. Madison (p. 237)
Louisiana Purchase (p. 237)
expedition of Lewis and Clark (p. 239)
Barbary Wars (p. 241)
Embargo Act (p. 242)
Tecumseh and Tenskwatawa (p. 243)
Hartford Convention (p. 247)

wwnorton.com
/studyspace

VISIT STUDYSPACE FOR THESE
RESOURCES AND MORE

- A chapter outline
- A diagnostic chapter quiz
- Interactive maps
- Map worksheets
- Multimedia documents

CHAPTER 9

THE MARKET REVOLUTION

★

1800–1840

1793	Eli Whitney's cotton gin
1790s–1830s	Second Great Awakening
1806	Congress approves funds for the National Road
1807	Robert Fulton's steamboat
1814	Waltham textile factory
1819	*Dartmouth College v. Woodward*
	Adams-Onís Treaty with Spain
1825	Erie Canal opens
1831	Cyrus McCormick's reaper
1837	John Deere's steel plow
	Depression begins
	Ralph Waldo Emerson's "The American Scholar"
1844	Telegraph put into commercial operation
1845	John O'Sullivan coins phrase "manifest destiny"
1845–1851	Ireland's Great Famine
1854	Henry David Thoreau's *Walden*

A watercolor from 1829 depicts the Erie Canal five years after it opened. Boats carrying passengers and goods traverse the waterway, along whose banks farms and villages have sprung up.

FOCUS
QUESTIONS

- *What were the main elements of the market revolution?*

- *How did the market revolution spark social change?*

- *How did the meanings of American freedom change in this period?*

- *How did the market revolution affect the lives of workers, women, and African-Americans?*

In 1824, the Marquis de Lafayette visited the United States. Nearly fifty years had passed since, as a youth of twenty, the French nobleman fought at Washington's side in the War of Independence. Since 1784, when he had last journeyed to the United States, the nation's population had tripled to nearly 12 million, its land area had more than doubled, and its political institutions had thrived. The thirteen states of 1784 had grown to twenty-four, and Lafayette visited every one. He traveled up the Mississippi and Ohio rivers by steamboat, a recent invention that was helping to bring economic development to the trans-Appalachian West, and crossed upstate New York via the Erie Canal, the world's longest man-made waterway, which linked the region around the Great Lakes with the Atlantic coast via the Hudson River.

Americans in the first half of the nineteenth century were fond of describing liberty as the defining quality of their new nation, the unique genius of its institutions. Likenesses of the goddess of Liberty, a familiar figure in eighteenth-century British visual imagery, became even more common in the United States, appearing in paintings and sculpture and on folk art from weather vanes to quilts and tavern signs. In *Democracy in America*, the French historian and politician Alexis de Tocqueville wrote of the "holy cult of freedom" he encountered on his own visit to the United States during the early 1830s. "For fifty years," he wrote, "the inhabitants of the United States have been repeatedly and constantly told that they are the only religious, enlightened, and free people. They . . . have an immensely high opinion of themselves and are not far from believing that they form a species apart from the rest of the human race."

Even as Lafayette, Tocqueville, and numerous other visitors from abroad toured the United States, however, Americans' understandings of freedom were changing. Three historical processes unleashed by the Revolution accelerated after the War of 1812: the spread of market relations, the westward movement of the population, and the rise of a vigorous political democracy. (The first two will be discussed in this chapter, the third in Chapter 10.) All helped to reshape the idea of freedom, identifying it ever more closely with economic opportunity, physical mobility, and participation in a vibrantly democratic political system.

But American freedom also continued to be shaped by the presence of slavery. Lafayette, who had purchased a plantation in the West Indies and freed its slaves, once wrote, "I would never have drawn my sword in the cause of America if I could have conceived that thereby I was founding a land of slavery." Yet slavery was moving westward with the young republic. Half a century after the winning of independence, the coexistence of liberty and slavery, and their simultaneous expansion, remained the central contradiction of American life.

A NEW ECONOMY

In the first half of the nineteenth century, an economic transformation known to historians as the market revolution swept over the United States. Its catalyst was a series of innovations in transportation and communication. The market revolution was an acceleration of developments already under way in the colonial era. As noted in previous chapters, southern planters were selling the products of slave labor in the international market as early as the seventeenth century. By the eighteenth, many colonists had been drawn into Britain's commercial empire. Consumer goods like sugar and tea and market-oriented tactics like the boycott of British goods had been central to the political battles leading up to independence.

An economic transformation

Nonetheless, as Americans moved across the Appalachian Mountains and into interior regions of the states along the Atlantic coast, they found themselves more and more isolated from markets. In 1800, American farm families produced at home most of what they needed, from clothing to farm implements. What they could not make themselves, they obtained by bartering with their neighbors or purchasing from local stores and from rural craftsmen like blacksmiths and shoemakers. Those farmers not located near cities or navigable waterways found it almost impossible to market their produce. Many Americans devoted their energies to solving the technological problems that inhibited commerce within the country.

An early version of the great seal of Ohio, which entered the Union in 1803, depicts a canal boat.

Roads and Steamboats

In the first half of the nineteenth century, in rapid succession, the steamboat, canal, railroad, and telegraph wrenched America out of its economic past. These innovations opened new land to settlement, lowered transportation costs, and made it far easier for economic enterprises to sell their products. They linked farmers to national and world markets and made them major consumers of manufactured goods. Americans, wrote Tocqueville, had "annihilated space and time."

The Cumberland road

In 1806, Congress authorized the construction of the paved National Road from Cumberland, Maryland, to the Old Northwest. It reached Wheeling, on the Ohio River, in 1818 and by 1838 extended to Illinois, where it ended. But it was improved water transportation that most dramatically increased the speed and lowered the expense of commerce.

Robert Fulton, a Pennsylvania-born artist and engineer, had experimented with **steamboat** designs while living in France during the 1790s. But not until 1807, when Fulton's ship, the *Clermont*, navigated the Hudson River from New York City to Albany, was the steamboat's technological and commercial feasibility demonstrated. The invention made possible upstream commerce (that is, travel against the current) on the country's major rivers as well as rapid transport across the Great Lakes and, eventually, the Atlantic Ocean. By 1811, the first steamboat had been introduced on the Mississippi River; twenty years later some 200 plied its waters.

Advantages of the steamboat

The Erie Canal

The completion in 1825 of the 363-mile **Erie Canal** across upstate New York (a remarkable feat of engineering at a time when America's next largest canal was only twenty-eight miles long) allowed goods to flow between the Great Lakes and New York City. Almost instantaneously, the canal attracted an influx of farmers migrating from New England, giving birth to cities like Buffalo, Rochester, and Syracuse along its path.

Connecting New York City and the Old Northwest

New York governor DeWitt Clinton, who oversaw the construction of the state-financed canal, predicted that it would make New York City "the granary of the world, the emporium of commerce, the seat of manufactures, the focus of great moneyed operations." And, indeed, the canal gave

A view of New York City, in 1849, by the noted lithographer Nathaniel Currier. Steamships and sailing vessels of various sizes crowd the harbor of the nation's largest city and busiest port.

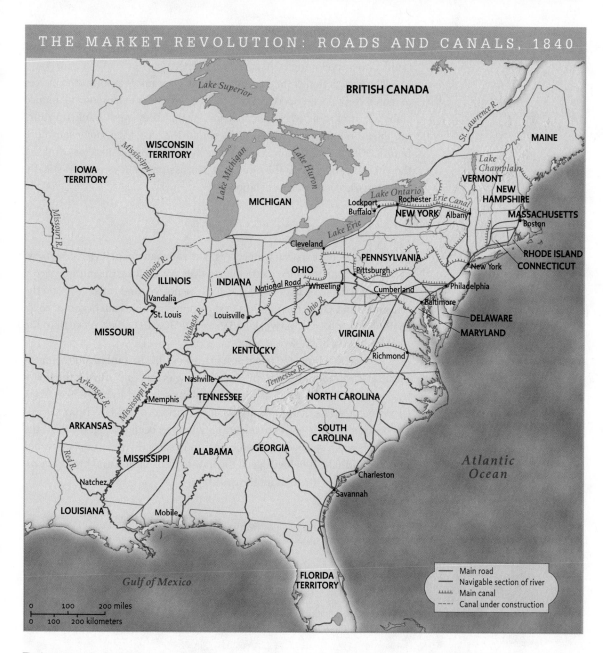

THE MARKET REVOLUTION: ROADS AND CANALS, 1840

The improvement of existing roads and building of new roads and canals sharply reduced transportation times and costs and stimulated the growth of the market economy.

New York City primacy over competing ports in access to trade with the Old Northwest. In its financing by the state government, the Erie Canal typified the developing transportation infrastructure.

The completion of the Erie Canal set off a scramble among other states to match New York's success. Several borrowed so much money to finance elaborate programs of canal construction that they went bankrupt during the economic depression that began in 1837. By then, however, more than 3,000 miles of canals had been built, creating a network linking the Atlantic states with the Ohio and Mississippi valleys and drastically reducing the cost of transportation.

State spending for internal improvements

Railroads and the Telegraph

Canals connected existing waterways. The **railroad** opened vast new areas of the American interior to settlement, while stimulating the mining of coal for fuel and the manufacture of iron for locomotives and rails. Work on the Baltimore and Ohio, the nation's first commercial railroad, began in 1828. By 1860, the railroad network had grown to 30,000 miles, more than the total in the rest of the world combined.

At the same time, the **telegraph** made possible instantaneous communication throughout the nation. The device was invented during the 1830s by Samuel F. B. Morse, an artist and amateur scientist living in New York City, and it was put into commercial operation in 1844. Within sixteen years, some 50,000 miles of telegraph wire had been strung. Initially, the telegraph was a service for businesses, and especially newspapers, rather than individuals. It helped speed the flow of information and brought uniformity to prices throughout the country.

An 1827 engraving designed to show the feasibility of railroads driven by steam-powered locomotives, and dedicated to the president of the Baltimore and Ohio Railroad, which began construction in the following year. The engraver placed passengers as far from the locomotive as possible to ensure their safety in case of an explosion.

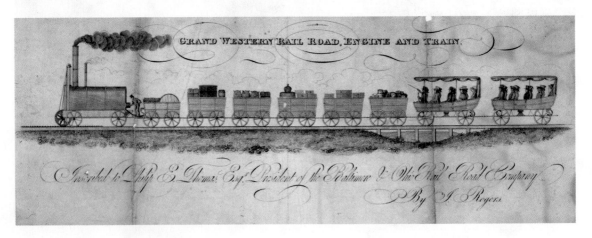

GRAND WESTERN RAIL ROAD, ENGINE AND TRAIN.

The Rise of the West

Improvements in transportation and communication made possible the rise of the West as a powerful, self-conscious region of the new nation. Between 1790 and 1840, some 4.5 million people crossed the Appalachian Mountains—more than the entire U.S. population at the time of Washington's first inauguration. Most of this migration took place after the end of the War of 1812, which unleashed a flood of land-hungry settlers moving from eastern states. In the six years following the end of the war in 1815, six new states entered the Union (Indiana, Illinois, Missouri, Alabama, Mississippi, and Maine—the last an eastern frontier for New England).

Migration west

Few Americans moved west as lone pioneers. More frequently, people traveled in groups and, once they arrived in the West, cooperated with each other to clear land, build houses and barns, and establish communities. One stream of migration, including both small farmers and planters with their slaves, flowed out of the South to create the new Cotton Kingdom of Alabama, Mississippi, Louisiana, and Arkansas. Many farm families from the Upper South crossed into southern Ohio, Indiana, and Illinois. A third population stream moved from New England across New York to the Upper Northwest—northern Ohio, Indiana, and Illinois, and Michigan and Wisconsin.

Some western migrants became "**squatters**," setting up farms on unoccupied land without a clear legal title. Those who purchased land acquired it either from the federal government, at the price, after 1820, of $1.25 per acre payable in cash or from land speculators on long-term credit. The West became the home of regional cultures very much like those the migrants

Regional cultures in the West

A watercolor by the artist Edwin Whitefield depicts a squatter's cabin in the Minnesota woods.

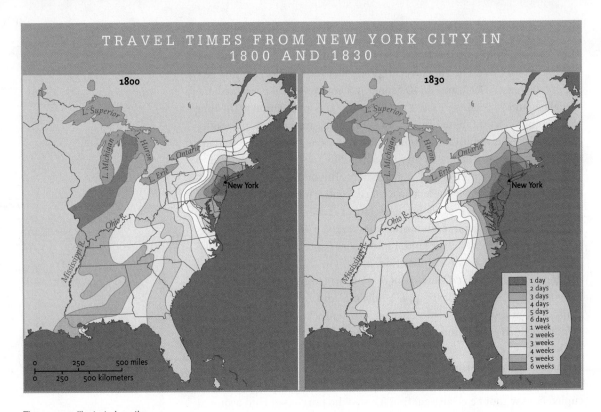

TRAVEL TIMES FROM NEW YORK CITY IN 1800 AND 1830

1800

1830

L. Superior
L. Michigan
L. Huron
L. Ontario
L. Erie
New York
Ohio R.
Mississippi R.

L. Superior
L. Michigan
Huron
L. Ontario
L. Erie
New York
Ohio R.
Mississippi R.

1 day
2 days
3 days
4 days
5 days
6 days
1 week
2 weeks
3 weeks
4 weeks
5 weeks
6 weeks

0   250   500 miles
0   250   500 kilometers

These maps illustrate how the transportation revolution of the early nineteenth century made possible much more rapid travel within the United States.

Expansion into Florida

had left behind. Upstate New York and the Upper Northwest resembled New England, with its small towns, churches, and schools, while the Lower South replicated the plantation-based society of the southern Atlantic states.

National boundaries made little difference to territorial expansion—in Florida, and later in Texas and Oregon, American settlers rushed in to claim land under the jurisdiction of foreign countries (Spain, Mexico, and Britain) or Indian tribes, confident that American sovereignty would soon follow in their wake. In 1810, American residents of West Florida rebelled and seized Baton Rouge, and the United States soon annexed the area. The drive for the acquisition of East Florida was spurred by Georgia and Alabama planters who wished to eliminate a refuge for fugitive slaves and hostile Seminole Indians. Andrew Jackson led troops into the area in 1818. While on foreign soil, he created an international crisis by executing two British traders and a number of Indian chiefs. Although Jackson withdrew, Spain, aware that it could not defend the territory, sold it to the United States in the Adams-Onís Treaty of 1819 negotiated by John Quincy Adams.

Successive censuses told the remarkable story of western growth. In 1840, by which time the government had sold to settlers and land companies nearly 43 million acres of land, 7 million Americans—two-fifths of the total population—lived beyond the Appalachian Mountains. Between 1810 and 1830, Ohio's population grew from 231,000 to more than 900,000. It reached nearly 2 million in 1850, when it ranked third among all the states. The careers of the era's leading public figures reflected the westward movement. Andrew Jackson, Henry Clay, and many other statesmen were born in states along the Atlantic coast but made their mark in politics after moving west.

40 percent of Americans west of the Appalachian Mountains

The Cotton Kingdom

Although the market revolution and westward expansion occurred simultaneously in the North and the South, their combined effects heightened the nation's sectional divisions. In some ways, the most dynamic feature of the American economy in the first thirty years of the nineteenth century was the rise of the **Cotton Kingdom**. The early industrial revolution, which began in England and soon spread to parts of the North, centered on factories producing cotton textiles with water-powered spinning and weaving machinery. These factories generated an immense demand for cotton, a crop the Deep South was particularly suited to growing because of its climate and soil fertility. Until 1793, the marketing of cotton had been slowed by the laborious task of removing seeds from the plant itself. But

Cotton and industry

TABLE 9.1 Population Growth of Selected Western States, 1800–1850 (Excluding Indians)

STATE	1810	1830	1850
Alabama	9,000	310,000	772,000
Illinois	12,000	157,000	851,000
Indiana	25,000	343,000	988,000
Louisiana	77,000	216,000	518,000
Mississippi	31,000	137,000	607,000
Missouri	20,000	140,000	682,000
Ohio	231,000	938,000	1,980,000

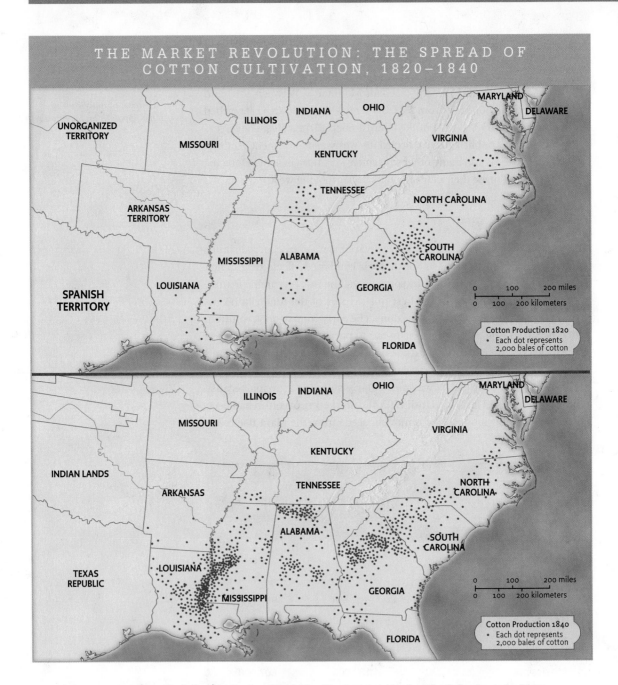

THE MARKET REVOLUTION: THE SPREAD OF COTTON CULTIVATION, 1820–1840

UNORGANIZED TERRITORY

ILLINOIS · INDIANA · OHIO · MARYLAND · DELAWARE

MISSOURI · KENTUCKY · VIRGINIA

ARKANSAS TERRITORY

TENNESSEE · NORTH CAROLINA

SPANISH TERRITORY

LOUISIANA · MISSISSIPPI · ALABAMA · GEORGIA · SOUTH CAROLINA

FLORIDA

0   100   200 miles
0   100   200 kilometers

Cotton Production 1820
• Each dot represents 2,000 bales of cotton

ILLINOIS · INDIANA · OHIO · MARYLAND · DELAWARE

MISSOURI · KENTUCKY · VIRGINIA

INDIAN LANDS

ARKANSAS · TENNESSEE · NORTH CAROLINA

TEXAS REPUBLIC

LOUISIANA · MISSISSIPPI · ALABAMA · GEORGIA · SOUTH CAROLINA

FLORIDA

0   100   200 miles
0   100   200 kilometers

Cotton Production 1840
• Each dot represents 2,000 bales of cotton

Maps of cotton production graphically illustrate the rise of the Cotton Kingdom stretching from South Carolina to Louisiana.

in that year, Eli Whitney, a Yale graduate working in Georgia as a private tutor, invented the **cotton gin**. A fairly simple device consisting of rollers and brushes, the gin quickly separated the seed from the cotton. Coupled with rising demand for cotton and the opening of new lands in the West, Whitney's invention revolutionized American slavery, an institution that many Americans had expected to die out because its major crop, tobacco, exhausted the soil.

After the War of 1812, the federal government moved to consolidate American control over the Deep South, forcing defeated Indians to cede land, encouraging white settlement, and acquiring Florida. Settlers from the older southern states flooded into the region. Planters monopolized the most fertile land, whereas poorer farmers were generally confined to less productive and less accessible areas in the "hill country" and piney woods. After Congress prohibited the Atlantic slave trade in 1808—the earliest date allowed by the Constitution—a massive trade in slaves developed within the United States, supplying the labor force required by the new Cotton Kingdom.

Slave trading became a well-organized business, with firms gathering slaves in Maryland, Virginia, and South Carolina and shipping them to markets in Mobile, Natchez, and New Orleans. Slave coffles—groups chained to one another on forced marches to the Deep South—became a common sight. Indeed, historians estimate that around 1 million slaves were shifted from the older slave states to the Deep South between 1800 and 1860. A source of greater freedom for many whites, the westward movement meant to African-Americans the destruction of family ties, the breakup of long-standing communities, and receding opportunities for liberty.

In 1793, when Whitney designed his invention, the United States produced 5 million pounds of cotton. By 1820, the crop had grown to nearly 170 million pounds.

Slave Trader, Sold to Tennessee, a watercolor sketch by the artist Lewis Miller from the mid-1850s. Miller depicts a group of slaves being marched from Virginia to Tennessee. Once Congress voted to prohibit the further importation of slaves into the country, slaveowners in newly opened areas of the country had to obtain slaves from other parts of the United States.

Surge in cotton production

MARKET SOCIETY

Since cotton was produced solely for sale in national and international markets, the South was in some ways the most commercially oriented region of the United States. Yet rather than spurring economic change, the South's expansion westward simply reproduced the same agrarian,

A trade card depicts the interior of a chair-manufacturing workshop in New York City. The owner stands at the center, dressed quite differently from his employees. The men are using traditional hand tools; furniture manufacturing had not yet been mechanized.

slave-based social order of the older states. The region remained overwhelmingly rural. In 1860, roughly 80 percent of southerners worked the land—the same proportion as in 1800.

Commercial Farmers

In the North, however, the market revolution and westward expansion set in motion changes that transformed the region into an integrated economy of commercial farms and manufacturing cities. As the Old Northwest became a more settled society, bound by a web of transportation and credit to eastern centers of commerce and banking, farmers found themselves drawn into the new market economy. They increasingly concentrated on growing crops and raising livestock for sale, while purchasing at stores goods previously produced at home.

Western farmers found in the growing cities of the East a market for their produce and a source of credit. Loans originating with eastern banks and insurance companies financed the acquisition of land and supplies and, in the 1840s and 1850s, the purchase of fertilizer and new agricultural machinery to expand production. The **steel plow**, invented by John Deere in 1837 and mass-produced by the 1850s, made possible the rapid subduing of the western prairies. The **reaper**, a horse-drawn machine that greatly increased the amount of wheat a farmer could harvest, was invented by Cyrus McCormick in 1831 and produced in large quantities soon afterward. Eastern farmers, unable to grow wheat and corn as cheaply as their western counterparts, increasingly concentrated on producing dairy products, fruits, and vegetables for nearby urban centers.

The Growth of Cities

From the beginning, cities formed part of the western frontier. Cincinnati was known as "porkopolis," after its slaughterhouses where hundreds of thousands of pigs were butchered each year and processed for shipment to eastern consumers of meat. The greatest of all the western cities was Chicago. In the early 1830s, it was a tiny settlement on the shore of Lake Michigan. By 1860, thanks to the railroad, Chicago had become the nation's fourth largest city, where farm products from throughout the Northwest were gathered to be sent east.

Like rural areas, urban centers witnessed dramatic changes due to the market revolution. Urban merchants, bankers, and master craftsmen took advantage of the economic opportunities created by the expanding market among commercial farmers. The drive among these businessmen

Western cities

A painting of Cincinnati, self-styled Queen City of the West, from 1835. Steamboats line the Ohio River waterfront.

to increase production and reduce labor costs fundamentally altered the nature of work. Traditionally, skilled artisans had manufactured goods at home, where they controlled the pace and intensity of their own labor. Now, entrepreneurs gathered artisans into large workshops in order to oversee their work and subdivide their tasks. Craftsmen who traditionally produced an entire pair of shoes or piece of furniture saw the labor process broken down into numerous steps requiring far less skill and training. They found themselves subjected to constant supervision by their employers and relentless pressure for greater output and lower wages.

A broadside from 1853 illustrates the long hours of work (from 5 AM to 6:30 PM with brief breaks for meals) in the textile mills of Holyoke, Massachusetts. Factory labor was strictly regulated by the clock.

The Factory System

In some industries, most notably textiles, the factory superseded traditional craft production altogether. Factories gathered large groups of workers under central supervision and replaced hand tools with power-driven machinery. Samuel Slater, an immigrant from England, established America's first factory in 1790 at Pawtucket, Rhode Island. Since British law made it illegal to export the plans for industrial machinery, Slater, a skilled mechanic, built from memory a power-driven spinning jenny, one of the key inventions of the early industrial revolution.

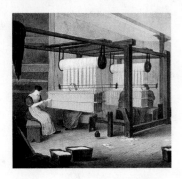

Women at work tending machines in the Lowell textile mills.

Steam power and factories

Interchangable parts

Female and child labor

Spinning factories such as Slater's produced yarn, which was then sent to traditional hand-loom weavers and farm families to be woven into cloth. This "outwork" system, in which rural men and women earned money by taking in jobs from factories, typified early industrialization. Eventually, however, the entire manufacturing process in textiles, shoes, and many other products was brought under a single factory roof.

The cutoff of British imports because of the Embargo of 1807 and the War of 1812 stimulated the establishment of the first large-scale American factory utilizing power looms for weaving cotton cloth. This was constructed in 1814 at Waltham, Massachusetts, by a group of merchants who came to be called the Boston Associates. In the 1820s, they expanded their enterprise by creating an entirely new factory town (incorporated as the city of Lowell in 1836) on the Merrimack River, twenty-seven miles from Boston. Here they built a group of modern textile factories that brought together all phases of production from the spinning of thread to the weaving and finishing of cloth.

The earliest factories, including those at Pawtucket, Waltham, and Lowell, were located along the "fall line," where waterfalls and river rapids could be harnessed to provide power for spinning and weaving machinery. By the 1840s, steam power made it possible for factory owners to locate in towns like New Bedford that were nearer to the coast, and in large cities like Philadelphia and Chicago with their immense local markets. In 1850, manufacturers produced in factories not only textiles but also a wide variety of other goods, including tools, firearms, shoes, clocks, ironware, and agricultural machinery. What came to be called the "**American system of manufactures**" relied on the mass production of interchangeable parts that could be rapidly assembled into standardized finished products. More impressive, in a way, than factory production was the wide dispersion of mechanical skills throughout northern society. Every town, it seemed, had its sawmill, paper mill, iron works, shoemaker, hatmaker, tailor, and a host of other such small enterprises.

The "Mill Girls"

Although some factories employed entire families, the early New England textile mills relied largely on female and child labor. At Lowell, the most famous center of early textile manufacturing, young unmarried women from Yankee farm families dominated the workforce that tended the spinning machines. To persuade parents to allow their daughters to leave home to work in the mills, Lowell owners set up boarding houses with strict rules regulating personal behavior. They also established lecture halls and churches to occupy the women's free time.

COTTON MILLS, 1820s

The early industrial revolution was concentrated in New England, where factories producing textiles from raw cotton sprang up along the region's many rivers, taking advantage of water power to drive their machinery.

This was the first time in history that large numbers of women left their homes to participate in the public world. Most valued the opportunity to earn money independently at a time when few other jobs were open to women. But these women did not become a permanent class of factory workers. They typically remained in the factories for only a few years, after which they left to return home, marry, or move west.

The Growth of Immigration

Economic expansion fueled a demand for labor, which was met, in part, by increased **immigration** from abroad. Between 1790 and 1830, immigrants contributed only marginally to American population growth. But between

Young women workers from the Amoskeag textile mills in Manchester, New Hampshire, photographed in 1854.

1840 and 1860, over 4 million people (more than the entire population in 1790) entered the United States, the majority from Ireland and Germany. About 90 percent headed for the northern states, where job opportunities were most abundant and the new arrivals would not have to compete with slave labor. In 1860, the 814,000 residents of New York City, the major port of entry, included more than 384,000 immigrants, and one-third of the population of Wisconsin was foreign-born.

Numerous factors inspired this massive flow of population across the Atlantic. In Europe, the modernization of agriculture and the industrial revolution disrupted centuries-old patterns of life, pushing peasants off the land and eliminating the jobs of traditional craft workers. The introduction of the oceangoing steamship and the railroad made long-distance travel more practical. Moreover, America's political and religious freedoms attracted Europeans, including political refugees from the failed revolutions of 1848, who chafed under the continent's repressive governments and rigid social hierarchies.

The largest number of immigrants, however, were refugees from disaster—Irish men and women fleeing the Great Famine of 1845–1851, when a blight destroyed the potato crop on which the island's diet relied. An estimated 1 million persons starved to death and another million emigrated in those years, most of them to the United States. Lacking industrial skills and capital, these impoverished agricultural laborers and small farmers ended up filling the low-wage unskilled jobs native-born Americans sought to avoid. Male Irish immigrants built America's railroads, dug canals, and worked as common laborers, servants, longshoremen, and factory operatives. Irish women frequently went to work as servants in the homes of native-born Americans, although some preferred factory work to domestic service. By the end of the 1850s, the Lowell textile mills had largely replaced Yankee farm women with immigrant Irish families. Four-fifths of Irish immigrants remained in the Northeast.

The second-largest group of immigrants, Germans, included a considerably larger number of skilled craftsmen than the Irish. Germans also settled in tightly knit neighborhoods in eastern cities, but many were able to move to the West, where they established themselves as craftsmen, shopkeepers, and farmers. The "German triangle," as the cities of Cincinnati, St. Louis, and Milwaukee were sometimes called, all attracted large German populations.

Some 40,000 Scandinavians also emigrated to the United States in these years, most of whom settled on farms in the Old Northwest.

TABLE 9.2 Total Number of Immigrants by Five-Year Period	
YEARS	NUMBER OF IMMIGRANTS
1841–1845	430,000
1846–1850	1,283,000
1851–1855	1,748,000
1856–1860	850,000

The Rise of Nativism

The idea of the United States as a refuge for those seeking economic opportunity or as an escape from oppression has always coexisted with suspicion of and hostility to foreign newcomers. American history has witnessed periods of intense anxiety over immigration. The Alien Act of 1798 reflected fear of immigrants with radical political views. During the early twentieth century, as will be discussed below, there was widespread hostility to the "new immigration" from southern and eastern Europe. In the early twenty-first century, the question of how many persons should be allowed to enter the United States, and under what circumstances, remains a volatile political issue.

Archbishop John Hughes of New York City made the Catholic Church a more assertive institution. He condemned the use of the Protestant King James Bible in the city's public schools, pressed Catholic parents to send their children to an expanding network of parochial schools, and sought government funding to pay for them. He aggressively sought to win converts from Protestantism.

Many Protestants found such activities alarming. Catholicism, they feared, threatened American institutions and American freedom. In 1834, Lyman Beecher, a prominent Presbyterian minister (and father of the religious leader Henry Ward Beecher and the writers Harriet Beecher Stowe and Catharine Beecher), delivered a sermon in Boston, soon published as "A Plea for the West." Beecher warned that Catholics were seeking to dominate the American West, where the future of Christianity in the

FIGURE 9.1
Sources of
Immigration, 1850

Other 21% (77,700)
England 14% (51,800)
Germany 21% (77,700)
Ireland 44% (162,800)

Lyman Beecher

Riot in Philadelphia, an 1844 lithograph, depicts street battles between nativists and Irish Catholics that left fifteen persons dead. The violence originated in a dispute over the use of the Protestant King James Bible in the city's public schools.

world would be worked out. His sermon inspired a mob to burn a Catholic convent in the city.

The Irish influx of the 1840s and 1850s thoroughly alarmed many native-born Americans and led to violent anti-immigrant riots in New York City and Philadelphia. Those who feared the impact of immigration on American political and social life were called "**nativists**." They blamed immigrants for urban crime, political corruption, and a fondness for intoxicating liquor, and they accused them of undercutting native-born skilled laborers by working for starvation wages. Stereotypes similar to those directed at blacks flourished regarding the Irish as well—childlike, lazy, and slaves of their passions, they were said to be unsuited for republican freedom.

Nativist stereotypes

The Transformation of Law

American law increasingly supported the efforts of entrepreneurs to participate in the market revolution, while shielding them from interference by local governments and liability for some of the less desirable results of economic growth. The corporate form of business organization became central to the new market economy. A corporate firm enjoys special privileges and powers granted in a charter from the government, among them that investors and directors are not personally liable for the company's debts. Unlike companies owned by an individual, family, or limited partnership, in other words, a corporation can fail without ruining its directors and stockholders.

Corporations

Many Americans distrusted corporate charters as a form of government-granted special privilege. But the courts upheld their validity, while opposing efforts by established firms to limit competition from newcomers. In ***Dartmouth College v. Woodward*** (1819), John Marshall's Supreme Court defined corporate charters issued by state legislatures as contracts, which future lawmakers could not alter or rescind. Five years later, in *Gibbons v. Ogden*, the Court struck down a monopoly the New York legislature had granted for steamboat navigation. And in 1837, with Roger B. Taney now the chief justice, the Court ruled that the Massachusetts legislature did not infringe the charter of an existing company that had constructed a bridge over the Charles River when it empowered a second company to build a competing bridge. The community, Taney declared, had a legitimate interest in promoting transportation and prosperity.

Court decisions on the economy

THE FREE INDIVIDUAL

By the 1830s, the market revolution and westward expansion had produced a society that amazed European visitors: energetic, materialistic,
and seemingly in constant motion. Alexis de Tocqueville was struck by
Americans' restless energy and apparent lack of attachment to place. "No
sooner do you set foot on American soil," he observed, "than you find your-
self in a sort of tumult. All around you, everything is on the move."

An energetic society

The West and Freedom

Westward expansion and the market revolution reinforced some older
ideas of freedom and helped to create new ones. American freedom, for
example, had long been linked with the availability of land in the West.
A New York journalist, John L. O'Sullivan, first employed the phrase
"**manifest destiny**," meaning that the United States had a divinely appointed
mission, so obvious as to be beyond dispute, to occupy all of North America.
Americans, he proclaimed, had a far better title to western lands than could
be provided by any international treaty, right of discovery, or long-term
settlement.

O'Sullivan wrote these words in 1845, but the essential idea was
familiar much earlier. Many Americans believed that the settlement and
economic exploitation of the West would prevent the United States from
following the path of Europe and becoming a society with fixed social
classes and a large group of wage-earning poor. In the West, where land
was more readily available and oppressive factory labor far less common, there continued to be the chance to achieve economic independence,
the social condition of freedom. In national myth and ideology, the West
would long remain, as the writer Wallace Stegner would later put it, "the
last home of the freeborn American."

The West and economic independence

The Transcendentalists

The restless, competitive world of the market revolution strongly encouraged the identification of American freedom with the absence of restraints
on self-directed individuals seeking economic advancement and personal
development. The "one important revolution" of the day, the philosopher
Ralph Waldo Emerson wrote in the 1830s, was "the new value of the private man." In Emerson's definition, rather than a preexisting set of rights

Individual freedom

or privileges, freedom was an open-ended process of self-realization by which individuals could remake themselves and their own lives.

Emerson was perhaps the most prominent member of a group of New England intellectuals known as the **transcendentalists**, who insisted on the primacy of individual judgment over existing social traditions and institutions. Emerson's Concord, Massachusetts, neighbor, the writer Henry David Thoreau, echoed his call for individual self-reliance. "Any man more right than his neighbors," Thoreau wrote, "is a majority of one."

Emerson and Thoreau

In his own life, Thoreau illustrated Emerson's point about the primacy of individual conscience in matters political, social, and personal, and the need to find one's own way rather than following the crowd. Thoreau became persuaded that modern society stifled individual judgment by making men "tools of their tools," trapped in stultifying jobs by their obsession with acquiring wealth. Even in "this comparatively free country," he wrote, most persons were so preoccupied with material things that they had no time to contemplate the beauties of nature.

To escape this fate, Thoreau retreated for two years to a cabin on Walden Pond near Concord, where he could enjoy the freedom of isolation from the "economical and moral tyranny" he believed ruled American society. He subsequently published *Walden* (1854), an account of his experiences and a critique of how the market revolution was, in his opinion, degrading both Americans' values and the natural environment. An area that had been covered with dense forest in his youth, he observed, had been so transformed by woodcutters and farmers that it had become almost completely devoid of trees and wild animals. Thoreau appealed to Americans to "simplify" their lives rather than become obsessed with the accumulation of wealth. Genuine freedom, he insisted, lay within.

The daguerreotype, an early form of photography, required the sitter to remain perfectly still for twenty seconds or longer. The philosopher Ralph Waldo Emerson, depicted here, did not like the result. He complained in his journal that in his "zeal not to blur the image," every muscle had become "rigid" and his face was fixed in a frown as "in madness, or in death."

The Second Great Awakening

The popular religious revivals that swept the country during the **Second Great Awakening** added a religious underpinning to the celebration of personal self-improvement, self-reliance, and self-determination. These revivals, which began at the turn of the century, were originally organized by established religious leaders alarmed by low levels of church attendance in the young republic (perhaps as few as 10 percent of white Americans regularly attended church during the 1790s). But they quickly expanded far beyond existing churches. They reached a crescendo in the 1820s and early 1830s, when the Reverend Charles Grandison Finney held months-long revival meetings in upstate New York and New York City.

Religious Camp Meeting, a watercolor from the late 1830s depicting an evangelical preacher at a revival meeting. Some of the audience members seem inattentive, while others are moved by his fiery sermon.

Like the evangelists (traveling preachers) of the first Great Awakening of the mid-eighteenth century discussed in Chapter 4, Finney warned of hell in vivid language while offering the promise of salvation to converts who abandoned their sinful ways.

The Second Great Awakening democratized American Christianity, making it a truly mass enterprise. At the time of independence, fewer than 2,000 Christian ministers preached in the United States. In 1845, they numbered 40,000. Evangelical denominations such as the Methodists and Baptists enjoyed explosive growth in membership, and smaller sects proliferated. By the 1840s, Methodism, with more than 1 million members, had become the country's largest denomination. At large camp meetings, especially prominent on the frontier, fiery revivalist preachers rejected the idea that man is a sinful creature with a preordained fate, promoting instead the doctrine of human free will. At these gatherings, rich and poor, male and female, and in some instances whites and blacks worshiped alongside one another and pledged to abandon worldly sins in favor of the godly life.

Democratizing American Christianity

Camp meetings

The Awakening's Impact

Even more than its predecessor of several decades earlier, the Second Great Awakening stressed the right of private judgment in spiritual matters and the possibility of universal salvation through faith and good

VOICES OF FREEDOM

From Ralph Waldo Emerson,
"The American Scholar" (1837)

Ralph Waldo Emerson was perhaps the most prominent intellectual in mid-nineteenth-century America. In this famous address, delivered at Harvard College, he insisted on the primacy of individual judgment over existing social traditions as the essence of freedom.

Perhaps the time is already come, when . . . the sluggard intellect of this continent will look from under its iron lids and fill the postponed expectation of the world with something better than the exertions of mechanical skill. Our day of dependence, our long apprenticeship to the learning of other lands, draws to a close. . . .

In self-trust, all the virtues are comprehended. Free should the scholar be—free and brave. Free even to the definition of freedom. . . . Not he is great who can alter matter, but he who can alter my state of mind. They are the kings of the world who give the color of their present thought to all nature and all art. . . .

[A] sign of the times . . . is the new importance given to the single individual. Every thing that tends to insulate the individual—to surround him with barriers of natural respect, so that each man shall feel the world is his, and man shall treat with man as a sovereign state with a sovereign state—tends to true union as well as greatness. 'I learned,' said the melancholy Pestalozzi [a Swiss educator], "that no man in God's wide earth is either willing or able to help any other man." Help must come from his bosom alone. . . .

We have listened too long to the courtly muses of Europe. The spirit of the American freeman is already suspected to be timid, imitative, tame. . . . The scholar is decent, indolent, complaisant. See already the tragic consequence. The mind of this country taught to aim at low objects, eats upon itself. Young men . . . do not yet see, that if the single man [should] plant himself indomitably on his instincts, and there abide, the huge world will come round to him. . . . We will walk on our own feet; we will work with our own hands; we will speak our own minds.

From "Factory Life as It Is, by an Operative" (1845)

Beginning in the 1830s, young women who worked in the cotton textile factories in Lowell, Massachusetts, organized to demand shorter hours of work and better labor conditions. In this pamphlet from 1845, a factory worker details her grievances as well as those of female domestic workers, the largest group of women workers.

Philanthropists of the nineteenth century!—shall not the operatives of our country be permitted to speak for themselves? Shall the worthy laborer be awed into silence by wealth and power, and for fear of being deprived of the means of procuring his daily bread? Shall tyranny and cruel oppression be allowed to rivet the chains of physical and mental slavery on the millions of our country who are the real producers of all its improvements and wealth, and they fear to speak out in noble self-defense? Shall they fear to appeal to the sympathies of the people, or the justice of this far-famed republican nation? God forbid!

Much has been written and spoken in woman's behalf, especially in America; and yet a large class of females are, and have been, destined to a state of servitude as degrading as unceasing toil can make it. I refer to the female operatives of New England—the free states of our union—the states where no colored slave can breathe the balmy air, and exist as such—but yet there are those, a host of them, too, who are in fact nothing more nor less than slaves in every sense of the word! Slaves to a system of labor which requires them to toil from five until seven o'clock, with one hour only to attend to the wants of nature, allowed—slaves to ignorance—and how can it be otherwise? What time has the operative to bestow on moral, religious or intellectual culture? Common sense will teach every one the utter impossibility of improving the mind under these circumstances, however great the desire may be for knowledge.

Again, we hear much said on the subject of benevolence among the wealthy and so called, Christian part of community. Have we not cause to question the sincerity of those who, while they talk benevolence in the parlor, compel their help to labor for a mean, paltry pittance in the kitchen? And while they manifest great concern for the souls of the heathen in distant lands, care nothing for the bodies and intellects of those within their own precincts? . . .

In the strength of our united influence we will soon show these drivelling cotton lords, this mushroom aristocracy of New England, who so arrogantly aspire to lord it over God's heritage, that our rights cannot be trampled upon with impunity; that our rights cannot be trampled upon with impunity; that we WILL not longer submit to that arbitrary power which has for the last ten years been so abundantly exercised over us.

QUESTIONS

1. *How does Emerson define the freedom of what he calls "the single individual"?*

2. *Why does the female factory worker compare her conditions with those of slaves?*

3. *What does the contrast between these two documents suggest about the impact of the market revolution on American thought?*

Das neue Jerusalem (The New Jerusalem), an early-nineteenth-century watercolor, in German, illustrates the narrow gateway to heaven and the fate awaiting sinners in hell. These were common themes of preachers in the Second Great Awakening.

works. Every person, Finney insisted, was a "moral free agent"—that is, a person free to choose between a Christian life and sin.

Revivalist ministers seized the opportunities offered by the market revolution to spread their message. They raised funds, embarked on lengthy preaching tours by canal, steamboat, and railroad, and flooded the country with mass-produced, inexpensive religious tracts. The revivals' opening of religion to mass participation and their message that ordinary Americans could shape their own spiritual destinies resonated with the spread of market values.

To be sure, evangelical preachers can hardly be described as cheerleaders for a market society. They regularly railed against greed and indifference to the welfare of others as sins. Yet the revivals thrived in areas caught up in the rapid expansion of the market economy, such as the region of upstate New York along the path of the Erie Canal. Most of Finney's converts here came from the commercial and professional classes. Evangelical ministers promoted what might be called a controlled individualism as the essence of freedom. In stressing the importance of industry, sobriety, and self-discipline as examples of freely chosen moral behavior, evangelical preachers promoted the very qualities necessary for success in a market culture.

The Emergence of Mormonism

The end of governmental support for established churches promoted competition among religious groups that kept religion vibrant and promoted the emergence of new denominations. Among the most successful of the religions that sprang up was the **Church of Latter-Day Saints, or Mormons**, which hoped to create a Kingdom of God on earth. The Mormons were founded in the 1820s by Joseph Smith, a farmer in upstate New York who as a youth began to experience religious visions. He claimed to have been led by an angel to a set of golden plates covered with strange writing. Smith translated and published them as *The Book of Mormon*, after a fourth-century prophet.

The Book of Mormon tells the story of three families who traveled from the ancient Middle East to the Americas, where they eventually evolved into Native American tribes. Jesus Christ plays a prominent role in the

Joseph Smith

book, appearing to one of the family groups in the Western Hemisphere after his death and resurrection. The second coming of Christ would take place in the New World, where Smith was God's prophet.

Mormonism emerged in a center of the Second Great Awakening, upstate New York. The church founded by Smith shared some features with other Christian denominations including a focus on the family and community as the basis of social order and a rejection of alcohol. Gradually, however, Smith began to receive visions that led to more con-

In this 1846 photograph, the massive Mormon temple in Nauvoo, Illinois, towers over the ramshackle wooden buildings of this town along the Mississippi River.

troversial doctrines, notably polygamy, which allows one man to have more than one wife. By the end of his life, Smith had married no fewer than thirty women. Along with the absolute authority Smith exercised over his followers, this doctrine outraged the Mormons' neighbors. Mobs drove Smith and his followers out of New York, Ohio, and Missouri before they settled in 1839 in Nauvoo, Illinois. There, five years later, Smith was arrested on the charge of inciting a riot that destroyed an anti-Mormon newspaper. While in jail awaiting trial, Smith was murdered by a group of intruders. In 1847, his successor as Mormon leader, Brigham Young, led more than 2,000 followers across the Great Plains and Rocky Mountains to the shores of the Great Salt Lake in present-day Utah. By 1852, the number of Mormons in various settlements in Utah reached 16,000. The Mormons' experience revealed the limits of religious toleration in nineteenth-century America but also the opportunities offered by religious pluralism. Today, Mormons constitute the fourth largest church in the United States, and *The Book of Mormon* has been translated into over 100 languages.

Brigham Young

THE LIMITS OF PROSPERITY

Liberty and Prosperity

As the market revolution progressed, the right to compete for economic advancement became a touchstone of American freedom. Americans celebrated the opportunities open to the "**self-made man**," a term that came

Pat Lyon at the Forge, an 1826–1827 painting of a prosperous blacksmith. Proud of his accomplishments as a self-made man who had achieved success through hard work and skill rather than inheritance, Lyon asked the artist to paint him in his shop wearing his work clothes.

into use at this time. According to this idea, those who achieved success in America did so not as a result of hereditary privilege or government favoritism as in Europe, but through their own intelligence and hard work. The market revolution enriched numerous bankers, merchants, industrialists, and planters. It produced a new middle class—an army of clerks, accountants, and other office employees who staffed businesses in Boston, New York, and elsewhere. It created new opportunities for farmers who profited from the growing demand at home and abroad for American agricultural products, and for skilled craftsmen such as Thomas Rodgers, a machine builder who established a successful locomotive factory in Paterson, New Jersey. New opportunities for talented men opened in professions such as law, medicine, and teaching. By the early 1820s, there were an estimated 10,000 physicians in the United States.

Race and Opportunity

The market revolution affected the lives of all Americans. But not all were positioned to take advantage of its benefits. Most blacks, of course, were slaves, but even free blacks found themselves excluded from the new economic opportunities. The 220,000 blacks living in the free states on the eve of the Civil War (less than 2 percent of the North's population) suffered discrimination in every phase of their lives. The majority of blacks lived in the poorest, unhealthiest sections of cities like New York, Philadelphia, and Cincinnati. And even these neighborhoods were subject to occasional violent assault by white mobs, like the armed bands that attacked blacks and destroyed their homes and businesses in Cincinnati in 1829.

Black institutions

Barred from schools and other public facilities, free blacks laboriously constructed their own institutional life, centered on mutual-aid and educational societies, as well as independent churches, most notably the African Methodist Episcopal Church. Richard Allen of Philadelphia, a Methodist preacher, had been spurred to found the church after being forcibly removed from his former church for praying at the altar rail, a place reserved for whites.

Downward mobility of free blacks

Whereas many white Americans could look forward to a life of economic accumulation and individual advancement, large numbers of free blacks experienced downward mobility. At the time of abolition in the North, because of widespread slave ownership among eighteenth-century artisans, a considerable number of northern blacks possessed craft skills. But it became more and more difficult for blacks to utilize these skills once they became free. Although many white artisans criticized slavery, most viewed the freed slaves as low-wage competitors and sought to bar them from skilled employment.

Hostility from white craftsmen, however, was only one of many obstacles that kept blacks confined to the lowest ranks of the labor market. White employers refused to hire them in anything but menial positions, and white customers did not wish to be served by them. The result was a rapid decline in economic status until by mid-century, the vast majority of northern blacks labored for wages in unskilled jobs and as domestic servants. The state census of 1855 revealed 122 black barbers and 808 black servants in New York City, but only 1 lawyer and 6 doctors. Nor could free blacks take advantage of the opening of the West to improve their economic status, a central component of American freedom. Federal law barred them from access to public land, and by 1860 four states—Indiana, Illinois, Iowa, and Oregon—prohibited them from entering their territory altogether.

Limited opportunity for free blacks

The Cult of Domesticity

Women, too, found many of the opportunities opened by the market revolution closed to them. As the household declined as a center of economic production, many women saw their traditional roles undermined by the availability of mass-produced goods previously made at home. Some women, as noted above, followed work as it moved from household to factory. Others embraced a new definition of femininity, which glorified not a woman's contribution to the family's economic well-being, but her ability to create a private environment shielded from the competitive tensions of the market economy. Woman's "place" was in the home, a site increasingly emptied of economically productive functions as work moved from the household to workshops and factories. Her role was to sustain nonmarket values like love, friendship, and mutual obligation, providing men with a shelter from the competitive marketplace.

The earlier ideology of "republican motherhood," which allowed women a kind of public role as mothers of future citizens, subtly evolved into the mid-nineteenth-century "**cult of domesticity**." "In whatever situation of life a woman is placed from her cradle to her grave," declared *The Young Lady's Book*, one of numerous popular magazines addressed to female audiences of the 1820s and 1830s, "a spirit of obedience and submission, pliability of temper, and humility of mind, are required from her."

With more and more men leaving the home for work, women did exercise considerable power over personal affairs within the family. The rapid decline in the American birthrate during the nineteenth century

Married, a lithograph from around 1849, depicts a young, middle-class family at home. It exemplifies the cult of domesticity, in which women's social role was to fulfill their family responsibilities.

An image from a female infant's 1830 birth and baptismal certificate depicts a domestic scene, with women at work while men relax.

Expanding middle class

A "family wage"

(from an average of seven children per woman in 1800 to four in 1900) cannot be explained except by the conscious decision of millions of women to limit the number of children they bore. But the idea of domesticity minimized women's even indirect participation in the outside world. Men moved freely between the public and private "spheres"; women were supposed to remain cloistered in the private realm of the family.

Women and Work

Prevailing ideas concerning gender bore little relation to the experience of those women who worked for wages at least some time in their lives. They did so despite severe disadvantages. Women could not compete freely for employment, since only low-paying jobs were available to them. Married women still could not sign independent contracts or sue in their own names, and not until after the Civil War did they, not their husbands, control the wages they earned. Nonetheless, for poor city dwellers and farm families, the labor of all family members was essential to economic survival. Thousands of poor women found jobs as domestic servants, factory workers, and seamstresses.

For the expanding middle class, however, it became a badge of respectability for wives to remain at home, outside the disorderly new market economy, while husbands conducted business in their offices, shops, and factories. In larger cities, where families of different social classes had previously lived alongside one another, fashionable middle-class neighborhoods populated by merchants, factory owners, and professionals like lawyers and doctors began to develop. Work in middle-class homes was done by domestic servants, the largest employment category for women in nineteenth-century America. The freedom of the middle-class woman—defined in part as freedom from labor—rested on the employment of other women within her household.

Even though most women were anything but idle, in a market economy where labor increasingly meant work that created monetary value, it became more and more difficult to think of labor as encompassing anyone but men. Discussions of labor rarely mentioned housewives, domestic servants, and female outworkers, except as an indication of how the spread of capitalism was degrading men. The idea that the male head of household should command a "family wage" that enabled him to support his wife and children became a popular definition of social justice. It sank deep roots not only among middle-class Americans but among working-class men as well.

The Early Labor Movement

Although many Americans welcomed the market revolution, others felt threatened by its consequences. Surviving members of the revolutionary generation feared that the obsession with personal economic gain was undermining devotion to the public good.

Many Americans experienced the market revolution not as an enhancement of the power to shape their own lives, but as a loss of freedom. The period between the War of 1812 and 1840 witnessed a sharp economic downturn in 1819, a full-fledged depression starting in 1837, and numerous ups and downs in between, during which employment was irregular and numerous businesses failed. The economic transformation significantly widened the gap between wealthy merchants and industrialists on the one hand and impoverished factory workers, unskilled dockworkers, and seamstresses laboring at home on the other. In Massachusetts, the most industrialized state in the country, the richest 5 percent of the population owned more than half the wealth.

The Shoemakers' Strike in Lynn—Procession in the Midst of a Snow-Storm, of Eight Hundred Women Operatives, an engraving from *Frank Leslie's Illustrated Newspaper*, March 17, 1860. The striking women workers carry a banner comparing their condition to that of slaves.

Alarmed at the erosion of traditional skills and the threat of being reduced to the status of dependent wage earners, skilled craftsmen in the late 1820s created the world's first Workingmen's Parties, short-lived political organizations that sought to mobilize lower-class support for candidates who would press for free public education, an end to imprisonment for debt, and legislation limiting work to ten hours per day. In the 1830s, a time of rapidly rising prices, union organization spread and strikes became commonplace. Along with demands for higher wages and shorter hours, the early labor movement called for free homesteads for settlers on public land and an end to the imprisonment of union leaders for conspiracy.

Demands of early labor movement

The "Liberty of Living"

But over and above these specific issues, workers' language of protest drew on older ideas of freedom linked to economic autonomy, public-spirited virtue, and social equality. The conviction of twenty New York tailors in 1835 under the common law of conspiracy for combining to seek higher wages inspired a public procession marking the "burial of liberty." Such actions and language were not confined to male workers. The young mill women of Lowell walked off their jobs in 1834 to protest a reduction in wages and again two years later when employers raised rents at their

Labor actions

boardinghouses. They carried banners affirming their rights as "daughters of free men," and, addressing the factory owners, they charged that "the oppressive hand of avarice [greed] would enslave us."

Rooted in the traditions of the small producer and the identification of freedom with economic independence, labor's critique of the market economy directly challenged the idea that individual improvement—Emerson's "self-trust, self-reliance, self-control, self-culture"—offered an adequate response to social inequality. Orestes Brownson, in his influential essay "The Laboring Classes" (1840), argued that the solution to workers' problems did not require a more complete individualism. What was needed instead, he believed, was a "radical change [in] existing social arrangements" so as to produce "equality between man and man." Here lay the origins of the idea, which would become far more prominent in the late nineteenth and twentieth centuries, that economic security—a standard of life below which no person would fall—formed an essential part of American freedom.

The idea of economic security

Thus, the market revolution transformed and divided American society and its conceptions of freedom. It encouraged a new emphasis on individualism and physical mobility among white men while severely limiting the options available to women and African-Americans. It opened new opportunities for economic freedom for many Americans while leading others to fear that their traditional economic independence was being eroded. In a democratic society, it was inevitable that the debate over the market revolution and its consequences for freedom would be reflected in American politics.

Tensions in the market revolution

CHAPTER REVIEW AND ONLINE RESOURCES

REVIEW QUESTIONS

1. *Identify the major transportation improvements in this period, and explain how they influenced the market economy.*

2. *How did state and local governments promote the national economy in this period?*

3. *How did the market economy and westward expansion entrench the institution of slavery?*

4. *How did westward expansion and the market revolution drive each other?*

5. *What role did immigrants play in the new market society?*

6. *How did changes in the law promote development in the economic system?*

7. *As it democratized American Christianity, the Second Great Awakening both took advantage of the market revolution and criticized its excesses. Explain.*

8. *How did the market revolution change women's work and family roles?*

9. *Give some examples of the rise of individualism in these years.*

KEY TERMS

steamboats (p. 252)
Erie Canal (p. 252)
railroads (p. 254)
telegraph (p. 254)
squatters (p. 255)
Cotton Kingdom (p. 257)
cotton gin (p. 259)
John Deere steel plow (p. 260)
Cyrus McCormick reaper (p. 260)
factory system (p. 261)
"American system of manufactures" (p. 262)
mill girls (p. 262)
immigration (p. 263)
nativists (p. 266)
Dartmouth College v. Woodward (p. 266)
manifest destiny (p. 267)
transcendentalists (p. 268)
Second Great Awakening (p. 268)
Church of Latter-Day Saints, or Mormons (p. 272)
"self-made man" (p. 273)
cult of domesticity (p. 275)

wwnorton.com /studyspace

VISIT STUDYSPACE FOR THESE RESOURCES AND MORE

- A chapter outline
- A diagnostic chapter quiz
- Interactive maps
- Map worksheets
- Multimedia documents

1811	Bank of the United States charter expires
1816	Second Bank of the United States established
1817	Inauguration of James Monroe
1819	Panic of 1819
	McCulloch v. Maryland
1820	Missouri Compromise
1823	Monroe Doctrine
1825	Inauguration of John Quincy Adams
1828	"Tariff of abominations"
1829	Inauguration of Andrew Jackson
1830	Indian Removal Act
1831	*Cherokee Nation v. Georgia*
1832	Nullification crisis
	Worcester v. Georgia
1833	Force Act
1835	Tocqueville's *Democracy in America*
1835– 1842	Second Seminole War
1837	Inauguration of Martin Van Buren
1837– 1843	Panic of 1837 and ensuing depression
1838– 1839	Trail of Tears
1841	Inauguration of William Henry Harrison
	Dorr War

CHAPTER 10

DEMOCRACY IN AMERICA

★

1815–1840

Justice's Court in the Back Woods, an 1852 painting by Tompkins Harrison Matteson, depicts the expansion of the public sphere to include ordinary Americans. A court is in session in a local tavern. The justice of the peace, who presides, is a shoemaker who has set aside his tools but still wears his leather work apron. A lawyer appeals to the jury, composed of average (male) citizens. The case has to do with an assault. The plaintiff, his head bandaged, leans on the table at the right, while a woman consoles the defendant on the far left.

he inauguration of Andrew Jackson on March 4, 1829, made it clear that something had changed in American politics. The swearing-in of the president had previously been a small, dignified event. Jackson's inauguration attracted a crowd of some 20,000 people who poured into the White House after the ceremony, ruining furniture and breaking china and glassware in the crush. It was "the reign of King Mob," lamented Justice Joseph Story of the Supreme Court.

Jackson's career embodied the major developments of his era—the market revolution, the westward movement, the expansion of slavery, and the growth of democracy. He was a symbol of the self-made man. Unlike previous presidents, Jackson rose to prominence from a humble background, reflecting his era's democratic opportunities. Born in 1767 on the South Carolina frontier, he had been orphaned during the American Revolution. While still a youth, he served as a courier for patriotic forces during the War of Independence. His military campaigns against the British and Indians during the War of 1812 helped to consolidate American control over the Deep South, making possible the rise of the Cotton Kingdom. He himself acquired a large plantation in Tennessee. But more than anything else, to this generation of Americans Andrew Jackson symbolized one of the most crucial features of national life—the triumph of political democracy.

Americans pride themselves on being the world's oldest democracy. New Zealand, whose constitution of 1893 gave women and Maoris (the native population) the right to vote, may have a better claim. Europe, however, lagged far behind. Britain did not achieve universal male suffrage until the 1880s. France instituted it in 1793, abandoned it in 1799, reintroduced it in 1848, and abandoned it again a few years later. More to the point, perhaps, democracy became part of the definition of American nationality and the American idea of freedom.

FOCUS QUESTIONS

- *What were the social bases for the flourishing democracy of the early mid-nineteenth century?*

- *What efforts strengthened or hindered the economic integration of the nation?*

- *What were the major areas of conflict between nationalism and sectionalism?*

- *In what ways did Andrew Jackson embody the contradictions of democratic nationalism?*

- *How did the Bank War influence the economy and party competition?*

THE TRIUMPH OF DEMOCRACY

Property and Democracy

The market revolution and territorial expansion were intimately connected with a third central element of American freedom—political democracy. The challenge to property qualifications for voting, begun during

An anti-Jackson cartoon from 1832 portrays Andrew Jackson as an aspiring monarch, wielding the veto power while trampling on the Constitution.

the American Revolution, reached its culmination in the early nineteenth century. Not a single state that entered the Union after the original thirteen required ownership of property to vote. In the older states, by 1860 all but one had ended property requirements for voting (though several continued to bar persons accepting poor relief, on the grounds that they lacked genuine independence). The personal independence necessary in the citizen now rested not on ownership of property but on ownership of one's self—a reflection of the era's individualism.

The Dorr War

The lone exception to the trend toward democratization was Rhode Island, which required voters to own real estate valued at $134 or rent property for at least $7 per year. A center of factory production, Rhode Island had a steadily growing population of propertyless wage earners unable to vote. In October 1841, proponents of democratic reform organized a People's Convention, which drafted a new state constitution. It enfranchised all adult white men while eliminating entirely blacks (although in a subsequent referendum, blacks' right to vote was restored). When the reformers ratified their constitution in an extralegal referendum and proceeded to inaugurate Thomas Dorr, a prominent Rhode Island lawyer, as governor, President John Tyler dispatched federal troops to the state. The movement collapsed, and Dorr subsequently served nearly two years in prison for treason.

Tocqueville on Democracy

White male suffrage

By 1840, more than 90 percent of adult white men were eligible to vote. A flourishing democratic system had been consolidated. American politics was boisterous, highly partisan, and sometimes violent, and it engaged the energies of massive numbers of citizens. In a country that lacked more traditional bases of nationality—a powerful and menacing neighbor, historic ethnic, religious, or cultural unity—democratic political institutions came to define the nation's sense of its own identity.

Alexis de Tocqueville

Alexis de Tocqueville, the French writer who visited the United States in the early 1830s, returned home to produce ***Democracy in America***, a classic account of a society in the midst of a political transformation. Tocqueville had come to the United States to study prisons. But he soon realized that to understand America, he must understand democracy (which as a person of aristocratic background he rather disliked). His key

Independence Day Celebration in Centre Square, an 1819 painting by John Lewis Krimmel, a German-American artist, depicts a gathering to celebrate the Fourth of July in Philadelphia. On the left, beneath a portrait of George Washington, is a depiction of a naval battle from the War of 1812; on the right, beneath the state flag of Pennsylvania, is an image of the Battle of New Orleans. The celebration, an example of rising American nationalism, includes men and women, soldiers, merchants, and ordinary citizens but is entirely white except for a young black boy in the lower left.

insight was that democracy by this time meant far more than either the right to vote or a particular set of political institutions. It was what scholars call a "habit of the heart," a culture that encouraged individual initiative, belief in equality, and an active public sphere populated by numerous voluntary organizations that sought to improve society. Democracy, Tocqueville saw, had become an essential attribute of American freedom.

Democratic culture

As Tocqueville recognized, the idea that sovereignty belongs to the mass of ordinary citizens was a profound shift in political thought. The founders of the republic, who believed that government must rest on the consent of the governed, also sought to shield political authority from excessive influence by ordinary people (hence the Electoral College, Supreme Court, and other undemocratic features of the Constitution). Nonetheless, thanks to persistent pressure from those originally excluded from political participation, democracy—for white males—had triumphed by the Age of Jackson.

Popular sovereignty

The Information Revolution

The market revolution and political democracy produced a large expansion of the public sphere and an explosion in printing sometimes called the "**information revolution**." The application of steam power to newspaper printing led to a great increase in output and the rise of the mass-circulation "penny press," priced at one cent per issue instead of the traditional six. Newspapers such as the *New York Sun* and *New York Herald* introduced a new style of journalism, appealing to a mass audience by emphasizing sensationalism,

The rise of the mass-circulation press

crime stories, and exposés of official misconduct. By 1840, according to one estimate, the total weekly circulation of newspapers in the United States, whose population was 17 million, exceeded that of Europe, with 233 million people.

Alternative journalism

The reduction in the cost of printing also made possible the appearance of "alternative" newspapers in the late 1820s and early 1830s, including *Freedom's Journal* (the first black newspaper), *Philadelphia Mechanic's Advocate* and other labor publications, the abolitionist weekly *The Liberator*, and *Cherokee Phoenix*, the first Native American newspaper.

The Limits of Democracy

By the 1830s, the time of Andrew Jackson's presidency, the axiom that "the people" ruled had become a universally accepted part of American politics. Those who opposed this principle, wrote Tocqueville, "hide their heads." But the very centrality of democracy to the definition of both freedom and nationality made it all the more necessary to define the boundaries of the political nation. As older economic exclusions fell away, others survived and new ones were added.

"Universal suffrage"

The "principle of universal suffrage," declared the *United States Magazine and Democratic Review* in 1851, meant that "white males of age constituted the political nation." How could the word "universal" be reconciled with barring blacks and women from political participation? As democracy triumphed, the intellectual grounds for exclusion shifted from economic

Democracy, gender, and race

dependency to natural incapacity. Gender and racial differences were widely understood as part of a single, natural hierarchy of innate endowments. White males were considered inherently superior in character and abilities to non-whites and women. The debate over which people are and are not qualified to take part in American democracy lasted well into the twentieth century. Not until 1920 was the Constitution amended to require states to allow women to vote. The Voting Rights Act of 1965 swept away restrictions on black voting imposed by many southern states.

A Racial Democracy

If the exclusion of women from political freedom continued a long-standing practice, the increasing identification of democracy and whiteness marked something of a departure. Blacks were increasingly considered a group apart. Racist imagery became the stock-in-trade of popular theatrical presentations like minstrel shows, in which white actors in blackface entertained the audience by portraying African-Americans as stupid, dishonest, and altogether ridiculous. With the exception of Herman Melville, who portrayed complex, sometimes heroic black characters in works like *Moby Dick* and *Benito Cereno* (the latter a fictionalized account of a shipboard slave rebellion), American authors either ignored blacks entirely or presented them as stereotypes—happy slaves prone to super- stition or long-suffering but devout Christians. Meanwhile, the somewhat tentative thinking of the revolutionary era about the status of non-whites flowered into an elaborate ideology of racial superiority and inferiority, complete with "scientific" underpinnings. These developments affected the boundaries of the political nation.

In the revolutionary era, only Virginia, South Carolina, and Georgia explicitly confined the vote to whites, although elsewhere, custom often made it difficult for free blacks to exercise the franchise. As late as 1800, no northern state barred blacks from voting. But every state that entered the Union after that year, with the single exception of Maine, limited the right to vote to white males. And, beginning with Kentucky in 1799 and Maryland two years later, many states that had allowed blacks to vote rescinded the privilege. By 1860, blacks could vote on the same basis as whites in only five New England states, which contained only 4 percent of the nation's free black population.

In effect, race had replaced class as the boundary between those American men who were entitled to enjoy political freedom and those who were not. Even as this focus on race limited America's political com- munity as a whole, it helped to solidify a sense of national identity among the diverse groups of European origin. In a country where the right to vote had become central to the meaning of freedom, it is difficult to overstate the importance of the fact that white male immigrants could vote in some states almost from the moment they landed in America, whereas nearly all free blacks (and, of course, slaves), whose ancestors had lived in the coun- try for centuries, could not vote at all.

"Dandy Jim," a piece of sheet music from 1843. Minstrel shows were a form of nineteenth-century entertainment in which white actors impersonated blacks. Here, the actor makes fun of a black man attempting to adopt the style of middle-class white Americans.

NATIONALISM AND ITS DISCONTENTS

The American System

The War of 1812, which the United States and Great Britain—the world's foremost military power—fought to a draw, inspired an outburst of nationalist pride. But the war also revealed how far the United States still was from being a truly integrated nation. With the Bank of the United

War of 1812 and American nationalism

States having gone out of existence when its charter expired in 1811, the country lacked a uniform currency and found it almost impossible to raise funds for the war effort. Given the primitive state of transportation, it proved very difficult to move men and goods around the country. One shipment of supplies from New England had taken seventy-five days to reach New Orleans. With the coming of peace, the manufacturing enterprises that sprang up while trade with Britain had been suspended faced intense competition from low-cost imported goods. A younger generation of Republicans, led by Henry Clay and John C. Calhoun, believed these **"infant industries"** deserved national protection.

Madison's blueprint for economic development

In his annual message (now known as the State of the Union address) to Congress in December 1815, President James Madison put forward a blueprint for government-promoted economic development that came to be known as the **American System**, a label coined by Henry Clay. The plan rested on three pillars: a new national bank, a tariff on imported manufactured goods to protect American industry, and federal financing of improved roads and canals. The last was particularly important to those worried about the dangers of disunity. "Let us bind the nation together, with a perfect system of roads and canals," John C. Calhoun implored Congress in 1815. "Let us conquer space."

Madison's veto

Congress enacted an **internal-improvements** program drafted by Calhoun, only to be astonished when the president, on the eve of his retirement from office in March 1817, vetoed the bill. Since calling for its enactment, Madison had become convinced that allowing the national government to exercise powers not mentioned in the Constitution would prove dangerous to individual liberty and southern interests. The other

An image from a broadside from the campaign of 1824, promoting the American System of government-sponsored economic development. The illustrations represent industry, commerce, and agriculture. The ship at the center is named the *John Quincy Adams*. Its flag, "No Colonial Subjection," suggests that without a balanced economy, the United States will remain economically dependent on Great Britain.

two parts of his plan, however, became law. The tariff of 1816 offered protection to goods that could be produced in the United States, especially
cheap cotton textiles, while admitting tax-free those that could not be
manufactured at home. Many southerners supported the tariff, believing
that it would enable their region to develop a manufacturing base to rival
New England's. And in 1816, a new Bank of the United States was created,
with a twenty-year charter from Congress.

Tariff of 1816

Banks and Money

The **Second Bank of the United States** soon became the focus of public
resentment. Like its predecessor, it was a private, profit-making corporation that acted as the government's financial agent, issuing paper money,
collecting taxes, and paying the government's debts. It was also charged
with ensuring that paper money issued by local banks had real value. In
the nineteenth century, paper money consisted of notes promising to pay
the bearer on demand a specified amount of "specie" (gold or silver). Since
banks often printed far more money than the specie in their vaults, the value
of paper currency fluctuated wildly. The Bank of the United States was
supposed to correct this problem by preventing the overissuance of money.

Regulating local banks

The Panic of 1819

But instead of effectively regulating the currency and loans issued by local
banks, the Bank of the United States participated in a speculative fever
that swept the country after the end of the War of 1812. The resumption
of trade with Europe created a huge overseas market for American cotton
and grain. Coupled with the rapid expansion of settlement into the West,
this stimulated demand for loans to purchase land, which local banks and
branches of the Bank of the United States were only too happy to meet by
printing more money. The land boom was especially acute in the South,
where the Cotton Kingdom was expanding.

Land boom

Early in 1819, as European demand for American farm products
declined to normal levels, the economic bubble burst. The Bank of the
United States, followed by state banks, began asking for payments from
those to whom it had loaned money. Farmers and businessmen who could
not repay declared bankruptcy, and unemployment rose in eastern cities.

The economic bubble bursts

The **Panic of 1819** lasted little more than a year, but it severely disrupted
the political harmony of the previous years. To the consternation of creditors, many states, especially in the West, suspended the collection of debts.
Kentucky went even further, establishing a state bank that flooded the state
with paper money that creditors were required to accept in repayment of

loans. This eased the burden on indebted farmers but injured those who had loaned them the money. Overall, the panic deepened many Americans' traditional distrust of banks. It undermined the reputation of the Second Bank of the United States, which was widely blamed for causing the panic. Several states retaliated against the national bank by taxing its local branches.

These tax laws produced another of John Marshall's landmark Supreme Court decisions, in the case of **McCulloch v. Maryland** (1819). Reasserting his broad interpretation of governmental powers, Marshall declared the Bank a legitimate exercise of congressional authority under the Constitution's clause that allowed Congress to pass "necessary and proper" laws. Marshall's interpretation of the Constitution directly contradicted the "strict construction" view that limited Congress to powers specifically granted in the Constitution.

The Missouri Controversy

In 1816, James Monroe handily defeated the Federalist candidate Rufus King, becoming the last of the Virginia presidents. By 1820, the Federalists fielded electoral tickets in only two states, and Monroe carried the entire country. Monroe's two terms in office were years of one-party government, sometimes called the Era of Good Feelings. Plenty of bad feelings, however, surfaced during his presidency. In the absence of two-party competition, politics was organized along lines of competing sectional interests.

In 1819, Congress considered a request from Missouri, an area carved out of the Louisiana Purchase, to draft a constitution in preparation for admission to the Union as a state. Missouri's slave population already exceeded 10,000. James Tallmadge, a Republican congressman from New York, moved that the introduction of further slaves be prohibited and that children of those already in Missouri be freed at age twenty-five.

Tallmadge's proposal sparked two years of controversy, during which Republican unity shattered along sectional lines. His restriction passed the House, where most northern congressmen supported it over the objections of southern representatives. It died in the Senate, however. When Congress reconvened in 1820, Senator Jesse Thomas of Illinois proposed a compromise. Missouri would be authorized to draft a constitution without Tallmadge's restriction. Maine, which prohibited slavery, would be admitted to the Union to maintain the sectional balance between free and slave states. And slavery would be prohibited in all remaining territory within the Louisiana Purchase north of latitude 36°30' (Missouri's southern boundary). Congress adopted Thomas's plan as the **Missouri Compromise**.

The Missouri controversy raised for the first time what would prove to be a fatal issue—the westward expansion of slavery. The sectional division

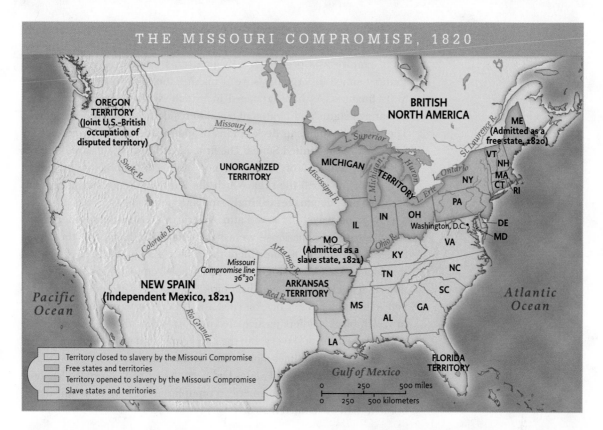

THE MISSOURI COMPROMISE, 1820

Territory closed to slavery by the Missouri Compromise
Free states and territories
Territory opened to slavery by the Missouri Compromise
Slave states and territories

it revealed aroused widespread feelings of dismay. "This momentous question," wrote Jefferson, "like a fire bell in the night, awakened and filled me with terror. I considered it at once as the knell of the union." For the moment, however, the slavery issue faded once again from national debate.

The Missouri Compromise temporarily settled the question of the expansion of slavery by dividing the Louisiana Purchase into free and slave areas.

NATION, SECTION, AND PARTY

The United States and the Latin American Wars of Independence

Between 1810 and 1822, Spain's Latin American colonies rose in rebellion and established a series of independent nations, including Mexico, Venezuela, Ecuador, and Peru. By 1825, Spain's once vast American empire had been reduced to the islands of Cuba and Puerto Rico. The uprisings inspired a wave of sympathy in the United States. In 1822, the Monroe administration became the first government to extend diplomatic recognition to the new Latin American republics.

The new Latin American republics

Parallels existed between the Spanish-American revolutions and the one that had given birth to the United States. In both cases, the crisis of empire was precipitated by programs launched by the imperial country aimed in large measure at making the colonies contribute more to its finances. As had happened in British North America, local elites demanded status and treatment equal to residents of the imperial power. The Spanish-American declarations of independence borrowed directly from that of the United States. The first, issued in 1811, declared that the "United Provinces" of Venezuela now enjoyed "among the sovereign nations of the earth the rank which the Supreme Being and nature has assigned us"—language strikingly similar to Jefferson's.

Latin American constitutions

In some ways, the new Latin American constitutions—adopted by seventeen different nations—were more democratic than that of the United States. Most sought to implement the trans-Atlantic ideals of rights and freedom by creating a single national "people" out of the diverse populations that made up the Spanish empire. To do so, they extended the right to vote to Indians and free blacks. The Latin American wars of independence, in which black soldiers participated on both sides, also set in motion the gradual abolition of slavery. But the Latin American wars of independence lasted longer—sometimes more than a decade—and were more destructive than the one in the United States had been. As a result, it proved far more difficult for the new Latin American republics to achieve economic development than the United States.

The Monroe Doctrine

John Quincy Adams

John Quincy Adams, who was serving as James Monroe's secretary of state, was devoted to consolidating the power of the national government at home and abroad. Adams feared that Spain would try to regain its Latin American colonies. In 1823, he drafted a section of the president's annual message to Congress that became known as the **Monroe Doctrine**. It expressed three principles. First, the United States would oppose any further efforts at colonization by European powers in the Americas. Second, the United States would abstain from involvement in the wars of Europe. Finally, Monroe warned European powers not to interfere with the newly independent states of Latin America.

America's diplomatic declaration of independence

The Monroe Doctrine is sometimes called America's diplomatic declaration of independence. For many decades, it remained a cornerstone of American foreign policy. Based on the assumption that the Old and New Worlds formed separate political and diplomatic systems, it claimed for the United States the role of dominant power in the Western Hemisphere.

The Election of 1824

The Monroe Doctrine reflected a rising sense of American nationalism. But sectionalism seemed to rule domestic politics. As the election of 1824 approached, only Andrew Jackson could claim truly national support. Jackson's popularity rested not on any specific public policy—few voters knew his views—but on military victories over the British at the Battle of New Orleans, and over the Creek and Seminole Indians. Other candidates included John Quincy Adams, Secretary of the Treasury William H. Crawford of Georgia, and Henry Clay of Kentucky. Adams's support was concentrated in New England and, more generally, in the North, where Republican leaders insisted the time had come for the South to relinquish the presidency. Crawford represented the South's Old Republicans, who wanted the party to reaffirm the principles of states' rights and limited government. Clay was one of the era's most popular politicians, but his support in 1824 lay primarily in the West.

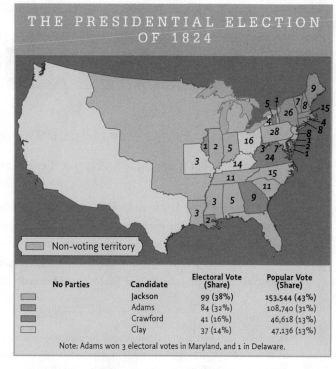

THE PRESIDENTIAL ELECTION OF 1824

Non-voting territory

No Parties	Candidate	Electoral Vote (Share)	Popular Vote (Share)
	Jackson	99 (38%)	153,544 (43%)
	Adams	84 (32%)	108,740 (31%)
	Crawford	41 (16%)	46,618 (13%)
	Clay	37 (14%)	47,136 (13%)

Note: Adams won 3 electoral votes in Maryland, and 1 in Delaware.

Jackson received 153,544 votes and carried states in all the regions outside of New England. But with four candidates in the field, none received a majority of the electoral votes. As required by the Constitution, Clay, who finished fourth, was eliminated, and the choice among the other three fell to the House of Representatives. Sincerely believing Adams to be the most qualified candidate and the one most likely to promote the American System, and probably calculating that the election of Jackson, a westerner, would impede his own presidential ambitions, Clay gave his support to Adams, helping to elect him. He soon became secretary of state in Adams's cabinet. The charge that he had made a "corrupt bargain"—bartering critical votes in the presidential contest for a public office—clung to Clay for the rest of his career, making it all but impossible for him to reach the White House. The election of 1824 laid the groundwork for a new system of political parties. Supporters of Jackson and Crawford would soon unite in the Democratic Party. The alliance of Clay and Adams became the basis for the Whig Party of the 1830s.

The "corrupt bargain"

VOICES OF FREEDOM

From President James Monroe,
Annual Message to Congress (1823)

In the wake of the Latin American struggle for independence, President James Monroe included in his annual message a passage that became known as the Monroe Doctrine. It outlined principles that would help to govern the country's relations with the rest of the world for nearly a century—that the Western Hemisphere was no longer open to European colonization and that the United States would remain uninvolved in the wars of Europe.

[This] occasion has been judged proper for asserting, as a principle, . . . that the American continents, by the free and independent condition which they have assumed and maintain, are henceforth not to be considered as subjects for future colonization by any European powers. . . .

It was stated at the commencement of the last session that a great effort was then making in Spain and Portugal to improve the condition of the people of those countries, and that it appeared to be conducted with extraordinary moderation. It need scarcely be remarked that the results have been so far very different from what was then anticipated. Of events in that quarter of the globe, with which we have so much intercourse and from which we derive our origin, we have always been anxious and interested spectators. The citizens of the United States cherish sentiments the most friendly in favor of the liberty and happiness of their fellow-men on that side of the Atlantic. In the wars of the European powers in matters relating to themselves we have never taken any part, nor does it comport with our policy to do so. It is only when our rights are invaded or seriously menaced that we resent injuries or make preparation for our defense. With the movements in this hemisphere we are of necessity more immediately connected, and by causes which must be obvious to all enlightened and impartial observers. The political system of the allied powers [of Europe] is essentially different in this respect from that of America. . . .

We owe it, therefore, to candor and to the amicable relations existing between the United States and those powers to declare that we should consider any attempt on their part to extend their system to any portion of this hemisphere as dangerous to our peace and safety. With the existing colonies or dependencies of any European power we have not interfered and shall not interfere. But with the Governments who have declared their independence and maintain it, and whose independence we have, on great consideration and on just principles, acknowledged, we could not view any interposition for the purpose of oppressing them, or controlling in any other manner their destiny, by any European power in any other light than as the manifestation of an unfriendly disposition toward the United States.

From John C. Calhoun, "A Disquisition on Government" (ca. 1845)

The most prominent political philosopher in the pre–Civil War South, John C. Calhoun sought to devise ways that the South could retain the power to protect its interests within the Union (especially the institution of slavery) as it fell behind the North in population and political power.

There are two different modes in which the sense of the community may be taken; one, simply by the right of suffrage, unaided; the other, by the right through a proper organism. Each collects the sense of the majority. But one regards numbers only, and considers the whole community as a unit, having but one common interest throughout; and collects the sense of the greater number of the whole, as that of the community. The other, on the contrary, regards interests as well as numbers;—considering the community as made up of different and conflicting interests, as far as the action of the government is concerned; and takes the sense of each, through its majority or appropriate organ, and the united sense of all, as the sense of the entire community. The former of these I shall call the numerical, or absolute majority; and the latter, the concurrent, or constitutional majority. I call it the constitutional majority, because it is an essential element in every constitutional government,—be whatever form it takes. So great is the difference, politically speaking, between the two majorities, that they cannot be confounded, without leading to great and fatal errors; and yet the distinction between them has been so entirely overlooked, that when the term *majority* is used in political discussions, it is applied exclusively to designate the numerical,—as if there were no other. . . .

The first and leading error which naturally arises from overlooking the distinction referred to, is, to confound the numerical majority with the people, and this is so completely as to regard them as identical. This is a consequence that necessarily results from considering the numerical as the only majority. All admit, that a popular government, or democracy, is the government of the people. . . . Those who regard the numerical as the only majority . . . [are] forced to regard the numerical majority as, in effect, the entire people. . . .

The necessary consequence of taking the sense of the community by the concurrent majority is . . . to give to each interest or portion of the community a negative on the others. It is this mutual negative among its various conflicting interests, which invests each with the power of protecting itself; . . . Without this, there can be no constitution.

QUESTIONS

1. *Why does Monroe think that the "systems" of Europe and the Western Hemisphere are fundamentally different?*

2. *Which Americans would be most likely to object to Calhoun's political system?*

3. *How do the two documents differ in their conception of how powerful the national government ought to be?*

The Nationalism of John Quincy Adams

John Quincy Adams enjoyed one of the most distinguished pre-presidential careers of any American president. The son of John Adams, he had witnessed the Battle of Bunker Hill at age eight and at fourteen had worked as private secretary and French interpreter for an American envoy in Europe. He had gone on to serve as ambassador to Prussia, the Netherlands, Britain, and Russia, and as a senator from Massachusetts.

John Quincy Adams in an 1843 daguerreotype.

Adams was not an engaging figure. He described himself as "a man of cold, austere, and foreboding manners." But he had a clear vision of national greatness. At home, he strongly supported the American System of government-sponsored economic development. Abroad, he hoped to encourage American commerce throughout the world and, as illustrated by his authorship of the Monroe Doctrine, enhance American influence in the Western Hemisphere. An ardent expansionist, Adams was certain that the United States would eventually, and peacefully, absorb Canada, Cuba, and at least part of Mexico.

"Liberty Is Power"

Adams held a view of federal power far more expansive than did most of his contemporaries. In his first message to Congress, in December 1825, he set forth a comprehensive program for an activist national state. "The spirit of improvement is abroad in the land," Adams announced, and the federal government should be its patron. He called for legislation promoting agriculture, commerce, manufacturing, and "the mechanical and elegant arts." His plans included the establishment of a national university, an astronomical observatory, and a naval academy. At a time when many Americans felt that governmental authority posed the greatest threat to freedom, Adams astonished many listeners with the bold statement "liberty is power."

Adams's nationalism

Adams's proposals alarmed all believers in strict construction of the Constitution. His administration spent more on internal improvements than those of his five predecessors combined, and it enacted a steep increase in tariff rates in 1828. But the rest of Adams's ambitious ideas received little support in Congress.

Martin Van Buren and the Democratic Party

Adams's program handed his political rivals a powerful weapon. With individual liberty, states' rights, and limited government as their rallying cries, Jackson's supporters began to organize for the election of 1828 almost as soon as Adams assumed office. Martin Van Buren, a senator from New York, supervised the task. The clash between Adams and Van Buren demonstrated how democracy was changing the nature of American politics. Adams typified the old politics—he was the son of a president and, like Jefferson and Madison, a man of sterling intellectual accomplishments. Van Buren represented the new political era. The son of a tavern keeper, he was a talented party manager, not a person of great vision or intellect.

But Van Buren did have a compelling idea. Rather than being danger-ous and divisive, as the founding generation had believed, political parties, he insisted, were necessary and desirable. Party competition provided a check on those in power and offered voters a real choice in elections. And by bringing together political leaders from different regions in support of common candidates and principles, national parties could counteract the sectionalism that had reared its head during the 1820s. National political parties, Van Buren realized, formed a bond of unity in a divided nation. He set out to reconstruct the Jeffersonian political alliance between "the planters of the South and the plain republicans [the farmers and urban workers] of the North."

The Election of 1828

By 1828, Van Buren had established the political apparatus of the Democratic Party, complete with local and state party units overseen by a national committee and a network of local newspapers devoted to the party and to the election of Andrew Jackson. Apart from a general com-mitment to limited government, Jackson's supporters made few campaign promises, relying on their candidate's popularity and the workings of party machinery to get out the vote. The 1828 election campaign was scurrilous. Jackson's supporters praised their candidate's frontier manli-ness and ridiculed Adams's intellectual attainments. ("Vote for Andrew Jackson who can fight, not John Quincy Adams who can write," declared one campaign slogan.) Jackson's opponents condemned him as a murderer for having executed army deserters and killing men in duels. They ques-tioned the morality of his wife, Rachel, because she had married Jackson before her divorce from her first husband had become final.

Nearly 57 percent of the eligible electorate cast ballots, more than double the percentage four years earlier. Jackson won a resounding vic-tory, carrying the entire South and West, along with Pennsylvania. His election was the first to demonstrate how the advent of universal white

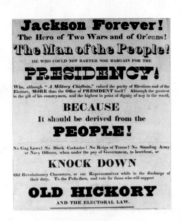

A broadside from the 1828 campaign illustrates how Andrew Jackson's supporters promoted him as a military hero and "man of the people."

male voting, organized by national political parties, had transformed American politics. For better or worse, the United States had entered the Age of Jackson.

THE AGE OF JACKSON

Andrew Jackson was a man of many contradictions. Although he had little formal education, Jackson was capable of genuine eloquence in his public statements. A self-proclaimed champion of the common man, he held a vision of democracy that excluded any role for Indians, who he believed should be pushed west of the Mississippi River, and African-Americans, who should remain as slaves or be freed and sent abroad. A strong nationalist, Jackson nonetheless believed that the states, not Washington, D.C., should be the focal point of governmental activity.

The Party System

By the time of Jackson's presidency, politics had become more than a series of political contests—it was a spectacle, a form of mass entertainment, a part of Americans' daily lives. Every year witnessed elections to some office—local, state, or national—and millions took part in the parades and rallies organized by the parties. Politicians were popular heroes with mass followings and popular nicknames. Jackson was Old Hickory, Clay was Harry of the West, and Van Buren the Little Magician (or, to his critics, the Sly Fox). Thousands of Americans willingly attended lengthy political orations and debates.

Party machines, headed by professional politicians, reached into every neighborhood, especially in cities. They provided benefits like jobs to constituents and ensured that voters went to the polls on election day. Government posts, Jackson declared, should be open to the people, not reserved for a privileged class of permanent bureaucrats. He introduced

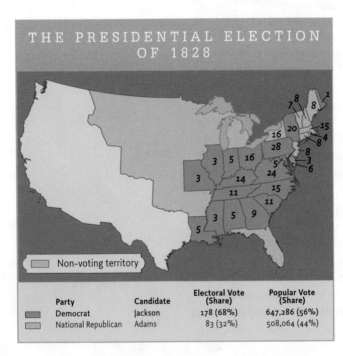

THE PRESIDENTIAL ELECTION OF 1828

Non-voting territory

Party	Candidate	Electoral Vote (Share)	Popular Vote (Share)
Democrat	Jackson	178 (68%)	647,286 (56%)
National Republican	Adams	83 (32%)	508,064 (44%)

the principle of rotation in office (called the "**spoils system**" by opponents) into national government, making loyalty to the party the main qualification for jobs like postmaster and customs official.

Large national conventions where state leaders gathered to hammer out a platform now chose national candidates. Newspapers played a greater and greater role in politics. Every significant town, it seemed, had its Democratic and Whig papers whose job was not so much to report the news as to present the party's position on issues of the day. Jackson's Kitchen Cabinet—an informal group of advisers who helped to write his speeches and supervise communication between the White House and local party officials—mostly consisted of newspaper editors.

Political innovations

Democrats and Whigs

There was more to party politics, however, than spectacle and organization. Jacksonian politics revolved around issues spawned by the market revolution and the continuing tension between national and sectional loyalties. **Democrats** tended to be alarmed by the widening gap between social classes. They warned that "nonproducers"—bankers, merchants, and speculators—were seeking to use connections with government to enhance their wealth to the disadvantage of the "producing classes" of farmers, artisans, and laborers. They believed the government should adopt a hands-off attitude toward the economy and not award special favors to entrenched economic interests. This would enable ordinary Americans to test their abilities in the fair competition of the self-regulating market. The Democratic Party attracted aspiring entrepreneurs who resented government aid to established businessmen, as well as large numbers of farmers and city workingmen suspicious of new corporate enterprises. Poorer farming regions isolated from markets, like the lower Northwest and the southern backcountry, tended to vote Democratic.

Issues for the Democratic Party

Whigs united behind the American System, believing that via a protective tariff, a national bank, and aid to internal improvements, the federal government could guide economic development. They were strongest in the Northeast, the most rapidly modernizing region of the country. Most established businessmen and bankers supported their program of government-promoted economic growth, as did farmers in regions near rivers, canals, and the Great Lakes, who benefited from economic changes or hoped to do so. The counties of upstate New York along the Erie Canal, for example, became a Whig stronghold, whereas more isolated rural communities tended to vote Democratic. Many slaveholders supported

Issues for the Whig Party

the Democrats, believing states' rights to be slavery's first line of defense. But like well-to-do merchants and industrialists in the North, the largest southern planters generally voted Whig.

Public and Private Freedom

The party battles of the Jacksonian era reflected the clash between "public" and "private" definitions of American freedom and their relationship to governmental power, a persistent tension in the nation's history. For Democrats, liberty was a set of private rights best secured by local governments and endangered by powerful national authority. "The limitation of power, in every branch of our government," wrote a Democratic newspaper in 1842, "is the only safeguard of liberty." During Jackson's presidency, Democrats reduced expenditures, lowered the tariff, killed the national bank, and refused pleas for federal aid to internal improvements. By 1835, Jackson had even managed to pay off the national debt. As a result, states replaced the federal government as the country's main economic actors, planning systems of canals and roads and chartering banks and other corporations.

The Democrats: power a threat to liberty

Democrats, moreover, considered individual morality a private matter, not a public concern. They opposed attempts to impose a unified moral vision on society, such as "temperance" legislation, which restricted or outlawed the production and sale of liquor, and laws prohibiting various kinds of entertainment on Sundays. "In this country," declared the New York *Journal of Commerce* in 1848, "liberty is understood to be the *absence* of government from private affairs."

Whigs, for their part, insisted that liberty and power reinforced each other. "A weak government," wrote Francis Lieber, the founding father of American political science, was "a negation of liberty." An activist national government, on the other hand, could enhance the realm of freedom. The government, Whigs believed, should create the conditions for balanced and regulated economic development, thereby promoting a prosperity in which all classes and regions would share.

The Whigs: power allied with liberty

Whigs, moreover, rejected the premise that the government must not interfere in private life. To function as free—that is, self-directed and self-disciplined—moral agents, individuals required certain character traits, which government could help to instill. Many evangelical Protestants supported the Whigs, convinced that via public education, the building of schools and asylums, temperance legislation, and the like, democratic governments could inculcate the "principles of morality." And during the

Government and private life

Jacksonian era, popularly elected local authorities enacted numerous laws, ordinances, and regulations that tried to shape public morals by banning prostitution and the consumption of alcohol, and regulating other kinds of personal behavior. Pennsylvania was as renowned in the nineteenth century for its stringent laws against profanity and desecrating the Sabbath as it had been in the colonial era for its commitment to religious liberty.

Shaping public morals

South Carolina and Nullification

Andrew Jackson, it has been said, left office with many more principles than he came in with. Elected as a military hero backed by an efficient party machinery, he was soon forced to define his stance on public issues. Despite his commitment to states' rights, Jackson's first term was dominated by a battle to uphold the supremacy of federal over state law. The tariff of 1828, which raised taxes on imported manufactured goods made of wool as well as on raw materials such as iron, had aroused considerable opposition in the South, nowhere more than in South Carolina, where it was called the **"tariff of abominations."** The state's leaders no longer believed it possible or desirable to compete with the North in industrial development. Insisting that the tariff on imported manufactured goods raised the prices paid by southern consumers to benefit the North, the legislature threatened to "nullify" it—that is, declare it null and void within their state.

Tariff of 1828

Sectional economic differences

The state with the largest proportion of slaves in its population (55 percent in 1830), South Carolina was controlled by a tightly knit group of large planters. They maintained their grip on power by a state constitution that gave plantation counties far greater representation in the legislature than their population warranted, as well as through high property qualifications for officeholders. Behind their economic complaints against the tariff lay the conviction that the federal government must be weakened lest it one day take action against slavery.

Calhoun's Political Theory

John C. Calhoun soon emerged as the leading theorist of nullification. As the South began to fall behind the rest of the country in population, Calhoun had evolved from the nationalist of 1812 into a powerful defender of southern sectionalism. Having been elected vice president in 1828, Calhoun at first remained behind the scenes, secretly drafting the *Exposition and Protest* in which the South Carolina legislature justified nullification. The national government, Calhoun insisted, had been created by

Calhoun's Exposition and Protest

an agreement, or compact, among sovereign states, each of which retained the right to prevent the enforcement within its borders of acts of Congress that exceeded the powers specifically spelled out in the Constitution.

Almost from the beginning of Jackson's first term, Calhoun's influence in the administration waned, while Secretary of State Martin Van Buren emerged as the president's closest adviser. One incident that helped set Jackson against Calhoun occurred a few weeks after the inauguration. Led by Calhoun's wife, Floride, Washington society women ostracized Peggy Eaton, the wife of Jackson's secretary of war, because she was the daughter of a Washington tavern keeper and, allegedly, a woman of "easy virtue." Jackson identified the criticism of Peggy Eaton with the abuse his own wife had suffered during the campaign of 1828.

Far weightier matters soon divided Jackson and Calhoun. Debate over nullification raged in Washington. In a memorable exchange in the Senate in January 1830, Daniel Webster, a senator from Massachusetts, responded to South Carolina senator Robert Y. Hayne, a disciple of Calhoun. The people, not the states, declared Webster, created the Constitution, making the federal government sovereign. He called nullification illegal, unconstitutional, and treasonous. Webster's ending was widely hailed throughout the country—"Liberty *and* Union, now and forever, one and inseparable." A few weeks later, at a White House dinner, Jackson delivered a toast while fixing his gaze on Calhoun: "Our Federal Union—it must be preserved." Calhoun's reply came immediately: "The Union—next to our liberty most dear." By 1831, Calhoun had publicly emerged as the leading theorist of states' rights.

Eaton affair

Webster-Hayne debate

An 1834 print portrays the United States as a Temple of Liberty. At the center, a figure of liberty rises from the flames, holding the Bill of Rights and a staff with a liberty cap. Justice and Minerva (Roman goddess of war and wisdom) flank the temple, above which flies a banner, "The Union Must and Shall Be Preserved."

The Nullification Crisis

Nullification was not a purely sectional issue. South Carolina stood alone during the crisis, and several southern states passed resolutions condemning its action. Nonetheless, the elaboration of the compact theory of the Constitution gave the South a well-developed political philosophy to which it would turn when sectional conflict became more intense.

To Jackson, nullification amounted to nothing less than disunion. He dismissed Calhoun's constitutional arguments out of hand: "Can anyone of common sense believe the absurdity, that a faction of any state, or a state, has a right to secede and destroy this union, and the liberty of the country with it?" The issue came to a head in 1832, when a new tariff was enacted. Despite a reduction in tariff rates, South Carolina declared the tax on imported goods null and void in the state after the following February. In response, Jackson persuaded Congress to enact a Force Bill authorizing him to use the army and navy to collect customs duties. To avert a confrontation, Henry Clay, with Calhoun's assistance, engineered the passage of a new tariff, in 1833, further reducing duties. South Carolina then rescinded the ordinance of nullification, although it proceeded to "nullify" the **Force Act**. Calhoun abandoned the Democratic Party for the Whigs, where, with Clay and Webster, he became part of a formidable trio of political leaders (even though the three agreed on virtually nothing except hostility toward Jackson).

Jackson's stance

South Carolina and the tariff of 1832

Indian Removal

The nullification crisis underscored Jackson's commitment to the sovereignty of the nation. His exclusion of Indians from the era's assertive democratic nationalism led to the final act in the centuries-long conflict between white Americans and Indians east of the Mississippi River. In the slave states, the onward march of cotton cultivation placed enormous pressure on remaining Indian holdings. One of the early laws of Jackson's administration, the **Indian Removal Act** of 1830, provided funds for uprooting the so-called Five Civilized Tribes—the Cherokee, Chickasaw, Choctaw, Creek, and Seminole—with a population of around 60,000 living in North Carolina, Georgia, Florida, Alabama, and Mississippi.

The law marked a repudiation of the Jeffersonian idea that "civilized" Indians could be assimilated into the American population. These tribes had made great efforts to become everything republican citizens should be. The Cherokee had taken the lead, establishing schools, adopting written laws and a constitution modeled on that of the United States, and becoming

Shift in Indian policy

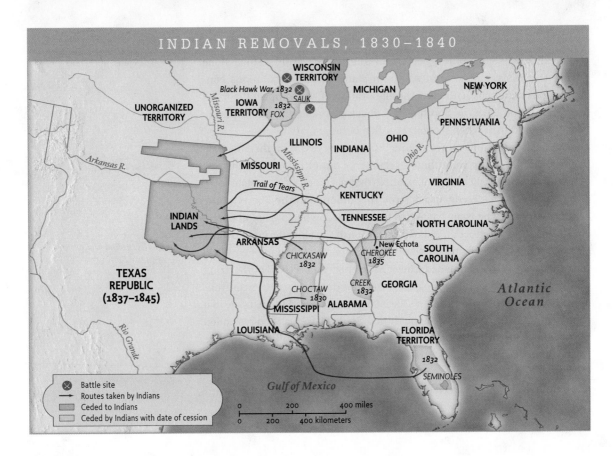

INDIAN REMOVALS, 1830–1840

The removal of the so-called Five Civilized Tribes from the Southeast all but ended the Indian presence east of the Mississippi River.

successful farmers, many of whom owned slaves. But in his messages to Congress, Jackson repeatedly referred to them as "savages" and supported Georgia's effort to seize Cherokee land and nullify the tribe's laws. In good American fashion, Cherokee leaders went to court to protect their rights, guaranteed in treaties with the federal government. Their appeals forced the Supreme Court to clarify the unique status of American Indians.

The Supreme Court and the Indians

In a crucial case involving Indians in 1823, *Johnson v. M'Intosh*, the Court had proclaimed that Indians were not in fact owners of their land but merely had a "right of occupancy." Chief Justice John Marshall claimed that from the early colonial era, Indians had lived as nomads and hunters, not farmers. Entirely inaccurate as history, the decision struck a serious blow against Indian efforts to retain their lands. In *Cherokee Nation v. Georgia* (1831), Marshall described Indians as "wards" of the federal government.

"Right of occupancy"

They deserved paternal regard and protection, but they lacked the standing as citizens that would allow the Supreme Court to enforce their rights. The justices could not, therefore, block Georgia's effort to extend its jurisdiction over the tribe.

Marshall, however, believed strongly in the supremacy of the federal government over the states. In 1832, in **Worcester v. Georgia**, the Court seemed to change its mind, holding that Indian nations were a distinct people with the right to maintain a separate political identity. They must be dealt with by the federal government, not the states, and Georgia's actions violated the Cherokees' treaties with Washington. Jackson, however, refused to recognize the validity of the *Worcester* ruling. "John Marshall has made his decision," he supposedly declared, "now let him enforce it."

With legal appeals exhausted, one faction of the tribe agreed to cede their lands, but the majority, led by John Ross, who had been elected "principal chief" under the Cherokee constitution, adopted a policy of passive resistance. Federal soldiers forcibly removed them during the presidency of Jackson's successor, Martin Van Buren. The army herded 18,000 Cherokee men, women, and children into stockades and then forced them to move west. At least one-quarter perished during the winter of 1838–1839 on the **Trail of Tears**, as the removal route from Georgia to the area of present-day Oklahoma came to be called. (In the Cherokee language, it literally meant "the trail on which we cried.")

A lithograph from 1836 depicts Sequoia, with the alphabet of the Cherokee language that he developed. Because of their written language and constitution, the Cherokee were considered by many white Americans to be a "civilized tribe."

Buffalo Chase over Prairie Bluffs, a painting from the 1830s by George Catlin, who created dozens of works depicting Native Americans in the trans-Mississippi West. Catlin saw himself as recording for posterity a vanishing way of life. At the time, millions of buffalo inhabited the West, providing food and hides for Native Americans.

During the 1830s, most of the other southern tribes bowed to the inevitable and departed peacefully. But with the assistance of escaped slaves, the Seminoles of sparsely settled Florida resisted. In the Second Seminole War, which lasted from 1835 to 1842 (the first had followed American acquisition of Florida in 1819), some 1,500 American soldiers and the same number of Seminoles were killed, and perhaps 3,000 Indians and 500 blacks were forced to move to the West. A small number of Seminoles managed to remain in Florida, a tiny remnant of the once sizable Indian population east of the Mississippi River.

Seminole resistance

Effects of Indian removal

Removal of the Indians powerfully reinforced the racial definition of American nationhood and freedom. At the time of independence, Indians had been a familiar presence in many parts of the United States. But by 1840, in the eyes of most whites east of the Mississippi River, they were simply a curiosity, a relic of an earlier period of American history. Although Indians still dominated the trans-Mississippi West, as American settlement pushed relentlessly westward it was clear that their days of freedom there also were numbered.

THE BANK WAR AND AFTER

Biddle's Bank

The central political struggle of the Age of Jackson was the president's war on the Bank of the United States. The Bank symbolized the hopes and fears inspired by the market revolution. The expansion of banking helped to finance the nation's economic development. But many Americans, including Jackson, distrusted bankers as "nonproducers" who contributed nothing to the nation's wealth but profited from the labor of others. The tendency of banks to overissue paper money, whose deterioration in value reduced the real income of wage earners, reinforced this conviction.

Distrust of banks

Heading the Bank was Nicholas Biddle of Pennsylvania, who during the 1820s had effectively used the institution's power to curb the overissuing of money by local banks and to create a stable currency throughout the nation. A snobbish, aristocratic Philadelphian, Biddle was as strong-willed as Jackson and as unwilling to back down in a fight. In 1832, he told a congressional committee that his Bank had the ability to "destroy" any state bank. He hastened to add that he had never "injured" any of them. But Democrats wondered whether any institution, public or private, ought

Nicholas Biddle

to possess such power. Many called it the Monster Bank, an illegitimate union of political authority and entrenched economic privilege. The issue of the Bank's future came to a head in 1832. Although the institution's charter would not expire until 1836, Biddle's allies persuaded Congress to approve a bill extending it for another twenty years. Jackson saw the tactic as a form of blackmail—if he did not sign the bill, the Bank would use its considerable resources to oppose his reelection.

Jackson's veto message is perhaps the central document of his presidency. In a democratic government, Jackson insisted, it was unacceptable for Congress to create a source of concentrated power and economic privilege unaccountable to the people. "It is to be regretted," he declared, "that the rich and powerful too often bend the acts of government to their selfish purposes." Exclusive privileges like the Bank's charter widened the gap between the wealthy and "the humble members of society—the farmers, mechanics, and laborers." Jackson presented himself as the defender of these "humble" Americans.

Jackson's veto of the bank bill

The **Bank War** reflected how Jackson enhanced the power of the presidency during his eight years in office, proclaiming himself the symbolic representative of all the people. He was the first president to use the veto power as a major weapon and to appeal directly to the public for political support, over the head of Congress. Whigs denounced him for usurping the power of the legislature. But Jackson's effective appeal to democratic popular sentiments helped him win a sweeping reelection victory in 1832 over the Whig candidate, Henry Clay. His victory ensured the death of the Bank of the United States.

Enhancing the power of the presidency

The Downfall of Mother Bank, a Democratic cartoon celebrating the destruction of the Second Bank of the United States. President Andrew Jackson topples the building by brandishing his order removing federal funds from the Bank. Led by Nicholas Biddle, with the head of a demon, the Bank's corrupt supporters flee, among them Henry Clay, Daniel Webster, and newspaper editors allegedly paid by the institution.

Pet Banks, the Economy, and the Panic of 1837

What, however, would take the Bank's place? Not content to wait for the charter of the Bank of the United States to expire in 1836, Jackson authorized the removal of federal funds from its vaults and their deposit in select local banks. Not surprisingly, political and personal connections often determined the choice of these "**pet banks**." Two secretaries of the Treasury refused to transfer federal money to the pet banks, since the law creating the Bank had specified that government funds could not be removed except for a good cause as communicated to Congress. Jackson finally appointed Attorney General Roger B. Taney, a loyal Maryland Democrat, to the Treasury post, and he carried out the order. When John Marshall died in 1835, Jackson rewarded Taney by appointing him chief justice.

Consequences of the removal of federal deposits

Without government deposits, the Bank of the United States lost its ability to regulate the activities of state banks. The value of bank notes in circulation rose from $10 million in 1833 to $149 million in 1837. As prices rose dramatically, "real wages"—the actual value of workers' pay—declined. Numerous labor unions emerged, which attempted to protect the earnings of urban workers. Meanwhile, speculators hastened to cash in on rising land prices. Using paper money, they bought up huge blocks of public land, which they resold to farmers or to eastern purchasers of lots in entirely nonexistent western towns.

The Specie Circular

Inevitably, the speculative boom collapsed. The government sold 20 million acres of federal land in 1836, ten times the amount sold in 1830, nearly all of it paid for in paper money, often of questionable value. In July 1836, the Jackson administration issued the Specie Circular, declaring that henceforth it would only accept gold and silver as payment for public land. At the same time, the Bank of England, increasingly suspicious about the value of American bank notes, demanded that American merchants pay their creditors in London in gold or silver. Then, an economic downturn in Britain dampened demand for American cotton, the country's major export.

Economic collapse

Taken together, these events triggered an economic collapse in the United States, the **Panic of 1837**, followed by a depression that lasted to 1843. Businesses throughout the country failed, and many farmers, unable to meet mortgage payments because of declining income, lost their land. Tens of thousands of urban workers saw their jobs disappear. The fledgling labor movement collapsed as strikes became impossible, given the surplus of unemployed labor.

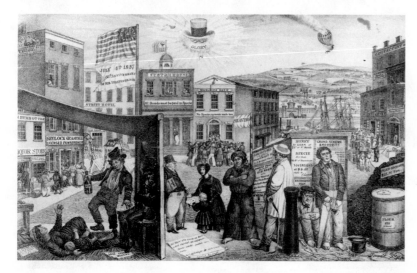

The Times, an 1837 engraving that blames Andrew Jackson's policies for the economic depression. The Custom House is idle, while next door a bank is mobbed by worried depositors. Beneath Jackson's hat, spectacles, and clay pipe (with the ironic word "glory"), images of hardship abound.

Van Buren in Office

The president forced to deal with the depression was Martin Van Buren, who had been elected in 1836 over three regional candidates put forward by the Whigs. Under Van Buren, the hard money, anti-bank wing of the Democratic Party came to power. In 1837, the administration announced its intention to remove federal funds from the pet banks and hold them in the Treasury Department in Washington, under the control of government officials. Not until 1840 did Congress approve the new policy, known as the Independent Treasury, which completely separated the federal government from the nation's banking system. It would be repealed in 1841 when the Whigs returned to power, but it was reinstated under President James K. Polk in 1846.

The Independent Treasury

The Election of 1840

Despite his reputation as a political magician, Van Buren found that without Jackson's personal popularity he could not hold the Democratic coalition together. In 1840, he also discovered that his Whig opponents had mastered the political techniques he had helped to pioneer. Confronting an unprecedented opportunity for victory because of the continuing economic depression, the Whigs abandoned their most prominent leader, Henry Clay, and nominated William Henry Harrison. Harrison's main claim to fame was military success against the British and Indians during the War of 1812.

William Henry Harrison

A political cartoon from the 1840 presidential campaign shows public opinion as the "almighty lever" of politics in a democracy. Under the gaze of the American eagle, "Loco-Foco" Democrats slide into an abyss, while the people are poised to lift William Henry Harrison, the Whig candidate, to victory.

THE ALMIGHTY LEVER

The party nominated Harrison without a platform. In a flood of publications, banners, parades, and mass meetings, they promoted him as the "log cabin" candidate, the champion of the common man. This tactic proved enormously effective, even though it bore little relationship to the actual life of the wealthy Harrison. His running mate was John Tyler, a states'-rights Democrat from Virginia who had joined the Whigs after the nullification crisis and did not follow Calhoun back to the Democrats. On almost every issue of political significance, Tyler held views totally opposed to those of other Whigs. But party leaders hoped he could expand their base in the South.

By 1840, the mass democratic politics of the Age of Jackson had absorbed the logic of the marketplace. Selling candidates and their images was as important as the positions for which they stood. With two highly organized parties competing throughout the country, voter turnout soared to 80 percent of those eligible. Harrison won a sweeping victory. "We have taught them how to conquer us," lamented a Democratic newspaper.

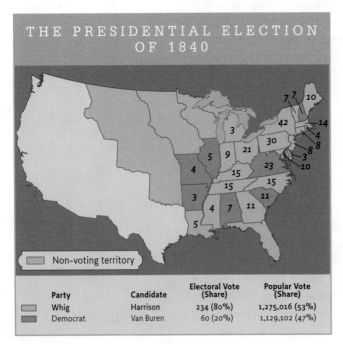

THE PRESIDENTIAL ELECTION OF 1840

Non-voting territory

Party	Candidate	Electoral Vote (Share)	Popular Vote (Share)
Whig	Harrison	234 (80%)	1,275,016 (53%)
Democrat	Van Buren	60 (20%)	1,129,102 (47%)

Whig success proved short-lived. Immediately on assuming office, Harrison contracted pneumonia. He died a month later, and John Tyler succeeded him. When the Whig majority in Congress tried to enact the American System into law, Tyler vetoed nearly every measure, including a new national bank and higher tariff. Most of the cabinet resigned, and his party repudiated him. Tyler's four years in office were nearly devoid of accomplishment. If the campaign that resulted in the election of Harrison and Tyler demonstrated how a flourishing system of democratic politics had come into existence, Tyler's lack of success showed that political parties had become central to American government. Without a party behind him, a president could not govern. But a storm was now gathering that would test the stability of American democracy and the statesmanship of its political leaders.

Importance of political parties

CHAPTER REVIEW AND ONLINE RESOURCES

REVIEW QUESTIONS

1. *What global changes prompted the Monroe Doctrine? What were its key provisions? How does it show America's growing international presence?*

2. *How did Andrew Jackson represent the major developments of the era: westward movement, the market revolution, and the expansion of democracy for some alongside the limits on it for others?*

3. *How did the expansion of white male democracy run counter to the ideals of the founders, who believed government should be sheltered from excessive influence by ordinary people?*

4. *What were the components of the American System, and how were they designed to promote the national economy under the guidance of the federal government?*

5. *How did the Missouri Compromise and the nullification crisis demonstrate increasing sectional competition and disagreements over slavery?*

6. *According to Martin Van Buren, why were political parties a desirable element of public life? What did he do to build the party system?*

7. *What were the major economic, humanitarian, political, and social arguments for and against Indian Removal?*

8. *What were the key issues that divided the Democratic and Whig Parties? Where did each party stand on those issues?*

9. *Explain the causes and effects of the Panic of 1837.*

KEY TERMS

Dorr War (p. 282)

Democracy in America (p. 282)

"information revolution" (p. 283)

"infant industries" (p. 286)

American System (p. 286)

internal improvements (p. 286)

Second Bank of the United States (p. 287)

Panic of 1819 (p. 287)

McCulloch v. Maryland (p. 288)

Missouri Compromise (p. 288)

Monroe Doctrine (p. 290)

"spoils system" (p. 297)

Democratic Party and Whig Party (p. 297)

"tariff of abominations" (p. 299)

nullification crisis (p. 301)

Force Act (p. 301)

Indian Removal Act (p. 301)

Worcester v. Georgia (p. 303)

Trail of Tears (p. 303)

Bank War (p. 305)

"pet banks" (p. 306)

Panic of 1837 (p. 306)

wwnorton.com
/studyspace

VISIT STUDYSPACE FOR THESE RESOURCES AND MORE

- A chapter outline
- A diagnostic chapter quiz
- Interactive maps
- Map worksheets
- Multimedia documents

CHAPTER 11

THE PECULIAR INSTITUTION

★

1791–1804	Haitian Revolution
1800	Gabriel's Rebellion
1811	Slave revolt in Louisiana
1822	Denmark Vesey's slave conspiracy
1830s	States legislate against teaching slaves to read or write
1831	William Lloyd Garrison's *The Liberator* debuts
	Nat Turner's Rebellion
1831–1832	Slave revolt in Jamaica
1832	Virginia laws tighten the slave system
1833	Great Britain abolishes slavery within its empire
1838	Frederick Douglas escapes slavery
1839	Slaves take control of the *Amistad*
1841	Slave uprising on the *Creole*
1849	Harriet Tubman escapes slavery
1855	Trial of Celia

Richmond's Slave Market Auction, by the British artist Eyre Crowe, depicts a scene in an auction house. A slave sale is in progress, while on the right, slaves wait apprehensively for their turn to be sold. A child clings to her mother, perhaps for the last time, while potential buyers examine the seated women. Crowe entered the auction house in March 1853 after seeing an advertisement for a slave sale, and began sketching. When the white crowd realized what he was doing, they "rushed on him savagely and obliged him to quit," Crowe's traveling companion wrote to a friend. The painting is based on his sketches.

FOCUS QUESTIONS

- How did slavery shape social and economic relations in the Old South?

- What were the legal and material constraints on slaves' lives and work?

- How did distinct slave cultures emerge in the Old South?

- What were the major forms of resistance to slavery?

I n an age of "self-made" men, no American rose more dramatically from humble origins to national and international distinction than Frederick Douglass. Born into slavery in 1818, he became a major figure in the crusade for abolition, the drama of emancipation, and the effort during Reconstruction to give meaning to black freedom.

Douglass was the son of a slave mother and an unidentified white man, possibly his owner. As a youth in Maryland, he gazed out at the ships in Chesapeake Bay, seeing them as "freedom's swift-winged angels." In violation of Maryland law, Douglass learned to read and write, initially with the assistance of his owner's wife and then, after her husband forbade her to continue, with the help of local white children. "From that moment," he later wrote, he understood that knowledge was "the pathway from slavery to freedom." In 1838, having borrowed the free papers of a black sailor, he escaped to the North.

Frederick Douglass went on to become the most influential African-American of the nineteenth century and the nation's preeminent advocate of racial equality. He also published a widely read autobiography that offered an eloquent condemnation of slavery and racism. Indeed, his own accomplishments testified to the incorrectness of prevailing ideas about blacks' inborn inferiority. Douglass was also active in other reform movements, including the campaign for women's rights. Douglass argued that in their desire for freedom, the slaves were truer to the nation's underlying principles than the white Americans who annually celebrated the Fourth of July while allowing the continued existence of slavery.

THE OLD SOUTH

When Frederick Douglass was born, slavery was already an old institution in America. Two centuries had passed since the first twenty Africans were landed in Virginia from a Dutch ship. After abolition in the North, slavery had become the "**peculiar institution**" of the South—that is, an institution unique to southern society. The Mason-Dixon Line, drawn by two surveyors in the eighteenth century to settle a boundary dispute between Maryland and Pennsylvania, eventually became the dividing line between slavery and freedom.

Despite the hope of some of the founders that slavery might die out, in fact the institution survived the crisis of the American Revolution and rapidly expanded westward. On the eve of the Civil War, the slave population had risen to nearly 4 million, its high rate of natural increase more than

Mason-Dixon line

The expansion of slavery

making up for the prohibition in 1808 of further slave imports from Africa. In the South as a whole, slaves made up one-third of the total population, and in the cotton-producing states of the Deep South, around half. By the 1850s, slavery had crossed the Mississippi River and was expanding rapidly in Arkansas, Louisiana, and eastern Texas.

Cotton Is King

In the nineteenth century, cotton replaced sugar as the world's major crop produced by slave labor. And although slavery survived in Brazil and the Spanish and French Caribbean, its abolition in the British empire in 1833 made the United States indisputably the center of New World slavery.

Because the early industrial revolution centered on factories using cotton as the raw material to manufacture cloth, cotton had become by far the most important commodity in international trade. And three-fourths of the world's cotton supply came from the southern United States. Textile manufacturers in places as far flung as Massachusetts, Lancashire in Great Britain, Normandy in France, and the suburbs of Moscow depended on a regular supply of American cotton.

As early as 1803, cotton had become the most important American export. Cotton sales earned the money from abroad that allowed the United States to pay for imported manufactured goods. On the eve of the Civil War, it accounted for well over half of the total value of American exports. In 1860, the economic investment represented by the slave population exceeded the value of the nation's factories, railroads, and banks combined.

A photograph of Frederick Douglass, the fugitive slave who became a prominent abolitionist, taken between 1847 and 1852. As a fellow abolitionist noted at the time, "The very look and bearing of Douglass are an irresistible logic against the oppression of his race."

Economic value of slavery

COTTON PRESSING IN LOUISIANA

"Cotton Pressing in Louisiana," from *Ballou's Magazine* in 1856, illustrates how slaves were used to supply power for a partially mechanized work process.

The Second Middle Passage

As noted in Chapter 9, to replace the slave trade from Africa, which had been prohibited by Congress in 1808, a massive trade in slaves developed within the United States. More than 2 million slaves were sold between 1820 and 1860. The main business districts of southern cities contained the offices of slave traders, complete with signs reading "Negro Sales" or "Negroes Bought Here." Auctions of slaves took place at public slave markets, as in New Orleans, or at courthouses. Southern newspapers carried advertisements for slave sales, southern banks financed slave trading, southern ships and railroads carried slaves from buyers to sellers, and southern states and municipalities earned revenue by taxing the sale of slaves.

Slave trade in the South

Slavery and the Nation

Slavery shaped the lives of all Americans, white as well as black. It helped to determine where they lived, how they worked, and under what conditions they could exercise their freedoms of speech, assembly, and the press.

Northern participation

Northern merchants and manufacturers participated in the slave economy and shared in its profits. Money earned in the cotton trade helped to finance industrial development and internal improvements in the North. Northern ships carried cotton to New York and Europe, northern bankers financed cotton plantations, northern companies insured slave property, and northern factories turned cotton into cloth. New York City's rise to commercial prominence depended as much on the establishment of shipping lines that gathered the South's cotton and transported it to Europe as on the Erie Canal.

TABLE 11.1   Growth of the Slave Population

YEAR	SLAVE POPULATION
1790	697,624
1800	893,602
1810	1,191,362
1820	1,538,022
1830	2,009,043
1840	2,487,355
1850	3,204,313
1860	3,953,760

The Southern Economy

There was no single South before the Civil War. In the eight slave states of the Upper South, slaves and slaveowners made up a smaller percentage of the total population than in the seven Deep South states, which stretched from South Carolina west to Texas. The Upper South had major centers of industry in Baltimore, Richmond,

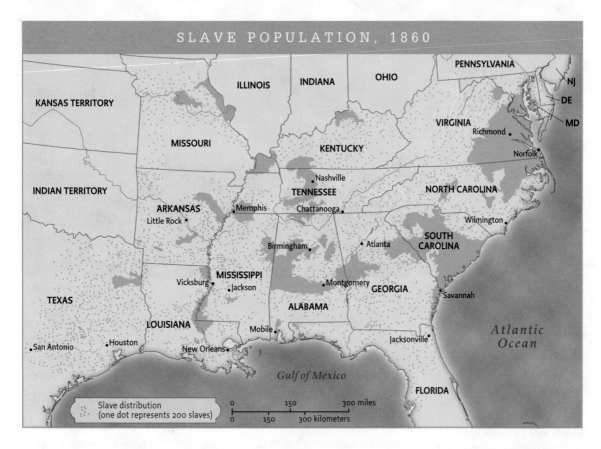

SLAVE POPULATION, 1860

Slave distribution
(one dot represents 200 slaves)

and St. Louis, and its economies were more diversified than those in the Deep South, which was heavily dependent on cotton. Not surprisingly, during the secession crisis of 1860–1861, the Deep South states were the first to leave the Union.

Nonetheless, slavery led the South down a very different path of economic development than the North's, limiting the growth of industry, discouraging immigrants from entering the region, and inhibiting technological progress. The South did not share in the urban growth experienced by the rest of the country. In the Cotton Kingdom, the only city of significant size was New Orleans. With a population of 168,000 in 1860, New Orleans ranked as the nation's sixth-largest city. As the gathering point for cotton grown along the Mississippi River and sugar from the plantations of southeastern Louisiana, it was the world's leading exporter of slave-grown crops.

Rather than being evenly distributed throughout the South, the slave population was concentrated in areas with the most fertile soil and easiest access to national and international markets. By 1860, a significant percentage of the slave population had been transported from the Atlantic coast to the Deep South via the internal slave trade.

New Orleans

This 1860 view of New Orleans captures the size and scale of the cotton trade in the South's largest city. More than 3,500 steamboats arrived in New Orleans in 1860.

In 1860, the South produced less than 10 percent of the nation's manufactured goods. Many northerners viewed slavery as an obstacle to American economic progress. But as New Orleans showed, slavery and economic growth could go hand in hand. In general, the southern economy was hardly stagnant, and slavery proved very profitable for most owners. The profits produced by slavery for the South and the nation as a whole formed a powerful obstacle to abolition. Speaking of cotton, Senator James Henry Hammond of South Carolina declared, "No power on earth dares to make war upon it. Cotton is king."

Plain Folk of the Old South

An upcountry family, dressed in homespun, in Cedar Mountain, Virginia. Many white families in the pre–Civil War South were largely isolated from the market economy. This photograph was taken in 1862 but reflects the prewar way of life.

The foundation of the Old South's economy, slavery powerfully shaped race relations, politics, religion, and the law. Its influence was pervasive: "Nothing escaped," writes one historian, "nothing and no one." This was true despite the fact that the majority of white southerners—three out of four white families—owned no slaves. Many southern farmers lived outside the plantation belt in hilly areas unsuitable for cotton production. Using family labor, they raised livestock and grew food for their own use, purchasing relatively few goods at local stores. Unlike northern farmers, therefore, they did not provide a market for manufactured goods. This was one of the main reasons that the South did not develop an industrial base.

Lack of southern market for manufactures

Some poorer whites resented the power and privileges of the great planters. Politicians such as Andrew Johnson of Tennessee and Joseph Brown of Georgia rose to power as self-proclaimed spokesmen of the common man against the "slaveocracy." But most poor whites made their peace with the planters in whose hands economic and social power was concentrated. Racism, kinship ties, common participation in a democratic political culture, and regional loyalty in the face of outside criticism all served to cement bonds between planters and the South's "**plain folk**." Like other white southerners, most small farmers believed their economic and personal freedom rested on slavery. Not until the Civil War would class tensions among the white population threaten the planters' domination.

Planters and "plain folk"

The Planter Class

Even among slaveholders, the planter was far from typical. In 1850, a majority of slaveholding families owned five or fewer slaves. Fewer than 40,000 families possessed the twenty or more slaves that qualified them as planters. Fewer than 2,000 families owned a hundred slaves or more. Nonetheless, even though the planter was not the typical slaveholder or white southerner, his values and aspirations dominated southern life. The plantation, wrote Frederick Douglass, was "a little nation by itself, with its own language, its own rules, regulations, and customs." These rules and customs set the tone for southern society.

Ownership of slaves provided the route to wealth, status, and influence. Planters not only held the majority of slaves but also controlled the most fertile land, enjoyed the highest incomes, and dominated state and local offices and the leadership of both political parties. Slavery, of course, was a profit-making system, and slaveowners kept close watch on world prices for their products, invested in enterprises such as railroads and canals, and carefully supervised their plantations. Their wives—the "plantation mistresses" idealized in southern lore for femininity, beauty, and dependence on men—were hardly idle. They cared for sick slaves, directed the domestic servants, and supervised the entire plantation when their husbands were away. The wealthiest Americans before the Civil War were planters in the South Carolina low country and the cotton region around Natchez, Mississippi.

A slave dealer's place of business in Atlanta. The buying and selling of slaves was a regularized part of the southern economy, and such businesses were a common sight in every southern town.

On the cotton frontier, many planters lived in crude log homes. But in the older slave states, and as settled society developed in the Deep South, they constructed elegant mansions adorned with white columns in the Greek Revival style of architecture. Planters discouraged their sons from entering "lowly" trades such as commerce and manufacturing, one reason that the South remained overwhelmingly agricultural.

The Paternalist Ethos

Plantation hierarchy

The slave plantation was deeply embedded in the world market, and planters sought to accumulate land, slaves, and profits. However, planters' values glorified not the competitive capitalist marketplace but a hierarchical, agrarian society in which slaveholding gentlemen took personal responsibility for the physical and moral well-being of their dependents—women, children, and slaves.

This outlook, known as "**paternalism**" (from the Latin word for "father"), had been a feature of American slavery even in the eighteenth century. But it became more ingrained after the closing of the African slave trade in 1808, which narrowed the cultural gap between master and slave and gave owners an economic interest in the survival of their human property. Unlike the absentee planters of the West Indies, many of whom resided in Great Britain, southern slaveholders lived on their plantations and thus had year-round contact with their slaves.

The paternalist outlook both masked and justified the brutal reality of slavery. It enabled slaveowners to think of themselves as kind, responsible masters even as they bought and sold their human property—a practice at odds with the claim that slaves formed part of the master's "family."

The Proslavery Argument

In the thirty years before the outbreak of the Civil War, even as northern criticism of the "peculiar institution" began to deepen, proslavery thought came to dominate southern public life. Fewer and fewer white southerners shared the view, common among the founding fathers, that slavery was, at best, a "necessary evil."

TABLE 11.2 Slaveholding, 1850 (in Round Numbers)

NUMBER OF SLAVES OWNED	SLAVEHOLDERS
1	68,000
2–4	105,000
5–9	80,000
10–19	55,000
20–49	30,000
50–99	6,000
100–199	1,500
200+	250

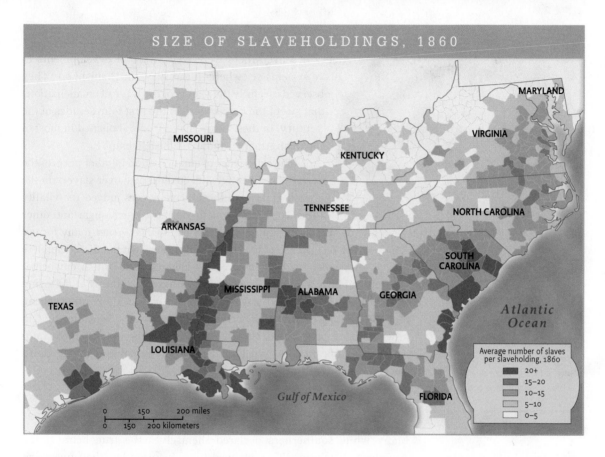

SIZE OF SLAVEHOLDINGS, 1860

Average number of slaves
per slaveholding, 1860

- 20+
- 15–20
- 10–15
- 5–10
- 0–5

Even those who had no direct stake in slavery shared with planters a deep commitment to white supremacy. Indeed, racism—the belief that blacks were innately inferior to whites and unsuited for life in any condition other than slavery—formed one pillar of the proslavery ideology. Most slaveholders also found legitimation for slavery in biblical passages such as the injunction that servants should obey their masters. Others argued that slavery was essential to human progress. Without slavery, they believed, planters would be unable to cultivate the arts, sciences, and other civilized pursuits.

Still other defenders of slavery insisted that the institution guaranteed equality for whites by preventing the growth of a class doomed to a life of unskilled labor. Like northerners, they claimed to be committed to the ideal of freedom. Slavery for blacks, they declared, was the surest guarantee of "perfect equality" among whites, liberating them from the "low, menial" jobs such as factory labor and domestic service performed by wage laborers in the North.

Most southern slaveholders owned fewer than five slaves. The largest plantations were concentrated in coastal South Carolina and along the Mississippi River.

Slavery and white supremacy

Equality for whites

Abolition in the Americas

American slaveowners were well aware of developments in slave systems elsewhere in the Western Hemisphere. They observed carefully the results of the wave of emancipations that swept the hemisphere in the first four decades of the century. In these years, slavery was abolished in most of Spanish America and in the British empire.

The experience of emancipation in other parts of the hemisphere strongly affected debates over slavery in the United States. Southern slaveowners judged the vitality of the Caribbean economy by how much sugar and other crops it produced for the world market. Since many former slaves preferred to grow food for their own families, defenders of slavery in the United States charged that British emancipation had been a failure. Abolitionists disagreed, pointing to the rising standard of living of freed slaves, the spread of education among them, and other improvements in their lives. But the stark fact remained that, in a hemispheric perspective, slavery was a declining institution. At mid-century, significant New World slave systems remained only in Cuba, Puerto Rico, Brazil—and the United States.

A plate manufactured in England to celebrate emancipation in the British empire. After a brief period of apprenticeship, the end of slavery came on August 1,1838. At the center, a family of former slaves celebrates outside their cabin.

Slavery and Liberty

Many white southerners declared themselves the true heirs of the American Revolution. They claimed to be inspired by "the same spirit of freedom and independence" that motivated the founding generation. Beginning in the 1830s, however, proslavery writers began to question the ideals of liberty, equality, and democracy so widely shared elsewhere in the nation. South Carolina, the only southern state where a majority of white families owned slaves, became the home of an aggressive defense of slavery that repudiated the idea that freedom and equality were universal entitlements. The language of the Declaration of Independence—that all men were created equal and entitled to liberty—was "the most false and dangerous of all political errors," insisted John C. Calhoun.

Questioning founding ideals

The Virginia writer George Fitzhugh took the argument to its most radical conclusion, repudiating not only Jeffersonian ideals but the notion of America's special mission in the world. Far from being the natural condition of mankind, Fitzhugh wrote, "universal liberty" was the exception, an experiment carried on "for a little while" in "a corner of Europe" and the northern United States. Taking the world and its history as a whole,

George Fitzhugh

slavery, "without regard to race and color," was "the general, . . . normal, natural" basis of "civilized society."

After 1830, southern writers, newspaper editors, politicians, and clergymen increasingly devoted themselves to spreading the defense of slavery. The majority of white southerners came to believe that freedom for whites rested on the power to command the labor of blacks. In the words of the Richmond *Enquirer*, "freedom is not possible without slavery."

Spreading defense of slavery

LIFE UNDER SLAVERY

Slaves and the Law

For slaves, the "peculiar institution" meant a life of incessant toil, brutal punishment, and the constant fear that their families would be destroyed by sale. Before the law, slaves were property. Although they had a few legal rights (all states made it illegal to kill a slave except in self-defense, and slaves accused of serious crimes were entitled to their day in court, before all-white judges and juries), these were haphazardly enforced. Slaves could be sold or leased by their owners at will and lacked any voice in the governments that ruled over them. They could not testify in court against a white person, sign contracts or acquire property, own firearms, hold meetings unless a white person was present, or leave the farm or plantation without the permission of their owner. By the 1830s, it was against the law to teach a slave to read or write.

Slaves as property

Legal restrictions on slaves

Not all of these laws were rigorously enforced. Some members of slaveholding families taught slave children to read (although rather few, since well over 90 percent of the slave population was illiterate in 1860). It was quite common throughout the South for slaves to gather without white supervision at crossroads villages and country stores on Sunday, their day of rest.

A poster advertising the raffle of a horse and a slave, treated as equivalents, at a Missouri store.

The slave, declared a Louisiana law, "owes to his master . . . a respect without bounds, and an absolute obedience." No aspect of slaves' lives, from the choice of marriage partners to how they spent their free time, was immune from his interference. The entire system of southern justice, from the state militia and courts down to armed patrols in each locality, was designed to enforce the master's control over the persons and labor of his slaves.

In one famous case, a Missouri court considered the "crime" of Celia, a slave who had killed her master in 1855 while resisting a sexual assault.

State law deemed "any woman" in such circumstances to be acting in self-defense. But Celia, the court ruled, was not a "woman" in the eyes of the law. She was a slave, whose master had complete power over her person. The court sentenced her to death. However, since Celia was pregnant, her execution was postponed until the child was born, so as not to deprive her owner's heirs of their property rights.

Slaves outside their cabin on a South Carolina plantation, probably photographed in the 1850s. They had brought their furniture outdoors to be included in the photo.

Conditions of Slave Life

Compared with their counterparts in the West Indies and Brazil, American slaves enjoyed better diets, lower rates of infant mortality, and longer life expectancies. Many factors contributed to improving material conditions. Most of the South lies outside the geographical area where tropical diseases like malaria, yellow fever, and typhoid fever flourish, so health among all southerners was better than in the Caribbean. And with the price of slaves rising dramatically after the closing of the African slave trade, it made economic sense for owners to become concerned with the health and living conditions of their human property.

Although slaves in the United States enjoyed better material lives than elsewhere in the Western Hemisphere, they had far less access to freedom. In Brazil, it was not uncommon for an owner to free slaves as a form of celebration—on the occasion of a wedding in the owner's family, for example—or to allow slaves to purchase their freedom. In the nineteenth-century South, however, more and more states set limits on voluntary manumission, requiring that such acts be approved by the legislature. Few slave societies in history have so systematically closed off all avenues to freedom as the Old South.

Limiting voluntary manumission

Free Blacks in the Old South

The existence of slavery helped to define the status of those blacks who did enjoy freedom. On the eve of the Civil War, nearly half a million free blacks lived in the United States, a majority in the South. Most were the descendants of slaves freed by southern owners in the aftermath of the Revolution or by the gradual emancipation laws of the northern states. Their numbers were supplemented by slaves who had been voluntarily liberated by their masters, who had been allowed to purchase their freedom, or who succeeded in running away.

When followed by "black" or "Negro," the word "free" took on an entirely new meaning. Free blacks in the South could legally own property and marry and, of course, could not be bought and sold. But many regulations restricting the lives of slaves also applied to them. Free blacks had no voice in selecting public officials. They were not allowed to testify in court or serve on juries, and they had to carry at all times a certificate of freedom. Poor free blacks who required public assistance could be bound out to labor alongside slaves. By the 1850s, most southern states prohibited free blacks from entering their territory. A few states even moved to expel them altogether, offering the choice of enslavement or departure.

In New Orleans and Charleston, on the other hand, relatively prosperous free black communities developed, mostly composed of mixed-race descendants of unions between white men and slave women. Many free blacks in these cities acquired an education and worked as skilled craftsmen such as tailors, carpenters, and mechanics. They established churches for their communities and schools for their children. In the Upper South, where the large majority of southern free blacks lived, they generally worked for wages as farm laborers. Overall, in the words of Willis A. Hodges, a member of a free Virginia family that helped runaways to reach the North, free blacks and slaves were "one man of sorrow."

Slaves were an ever-present part of southern daily life. In this 1826 portrait of the five children of Commodore John Daniel Daniels, a wealthy Baltimore shipowner, a young slave lies on the floor at their side, holding the soap for a game of blowing bubbles, while another hovers in the background, almost depicted as part of the room's design.

Slave Labor

First and foremost, slavery was a system of labor; "from sunup to first dark," with only brief interruptions for meals, work occupied most of the slaves' time. Large plantations were diversified communities, where slaves performed all kinds of work. The 125 slaves on one plantation, for instance, included a butler, two waitresses, a nurse, a dairymaid, a gardener, ten carpenters, and two shoemakers. Other plantations counted among their slaves engineers, blacksmiths, and weavers, as well as domestic workers from cooks to coachmen.

The large majority of slaves—75 percent of women and nearly 90 percent of men, according to one study—worked in the fields. The precise organization of their labor varied according to the crop and the size of

Varieties of slave labor

In this undated photograph, men, women, and children pick cotton under the watchful eye of an overseer. Unlike sugarcane, cotton does not grow to a great height, allowing an overseer to supervise a large number of slaves.

the holding. On small farms, the owner often toiled side by side with his slaves. The largest concentration of slaves, however, lived and worked on plantations in the Cotton Belt, where men, women, and children labored in gangs, often under the direction of an overseer and perhaps a slave "driver" who assisted him. Among slaves, overseers had a reputation for meting out brutal treatment.

The 150,000 slaves who worked in the sugar fields of southern Louisiana also labored in large gangs. Conditions here were among the harshest in the South, for the late fall harvest season required round-the-clock labor to cut and process the sugarcane before it spoiled. On the rice plantations of South Carolina and Georgia, the system of task labor, which had originated in the colonial era, prevailed. With few whites willing to venture into the malaria-infested swamps, slaves were assigned daily tasks and allowed to set their own pace of work. Once a slave's task had been completed, he or she could spend the rest of the day hunting, fishing, or cultivating garden crops.

Slavery in the Cities

Businessmen, merchants, lawyers, and civil servants owned slaves, and by 1860 some 200,000 worked in industry, especially in the ironworks and tobacco factories of the Upper South. In southern cities, thousands were employed as unskilled laborers and skilled artisans. Most city slaves were servants, cooks, and other domestic laborers. But owners sometimes allowed those with craft skills to "hire their own time." This meant that they could make work arrangements individually with employers, with most of the wages going to the slave's owner. Many urban slaves even lived on their own. But slaveholders increasingly became convinced that, as one wrote, the growing independence of skilled urban slaves "exerts a most injurious influence upon the relation of master and servant." For this reason, many owners in the 1850s sold city slaves to the countryside and sought replacements among skilled white labor.

Skilled labor

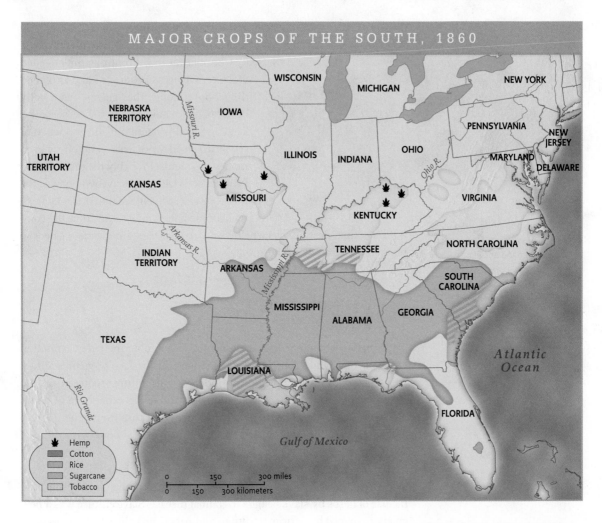

MAJOR CROPS OF THE SOUTH, 1860

Legend:
- Hemp
- Cotton
- Rice
- Sugarcane
- Tobacco

0   150   300 miles
0   150   300 kilometers

Cotton was the major agricultural crop of the South, and, indeed, the nation, but slaves also grew rice, sugarcane, tobacco, and hemp.

Maintaining Order

Slaveowners employed a variety of means in their attempts to maintain order and discipline among their human property and persuade them to labor productively. At base, the system rested on force. Masters had almost complete discretion in inflicting punishment, and rare was the slave who went through his or her life without experiencing a whipping. Any infraction of plantation rules, no matter how minor, could be punished by the lash. One Georgia planter recorded in his journal that he had whipped

A system based on force

A Public Whipping of Slaves in Lexington, Missouri, in 1856, an illustration from the abolitionist publication *The Suppressed Book about Slavery*. Whipping was a common form of punishment for slaves.

a slave "for not bringing over milk for my coffee, being compelled to take it without."

Subtler means of control supplemented violence. Owners encouraged and exploited divisions among the slaves, especially between field hands and house servants. They created systems of incentives that rewarded good work with time off or even money payments. Probably the most powerful weapon wielded by slaveowners was the threat of sale, which separated slaves from their immediate families and from the communities that, despite overwhelming odds, African-Americans created on plantations throughout the South.

SLAVE CULTURE

Slaves never abandoned their desire for freedom or their determination to resist total white control over their lives. In the face of grim realities, they succeeded in forging a semi-independent culture, centered on the family and church. This enabled them to survive the experience of bondage without surrendering their self-esteem and to pass from generation to generation a set of ideas and values fundamentally at odds with those of their masters.

African heritage

Slave culture drew on the African heritage. African influences were evident in the slaves' music and dances, their style of religious worship, and the use of herbs by slave healers to combat disease. Slave culture was a new creation, shaped by African traditions and American values and experiences.

The Slave Family

Slave marriages

At the center of the slave community stood the family. On the sugar plantations of the West Indies, the number of males far exceeded that of females, the workers lived in barracks-type buildings, and settled family life was nearly impossible. The United States, where the slave population grew from natural increase rather than continued importation from Africa, had an even male-female ratio, making the creation of families far more possible. To be sure, the law did not recognize the legality of slave marriages. The master had to consent before a man and woman could "jump over the broomstick" (the slaves' marriage ceremony), and families stood in constant danger of being broken up by sale.

Nonetheless, most adult slaves married, and their unions, when not disrupted by sale, typically lasted for a lifetime. To solidify a sense of family continuity, slaves frequently named children after cousins, uncles, grandparents, and other relatives. Most slaves lived in two-parent families. But because of constant sales, the slave community had a significantly higher number of female-headed households than among whites, as well as families in which grandparents, other relatives, or even non-kin assumed responsibility for raising children.

The Threat of Sale

As noted above, the threat of sale, which disrupted family ties, was perhaps the most powerful disciplinary weapon slaveholders possessed. As the domestic slave trade expanded with the rise of the Cotton Kingdom, about one slave marriage in three in slave-selling states like Virginia was broken by sale. Many children were separated from their parents by sale.

Slave traders gave little attention to preserving family ties. A public notice, "Sale of Slaves and Stock," announced the 1852 auction of property belonging to a recently deceased Georgia planter. It listed thirty-six individuals ranging from an infant to a sixty-nine-year-old woman and ended with the proviso: "Slaves will be sold separate, or in lots, as best suits the purchaser." Sales like this were a human tragedy.

Gender Roles among Slaves

In some ways, gender roles under slavery differed markedly from those in the larger society. Slave men and women experienced, in a sense, the equality of powerlessness. The nineteenth century's "cult of domesticity," which defined the home as a woman's proper sphere, did not apply to slave women, who regularly worked in the fields. Slave men could not act as the economic providers for their families. Nor could they protect their

Sale of Slaves and Stock.

The Negroes and Stock listed below, are a Prime Lot, and belong to the ESTATE OF THE LATE LUTHER McGOWAN, and will be sold on Monday, Sept. 22nd, 1852, at the Fair Grounds, in Savannah, Georgia, at 1:00 P. M. The Negroes will be taken to the grounds two days previous to the Sale, so that they may be inspected by prospective buyers.

On account of the low prices listed below, they will be sold for cash only, and must be taken into custody within two hours after sale.

No.	Name.	Age.	Remarks.	Price.
1	Lunesta	27	Prime Rice Planter,	$1,275.00
2	Violet	16	Housework and Nursemaid,	900.00
3	Lizzie	30	Rice, Unsound,	300.00
4	Minda	27	Cotton, Prime Woman,	1,200.00
5	Adam	28	Cotton, Prime Young Man,	1,100.00
6	Abel	41	Rice Hand, Eyesight Poor,	675.00
7	Tanney	22	Prime Cotton Hand,	950.00
8	Flementina	39	Good Cook. Stiff Knee,	400.00
9	Lanney	34	Prime Cottom Man,	1,000.00
10	Sally	10	Handy in Kitchen,	675.00
11	Maccabey	35	Prime Man, Fair Carpenter,	980.00
12	Dorcas Judy	25	Seamstress, Handy in House,	800.00
13	Happy	60	Blacksmith,	575.00
14	Mowden	15	Prime Cotton Boy,	700.00
15	Bills	21	Handy with Mules,	900.00
16	Theopolis	39	Rice Hand, Gets Fits,	575.00
17	Coolidge	29	Rice Hand and Blacksmith,	1,275.00
18	Bessie	69	Infirm, Sews,	250.00
19	Infant	1	Strong Likely Boy	400.00
20	Samson	41	Prime Man, Good with Stock,	975.00
21	Callie May	27	Prime Woman, Rice,	1,000.00
22	Honey	14	Prime Girl, Hearing Poor,	850.00
23	Angelina	16	Prime Girl, House or Field,	1,000.00
24	Virgil	21	Prime Field Hand,	1,100.00
25	Tom	40	Rice Hand, Lame Leg,	750.00
26	Noble	11	Handy Boy,	900.00
27	Judge Lesh	55	Prime Blacksmith,	800.00
28	Booster	43	Fair Mason, Unsound,	600.00
29	Big Kate	37	Housekeeper and Nurse,	950.00
30	Melie Ann	19	Housework, Smart Yellow Girl,	1,250.00
31	Deacon	26	Prime Rice Hand,	1,000.00
32	Coming	19	Prime Cotton Hand,	1,000.00
33	Mabel	47	Prime Cotton Hand,	800.00
34	Uncle Tim	60	Fair Hand with Mules,	600.00
35	Abe	27	Prime Cotton Hand,	1,000.00
36	Tennes	29	Prime Rice Hand and Coachman,	1,250.00

There will also be offered at this sale, twenty head of Horses and Mules with harness, along with thirty head of Prime Cattle. Slaves will be sold separate, or in lots, as best suits the purchaser. Sale will be held rain or shine.

A broadside advertising the public sale of slaves, along with horses, mules, and cattle, after the death of their owner. The advertisement notes that the slaves will be sold individually or in groups "as best suits the purchaser," an indication that families were likely to be broken up. The prices are based on each slave's sex, age, and skill.

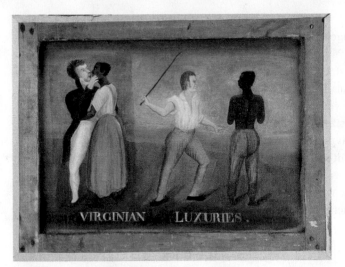

Virginian Luxuries. Originally painted on the back panel of a formal portrait, this image illustrates two "luxuries" of a Virginia slaveowner—the power to sexually abuse slave women and to whip slaves.

wives from physical or sexual abuse by owners and overseers (a frequent occurrence on many plantations) or determine when and under what conditions their children worked.

When slaves worked "on their own time," however, more conventional gender roles prevailed. Slave men chopped wood, hunted, and fished, while women washed, sewed, and assumed primary responsibility for the care of children. Some planters allowed their slaves small plots of land on which to grow food to supplement the rations provided by the owner; women usually took charge of these "garden plots."

Slave Religion

A distinctive version of Christianity also offered solace to slaves in the face of hardship and hope for liberation from bondage. Some blacks, free and slave, had taken part in the Great Awakening of the colonial era, and even more were swept into the South's Baptist and Methodist churches during the religious revivals of the late eighteenth and early nineteenth centuries. As one preacher recalled of the great camp meeting that drew thousands of worshipers to Cane Ridge, Kentucky, in 1801, no distinctions were made "as to age, sex, color, or anything of a temporary nature; old and young, male and female, black and white, had equal privilege to minister the light which they received, in whatever way the Spirit directed."

Black preachers

Even though the law prohibited slaves from gathering without a white person present, every plantation, it seemed, had its own black preacher. Usually the preacher was a "self-called" slave who possessed little or no formal education but whose rhetorical abilities and familiarity with the Bible made him one of the most respected members of the slave community. Especially in southern cities, slaves also worshiped in biracial congregations with white ministers, where they generally were required to sit in the back pews or in the balcony. Urban free blacks established their own churches, sometimes attended by slaves.

Religion and social control

To masters, Christianity offered another means of social control. Many required slaves to attend services conducted by white ministers, who preached that theft was immoral and that the Bible required servants to obey their masters. One slave later recalled being told in a white minister's sermon "how good God was in bringing us over to this country from dark and benighted Africa, and permitting us to listen to the sound of the gospel."

In their own religious gatherings, slaves transformed the Christianity they had embraced, turning it to their own purposes. The biblical story of Exodus, for example, in which God chose Moses to lead the enslaved Jews of Egypt into a promised land of freedom, played a central role in black Christianity. Slaves iden-

Kitchen Ball at White Sulphur Springs, Virginia, an 1838 painting by the German-born American artist Christian Mayr. Fashionably dressed domestic slaves celebrate the wedding of a couple, dressed in white at the center.

tified themselves as a chosen people whom God in the fullness of time would deliver from bondage. At the same time, the figure of Jesus Christ represented to slaves a personal redeemer, one who truly cared for the oppressed. And in the slaves' eyes, the Christian message of brotherhood and the equality of all souls before the Creator offered an irrefutable indictment of the institution of slavery.

The Desire for Liberty

Despite their masters' elaborate ideology defending the South's "peculiar institution," slave culture rested on a conviction of the injustices of bondage and the desire for freedom. When slaves sang, "I'm bound for the land of Canaan," they meant not only relief from worldly woes in an afterlife but also escaping to the North or witnessing the breaking of slavery's chains. A fugitive who reached the North later recalled that the "desire for freedom" was the "constant theme" of conversations in the slave quarters.

Most slaves, however, fully understood the impossibility of directly confronting such an entrenched system. Their folk tales had no figures equivalent to Paul Bunyan, the powerful, larger-than-life backwoodsman popular in white folklore. Slaves' folklore, such as the Brer Rabbit stories, glorified the weak hare who outwitted stronger foes like the bear and fox, rather than challenging them outright. Their religious songs, or spirituals, spoke of lives of sorrow ("I've been 'buked and I've been scorned"), while holding out hope for ultimate liberation ("Didn't my Lord deliver Daniel?").

Slave culture

Owners attempted to prevent slaves from learning about the larger world. But slaves created neighborhood networks that transmitted information between plantations. Skilled craftsmen, preachers, pilots

Neighborhood networks

Plantation Burial, a painting from around 1860 by John Antrobus, an English artist who emigrated to New Orleans in 1850 and later married the daughter of a plantation owner. A slave preacher conducts a funeral service while black men, women, and children look on. The well-dressed white man and woman on the far right are, presumably, the plantation owner and his wife. This is a rare eyewitness depiction of black culture under slavery.

on ships, and other privileged slaves spread news of local and national events. James Henry Hammond of South Carolina was "astonished and shocked" to find that his slaves understood the political views of the presidential candidates of 1844, Henry Clay and James K. Polk, and knew "most of what the abolitionists are doing."

The world of most rural slaves was bounded by their local communities and kin. Nor could slaves remain indifferent to the currents of thought unleashed by the American Revolution or to the language of freedom in the society around them. "I am in a land of liberty," wrote Joseph Taper, a Virginia slave who escaped to Canada around 1840. "Here man is as God intended he should be."

RESISTANCE TO SLAVERY

Confronted with federal, state, and local authorities committed to preserving slavery, and outnumbered within the South as a whole by the white population, slaves could only rarely express their desire for freedom by outright rebellion. Compared with revolts in Brazil and the West Indies, which experienced numerous uprisings, involving hundreds or even thousands of slaves, revolts in the United States were smaller and less frequent. Resistance to slavery took many forms in the Old South, from individual acts of defiance to occasional uprisings. These actions posed a constant challenge to the slaveholders' self-image as benign paternalists and their belief that slaves were obedient subjects grateful for their owners' care.

Forms of Resistance

Everyday resistance

The most widespread expression of hostility to slavery was "day-to-day resistance" or "**silent sabotage**"—doing poor work, breaking tools, abusing animals, and in other ways disrupting the plantation routine. Then there was the theft of food, a form of resistance so common that one southern physician diagnosed it as a hereditary disease unique to blacks. Less frequent, but more dangerous, were serious crimes committed by slaves, including arson, poisoning, and armed assaults against individual whites.

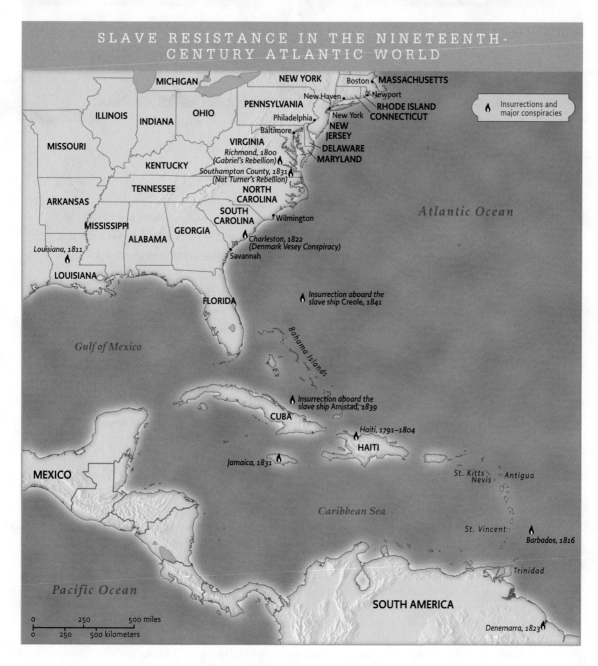

SLAVE RESISTANCE IN THE NINETEENTH-CENTURY ATLANTIC WORLD

Insurrections and major conspiracies

MICHIGAN

NEW YORK

Boston MASSACHUSETTS

New Haven Newport

PENNSYLVANIA

ILLINOIS INDIANA OHIO

Philadelphia RHODE ISLAND CONNECTICUT

New York

Baltimore NEW JERSEY

MISSOURI DELAWARE

VIRGINIA MARYLAND

Richmond, 1800 (Gabriel's Rebellion)

KENTUCKY Southampton County, 1831 (Nat Turner's Rebellion)

TENNESSEE NORTH CAROLINA

ARKANSAS SOUTH CAROLINA

Wilmington

MISSISSIPPI GEORGIA Charleston, 1822 (Denmark Vesey Conspiracy)

ALABAMA Savannah

Louisiana, 1811

LOUISIANA

FLORIDA

Atlantic Ocean

Insurrection aboard the slave ship Creole, 1841

Gulf of Mexico

Bahama Islands

Insurrection aboard the slave ship Amistad, 1839

CUBA

Haiti, 1791–1804

HAITI

Jamaica, 1831

MEXICO

St. Kitts Nevis Antigua

Caribbean Sea

St. Vincent Barbados, 1816

Trinidad

Pacific Ocean

SOUTH AMERICA

0   250   500 miles
0   250   500 kilometers

Denemarra, 1823

Instances of slave resistance occurred throughout the Western Hemisphere, on land and at sea. This map shows the location of major events in the nineteenth century.

VOICES OF FREEDOM

From Letter by Joseph Taper to Joseph Long (1840)

No one knows how many slaves succeeded in escaping from bondage before the Civil War. Some settled in northern cities like Boston, Cincinnati, and New York. But because the Constitution required that fugitives be returned to slavery, many continued northward until they reached Canada.

One successful fugitive was Joseph Taper, a slave in Frederick County, Virginia, who in 1837 ran away to Pennsylvania with his wife and children. Two years later, learning that a "slave catcher" was in the neighborhood, the Tapers fled to Canada. In 1840, Taper wrote to a white acquaintance in Virginia recounting some of his experiences.

The biblical passage to which Taper refers reads: "And I will come near to you to judgment; and I will be a swift witness against the sorcerers, and against the adulterers, and against false swearers, and against those that oppress the hireling in his wages, the widow, and the fatherless, and that turn aside the stranger from his right, and fear not me, saith the Lord of hosts."

Dear sir,

I now take the opportunity to inform you that I am in a land of liberty, in good health. . . . Since I have been in the Queen's dominions I have been well contented, Yes well contented for Sure, man is as God intended he should be. That is, all are born free and equal. This is a wholesome law, not like the Southern laws which puts man made in the image of God, on level with brutes. O, what will become of the people, and where will they stand in the day of Judgment. Would that the 5th verse of the 3d chapter of Malachi were written as with the bar of iron, and the point of a diamond upon every oppressor's heart that they might repent of this evil, and let the oppressed go free. . . .

We have good schools, and all the colored population supplied with schools. My boy Edward who will be six years next January, is now reading, and I intend keeping him at school until he becomes a good scholar.

I have enjoyed more pleasure within one month here than in all my life in the land of bondage. . . . My wife and self are sitting by a good comfortable fire happy, knowing that there are none to molest [us] or make [us] afraid. God save Queen Victoria. The Lord bless her in this life, and crown her with glory in the world to come is my prayer,

Yours With much respect

most obt, Joseph Taper

From "Slavery and the Bible" (1850)

White southerners developed an elaborate set of arguments defending slavery in the period before the Civil War. One pillar of proslavery thought was the idea that the institution was sanctioned by the Bible, as in this essay from the influential southern magazine *De Bow's Review*.

A very large party in the United States believe that holding slaves is morally wrong; this party founds its belief upon precepts taught in the Bible, and takes that book as the standard of morality and religion.

. . . We think we can show, that the Bible teaches clearly and conclusively that the holding of slaves is right; and if so, no deduction from general principles can make it wrong, if that book is true. . . .

Slavery has existed in some form or under some name, in almost every country of the globe. It existed in every country known, even by name, to any one of the sacred writers, at the time of his writing; yet none of them condemns it in the slightest degree. Would this have been the case had it been wrong in itself? Would not some one of the host of sacred writers have spoken of this alleged crime, in such terms as to show, in a manner not to be misunderstood, that God wished all men to be equal?

Abraham, the chosen servant of God, had his bond servants, whose condition was similar to, or worse than, that of our slaves. He considered them as his property, to be bought and sold as any other property which he owned. . . .

We find . . . that both the Old and New Testaments speak of slavery—that they do not condemn the relation, but, on the contrary, expressly allow it or create it; and they give commands and exhortations, which are based upon its legality and propriety. It can not, then, be wrong.

QUESTIONS

1. *How does Taper's letter reverse the rhetoric, common among white Americans, which saw the United States as a land of freedom and the British empire as lacking in liberty?*

2. *Why does De Bow feel that it is important to show that the Bible sanctions slavery?*

3. *How do Taper and De Bow differ in their understanding of the relationship of slavery and Christianity?*

Even more threatening to the stability of the slave system were slaves who ran away. Formidable obstacles confronted the prospective fugitive. Patrols were constantly on the lookout for runaway slaves. Slaves had little or no knowledge of geography, apart from understanding that following the north star led to freedom. No one knows how many slaves succeeded in reaching the North or Canada—the most common rough estimate is around 1,000 per year. Not surprisingly, most of those who succeeded lived, like Frederick Douglass, in the Upper South, especially Maryland, Virginia, and Kentucky, which bordered on the free states. Douglass, who escaped at age twenty, was also typical in that the large majority of fugitives were young men. Most slave women were not willing to leave children behind, and taking them along on the arduous escape journey was nearly impossible.

Fugitive destinations

In the Deep South, fugitives tended to head for cities like New Orleans or Charleston, where they hoped to lose themselves in the free black community. Other escapees fled to remote areas like the Great Dismal Swamp of Virginia or the Florida Everglades, where the Seminole Indians offered refuge before they were forced to move west. Even in Tennessee, a study of newspaper advertisements for runaways finds that around 40 percent were thought to have remained in the local neighborhood and 30 percent to have headed to other locations in the South, while only 25 percent tried to reach the North.

The **Underground Railroad**, a loose organization of sympathetic abolitionists who hid fugitives in their homes and sent them on to the next "station," assisted some runaway slaves. A few courageous individuals made forays into the South to liberate slaves. The best known was **Harriet Tubman**. Born in Maryland in 1820, Tubman escaped to Philadelphia in 1849 and during the next decade risked her life by making some twenty trips back to her state of birth to lead relatives and other slaves to freedom.

The top part of a typical broadside offering a reward for the capture of four runaway slaves. This was distributed in Mississippi County, Missouri, in 1852. The high reward for George, $1,000, suggests that he is an extremely valued worker.

The *Amistad*

In a few instances, large groups of slaves collectively seized their freedom. The most celebrated instance involved fifty-three slaves who in 1839 took control of **the *Amistad***, a ship transporting them from one port in Cuba to another, and tried to force the navigator to steer it to Africa. The *Amistad* wended its way up the Atlantic coast until an American vessel seized it off the coast of Long Island. President Martin Van Buren favored returning the slaves to Cuba. But abolitionists brought their case to the Supreme Court, where the former president John Quincy Adams argued that since

A painting depicting an incident in the Maroon War of 1795 on the island of Jamaica, when British troops were ambushed near a sugar plantation. Maroons were runaway slaves who established independent communities in the mountains, and fought to prevent being returned to slavery.

they had been recently brought from Africa in violation of international treaties banning the slave trade, the captives should be freed. The Court accepted Adams's reasoning, and most of the captives made their way back to Africa.

Success of Amistad *case*

The *Amistad* case had no legal bearing on slaves within the United States. But it may well have inspired a similar uprising in 1841, when 135 slaves being transported by sea from Norfolk, Virginia, to New Orleans seized control of the ship *Creole* and sailed for Nassau in the British Bahamas. Their leader had the evocative name Madison Washington. To the dismay of the Tyler administration, the British gave refuge to the *Creole* slaves.

Slave Revolts

Resistance to slavery occasionally moved beyond such individual and group acts of defiance to outright rebellion. The four largest conspiracies in American history occurred within the space of thirty-one years in the early nineteenth century. The first, organized by the Virginia slave Gabriel in 1800, was discussed in Chapter 8. It was followed eleven years later by an uprising on sugar plantations upriver from New Orleans. Somewhere between 200 and 500 men and women, armed with sugarcane knives, axes, clubs, and a few guns, marched toward the city, destroying property as they proceeded. The white population along the route fled in panic to

Uprising near New Orleans

New Orleans. Within two days, the militia and regular army troops met the rebels and dispersed them in a pitched battle, killing sixty-six.

The next major conspiracy was organized in 1822 by **Denmark Vesey,** a slave carpenter in Charleston, South Carolina, who had purchased his freedom after winning a local lottery. His conspiracy reflected the combination of American and African influences then circulating in the Atlantic world and coming together in black culture. "He studied the Bible a great deal," recalled one of his followers, "and tried to prove from it that slavery and bondage is against the Bible." Vesey also quoted the Declaration of Independence, pored over newspaper reports of the debates in Congress regarding the Missouri Compromise, and made pronouncements like "all men had equal rights, blacks as well as whites." And he read to his conspirators accounts of the successful slave revolution in Haiti. The African heritage was present in the person of Vesey's lieutenant Gullah Jack, a religious "conjurer" from Angola who claimed to be able to protect the rebels against injury or death. The plot was discovered before it could reach fruition.

Vesey's influences

As with many slave conspiracies, evidence about the Vesey plot is contradictory and disputed. Much of it comes from a series of trials in which the court operated in secret and failed to allow the accused to confront those who testified against them.

Nat Turner's Rebellion

The most prominent slave revolt

The best known of all slave rebels was Nat Turner, a slave preacher and religious mystic in Southampton County, Virginia, who came to believe that God had chosen him to lead a black uprising. Turner traveled widely in the county, conducting religious services. He told of seeing black and white angels fighting in the sky and the heavens running red with blood. Perhaps from a sense of irony, Turner initially chose July 4, 1831, for his rebellion, only to fall ill on the appointed day. On August 22, he and a handful of followers marched from farm to farm assaulting the white inhabitants. By the time the militia put down the uprising, about eighty slaves had joined Turner's band, and some sixty whites had been killed. Turner was subsequently captured and, with seventeen other rebels, condemned to die. Asked before his execution whether he regretted what he had done, Turner responded, "Was not Christ crucified?"

Panic among whites

Turner's rebellion sent shock waves through the entire South. "A Nat Turner," one white Virginian warned, "might be in any family." In the panic that followed the revolt, hundreds of innocent slaves were whipped, and scores executed. For one last time, Virginia's leaders openly debated whether steps ought to be taken to do away with the "peculiar institution." But a proposal to commit the state to gradual emancipation and the removal of the black population from the state failed to win legislative approval. The measure gained overwhelming support in the western part of Virginia, where slaves represented less than 10 percent of the population, but it failed to win sufficient votes in the eastern counties, where slavery was centered.

Instead of moving toward emancipation, the Virginia legislature of 1832 decided to fasten even more tightly the chains of bondage. New laws prohibited blacks, free or slave, from acting as preachers (a measure that proved impossible to enforce), strengthened the militia and patrol systems, banned free blacks from owning firearms, and prohibited teaching slaves to read. Other southern states followed suit.

In some ways, 1831 marked a turning point for the Old South. In that year, Parliament launched a program for abolishing slavery throughout the British empire (a process completed in 1838), underscoring the South's growing isolation in the Western world. Turner's rebellion, following only a few months after the appearance in Boston of William Lloyd Garrison's abolitionist journal, *The Liberator* (discussed in the next chapter), suggested that American slavery faced enemies both within and outside the South. The proslavery argument increasingly permeated southern intellectual and political life, while dissenting opinions were suppressed. Some states made membership in an abolitionist society a criminal offense, while mobs drove critics of slavery from their homes. The South's "great reaction" produced one of the most thoroughgoing suppressions of freedom of speech in American history. Even as reform movements arose in the North that condemned slavery as contrary to Christianity and to basic American values, and national debate over the peculiar institution intensified, southern society closed in defense of slavery.

An engraving depicting Nat Turner's slave rebellion of 1831, from a book published soon after the revolt.

A turning point

An intensifying debate

CHAPTER REVIEW AND ONLINE RESOURCES

REVIEW QUESTIONS

1. *Given that most northern states had abolished slavery by the 1830s, how is it useful to think of slavery as a national—rather than regional—economic and political system?*

2. *Although some poor southern whites resented the dominance of the "slavocracy," most supported the institution and accepted the power of the planter class. Why did the "plain folk" continue to support slavery?*

3. *How did the planters' paternalism serve to justify the system of slavery? How did it hide the reality of life for slaves?*

4. *Identify the basic elements of the proslavery defense and those points aimed especially at non-southern audiences.*

5. *Compare slaves in the Old South with those elsewhere in the world, focusing on health, diet, and opportunities for freedom.*

6. *Describe the difference between gang labor and task labor for slaves, and explain how slaves' tasks varied by region across the Old South.*

7. *How did enslaved people create community and a culture that allowed them to survive in an oppressive society?*

8. *Identify the different types of resistance to slavery. Which ones were the most common, the most effective, and the most demonstrative?*

KEY TERMS

the "peculiar institution" (p. 312)

Cotton Is King (p. 313)

Second Middle Passage (p. 314)

"plain folk" (p. 317)

paternalism (p. 318)

proslavery argument (p. 318)

slave family (p. 326)

slave religion (p. 328)

silent sabotage (p. 330)

Underground Railroad (p. 334)

Harriet Tubman (p. 334)

the *Amistad* (p. 334)

Denmark Vesey (p. 336)

Nat Turner's Rebellion (p. 336)

wwnorton.com /studyspace

VISIT STUDYSPACE FOR THESE RESOURCES AND MORE

- A chapter outline
- A diagnostic chapter quiz
- Interactive maps
- Map worksheets
- Multimedia documents

CHAPTER 12

AN AGE OF REFORM

★

1820–1840

1816 American Colonization Society founded

1825 Owenite community established at New Harmony, Indiana

1826 American Temperance Society founded

1827 First U.S. black newspaper, *Freedom's Journal*, established

1829 David Walker's *An Appeal to the Coloured Citizens of the World*

1833 American Anti-Slavery Society founded

1836 Congress adopts the "gag rule"

1837 Elijah Lovejoy killed

1845 Margaret Fuller's *Woman in the Nineteenth Century*

1848 John Humphrey Noyes founds Oneida, New York

Seneca Falls Convention held

1852 Harriet Beecher Stowe's *Uncle Tom's Cabin*

Frederick Douglass's speech "What, to the Slave, is the Fourth of July?"

1860 Tax-supported school systems established in all northern states

An abolitionist banner. Antislavery organizations adopted the Liberty Bell as a symbol of their campaign to extend freedom to black Americans. Previously, the bell, forged in Philadelphia in the eighteenth century, had simply been known as the Old State House Bell.

Among the many Americans who devoted their lives to the crusade against slavery, few were as selfless or courageous as Abby Kelley. As a teacher in Lynn, Massachusetts, she joined the Female Anti-Slavery Society and, like thousands of other northern women, threw herself into the abolitionist movement. In 1838, Kelley began to give public speeches about slavery. Her first lecture outside of Lynn was literally a baptism of fire. Enraged by reports that abolitionists favored "amalgamation" of the races—that is, sexual relations between whites and blacks—residents of Philadelphia stormed the meeting hall and burned it to the ground.

For two decades, Kelley traveled throughout the North, speaking almost daily in churches, public halls, and antislavery homes on "the holy cause of human rights." Her career illustrated the interconnections of the era's reform movements. In addition to abolitionism, she was active in pacifist organizations—which opposed the use of force, including war, to settle disputes—and was a pioneer in the early struggle for women's rights. She forthrightly challenged her era's assumption that woman's "place" was in the home. More than any other individual, remarked Lucy Stone, another women's rights advocate, Kelley "earned for us all the right of free speech."

Abby Kelley's private life was as unconventional as her public career. Happily married to the ardent abolitionist Stephen S. Foster, she gave birth to a daughter in 1847 but soon returned to lecturing. When criticized for not devoting herself to the care of her infant, Kelley replied: "I have done it for the sake of the mothers whose babies are sold away from them. The most precious legacy I can leave my child is a free country."

THE REFORM IMPULSE

"In the history of the world," wrote Ralph Waldo Emerson in 1841, "the doctrine of reform has never such hope as at the present hour." Abolitionism was only one of this era's numerous efforts to improve American society. Americans established voluntary organizations that worked to prevent the manufacture and sale of liquor, end public entertainments and the delivery of the mail on Sunday, improve conditions in prisons, expand public education, uplift the condition of wage laborers, and reorganize society on the basis of cooperation rather than competitive individualism.

Goals of reformers

Nearly all these groups worked to convert public opinion to their cause. They sent out speakers, gathered signatures on petitions, and published

A rare photograph of an abolitionist meeting in New York State around 1850. Frederick Douglass is to the left of the woman at the center.

pamphlets. Some reform movements, like restraining the consumption of liquor and alleviating the plight of the blind and insane, flourished through-out the nation. Others, including women's rights, labor unionism, and educational reform, were weak or nonexistent in the South, where they were widely associated with antislavery sentiment. Reform was an international crusade. Peace, temperance, women's rights, and antislavery advocates regularly crisscrossed the Atlantic to promote their cause.

Reformers adopted a wide variety of tactics to bring about social change. Some relied on "moral suasion" to convert people to their cause. Others, such as opponents of "demon rum," sought to use the power of the government to force sinners to change their ways. Some reformers decided to withdraw altogether from the larger society and establish their own cooperative settlements. They hoped to change American life by creating "heavens on earth," where they could demonstrate by example the superi-ority of a collective way of life.

Reform tactics

Utopian Communities

About 100 reform communities were established in the decades before the Civil War. Historians call them "utopian" after Thomas More's sixteenth-century novel *Utopia*, an outline of a perfect society. (The word has also

Thomas More

come to imply that such plans are impractical and impossible to realize.) Most communities arose from religious conviction, but others were inspired by the secular desire to counteract the social and economic changes set in motion by the market revolution.

Nearly all the communities set out to reorganize society on a cooperative basis, hoping to restore social harmony to a world of excessive individualism and to narrow the widening gap between rich and poor. Through their efforts, the words "socialism" and "communism," meaning a social organization in which productive property is owned by the community rather than private individuals, entered the language of politics. Most **utopian communities** also tried to find substitutes for conventional gender relations and marriage patterns. Some prohibited sexual relations between men and women altogether; others allowed them to change partners at will. But nearly all insisted that the abolition of private property must be accompanied by an end to men's "property" in women.

> *Social harmony*

In the first half of the nineteenth century, dozens of utopian communities were established in the United States, where small groups of men and women attempted to establish a more perfect social order within the larger society.

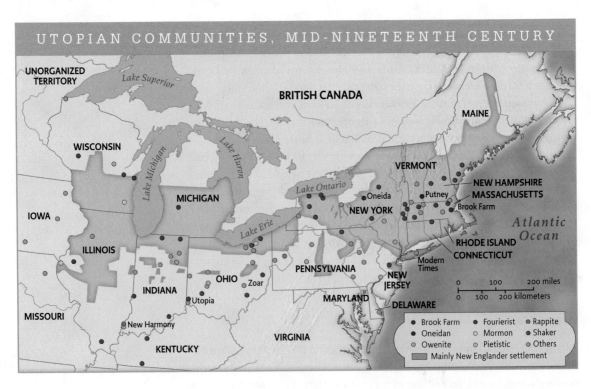

UTOPIAN COMMUNITIES, MID-NINETEENTH CENTURY

An engraving of a Shaker dance, drawn by Benson Lossing, an artist who visited a Shaker community and reported on life there for *Harper's Magazine* in 1857.

The Shakers

Religious communities attracted those who sought to find a retreat from a society permeated by sin. But the Shakers, the most successful of the religious communities, also had a significant impact on the outside world. At their peak during the 1840s, cooperative Shaker settlements, which stretched from Maine to Kentucky, included more than 5,000 members.

God, the Shakers believed, had a "dual" personality, both male and female, and thus the two sexes were spiritually equal. "Virgin purity" formed a pillar of the Shakers' faith. They completely abandoned traditional family life. Men and women lived separately in large dormitory-like structures and ate in communal dining rooms. They increased their numbers by attracting converts and adopting children from orphanages, rather than through natural increase. Although they rejected the individual accumulation of private property, the Shakers proved remarkably successful economically. They were among the first to market vegetable and flower seeds and herbal medicines commercially and to breed cattle for profit. Their beautifully crafted furniture is still widely admired today.

Shaker beliefs

Oneida

Another influential and controversial community was Oneida, founded in 1848 in upstate New York by John Humphrey Noyes, the Vermont-born son of a U.S. congressman. In 1836, Noyes and his followers formed a small

John Humphrey Noyes

"Complex marriage"

community in Putney, Vermont. His community became notorious for what Noyes called "complex marriage," whereby any man could propose sexual relations to any woman, who had the right to reject or accept his invitation, which would then be registered in a public record book. The great danger was "exclusive affections," which, Noyes felt, destroyed the harmony of the community.

After being indicted for adultery by local officials, Noyes in 1848 moved his community to Oneida, where it survived until 1881. Oneida was an extremely dictatorial environment. To become a member of the community, one had to demonstrate command of Noyes's religious teachings and live according to his rules.

Worldly Communities

To outside observers, utopian communities like Oneida seemed cases of "voluntary slavery." But because of their members' selfless devotion to the teachings and rules laid down by their leader, spiritually oriented communities often achieved remarkable longevity. The Shakers survived well into the twentieth century. Communities with a more worldly orientation tended to be beset by internal divisions and therefore lasted for much shorter periods.

The most important secular communitarian (meaning a person who plans or lives in a cooperative community) was Robert Owen, a British factory owner. Appalled by the degradation of workers in the early industrial revolution, Owen created a model factory village at New Lanark, Scotland, which combined strict rules of work discipline with comfortable housing and free public education. Around 1815, its 1,500 employees made New Lanark the largest center of cotton manufacturing in the world. In 1824, he purchased the Harmony community in Indiana—originally founded by the German Protestant religious leader George Rapp, who had emigrated to America with his followers at the beginning of the nineteenth century. Here, Owen established New Harmony, where he hoped to create a "new moral world."

In Owen's scheme, children would be removed at an early age from the care of their parents to be educated in schools where they would be trained to subordinate individual ambition to the common good. Owen also defended women's rights, especially access to education and the right to divorce. At New Harmony, he promised, women would no longer be "enslaved" to their husbands, and "false notions" about innate differences between the sexes would be abandoned.

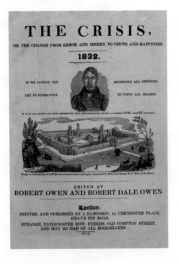

The Crisis, a publication by the communitarian Robert Owen and his son, Robert Dale Owen. The cover depicts Owen's vision of a planned socialist community.

Harmony eluded the residents of New Harmony. They squabbled about everything from the community's constitution to the distribution of property. Owen's settlement survived for only a few years, but it strongly influenced the labor movement, educational reformers, and women's rights advocates. Owen's vision resonated with the widely held American belief that a community of equals could be created in the New World.

Robert Owen's New Harmony

Religion and Reform

Most Americans saw the ownership of property as the key to economic independence—and, therefore, to freedom—and marriage as the foundation of the social order. Few were likely to join communities that required them to surrender both. Far more typical of the reform impulse were movements that aimed at liberating men and women either from restraints external to themselves, such as slavery and war, or from forms of internal "servitude" like drinking, illiteracy, and a tendency toward criminality. Many of these reform movements drew their inspiration from the religious revivalism of the Second Great Awakening, discussed in Chapter 9. If, as the revivalist preachers maintained, God had created man as a "free moral agent," sinners could not only reform themselves but could also remake the world.

Mainstream reform

The revivals popularized the outlook known as **"perfectionism,"** which saw both individuals and society at large as capable of indefinite improvement. Under the impact of the revivals, older reform efforts moved in a new, radical direction. **Temperance** (which literally means moderation in the consumption of liquor) was transformed into a crusade to eliminate drinking entirely. Criticism of war became outright pacifism. And, as will be related below, critics of slavery now demanded not gradual emancipation but immediate and total abolition.

A temperance banner from around 1850 depicts a young man torn between a woman in white, who illustrates female purity, and a temptress, who offers him a drink of liquor.

To members of the North's emerging middle-class culture, reform became a badge of respectability, an indication that individuals had taken control of their own lives and had become morally accountable human beings. The American Temperance Society, founded in 1826, directed its efforts to redeeming not only habitual drunkards but also the occasional drinker. It claimed by the 1830s to have persuaded hundreds of thousands of Americans to renounce liquor. By 1840, the consumption of alcohol per person had fallen to less than half the level of a decade earlier. (It had peaked in 1830 at seven gallons per person per year, compared with around two gallons today.)

Critics of Reform

Taverns

Many Americans saw the reform impulse as an attack on their own freedom. Taverns were popular meeting places for urban workingmen, sites not only of drinking but also of political discussions, organizational meetings, and recreation. Drinking was a prominent feature of festive celebrations and events like militia gatherings. A "Liberty Loving Citizen" of Worcester, Massachusetts, wondered what gave one group of citizens the right to dictate to others how to conduct their personal lives.

Catholics on reform

American Catholics, their numbers growing because of Irish and German immigration, proved hostile to the reform impulse. Catholics understood freedom in ways quite different from how Protestant reformers did. They viewed sin as an inescapable burden of individuals and society. The perfectionist idea that evil could be banished from the world struck them as an affront to genuine religion, and they bitterly opposed what they saw as reformers' efforts to impose their own version of Protestant morality on their neighbors. Whereas reformers spoke of man as a free moral agent, Catholics tended to place less emphasis on individual independence and more on the importance of communities centered on family and church.

Reformers and Freedom

Tension between liberation and control

Reformers had to reconcile their desire to create moral order and their quest to enhance personal freedom. They did this through a vision of freedom that was liberating and controlling at the same time. On the one hand, reformers insisted that their goal was to enable Americans to enjoy genuine liberty. In a world in which personal freedom increasingly meant the opportunity to compete for economic gain and individual self-improvement, they spoke of liberating Americans from various forms of "slavery" that made it impossible to succeed—slavery to drink, to poverty, to sin.

On the other hand, reformers insisted that self-fulfillment came through **self-discipline**. Their definition of the free individual was the person who internalized the practice of self-control. In some ways, reformers believed, American society suffered from an excess of liberty—the anarchic "natural liberty" John Winthrop had warned against in the early days of Puritan Massachusetts, as opposed to the "Christian liberty" of the morally upright citizen.

Many religious groups in the East worried that settlers in the West and immigrants from abroad lacked self-control and led lives of vice, exhibited by drinking, violations of the Sabbath, and lack of Protestant devotion. They formed the American Tract Society, the American Bible Society, and other groups that flooded eastern cities and the western frontier with copies of the gospel and pamphlets promoting religious virtue. Between 1825 and 1835, the pamphlets distributed by the Tract Society amounted to more than 500 million pages.

American Tract Society

The Invention of the Asylum

The tension between liberation and control in the era's reform movements was vividly evident in the proliferation of new institutions that reformers hoped could remake human beings into free, morally upright citizens. In colonial America, crime had mostly been punished by whipping, fines, or banishment. The poor received relief in their own homes, orphans lived with neighbors, and families took care of mentally ill members.

During the 1830s and 1840s, Americans embarked on a program of institution building—jails for criminals, poorhouses for the destitute, asylums for the insane, and orphanages for children without families. These institutions differed in many respects, but they shared with communitarians and religious believers in "perfectionism" the idea that social ills once considered incurable could in fact be eliminated. Prisons and **asylums** would eventually become overcrowded places where rehabilitating the inmates seemed less important than simply holding them at bay, away from society. At the outset, however, these institutions were inspired by the conviction that those who passed through their doors could eventually be released to become productive, self-disciplined citizens.

Reform institutions

The Common School

The largest effort at institution building before the Civil War came in the movement to establish **common schools**—that is, tax-supported state school systems open to all children. In the early nineteenth century, most children were educated in locally supported schools, private academies, charity schools, or at home. Many had no access to learning at all. School reform reflected the numerous purposes that came together in the era's reform impulse. Horace Mann, a Massachusetts lawyer and Whig politician who served as director of the state's board of education, was the era's leading educational reformer. He hoped that universal **public education** could restore equality to a fractured society by bringing the children of all classes together in a common learning experience and equipping the less fortunate to advance in the social scale.

Horace Mann

With labor organizations, factory owners, and middle-class reformers all supporting the idea, every northern state by 1860 had established tax-supported school systems for its children. The common-school movement created the first real career opportunity for women, who quickly came to dominate the ranks of teachers. The South, where literate blacks were increasingly viewed as a danger to social order and planters had no desire to tax themselves to pay for education for poor white children, lagged far behind in public education. This was one of many ways in which North and South seemed to be growing apart.

The rise of public education

THE CRUSADE AGAINST SLAVERY

Compared with drinking, Sabbath-breaking, and illiteracy, the greatest evil in American society at first appeared to attract the least attention from reformers. For many years, it seemed that the only Americans willing to challenge the existence of slavery were Quakers, slaves, and free blacks.

Colonization

Before the 1830s, those white Americans willing to contemplate an end to bondage almost always coupled calls for abolition with the "colonization" of freed slaves—their deportation to Africa, the Caribbean, or Central America. In 1816, proponents of this idea founded the **American Colonization Society**, which promoted the gradual abolition of slavery and the settlement of black Americans in Africa. It soon established Liberia on the coast of West Africa, an outpost of American influence whose capital, Monrovia, was named for President James Monroe.

Liberia

Colonization struck many observers as totally impractical. Nonetheless, numerous prominent political leaders of the Jacksonian era—including Henry Clay, John Marshall, Daniel Webster, and Jackson himself—supported the Colonization Society. Many colonizationists believed that slavery and racism were so deeply embedded in American life that blacks could never achieve equality if freed and allowed to remain in the country. Like Indian removal, colonization rested on the premise that America is fundamentally a white society.

Beliefs of colonizationists

In the decades before the Civil War, several thousand black Americans did emigrate to Liberia with the aid of the Colonization Society. Some were slaves emancipated by their owners on the condition that they depart, while others left voluntarily, motivated by a desire to spread Christianity in Africa or to enjoy rights denied them in the United States. Having experienced "the legal slavery of the South and the social slavery of the North," wrote one emigrant on leaving for Liberia, he knew he could "never be a free man in this country."

But most African-Americans adamantly opposed the idea of colonization. In fact, the formation of the American Colonization Society galvanized free blacks to claim their rights as Americans. Early in 1817, some 3,000 free blacks assembled in Philadelphia for the first national black convention. Their resolutions insisted that blacks were Americans, entitled to the same freedom and rights enjoyed by whites.

African-American responses to colonization

Militant Abolitionism

The abolitionist movement that arose in the 1830s differed profoundly from its genteel, conservative predecessor. Drawing on the religious conviction that slavery was an unparalleled sin and the secular one that it contradicted the values enshrined in the Declaration of Independence, a new generation of reformers rejected the traditional approach of gradual emancipation and demanded immediate abolition. Also unlike their predecessors, they directed explosive language against slavery and slaveholders and insisted that blacks, once free, should be incorporated as equal citizens of the republic rather than being deported. Perfecting American society, they insisted, meant rooting out not just slavery, but racism in all its forms.

Immediate abolition

The first indication of the new spirit of abolitionism came in 1829 with the appearance of *An Appeal to the Coloured Citizens of the World* by David Walker, a free black who had been born in North Carolina and now operated a used-clothing store in Boston. A passionate indictment of slavery and racial prejudice, the *Appeal* called on black Americans to mobilize for abolition—by force if necessary—and warned whites that the nation faced divine punishment if it did not mend its sinful ways. Walker called on blacks to take pride in the achievements of ancient African civilizations and to claim all their rights as Americans. "Tell us no more about colonization," Walker wrote, addressing white readers, "for America is as much our country as it is yours." Like other reformers, Walker used both secular and religious language. He warned that God would wreak vengeance on the United States for violating the principles of justice and heaped scorn on ministers who defended slavery for violating the golden rule espoused by Jesus Christ ("whatsoever ye would that men should do unto you, do yet even so unto them").

Walker died in mysterious circumstances in 1830. Not until the appearance in 1831 of *The Liberator*, William Lloyd Garrison's weekly

William Lloyd Garrison, editor of *The Liberator* and probably the nation's most prominent abolitionist, in a daguerreotype from around 1850.

journal published in Boston, did the new breed of abolitionism find a permanent voice. "I will be as harsh as truth," Garrison announced, "and as uncompromising as justice. On this subject, I do not wish to think, or speak, or write, with moderation. . . . I will not equivocate—I will not excuse—I will not retreat a single inch—and I will be heard."

And heard he was. Some of Garrison's ideas, such as his suggestion that the North abrogate the Constitution and dissolve the Union to end its complicity in the evil of slavery, were rejected by many abolitionists. But his call for the immediate abolition of slavery echoed throughout antislavery circles. Garrison's pamphlet, *Thoughts on African Colonization*, persuaded many foes of slavery that blacks must be recognized as part of American society, not viewed as aliens to be shipped overseas.

Garrison's Thoughts on African Colonization

Spreading the Abolitionist Message

Beginning with a handful of activists, the abolitionist movement expanded rapidly throughout the North. Antislavery leaders took advantage of the rapid development of print technology and the expansion of literacy due to common-school education to spread their message. Like radical pamphleteers of the American Revolution and evangelical ministers of the Second Great Awakening, they recognized the democratic potential

Pamphlets, broadsides, newspapers

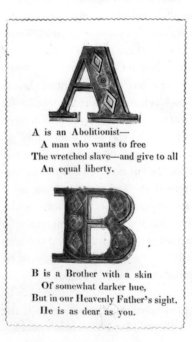

A is an Abolitionist—
A man who wants to free
The wretched slave—and give to all
An equal liberty.

B is a Brother with a skin
Of somewhat darker hue,
But in our Heavenly Father's sight,
He is as dear as you.

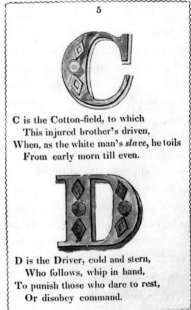

C is the Cotton-field, to which
This injured brother's driven,
When, as the white man's *slave*, he toils
From early morn till even.

D is the Driver, cold and stern,
Who follows, whip in hand,
To punish those who dare to rest,
Or disobey command.

Pages from an abolitionist book for children. Abolitionists sought to convince young and old of the evils of slavery.

in the production of printed material. Abolitionists seized on the recently invented steam printing press to produce millions of copies of pamphlets, newspapers, petitions, novels, and broadsides. Between the formation of the **American Anti-Slavery Society** in 1833 and the end of the decade, some 100,000 northerners joined local groups devoted to abolition. Most were ordinary citizens—farmers, shopkeepers, craftsmen, laborers, along with a few prominent businessmen like the merchants Arthur and Lewis Tappan of New York.

If Garrison was the movement's most notable propagandist, Theodore Weld, a young minister who had been converted by the evangelical preacher Charles G. Finney, helped to create its mass constituency. A brilliant orator, Weld trained a band of speakers who brought the abolitionist message into the heart of the rural and small-town North. Their methods were those of the revivalists—fervent preaching, lengthy meetings, calls for individuals to renounce their immoral ways—and their message was a simple one: slavery was a sin.

Theodore Weld

Slavery and Moral Suasion

Many southerners feared that the abolitionists intended to spark a slave insurrection, a belief strengthened by the outbreak of Nat Turner's Rebellion a few months after *The Liberator* made its appearance. Yet not only was Garrison completely unknown to Turner, but nearly all abolitionists, despite their militant language, rejected violence as a means of ending

Slave Market of America, an engraving produced by the American Anti-Slavery Society in 1836, illustrates how abolitionists sought to identify their cause with American traditions, even as they mocked the nation's claim to be a "land of the free."

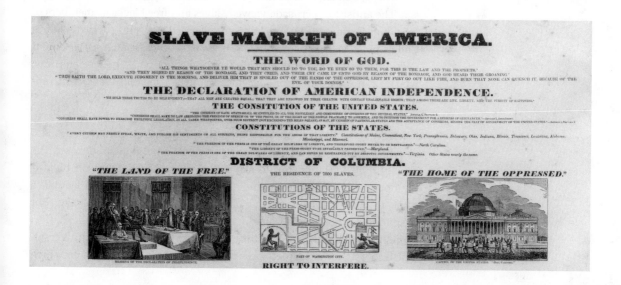

slavery. Many were pacifists or "non-resistants," who believed that coercion should be eliminated from all human relationships and institutions. Their strategy was "**moral suasion**" and their arena the public sphere. Slaveholders must be convinced of the sinfulness of their ways, and the North of its complicity in the peculiar institution.

Among the first to appreciate the key role of public opinion in a mass democracy, abolitionists focused their efforts not on infiltrating the existing political parties, but on awakening the nation to the moral evil of slavery. Their language was deliberately provocative, calculated to seize public attention. "Slavery," said Garrison, "will not be overthrown without excitement, without a most tremendous excitement." Abolitionists argued that slavery was so deeply embedded in American life that its destruction would require fundamental changes in the North as well as the South. They insisted that the inherent, natural, and absolute right to personal liberty, regardless of race, took precedence over other forms of freedom, such as the right of citizens to accumulate and hold property or self-government by local political communities.

Awakening the nation

A New Vision of America

An American people unbounded by race

In a society in which the rights of citizenship had become more and more closely associated with whiteness, the antislavery movement sought to reinvigorate the idea of freedom as a truly universal entitlement. The origins of the idea of an American people unbounded by race lies not with the founders, who by and large made their peace with slavery, but with the abolitionists. The antislavery crusade viewed slaves and free blacks as members of the national community, a position summarized in the title of Lydia Maria Child's popular treatise of 1833, *An Appeal in Favor of That Class of Americans Called Africans*. The idea that birthplace alone, not race, should determine who was an American, later enshrined in the Fourteenth Amendment, represented a radical departure from the traditions of American life.

Angelina Grimké

The crusade against slavery, wrote Angelina Grimké, who became a leading abolitionist speaker, was the nation's preeminent "school in which human rights are . . . investigated." Abolitionists debated the Constitution's relationship to slavery. William Lloyd Garrison burned the document, calling it a covenant with the devil; Frederick Douglass came to believe that it offered no national protection to slavery. But despite this difference of opinion, abolitionists developed an alternative, rights-oriented view of constitutional law, grounded in their universalistic understanding of liberty. Seeking to define the core rights to which all Americans were entitled—the meaning of freedom in concrete legal terms—abolitionists invented the concept of equality before the law regardless of race, one all but unknown in American life before the Civil War. Abolitionist literature also helped to expand the definition of cruelty. The graphic descriptions of the beatings, brandings, and other physical sufferings of the slaves helped to popularize the idea of bodily integrity as a basic right that slavery violated.

Abolitionism and the Constitution

Despite being denounced by their opponents as enemies of American principles, abolitionists consciously identified their movement with the revolutionary heritage. The Declaration of Independence was not as fundamental to public oratory in the early republic as it would later become. Abolitionists seized upon it, interpreting the document's preamble as a condemnation of slavery. The Liberty Bell, later one of the nation's most venerated emblems of freedom, did not achieve that status until abolitionists adopted it as a symbol and gave it its name as part of an effort to identify their principles with those of the founders. Of course, Americans of all regions and political beliefs claimed the Revolution's legacy. Abolitionists never represented more than a small part of the North's population. But as the slavery controversy intensified, the belief spread far beyond abolitionist circles that slavery contradicted the nation's heritage of freedom.

Abolitionism and the revolutionary heritage

BLACK AND WHITE ABOLITIONISM

Black Abolitionists

Blacks played a leading role in the antislavery movement. Frederick Douglass was only one among many former slaves who published accounts of their lives in bondage; these accounts convinced thousands of northerners of the evils of slavery. Indeed, the most effective piece of antislavery literature of the entire period, Harriet Beecher Stowe's novel *Uncle Tom's Cabin*, was to some extent modeled on the autobiography of the fugitive slave Josiah Henson. Serialized in 1851 in a Washington antislavery newspaper and published as a book the following year, **Uncle Tom's Cabin** sold more than 1 million copies by 1854, and it also inspired numerous stage versions. By portraying slaves as sympathetic men and women, and as Christians at the mercy of slaveholders who split up families and set bloodhounds on innocent mothers and children, Stowe's melodrama gave the abolitionist message a powerful human appeal.

One of many popular lithographs illustrating scenes from Harriet Beecher Stowe's novel *Uncle Tom's Cabin*, the most widely read of all antislavery writings. This depicts the slave Eliza escaping with her child across the ice floes of the Ohio River.

PERILOUS ESCAPE OF ELIZA AND CHILD

By the 1840s, black abolitionists sought an independent role within the movement, regularly holding their own conventions. The black abolitionist Henry Highland Garnet, who as a child had escaped from slavery in Maryland with his father, proclaimed at one such gathering in 1843 that slaves should rise in rebellion to throw off their shackles. His position was so at odds with the prevailing belief in moral suasion that the published proceedings entirely omitted the speech.

At every opportunity, black abolitionists rejected the nation's pretensions as a land of liberty. Free black communities in the North devised an alternative calendar of "freedom celebrations" centered on January 1, the date in 1808 on which the slave trade became illegal, and August 1, the anniversary of West Indian emancipation, rather than July 4. In doing so, they offered a stinging rebuke to white Americans' claims to live in a land of freedom.

Color-blind citizenship

Even more persistently than their white counterparts, black abolitionists articulated the ideal of color-blind citizenship. "The real battleground between liberty and slavery," wrote Samuel Cornish, "is prejudice against color." (Cornish, a Presbyterian minister, had helped to establish the nation's first black newspaper, *Freedom's Journal*, in New York City in 1827. The first editor, John B. Russwurm, closed the paper after two years and moved to Liberia, explaining, "we consider it a waste of mere words to talk of ever enjoying citizenship in this country.")

Frederick Douglass's Fourth of July speech

The greatest oration on American slavery and American freedom was delivered in Rochester in 1852 by Frederick Douglass. Speaking just after the annual Independence Day celebration, Douglass posed the question, "What, to the Slave, is the Fourth of July?" He answered that Fourth of July festivities revealed the hypocrisy of a nation that proclaimed its belief in liberty yet daily committed "practices more shocking and bloody" than did any other country on earth. Like other abolitionists, however, Douglass also laid claim to the founders' legacy. The Revolution had left a "rich inheritance of justice, liberty, prosperity, and independence" from which subsequent generations had tragically strayed. Only by abolishing slavery and freeing the "great doctrines" of the Declaration of Independence from the "narrow bounds" of race could the United States recapture its original mission.

Gentlemen of Property and Standing

Opposition to abolitionism

At first, abolitionism aroused violent hostility from northerners who feared that the movement threatened to disrupt the Union, interfere with profits wrested from slave labor, and overturn white supremacy. Led by "**gentlemen of property and standing**" (often merchants with close commercial ties to the South), mobs disrupted abolitionist meetings in northern cities.

Destruction by Fire of Pennsylvania Hall, a lithograph depicting the burning of the abolitionist meeting hall by a Philadelphia mob in 1838.

In 1837, antislavery editor Elijah P. Lovejoy became the movement's first martyr when he was killed by a mob in Alton, Illinois, while defending his press. In 1838, a mob in Philadelphia burned to the ground Pennsylvania Hall, which abolitionists had built to hold their meetings. Before starting the fire, however, the mob patriotically carried a portrait of George Washington to safety.

Elijah P. Lovejoy

Elsewhere, crowds of southerners, with the unspoken approval of Andrew Jackson's postmaster general, Amos Kendall, burned abolitionist literature that they had removed from the mails. In 1836, when abolitionists began to flood Washington with petitions calling for emancipation in the nation's capital, the House of Representatives adopted the notorious "**gag rule**," which prohibited their consideration. The rule was repealed in 1844, thanks largely to the tireless opposition of former president John Quincy Adams, who since 1831 had represented Massachusetts in the House.

Far from stemming the movement's growth, however, mob attacks and attempts to limit abolitionists' freedom of speech convinced many northerners that slavery was incompatible with the democratic liberties of white Americans. "We commenced the present struggle," announced abolitionist William Jay, "to obtain the freedom of the slave; we are compelled to continue it to preserve our own. We are now contending . . . for the liberty of speech, of the press, and of conscience."

The abolitionist movement now broadened its appeal so as to win the support of northerners who cared little about the rights of blacks but could be convinced that slavery endangered their own cherished freedoms. The gag rule aroused considerable resentment in the North. "If the government

Am I Not a Man and a Brother? The most common abolitionist depiction of a slave, this image not only presents African-Americans as unthreatening individuals seeking white assistance but also calls upon white Americans to recognize blacks as fellow men unjustly held in bondage.

once begins to discriminate as to what is orthodox and what heterodox in opinion," wrote the *New York Evening Post*, hardly a supporter of abolitionism, "farewell, a long farewell to our freedom."

THE ORIGINS OF FEMINISM

The Rise of the Public Woman

Northern women in abolitionism

"When the true history of the antislavery cause shall be written," Frederick Douglass later recalled, "women will occupy a large space in its pages." Much of the movement's grassroots strength derived from northern women, who joined by the thousands. Most were evangelical Protestants, New England Congregationalists, or Quakers convinced, as Martha Higginson of Vermont wrote, that slavery was "a disgrace in this land of Christian light and liberty."

Women and politics

The public sphere was open to women in ways government and party politics were not. Women's letters and diaries reveal a keen interest in political issues, from slavery to presidential campaigns. Long before they could vote, women circulated petitions, attended mass meetings, marched in political parades, delivered public lectures, and raised money for political causes. They became active in the temperance movement, the building of asylums, and other reform activities. **Dorothea Dix**, a Massachusetts schoolteacher, for example, was the leading advocate of more humane treatment of the insane, who at the time generally were placed in jails alongside debtors and hardened criminals. Thanks to her efforts, twenty-eight states constructed mental hospitals before the Civil War.

Women and Free Speech

Abolitionism and women's rights

All these activities enabled women to carve out a place in the public sphere. But it was participation in abolitionism that inspired the early movement for women's rights. In working for the rights of the slave, not a few women developed a new understanding of their own subordinate social and legal status. The daughters of a prominent South Carolina slaveholder, Angelina and Sarah Grimké had been converted first to Quakerism and then abolitionism while visiting Philadelphia. During the 1830s, they began to deliver popular lectures that offered a scathing condemnation of slavery from the perspective of those who had witnessed its evils firsthand.

Outraged by the sight of females sacrificing all "modesty and delicacy" by appearing on the public lecture platform, a group of Massachusetts clergymen denounced the sisters. In reply, they forthrightly defended not only the right of women to take part in political debate but also their right to share the social and educational privileges enjoyed by men. "Since I engaged in the investigation of the rights of the slave," declared Angelina Grimké, "I have necessarily been led to a better understanding of my own." Her sister Sarah proceeded to publish *Letters on the Equality of the Sexes* (1838), a powerful call for equal rights for women and a critique of the notion of separate spheres. The book raised numerous issues familiar even today, including what later generations would call "equal pay for equal work." Why, Sarah Grimké wondered, did male teachers invariably receive higher wages than women, and a male tailor earn "two or three times as much" as a female counterpart "although the work done by each may be equally good?"

The Grimké sisters

Women's Rights

The Grimké sisters were the first to apply the abolitionist doctrine of universal freedom and equality to the status of women. Although they soon retired from the fray, unwilling to endure the intense criticism to which they were subjected, their writings helped to spark the movement for women's rights, which arose in the 1840s.

Elizabeth Cady Stanton and Lucretia Mott, the key organizers of the Seneca Falls Convention of 1848, were veterans of the antislavery crusade. In 1840, they had traveled to London as delegates to the World Anti-Slavery Convention, only to be barred from participating because of their sex. The Seneca Falls Convention, a gathering on behalf of women's rights held in the upstate New York town where Stanton lived, raised the issue of **woman suffrage** for the first time. Stanton, the principal author, modeled the Seneca Falls Declaration of Sentiments on the Declaration of Independence (see the Appendix for the full text). But the document added "women" to Jefferson's axiom "all men are created equal," and in place of a list of injustices committed by George III, it condemned the "injuries and usurpations on the part of man toward woman." The first to be listed was denying her the right to vote. As Stanton told the convention, only the vote would make woman "free as man is free," since in a democratic society, freedom was impossible without access to the ballot. The argument was simple and irrefutable: in the words of Lydia Maria Child, "either the theory of our government [the democratic principle that government rests on the will of the people] is *false*, or women have a right to vote."

The Seneca Falls Convention

The Declaration of Sentiments

Seneca Falls marked the beginning of the seventy-year struggle for woman suffrage. The vote, however, was hardly the only issue raised at the convention. The Declaration of Sentiments condemned the entire structure of inequality that denied women access to education and employment, gave husbands control over the property and wages of their wives and custody of children in the event of divorce, deprived women of independent legal status after they married, and restricted them to the home as their "sphere of action." Equal rights became the rallying cry of the early movement for women's rights, and equal rights meant claiming access to all the prevailing definitions of freedom.

Feminism and Freedom

Like abolitionism, temperance, and other reforms, women's rights was an international movement. Lacking broad backing at home, early feminists found allies abroad. "Women alone will say what freedom they want," declared an article in *The Free Woman*, a journal established in Paris in 1832.

Women, wrote Margaret Fuller, had the same right as men to develop their talents, to "grow . . . to live freely and unimpeded." The daughter of a Jeffersonian congressman, Fuller was educated at home, at first under her father's supervision (she learned Latin before the age of six) and later on her own. She became part of New England's transcendentalist circle (discussed in Chapter 9) and from 1840 to 1842 edited *The Dial*, a magazine that reflected the group's views. In 1844, Fuller became literary editor of the *New York Tribune*, the first woman to achieve so important a position in American journalism.

Margaret Fuller

In **Woman in the Nineteenth Century**, published in 1845, Fuller sought to apply to women the transcendentalist idea that freedom meant a quest for personal development. "Every path" to self-fulfillment, she insisted, should be "open to woman as freely as to man." Fuller traveled to Europe as a correspondent for the *Tribune*, and there she married an Italian patriot. Along with her husband and baby, she died in a shipwreck in 1850 while returning to the United States.

Portrait of feminist Margaret Fuller (1810–1850) from an undated daguerreotype.

Women and Work

Women also demanded the right to participate in the market revolution. At an 1851 women's rights convention, the black abolitionist Sojourner Truth insisted that the movement devote attention to the plight of poor and working-class women and repudiate the idea that women were too delicate to engage in work outside the home. Born a slave in New York State around 1799, Truth did not obtain her freedom until the state's emancipation law of 1827. A listener at her 1851 speech (which was not recorded at the time) later recalled that Truth had spoken of her years of hard physical labor, had flexed her arm to show her strength, and exclaimed, "and aren't I a woman?"

Although those who convened at Seneca Falls were predominantly from the middle class—no representatives of the growing number of "factory girls" and domestic servants took part— the participants rejected the identification of the home as the women's "sphere." During the 1850s, some feminists tried to popularize a new style of dress, devised by Amelia Bloomer, consisting of a loose-fitting tunic and trousers. The target of innumerable male jokes, the "bloomer" costume attempted to make a serious point—that the long dresses, tight corsets, and numerous petticoats considered to be appropriate female attire were so confining that they made it almost impossible for women to claim a place in the public sphere or to work outside the home.

Woman's Emancipation, a satirical engraving from *Harper's Monthly*, August 1851, illustrating the much-ridiculed "Bloomer" costume.

The Slavery of Sex

The dichotomy between freedom and slavery powerfully shaped early feminists' political language. Just as the idea of "wage slavery" enabled northern workers to challenge the inequalities inherent in market definitions of freedom, the concept of the **"slavery of sex"** empowered the women's movement to develop an all-encompassing critique of male authority and their own subordination. Feminists of the 1840s and 1850s pointed out that the law of marriage made nonsense of the description of the family as a "private" institution independent of public authority. When the abolitionists and women's rights activists Lucy Stone and Henry Blackwell married, they felt obliged to repudiate New York's laws that clothed the husband "with legal powers which . . . no man should possess." The analogy between free women and slaves gained prominence as it was swept up in the accelerating debate over slavery. For their part, southern defenders of slavery frequently linked slavery and marriage as natural and just forms of inequality. Eliminating the former institution, they charged, would threaten the latter.

Feminists and marriage

VOICES OF FREEDOM

From Angelina Grimké, Letter in
The Liberator (August 2, 1837)

The daughters of a prominent South Carolina slaveholder, Angelina and Sarah Grimké became abolitionists after being sent to Philadelphia for education. In this article, Angelina Grimké explains how participation in the movement against slavery led her to a greater recognition of women's lack of basic freedoms.

Since I engaged in the investigation of the rights of the slave, I have necessarily been led to a better understanding of my own; for I have found the Anti-Slavery cause to be . . . the school in which human rights are more fully investigated, and better understood and taught, than in any other [reform] enterprise. . . . Here we are led to examine why human beings have any rights. It is because they are moral beings. . . . Now it naturally occurred to me, that if rights were founded in moral being, then the circumstance of sex could not give to man higher rights and responsibilities, than to woman. . . .

When I look at human beings as moral beings, all distinction in sex sinks to insignificance and nothingness; for I believe it regulates rights and responsibilities no more than the color of the skin or the eyes. My doctrine, then is, that whatever it is morally right for man to do, it is morally right for woman to do. . . . This regulation of duty by the mere circumstance of sex . . . has led to all that [numerous] train of evils flowing out of the anti-christian doctrine of masculine and feminine virtues. By this doctrine, man has been converted into the warrior, and clothed in sternness . . . whilst woman has been taught to lean upon an arm of flesh, to . . . be admired for her personal charms, and caressed and humored like a spoiled child, or converted into a mere drudge to suit the convenience of her lord and master. . . . It has robbed woman of . . . the right to think and speak and act on all great moral questions, just as men think and speak and act. . . .

The discussion of the wrongs of slavery has opened the way for the discussion of other rights, and the ultimate result will most certainly be . . . the letting of the oppressed of every grade and description go free.

From Frederick Douglass, Speech on July 5, 1852, Rochester, New York

One of the most prominent reform leaders of his era, Frederick Douglass escaped from slavery in 1838 and soon became an internationally known writer and orator against slavery. His speech of July 1852 condemned the hypocrisy of a nation that proclaimed its devotion to freedom while practicing slavery. It was reprinted in 1855 in his autobiography, *My Bondage and My Freedom*.

Fellow-citizens, pardon me, allow me to ask, why am I called upon to speak here to-day? What have I, or those I represent, to do with your national independence? Are the great principles of political freedom and of natural justice, embodied in that Declaration of Independence, extended to us? . . . Such is not the case. I say it with a sad sense of the disparity between us. I am not included within the pale of this glorious anniversary! Your high independence only reveals the immeasurable distance between us. . . . The rich inheritance of justice, liberty, prosperity and independence, bequeathed by your fathers, is shared by you, not by me. . . .

For the present, it is enough to affirm the equal manhood of the negro race. Is it not astonishing that, while we are ploughing, planting and reaping, using all kinds of mechanical tools, erecting houses, constructing bridges, building ships, . . . acting as clerks, merchants and secretaries . . . confessing and worshiping the Christian's God, and looking hopefully for life and immortality beyond the grave, we are called upon to prove that we are men! . . .

Would you have me argue that man is entitled to liberty? That he is the rightful owner of his body? You have already declared it. Must I argue the wrongfulness of slavery? . . . that men have a natural right to freedom? . . . To do so, would be to make myself ridiculous, and to offer an insult to your understanding. There is not a man beneath the canopy of heaven, that does not know that slavery is wrong *for him*. . . .

What, to the American slave, is your 4th of July? I answer: a day that reveals to him, more than all other days in the year, the gross injustice and cruelty to which he is the constant victim. To him, your celebration is a sham; your boasted liberty, an unholy license; your national greatness, swelling vanity; your sounds of rejoicing are empty and heartless; your denunciations of tyrants, brass fronted impudence; your shouts of liberty and equality, hollow mockery—a thin veil to cover up crimes that would disgrace a nation of savages. There is not a nation on the earth guilty of practices, more shocking and bloody, than are the people of these United States, at this very hour.

QUESTIONS

1. *What consequences does Grimké believe follow from the idea of rights being founded in the individual's "moral being"?*

2. *How does Douglass turn the ideals proclaimed by white Americans into weapons against slavery?*

3. *What do these documents suggest about the language and arguments employed by abolitionists?*

Marriage was not, literally speaking, equivalent to slavery. The married woman, however, did not enjoy the fruits of her own labor—a central element of freedom. Beginning with Mississippi in 1839, numerous states enacted married women's property laws, shielding from a husband's creditors property brought into a marriage by his wife. Such laws initially aimed not to expand women's rights so much as to prevent families from losing their property during the depression that began in 1837. But in 1860, New York enacted a more far-reaching measure, allowing married women to sign contracts, buy and sell property, and keep their own wages. In most states, however, property accumulated after marriage, as well as wages earned by the wife, still belonged to the husband.

Married women's property and the law

"Social Freedom"

Influenced by abolitionism, women's rights advocates turned another popular understanding of freedom—self-ownership, or control over one's own person—in an entirely new direction. The law of domestic relations presupposed the husband's right of sexual access to his wife and to inflict corporal punishment on her. Courts proved reluctant to intervene in cases of physical abuse so long as it was not "extreme" or "intolerable." "Women's Rights," declared a Boston meeting in 1859, included "freedom and equal rights in the family." The demand that women should enjoy the rights to regulate their own sexual activity and procreation and to be protected by the state against violence at the hands of their husbands challenged the notion that claims for justice, freedom, and individual rights should stop at the household's door.

Rights within the family

The issue of women's private freedom revealed underlying differences within the movement for women's rights. Belief in equality between the sexes and in the sexes' natural differences coexisted in antebellum feminist thought. Even as they entered the public sphere and thereby challenged some aspects of the era's "cult of domesticity" (discussed in Chapter 9), many early feminists accepted other elements. Allowing women a greater role in the public sphere, many female reformers argued, would bring their "inborn" maternal instincts to bear on public life, to the benefit of the entire society.

Even feminists critical of the existing institution of marriage generally refrained from raising in public the explosive issue of women's "private" freedom. Not until the twentieth century would the demand that freedom be extended to intimate aspects of life inspire a mass movement. But the dramatic fall in the birthrate over the course of the nineteenth century

Women's private freedom

suggests that many women were quietly exercising "personal freedom" in their most intimate relationships.

The Abolitionist Schism

Even in reform circles, the demand for a greater public role for women remained extremely controversial. Massachusetts physician Samuel Gridley Howe pioneered humane treatment of the blind and educational reform, and he was an ardent abolitionist. But Howe did not support his wife's participation in the movement for female suffrage, which, he complained, caused her to "neglect domestic relations." When organized abolitionism split into two wings in 1840, the immediate cause was a dispute over the proper role of women in antislavery work. Abby Kelley's appointment to the business committee of the American Anti-Slavery Society sparked the formation of a rival abolitionist organization, the American and Foreign Anti-Slavery Society, which believed it wrong for a woman to occupy so prominent a position. The antislavery poet John Greenleaf Whittier compared Kelley to Eve, Delilah, and Helen of Troy, women who had sown the seeds of male destruction.

> *The role of women in abolitionism*

Behind the split lay the fear among some abolitionists that Garrison's radicalism on issues like women's rights, as well as his refusal to support the idea of abolitionists voting or running for public office, impeded

This image appeared on the cover of the sheet music for "Get Off the Track!", a song popularized by the Hutchinson singers, who performed antislavery songs. The trains *Immediate Emancipation* (with *The Liberator* as its front wheel) and *Liberty Party* pull into a railroad station. *The Herald of Freedom* and *American Standard* were antislavery newspapers. The song's lyrics praised William Lloyd Garrison and criticized various politicians, among them Henry Clay. The chorus went: "Roll it along! Through the nation / Freedom's car, Emancipation."

the movement's growth. Determined to make abolitionism a political movement, the seceders formed the **Liberty Party**, which nominated James G. Birney as its candidate for president. He received only 7,000 votes (about one-third of 1 percent of the total). In 1840, antislavery northerners saw little wisdom in "throwing away" their ballots on a third-party candidate.

Achievements of feminism and abolitionism

Although the achievement of most of their demands lay far in the future, the women's rights movement succeeded in making "the woman question" a permanent part of the transatlantic discussion of social reform. As for abolitionism, although it remained a significant presence in northern public life until emancipation was achieved, by 1840 the movement had accomplished its most important work. More than 1,000 local antislavery societies were now scattered throughout the North, representing a broad constituency awakened to the moral issue of slavery. The "great duty of freedom," Ralph Waldo Emerson had declared in 1837, was "to open our halls to discussion of this question." The abolitionists' greatest achievement lay in shattering the conspiracy of silence that had sought to preserve national unity by suppressing public debate over slavery.

CHAPTER REVIEW AND ONLINE RESOURCES

REVIEW QUESTIONS

1. How did the utopian communities challenge existing ideas about property and marriage?

2. How did the supporters and opponents of temperance understand the meaning of freedom differently?

3. What were the similarities and differences between the common school and the institutions like asylums, orphanages, and prisons that were created by reformers?

4. Why did so many prominent white Americans, from both the North and South, support the colonization of freed slaves?

5. How was the abolition movement affected by other social and economic changes such as the rise in literacy, new print technology, and ideas associated with the market revolution?

6. How was racism evident even in the abolitionist movement? What steps did some abolitionists take to fight racism in American society?

7. How could antebellum women participate in the public sphere even though they were excluded from government and politics?

8. How did white women's participation in the abolitionist movement push them to a new understanding of their own rights and oppression?

9. How did advocates for women's rights in these years both accept and challenge existing gender beliefs and social roles?

10. To what degree was antebellum reform international in scope?

KEY TERMS

utopian communities (p. 342)

"perfectionism" (p. 345)

temperance (p. 345)

self-discipline (p. 346)

asylums (p. 347)

common schools (p. 347)

public education (p. 347)

American Colonization Society (p. 348)

American Anti-Slavery Society (p. 351)

"moral suasion" (p. 352)

Uncle Tom's Cabin (p. 353)

"gentlemen of property and standing" (p. 354)

"Am I Not a Man and a Brother?" (p. 355)

gag rule (p. 355)

Dorothea Dix (p. 356)

woman suffrage (p. 357)

Woman in the Nineteenth Century (p. 358)

"slavery of sex" (p. 359)

Liberty Party (p. 364)

wwnorton.com
/studyspace

VISIT STUDYSPACE FOR THESE RESOURCES AND MORE

- A chapter outline
- A diagnostic chapter quiz
- Interactive maps
- Map worksheets
- Multimedia documents

1820	Moses Austin receives Mexican land grant
1836	Texas independence from Mexico
1845	Inauguration of James Polk
	United States annexes Texas
1846–1848	Mexican War
1846	Wilmot Proviso
1848	Treaty of Guadalupe Hidalgo
	Gold discovered in California
	Free Soil Party organized
1849	Inauguration of Zachary Taylor
1850	Compromise of 1850
	Fugitive Slave Act
1853	Inauguration of Franklin Pierce
1854	Kansas-Nebraska Act
	Know-Nothing Party established
	Ostend Manifesto
	Republican Party organized
1856	"Bleeding Kansas"
1857	Inauguration of James Buchanan
	Dred Scott decision
1858	Lincoln-Douglas debates
1859	John Brown's raid on Harpers Ferry
1860	South Carolina secedes
1861	Inauguration of Abraham Lincoln
	Fort Sumter fired on

Abraham Lincoln's nickname, "The Railsplitter," recalled his humble origins. An unknown artist created this larger-than-life portrait. The White House is visible in the distance. The painting is said to have been displayed during campaign rallies in 1860.

CHAPTER 13

A HOUSE DIVIDED

★

1840-1861

In 1855, Thomas Crawford, one of the era's most prominent American sculptors, was asked to design a statue to adorn the Capitol's dome, still under construction in Washington, D.C. He proposed a statue of Freedom, a female figure wearing a liberty cap. Secretary of War Jefferson Davis of Mississippi, one of the country's largest slaveholders, objected to Crawford's plan. Ancient Romans, he noted, regarded the cap as "the badge of the freed slave." Its use, he feared, might suggest that there was a connection between the slaves' longing for freedom and the liberty of freeborn Americans. Davis ordered the liberty cap replaced with a less controversial military symbol, a feathered helmet.

In 1863, the colossal Statue of Freedom was installed atop the Capitol, where it can still be seen today. By the time it was put in place, the country was immersed in the Civil War and Jefferson Davis had become president of the Confederate States of America. The dispute over the Statue of Freedom offers a small illustration of how, by the mid-1850s, nearly every public question was being swept up into the gathering storm over slavery.

FOCUS QUESTIONS

• *What were the major factors contributing to U.S. territorial expansion in the 1840s?*

• *Why did the expansion of slavery become the most divisive political issue in the 1840s and 1850s?*

• *What combination of issues and events fueled the creation of the Republican Party in the 1850s?*

• *What enabled Lincoln to emerge from the divisive party politics of the 1850s?*

• *What were the final steps on the road to secession?*

The original and final designs for Thomas Crawford's *Statue of Freedom* for the dome of the Capitol building. Secretary of War Jefferson Davis of Mississippi insisted that the liberty cap in the first design, a symbol of the emancipated slave in ancient Rome, be replaced.

FRUITS OF MANIFEST DESTINY

Continental Expansion

In the 1840s, slavery moved to the center stage of American politics. It did so not in the moral language or with the immediatist program of abolitionism, but as a result of the nation's territorial expansion. Between 1840 and 1860, nearly 300,000 men, women, and children had braved disease, starvation, the natural barrier of the Rocky Mountains, and occasional Indian attacks to travel overland to Oregon and California.

During most of the 1840s, the United States and Great Britain jointly administered Oregon, and Utah was part of Mexico. This did not stop Americans from settling in either region. National boundaries meant little to those who moved west. The 1840s witnessed an intensification of the old belief that God intended the American nation to reach all the way to the Pacific Ocean. As noted in Chapter 9, the term that became a shorthand for this expansionist spirit was "manifest destiny."

"Manifest destiny"

The Mexican Frontier: New Mexico and California

Settlement of Oregon did not directly raise the issue of slavery. But the nation's acquisition of part of Mexico did. When Mexico achieved its independence from Spain in 1821, it was nearly as large as the United

A watercolor of a scene on a ranch near Monterey, California, in 1849 depicts *Californios* supervising the work of Native Americans.

States, and its population of 6.5 million was about two-thirds that of its northern neighbor. However, Mexico's northern provinces—California, New Mexico, and Texas—were isolated and sparsely settled outposts surrounded by Indian country. California's non-Indian population in 1821, some 3,200 missionaries, soldiers, and settlers, was vastly outnumbered by about 20,000 Indians living and working on land owned by religious missions and by 150,000 members of unsubdued tribes in the interior. By 1840, California was already linked commercially with the United States, and New England ships were trading with the region. In 1846, Alfred Robinson, who had moved from Boston, published *Life in California*. "In this age of annexation," he wondered, "why not extend the 'area of freedom' by the annexation of California?"

Mexican California

Westward migration in the early and mid-1840s took American settlers across Indian country into the Oregon Territory, ownership of which was disputed with Great Britain. The Mormons migrated west to Salt Lake City, then part of Mexico.

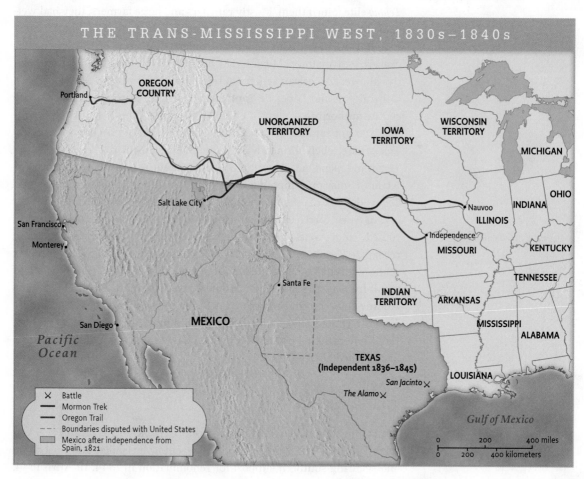

THE TRANS-MISSISSIPPI WEST, 1830s–1840s

Legend:
- ✗ Battle
- — Mormon Trek
- — Oregon Trail
- --- Boundaries disputed with United States
- Mexico after independence from Spain, 1821

The Texas Revolt

The first part of Mexico to be settled by significant numbers of Americans was Texas, whose non-Indian population of Spanish origin (called *Tejanos*) numbered only about 2,000 when Mexico became independent. In order to develop the region, the Spanish government had accepted an offer by Moses Austin, a Connecticut-born farmer, to colonize it with Americans. In 1820, Austin received a large land grant. He died soon afterward, and his son Stephen continued the plan, now in independent Mexico, reselling land in smaller plots to American settlers at twelve cents per acre.

Moses and Stephen Austin

Alarmed that its grip on the area was weakening, the Mexican government in 1830 annulled existing land contracts and barred future emigration from the United States. Led by Stephen Austin, American settlers demanded greater autonomy within Mexico. Part of the area's tiny *Tejano* elite joined them. Mostly ranchers and large farmers, they had welcomed the economic boom that accompanied the settlers and had formed economic alliances with American traders. The issue of slavery further exacerbated matters. Mexico had abolished slavery, but local authorities allowed American settlers to bring slaves with them. Mexico's ruler, General Antonio López de **Santa Anna**, sent an army in 1835 to impose central authority.

Reasons for the Texas revolt

The appearance of Santa Anna's army sparked a chaotic revolt in Texas. The rebels formed a provisional government that soon called for Texan independence. On March 6, 1836, Santa Anna's army stormed the Alamo, a mission compound in San Antonio, killing its 187 American and *Tejano* defenders. "Remember the Alamo" became the Texans' rallying cry. In April, forces under Sam Houston, a former governor of Tennessee, routed Santa Anna's army at the Battle of San Jacinto and forced him to recognize Texan independence. In 1837, the Texas Congress called for union with the United States. But fearing the political disputes certain to result from an attempt to add another slave state to the Union, Presidents Andrew Jackson and Martin Van Buren shelved the question. Settlers from the United States nonetheless poured into the region, many of them slaveowners taking up fertile cotton land. By 1845, the population of Texas had reached nearly 150,000.

Battle of San Jacinto

The Election of 1844

Texas annexation remained on the political back burner until President John Tyler revived it in the hope of rescuing his failed administration and securing southern support for renomination in 1844. In April 1844,

The Tyler administration and Texas

The plaza in San Antonio not long after the United States annexed Texas in 1845.

a letter by John C. Calhoun, whom Tyler had appointed secretary of state, was leaked to the press. It linked the idea of absorbing Texas directly to the goal of strengthening slavery in the United States. Some southern leaders, indeed, hoped that Texas could be divided into several states, thus further enhancing the South's power in Congress. Late that month, Henry Clay and former president Van Buren, the prospective Whig and Democratic candidates for president and two of the party system's most venerable leaders, met at Clay's Kentucky plantation. They agreed to issue letters rejecting immediate annexation on the grounds that it might provoke war with Mexico.

Slavery and expansion

Clay went on to receive the Whig nomination, but for Van Buren the letters proved to be a disaster. At the Democratic convention, southerners bent on annexation deserted Van Buren's cause, and he failed to receive the two-thirds majority necessary for nomination. The delegates then turned to the little-known James K. Polk, a former governor of Tennessee whose main assets were his support for annexation and his close association with Andrew Jackson, still the party's most popular figure. To soothe injured feelings among northern Democrats over the rejection of Van Buren, the party platform called not only for the "**reannexation**" of Texas (implying that Texas had been part of the Louisiana Purchase and therefore had once belonged to the United States) but also the "**reoccupation**" of all of Oregon. "Fifty-four forty or fight"—American control of Oregon all the way to its northern boundary at north latitude 54°40'—became a popular campaign slogan.

Emergence of Polk

Polk was the first "dark horse" candidate for president—that is, one whose nomination was completely unexpected. In the fall, he defeated

Clay in an extremely close election. Polk's margin in the popular vote was less than 2 percent. Had not James G. Birney, running again as the Liberty Party candidate, received 16,000 votes in New York, mostly from anti-slavery Whigs, Clay would have been elected. In March 1845, only days before Polk's inauguration, Congress declared Texas part of the United States.

Polk's election

The Road to War

Polk's goals

James K. Polk may have been virtually unknown, but he assumed the presidency with a clearly defined set of goals: to reduce the tariff, reestablish the independent Treasury system, settle the dispute over ownership of Oregon, and bring California into the Union. Congress soon enacted the first two goals, and the third was accomplished in an agreement with Great Britain dividing Oregon at the forty-ninth parallel.

Acquiring California proved more difficult. Polk dispatched an emissary to Mexico offering to purchase the region, but the Mexican government refused to negotiate. By the spring of 1846, Polk was planning for military action. In April, American soldiers under Zachary Taylor moved into the region between the Nueces River and the Rio Grande, land claimed by both countries on the disputed border between Texas and Mexico. This action made conflict with Mexican forces inevitable. When fighting broke out, Polk claimed that the Mexicans had "shed blood upon American soil" and called for a declaration of war.

War News from Mexico, an 1848 painting by Richard C. Woodville, shows how Americans received war news through the popular press.

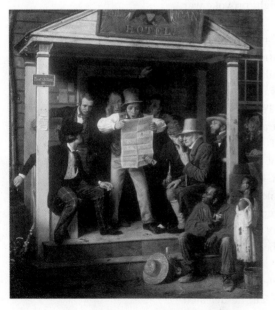

The War and Its Critics

The Mexican War was the first American conflict to be fought primarily on foreign soil and the first in which American troops occupied a foreign capital. Inspired by the expansionist fervor of manifest destiny, a majority of Americans supported the war. But a significant minority in the North dissented, fearing that far from expanding the "great empire of liberty," the administration's real aim was to acquire new land for the expansion of slavery. Henry David Thoreau was jailed in Massachusetts in 1846 for refusing to pay taxes as a protest against the war. Defending his action, Thoreau wrote an important essay, "On Civil Disobedience," which inspired such later advocates of nonviolent resistance to unjust laws as Martin Luther King Jr.

Among the war's critics was Abraham Lincoln, who had been elected to Congress in 1846 from Illinois. Like many Whigs, Lincoln questioned whether the Mexicans had actually inflicted casualties on American soil, as Polk claimed. But Lincoln was also disturbed by Polk's claiming the right to initiate an invasion of Mexico. Lincoln's stance proved unpopular in Illinois. He had already agreed to serve only one term in Congress, but when Democrats captured his seat in 1848, many blamed the result on Lincoln's criticism of the war. Nonetheless, the concerns he raised regarding the president's power to "make war at pleasure" would continue to echo in the twentieth and twenty-first centuries.

Lincoln as war critic

Combat in Mexico

More than 60,000 volunteers enlisted and did most of the fighting. Combat took place on three fronts. In June 1846, a band of American insurrectionists proclaimed California freed from Mexican control and named Captain John C. Frémont, head of a small scientific expedition in the West, its ruler. Their aim was California's incorporation into the United States, but for the moment they adopted a flag depicting a large bear as the symbol of the area's independence. A month later, the U.S. Navy sailed into Monterey and San Francisco harbors, raised the American flag, and put an end to the "bear flag republic." At almost the same time, 1,600 American troops under General Stephen W. Kearney occupied Sante Fe without resistance and then set out for southern California, where they helped to put down a Mexican uprising against American rule.

The war's three fronts

The bulk of the fighting occurred in central Mexico. In February 1847, Taylor defeated Santa Anna's army at the Battle of Buena Vista. When the Mexican government still refused to negotiate, Polk ordered American forces under Winfield Scott to march inland from the port of Veracruz toward Mexico City. Scott's forces routed Mexican defenders and in September occupied the country's capital. In February 1848, the two governments agreed to the Treaty of Guadalupe Hidalgo, which confirmed the annexation of Texas and ceded California and present-day New Mexico, Arizona, Nevada, and Utah to the United States.

The defeat of Mexico and its consequences

The Mexican War is only a footnote in most Americans' historical memory. Unlike for other wars, few public monuments celebrate the conflict. Mexicans, however, regard the war (or "the dismemberment," as it is called in that country) as a central event of their national history

THE MEXICAN WAR, 1846–1848

The Mexican War was the first in which an American army invaded another country and occupied its capital. As a result of the war, the United States acquired a vast new area in the modern-day Southwest.

and a source of continued resentment over a century and a half after it was fought.

Race and Manifest Destiny

With the end of the Mexican War, the United States absorbed half a million square miles of Mexico's territory, one-third of that nation's total area. A region that for centuries had been united was suddenly split in two, dividing families and severing trade routes. An estimated 75,000 to 100,000 Spanish-speaking Mexicans and more than 150,000 Indians inhabited the land annexed from Mexico, known as the Mexican Cession. The Treaty of Guadalupe Hidalgo guaranteed to "male citizens" of the area "the free enjoyment of their liberty and property" and "all the rights" of Americans—a provision designed to protect the property of large Mexican landowners in California. Thus, in the first half of the nineteenth century, some residents of the area went from being Spaniards to Mexicans to Americans. Although not newcomers, they had to adjust to a new identity as if they were immigrants. As for Indians whose homelands and hunting grounds suddenly became part of the United States, the treaty referred to them only as "savage tribes" whom the United States must prevent from launching incursions into Mexico across the new border.

During the 1840s, territorial expansion came to be seen as proof of the innate superiority of the "Anglo-Saxon race" (a mythical construct defined largely by its opposites: blacks, Indians, Hispanics, and Catholics). "*Race*,"

The Mexican Cession

Status of Mexicans and Indians

By 1853, with the Gadsden Purchase, the present boundaries of the United States in North America, with the exception of Alaska, had been created.

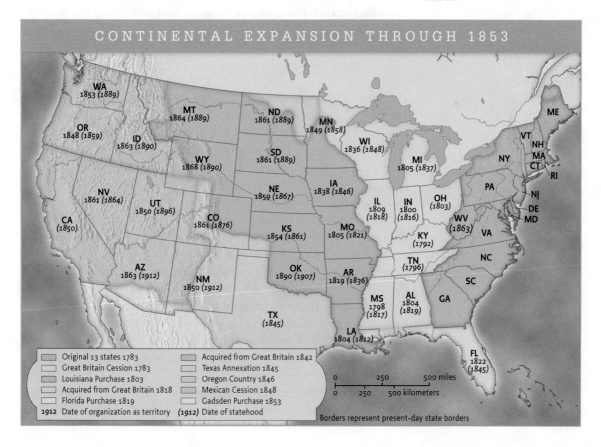

CONTINENTAL EXPANSION THROUGH 1853

WA 1853 (1889)
OR 1848 (1859)
MT 1864 (1889)
ID 1863 (1890)
ND 1861 (1889)
MN 1849 (1858)
ME
WI 1836 (1848)
VT
NH
MA
NY
CT
RI
WY 1868 (1890)
SD 1861 (1889)
MI 1805 (1837)
NV 1861 (1864)
UT 1850 (1896)
NE 1859 (1867)
IA 1838 (1846)
PA
NJ
CA (1850)
CO 1861 (1876)
IL 1809 (1818)
IN 1800 (1816)
OH (1803)
WV (1863)
DE
MD
KS 1854 (1861)
MO 1805 (1821)
KY (1792)
VA
AZ 1863 (1912)
OK 1890 (1907)
AR 1819 (1836)
TN (1796)
NC
NM 1850 (1912)
SC
TX (1845)
MS 1798 (1817)
AL 1804 (1819)
GA
LA 1804 (1812)
FL 1822 (1845)

Legend:
- Original 13 states 1783
- Great Britain Cession 1783
- Louisiana Purchase 1803
- Acquired from Great Britain 1818
- Florida Purchase 1819
- Acquired from Great Britain 1842
- Texas Annexation 1845
- Oregon Country 1846
- Mexican Cession 1848
- Gadsden Purchase 1853
- **1912** Date of organization as territory (*1912*) Date of statehood

0   250   500 miles
0   250   500 kilometers

Borders represent present-day state borders

FRUITS OF MANIFEST DESTINY | 375

declared John L. O'Sullivan's *Democratic Review*, was the "key" to the "history of nations" and the rise and fall of empires. Newspapers, magazines, and scholarly works popularized the link between American freedom and the supposedly innate liberty-loving qualities of Anglo-Saxon Protestants. Indeed, calls by some expansionists for the United States to annex all of Mexico failed in part because of fear that the nation could not assimilate its large non-white Catholic population, supposedly unfit for citizenship in a republic.

The Texas constitution

Local circumstances affected racial definitions in the former Mexican territories. Although Mexico had abolished slavery and considered all persons equal before the law, the Texas constitution adopted after independence protected slavery and denied civil rights to Indians and persons of African origin. Texas defined "Spanish" Mexicans, however, especially those who occupied important social positions, as white. The residents of New Mexico of both Mexican and Indian origin, on the other hand, were long deemed "too Mexican" for democratic self-government. With white migration lagging, Congress did not allow New Mexico to become a state until 1912.

Gold-Rush California

California had a non-Indian population of less than 15,000 when the Mexican War ended. For most of the 1840s, ten times as many Americans emigrated to Oregon as to California. But this changed dramatically after

Sutter's mill

January 1848, when gold was discovered in the foothills of the Sierra Nevada Mountains at a sawmill owned by the Swiss immigrant Johann A. Sutter. By ship and land, newcomers poured into California. The non-Indian population rose to 200,000 by 1852 and more than 360,000 eight years later.

California's gold-rush population was incredibly diverse. Experienced miners flooded in from Mexico and South America. Tens of thousands

Diversity of the gold-rush population

of Americans who had never seen a mine arrived from the East, and from overseas came Irish, Germans, Italians, and Australians. Nearly 25,000 Chinese landed between 1849 and 1852. Unlike the families who settled farming frontiers, most of the gold-rush migrants were young men. Women played many roles in western mining communities, running restaurants and boardinghouses and working as laundresses, cooks, and prostitutes. But as late as 1860, California's male population outnumbered females by nearly three to one.

As early surface mines quickly became exhausted, they gave way to underground mining that required a large investment of capital. This economic development worsened conflicts among California's many racial and ethnic groups engaged in fierce competition for gold. White miners organized extralegal groups that expelled "foreign miners"—Mexicans, Chileans, Chinese, French, and American Indians—from areas with gold. The state legislature imposed a tax of twenty dollars per month on foreign miners, driving many of them from the state.

Conflicts over gold

For California's Indians, the gold rush and absorption into the United States proved to be disastrous. Gold seekers overran Indian communities. Miners, ranchers, and vigilantes murdered thousands of Indians. Determined to reduce the native population, state officials paid millions in bounties to private militias that launched attacks on the state's Indians. Although California was a free state, thousands of Indian children, declared orphans or vagrants by local courts, were bought and sold as slaves. By 1860, California's Indian population, nearly 150,000 when the Mexican War ended, had been reduced to around 30,000.

The gold rush and California's Indians

In a remarkable coincidence, the California gold rush took place almost simultaneously with another located halfway around the world. In 1851, gold was discovered in Australia, then a collection of British colonies. During the 1850s, California and Australia together produced 80 percent of the world's gold. Like California, Australia attracted gold-seekers from across the globe. As in California, the gold rush was a disaster for the aboriginal peoples (as native Australians are called), whose population, already declining, fell precipitously.

Transportation of Cargo by Westerners at the Port of Yokohama, 1861, by the Japanese artist Utagawa Sadahide, depicts ships in port, including an American one on the left, eight years after Commodore Perry's first voyage to Japan.

Opening Japan

The Mexican War ended with the United States in possession of the magnificent harbors of San Diego and San Francisco, long seen as jumping-off points for trade with the Far East. In the 1850s, the United States took the lead in opening Japan, a country that had closed itself to nearly all foreign contact for more than two centuries. In 1853 and 1854, American warships under the command of **Commodore Matthew Perry** (the younger brother of Oliver Perry, a hero of the War of 1812) sailed into Tokyo Harbor. Perry, who had been sent by President Millard Fillmore to negotiate a trade treaty, demanded that the Japanese deal with him. Alarmed by European intrusions into China and impressed by Perry's armaments as well as a musical pageant he presented that included a blackface minstrel show, Japanese leaders agreed to

do so. In 1854, they opened two ports to American shipping. As a result, the United States acquired refueling places on the route to China—seen as Asia's most important trading partner. And Japan soon launched a process of modernization that transformed it into the region's major military power.

A DOSE OF ARSENIC

Slavery in the West

Victory over Mexico added more than 1 million square miles to the United States—an area larger than the Louisiana Purchase. But the acquisition of this vast territory raised the fatal issue that would disrupt the political system and plunge the nation into civil war—whether slavery should be allowed to expand into the West. Events soon confirmed Ralph Waldo Emerson's prediction that if the United States gobbled up part of Mexico, "it will be as the man who swallows arsenic. . . . Mexico will poison us."

Already, the bonds of Union were fraying. In 1844 and 1845, the Methodists and Baptists, the two largest evangelical churches, divided into northern and southern branches. Once the churches were divided by section, it was easier for the southern branch to move toward a stronger biblical defense of slavery, and the northern toward antislavery, if not necessarily abolitionism. But it was the entrance of the slavery issue into the heart of American politics as the result of the Mexican War that eventually dissolved perhaps the strongest force for national unity—the two-party system.

The Wilmot Proviso

Party vs. section

Before 1846, the status of slavery in all parts of the United States had been settled, either by state law or by the Missouri Compromise, which determined slavery's status in the Louisiana Purchase. The acquisition of new land reopened the question of slavery's expansion. The divisive potential of this issue became clear in 1846, when Congressman David Wilmot of Pennsylvania proposed a resolution prohibiting slavery from all territory acquired from Mexico. Party lines crumbled as every northerner, Democrat and Whig alike, supported what came to be known as the **Wilmot Proviso**, while nearly all southerners opposed it. The measure passed the House, where the more populous North possessed a majority, but failed in the Senate, with its even balance of free and slave states.

In 1848, opponents of slavery's expansion organized the **Free Soil Party** and nominated Martin Van Buren for president and Charles Francis Adams, the son of John Quincy Adams, as his running mate. Democrats nominated Lewis Cass of Michigan, who proposed that the decision on whether to allow slavery should be left to settlers in the new territories (an idea later given the name "popular sovereignty"). Van Buren was motivated in part by revenge against the South for jettisoning him in 1844. But his campaign struck a chord among northerners opposed to the expansion of slavery, and he polled some 300,000 votes, 14 percent of the northern total. Victory in 1848 went to the Whig candidate, Zachary Taylor, a hero of the Mexican War and a Louisiana sugar planter. But the fact that a former president and the son of another abandoned their parties to run on a Free Soil platform showed that antislavery sentiment had spread far beyond abolitionist ranks.

Zachary Taylor

The Free Soil Appeal

The Free Soil position had a popular appeal in the North that far exceeded the abolitionists' demand for immediate emancipation and equal rights for blacks. Many northerners had long resented what they considered southern domination of the federal government. The idea of preventing the creation of new slave states appealed to those who favored policies, such as the protective tariff and government aid to internal improvements, that the majority of southern political leaders opposed.

Economic betterment

For thousands of northerners, moreover, the ability to move to the new western territories held out the promise of economic betterment. "Freedom of the soil," declared George Henry Evans, the editor of a pro-labor newspaper, offered the only alternative to permanent economic dependence for American workers.

Such views merged easily with opposition to the expansion of slavery. If slave plantations were to occupy the fertile lands of the West, northern migration would be effectively blocked. The term "free soil" had a double meaning. The Free Soil platform of 1848 called both for barring slavery from western territories and for the federal government to provide free homesteads to settlers in the new territories. Unlike abolitionism, the "free soil" idea also appealed to the racism so widespread in northern society. Wilmot himself insisted that his controversial proviso was motivated to advance "the cause and rights of the free white man," in part by preventing him from having to compete with "black labor."

The Free Soil platform of 1848

To white southerners, the idea of barring slavery from territory acquired from Mexico seemed a violation of their equal rights as members of the Union. Just as northerners believed westward expansion essential to their economic well-being, southern leaders became convinced that slavery must expand or die. Moreover, the admission of new free states would overturn the delicate political balance between the sections and make the South a permanent minority. Southern interests would not be secure in a Union dominated by non-slaveholding states.

Crisis and Compromise

In world history, the year 1848 is remembered as the "springtime of nations," a time of democratic uprisings against the monarchies of Europe and demands by ethnic minorities for national independence. American principles of liberty and self-government appeared to be triumphing in the Old World. The Chartist movement in Great Britain organized massive demonstrations in support of a proposed Charter that demanded democratic reforms. The French replaced their monarchy with a republic. Hungarians proclaimed their independence from Austrian rule. Patriots in Italy and Germany, both divided into numerous states, demanded national unification. But the revolutionary tide receded. Chartism faded away, Emperor Napoleon III soon restored the French monarchy, and revolts in Budapest, Rome, and other cities were crushed. Would their own experiment in self-government, some Americans wondered, suffer the same fate as the failed revolutions of Europe?

With the slavery issue appearing more and more ominous, established party leaders moved to resolve differences between the sections. In 1850, California asked to be admitted to the Union as a free state. Many southerners opposed the measure, fearing that it would upset the sectional balance in Congress. Senator Henry Clay offered a plan with four main provisions that came to be known as the **Compromise of 1850**. California would enter the Union as a free state. The slave trade, but not slavery itself, would be abolished in the nation's capital. A stringent new law would allow southerners to reclaim runaway slaves. And the status of slavery in the remaining territories acquired from Mexico would be left to the decision of the local white inhabitants. The United States would also agree to pay off the massive debt Texas had accumulated while independent.

The Great Debate

In the Senate debate on the Compromise, the divergent sectional positions received eloquent expression. Powerful leaders spoke for and against compromise. Daniel Webster of Massachusetts announced his willingness to abandon the Wilmot Proviso and accept a new fugitive slave law if this were the price of sectional peace. John C. Calhoun, again representing South Carolina, was too ill to speak. A colleague read his remarks rejecting the very idea of compromise. The North must yield, Calhoun insisted, or the Union could not survive. William H. Seward of New York also opposed compromise. To southerners' talk of their constitutional rights, Seward responded that a "higher law" than the Constitution condemned slavery—the law of morality. Here was the voice of abolitionism, now represented in the U.S. Senate.

President Zachary Taylor, like Andrew Jackson a southerner but a strong nationalist, insisted that all Congress needed to do was admit California to the Union. But Taylor died suddenly of an intestinal infection on July 9, 1850. His successor, Millard Fillmore of New York, threw his support to Clay's proposals. Fillmore helped to break the impasse in Congress and secure adoption of the Compromise of 1850.

Senator Daniel Webster of Massachusetts in a daguerreotype from 1850, the year his speech in support of the Compromise of 1850 contributed to its passage.

The Fugitive Slave Issue

For one last time, political leaders had removed the dangerous slavery question from congressional debate. The new **Fugitive Slave Act**, however, made further controversy inevitable. The law allowed special federal commissioners to determine the fate of alleged fugitives without benefit of a jury trial or even testimony by the accused individual. It prohibited local authorities from interfering with the capture of fugitives and required individual citizens to assist in such capture when called upon by federal agents. Thus, southern leaders, usually strong defenders of states' rights and local autonomy, supported a measure that brought federal agents into communities throughout the North, armed with the power to override local law enforcement and judicial procedures to secure the return of runaway slaves. The security of slavery was more important to them than states'-rights consistency.

During the 1850s, federal tribunals heard more than 300 cases throughout the free states and ordered 157 fugitives returned to the South, many at the government's expense. But the law further widened sectional divisions. In a series of dramatic confrontations, fugitives, aided by abolitionist allies, violently resisted recapture. A large crowd in 1851 rescued the escaped slave Jerry from jail in Syracuse, New York, and spirited him off to Canada. In the same year, an owner who attempted to recapture a fugitive was killed in Christiana, Pennsylvania.

In the North, several thousand fugitives and freeborn blacks, worried that they might be swept up in the stringent provisions of the Fugitive Slave Act, fled to safety in Canada. The sight of so many refugees seeking

An 1855 broadside depicting the life of Anthony Burns, a runaway slave captured in Boston and returned to the South in 1854 by federal officials enforcing the Fugitive Slave Act.

liberty in a foreign land challenged the familiar image of the United States as an asylum for freedom.

Douglas and Popular Sovereignty

At least temporarily, the Compromise of 1850 seemed to have restored sectional peace and party unity. In the 1852 presidential election, Democrat Franklin Pierce won a sweeping victory over the Whig Winfield Scott on a platform that recognized the Compromise as a final settlement of the slavery controversy.

Kansas, Nebraska, and slavery

In 1854, however, the old political order finally succumbed to the disruptive pressures of sectionalism. Early in that year, Illinois senator Stephen A. Douglas introduced a bill to provide territorial governments for Kansas and Nebraska, located within the Louisiana Purchase. A strong believer in western development, he hoped that a transcontinental railroad could be constructed through Kansas or Nebraska. Southerners in Congress, however, seemed adamant against allowing the organization of new free territories that might further upset the sectional balance. Douglas hoped to satisfy them by applying the principle of **popular sovereignty**, whereby the status of slavery would be determined by the votes of local settlers, not Congress. To Douglas, popular sovereignty embodied the idea of local self-government and offered a middle ground between the extremes of North and South.

The Kansas-Nebraska Act

Unlike the lands taken from Mexico, Kansas and Nebraska lay in the nation's heartland, directly in the path of westward migration. Slavery, moreover, was prohibited there under the terms of the Missouri Compromise, which Douglas's bill repealed. In response to Douglas's

The Appeal of the Independent Democrats

proposal, a group of antislavery congressmen issued the *Appeal of the Independent Democrats*. It arraigned Douglas's bill as a "gross violation of a sacred pledge," part and parcel of "an atrocious plot" to convert free territory into a "dreary region of despotism, inhabited by masters and slaves." It helped to convince millions of northerners that southern leaders aimed at nothing less than extending their peculiar institution throughout the West.

Political transformation

Thanks to Douglas's energetic leadership, the **Kansas-Nebraska Act** became law in 1854. But it shattered the Democratic Party's unity and sparked a profound reorganization of American politics. During the next two years, the Whig Party, unable to develop a unified response to the political crisis, collapsed. From a region divided between the two parties,

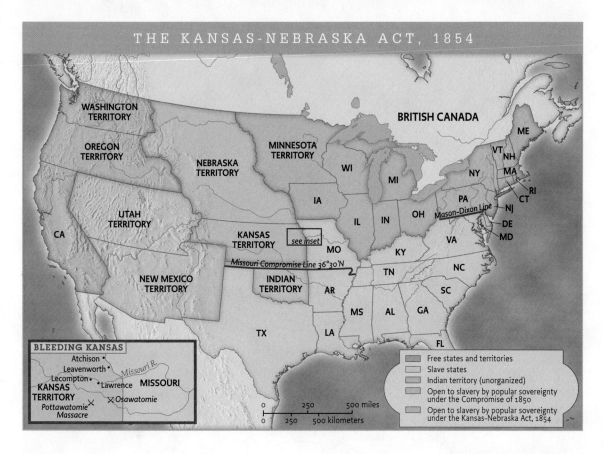

THE KANSAS-NEBRASKA ACT, 1854

WASHINGTON TERRITORY

OREGON TERRITORY

NEBRASKA TERRITORY

MINNESOTA TERRITORY

BRITISH CANADA

ME

VT
NH

WI

MI

NY

MA

RI
CT

UTAH TERRITORY

IA

PA

NJ

Mason-Dixon Line

DE

CA

IL   IN   OH

MD

KANSAS TERRITORY

see inset

MO

KY

VA

Missouri Compromise Line 36°30'N

NEW MEXICO TERRITORY

INDIAN TERRITORY

TN

NC

AR

SC

MS   AL   GA

TX

LA

FL

BLEEDING KANSAS

Atchison •

Leavenworth •

Missouri R.

Lecompton •

• Lawrence   **MISSOURI**

KANSAS TERRITORY

× Osawatomie

Pottawatomie × Massacre

0   250   500 miles

0   250   500 kilometers

- Free states and territories
- Slave states
- Indian territory (unorganized)
- Open to slavery by popular sovereignty under the Compromise of 1850
- Open to slavery by popular sovereignty under the Kansas-Nebraska Act, 1854

the South became solidly Democratic. Most northern Whigs, augmented by thousands of disgruntled Democrats, joined a new organization, the Republican Party, dedicated to preventing the further expansion of slavery.

The Kansas-Nebraska Act opened a vast area in the nation's heartland to the possible spread of slavery by repealing the Missouri Compromise and providing that settlers would determine the status of slavery in these territories.

THE RISE OF THE REPUBLICAN PARTY

The Northern Economy

The disruptive impact of slavery on the traditional parties was the immediate cause of political transformation in the mid-1850s. But the rise of the Republican Party also reflected underlying economic and social changes, notably the completion of the market revolution and the beginning of mass immigration from Europe.

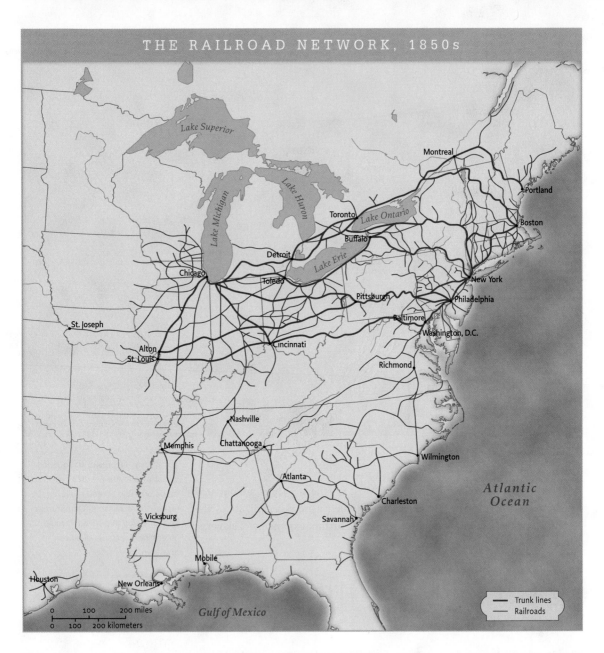

THE RAILROAD NETWORK, 1850s

The rapid expansion of the railroad network in the 1850s linked the Northeast and Old Northwest in a web of commerce. The South's rail network was considerably less developed, accounting for only 30 percent of the nation's track mileage.

The period from 1843 to 1857 witnessed explosive economic growth, especially in the North. The catalyst was the completion of the railroad network. From 5,000 miles in 1848, railroad track mileage grew to 30,000 by 1860, with most of the construction occurring in Ohio, Illinois, and other states of the Old Northwest. Four great trunk railroads now linked eastern cities with western farming and commercial centers. The railroads completed the reorientation of the Northwest's trade from the South to the East. As late as 1850, most western farmers still shipped their produce down the Mississippi River. Ten years later, however, railroads transported nearly all their crops to the East, at a fraction of the previous cost. Eastern industrialists marketed manufactured goods to the commercial farmers of the West, while residents of the region's growing cities consumed the food westerners produced. The economic integration of the Northwest and Northeast created the groundwork for their political unification in the Republican Party.

The railroad network in the North

Although most northerners still lived in small towns and rural areas, the majority of the workforce no longer labored in agriculture. Two great areas of industrial production had arisen. One, along the Atlantic coast, stretched from Boston to Philadelphia and Baltimore. A second was centered on or near the Great Lakes, in inland cities like Buffalo, Cleveland, Pittsburgh, and Chicago. Driven by railroad expansion, coal mining and iron manufacturing were growing rapidly. Chicago, the Old Northwest's major rail center and the jumping-off place for settlers heading for the Great Plains, had become a complex manufacturing center. Although the southern economy was also growing and the continuing expansion of cotton production brought wealth to slaveholders, the South did not share in these broad economic changes.

Integration of Northwest and Northeast

A lithograph from around 1860 depicts the town of Bridgewater, Massachusetts, home of a major iron works. A railroad speeds along in the foreground, while factory smokestacks dot the horizon. The tidy buildings in the center suggest that industrialization has not upset social harmony. Industrial development in the north widened the gap between the sections.

The Rise and Fall of the Know-Nothings

Nativism—hostility to immigrants, especially Catholics—became a national political movement with the sudden appearance in 1854 of the American, or **Know-Nothing, Party** (so called because it began as a secret organization whose members, when asked about its existence, were supposed to respond, "I know nothing"). The party trumpeted its dedication to reserving

The Propagation Society—More Free than Welcome, an anti-Catholic cartoon from the 1850s, illustrates the nativist fear that the Catholic Church poses a threat to American society. Pope Pius IX, cross in hand, steps ashore from a boat that also holds five bishops. Addressing "Young America," who holds a Bible, he says that he has come to "take charge of your spiritual welfare." A bishop adds, "I cannot bear to see that boy, with that horrible book."

political office for native-born Americans and to resisting the "aggressions" of the Catholic Church, such as its supposed efforts to undermine public school systems. The Know-Nothings swept the 1854 state elections in Massachusetts, electing the governor, all of the state's congressmen, and nearly every member of the state legislature. In many states, nativists emerged as a major component of victorious "anti-Nebraska" coalitions of voters opposed to the Kansas-Nebraska Act. In the North, the Know-Nothings' appeal combined anti-Catholic and antislavery sentiment, with opposition to the sale of liquor often added to the equation.

Nativism and antislavery

Despite severe anti-Irish discrimination in jobs, housing, and education, however, it is remarkable how little came of demands that immigrants be barred from the political nation. All European immigrants benefited from being white. The newcomers had the good fortune to arrive after white male suffrage had become the norm and automatically received the right to vote.

Suffrage for European immigrants

The Free Labor Ideology

By 1856, it was clear that the Republican Party—a coalition of antislavery Democrats, northern Whigs, Free Soilers, and Know-Nothings opposed to the further expansion of slavery—would become the major alternative to the Democratic Party in the North. The party's appeal rested on the idea of "free labor." In Republican hands, the antithesis between "free society" and

The Republican Party and free labor

George Catlin's 1827 painting *Five Points* depicts a working-class immigrant neighborhood in New York City that gained a reputation for crime, drinking, and overcrowding.

"slave society" coalesced into a comprehensive worldview that glorified the North as the home of progress, opportunity, and freedom.

The defining quality of northern society, Republicans declared, was the opportunity it offered each laborer to move up to the status of land-owning farmer or independent craftsman, thus achieving the economic independence essential to freedom. Slavery, by contrast, spawned a social order consisting of degraded slaves, poor whites with no hope of advancement, and idle aristocrats. If slavery were to spread into the West, northern free laborers would be barred, and their chances for social advancement severely diminished. Slavery, Republicans insisted, must be kept out of the territories so that free labor could flourish. The Republican platform of 1856 condemned slavery as one of the "twin relics of barbarism" in the United States (the other being Mormon polygamy).

Free labor versus slavery

Republicans were not abolitionists—they focused on preventing the spread of slavery, not attacking it where it existed. Nonetheless, many party leaders viewed the nation's division into free and slave societies as an "irrepressible conflict," as Senator William H. Seward of New York put it in 1858, that eventually would have to be resolved.

Spread of slavery

"Bleeding Kansas" and the Election of 1856

Their free labor outlook, which resonated so effectively with deeply held northern values, helps to explain the Republicans' rapid rise to prominence. But dramatic events in 1855 and 1856 also fueled the party's growth. When

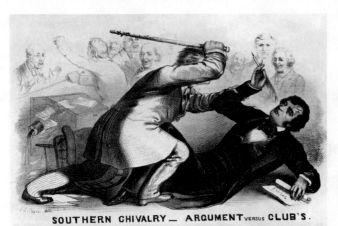

SOUTHERN CHIVALRY— ARGUMENT versus CLUB'S.

A contemporary print denounces South Carolina congressman Preston S. Brooks's assault on Massachusetts senator Charles Sumner in May 1856. The attack on the floor of the Senate was in retaliation for Sumner's speech accusing Senator Andrew P. Butler (Brooks's distant cousin) of having taken "the harlot slavery" as his mistress.

Parties along sectional lines

Kansas held elections in 1854 and 1855, hundreds of proslavery Missourians crossed the border to cast fraudulent ballots. President Franklin Pierce recognized the legitimacy of the resulting proslavery legislature, but settlers from free states soon established a rival government. A sporadic civil war broke out in Kansas in which some 200 persons eventually lost their lives. In one incident, in May 1856, a proslavery mob attacked the free-soil stronghold of Lawrence, burning public buildings and pillaging private homes.

"**Bleeding Kansas**" seemed to discredit Douglas's policy of leaving the decision on slavery up to the local population, thus aiding the Republicans. The party also drew strength from an unprecedented incident in the halls of Congress. South Carolina representative Preston Brooks, wielding a gold-tipped cane, beat the antislavery senator Charles Sumner of Massachusetts unconscious.

In the election of 1856, the Republican Party chose as its candidate John C. Frémont and drafted a platform that strongly opposed the further expansion of slavery. Stung by the northern reaction to the Kansas-Nebraska Act, the Democrats nominated James Buchanan, who had been minister to Great Britain in 1854 and thus had no direct connection with that divisive measure. The Democratic platform endorsed the principle of popular sovereignty as the only viable solution to the slavery controversy. Meanwhile, the Know-Nothings presented ex-president Millard Fillmore as their candidate. Frémont outpolled Buchanan in the North, carrying eleven of sixteen free states—a remarkable achievement for an organization that had existed for only two years. But Buchanan won the entire South and the key northern states of Illinois, Indiana, and Pennsylvania, enough to ensure his victory. Fillmore carried only Maryland. The 1856 election returns made starkly clear that political parties had reoriented themselves along sectional lines. One major party had been destroyed, another seriously weakened, and a new one had arisen, devoted entirely to the interests of the North.

THE EMERGENCE OF LINCOLN

The final collapse of the party system took place during the administration of a president who epitomized the old political order. Born during George Washington's presidency, James Buchanan had served in Pennsylvania's legislature, in both houses of Congress, and as secretary of state under James K. Polk. A staunch believer in the Union, he committed himself to pacifying inflamed sectional emotions. Few presidents have failed more disastrously in what they set out to accomplish.

The Dred Scott Decision

Even before his inauguration, Buchanan became aware of an impending Supreme Court decision that held out the hope of settling the slavery controversy once and for all. This was the case of Dred Scott. During the 1830s, Scott had accompanied his owner, Dr. John Emerson of Missouri, to Illinois, where slavery had been prohibited by the Northwest Ordinance of 1787 and by state law, and to Wisconsin Territory, where it was barred by the Missouri Compromise. After returning to Missouri, Scott sued for his freedom, claiming that residence on free soil had made him free.

THE PRESIDENTIAL ELECTION OF 1856

Party	Candidate	Electoral Vote (Share)	Popular Vote (Share)
Democrat	Buchanan	174 (59%)	1,838,169 (45%)
Republican	Frémont	114 (39%)	1,341,264 (33%)
American	Fillmore	8 (3%)	874,534 (22%)

Non-voting territory

The **Dred Scott decision**, one of the most famous—or infamous—rulings in the long history of the Supreme Court, was announced in March 1857, two days after Buchanan's inauguration. Speaking for the majority, Chief Justice Roger B. Taney declared that only white persons could be citizens of the United States. The nation's founders, Taney insisted, believed that blacks "had no rights which the white man was bound to respect."

As for Scott's residence in Wisconsin, the ruling stated that Congress possessed no power under the Constitution to bar slavery from a territory. The Missouri Compromise, recently repealed by the Kansas-Nebraska Act, had been unconstitutional, and so was any measure interfering with southerners' right to bring slaves into the western territories. The decision in effect declared unconstitutional the Republican platform of restricting slavery's expansion. It also seemed to undermine Douglas's doctrine of popular sovereignty. For if Congress lacked the power to prohibit slavery in a territory, how could a territorial legislature created by Congress do so?

Slavery, announced President Buchanan, henceforth existed in all the territories, "by virtue of the Constitution." In 1858, his administration attempted to admit Kansas as a slave state under the Lecompton

Chief Justice Taney

The Lecompton battle

Dred Scott as painted in 1857, the year the Supreme Court ruled that he and his family must remain in slavery. (Collection of the New York Historical Society)

Constitution, which had been drafted by a pro-southern convention and never submitted to a popular vote. Outraged by this violation of popular sovereignty, Douglas formed an unlikely alliance with congressional Republicans to block the attempt. The Lecompton battle convinced southern Democrats that they could not trust their party's most popular northern leader.

Lincoln and Slavery

The depth of Americans' divisions over slavery was brought into sharp focus in 1858 in one of the most storied election campaigns in the nation's history. Seeking reelection to the Senate as both a champion of popular sovereignty and the man who had prevented the administration from forcing slavery on the people of Kansas, Douglas faced an unexpectedly strong challenge from Abraham Lincoln, then little known outside of Illinois. Born into a modest farm family in Kentucky in 1809, Lincoln had moved as a youth to frontier Indiana and then Illinois. He had served four terms as a Whig in the state legislature and one in Congress from 1847 to 1849.

Lincoln developed a critique of slavery and its expansion that gave voice to the central values of the emerging Republican Party and the millions of northerners whose loyalty it commanded. His speeches combined the moral fervor of the abolitionists with the respect for order and the Constitution of more conservative northerners. If slavery were allowed to expand, he warned, the "love of liberty" would be extinguished and with it America's special mission to be a symbol of democracy for the entire world.

Lincoln was fascinated and disturbed by the writings of proslavery ideologues like George Fitzhugh (discussed in Chapter 11), and he rose to the defense of northern society. "I want every man to have the chance," said Lincoln, "and I believe a black man is entitled to it, in which he *can* better his condition." Blacks might not be the equal of whites in all respects, but in their "natural right" to the fruits of their labor, they were "my equal and the equal of all others."

The Lincoln-Douglas Campaign

The campaign against Douglas, the North's preeminent political leader, created Lincoln's national reputation. Accepting his party's nomination for the Senate in June 1858, Lincoln announced, "A house divided against itself cannot stand. I believe this government cannot endure, permanently half

"A house divided"

slave and half *free*." Lincoln's point was not that civil war was imminent, but that Americans must choose between favoring and opposing slavery.

The **Lincoln-Douglas debates**, held in seven Illinois towns and attended by tens of thousands of listeners, remain classics of American political oratory. Clashing definitions of freedom lay at their heart. To Lincoln, freedom meant opposition to slavery. Douglas argued, on the other hand, that the essence of freedom lay in local self-government and individual self-determination. A large and diverse nation could only survive by respecting the right of each locality to determine its own institutions. In response to a question posed by Lincoln during the Freeport debate, Douglas insisted that popular sovereignty was not incompatible with the Dred Scott decision. Although territorial legislatures could no longer exclude slavery directly, he argued, if the people wished to keep slaveholders out all they needed to do was refrain from giving the institution legal protection.

Lincoln shared many of the racial prejudices of his day. He opposed giving Illinois blacks the right to vote or serve on juries and spoke frequently of colonizing blacks overseas as the best solution to the problems of slavery and race. Yet, unlike Douglas, Lincoln did not use appeals to racism to garner votes. And he refused to exclude blacks from the human family. No less than whites, they were entitled to the inalienable rights of the Declaration of Independence, which applied to "all men, in all lands, everywhere," not merely to Europeans and their descendants.

The 1858 Illinois election returns revealed a state sharply divided, like the nation itself. Southern Illinois, settled from the South, voted strongly Democratic, while the rapidly growing northern part of the state was firmly in the Republican column. Until the adoption of the Seventeenth Amendment in the early twentieth century, each state's legislature chose its U.S. senators. The Democrats emerged with a narrow margin in the legislature, and Douglas was reelected. His victory was remarkable because elsewhere in the North Republicans swept to victory in 1858.

John Brown at Harpers Ferry

An armed assault by the abolitionist John Brown on the federal arsenal at **Harpers Ferry**, Virginia, further heightened sectional tensions. During the civil war in Kansas, Brown traveled to the territory. In May 1856, after the attack on Lawrence, he and a few followers murdered five proslavery settlers at Pottawatomie Creek. For the next two years, he traveled through the North and Canada, raising funds and enlisting followers for a war against slavery.

Abraham Lincoln in 1858, the year of the Lincoln-Douglas debates.

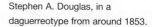

Stephen A. Douglas, in a daguerreotype from around 1853.

VOICES OF FREEDOM

From the Lincoln-Douglas Debates (1858)

The most famous political campaign in American history, the 1858 race for the U.S. Senate between Senator Stephen A. Douglas (a former Illinois judge) and Abraham Lincoln was highlighted by seven debates in which they discussed the politics of slavery and contrasting understandings of freedom.

DOUGLAS: Mr. Lincoln says that this government cannot endure permanently in the same condition in which it was made by its framers—divided into free and slave states. He says that it has existed for about seventy years thus divided, and yet he tells you that it cannot endure permanently on the same principles and in the same relative conditions in which our fathers made it. . . . One of the reserved rights of the states, was the right to regulate the relations between master and servant, on the slavery question.

Now, my friends, if we will only act conscientiously upon this great principle of popular sovereignty which guarantees to each state and territory the right to do as it pleases on all things local and domestic instead of Congress interfering, we will continue to be at peace one with another.

LINCOLN: Judge Douglas says, "Why can't this Union endure permanently, half slave and half free?" "Why can't we let it stand as our fathers placed it?" That is the exact difficulty between us. . . . I say when this government was first established it was the policy of its founders to prohibit the spread of slavery into the new territories of the United States, where it had not existed. But Judge Douglas and his friends have broken up that policy and placed it upon a new basis by which it is to become national and perpetual. All I have asked or desired anywhere is that it should be placed back again upon the basis that the founders of our government originally placed it—restricting it from the new territories. . . .

Judge Douglas assumes that we have no interest in them—that we have no right to interfere. . . . Do we not wish for an outlet for our surplus population, if I may so express myself? Do we not feel an interest in getting to that outlet with such institutions as we would like to have prevail there? Now irrespective of the moral aspect of this question as to whether there is a right or wrong in enslaving a negro, I am still in favor of our new territories being in such a condition that white men may find a home. I am in favor of this not merely for our own people, but as an outlet for *free white people everywhere*, the world over—in which Hans and Baptiste and Patrick, and all other men from all the world, may find new homes and better their conditions in life.

DOUGLAS: For one, I am opposed to negro citizenship in any and every form. I believe this government was made on the white basis. I believe it was made by white men, for the benefit of white men and their posterity forever . . . I do not believe that the Almighty made the negro capable of self-government. I say to you, my fellow-citizens, that in my opinion the signers of the Declaration of Independence had no reference to the negro whatever when they declared all men to be created equal. They desired to express by that phrase, white men, men of European birth and European descent . . . when they spoke of the equality of men.

LINCOLN: I have no purpose to introduce political and social equality between the white and the black races. There is a physical difference between the two, which in my judgment will probably forever forbid their living together upon the footing of perfect equality, and inasmuch as it becomes a necessity that there must be a difference, I, as well as Judge Douglas, am in favor of the race to which I belong, having the superior position. . . . But I hold that notwithstanding all this, there is no reason in the world why the negro is not entitled to all the natural rights enumerated in the Declaration of Independence, the right to life, liberty, and the pursuit of happiness. I hold that he is as much entitled to these as the white man. I agree with Judge Douglas he is not my equal in many respects—certainly not in color, perhaps not in moral or intellectual endowment. But in the right to eat the bread, without leave of anybody else, which his own hand earns, *he is my equal and the equal of Judge Douglas, and the equal of every living man.*

DOUGLAS: He tells you that I will not argue the question whether slavery is right or wrong. I tell you why I will not do it. . . . I hold that the people of the slaveholding states are civilized men as well as ourselves, that they bear consciences as well as we, and that they are accountable to God and their posterity and not to us. It is for them to decide therefore the moral and religious right of the slavery question for themselves within their own limits. . . . He says that he looks forward to a time when slavery shall be abolished everywhere. I look forward to a time when each state shall be allowed to do as it pleases.

LINCOLN: I suppose that the real difference between Judge Douglas and his friends, and the Republicans, is that the Judge is not in favor of making any difference between slavery and liberty . . . and consequently every sentiment he utters discards the idea that there is any wrong in slavery. . . . That is the real issue. That is the issue that will continue in this country when these poor tongues of Judge Douglas and myself shall be silent. It is the eternal struggle between these two principles—right and wrong—throughout the world.

QUESTIONS

1. *How do Lincoln and Douglas differ on what rights black Americans are entitled to enjoy?*

2. *Why does Lincoln believe the nation cannot exist forever half slave and half free, whereas Douglas believes it can?*

3. *How does each of the speakers balance the right of each state to manage its own affairs against the right of every person to be free?*

John Brown in an 1856 photograph.

On October 16, 1859, with twenty-one men, five of them black, Brown seized Harpers Ferry. The plan made little military sense. Brown's band was soon surrounded and killed or captured by a detachment of federal soldiers headed by Colonel Robert E. Lee. Placed on trial for treason against the state of Virginia, Brown conducted himself with dignity and courage. When Virginia's governor, Henry A. Wise, spurned pleas for clemency and ordered Brown executed, he turned Brown into a martyr to much of the North.

To the South, the failure of Brown's assault seemed less significant than the adulation he seemed to arouse from much of the northern public. His raid and execution further widened the breach between the sections. Brown's last letter was a brief, prophetic statement: "I, John Brown, am quite certain that the crimes of this guilty land will never be purged away but with blood."

The Rise of Southern Nationalism

With the Republicans continuing to gain strength in the North, Democrats might have been expected to put a premium on party unity as the election of 1860 approached. By this time, however, a sizable group of southerners now viewed their region's prospects as more favorable outside the Union than within it. To remain in the Union, secessionists argued, meant to accept "bondage" to the North. But an independent South could become the foundation of a slave empire ringing the Caribbean and embracing Cuba, other West Indian islands, Mexico, and parts of Central America.

Secessionists

More and more southerners were speaking openly of southward expansion. In 1854, Pierre Soulé of Louisiana, the American ambassador to Spain, had persuaded the ministers to Britain and France to join him in signing the Ostend Manifesto, which called on the United States to purchase or seize Cuba, where slavery was still legal, from Spain. Meanwhile, the military adventurer William Walker led a series of **"filibustering" expeditions** (the term derived from the Spanish word for pirate, *filibustero*) in Central America.

Ostend Manifesto

By the late 1850s, southern leaders were bending every effort to strengthen the bonds of slavery. "Slavery is our king," declared a South Carolina politician in 1860. "Slavery is our truth, slavery is our divine right." By early 1860, seven states of the Deep South had gone on record demanding that the Democratic platform pledge to protect slavery in all the territories that had not yet been admitted to the Union as states.

An 1835 painting of the federal arsenal at Harpers Ferry, Virginia (now West Virginia). John Brown's raid on Harpers Ferry in October 1859 helped to bring on the Civil War.

Virtually no northern politician could accept this position. For southern leaders to insist on it would guarantee the destruction of the Democratic Party as a national institution. But southern nationalists, known as **"fire-eaters,"** hoped to split the party and the country and form an independent Southern Confederacy.

The Election of 1860

When the Democratic convention met in April 1860, Douglas's supporters commanded a majority but not the two-thirds required for a presidential nomination. When the convention adopted a platform reaffirming the doctrine of popular sovereignty, delegates from the seven slave states of the Lower South walked out, and the gathering recessed in confusion. Six weeks later, it reconvened, replaced the bolters with Douglas supporters, and nominated him for president. In response, southern Democrats placed their own ticket in the field, headed by John C. Breckinridge of Kentucky. Breckinridge insisted that slavery must be protected in the western territories.

The Democratic Party, the last great bond of national unity, had been shattered. National conventions had traditionally been places where party managers, mindful of the need for unity in the fall campaign, reconciled their differences. But in 1860, neither northern nor southern Democrats were interested in conciliation. Southern Democrats no longer trusted

Democratic Party shattered

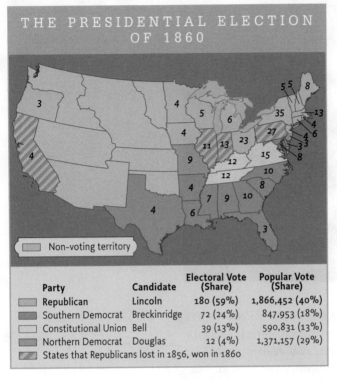

THE PRESIDENTIAL ELECTION OF 1860

Non-voting territory

Party	Candidate	Electoral Vote (Share)	Popular Vote (Share)
Republican	Lincoln	180 (59%)	1,866,452 (40%)
Southern Democrat	Breckinridge	72 (24%)	847,953 (18%)
Constitutional Union	Bell	39 (13%)	590,831 (13%)
Northern Democrat	Douglas	12 (4%)	1,371,157 (29%)
States that Republicans lost in 1856, won in 1860			

The election of Lincoln

their northern counterparts. Douglas's backers, for their part, would not accept a platform that doomed their party to certain defeat in the North.

Meanwhile, Republicans gathered in Chicago and chose Lincoln as their standard-bearer. The party platform denied the validity of the Dred Scott decision, reaffirmed Republicans' opposition to slavery's expansion, and added economic planks designed to appeal to a broad array of northern voters—free homesteads in the West, a protective tariff, and government aid in building a transcontinental railroad.

In effect, two presidential campaigns took place in 1860. In the North, Lincoln and Douglas were the combatants. In the South, the Republicans had no presence, and three candidates contested the election—Douglas, Breckinridge, and John Bell of Tennessee, the candidate of the hastily organized Constitutional Union Party. A haven for Unionist former Whigs, this new party adopted a platform consisting of a single pledge—to preserve "the Constitution as it is [that is, with slavery] and the Union as it was [without sectional discord]."

The most striking thing about the election returns was their sectional character. Lincoln carried all of the North except New Jersey, receiving 1.8 million popular votes (54 percent of the regional total and 40 percent of the national) and 180 electoral votes (a clear majority). Breckinridge captured most of the slave states, although Bell carried three Upper South states and about 40 percent of the southern vote as a whole. Douglas placed first only in Missouri, but he was the only candidate with significant support in all parts of the country. His failure to carry either section, however, suggested that a traditional political career based on devotion to the Union was no longer possible. Without a single vote in ten southern states, Lincoln was elected the nation's sixteenth president. But because of the North's superiority in population, Lincoln would still have carried the electoral college and thus been elected president even if the votes of his three opponents had all been cast for a single candidate.

An 1860 engraving of a mass meeting in Savannah, Georgia, shortly after Lincoln's election as president, which called for the state to secede from the Union. The banner on the obelisk at the center reads, "Our Motto Southern Rights, Equality of the States, Don't Tread on Me"—the last a slogan from the American Revolution.

THE IMPENDING CRISIS

The Secession Movement

In the eyes of many white southerners, Lincoln's victory placed their future at the mercy of a party avowedly hostile to their region's values and interests. Those advocating secession did not believe Lincoln's administration would take immediate steps against slavery in the states. But if, as seemed quite possible, the election of 1860 marked a fundamental shift in power, the beginning of a long period of Republican rule, who could say what the North's antislavery sentiment would demand in five years, or ten? Slaveowners, moreover, feared Republican efforts to extend their party into the South by appealing to non-slaveholders. Rather than accept permanent minority status, Deep South political leaders boldly struck for their region's independence.

Southern response to Lincoln's victory

In the months that followed Lincoln's election, seven states stretching from South Carolina to Texas seceded from the Union. These were the states of the Cotton Kingdom, where slaves represented a larger part of the total population than in the Upper South. First to secede was South Carolina, the state with the highest percentage of slaves in its population and a long history of political radicalism. On December 20, 1860, the legislature unanimously voted to leave the Union. Its *Declaration of the Immediate*

South Carolina

Causes of Secession placed the issue of slavery squarely at the center of the crisis. Experience had proved "that slaveholding states cannot be safe in subjection to nonslaveholding states."

The Secession Crisis

As the Union unraveled, President Buchanan seemed paralyzed. He denied that a state could secede, but he also insisted that the federal government had no right to use force against it. Other political leaders struggled to find a formula to resolve the crisis. Senator John J. Crittenden of Kentucky, a slave state on the border between North and South, offered the most widely supported compromise plan of the secession winter. Embodied in a series of unamendable constitutional amendments, Crittenden's proposal would have guaranteed the future of slavery in the states where it existed and extended the Missouri Compromise line to the Pacific Ocean, dividing between slavery and free soil all territories "now held, or hereafter acquired." The seceding states rejected the compromise as too little, too late. But many in the Upper South and North saw it as a way to settle sectional differences and prevent civil war.

Crittenden compromise

Crittenden's plan, however, foundered on the opposition of Abraham Lincoln. Willing to conciliate the South on issues like the return of fugitive slaves, Lincoln took an unyielding stand against the expansion of slavery. "We have just carried an election," he wrote, "on principles fairly stated to the people. Now we are told in advance that the government shall be broken up unless we surrender to those we have beaten, before we take the offices. . . . If we surrender, it is the end of us and the end of the government."

Lincoln's opposition to the Crittenden plan

Before Lincoln assumed office on March 4, 1861, the seven seceding states formed the Confederate States of America, adopted a constitution, and chose as their president Jefferson Davis of Mississippi. With a few alterations—the president served a single six-year term; cabinet members, as in Britain, could sit in Congress—the Confederate constitution was modeled closely on that of the United States. It departed from the federal Constitution, however, in explicitly guaranteeing slave property both in the states and in any territories the new nation acquired. The "cornerstone" of the Confederacy, announced Davis's vice president, Alexander H. Stephens of Georgia, was "the great truth that the negro is not equal to the white man, that slavery, subordination to the superior race, is his natural and normal condition."

The Confederate States of America

And the War Came

In his inaugural address, delivered on March 4, 1861, Lincoln tried to be conciliatory. He rejected the right of secession but denied any intention of interfering with slavery in the states. He said nothing of retaking the forts, arsenals, and customs houses the Confederacy had seized, although he did promise to "hold" remaining federal property in the seceding states. But Lincoln also issued a veiled warning: "In your hands, my dissatisfied fellow countrymen, and not in mine, is the momentous issue of civil war."

In his first month as president, Lincoln walked a tightrope. He avoided any action that might drive more states from the Union, encouraged southern Unionists to assert themselves within the Confederacy, and sought to quiet a growing clamor in the North for forceful action against secession. Knowing that the risk of war existed, Lincoln strove to ensure that if hostilities did break out, the South, not the Union, would fire the first shot. And that is precisely what happened on April 12, 1861, at Fort Sumter, an enclave of Union control in the harbor of Charleston, South Carolina.

A few days earlier, Lincoln had notified South Carolina's governor that he intended to replenish the garrison's dwindling food supplies. Viewing Fort Sumter's presence as an affront to southern nationhood and perhaps hoping to force the wavering Upper South to join the

Lincoln's response to secession

Fort Sumter

Inauguration of Mr. Lincoln, a photograph taken on March 4, 1861. The unfinished dome of the Capitol building symbolizes the precarious state of the Union at the time Lincoln assumed office.

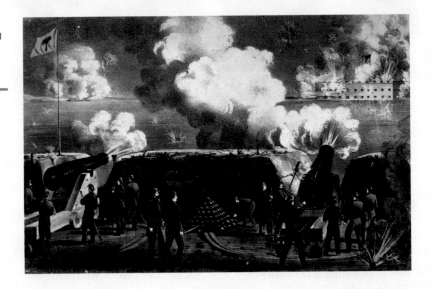

Bombardment of Fort Sumter,
a lithograph by Nathaniel Currier and
James Ives depicting the beginning
of the Civil War.

Confederacy, Jefferson Davis ordered batteries to fire on the fort. On April
14, its commander surrendered. The following day, Lincoln proclaimed
that an insurrection existed in the South and called for 75,000 troops to
suppress it. Civil war had begun. Within weeks, Virginia, North Carolina,
Tennessee, and Arkansas joined the Confederacy. "Both sides deprecated
war," Lincoln later said, "but one of them would *make* war rather than let
the nation survive; and the other would *accept* war rather than let it perish.
And the war came."

The Union created by the founders lay in ruins. The struggle to
rebuild it would bring about a new birth of American freedom.

CHAPTER REVIEW AND ONLINE RESOURCES

REVIEW QUESTIONS

1. *Explain the justifications for the doctrine of manifest destiny, including material and idealistic motivations.*

2. *Why did many Americans criticize the Mexican War? How did they see expansion as a threat to American liberties?*

3. *How did the concept of "race" develop by the mid-nineteenth century? How did it enter into the manifest destiny debate?*

4. *How did western expansion affect the sectional tensions between the North and South?*

5. *How did the market revolution contribute to the rise of the Republican Party? How did those economic and political factors serve to unite groups in the Northeast and in the Northwest, and why was that unity significant?*

6. *Based on the Lincoln-Douglas debates, how did the two differ on the expansion of slavery, equal rights, and the role of the national government? Use examples of their words to illustrate your points.*

7. *Why did Stephen Douglas, among others, believe that "popular sovereignty" could resolve sectional divisions of the 1850s? Why did the idea not work out?*

8. *Explain how sectional voting patterns in the 1860 presidential election allowed southern "fire-eaters" to justify secession.*

9. *What do the California gold rush and the opening of Japan reveal about the United States involvement in a global economic system?*

KEY TERMS

Tejanos (p. 370)

Texas revolt (p. 370)

Santa Anna (p. 370)

"reannexation" of Texas and "reoccupation" of Oregon (p. 371)

gold rush (p. 376)

Commodore Matthew Perry (p. 377)

Wilmot Proviso (p. 378)

Free Soil Party (p. 379)

Compromise of 1850 (p. 380)

Fugitive Slave Act (p. 381)

popular sovereignty (p. 382)

Kansas-Nebraska Act (p. 382)

Know-Nothing Party (p. 385)

"Bleeding Kansas" (p. 388)

Dred Scott decision (p. 389)

Lincoln-Douglas debates (p. 391)

Harpers Ferry (p. 391)

"filibustering" expeditions (p. 394)

"fire-eaters" (p. 395)

wwnorton.com
/studyspace

VISIT STUDYSPACE FOR THESE
RESOURCES AND MORE

- A chapter outline
- A diagnostic chapter quiz
- Interactive maps
- Map worksheets
- Multimedia documents

1861   Civil War begins at Fort Sumter

First Battle of Bull Run

1862   Forts Henry and Donelson captured

Monitor v. *Merrimac* sea battle

Battle of Shiloh

Confederacy institutes the draft Homestead Act

Seven Days' Campaign

Second Battle of Bull Run

Union Pacific and Central Pacific chartered

Morrill Act of 1862

Battle at Antietam

1863   Emancipation Proclamation

Siege of Vicksburg

Battle at Gettysburg

New York draft riots

Lincoln introduces his Ten-Percent Plan

1864   General Grant begins a war of attrition

Wade-Davis Bill

General Sherman marches to the sea

1865   Thirteenth Amendment

Union capture of Richmond

General Lee surrenders to General Grant at Appomattox Courthouse

Lincoln assassinated

1866   *Ex parte Milligan* ruling

Departure of the 7th Regiment, a lithograph from 1861 illustrating the departure of a unit of the New York State militia for service in the Civil War. A contemporary writer captured the exuberant spirit of the early days of the war: "New York was certainly raving mad with excitement. The ladies laughed, smiled, sighed, sobbed, and wept. The men cheered and shouted as never men cheered and shouted before."

CHAPTER 14

A NEW BIRTH OF FREEDOM

THE CIVIL WAR, 1861-1865

L ike hundreds of thousands of other Americans, Marcus M. Spiegel volunteered in 1861 to fight in the Civil War. Born into a Jewish family in Germany in 1829, Spiegel emigrated to Ohio, where he married the daughter of a local farmer. When the Civil War broke out, the nation's 150,000 Jews represented less than 1 percent of the total population. But Spiegel shared wholeheartedly in American patriotism. He went to war, he wrote to his brother-in-law, to defend "the flag that was ever ready to protect you and me and every one who sought its protection from oppression." He never wavered in his commitment to the "glorious cause" of preserving the Union and its heritage of freedom.

What one Pennsylvania recruit called "the magic word *Freedom*" shaped how many Union soldiers understood the conflict. But as the war progressed, prewar understandings of liberty gave way to something new. Millions of northerners who had not been abolitionists became convinced that preserving the Union required the destruction of slavery. Marcus Spiegel's changing views mirrored this transformation. Spiegel was an ardent Democrat. He shared the era's racist attitudes and thought Lincoln's Emancipation Proclamation a serious mistake. Yet as the Union army penetrated the heart of the Deep South, Spiegel became increasingly opposed to slavery. "Since I am here," he wrote to his wife from Louisiana in January 1864, "I have learned and seen . . . the horrors of slavery. . . . Never hereafter will I either speak or vote in favor of slavery."

Marcus Spiegel was killed in a minor engagement in Louisiana in May 1864, one of hundreds of thousands of Americans to perish in the Civil War.

FOCUS QUESTIONS

- *Why is the Civil War considered the first modern war?*

- *How did a war to preserve the Union become a war to end slavery?*

- *How did the Civil War transform the national economy and create a stronger nation-state?*

- *How did the war effort affect the society and economy of the Confederacy?*

- *What were the military and political turning points of the war?*

- *What were the most important wartime "rehearsals for Reconstruction"?*

THE FIRST MODERN WAR

The American Civil War is often called the **first modern war**. Never before had mass armies confronted each other on the battlefield with the deadly weapons created by the industrial revolution. The resulting casualties dwarfed anything in the American experience. Beginning as a battle of army versus army, the war became a conflict of society against society, in which the distinction between military and civilian targets often disappeared. In a war of this kind, the effectiveness of political leadership, the ability to mobilize economic resources, and a society's willingness to keep up the fight despite setbacks are as crucial to the outcome as success or failure on individual battlefields.

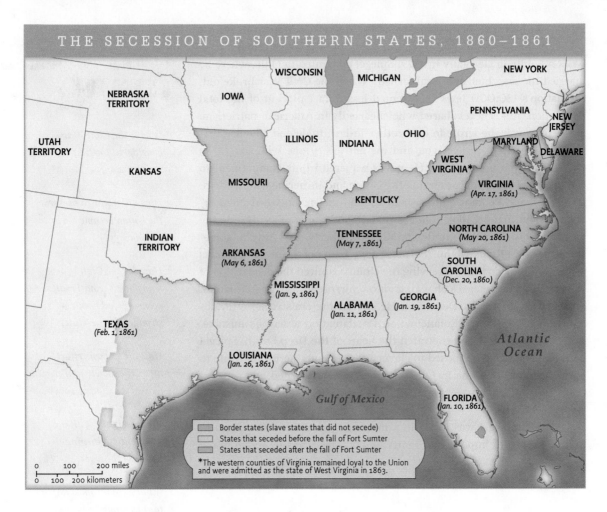

THE SECESSION OF SOUTHERN STATES, 1860–1861

Border states (slave states that did not secede)
States that seceded before the fall of Fort Sumter
States that seceded after the fall of Fort Sumter

*The western counties of Virginia remained loyal to the Union and were admitted as the state of West Virginia in 1863.

By the time secession ran its course, eleven slave states had left the Union.

Advantages of the North and South

The Two Combatants

Almost any comparison between Union and Confederacy seemed to favor the Union. The population of the North and the loyal border slave states numbered 22 million in 1860, whereas only 9 million persons lived in the Confederacy, 3.5 million of them slaves. In manufacturing, railroad mileage, and financial resources, the Union far outstripped its opponent. On the other hand, the Union confronted by far the greater task. To restore the shattered nation, it had to invade and conquer an area larger than western Europe. Moreover, Confederate soldiers were highly motivated fighters, defending their homes and families.

On both sides, the outbreak of war stirred powerful feelings of patriotism. Recruits rushed to enlist, expecting a short, glorious war. Later, as enthusiasm waned, both sides resorted to a **draft**. By 1865, more

Sergeant James W. Travis, Thirty-eighth Illinois Infantry, Union army, and Private Edwin Francis Jemison, Second Louisiana Regiment, Confederate army, two of the nearly 3 million Americans who fought in the Civil War. Before going off to war, many soldiers sat for photographs like these, reproduced on small cards called *cartes de visite*, which they distributed to friends and loved ones. Jemison was killed in the Battle of Malvern Hill in July 1862.

than 2 million men had served in the Union army and 900,000 in the Confederate army. Each was a cross section of its society: the North's was composed largely of farm boys, shopkeepers, artisans, and urban workers, while the South's consisted mostly of non-slaveholding small farmers, with slaveowners dominating the officer corps.

> *Soldiers North and South*

The Technology of War

Neither the soldiers nor their officers were prepared for the way technology had transformed warfare. The Civil War was the first major conflict in which the railroad transported troops and supplies and the first to see railroad junctions such as Atlanta and Petersburg become major military objectives. The famous sea battle between the Union vessel ***Monitor*** and the Confederate ***Merrimac*** in 1862 was the first demonstration of the superiority of ironclads over wooden ships, revolutionizing naval warfare. The war saw the use of the telegraph for military communication, the introduction of observation balloons to view enemy lines, and even primitive hand grenades and submarines.

> *Ironclad ships*

Perhaps most important, a revolution in arms manufacturing had replaced the traditional musket, accurate at only a short range, with the more modern rifle, deadly at 600 yards or more because of its grooved (or "rifled") barrel. This development changed the nature of combat, emphasizing the importance of heavy fortifications and elaborate trenches and giving those on the defensive—usually southern armies—a significant advantage over attacking forces. The war of rifle and trench produced the appalling casualty statistics of Civil War battles. The most recent estimate

> *The rifle*

An eight-inch cannon, one of the weapons forged in the industrial revolution and deployed in the Civil War.

of those who perished in the war—around 750,000 men—represents the equivalent, in terms of today's population, of more than 7 million men. The death toll in the Civil War nearly equals the total number of Americans who died in all the nation's other wars, from the Revolution to the war in Iraq.

Nor was either side ready for other aspects of modern warfare. Medical care remained primitive. Diseases such as measles, dysentery, malaria, and typhus swept through army camps, killing more men than did combat. The Civil War was the first war in which large numbers of Americans were captured by the enemy and held in dire conditions in military prisons. Some 50,000 men died in these prisons, victims of starvation and disease, including 13,000 Union soldiers at Andersonville, Georgia.

The Public and the War

Propaganda

Another modern feature of the Civil War was that both sides were assisted by a vast propaganda effort to mobilize public opinion. In the Union, an outpouring of lithographs, souvenirs, sheet music, and pamphlets issued

War Spirit at Home, an 1866 painting by the New Jersey artist Lilly M. Spencer, depicts a family reading the news of the Union capture of Vicksburg in 1863. The household is now composed of women and children; the husband may be off in the army. While the children play as soldiers, the cross in the folds of the newspaper suggests a less celebratory reflection on the conflict. Newspapers brought news of the war into American homes.

by patriotic organizations and the War Department reaffirmed northern values, tarred the Democratic Party with the brush of treason, and accused the South of numerous crimes against Union soldiers and loyal civilians. Comparable items appeared in the Confederacy.

At the same time, the war's brutal realities were brought home with unprecedented immediacy to the public at large. War correspondents accompanied the armies, and newspapers reported the results of battles on the following day and quickly published long lists of casualties. The infant art of photography carried images of war into millions of American living rooms.

Mobilizing Resources

The outbreak of the war found both sides unprepared. In 1861, there was no national railroad gauge (the distance separating the two tracks), so trains built for one line could not run on another. There was no national banking system, no tax system capable of raising the enormous funds needed to finance the war, and not even accurate maps of the southern states. Soon after the firing on Fort Sumter, Lincoln proclaimed a naval blockade of the South, part of the so-called Anaconda Plan, which aimed to strangle the South economically. But the navy charged with patrolling the 3,500-mile coastline consisted of only ninety vessels, fewer than half of them steam powered. Not until late in the war did the blockade become effective.

Then there was the problem of purchasing and distributing the food, weapons, and other supplies required by the soldiers. The Union army eventually became the best-fed and best-supplied military force in history. By the war's third year, on the other hand, southern armies were suffering from acute shortages of food, uniforms, and shoes.

Military Strategies

Each side tried to find ways to maximize its advantages. Essentially, the Confederacy adopted a defensive strategy, with occasional thrusts into the North. General Robert E. Lee, the leading southern commander, was a brilliant battlefield tactician who felt confident of his ability to fend off

FIGURE 14.1 Resources for War: Union versus Confederacy

Population: 22 million / 9 million (including 3.5 million slaves)

Factories: 110,000 / 18,000 — Union / Confederacy

Value of goods produced: 1.5 billion / 155 million

Railroad tracks (% of total U.S. mileage): 70% / 30%

Textiles (including cotton cloth and woolen goods): Ratio 17:1

Firearms: Ratio 32:1

Pig iron: Ratio 20:1

In nearly every resource for warfare, the Union enjoyed a distinct advantage. But this did not make Union victory inevitable; as in the War of Independence, the stronger side sometimes loses.

A defensive strategy

Union army wagons crossing the Rapidan River in Virginia in May 1864. Supplying Civil War armies required an immense mobilization of economic resources.

attacks by larger Union forces. He hoped that a series of defeats would weaken the North's resolve and lead it eventually to abandon the conflict and recognize southern independence.

Changing northern strategy

Lincoln's early generals initially concentrated on occupying southern territory and attempting to capture Richmond, the Confederate capital. They attacked sporadically and withdrew after a battle, thus sacrificing the North's manpower superiority and allowing the South to concentrate its smaller forces when an engagement impended. Well before his generals did, Lincoln realized that simply capturing and occupying territory would not win the war, and that defeating the South's armies, not capturing its capital, had to be the North's battlefield objective. And when he came to adopt the policy of emancipation, Lincoln acknowledged what Confederate vice president Alexander H. Stephens had already affirmed: slavery was the "cornerstone" of the Confederacy. To win the war, therefore, the Union must make the institution that lay at the economic and social foundation of southern life a military target.

The War Begins

In the East, most of the war's fighting took place in a narrow corridor between Washington and Richmond—a distance of only 100 miles—as a succession of Union generals led the Army of the Potomac (as the main northern force in the East was called) toward the Confederate capital, only to be turned back by southern forces. The first significant engagement, the

First Bull Run

first Battle of Bull Run, took place in northern Virginia on July 21, 1861. It ended with the chaotic retreat of the Union soldiers, along with the sight-seers and politicians who had come to watch the battle.

McClellan

In the wake of Bull Run, George B. McClellan, an army engineer who had recently won a minor engagement with Confederate troops in western Virginia, assumed command of the Union's Army of the Potomac. A brilliant organizer, McClellan succeeded in welding his men into a superb fighting force. He seemed reluctant, however, to commit them to

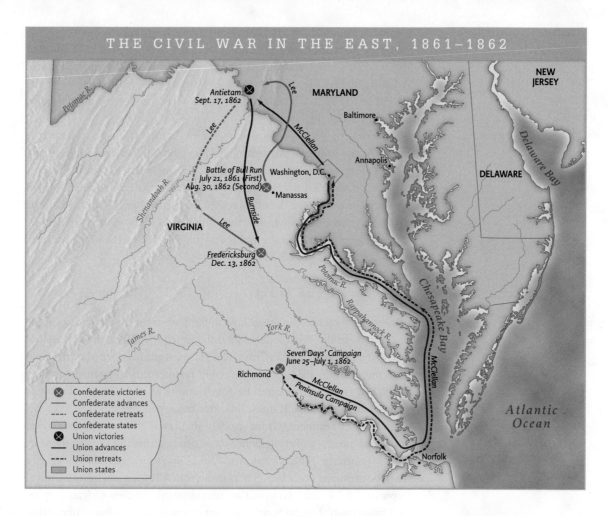

THE CIVIL WAR IN THE EAST, 1861–1862

Antietam
Sept. 17, 1862

MARYLAND

Baltimore

Lee

McClellan

Annapolis

NEW JERSEY

DELAWARE

Delaware Bay

Battle of Bull Run
July 21, 1861 (First)
Aug. 30, 1862 (Second)

Washington, D.C.

Manassas

Burnside

VIRGINIA

Lee

Fredericksburg
Dec. 13, 1862

Shenandoah R.

Potomac R.

Rappahannock R.

Chesapeake Bay

James R.

York R.

Seven Days' Campaign
June 25–July 1, 1862

Richmond

McClellan
Peninsula Campaign

McClellan

Norfolk

Atlantic Ocean

Confederate victories
Confederate advances
Confederate retreats
Confederate states
Union victories
Union advances
Union retreats
Union states

battle, since he tended to overestimate the size of enemy forces. And as a Democrat, he hoped that compromise might end the war without large-scale loss of life or a weakening of slavery. Months of military inactivity followed.

During the first two years of the war, most of the fighting took place in Virginia and Maryland.

The War in the East, 1862

Not until the spring of 1862, after a growing clamor for action by Republican newspapers, members of Congress, and an increasingly impatient Lincoln, did McClellan lead his army of more than 100,000 men into Virginia. Here they confronted the smaller Army of Northern Virginia under the command of the Confederate general Joseph E. Johnston, and after he was wounded, Robert E. Lee. In the Seven Days' Campaign, a series of engagements in June 1862 on the peninsula south of Richmond, Lee blunted McClellan's attacks and forced him to withdraw back to the vicinity of Washington, D.C. In August 1862, Lee again emerged victorious at the second Battle of Bull Run against Union forces under the command of General John Pope.

Successful on the defensive, Lee now launched an invasion of the North. At the **Battle of Antietam**, in Maryland, McClellan and the Army of the Potomac repelled Lee's advance. In a single day of fighting, nearly 4,000 men were killed and 18,000 wounded (2,000 of whom later died of their injuries). More Americans died on September 17, 1862, when the Battle of Antietam was fought, than on any other day in the nation's history, including Pearl Harbor and D-Day in World War II and the terrorist attacks of September 11, 2001.

The War in the West

While the Union accomplished little in the East in the first two years of the war, events in the West followed a different course. Here, the architect of early success was Ulysses S. Grant. A West Point graduate who had resigned from the army in 1854, Grant had been notably unsuccessful in civilian life. When the war broke out, he was working as a clerk in his brother's leather store in Galena, Illinois. But after being commissioned as a colonel in an Illinois regiment, Grant quickly displayed the daring, the logical mind, and the grasp of strategy he would demonstrate throughout the war.

In February 1862, Grant won the Union's first significant victory when he captured Forts Henry and Donelson in Tennessee. In April, naval forces under Admiral David G. Farragut steamed into New Orleans, giving the Union control of the South's largest city and the rich sugar plantation parishes to its south and west. At the same time, Grant withstood a surprise Confederate attack at Shiloh, Tennessee. But Union momentum in the West then stalled.

THE COMING OF EMANCIPATION

Slavery and the War

War, it has been said, is the midwife of revolution. And the Civil War produced far-reaching changes in American life. The most dramatic of these was the destruction of slavery, the central institution of southern society.

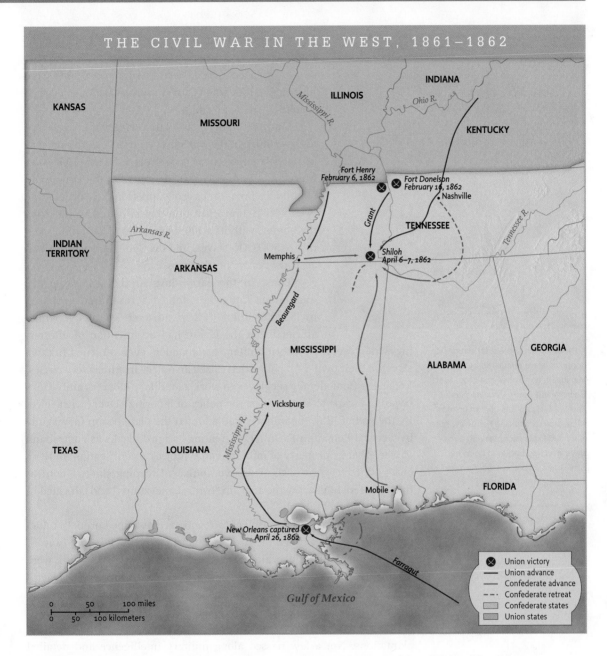

THE CIVIL WAR IN THE WEST, 1861–1862

Most of the Union's victories in the first two years of the war occurred in the West, especially at Shiloh and New Orleans.

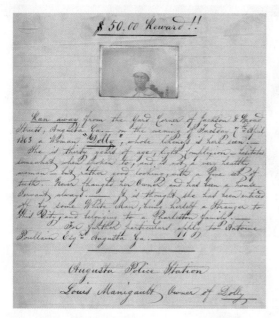

An 1863 advertisement for a runaway domestic slave circulated by Louis Manigault, a member of a prominent Georgia and South Carolina planter family. Manigault blamed an unknown white man for enticing her away, but she most likely escaped with a male slave who had begun to court her. Slaves fled to Union lines from the first days of the Civil War.

The "freedom war"

In numbers, scale, and the economic power of the institution of slavery, American emancipation dwarfed that of any other country (although far more people were liberated in 1861 when Czar Alexander II abolished serfdom in the Russian empire).

Lincoln initially insisted that slavery was irrelevant to the conflict. In the war's first year, his paramount concerns were to keep the border slave states—Delaware, Maryland, Kentucky, and Missouri—in the Union and to build the broadest base of support in the North for the war effort. Action against slavery, he feared, would drive the border, with its white population of 2.6 million and nearly 500,000 slaves, into the Confederacy and alienate conservative northerners.

Thus, in the early days of the war, a nearly unanimous Congress adopted a resolution proposed by Senator John J. Crittenden of Kentucky, which affirmed that the Union had no intention of interfering with slavery. Northern military commanders even returned fugitive slaves to their owners, a policy that raised an outcry in antislavery circles. Yet as the Confederacy set slaves to work as military laborers and blacks began to escape to Union lines, the policy of ignoring slavery unraveled. By the end of 1861, the military had adopted the plan, begun in Virginia by General Benjamin F. Butler, of treating escaped blacks as contraband of war—that is, property of military value subject to confiscation. Butler's order added a word to the war's vocabulary. Escaping slaves ("**contrabands**") were housed by the army in "contraband camps" and educated in new "contraband schools."

Meanwhile, slaves themselves took actions that helped propel a reluctant white America down the road to emancipation. Well before Lincoln made emancipation a war aim, blacks, in the North and the South, were calling the conflict the "freedom war." In 1861 and 1862, as the federal army occupied Confederate territory, slaves by the thousands headed for Union lines. Unlike fugitives before the war, these runaways included large numbers of women and children, as entire families abandoned the plantations. Not a few passed along military intelligence and detailed knowledge of the South's terrain. In southern Louisiana, the arrival of the Union army in 1862 led slaves to sack plantation houses and refuse to work unless wages were paid. Slavery there, wrote a northern reporter, "is forever destroyed and worthless, no matter what Mr. Lincoln or anyone else may say on the subject."

Steps toward Emancipation

The most uncompromising opponents of slavery before the war, abolitionists and **Radical Republicans**, quickly concluded that the institution must
become a target of the Union war effort. Outside of Congress, few pressed
the case for emancipation more eloquently than Frederick Douglass. From
the outset, he insisted that it was futile to "separate the freedom of the slave
from the victory of the government."

These appeals won increasing support in a Congress frustrated by
lack of military success. In March 1862, Congress prohibited the army
from returning fugitive slaves. Then came abolition in the District of
Columbia (with monetary compensation for slaveholders) and the territories, followed in July by the Second Confiscation Act, which liberated
slaves of disloyal owners in Union-occupied territory, as well as slaves
who escaped to Union lines.

Congressional policy against slavery

Throughout these months, Lincoln struggled to retain control of
the emancipation issue. In August 1861, John C. Frémont, commanding Union forces in Missouri, a state racked by a bitter guerrilla war
between pro-northern and pro-southern bands, decreed the freedom of its
slaves. Fearful of the order's impact on the border states, Lincoln swiftly
rescinded it. In November, the president proposed that the border states
embark on a program of gradual emancipation with the federal government paying owners for their loss of property. He also revived the idea
of colonization. In August 1862, Lincoln met at the White House with a
delegation of black leaders and urged them to promote emigration from
the United States. "You and we are different races," he declared. "It is better
for us both to be separated." As late as December, the president signed an
agreement with a shady entrepreneur to settle former slaves on an island
off the coast of Haiti.

Lincoln's evolving policy

Abe Lincoln's Last Card, an
engraving from the British magazine
Punch, October 18, 1862, portrays
the Preliminary Emancipation
Proclamation as the last move of
a desperate gambler.

ABE LINCOLN'S LAST CARE OR, ROUGE-ET-NOIR.

Lincoln's Decision

Sometime during the summer of 1862, Lincoln concluded that emancipation had become a political and
military necessity. Many factors contributed to his
decision—lack of military success, hope that emancipated slaves might help meet the army's growing manpower needs, changing northern public opinion, and the
calculation that making slavery a target of the war effort
would counteract sentiment in Britain for recognition of
the Confederacy. But on the advice of Secretary of State

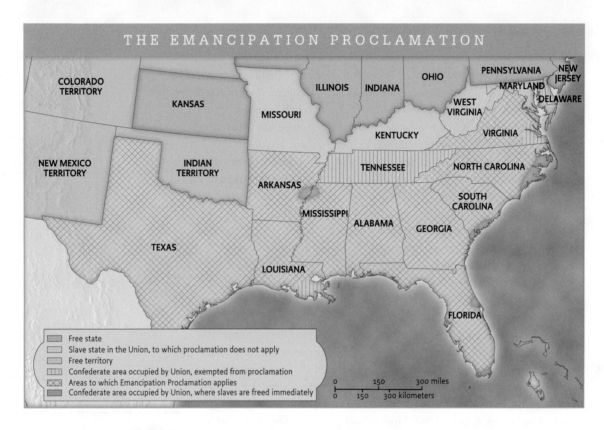

THE EMANCIPATION PROCLAMATION

Legend:
- Free state
- Slave state in the Union, to which proclamation does not apply
- Free territory
- Confederate area occupied by Union, exempted from proclamation
- Areas to which Emancipation Proclamation applies
- Confederate area occupied by Union, where slaves are freed immediately

0   150   300 miles
0   150   300 kilometers

With the exception of a few areas, the Emancipation Proclamation applied only to slaves in parts of the Confederacy not under Union control on January 1, 1863. Lincoln did not "free the slaves" with a stroke of his pen, but the proclamation did change the nature of the Civil War.

William H. Seward, Lincoln delayed his announcement until after a Union victory, lest it seem an act of desperation. On September 22, 1862, five days after McClellan's army forced Lee to retreat at Antietam, Lincoln issued the Preliminary Emancipation Proclamation. It warned that unless the South laid down its arms by the end of 1862, he would decree abolition.

The initial northern reaction was not encouraging. In the fall elections of 1862, Democrats made opposition to emancipation the centerpiece of their campaign. The Republicans suffered sharp reverses. In his annual message to Congress, early in December, Lincoln tried to calm northerners' racial fears: "In giving freedom to the slave, we assure freedom to the free—honorable alike in what we give, and what we preserve."

The Emancipation Proclamation

Effects of the Emancipation Proclamation

On January 1, 1863, after greeting visitors at the annual White House New Year's reception, Lincoln retired to his study to sign the **Emancipation Proclamation**. The document did not liberate all the slaves—indeed, on the day it was issued, it applied to very few. Because its legality derived from the president's authority as military commander-in-chief to combat the South's rebellion, the proclamation exempted areas firmly under Union control (where the war, in effect, had already ended). Thus, it did not apply to the loyal border slave states that had never seceded or to areas of the Confederacy occupied by Union soldiers, such as Tennessee and parts of Virginia and Louisiana. But the vast majority of the South's slaves—more than 3 million men, women, and children—it declared "henceforward shall be free." Since most of these slaves were still behind Confederate lines, however, their liberation would have to await Union victories.

Despite its limitations, the proclamation set off scenes of jubilation among free blacks and abolitionists in the North and "contrabands" and slaves in the South. "Sound the loud timbrel o'er Egypt's dark sea," intoned a black preacher at a celebration in Boston. "Jehovah hath triumphed, his people are free." By making the Union army an agent of emancipation and wedding the goals of Union and abolition, the proclamation sounded the eventual death knell of slavery.

Not only did the Emancipation Proclamation alter the nature of the Civil War and the course of American history, but it also marked a turning point in Lincoln's own thinking. For the first time, it committed the government to enlisting black soldiers in the Union army. He would later refuse suggestions that he rescind or modify the proclamation in the interest of peace. Were he to do so, he told one visitor, "I should be damned in time and eternity."

Like the end of slavery in Haiti and mainland Latin America, abolition in the United States came about as the result of war. But emancipation

Freed Negroes Celebrating President Lincoln's Decree of Emancipation, a fanciful engraving from the French periodical *Le Monde Illustré,* March 21, 1863.

in the United States differed from its counterparts elsewhere in the Western Hemisphere—it was immediate, not gradual, and offered no compensation to slaveholders for their loss of property (with the exception of those in Washington, D.C.). Not until 1888, when Brazil abolished the institution, did slavery come to an end in the entire Western Hemisphere.

The evolution of Lincoln's emancipation policy displayed the hallmarks of his wartime leadership—his capacity for growth and his ability to develop broad public support for his administration.

Enlisting Black Troops

Of the proclamation's provisions, few were more radical in their implications than the enrollment of blacks into military service. Since sailor had been one of the few occupations open to free blacks before the war, Secretary of the Navy Gideon Welles had already allowed African-Americans to serve on Union warships. But at the outset, the Union army refused to accept northern black volunteers. The administration feared that whites would not be willing to fight alongside blacks and that enlisting black soldiers would alienate the border slave states that remained in the Union.

By the end of the war, however, more than 180,000 black men had served in the Union army and 24,000 in the navy. One-third died in battle, or of wounds or disease. Some black units won considerable renown, among them the Fifty-fourth Massachusetts Volunteers, a company of free blacks from throughout the North commanded by Robert Gould Shaw, a young reformer from a prominent Boston family. The bravery of the Fifty-fourth in the July 1863 attack on Fort Wagner, South Carolina, where nearly half the unit, including Shaw, perished, helped to dispel widespread doubts about blacks' ability to withstand the pressures of the Civil War battlefield.

Most black soldiers were emancipated slaves who joined the army in the South. After Union forces in 1863 seized control of the rich plantation lands of the Mississippi Valley, General Lorenzo Thomas raised fifty regiments of black soldiers—some 76,000 men in all. Another large group hailed from the border states exempted from the Emancipation Proclamation, where enlistment was, for most of the war, the only route to freedom. Here black military service undermined slavery, for Congress expanded the Emancipation Proclamation to liberate black soldiers and their families.

The Black Soldier

For black soldiers themselves, military service proved to be a liberating experience. Out of the army came many of the leaders of the Reconstruction era. At least 130 former soldiers served in political office after the Civil

War. In time, the memory of black military service would fade from white America's collective memory. Of the hundreds of Civil War monuments that still dot the northern landscape, fewer than a dozen contain an image of a black soldier. But well into the twentieth century, it remained a point of pride in black families throughout the United States that their fathers and grandfathers had fought for freedom.

Within the army, however, black soldiers received treatment that was anything but equal to that of their white counterparts. Organized into segregated units under sometimes abusive white officers, they initially received lower pay (ten dollars per month, compared to sixteen dollars for white soldiers). They were disproportionately assigned to labor rather than combat, and they could not rise to the rank of commissioned officer until the very end of the war. In a notorious incident in 1864, 200 of 262 black soldiers died when southern troops under the command of Nathan B. Forrest overran Fort Pillow in Tennessee. Some of those who perished were killed after surrendering.

This is the only known photograph of a black Union soldier with his family.

Nonetheless, black soldiers played a crucial role not only in winning the Civil War but also in defining the war's consequences. Thanks in part to black military service, many Republicans in the last two years of the war came to believe that emancipation must bring with it equal protection of the laws regardless of race. One of the first acts of the federal government to recognize this principle was the granting of retroactive equal pay to black soldiers early in 1865.

The illustration accompanying *The American Flag*, a piece of patriotic Civil War sheet music, exemplifies how the war united the ideals of liberty and nationhood.

The service of black soldiers affected Lincoln's own outlook. In 1864, Lincoln, who before the war had never supported suffrage for African-Americans, urged the governor of Union-occupied Louisiana to work for the partial enfranchisement of blacks, singling out soldiers as especially deserving. At some future time, he observed, they might again be called upon to "keep the *jewel of Liberty* in the family of freedom."

THE SECOND AMERICAN REVOLUTION

The changing status of black Americans was only one dramatic example of what some historians call the **Second American Revolution**—the transformation of American government and society brought about by the Civil War.

THE AMERICAN FLAG,
A NEW NATIONAL LYRIC.

Liberty, Union, and Nation

A songbook compiled and illustrated by a Union soldier includes "John Brown's Body," sung to the melody of a Methodist hymn.

Never was freedom's contested nature more evident than during the Civil War. "We all declare for liberty," Lincoln observed in 1864, "but in using the same *word* we do not all mean the same *thing*." To the North, he continued, freedom meant for "each man" to enjoy "the product of his labor." To southern whites, it conveyed mastership—the power to do "as they please with other men, and the product of other men's labor." The Union's triumph consolidated the northern understanding of freedom as the national norm.

But it was Lincoln himself who linked the conflict with the deepest beliefs of northern society. It is sometimes said that the American Civil War was part of a broader nineteenth-century process of nation building. Throughout the world, powerful, centralized nation-states developed in old countries, and new nations emerged where none had previously existed. The Civil War took place as modern states were consolidating their power and reducing local autonomy. The Meiji Restoration in Japan saw the emperor reclaim power from local lords, or shoguns. Lincoln has been called the American equivalent of Giuseppe Mazzini or Otto von Bismarck, who during this same era created nation-states in Italy and Germany from disunited collections of principalities. But Lincoln's nation was different from those being constructed in Europe. They were based on the idea of unifying a particular people with a common ethnic, cultural, and linguistic heritage. To Lincoln, the American nation embodied a set of universal ideas, centered on political democracy and human liberty.

The Gettysburg Address

Lincoln summarized his conception of the war's meaning in November 1863 in brief remarks at the dedication of a military cemetery at the site of the war's greatest battle. The Gettysburg Address is considered his finest speech (see the Appendix for the full text). In less than three minutes, he identified the nation's mission with the principle that "all men are created equal," spoke of the war as bringing about a "new birth of freedom," and defined the essence of democratic government. The sacrifices of Union soldiers, he declared, would ensure that "government of the people, by the people, for the people, shall not perish from the earth."

Expansion of the American nation-state

The mobilization of the Union's resources for modern war brought into being a new American nation-state with greatly expanded powers and responsibilities. The United States remained a federal republic with sovereignty divided between the state and national governments. But the war forged a new national self-consciousness, reflected in the increasing use of the word "nation"—a unified political entity—in place of the older "Union" of separate states. In his inaugural address in 1861, Lincoln used the word "Union" twenty times, while making no mention of the "nation." By

1863, "Union" does not appear at all in the 269-word Gettysburg Address, while Lincoln referred five times to the "nation."

The War and American Religion

The upsurge of patriotism, and of national power, was reflected in many aspects of American life. Even as the war produced unprecedented casualties, the northern Protestant clergy strove to provide it with a religious justification and to reassure their congregations that the dead had not died in vain. The religious press now devoted more space to military and political developments than to spiritual matters. In numerous wartime sermons, Christianity and patriotism were joined in a **civic religion** that saw the war as God's mechanism for ridding the United States of slavery and enabling it to become what it had never really been—a land of freedom. Of course, the southern clergy was equally convinced that the Confederate cause represented God's will.

Religious beliefs enabled Americans to cope with the unprecedented mass death the war involved. Coping with death, moreover, required unprecedented governmental action, from notifying next of kin to accounting for the dead and missing. Both the Union and Confederacy established elaborate systems for gathering statistics and maintaining records of dead and wounded soldiers, an effort supplemented by private philanthropic organizations. After the war ended, the federal government embarked on

Lincoln and the Female Slave, by the free black artist David B. Bowser. Working in Philadelphia, Bowser painted flags for a number of black Civil War regiments. Lincoln confers freedom on a kneeling slave, an image that downplays blacks' role in their own emancipation.

A priest conducts mass for the Sixty-ninth New York State militia, stationed in Washington, D.C., in June 1861. The famed photographer Mathew Brady took this photo, which illustrates how the war mitigated the anti-Catholic bias so prominent in the 1850s.

VOICES OF FREEDOM

From Letter of Thomas F. Drayton
(April 17, 1861)

A South Carolina plantation owner and ardent supporter of secession, Thomas F. Drayton explained the Confederate cause in this letter to his brother Percival, an officer in the U.S. Navy, written from Charleston shortly after the firing on Fort Sumter. Drayton went on to serve as a brigadier general in the Confederate army.

My dear Percy

And so Sumter is at last ours, and this too without the loss of a *single* life upon either side.... Before this dispute is over however, I look for abundance of death & blood....

You say I don't yet understand the position you have taken. I do fully, but certainly differ from you when you say that to side with us, would be "battling for slavery against freedom." On the contrary, by siding with us, you likewise defend yourselves at the North against a far greater danger than we are threatened with, which is the enslavement of the *whites*; for the tendency with you is towards consolidation & the abrogation of State rights.... All these evils & horrors will be laid to your doors, because you have encouraged ... in the form of abolition lecturers, fanatical preachers, unscrupulous editors, selfish politicians; ... and by voting for men ... with the *avowed object* of abolishing slavery throughout the Southern States ... who made a merit of John Brown's murderous invasion; set at defiance all fugitive slave laws, ... and whose clergy denounced us indiscriminately as barbarians....

We are fighting for home & liberty. Can the North say as much? Good night. And don't say again, that in siding for us, you would be defending slavery and fighting for what is abhorrent to your feelings & convictions. On the contrary, in fighting on our side, you will be battling for law & order & against abstract fanatical ideas which will certainly bring about vastly greater evils upon our race, than could possibly result from the perpetuation of slavery among us.

From Abraham Lincoln, Address at Sanitary Fair, Baltimore (April 18, 1864)

Abraham Lincoln's speech at a Sanitary Fair (a grand bazaar that raised money for the care of Union soldiers) offers a dramatic illustration of the contested meaning of freedom during the Civil War.

The world has never had a good definition of the word liberty, and the American people, just now, are much in want of one. We all declare for liberty; but in using the same *word* we do not all mean the same *thing*. With some the word liberty may mean for each man to do as he pleases with himself, and the product of his labor; while with others the same word may mean for some men to do as they please with other men, and the product of other men's labor. Here are two, not only different, but incompatible things, called by the same name—liberty. And it follows that each of the things is, by the respective parties, called by two different and incompatible names—liberty and tyranny.

The shepherd drives the wolf from the sheep's throat, for which the sheep thanks the shepherd as a *liberator*, while the wolf denounces him for the same act as the destroyer of liberty, especially as the sheep was a black one. Plainly the sheep and the wolf are not agreed upon a definition of the word liberty; and precisely the same difference prevails today among us human creatures, even in the North, and all professing to love liberty. Hence we behold the process by which thousands are daily passing from under the yoke of bondage, hailed by some as the advance of liberty, and bewailed by others as the destruction of all liberty. Recently, as it seems, the people of Maryland have been doing something to define liberty [abolishing slavery in the state]; and thanks to them that, in what they have done, the wolf's dictionary, has been repudiated.

QUESTIONS

1. *Why does Drayton deny that the Confederacy is fighting to defend slavery?*

2. *What does Lincoln identify as the essential difference between northern and southern definitions of freedom?*

3. *How do Drayton and Lincoln differ in their definitions of liberty and whether it applies to African-Americans?*

A girl in mourning dress holds a framed photograph of her father, a cavalryman.

Arbitrary arrests and the suspension of habeas corpus

Northern prosperity in wartime

a program to locate and re-bury hundreds of thousands of Union soldiers in national military cemeteries. Between 1865 and 1871, the government reinterred more than 300,000 Union (but not Confederate) soldiers—including black soldiers, who were buried, as they had fought, in segregated sections of military cemeteries.

Liberty in Wartime

This intense new nationalism made criticism of the war effort—or of the policies of the Lincoln administration—seem to Republicans equivalent to treason. During the conflict, declared the Republican *New York Times*, "the safety of the nation is the supreme law." Arbitrary arrests numbered in the thousands. They included opposition newspaper editors, Democratic politicians, individuals who discouraged enlistment in the army, and ordinary civilians like the Chicago man briefly imprisoned for calling the president a "damned fool." With the Constitution unclear as to who possessed the power to suspend the writ of habeas corpus (thus allowing prisoners to be held without charge), Lincoln claimed the right under the presidential war powers and twice suspended the writ throughout the entire Union for those accused of "disloyal activities." Not until 1866, after the fighting had ended, did the Supreme Court, in the case **Ex parte Milligan**, declare it unconstitutional to bring accused persons before military tribunals where civil courts were operating. The Constitution, declared Justice David Davis, is not suspended in wartime—it remains "a law for rulers and people, equally in time of war and peace."

Lincoln was not a despot. Most of those arrested were quickly released, the Democratic press continued to flourish, and contested elections were held throughout the war. But the policies of the Lincoln administration offered proof—to be repeated during later wars—of the fragility of civil liberties in the face of assertive patriotism and wartime demands for national unity.

The North's Transformation

Even as he invoked traditional values, Lincoln presided over far-reaching changes in northern life. The effort to mobilize the resources of the Union greatly enhanced the power not only of the federal government but also of a rising class of capitalist entrepreneurs. Unlike the South, which suffered economic devastation, the North experienced the war as a time of prosperity.

Nourished by wartime inflation and government contracts, the profits of industry boomed. New England mills worked day and night to supply the army with blankets and uniforms, and Pennsylvania coal mines and ironworks rapidly expanded their production. Mechanization proceeded apace in many industries, especially those, such as boot and shoe production and meatpacking, that supplied the army's ever-increasing needs. Agriculture also flourished, for even as farm boys by the hundreds of thousands joined the army, the frontier of cultivation pushed westward, with machinery and immigrants replacing lost labor.

Government and the Economy

The new American nation-state that emerged during the Civil War was committed to rapid economic development. Congress adopted policies that promoted economic growth and permanently altered the nation's financial system. To spur agricultural development, the **Homestead Act** offered 160 acres of free public land to settlers in the West. It took effect on January 1, 1863, the same day as the Emancipation Proclamation, and like the proclamation, tried to implement a vision of freedom. By the 1930s, more than 400,000 families had acquired farms under its provisions. In addition, the Land Grant College Act assisted the states in establishing "agricultural and mechanic colleges."

Congress also made huge grants of money and land for internal improvements, including up to 100 million acres to the Union Pacific and Central Pacific, two companies chartered in 1862 and charged with building a railroad from the Missouri River to the Pacific coast. (These were the first corporate charters issued by the federal government since the Second Bank of the United States in 1816.) It required some 20,000 men to lay the tracks across prairies and mountains, a substantial number of them immigrant Chinese contract laborers, called "coolies" by many Americans. Hundreds of Chinese workers died blasting tunnels and building bridges through this treacherous terrain. When it was completed in 1869, the **transcontinental railroad**, which ran from Omaha, Nebraska, to San Francisco, expanded the national market, facilitated the spread of settlement and investment in the West, and heralded the doom of the Plains Indians.

The War and Native Americans

One of Lincoln's first orders as president was to withdraw federal troops from the West so that they could protect Washington, D.C. Recognizing that this would make it impossible for the army to keep white interlopers from intruding on Indian land, as treaties required it to do, Indian leaders

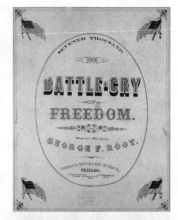

Sheet music for two of the best-known patriotic songs written during the Civil War.

Effects of the transcontinental railroad

A lithograph depicts the hanging of thirty-eight Sioux Indians in December 1862, the largest mass execution in American history.

begged Lincoln to reverse this decision, but to no avail. Inevitably, conflict flared in the West between Native Americans and white settlers, with disastrous results. During the Civil War, the Sioux killed hundreds of white farmers in Minnesota before being subdued by the army. After a military court sentenced more than 300 Indians to death, Lincoln commuted the sentences of all but 38. But their hanging in December 1862 remains the largest official execution in American history.

The Union army also launched a campaign against the Navajo in the Southwest, destroying their orchards and sheep and forcing 8,000 people to move to a reservation set aside by the government. The **Navajo's Long Walk** became as central to their historical experience as the Trail of Tears to the Cherokee (see Chapter 10). Unlike the eastern Indians, however, the Navajo were eventually allowed to return to a portion of their lands.

Some tribes that owned slaves, like the Cherokee, sided with the Confederacy. After 1865, they were forced to cede much of their land to the federal government and to accept former slaves into the Cherokee nation and give them land (the only slaveowners required to do so). Their status remains a point of controversy to this day. The Cherokee constitution was recently amended to exclude descendants of slaves from citizenship, leading to lawsuits that have yet to be resolved.

A Union soldier stands guard over a group of Indians during the Navajo's Long Walk, in which the army removed them from their New Mexico homeland to a reservation hundreds of miles away.

A New Financial System

The need to pay for the war produced dramatic changes in financial policy. To raise money, the government increased the tariff to unprecedented heights (thus promoting the further growth of northern industry), imposed new taxes on the production and consumption of goods, and enacted the nation's first income tax. It also borrowed more than $2 billion by selling interest-bearing bonds, thus creating an immense national debt. And it printed more than $400 million worth of paper money, called "greenbacks," declared to be legal tender—that is, money that must be accepted for nearly all public and private payments and debts. To rationalize the banking system, Congress established a system of nationally chartered banks, which were required to purchase government bonds and were given the right to issue bank notes as currency.

Financing the war

Numerous Americans who would take the lead in reshaping the nation's postwar economy created or consolidated their fortunes during the Civil War, among them the iron and steel entrepreneur Andrew Carnegie, the oil magnate John D. Rockefeller, the financiers Jay Gould and J. P. Morgan, and Philip D. Armour, who earned millions supplying beef to the Union army. These and other "captains of industry" managed to escape military service, sometimes by purchasing exemptions or hiring substitutes, as allowed by the draft law.

"Captains of industry"

Taken together, the Union's economic policies vastly increased the power and size of the federal government. The federal budget for 1865 exceeded $1 billion—nearly twenty times that of 1860. With its new army of clerks, tax collectors, and other officials, the government became the nation's largest employer. And although much of this expansion proved temporary, the government would never return to its weak and fragmented condition of the prewar period.

Women and the War

For many northern women, the conflict opened new doors of opportunity. Women took advantage of the wartime labor shortage to move into jobs in factories and into certain largely male professions, particularly nursing. The expansion of the activities of the national government opened new jobs for women as clerks in government offices. Many of these wartime gains were short lived, but in white-collar government jobs, retail sales, and nursing, women found a permanent place in the workforce.

Hundreds of thousands of northern women took part in organizations that gathered money and medical supplies for soldiers and sent

Filling Cartridges at the U.S. Arsenal of Watertown, Massachusetts, an engraving from *Harper's Weekly*, September 21, 1861. Both men and women were drawn to work in the booming war-related industries of the North.

books, clothing, and food to freedmen. The U.S. Sanitary Commission emerged as a centralized national relief agency to coordinate donations on the northern home front. Although control at the national level remained in male hands, patriotic women did most of the grassroots work. Women played the leading role in organizing **Sanitary Fairs**—grand bazaars that displayed military banners, uniforms, and other relics of the war and sold goods to raise money for soldiers' aid.

Northern women volunteers and the public sphere

Many men understood women's war work as an extension of their "natural" capacity for self-sacrifice. But the very act of volunteering for the war effort brought many northern women into the public sphere and offered them a taste of independence. From the ranks of this wartime mobilization came many of the leaders of the postwar movement for women's rights. Clara Barton, for example, organized supply lines and nursed wounded soldiers in northern Virginia. After the war, she became not only an advocate of woman suffrage but also, as president of the American National Red Cross, a strong proponent of the humane treatment of battlefield casualties.

The Divided North

Despite Lincoln's political skills, the war and his administration's policies divided northern society. Republicans labeled those opposed to the war Copperheads, after a poisonous snake that strikes without warning. Mounting casualties and rapid societal changes divided the North.

Copperheads

Whimsical potholders expressing hope for a better life for emancipated slaves were sold at the Chicago Sanitary Fair of 1865 to raise money for soldiers' aid.

Disaffection was strongest among the large southern-born population of states like Ohio, Indiana, and Illinois and working-class Catholic immigrants in eastern cities.

As the war progressed, it heightened existing social tensions and created new ones. The growing power of the federal government challenged traditional notions of local autonomy. The Union's draft law, which allowed individuals to provide a substitute or buy their way out of the army, caused widespread indignation. Workers resented manufacturers and financiers who reaped large profits while their own real incomes dwindled because of inflation. The prospect of a sweeping change in the status of blacks called forth a racist reaction in many parts of the North. Throughout the war, the Democratic Party subjected Lincoln's policies to withering criticism, although it remained divided between "War Democrats," who supported the military effort while criticizing emancipation and the draft, and those who favored immediate peace.

Social tensions in the North

On occasion, dissent degenerated into outright violence. In July 1863, the introduction of the draft provoked four days of rioting in New York City. The mob, composed largely of Irish immigrants, assaulted symbols of the new order being created by the war—draft offices, the mansions of wealthy Republicans, industrial establishments, and the city's black population, many of whom fled to New Jersey or took refuge in Central Park. Only the arrival of Union troops quelled the uprising, but not before more than 100 persons had died.

The New York City draft riots

The Riots in New York: The Mob Lynching a Negro in Clarkson Street, an engraving from the British magazine *Illustrated London News*, August 8, 1863, reveals how the New York City draft riots escalated from an attempt to obstruct the draft into an assault on the city's black population.

THE CONFEDERATE NATION

Leadership and Government

Jefferson Davis

The man charged with the task of rallying public support for the Confederacy proved unequal to the task. Jefferson Davis had moved to Mississippi as a youth, attended West Point, and acquired a large plantation. Aloof and stubborn, Davis lacked Lincoln's political flexibility and ability to communicate the war's meaning effectively to ordinary men and women.

Centralizing the South

Under Davis, the Confederate nation became far more centralized than the Old South had been. The government raised armies from scratch, took control of southern railroads, and built manufacturing plants. But it failed to find an effective way of utilizing the South's major economic resource, cotton. In the early part of the war, the administration tried to suppress cotton production, urging planters to grow food instead and banning cotton exports. This, it was hoped, would promote economic self-sufficiency and force Great Britain, whose textile mills could not operate without southern cotton, to intervene on the side of the Confederacy.

"**King Cotton diplomacy**" turned out to be ineffective. But the Confederate policy had far-reaching global consequences. Recognizing their overdependence on southern cotton, other nations moved to expand production. Britain promoted cultivation of the crop in Egypt and India, and Russia did the same in parts of Central Asia. As a result, the resumption of American cotton production after the war led directly to a worldwide crisis of overproduction that drove down the price of cotton, impoverishing farmers around the world.

The Inner Civil War

As the war progressed, social change and internal turmoil engulfed much of the Confederacy. At the outset, most white southerners rallied to the Confederate cause. No less fervently than northern troops, southern soldiers spoke of their cause in the language of freedom. "We are fighting for our liberty," wrote one volunteer, without any sense of contradiction, "against tyrants of the North . . . who are determined to destroy slavery."

Social change in the South

But even as it waged a desperate struggle for independence, the South found itself increasingly divided. One grievance was the draft. Like the Union, the Confederacy allowed individuals to provide a substitute.

Because of the accelerating disintegration of slavery, it also exempted one white male for every twenty slaves on a plantation (thus releasing many overseers and planters' sons from service). The "twenty-negro" provision convinced many yeomen that the struggle for southern independence had become "a rich man's war and a poor man's fight."

Economic Problems

Economic deprivation also sparked disaffection. As the blockade tight-ened, areas of the Confederacy came under Union occupation, and produc-tion by slaves declined, shortages arose of essential commodities such as salt, corn, and meat. The war left countless farms, plantations, businesses, and railroads in ruins. The economic crisis, which stood in glaring contrast to the North's boom, was an unavoidable result of the war. But Confederate policies exaggerated its effects. War requires sacrifice, and civilian support for war depends, in part, on the belief that sacrifice is being fairly shared. Many non-slaveholders, however, became convinced that they were bear-ing an unfair share of the war's burdens.

Declining southern production

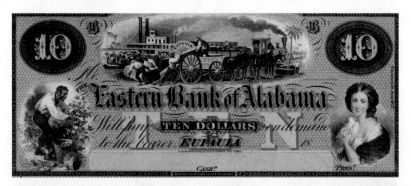

The centrality of slavery to the Confederacy is illustrated by the paper money issued by state governments and private banks, which frequently juxtaposed scenes of slaves at work with other revered images. The ten-dollar note of the Eastern Bank of Alabama depicts slaves working in the field and at a port, along with an idealized image of southern white womanhood. Alabama's five-dollar bill includes an overseer directing slaves in the field and a symbol of liberty.

An engraving in the *New York Illustrated News* depicts the bread riot that took place in Mobile, Alabama, in the fall of 1863.

Like the Union, the Confederacy borrowed heavily to finance the war. Unlike federal lawmakers, however, the planter-dominated Confederate Congress proved unwilling to levy heavy taxes that planters would have to pay. It relied on paper money, of which it issued $1.5 billion, far more than the North's greenbacks. The Confederate Congress also authorized military officers to seize farm goods to supply the army, paying with increasingly worthless Confederate money. Small farmers deeply resented this practice, known as "impressment." Food riots broke out in many places, including Richmond, Virginia, and Mobile, Alabama, where in 1863 large crowds of women plundered army food supplies. As the war progressed, desertion became what one officer called a "crying evil" for the southern armies. By the war's end, more than 100,000 men had deserted, almost entirely from among "the poorest class of nonslaveholders whose labor is indispensable to the daily support of their families."

By 1864, organized peace movements had appeared in several southern states, and secret pro-Union societies such as the Heroes of America were actively promoting disaffection.

Women and the Confederacy

Even more than in the North, the war placed unprecedented burdens on southern white women. Left alone on farms and plantations, they were often forced to manage business affairs and discipline slaves, previously the responsibility of men. As in the North, women mobilized to support soldiers in the field and stepped out of their traditional "sphere" to run commercial establishments and work in arms factories. In Richmond, "government girls" staffed many of the clerkships in the new Confederate bureaucracy.

Wartime roles for women in the Confederacy

All Confederate women struggled to cope as their loved ones were drawn off into the army. The war led to the political mobilization, for the first time, of non-slaveholding white women. Lacking the aid of slave labor, they found that the absence of their husbands from their previously self-sufficient farms made it impossible to feed their families. They flooded

Confederate authorities with petitions seeking assistance, not as charity but as a right. Politicians could not ignore the pleas of soldiers' wives, and state governments began to distribute supplies to needy families.

Southern women's self-sacrificing devotion to the cause became legendary. But as the war went on and the death toll mounted, increasing numbers of women came to believe that the goal of independence was not worth the cost. The growing disaffection of southern white women, conveyed in letters to loved ones at the front, contributed to the decline in civilian morale and encouraged desertion from the army.

Black Soldiers for the Confederacy

The growing shortage of white manpower eventually led Confederate authorities to a decision no one could have foreseen when the war began: they authorized the arming of slaves to fight for the South. Many slaveholders fiercely resisted this idea, and initially, the Confederate Senate rejected it. Not until March 1865, after Robert E. Lee had endorsed the plan, did the Confederate Congress authorize the arming of slaves.

Southern debate over arming the slaves

The war ended before the recruitment of black soldiers actually began. But the Confederate army did employ numerous blacks, nearly all of them slaves, as laborers. This later led to some confusion over whether blacks actually fought for the Confederacy—apart from a handful who "passed" for white, none in fact did. But the South's decision to raise black troops illustrates how the war undermined not only slavery but also the proslavery ideology. Declared Howell Cobb, a Georgia planter and politician, "If slaves make good soldiers, our whole theory of slavery is wrong."

TURNING POINTS

Gettysburg and Vicksburg

Despite the accelerating demise of slavery and the decline of morale in the South, the war's outcome remained very much in doubt for much of its third and fourth years. In April 1863, "Fighting Joe" Hooker, who had succeeded Ambrose E. Burnside as the Union commander in the East, brought the Army of the Potomac into central Virginia to confront Lee. Outnumbered two to one, Lee repelled Hooker's attack at Chancellorsville,

"Fighting Joe" Hooker

THE CIVIL WAR, 1863

In July 1863, the Union won major victories at Gettysburg and Vicksburg.

Gettysburg

although he lost his ablest lieutenant, "Stonewall" Jackson, mistakenly killed by fire from his own soldiers.

Lee now gambled on another invasion of the North, although his strategic objective remains unclear. Perhaps he believed a defeat on its own territory would destroy the morale of the northern army and public. In any event, the two armies, with Union soldiers now under the command of General George G. Meade, met at Gettysburg, Pennsylvania, on the first three days of July 1863. With 165,000 troops involved, Gettysburg remains the largest battle ever fought on the North American continent. On July 3, Confederate forces, led by Major General George E. Pickett's crack division, marched across an open field toward Union forces. Withering artillery and rifle fire met the charge, and most of Pickett's soldiers never reached Union lines. Pickett's Charge was Lee's greatest blunder. His army retreated to Virginia, never again to set foot on northern soil.

On the same day that Lee began his retreat from Gettysburg, the Union achieved a significant victory in the West. Late in 1862, Grant had moved into Mississippi toward the city of Vicksburg. From its heights, defended by miles of trenches and earthworks, the Confederacy commanded the central Mississippi River. When direct attacks failed, Grant launched a siege. On July 4, 1863, Vicksburg surrendered, and with it John C. Pemberton's army of 30,000 men, a loss the Confederacy could ill afford. The entire Mississippi Valley now lay in Union hands.

1864

Nearly two years, however, would pass before the war ended. Brought east to take command of Union forces, Grant in 1864 began a war of attrition against Lee's army in Virginia. That is, he was willing to accept high numbers of casualties, knowing that the North could replace its manpower losses, whereas the South could not. Grant understood that to bring the North's manpower advantage into play, he must attack continuously "all along the line," thereby preventing the enemy from concentrating its forces or retreating to safety after an engagement.

In May 1864, the 115,000-man Army of the Potomac crossed the Rapidan River to do battle with Lee's forces in Virginia. At the end of six weeks of fighting, Grant's casualties stood at 60,000—almost the size of Lee's entire army—while Lee had lost 30,000 men. The sustained fighting in Virginia was a turning point in modern warfare. With daily combat and a fearsome casualty toll, it had far more in common with the trench warfare of World War I (discussed in Chapter 19) than the almost gentlemanly fighting with which the Civil War began.

Grant had become the only Union general to maintain the initiative against Lee but at a cost that led critics to label him a "butcher of men." Victory still eluded him. Grant attempted to capture Petersburg, which controlled the railway link to Richmond, but Lee got to Petersburg first, and Grant settled in for a prolonged siege. Meanwhile, General William T. Sherman, who had moved his forces into Georgia from Tennessee, encountered dogged resistance from Confederate troops. Not until September 1864 did he finally enter Atlanta, seizing Georgia's main railroad center.

As casualty rolls mounted in the spring and summer of 1864, northern morale sank to its lowest point of the war. Lincoln for a time believed he would be unable to win reelection. In May, hoping to force Lincoln to

The surrender of Vicksburg

Generals Robert E. Lee and Ulysses S. Grant, leaders of the opposing armies in the East, 1864–1865.

A sketch by William Waud, an artist who covered the war for *Harper's Weekly*, depicts Pennsylvania soldiers voting in their army camp in the 1864 election.

step aside, Radical Republicans nominated John C. Frémont on a platform calling for a constitutional amendment to abolish slavery, federal protection of the freedmen's rights, and confiscation of the land of leading Confederates. The Democratic candidate for president, General George B. McClellan, was hampered from the outset of the campaign by a platform calling for an immediate cease-fire and peace conference—a plan that even war-weary northerners viewed as equivalent to surrender. In the end, Frémont withdrew, and buoyed by Sherman's capture of Atlanta, Lincoln won a sweeping victory. He captured every state but Kentucky, Delaware, and New Jersey. The result ensured that the war would continue until the Confederacy's defeat.

REHEARSALS FOR RECONSTRUCTION AND THE END OF THE WAR

As the war drew toward a close and more and more parts of the Confederacy came under Union control, federal authorities found themselves presiding over the transition from slavery to freedom. In South Carolina, Louisiana, and other parts of the South, debates took place over issues—access to land, control of labor, and the new structure of political power—that would reverberate in the postwar world.

The Sea Islands Experiment

The most famous "rehearsal for Reconstruction" took place on the Sea Islands just off the coast of South Carolina. The war was only a few months old when, in November 1861, the Union navy occupied the islands. Nearly the entire white population fled, leaving behind some 10,000 slaves. The navy was soon followed by other northerners—army officers, Treasury agents, prospective investors in cotton land, and a group known as Gideon's Band, which included black and white reformers and teachers committed to uplifting the freed slaves. Northern-born teachers like Charlotte Forten, a member of one of Philadelphia's most prominent black families, and Laura M. Towne, a white native of Pittsburgh, devoted themselves to teaching the freed blacks.

Gideon's Band

Many northerners believed that the transition from slave to free labor meant enabling blacks to work for wages in more humane conditions than under slavery. When the federal government put land on the islands up for sale, most was acquired not by former slaves but by northern investors bent on demonstrating the superiority of free wage labor and turning a tidy profit at the same time. By 1865, the **Sea Islands experiment** was widely held to be a success. But the experiment also bequeathed to postwar Reconstruction the contentious issue of whether landownership should accompany black freedom.

Wartime Reconstruction in the West

A very different rehearsal for Reconstruction, involving a far larger area and population than the Sea Islands, took place in Louisiana and the Mississippi Valley. After the capture of Vicksburg, the Union army established regulations for plantation labor. Military authorities insisted that the emancipated slaves must sign labor contracts with plantation owners who took an oath of loyalty. But, unlike before the war, they would be paid wages and provided with education, physical punishment was prohibited, and their families were safe from disruption by sale.

Teachers in the Freedmen's Schools in Norfolk, 1863, a photograph of a group of black and white teachers who brought education to former slaves in a Union-occupied part of Virginia.

Neither side was satisfied with the new labor system. Blacks resented having to resume working for whites and being forced to sign labor contracts. Planters complained that their workers were insubordinate. But only occasionally did army officers seek to implement a different vision of freedom. At Davis Bend, Mississippi, site of the cotton plantations of Jefferson Davis and his brother Joseph, the emancipated slaves saw the land divided among themselves. In addition, a system of government was established that allowed the former slaves to elect their own judges and sheriffs.

The Politics of Wartime Reconstruction

As the Civil War progressed, the future political status of African-Americans emerged as a key dividing line in public debates. Events in Union-occupied Louisiana brought the issue to national attention. Hoping to establish a functioning civilian government in the state, Lincoln in 1863 announced his **Ten-Percent Plan of Reconstruction**. He essentially offered an amnesty and full restoration of rights, including property except for slaves, to nearly all white southerners who took an oath affirming loyalty to the Union and support for emancipation. When 10 percent of the voters of 1860 had taken the oath, they could elect a new state government, which would be required to abolish slavery. Lincoln's plan offered no role to blacks in shaping the post-slavery order.

Lincoln's Ten-Percent Plan

Another group now stepped onto the stage of politics—the free blacks of New Orleans, who saw the Union occupation as a golden opportunity to press for equality before the law and a role in government for themselves. Their complaints at being excluded under Lincoln's Reconstruction plan won a sympathetic hearing from Radical Republicans in Congress. By the summer of 1864, dissatisfaction with events in Louisiana helped to inspire the Wade-Davis Bill, named for two leading Republican members of Congress. This bill required a majority (not one-tenth) of white male southerners to pledge support for the Union before Reconstruction could begin in any state, and it guaranteed blacks equality before the law, although not the right to vote. The bill passed Congress only to die when Lincoln refused to sign it and Congress adjourned. As the war drew to a close, it was clear that although slavery was dead, no agreement existed as to what social and political system should take its place.

Wade-Davis Bill

Victory at Last

After Lincoln's reelection, the war hastened to its conclusion. In November 1864, Sherman and his army of 60,000 set out from Atlanta on their March to the Sea. Cutting a sixty-mile-wide swath through the heart of Georgia, they destroyed railroads, buildings, and all the food and supplies they could not use. His aim, Sherman wrote, was "to whip the rebels, to humble their pride, to follow them to their innermost recesses, and make them fear and dread us." Here was modern war in all its destructiveness, even though few civilians were physically harmed. In January 1865, after capturing Savannah, Sherman moved into South Carolina, bringing even greater destruction.

Sherman's March to the Sea

On January 31, 1865, Congress approved the Thirteenth Amendment, which abolished slavery throughout the entire Union—and in so doing, introduced the word "slavery" into the Constitution for the first time. In March, in his second inaugural address, Lincoln called for reconciliation: "with malice toward none, with charity for all, . . . let us . . . bind up the nation's wounds." Yet he also leveled a harsh judgment on the nation's past. Perhaps, Lincoln suggested, God had brought on the war to punish the entire nation, not just the South, for the sin of slavery. And if God willed that the war continue until all the wealth created by 250 years of slave labor had been destroyed, and "every drop of blood drawn with the lash shall be paid by another drawn with the sword," this too would be an act of justice (see the Appendix for the full text).

April 1865 brought some of the most momentous events in American history. On April 2, Grant finally broke through Lee's lines at Petersburg,

General William T. Sherman photographed in 1864.

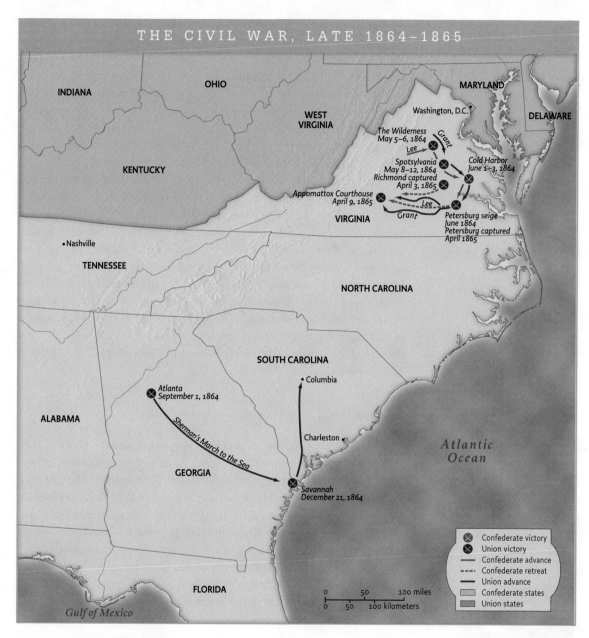

THE CIVIL WAR, LATE 1864–1865

The military defeat of the Confederacy came in the East, with Sherman's March to the Sea, Grant's occupation of Richmond, and the surrender of Robert E. Lee's army.

forcing the Army of Northern Virginia to abandon the city and leaving Richmond defenseless. The following day, Union soldiers occupied the southern capital. On April 4, heedless of his own safety, Lincoln walked the streets of Richmond accompanied only by a dozen sailors. At every step he was besieged by former slaves, some of whom fell on their knees before the embarrassed president, who urged them to remain standing. On April 9, realizing that further resistance was useless, Lee surrendered at Appomattox Courthouse, Virginia. Although some Confederate units remained in the field, the Civil War was over.

Surrender at Appomattox

Lincoln did not live to savor victory. On April 11, in what proved to be his last speech, he called publicly for the first time for limited black suffrage. Three days later, while attending a performance at Ford's Theatre in Washington, D.C., the president was mortally wounded by John Wilkes Booth, one of the nation's most celebrated actors. Lincoln died the next morning. A train carried the president's body to its final resting place in Illinois on a winding 1,600-mile journey that illustrated how tightly the railroad now bound the northern states. Grieving crowds lined the train route, and solemn processions carried the president's body to lie in state in major cities so that mourners could pay their respects. It was estimated that 300,000 persons passed by the coffin in Philadelphia, 500,000 in New York, and 200,000 in Chicago.

The assassination of Lincoln

The War and the World

In 1877, soon after retiring as president, Ulysses S. Grant embarked with his wife on a two-year tour of the world. At almost every location, he was greeted as a modern-day hero. What did America in the aftermath of the Civil War represent to the world? In England, the son of the duke of Wellington greeted Grant as a military genius. In Newcastle, parading English workers hailed him as the man whose military prowess had saved the world's leading experiment in democratic government and as a "Hero of Freedom." In Berlin, Otto von Bismarck, the chancellor of Germany, welcomed Grant as a nation-builder, who had accomplished on the battlefield something—national unity—that Bismarck was attempting to create for his own people.

A redesign of the American flag proposed in 1863 illustrates the linkage of nationalism and freedom that was solidified by the Civil War. The thirty-five stars forming the word "FREE" include the eleven Confederate states.

The War in American History

The Civil War laid the foundation for modern America, guaranteeing the Union's permanence, destroying slavery, and shifting power in the nation from the South to the North (and, more specifically, from slaveowning

Winslow Homer's painting, *The Veteran in a New Field*, completed in the fall of 1865, offers a reflection on the Civil War and its legacy. The one-armed former Union soldier, whose army jacket lies in the right corner, is at work cutting wheat. The scythe brings to mind the grim reaper, a symbol of death, perhaps a reference not only to war casualties but also Lincoln's assassination. But the bountiful field suggests national regeneration.

planters to northern capitalists). It dramatically increased the power of the federal government and accelerated the modernization of the northern economy. And it placed on the postwar agenda the challenge of defining and protecting African-American freedom. "Verily," as Frederick Douglass declared, "the work does not *end* with the abolition of slavery, but only *begins*."

Paradoxically, both sides lost something they had gone to war to defend. Slavery was the cornerstone of the Confederacy, but the war led inexorably to slavery's destruction. In the North, the war hastened the transformation of Lincoln's America—the world of free labor, of the small shop and independent farmer—into an industrial giant. Americans, in the words of the abolitionist Wendell Phillips, would "never again . . . see the republic in which we were born."

Slavery destroyed

CHAPTER REVIEW AND ONLINE RESOURCES

REVIEW QUESTIONS

1. What made the American Civil War the first modern war?

2. How was the North's victory over the South tied to the different ways the market revolution had developed in the North and South?

3. Describe how President Lincoln's war aims evolved between 1861 and 1863, changing from simply preserving the Union to also ending slavery.

4. How did the actions of slaves themselves, as well as northern military strategy and the Emancipation Proclamation, combine to end slavery?

5. What role did blacks play in both winning the Civil War and in defining the war's consequences?

6. How did federal policies undertaken during the Civil War transform the United States into a stronger nation-state—economically, politically, and ideologically?

7. What was the impact of the Civil War on civil liberties?

8. Compare and contrast women's efforts in the North and South to support the war effort and their families.

9. In what ways did the outcome of the Civil War change the United States' status in the world?

KEY TERMS

first modern war (p. 403)

the draft (p. 404)

Monitor v. *Merrimac* (p. 405)

Battle of Antietam (p. 410)

"contrabands" (p. 412)

Radical Republicans (p. 413)

Emancipation Proclamation (p. 414)

black soldiers and sailors (p. 416)

Second American Revolution (p. 417)

civic religion (p. 419)

Ex parte Milligan (p. 422)

Homestead Act (p. 423)

transcontinental railroad (p. 423)

Navajo's Long Walk (p. 424)

national banking system (p. 425)

women and war work (p. 425)

Sanitary Fairs (p. 426)

"King Cotton diplomacy" (p. 428)

Sea Islands experiment (p. 435)

Ten-Percent Plan of Reconstruction (p. 435)

wwnorton.com
/studyspace

VISIT STUDYSPACE FOR THESE RESOURCES AND MORE

- A chapter outline
- A diagnostic chapter quiz
- Interactive maps
- Map worksheets
- Multimedia documents

CHAPTER 15

" WHAT IS FREEDOM? "

★

RECONSTRUCTION, 1865 - 1877

1865	Special Field Order 15
	Freedmen's Bureau established
	Lincoln assassinated; Andrew Johnson becomes president
1865–1867	Presidential Reconstruction
	Black Codes
1866	Civil Rights Bill
	Ku Klux Klan established
1867	Reconstruction Act of 1867
	Tenure of Office Act
1867–1877	Radical Reconstruction
1868	Impeachment and trial of President Johnson
	Fourteenth Amendment ratified
1869	Inauguration of Ulysses S. Grant
1870	Hiram Revels, first black U.S. senator
	Fifteenth Amendment ratified
1870–1871	Enforcement Acts
1872	Liberal Republicans established
1873	Colfax Massacre
	Slaughterhouse Cases
	National economic depression begins
1876	*United States v. Cruikshank*
1877	Bargain of 1877

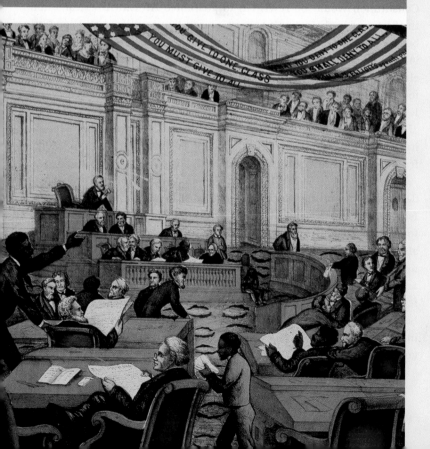

The Shackle Broken—by the Genius of Freedom. This 1874 lithograph depicts Robert B. Elliott, a black congressman from South Carolina, delivering celebrated speech supporting the bill that became the Civil Rights Act of 1875.

On the evening of January 12, 1865, less than a month after Union forces captured Savannah, Georgia, twenty leaders of the city's black community gathered for a discussion with General William T. Sherman and Secretary of War Edwin M. Stanton. The conversation revealed that the black leaders brought out of slavery a clear definition of freedom. Asked what he understood by slavery, Garrison Frazier, a Baptist minister chosen as the group's spokesman, responded that it meant one person's "receiving by irresistible power the work of another man, and not by his consent." Freedom he defined as "placing us where we could reap the fruit of our own labor, and take care of ourselves." The way to accomplish this was "to have land, and turn it and till it by our own labor."

Sherman's meeting with the black leaders foreshadowed some of the radical changes that would take place during the era known as Reconstruction (meaning, literally, the rebuilding of the shattered nation). In the years following the Civil War, former slaves and their white allies, North and South, would seek to redefine the meaning and boundaries of American freedom. Previously an entitlement of whites, freedom would be expanded to include black Americans. The laws and Constitution would be rewritten to guarantee African-Americans, for the first time in the nation's history, recognition as citizens and equality before the law. Black men would be granted the right to vote, ushering in a period of interracial democracy throughout the South. Black schools, churches, and other institutions would flourish, laying the foundation for the modern African-American community. Many of the advances of Reconstruction would prove temporary, swept away during a campaign of violence in the South and the North's retreat from the ideal of equality. But Reconstruction laid the foundation for future struggles to extend freedom to all Americans.

Four days after the meeting, Sherman responded to the black delegation by issuing Special Field Order 15. This set aside the Sea Islands and a large area along the South Carolina and Georgia coasts for the settlement of black families on forty-acre plots of land. He also offered them broken-down mules that the army could no longer use. In Sherman's order lay the origins of the phrase, "forty acres and a mule," which would reverberate across the South in the next few years. Among the emancipated slaves, Sherman's order raised hopes that the end of slavery would be accompanied by the economic independence that they, like other Americans, believed essential to genuine freedom.

THE MEANING OF FREEDOM

"What is freedom?" asked Congressman James A. Garfield in 1865. "Is it the bare privilege of not being chained? If this is all, then freedom is a bitter mockery, a cruel delusion." Did freedom mean simply the absence of slavery, or did it imply other rights for the former slaves, and if so, which ones? Equal civil rights, the vote, ownership of property? During Reconstruction, freedom became a terrain of conflict, its substance open to different, often contradictory interpretations.

African-Americans' understanding of freedom was shaped by their experiences as slaves and their observation of the free society around them. To begin with, freedom meant escaping the numerous injustices of slavery—punishment by the lash, the separation of families, denial of access to education, the sexual exploitation of black women by their owners—and sharing in the rights and opportunities of American citizens. "If I cannot do like a white man," Henry Adams, an emancipated slave in Louisiana, told his former master in 1865, "I am not free."

Conflicts over freedom

Family Record, a lithograph marketed to former slaves after the Civil War, centers on an idealized portrait of a middle-class black family, with scenes of slavery and freedom.

Families in Freedom

With slavery dead, institutions that had existed before the war, like the black family, free blacks' churches and schools, and the secret slave church, were strengthened, expanded, and freed from white supervision. The family was central to the postemancipation black community. Former slaves made remarkable efforts to locate loved ones from whom they had been separated under slavery. One northern reporter in 1865 encountered a freedman who had walked more than 600 miles from Georgia to North Carolina, searching for the wife and children from whom he had been sold away before the war.

While freedom helped to stabilize family life, it also subtly altered relationships within the family. Immediately after the Civil War, planters complained that freedwomen had "withdrawn" from field labor and work as house servants. Many black women preferred to devote more time to their families than had been possible under slavery, and men considered it a badge of

Five Generations of a Black Family, an 1862 photograph that suggests the power of family ties among emancipated slaves.

Mother and Daughter Reading, Mt. Meigs, Alabama, an 1890 photograph by Rudolph Eickemeyer. During Reconstruction and for years thereafter, former slaves exhibited a deep desire for education, and learning took place outside of school as well as within.

honor to see their wives remain at home. Eventually, the dire poverty of the black community would compel a far higher proportion of black women than white women to go to work for wages.

Church and School

At the same time, blacks abandoned white-controlled religious institutions to create churches of their own. On the eve of the Civil War, 42,000 black Methodists worshiped in biracial South Carolina churches; by the end of Reconstruction, only 600 remained. As the major institution independent of white control, the church played a central role in the black community. A place of worship, it also housed schools, social events, and political gatherings. Black ministers came to play a major role in politics. Some 250 held public office during Reconstruction.

Another striking example of the freedpeople's quest for individual and community improvement was their desire for education. The thirst for learning sprang from many sources—a desire to read the Bible, the need to prepare for the economic marketplace, and the opportunity, which arose in 1867, to take part in politics. Blacks of all ages flocked to the schools established by northern missionary societies, the Freedmen's Bureau, and groups of ex-slaves themselves. Reconstruction also witnessed the creation of the nation's first black colleges, including Fisk University in Tennessee, Hampton Institute in Virginia, and Howard University in the nation's capital.

Political Freedom

In a society that had made political participation a core element of freedom, the right to vote inevitably became central to the former slaves' desire for empowerment and equality. As Frederick Douglass put it soon after the South's surrender in 1865, "Slavery is not abolished until the black man has the ballot." In a "monarchial government," Douglass explained, no "special" disgrace applied to those denied the right to vote. But in a democracy, "where universal suffrage is the rule," excluding any group meant branding them with "the stigma of inferiority."

Anything less than full citizenship, black spokesmen insisted, would betray the nation's democratic promise and the war's meaning. To demonstrate their patriotism, blacks throughout the South organized Fourth of July celebrations. For years after the Civil War, white southerners would

The First African Church, Richmond, as depicted in *Harper's Weekly*, June 27, 1874. The establishment of independent black churches was an enduring accomplishment of Reconstruction.

"shut themselves within doors" on Independence Day, as a white resident of Charleston recorded in her diary, while former slaves commemorated the holiday themselves.

Land, Labor, and Freedom

Like those of rural people throughout the world, former slaves' ideas of freedom were directly related to landownership. On the land they would develop independent communities free of white control. Many former slaves insisted that through their unpaid labor, they had acquired a right to the land. "The property which they hold," declared an Alabama black convention, "was nearly all earned by the sweat of *our* brows." In some parts of the South, blacks in 1865 seized property, insisting that it belonged to them.

Freedom and landownership

In its individual elements and much of its language, former slaves' definition of freedom resembled that of white Americans—self-ownership, family stability, religious liberty, political participation, and economic autonomy. But these elements combined to form a vision very much their own. For whites, freedom, no matter how defined, was a given, a birthright to be defended. For African-Americans, it was an open-ended process, a transformation of every aspect of their lives and of the society and culture that had sustained slavery in the first place. Although the freedpeople failed to achieve full freedom as they understood it, their definition did much to shape national debate during the turbulent era of Reconstruction.

Freedom's meaning for former slaves

Masters without Slaves

Most white southerners reacted to military defeat and emancipation with dismay, not only because of the widespread devastation but also because they must now submit to northern demands. "The demoralization is

The southern white reaction to emancipation

Two maps of the Barrow plantation illustrate the effects of emancipation on rural life in the South. In 1860, slaves lived in communal quarters near the owner's house. Twenty years later, former slaves working as sharecroppers lived scattered across the plantation and had their own church and school.

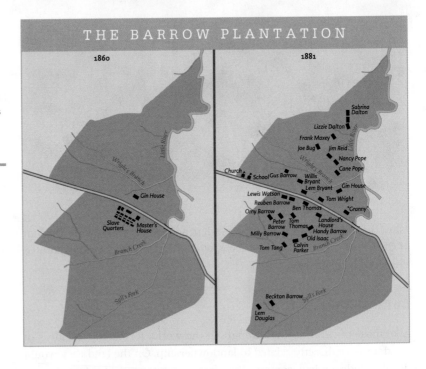

THE BARROW PLANTATION

1860

1881

complete," wrote a Georgia girl. "We are whipped, there is no doubt about it." The appalling loss of life, a disaster without parallel in the American experience, affected all classes of southerners. Nearly 260,000 men died for the Confederacy—more than one-fifth of the South's adult male white population. The widespread destruction of work animals, farm buildings, and machinery ensured that economic revival would be slow and painful. In 1870, the value of property in the South, not counting that represented by slaves, was 30 percent lower than before the war.

Confederate deaths

Planter families faced profound changes in the war's aftermath. Many lost not only their slaves but their life savings, which they had patriotically invested in now-worthless Confederate bonds. Some, whose slaves departed the plantation, for the first time found themselves compelled to do physical labor.

Planters

Southern planters sought to implement an understanding of freedom quite different from that of the former slaves. As they struggled to accept the reality of emancipation, most planters defined black freedom in the narrowest manner. As journalist Sidney Andrews discovered late in 1865, "The whites seem wholly unable to comprehend that freedom for the negro means the same thing as freedom for them."

The Free Labor Vision

Along with former slaves and former masters, the victorious Republican North tried to implement its own vision of freedom. Central to its definition was the antebellum principle of free labor, now further strengthened as a definition of the good society by the Union's triumph. In the free labor vision of a reconstructed South, emancipated blacks, enjoying the same opportunities for advancement as northern workers, would labor more productively than they had as slaves. At the same time, northern capital and migrants would energize the economy. The South would eventually come to resemble the "free society" of the North, complete with public schools, small towns, and independent farmers.

With planters seeking to establish a labor system as close to slavery as possible, and former slaves demanding economic autonomy and access to land, a long period of conflict over the organization and control of labor followed on plantations throughout the South. It fell to the **Freedmen's Bureau**, an agency established by Congress in March 1865, to attempt to establish a working free labor system.

The Freedmen's Bureau

Under the direction of O. O. Howard, a graduate of Bowdoin College in Maine and a veteran of the Civil War, the bureau took on responsibilities that can only be described as daunting. The bureau was an experiment in government social policy that seems to belong more comfortably to the New Deal of the 1930s or the Great Society of the 1960s (see Chapters 21 and 25, respectively) than to nineteenth-century America. Bureau agents were supposed to establish schools, provide aid to the poor and aged, settle disputes between whites and blacks and among the freedpeople, and secure for former slaves and white Unionists equal treatment before the courts. "It is not . . . in your power to fulfill one-tenth of the expectations of those who framed the Bureau," General William T. Sherman wrote to Howard. "I fear you have Hercules' task."

The bureau lasted from 1865 to 1870. Even at its peak, there were fewer than

Free labor and the good society

Winslow Homer's 1876 painting, *A Visit from the Old Mistress*, depicts an imaginary meeting between a southern white woman and her former slaves. Their stance and gaze suggest the tensions arising from the birth of a new social order. Homer places his subjects on an equal footing, yet maintains a space of separation between them. He exhibited the painting to acclaim at the Paris Universal Exposition in 1878.

THE MEANING OF FREEDOM | 447

The Freedmen's Bureau, an engraving from *Harper's Weekly*, July 25, 1868, depicts the bureau agent as a promoter of racial peace in the violent postwar South.

Achievements of the Freedmen's Bureau

1,000 agents in the entire South. Nonetheless, the bureau's achievements in some areas, notably education and health care, were striking. By 1869, nearly 3,000 schools, serving more than 150,000 pupils in the South, reported to the bureau. Bureau agents also ran hospitals established during the war and provided medical care and drugs to both black and white southerners.

The Failure of Land Reform

One provision of the law establishing the bureau gave it the authority to divide abandoned and confiscated land into forty-acre plots for rental and eventual sale to the former slaves. In the summer of 1865, however, President Andrew Johnson, who had succeeded Lincoln, ordered nearly all land in federal hands returned to its former owners. A series of confrontations followed, notably in South Carolina and Georgia, where the army forcibly evicted blacks who had settled on "Sherman land." When O. O. Howard, head of the Freedmen's Bureau, traveled to the Sea Islands to inform blacks of the new policy, he was greeted with disbelief and protest. A committee of former slaves drew up petitions to Howard and President Johnson. Land, the freedmen insisted, was essential to the meaning of freedom. Without it, they declared, "we have not bettered our condition" from the days of slavery—"you will see, this is not the condition of really free men."

Andrew Johnson and land reform

Because no land distribution took place, the vast majority of rural freedpeople remained poor and without property during Reconstruction.

They had no alternative but to work on white-owned plantations, often for their former owners. Far from being able to rise in the social scale through hard work, black men were largely confined to farm work, unskilled labor, and service jobs, and black women to positions in private homes as cooks and maids. The failure of land reform produced a deep sense of betrayal that survived among the former slaves and their descendants long after the end of Reconstruction. "No sir," Mary Gaffney, an elderly ex-slave, recalled in the 1930s, "we were not given a thing but freedom."

Out of the conflict on the plantations, new systems of labor emerged in the different regions of the South. **Sharecropping** came to dominate the Cotton Belt and much of the Tobacco Belt of Virginia and North Carolina. Sharecropping initially arose as a compromise between blacks' desire for land and planters' demand for labor discipline. The system allowed each black family to rent a part of a plantation, with the crop divided between worker and owner at the end of the year. Sharecropping guaranteed the planters a stable resident labor force. Former slaves preferred it to gang labor because it offered them the prospect of working without day-to-day white supervision. But as the years went on, sharecropping became more and more oppressive. Sharecroppers' economic opportunities were severely limited by a world market in which the price of farm products suffered a prolonged decline.

A nursemaid and her charge, from a daguerreotype around 1865.

The White Farmer

The plight of the small farmer was not confined to blacks in the postwar South. Wartime devastation set in motion a train of events that permanently altered the independent way of life of white yeomen, leading to what they considered a loss of freedom. To obtain supplies from merchants, farmers were forced to take up the growing of cotton and pledge a part of the crop as collateral (property the creditor can seize if a debt is not paid). This system became known as the "**crop lien.**" Since interest rates were extremely high and the price of cotton fell steadily, many farmers found themselves still in debt after marketing their portion of the crop at year's end. They had no choice but to continue to plant cotton to obtain new loans. By the mid-1870s, white farmers, who cultivated only 10 percent of the South's cotton crop in 1860, were growing 40 percent, and many who had owned their land had fallen into dependency as sharecroppers who now rented land owned by others.

The crop-lien system

Both black and white farmers found themselves caught in the sharecropping and crop-lien systems. The workings of sharecropping and the

The burden of debt

VOICES OF FREEDOM

From Petition of Committee in Behalf
of the Freedmen to Andrew Johnson (1865)

In the summer of 1865, President Andrew Johnson ordered land that had been distributed to freed slaves in South Carolina and Georgia returned to its former owners. A committee of freedmen drafted a petition asking for the right to obtain land. Johnson did not, however, change his policy.

We the freedmen of Edisto Island, South Carolina, have learned from you through Major General O. O. Howard . . . with deep sorrow and painful hearts of the possibility of [the] government restoring these lands to the former owners. We are well aware of the many perplexing and trying questions that burden your mind, and therefore pray to god (the preserver of all, and who has through our late and beloved President [Lincoln's] proclamation and the war made us a free people) that he may guide you in making your decisions and give you that wisdom that cometh from above to settle these great and important questions for the best interests of the country and the colored race.

Here is where secession was born and nurtured. Here is where we have toiled nearly all our lives as slaves and treated like dumb driven cattle. This is our home, we have made these lands what they were, we are the only true and loyal people that were found in possession of these lands. We have been always ready to strike for liberty and humanity, yea to fight if need be to preserve this glorious Union. Shall not we who are freedmen and have always been true to this Union have the same rights as are enjoyed by others? . . . Are not our rights as a free people and good citizens of these United States to be considered before those who were found in rebellion against this good and just government? . . .

[Are] we who have been abused and oppressed for many long years not to be allowed the privilege of purchasing land but be subject to the will of these large land owners? God forbid. Land monopoly is injurious to the advancement of the course of freedom, and if government does not make some provision by which we as freedmen can obtain a homestead, we have not bettered our condition. . . .

We look to you . . . for protection and equal rights with the privilege of purchasing a homestead—a homestead right here in the heart of South Carolina.

From a Sharecropping Contract (1866)

Few former slaves were able to acquire land in the post–Civil War South. Most ended up as sharecroppers, working on white-owned land for a share of the crop at the end of the growing season. This contract, typical of thousands of others, originated in Tennessee. The laborers signed with an X, as they were illiterate.

Thomas J. Ross agrees to employ the Freedmen to plant and raise a crop on his Rosstown Plantation. . . . On the following Rules, Regulations and Remunerations.

The said Ross agrees to furnish the land to cultivate, and a sufficient number of mules & horses and feed them to make and house said crop and all necessary farming utensils to carry on the same and to give unto said Freedmen whose names appear below one half of all the cotton, corn and wheat that is raised on said place for the year 1866 after all the necessary expenses are deducted out that accrues on said crop. Outside of the Freedmen's labor in harvesting, carrying to market and selling the same the said Freedmen . . . covenant and agrees to and with said Thomas J. Ross that for and in consideration of one half of the crop before mentioned that they will plant, cultivate, and raise under the management control and Superintendence of said Ross, in good faith, a cotton, corn and oat crop under his management for the year 1866. And we the said Freedmen agrees to furnish ourselves & families in provisions, clothing, medicine and medical bills and all, and every kind of other expenses that we may incur on said plantation for the year 1866 free of charge to said Ross. Should the said Ross furnish us any of the above supplies or any other kind of expenses, during said year, [we] are to settle and pay him out of the net proceeds of our part of the crop the retail price of the county at time of sale or any price we may agree upon—The said Ross shall keep a regular book account, against each and every one or the head of every family to be adjusted and settled at the end of the year.

We furthermore bind ourselves to and with said Ross that we will do good work and labor ten hours a day on an average, winter and summer. . . . We further agree that we will lose all lost time, or pay at the rate of one dollar per day, rainy days excepted. In sickness and women lying in childbed are to lose the time and account for it to the other hands out of his or her part of the crop. . . .

We furthermore bind ourselves that we will obey the orders of said Ross in all things in carrying out and managing said crop for said year and be docked for disobedience . . . and are also responsible to said Ross if we carelessly, maliciously maltreat any of his stock for said year to said Ross for damages to be assessed out of our wages.

Samuel (X) Johnson, Thomas (X) Richard, Tinny (X) Fitch, Jessie (X) Simmons, Sophe (X) Pruden, Henry (X) Pruden, Frances (X) Pruden, Elijah (X) Smith.

QUESTIONS

1. *Why do the black petitioners believe that owning land is essential to the enjoyment of freedom?*

2. *In what ways does the contract limit the freedom of the laborers?*

3. *What do these documents suggest about competing definitions of black freedom in the aftermath of slavery?*

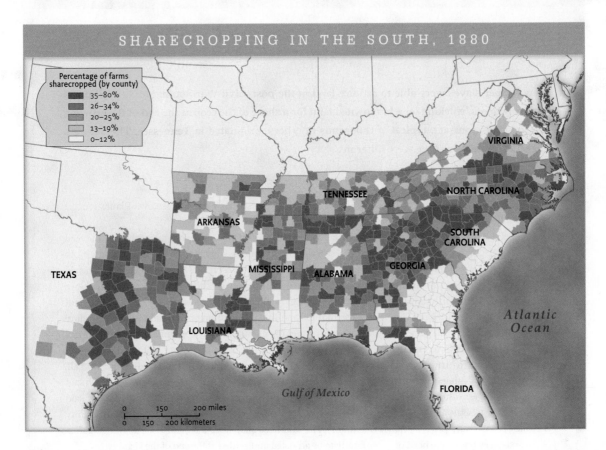

Percentage of farms sharecropped (by county)

- 35–80%
- 26–34%
- 20–25%
- 13–19%
- 0–12%

VIRGINIA

TENNESSEE

NORTH CAROLINA

ARKANSAS

SOUTH CAROLINA

GEORGIA

TEXAS

MISSISSIPPI

ALABAMA

LOUISIANA

Atlantic Ocean

Gulf of Mexico

FLORIDA

0   150   200 miles

0   150   200 kilometers

By 1880, sharecropping had become the dominant form of agricultural labor in large parts of the South. The system involved both white and black farmers.

Growth of southern cities

crop-lien system are illustrated by the case of Matt Brown, a Mississippi farmer who borrowed money each year from a local merchant. He began 1892 with a debt of $226 held over from the previous year. By 1893, although he produced cotton worth $171, Brown's debt had increased to $402, because he had borrowed $33 for food, $29 for clothing, $173 for supplies, and $112 for other items. Brown never succeeded in getting out of debt. He died in 1905; the last entry under his name in the merchant's account book is a coffin.

Even as the rural South stagnated economically, southern cities experienced remarkable growth after the Civil War. As railroads penetrated the interior, they enabled merchants in market centers like Atlanta to trade directly with the North, bypassing coastal cities that had traditionally monopolized southern commerce. A new urban middle class of merchants, railroad promoters, and bankers reaped the benefits of the spread of cotton production in the postwar South.

The cotton depot at Guthrie, Texas. Bales of cotton have been loaded onto trains for shipment. After the Civil War, more and more white farmers began growing cotton to support their families, permanently altering their formerly self-sufficient way of life.

Aftermath of Slavery

The United States, of course, was not the only society to confront the problem of the transition from slavery to freedom. Indeed, many parallels exist between the debates during Reconstruction and struggles that followed slavery in other parts of the Western Hemisphere over the same issues of land, control of labor, and political power. Planters elsewhere held the same stereotypical views of black laborers as were voiced by their counterparts in the United States—former slaves were supposedly lazy and lacking in ambition, and thought that freedom meant an absence of labor.

Emancipation in the Western Hemisphere

For their part, former slaves throughout the hemisphere tried to carve out as much independence as possible, both in their daily lives and in their labor. On small Caribbean islands like Barbados, where no unoccupied land existed, former slaves had no alternative but to return to plantation labor. Elsewhere, the plantations either fell to pieces, as in Haiti, or continued operating with a new labor force composed of indentured servants from India and China, as in Jamaica, Trinidad, and British Guiana. Southern planters in the United States brought in a few Chinese laborers in an attempt to replace freedmen, but since the federal government opposed such efforts, the Chinese remained only a tiny proportion of the southern workforce.

Chinese laborers at work on a Louisiana plantation during Reconstruction.

But if struggles over land and labor united its postemancipation experience with that of other societies, in one respect the United States was unique. Only in the United States were former slaves, within two years of the end of slavery, granted the right to vote and, thus, given a major share of political power. Few anticipated this development when the Civil War ended. It came about as the result of one of the greatest political crises of American history—the battle between President Andrew Johnson and Congress over Reconstruction. The struggle resulted in profound changes in the nature of citizenship, the structure of constitutional authority, and the meaning of American freedom.

THE MAKING OF RADICAL RECONSTRUCTION

Andrew Johnson

To Lincoln's successor, Andrew Johnson, fell the task of overseeing the restoration of the Union. Born in poverty in North Carolina, as a youth Johnson worked as a tailor's apprentice. Becoming a successful politician after moving to Tennessee, Johnson identified himself as the champion of his state's "honest yeomen" and a foe of large planters, whom he described as a "bloated, corrupted aristocracy." A strong defender of the Union, he became the only senator from a seceding state to remain at his post in Washington, D.C., when the Civil War began in 1861. When northern forces occupied Tennessee, Abraham Lincoln named him military governor. In 1864, Republicans nominated him to run for vice president as a symbol of the party's hope of extending its organization into the South.

In personality and outlook, Johnson proved unsuited for the responsibilities he shouldered after Lincoln's death. A lonely, stubborn man, he was intolerant of criticism and unable to compromise. He lacked Lincoln's political skills and keen sense of public opinion. Moreover, while Johnson had supported emancipation once Lincoln made it a goal of the war effort, he held deeply racist views. African-Americans, Johnson believed, had no role to play in Reconstruction.

The Failure of Presidential Reconstruction

A little over a month after Lee's surrender at Appomattox, and with Congress out of session until December, Johnson in May 1865 outlined his plan for reuniting the nation. He issued a series of proclamations that began the period of Presidential Reconstruction (1865–1867). Johnson offered a pardon (which restored political and property rights, except for slaves) to nearly all white southerners who took an oath of allegiance. He excluded Confederate leaders and wealthy planters whose prewar property had been valued at more than $20,000. Most of those exempted, however, soon received individual pardons from the president. Johnson also appointed provisional governors and ordered them to call state conventions, elected by whites alone, that would establish loyal governments in the South. Apart from the requirement that they abolish slavery, repudiate secession, and refuse to pay the Confederate debt—all unavoidable consequences of southern defeat—he granted the new governments a free hand in managing local affairs.

Johnson's program

The conduct of the southern governments elected under Johnson's program turned most of the Republican North against the president. By and large, white voters returned prominent Confederates and members of the old elite to power. Reports of violence directed against former slaves and northern visitors in the South further alarmed Republicans.

The Black Codes

But what aroused the most opposition to Johnson's Reconstruction policy were the **Black Codes**, laws passed by the new southern governments that attempted to regulate the lives of the former slaves. These laws granted blacks certain rights, such as legalized marriage, ownership of property, and limited access to the courts. But they denied them the rights to testify

Regulating former slaves

Selling a Freedman to Pay His Fine at Monticello, Florida, an engraving from *Frank Leslie's Illustrated Newspaper*, January 19, 1867. Under the Black Codes enacted by southern legislatures immediately after the Civil War, blacks convicted of "vagrancy"—often because they refused to sign contracts to work on plantations—were fined and, if unable to pay, auctioned off to work for the person who paid the fine.

against whites, to serve on juries or in state militias, or to vote. And in response to planters' demands that the freedpeople be required to work on the plantations, the Black Codes declared that those who failed to sign yearly labor contracts could be arrested and hired out to white landowners.

Clearly, the death of slavery did not automatically mean the birth of freedom. But the Black Codes so completely violated free labor principles that they called forth a vigorous response from the Republican North. In general, few groups of rebels in history have been treated more leniently than the defeated Confederates. A handful of southern leaders were arrested, but most were quickly released. Only one was executed—Henry Wirz, the commander of Andersonville prison, where thousands of Union prisoners of war had died. Most of the Union army was swiftly demobilized. What motivated the North's turn against Johnson's policies was not a desire to "punish" the white South, but the inability of the South's political leaders to accept the reality of emancipation as evidenced by the Black Codes.

Reaction to Black Codes

The Radical Republicans

When Congress assembled in December 1865, Johnson announced that with loyal governments functioning in all the southern states, the nation had been reunited. In response, Radical Republicans, who had grown increasingly disenchanted with Johnson during the summer and fall, called for the dissolution of these governments and the establishment of new ones with "rebels" excluded from power and black men guaranteed the right to vote. Radicals shared the conviction that Union victory created a golden opportunity to institutionalize the principle of equal rights for all, regardless of race.

The most prominent Radicals in Congress were Charles Sumner, a senator from Massachusetts, and Thaddeus Stevens, a lawyer and iron manufacturer who represented Pennsylvania in the House of Representatives. Before the Civil War, both had been outspoken foes of slavery and defenders of black rights. Stevens's most cherished aim was to confiscate the land of disloyal planters and divide it among former slaves and northern migrants to the South. But his plan to make "small independent landholders" of the former slaves proved too radical even for many of his Radical colleagues and failed to pass.

The Origins of Civil Rights

With the South unrepresented, Republicans enjoyed an overwhelming majority in Congress. Most Republicans were moderates, not Radicals. Moderates believed that Johnson's plan was flawed, but they desired to

Thaddeus Stevens, leader of the Radical Republicans in the House of Representatives during Reconstruction.

work with the president to modify it. They feared that neither northern nor southern whites would accept black suffrage. Moderates and Radicals joined in refusing to seat the southerners recently elected to Congress, but moderates broke with the Radicals by leaving the Johnson governments in place.

Radical Republicans versus moderates

Early in 1866, Senator Lyman Trumbull of Illinois proposed two bills that reflected the moderates' belief that Johnson's policy required modification. The first extended the life of the Freedmen's Bureau, which had originally been established for only one year. The second, the **Civil Rights Bill**, was described by one congressman as "one of the most important bills ever presented to the House for its action." It defined all persons born in the United States as citizens and spelled out rights they were to enjoy without regard to race. Equality before the law was central to the measure—no longer could states enact laws like the Black Codes discriminating between white and black citizens. So were free labor values. According to the law, no state could deprive any citizen of the right to make contracts, bring lawsuits, or enjoy equal protection of one's person and property. These, said Trumbull, were the "fundamental rights belonging to every man as a free man." The bill made no mention of the right to vote for blacks. In constitutional terms, the Civil Rights Bill represented the first attempt to define in law the essence of freedom.

The Civil Rights Bill of 1866

To the surprise of Congress, Johnson vetoed both bills. Both, he said, would centralize power in the national government and deprive the states of the authority to regulate their own affairs. Moreover, he argued, blacks did not deserve the rights of citizenship. Congress failed by a single vote to muster the two-thirds majority necessary to override the veto of the Freedmen's Bureau Bill (although later in 1866, it did extend the bureau's life to 1870). But in April 1866, the Civil Rights Bill became the first major law in American history to be passed over a presidential veto.

The Fourteenth Amendment

Congress now proceeded to adopt its own plan of Reconstruction. In June, it approved and sent to the states for ratification the **Fourteenth Amendment**, which placed in the Constitution the principle of citizenship for all persons born in the United States, and which empowered the federal government to protect the rights of all Americans. The amendment prohibited the states from abridging the "privileges and immunities" of citizens or denying them the "equal protection of the law." This broad language opened the door for future Congresses and the federal courts to breathe meaning into the guarantee of legal equality.

President Andrew Johnson, in an 1868 lithograph by Currier and Ives. Because of Johnson's stubborn opposition to the congressional Reconstruction policy, one disgruntled citizen drew a crown on his head with the words, "I am King."

In a compromise between the radical and moderate positions on black suffrage, the amendment did not grant blacks the right to vote. But it did provide that if a state denied the vote to any group of men, that state's representation in Congress would be reduced. (This provision did not apply when states barred women from voting.) The abolition of slavery threatened to increase southern political power, since now all blacks, not merely three-fifths as in the case of slaves, would be counted in determining a state's representation in Congress. The Fourteenth Amendment offered the leaders of the white South a choice—allow black men to vote and keep their state's full representation in the House of Representatives, or limit the vote to whites and sacrifice part of their political power.

Black suffrage and political power

By writing into the Constitution the principle that equality before the law regardless of race is a fundamental right of all American citizens, the amendment made the most important change in that document since the adoption of the Bill of Rights.

Significance of the Fourteenth Amendment

The Reconstruction Act

The Fourteenth Amendment became the central issue of the political campaign of 1866. Johnson embarked on a speaking tour of the North. Denouncing his critics, the president made wild accusations that the Radicals were plotting to assassinate him. His behavior further undermined public support for his policies, as did riots that broke out in Memphis and New Orleans, in which white policemen and citizens killed dozens of blacks.

In the northern congressional elections that fall, Republicans opposed to Johnson's policies won a sweeping victory. Nonetheless, at the president's urging, every southern state but Tennessee refused to ratify the Fourteenth Amendment. The intransigence of Johnson and the bulk of the white South pushed moderate Republicans toward the Radicals. In March 1867, over Johnson's veto, Congress adopted the **Reconstruction Act**, which temporarily divided the South into five military districts and called for the creation of new state governments, with black men given the right to vote. Thus began the period of Radical Reconstruction, which lasted until 1877.

Radical Reconstruction

Impeachment and the Election of Grant

In March 1867, Congress adopted the Tenure of Office Act, barring the president from removing certain officeholders, including cabinet members, without the consent of the Senate. Johnson considered this an unconstitutional restriction on his authority. In February 1868, he removed

A Democratic Party broadside from the election of 1866 in Pennsylvania uses racist imagery to argue that government assistance aids lazy former slaves at the expense of hardworking whites.

Secretary of War Edwin M. Stanton, an ally of the Radicals. The House of Representatives responded by approving articles of impeachment—that is, it presented charges against Johnson to the Senate, which had to decide whether to remove him from office.

That spring, for the first time in American history, a president was placed on trial before the Senate for "high crimes and misdemeanors." By this point, virtually all Republicans considered Johnson a failure as president. But some moderates feared that conviction would damage the constitutional separation of powers between Congress and the executive. Johnson's lawyers assured moderate Republicans that, if acquitted, he would stop interfering with Reconstruction policy. The final tally was 35-19 to convict Johnson, one vote short of the two-thirds necessary to remove him. Seven Republicans had joined the Democrats in voting to acquit the president.

The trial of Andrew Johnson

A few days after the vote, Republicans nominated Ulysses S. Grant, the Union's most prominent military hero, as their candidate for president. Grant's Democratic opponent was Horatio Seymour, the former governor of New York. Reconstruction became the central issue of the bitterly fought 1868 campaign. Democrats denounced Reconstruction as unconstitutional and condemned black suffrage as a violation of America's political traditions. They appealed openly to racism. Seymour's running mate, Francis P. Blair Jr., charged Republicans with placing the South under the rule of "a

Ulysses Grant

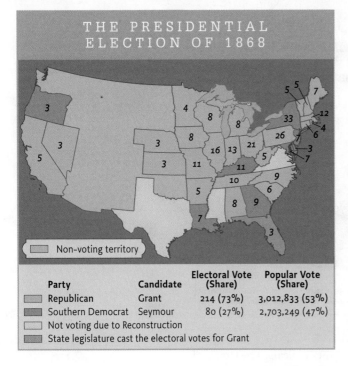

THE PRESIDENTIAL ELECTION OF 1868

Non-voting territory

Party	Candidate	Electoral Vote (Share)	Popular Vote (Share)
Republican	Grant	214 (73%)	3,012,833 (53%)
Southern Democrat	Seymour	80 (27%)	2,703,249 (47%)
Not voting due to Reconstruction			
State legislature cast the electoral votes for Grant			

semi-barbarous race" who longed to "subject the white women to their unbridled lust."

The Fifteenth Amendment

Grant won the election of 1868, although by a margin—300,000 of 6 million votes cast—that many Republicans found uncomfortably slim. The result led Congress to adopt the **Fifteenth Amendment**, which prohibited the federal and state governments from denying any citizen the right to vote because of race. Bitterly opposed by the Democratic Party, it was ratified in 1870.

Although the Fifteenth Amendment opened the door to suffrage restrictions not explicitly based on race—literacy tests, property qualifications, and poll taxes—and did not extend the right to vote to women, it marked the culmination of four decades of abolitionist agitation. "Nothing in all history," exclaimed veteran abolitionist William Lloyd Garrison, equaled "this wonderful, quiet, sudden transformation of four millions of human beings from . . . the auction-block to the ballot-box."

The Fifteenth Amendment, an 1870 lithograph marking the ratification of the constitutional amendment prohibiting states from denying citizens the right to vote because of race. Surrounding an image of a celebration parade are portraits of Abraham Lincoln; President Ulysses S. Grant and his vice president, Schuyler Colfax; the abolitionists John Brown, Martin R. Delany, and Frederick Douglass; and Hiram Revels, the first black to serve in the U.S. Senate. At the bottom are scenes of freedom—education, family, political representation, and church life.

The "Great Constitutional Revolution"

The laws and amendments of Reconstruction reflected the intersection of two products of the Civil War era—a newly empowered national state, and the idea of a national citizenry enjoying equality before the law. What Republican leader Carl Schurz called the "great Constitutional revolution" of Reconstruction transformed the federal system and with it, the language of freedom so central to American political culture.

Effects of Reconstruction amendments

Before the Civil War, American citizenship had been closely linked to race. But the laws and amendments of Reconstruction repudiated the idea that citizenship was an entitlement of whites alone. And, as one congressman noted, the amendments expanded the liberty of whites as well as blacks, including "the millions of people of foreign birth who will flock to our shores."

Race and citizenship

The new amendments also transformed the relationship between the federal government and the states. The Bill of Rights had linked civil liberties to the autonomy of the states. Its language—"Congress shall make no law"—reflected the belief that concentrated national power posed the greatest threat to freedom. The authors of the Reconstruction amendments assumed that rights required national power to enforce them. Rather than a threat to liberty, the federal government, in Charles Sumner's words, had become "the custodian of freedom."

The Reconstruction amendments transformed the Constitution from a document primarily concerned with federal-state relations and the rights of property into a vehicle through which members of vulnerable minorities could stake a claim to freedom and seek protection against misconduct by all levels of government. In the twentieth century, many of the Supreme Court's most important decisions expanding the rights of American citizens were based on the Fourteenth Amendment, perhaps most notably the 1954 *Brown* ruling that outlawed school segregation (see Chapter 24).

Constitutional significance

The Rights of Women

"The contest with the South that destroyed slavery," wrote the Philadelphia lawyer Sidney George Fisher in his diary, "has caused an immense increase in the popular passion for liberty and equality." But advocates of **women's rights** encountered the limits of the Reconstruction commitment to equality. Women activists saw Reconstruction as the moment to claim their own emancipation. The rewriting of the Constitution, declared suffrage leader Olympia Brown, offered the opportunity to sever the blessings of freedom from sex as well as race and to "bury the black man and the woman in the citizen."

Women and the limits of equality

A Delegation of Advocates of Woman Suffrage Addressing the House Judiciary Committee, an engraving from Frank Leslie's Illustrated Newspaper, February 4, 1871. The group includes Elizabeth Cady Stanton, seated just to the right of the speaker, and Susan B. Anthony, at the table on the extreme right.

Even Radical Republicans insisted that Reconstruction was the "Negro's hour" (the hour, that is, of the black male). The Fourteenth Amendment for the first time introduced the word "male" into the Constitution, in its clause penalizing a state for denying any group of men the right to vote. The Fifteenth Amendment outlawed discrimination in voting based on race but not gender. These measures produced a bitter split both between feminists and Radical Republicans, and within feminist circles. Some leaders, like Elizabeth Cady Stanton and Susan B. Anthony, denounced their former abolitionist allies and moved to sever the women's rights movement from its earlier moorings in the antislavery tradition.

Thus, even as it rejected the racial definition of freedom that had emerged in the first half of the nineteenth century, Reconstruction left the gender boundary largely intact. When women tried to use the rewritten legal code and Constitution to claim equal rights, they found the courts unreceptive. Myra Bradwell invoked the idea of free labor in challenging an Illinois statute limiting the practice of law to men, but the Supreme Court in 1873 rebuffed her claim. Free labor principles, the justices declared, did not apply to women, since "the law of the Creator" had assigned them to "the domestic sphere."

America's great departure

Despite their limitations, the Fourteenth and Fifteenth Amendments and the Reconstruction Act of 1867 marked a radical departure in American and world history. Alone among the nations that abolished slavery in the nineteenth century, the United States, within a few years of emancipation, clothed its former slaves with citizenship rights equal to those of whites. The Reconstruction Act of 1867 inaugurated America's first real experiment in interracial democracy.

RADICAL RECONSTRUCTION IN THE SOUTH

"The Tocsin of Freedom"

Political action by African-Americans

Among the former slaves, the passage of the Reconstruction Act inspired an outburst of political organization. At mass political meetings—community gatherings attended by men, women, and children—African-Americans

Electioneering at the South, an engraving from *Harper's Weekly,* July 25, 1868, depicts a speaker at a political meeting in the rural South. Women as well as men took part in these grassroots gatherings.

staked their claim to equal citizenship. Blacks, declared an Alabama meeting, deserved "exactly the same rights, privileges and immunities as are enjoyed by white men. We ask for nothing more and will be content with nothing less."

Determined to exercise their new rights as citizens, thousands joined the Union League, an organization closely linked to the Republican Party, and the vast majority of eligible African-Americans registered to vote. James K. Green, a former slave in Hale County, Alabama, and a League organizer, went on to serve eight years in the Alabama legislature. In the 1880s, Green looked back on his political career. Before the war, he declared, "I was entirely ignorant; I knew nothing more than to obey my master; and there were thousands of us in the same attitude. . . . But the tocsin [warning bell] of freedom sounded and knocked at the door and we walked out like free men and shouldered the responsibilities."

By 1870, all the former Confederate states had been readmitted to the Union, and in a region where the Republican Party had not existed before the war, nearly all were under Republican control. Their new state constitutions, drafted in 1868 and 1869 by the first public bodies in American history with substantial black representation, marked a considerable improvement over those they replaced. The constitutions greatly expanded public responsibilities. They established the region's first state-funded systems of free public education, and they created new penitentiaries, orphan asylums, and homes for the insane. The constitutions guaranteed equality of civil and political rights and abolished practices of the antebellum era such as whipping as a punishment for crime, property qualifications for officeholding, and imprisonment for debt. A few states initially barred former Confederates from voting, but this policy was quickly abandoned by the new state governments.

The First Vote, an engraving from *Harper's Weekly,* November 16, 1867, depicts the first biracial elections in southern history. The voters represent key sources of the black political leadership that emerged during Reconstruction—the artisan carrying his tools, the well-dressed city person (probably free before the war), and the soldier.

The Black Officeholder

Throughout Reconstruction, black voters provided the bulk of the Republican Party's support. But African-Americans did not control Reconstruction politics, as their opponents frequently charged. The highest offices remained almost entirely in white hands, and only in South Carolina, where blacks made up 60 percent of the population, did they form a majority of the legislature. Nonetheless, the fact that some 2,000 African-Americans held public office during Reconstruction marked a fundamental shift of power in the South and a radical departure in American government.

African-Americans were represented at every level of government. Fourteen were elected to the national House of Representatives. Two blacks served in the U.S. Senate during Reconstruction, both representing Mississippi. Hiram Revels, who had been born free in North Carolina, in 1870 became the first black senator in American history. The second, Blanche K. Bruce, a former slave, was elected in 1875. At state and local levels, the presence of black officeholders and their white allies made a real difference in southern life, ensuring that blacks accused of crimes would be tried before juries of their peers and enforcing fairness in such aspects of local government as road repair, tax assessment, and poor relief.

In South Carolina and Louisiana, homes of the South's wealthiest and best-educated free black communities, most prominent Reconstruction officeholders had never experienced slavery. In addition, a number of black Reconstruction officials, like Pennsylvania-born Jonathan J. Wright, who served on the South Carolina Supreme Court, had come from the North after the Civil War. The majority, however, were former slaves who had established their leadership in the black community by serving in the Union army; working as ministers, teachers, or skilled craftsmen; or engaging in Union League organizing.

A portrait of Hiram Revels, the first black U. S. senator, by Theodore Kaufmann, a German-born artist who emigrated to the United States in 1855. Lithograph copies sold widely in the North during Reconstruction. Frederick Douglass, commenting on the dignified image, noted that African-Americans "so often see ourselves described and painted as monkeys, that we think it a great piece of fortune to find an exception to this general rule."

Carpetbaggers and Scalawags

The new southern governments also brought to power new groups of whites. Many Reconstruction officials were northerners who for one reason or another had made their homes in the South after the war. Their opponents dubbed them "**carpetbaggers**," implying that they had packed all their belongings in a suitcase and left their homes in order to reap the spoils of office in the South. Some carpetbaggers were undoubtedly corrupt adventurers. The large majority, however, were former Union soldiers who decided to remain in the South when the war ended, before there was any prospect of going into politics.

Most white Republicans, however, had been born in the South. Former Confederates reserved their greatest scorn for these "**scalawags**," whom they considered traitors to their race and region. Some southern-born Republicans were men of stature and wealth, like James L. Alcorn, the owner of one of Mississippi's largest plantations and the state's first Republican governor. Most "scalawags," however, were non-slaveholding white farmers from the southern upcountry. Many had been wartime Unionists, and they now cooperated with the Republicans in order to prevent "rebels" from returning to power.

Southern Republicans

Southern Republicans in Power

In view of the daunting challenges they faced, the remarkable thing is not that Reconstruction governments in many respects failed, but how much they did accomplish. Perhaps their greatest achievement lay in establishing the South's first state-supported public schools. The new educational systems served both black and white children, although generally in schools segregated by race. Only in New Orleans were the public schools integrated during Reconstruction, and only in South Carolina did the state university admit black students (elsewhere, separate colleges were established). The new governments also pioneered civil rights legislation. Their laws made it illegal for railroads, hotels, and other institutions to discriminate on the basis of race. Enforcement varied considerably from locality to locality, but Reconstruction established for the first time at the state level a standard of equal citizenship and a recognition of blacks' right to a share of public services.

State-supported public schools

Civil rights legislation

Republican governments also took steps to strengthen the position of rural laborers and promote the South's economic recovery. They passed laws to ensure that agricultural laborers and sharecroppers had the first claim on harvested crops, rather than merchants to whom the landowner owed money. South Carolina created a state Land Commission, which by 1876 had settled 14,000 black families and a few poor whites on their own farms.

The Quest for Prosperity

Rather than on land distribution, however, the Reconstruction governments pinned their hopes for southern economic growth and opportunity for African-Americans and poor whites alike on regional economic development.

Economic development during Reconstruction

A group of black students and their teacher in a picture taken by an amateur photographer, probably a Union army veteran, while touring Civil War battlefields.

Railroad construction

Railroad construction, they believed, was the key to transforming the South into a society of booming factories, bustling towns, and diversified agriculture. Every state during Reconstruction helped to finance railroad construction, and through tax reductions and other incentives tried to attract northern manufacturers to invest in the region. The program had mixed results. Economic development in general remained weak.

To their supporters, the governments of Radical Reconstruction presented a complex pattern of disappointment and accomplishment. A revitalized southern economy failed to materialize, and most African-Americans remained locked in poverty. On the other hand, biracial demo-

Biracial democracy

cratic government, a thing unknown in American history, for the first time functioned effectively in many parts of the South. The conservative elite that had dominated southern government from colonial times to 1867 found itself excluded from political power, while poor whites, newcomers from the North, and former slaves cast ballots, sat on juries, and enacted and administered laws. It is a measure of how far change had progressed that the reaction against Reconstruction proved so extreme.

THE OVERTHROW OF RECONSTRUCTION

Reconstruction's Opponents

The South's traditional leaders—planters, merchants, and Democratic politicians—bitterly opposed the new governments. "Intelligence, virtue, and patriotism" in public life, declared a protest by prominent southern

Sources of opposition

Democrats, had given way to "ignorance, stupidity, and vice." Corruption did exist during Reconstruction, but it was confined to no race, region, or party. The rapid growth of state budgets and the benefits to be gained from public aid led in some states to a scramble for influence that produced bribery, insider dealing, and a get-rich-quick atmosphere. Southern frauds, however, were dwarfed by those practiced in these years by the Whiskey Ring, which involved high officials of the Grant administration, and by New York's Tweed Ring, controlled by the Democrats, whose thefts ran into the tens of millions of dollars. (These are discussed in the next chapter.) The rising taxes needed to pay for schools and other new public facilities and to assist railroad development were another cause of opposition to Reconstruction. Many poor whites who had initially supported the Republican Party turned against it when it became clear that their economic situation was not improving.

The most basic reason for opposition to Reconstruction, however, was that most white southerners could not accept the idea of former slaves voting, holding office, and enjoying equality before the law. Opponents launched a campaign of violence in an effort to end Republican rule. Their actions posed a fundamental challenge both for Reconstruction governments in the South and for policymakers in Washington, D.C.

A cartoon from around 1870 illustrates a key theme of the racist opposition to Reconstruction—that blacks had forced themselves upon whites and gained domination over them. A black school teacher inflicts punishment on a white student in an integrated classroom, and a racially mixed jury judges a white defendant.

"A Reign of Terror"

The Civil War ended in 1865, but violence remained widespread in large parts of the postwar South. In the early years of Reconstruction, violence was mostly local and unorganized. Blacks were assaulted and murdered for refusing to give way to whites on city sidewalks, using "insolent" language, challenging end-of-year contract settlements, and attempting to buy land. The violence that greeted the advent of Republican governments after 1867, however, was far more pervasive and more directly motivated by politics. In wide areas of the South, secret societies sprang up with the aim of preventing blacks from voting and destroying the organization of the Republican Party by assassinating local leaders and public officials.

Campaigns of violence

The most notorious such organization was the **Ku Klux Klan**, which in effect served as a military arm of the Democratic Party in the South. From its founding in 1866 in Tennessee, the Klan was a terrorist organization. It committed some of the most brutal criminal acts in American history. In many counties throughout the South, it launched what one victim called a "reign of terror" against Republican leaders, black and white.

The Klan's victims included white Republicans, among them wartime Unionists and local officeholders, teachers, and party organizers. But African-Americans—local political leaders, those who managed to acquire land, and others who in one way or another defied the norms of white supremacy—bore the brunt of the violence. On occasion, violence escalated from assaults on individuals to mass terrorism and even local insurrections. The bloodiest act of violence during Reconstruction took place in **Colfax**, Louisiana, in 1873, where armed whites assaulted the town with a small cannon. Hundreds of former slaves were murdered, including fifty members of a black militia unit after they had surrendered.

In 1870 and 1871, Congress adopted three **Enforcement Acts**, outlawing terrorist societies and allowing the president to use the army against them. These laws continued the expansion of national authority during Reconstruction. In 1871, President Grant dispatched federal marshals, backed up by troops in some areas, to arrest hundreds of accused Klansmen. Many Klan leaders fled the South. After a series of well-publicized trials, the Klan went out of existence. In 1872, for the first time since the Civil War, peace reigned in most of the former Confederacy.

A Prospective Scene in the City of Oaks, a cartoon in the September 1, 1868, issue of the *Independent Monitor,* a Democratic newspaper published in Tuscaloosa, Alabama. The cartoon sent a warning to the Reverend A. S. Lakin, who had moved from Ohio to become president of the University of Alabama, and Dr. N. B. Cloud, a southern-born Republican serving as Alabama's superintendent of public education. The Ku Klux Klan forced both men from their positions.

The Liberal Republicans

Despite the Grant administration's effective response to Klan terrorism, the North's commitment to Reconstruction waned during the 1870s. Northerners increasingly felt that the South should be able to solve its own problems without constant interference from Washington. The federal government had freed the slaves, made them citizens, and given them the right to vote. Now, blacks should rely on their own resources, not demand further assistance.

Waning commitment to the North

In 1872, an influential group of Republicans, alienated by corruption within the Grant administration and believing that the growth of federal power during and after the war needed to be curtailed, formed their own party. They included Republican founders like Lyman Trumbull and prominent editors and journalists such as E. L. Godkin of *The Nation*. Calling themselves Liberal Republicans, they nominated Horace Greeley, editor of the *New York Tribune*, for president.

Liberal Republicans

Democratic criticisms of Reconstruction found a receptive audience among the Liberals. As in the North, they became convinced, the "best men" of the South had been excluded from power while "ignorant" voters controlled politics, producing corruption and misgovernment. Greeley had spent most of his career, first as a Whig and then as a Republican, denouncing the Democratic Party. But with the

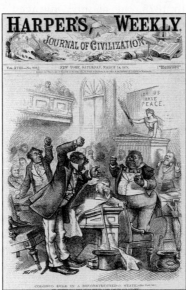

Changes in graphic artist Thomas Nast's depiction of blacks in *Harper's Weekly* mirrored the evolution of Republican sentiment in the North. *And Not This Man?* August 5, 1865, shows the black soldier as an upstanding citizen deserving of the vote. *Colored Rule in a Reconstructed (?) State*, March 14, 1874, suggests that Reconstruction legislatures had become travesties of democratic government.

1872 election

Republican split presenting an opportunity to repair their political fortunes, Democratic leaders endorsed Greeley as their candidate. But many rank-and-file Democrats, unable to bring themselves to vote for Greeley, stayed at home on election day. As a result, Greeley suffered a devastating defeat by Grant, whose margin of more than 700,000 popular votes was the largest in a nineteenth-century presidential contest. But Greeley's campaign placed on the northern agenda the one issue on which the Liberal reformers and the Democrats could agree—a new policy toward the South.

The North's Retreat

The Liberal attack on Reconstruction, which continued after 1872, contributed to a resurgence of racism in the North. Journalist James S. Pike, a leading Greeley supporter, in 1874 published *The Prostrate State*, an influential account of a visit to South Carolina. The book depicted a state engulfed by political corruption, drained by governmental extravagance, and under the control of "a mass of black barbarism." Resurgent racism offered a convenient explanation for the alleged "failure" of Reconstruction. The solution, for many, was to restore leading whites to political power.

Factors weakening Reconstruction

Other factors also weakened northern support for Reconstruction. In 1873, the country plunged into a severe economic depression. Distracted by economic problems, Republicans were in no mood to devote further attention to the South. The depression dealt the South a severe blow and further weakened the prospect that Republicans could revitalize the region's economy. Democrats made substantial gains throughout the nation in the elections of 1874. For the first time since the Civil War, their party took control of the House of Representatives. Before the new Congress met, the old one enacted a final piece of Reconstruction legislation, the **Civil Rights Act of 1875**. This outlawed racial discrimination in places of public accommodation like hotels and theaters. But it was clear that the northern public was retreating from Reconstruction.

The Supreme Court and Reconstruction

The Supreme Court whittled away at the guarantees of black rights Congress had adopted. In the ***Slaughterhouse Cases*** (1873), the justices ruled that the Fourteenth Amendment had not altered traditional federalism. Most of the rights of citizens, it declared, remained under state control. Three years later, in *United States v. Cruikshank*, the Court gutted the Enforcement Acts by throwing out the convictions of some of those responsible for the Colfax Massacre of 1873.

The Triumph of the Redeemers

By the mid-1870s, Reconstruction was clearly on the defensive. Democrats had already regained control of states with substantial white voting majorities such as Tennessee, North Carolina, and Texas. The victorious Democrats called themselves **Redeemers**, since they claimed to have "redeemed" the white South from corruption, misgovernment, and northern and black control.

Democratic victories at the polls

In those states where Reconstruction governments survived, violence again erupted. This time, the Grant administration showed no desire to intervene. In Mississippi, in 1875, armed Democrats destroyed ballot boxes and drove former slaves from the polls. The result was a Democratic landslide and the end of Reconstruction in Mississippi. Similar events

Return of violence

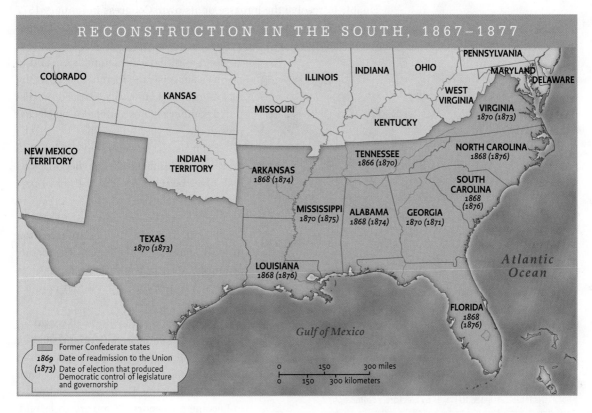

RECONSTRUCTION IN THE SOUTH, 1867–1877

Former Confederate states
1869 Date of readmission to the Union
(1873) Date of election that produced Democratic control of legislature and governorship

took place in South Carolina in 1876. Democrats nominated for governor former Confederate general Wade Hampton. Hampton promised to respect the rights of all citizens of the state, but his supporters, inspired by Democratic tactics in Mississippi, launched a wave of intimidation. Democrats intended to carry the election, one planter told a black official, "if we have to wade in blood knee-deep."

The Disputed Election and Bargain of 1877

Rutherford B. Hayes

Events in South Carolina directly affected the outcome of the presidential campaign of 1876. To succeed Grant, the Republicans nominated Governor Rutherford B. Hayes of Ohio. The Democrats chose as his opponent New York's governor, Samuel J. Tilden. By this time, only South Carolina, Florida, and Louisiana remained under Republican control. The election turned out to be so close that whoever captured these states—which both parties claimed to have carried—would become the next president.

Unable to resolve the impasse on its own, Congress in January 1877 appointed a fifteen-member Electoral Commission, composed of senators, representatives, and Supreme Court justices. Republicans enjoyed an 8-7 majority on the commission, and to no one's surprise, the members decided by that margin that Hayes had carried the disputed southern states and had been elected president.

Even as the commission deliberated, however, behind-the-scenes negotiations took place between leaders of the two parties. Hayes's representatives agreed to recognize Democratic control of the entire South and to avoid further intervention in local affairs. For their part, Democrats promised not to dispute Hayes's right to office and to respect the civil and political rights of blacks.

Thus was concluded the **Bargain of 1877**. Hayes became president and quickly ordered federal troops to stop guarding the state houses in Louisiana and South Carolina, allowing Democratic claimants to become governors. (Contrary to legend,

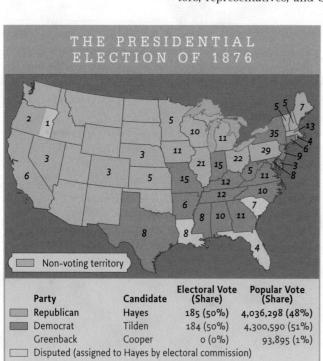

THE PRESIDENTIAL
ELECTION OF 1876

Non-voting territory

Party	Candidate	Electoral Vote (Share)	Popular Vote (Share)
Republican	Hayes	185 (50%)	4,036,298 (48%)
Democrat	Tilden	184 (50%)	4,300,590 (51%)
Greenback	Cooper	0 (0%)	93,895 (1%)
Disputed (assigned to Hayes by electoral commission)			

Hayes did not remove the last soldiers from the South—he simply ordered them to return to their barracks.) The triumphant southern Democrats failed to live up to their pledge to recognize blacks as equal citizens.

The End of Reconstruction

As a historical process—the nation's adjustment to the destruction of slavery—Reconstruction continued well after 1877. Blacks continued to vote and, in some states, hold office into the 1890s. But as a distinct era of national history—when Republicans controlled much of the South, blacks exercised significant political power, and the federal government accepted the responsibility for protecting the fundamental rights of all American citizens—Reconstruction had come to an end. Despite its limitations, Reconstruction was a remarkable chapter in the story of American freedom. Nearly a century would pass before the nation again tried to bring equal rights to the descendants of slaves. The civil rights era of the 1950s and 1960s would sometimes be called the Second Reconstruction.

Is This a Republican Form of Government?, a cartoon by Thomas Nast in *Harper's Weekly*, September 2, 1876, illustrates his conviction that the overthrow of Reconstruction meant that the United States was not prepared to live up to its democratic ideals or protect the rights of black citizens threatened by violence.

CHAPTER REVIEW AND ONLINE RESOURCES

REVIEW QUESTIONS

1. *In 1865, the former Confederate general Robert Richardson remarked that "the emancipated slaves own nothing, because nothing but freedom has been given to them." Explain whether this would be an accurate assessment of Reconstruction twelve years later.*

2. *The women's movement split into two separate national organizations in part because the Fifteenth Amendment did not give women the vote. Explain why the two groups split.*

3. *How did black families, churches, schools, and other institutions contribute to the development of African-American culture and political activism in this period?*

4. *Why did ownership of land and control of labor become major points of contention between former slaves and whites in the South?*

5. *By what methods did southern whites seek to limit African-American civil rights and liberties? How did the federal government respond?*

6. *How did the failure of land reform and continued poverty lead to new forms of servitude for both blacks and whites?*

7. *What caused the confrontation between President Johnson and Congress over Reconstruction policies?*

8. *What national issues and attitudes combined to bring an end to Reconstruction by 1877?*

9. *By 1877, how did the condition of former slaves in the United States compare with that of freedmen around the globe?*

KEY TERMS

Freedmen's Bureau (p. 447)

sharecropping (p. 449)

crop-lien system (p. 449)

Black Codes (p. 455)

Civil Rights Bill of 1866 (p. 457)

Fourteenth Amendment (p. 457)

Reconstruction Act (p. 458)

Fifteenth Amendment (p. 460)

women's rights (p. 461)

carpetbaggers and scalawags (p. 464)

Ku Klux Klan (p. 468)

Colfax Massacre (p. 468)

Enforcement Acts (p. 468)

Civil Rights Act of 1875 (p. 470)

Slaughterhouse Cases (p. 470)

Redeemers (p. 471)

Bargain of 1877 (p. 472)

wwnorton.com
/studyspace

VISIT STUDYSPACE FOR THESE RESOURCES AND MORE

- A chapter outline
- A diagnostic chapter quiz
- Interactive maps
- Map worksheets
- Multimedia documents

APPENDIX

DOCUMENTS

The Declaration of Independence (1776) A-2

The Constitution of the United States (1787) A-5

From George Washington's Farewell Address (1796) A-17

The Seneca Falls Declaration of Sentiments and
    Resolutions (1848) A-22

From Frederick Douglass's "What, to the Slave, Is the Fourth of
    July?" Speech (1852) A-25

The Gettysburg Address (1863) A-29

Abraham Lincoln's Second Inaugural Address (1865) A-30

The Populist Platform of 1892 A-31

Franklin D. Roosevelt's First Inaugural Address (1933) A-34

From The Program for the March on Washington for Jobs and
    Freedom (1963) A-37

Ronald Reagan's First Inaugural Address (1981) A-38

Barack Obama's First Inaugural Address (2009) A-42

TABLES AND FIGURES

Presidential Elections A-46

Admission of States A-54

Population of the United States A-55

Historical Statistics of the United States:
    Labor Force—Selected Characteristics Expressed as a
        Percentage of the Labor Force, 1800–2010 A-56
    Immigration, by Origin A-56
    Unemployment Rate, 1890–2013 A-57
    Voter Participation in Presidential Elections 1824–2012 A-57
    Union Membership as a Percentage of Nonagricultural
        Employment, 1880–2012 A-57
    Birthrate, 1820–2011 A-57

SUGGESTED READINGS ... A-59

GLOSSARY ... A-67

CREDITS ... A-95

INDEX ... A-99

THE DECLARATION OF INDEPENDENCE (1776)

When in the course of human events, it becomes necessary for one people to dissolve the political bands which have connected them with another, and to assume among the Powers of the earth, the separate and equal station to which the Laws of Nature and of Nature's God entitle them, a decent respect to the opinions of mankind requires that they should declare the causes which impel them to the separation.

We hold these truths to be self-evident, that all men are created equal, that they are endowed by their Creator with certain unalienable rights, that among these are Life, Liberty, and the pursuit of Happiness. That to secure these rights, Governments are instituted among Men, deriving their just powers from the consent of the governed. That whenever any Form of Government becomes destructive of these ends, it is the Right of the People to alter or to abolish it, and to institute new Government, laying its foundation on such principles and organizing its powers in such form, as to them shall seem most likely to effect their Safety and Happiness. Prudence, indeed, will dictate that Governments long established should not be changed for light and transient causes; and accordingly all experience hath shown, that mankind are more disposed to suffer, while evils are sufferable, than to right themselves by abolishing the forms to which they are accustomed. But when a long train of abuses and usurpations, pursuing invariably the same Object evinces a design to reduce them under absolute Despotism, it is their right, it is their duty, to throw off such Government, and to provide new Guards for their future security.—Such has been the patient sufferance of these Colonies; and such is now the necessity which constrains them to alter their former Systems of Government. The history of the present King of Great Britain is a history of repeated injuries and usurpations, all having in direct object the establishment of an absolute Tyranny over these States. To prove this, let Facts be submitted to a candid world.

He has refused his Assent to Laws, the most wholesome and necessary for the public good.

He has forbidden his Governors to pass Laws of immediate and pressing importance, unless suspended in their operation till his Assent should be obtained; and when so suspended, he has utterly neglected to attend to them.

He has refused to pass other Laws for the accommodation of large districts of people, unless those people would relinquish the right of Representation in the Legislature, a right inestimable to them and formidable to tyrants only.

He has called together legislative bodies at places unusual, uncomfortable, and distant from the depository of their public Records, for the sole purpose of fatiguing them into compliance with his measures.

He has dissolved Representative Houses repeatedly, for opposing with manly firmness his invasions on the rights of the people.

He has refused for a long time, after such dissolutions, to cause others to be elected; whereby the Legislative powers, incapable of Annihilation, have returned to the People at large for their exercise; the State remaining in the mean time exposed to all dangers of invasion from without, and convulsions within.

He has endeavoured to prevent the population of these States; for that purpose obstructing the Laws of Naturalization of Foreigners; refusing to pass others to encourage their migrations hither, and raising the conditions of new Appropriations of Lands.

He has obstructed the Administration of Justice, by refusing his Assent to Laws for establishing Judiciary powers.

He has made Judges dependent on his Will alone, for the tenure of their offices, and the amount and payment of their salaries.

He has erected a multitude of New Offices, and sent hither swarms of Officers to harass our People, and eat out their substance.

He has kept among us, in times of peace, Standing Armies without the Consent of our legislatures.

He has affected to render the Military independent of and superior to the Civil Power.

He has combined with others to subject us to a jurisdiction foreign to our constitution, and unacknowledged by our laws; giving his Assent to their Acts of pretended Legislation:

For quartering large bodies of armed troops among us:

For protecting them, by a mock Trial, from Punishment for any Murders which they should commit on the Inhabitants of these States:

For cutting off our Trade with all parts of the world:

For imposing taxes on us without our Consent:

For depriving us of many cases, of the benefits of Trial by jury:

For transporting us beyond Seas to be tried for pretended offences:

For abolishing the free System of English Laws in a neighbouring Province, establishing therein an Arbitrary government, and enlarging its Boundaries so as to render it at once an example and fit instrument for introducing the same absolute rule into these Colonies:

For taking away our Charters, abolishing our most valuable Laws, and altering fundamentally the Forms of our Governments:

For suspending our own Legislatures, and declaring themselves invested with Power to legislate for us in all cases whatsoever.

He has abdicated Government here, by declaring us out of his Protection and waging War against us.

He has plundered our seas, ravaged our Coasts, burnt our towns, and destroyed the lives of our people.

He is at this time transporting large armies of foreign mercenaries to compleat the works of death, desolation, and tyranny, already begun with circumstances of Cruelty & perfidy scarcely paralleled in the most barbarous ages, and totally unworthy the Head of a civilized nation.

He has constrained our fellow Citizens taken Captive on the high Seas to bear Arms against their Country, to become the executioners of their friends and Brethren, or to fall themselves by their Hands.

He has excited domestic insurrections amongst us, and has endeavoured to bring on the inhabitants of our frontiers, the merciless Indian Savages, whose known rule of warfare, is an undistinguished destruction of all ages, sexes, and conditions.

In every stage of these Oppressions We have Petitioned for Redress in the most humble terms: Our repeated Petitions have been answered only by repeated injury. A Prince, whose character is thus marked by every act which may define a Tyrant, is unfit to be the ruler of a free people.

Nor have We been wanting in attention to our British brethren. We have warned them from time to time of attempts by their legislature to extend an unwarrantable jurisdiction over us. We have reminded them of the circumstances of our emigration and settlement here. We have appealed to their native justice and magnanimity, and we have conjured them by the ties of our common kindred to disavow these usurpations, which, would inevitably interrupt our connections and correspondence. They too must have been deaf to the voice of justice and of consanguinity. We must, therefore, acquiesce in the necessity, which denounces our Separation, and hold them, as we hold the rest of mankind, Enemies in War, in Peace Friends.

WE, THEREFORE, the Representatives of the UNITED STATES OF AMERICA, in General Congress, Assembled, appealing to the Supreme Judge of the world for the rectitude of our intentions, do, in the Name, and by Authority of the good People of these Colonies, solemnly publish and declare, That these United Colonies are, and of Right ought to be FREE AND INDEPENDENT STATES; that they are Absolved from all Allegiance to the British Crown, and that all political connection between them and the State of Great Britain, is and ought to be totally dissolved; and that as Free and Independent States, they have full Power to levy War, conclude Peace, contract Alliances, establish Commerce, and to do all other Acts and Things which Independent States may of right do. And for the support of this Declaration, with a firm reliance on the Protection of Divine Providence, we mutually pledge to each other our Lives, our Fortunes, and our sacred Honor.

The foregoing Declaration was, by order of Congress, engrossed, and signed by the following members:

John Hancock

NEW HAMPSHIRE
Josiah Bartlett
William Whipple
Matthew Thornton

MASSACHUSETTS BAY
Samuel Adams
John Adams
Robert Treat Paine
Elbridge Gerry

RHODE ISLAND
Stephen Hopkins
William Ellery

CONNECTICUT
Roger Sherman
Samuel Huntington
William Williams
Oliver Wolcott

NEW YORK
William Floyd
Philip Livingston
Francis Lewis
Lewis Morris

NEW JERSEY
Richard Stockton
John Witherspoon
Francis Hopkinson
John Hart
Abraham Clark

PENNSYLVANIA
Robert Morris
Benjamin Rush
Benjamin Franklin
John Morton
George Clymer
James Smith
George Taylor
James Wilson
George Ross

DELAWARE
Caesar Rodney
George Read
Thomas M'Kean

MARYLAND
Samuel Chase
William Paca
Thomas Stone
Charles Carroll, of Carrollton

VIRGINIA
George Wythe
Richard Henry Lee
Thomas Jefferson
Benjamin Harrison
Thomas Nelson, Jr.
Francis Lightfoot Lee
Carter Braxton

NORTH CAROLINA
William Hooper
Joseph Hewes
John Penn

SOUTH CAROLINA
Edward Rutledge
Thomas Heyward, Jr.
Thomas Lynch, Jr.
Arthur Middleton

GEORGIA
Button Gwinnett
Lyman Hall
George Walton

Resolved, That copies of the Declaration be sent to the several assemblies, conventions, and committees, or councils of safety, and to the several commanding officers of the continental troops; that it be proclaimed in each of the United States, at the head of the army.

THE CONSTITUTION OF THE UNITED STATES (1787)

We the People of the United States, in order to form a more perfect Union, establish Justice, insure domestic Tranquility, provide for the common defence, promote the general Welfare, and secure the Blessings of Liberty to ourselves and our Posterity, do ordain and establish this Constitution for the United States of America.

ARTICLE. I.

Section. 1. All legislative Powers herein granted shall be vested in a Congress of the United States, which shall consist of a Senate and House of Representatives.

Section. 2. The House of Representatives shall be composed of Members chosen every second Year by the People of the several States, and the Electors in each State shall have the Qualifications requisite for Electors of the most numerous Branch of the State Legislature.

No Person shall be a Representative who shall not have attained to the Age of twenty five Years, and been seven Years a Citizen of the United States, and who shall not, when elected, be an Inhabitant of that State in which he shall be chosen.

Representatives and direct Taxes shall be apportioned among the several States which may be included within this Union, according to their respective Numbers, which shall be determined by adding to the whole Number of free Persons, including those bound to Service for a Term of Years, and excluding Indians not taxed, three fifths of all other Persons. The actual Enumeration shall be made within three Years after the first Meeting of the Congress of the United States, and within every subsequent Term of ten Years, in such Manner as they shall by Law direct. The Number of Representatives shall not exceed one for every thirty Thousand, but each State shall have at Least one Representative; and until such enumeration shall be made, the State of New Hampshire shall be entitled to chuse three, Massachusetts eight, Rhode-Island and Providence Plantations one, Connecticut five, New York six, New Jersey four, Pennsylvania eight, Delaware one, Maryland six, Virginia ten, North Carolina five, South Carolina five, and Georgia three.

When vacancies happen in the Representation from any state, the Executive Authority thereof shall issue Writs of Election to fill such Vacancies.

The House of Representatives shall chuse their Speaker and other Officers; and shall have the sole Power of Impeachment.

Section. 3. The Senate of the United States shall be composed of two Senators from each State, chosen by the legislature thereof, for six Years; and each Senator shall have one Vote.

Immediately after they shall be assembled in Consequence of the first Election, they shall be divided as equally as may be into three Classes. The Seats of the Senators of the first Class shall be vacated at the Expiration of the second Year, of the second Class at the Expiration of the fourth Year, and of the third Class at the Expiration of the sixth Year, so that one third may be chosen every second Year; and if Vacancies happen by Resignation, or otherwise, during the Recess of the Legislature of any State, the Executive thereof may make temporary Appointments until the next Meeting of the Legislature, which shall then fill such Vacancies.

No Person shall be a Senator who shall not have attained to the Age of thirty Years, and been nine Years a Citizen of the United States, and who shall not, when elected, be an Inhabitant of that State for which he shall be chosen.

The Vice President of the United States shall be President of the Senate, but shall have no Vote, unless they be equally divided.

The Senate shall chuse their other Officers, and also a President pro tempore, in the Absence of the

Vice President, or when he shall exercise the Office of President of the United States.

The Senate shall have the sole Power to try all Impeachments. When sitting for that Purpose, they shall be on Oath or Affirmation. When the President of the United States is tried, the Chief Justice shall preside: And no Person shall be convicted without the Concurrence of two thirds of the Members present.

Judgment in Cases of Impeachment shall not extend further than to removal from Office, and disqualification to hold and enjoy any Office of honor, Trust or Profit under the United States: but the Party convicted shall nevertheless be liable and subject to Indictment, Trial, Judgment and Punishment, according to Law.

Section. 4. The Times, Places and Manner of holding Elections for Senators and Representatives, shall be prescribed in each State by the Legislature thereof; but the Congress may at any time by Law make or alter such Regulations, except as to the Places of chusing Senators.

The Congress shall assemble at least once in every Year, and such Meeting shall be on the first Monday in December, unless they shall by Law appoint a different Day.

Section. 5. Each House shall be the Judge of the Elections, Returns and Qualifications of its own Members, and a Majority of each shall constitute a Quorum to do Business; but a smaller Number may adjourn from day to day, and may be authorized to compel the Attendance of absent Members, in such Manner, and under such Penalties as each House may provide.

Each House may determine the Rules of its Proceedings, punish its Members for disorderly Behaviour, and, with the Concurrence of two thirds, expel a Member.

Each House shall keep a Journal of its Proceedings, and from time to time publish the same, excepting such Parts as may in their Judgment require Secrecy; and the Yeas and Nays of the Members of either House on any question shall, at the Desire of one fifth of those Present, be entered on the Journal.

Neither House, during the Session of Congress, shall, without the Consent of the other, adjourn for more than three days, not to any other Place than that in which the two Houses shall be sitting.

Section. 6. The Senators and Representatives shall receive a Compensation for their Services, to be ascertained by Law, and paid out of the Treasury of the United States. They shall in all Cases, except Treason, Felony and Breach of the Peace, be privileged from Arrest during their Attendance at the Session of their respective Houses, and in going to and returning from the same; and for any Speech or Debate in either House, they shall not be questioned in any other Place.

No Senator or Representative shall, during the Time for which he was elected, be appointed to any civil Office under the Authority of the United States, which shall have been created, or the Emoluments whereof shall have been encreased during such time; and no Person holding any Office under the United States, shall be a Member of either House during his Continuance in Office.

Section. 7. All Bills for raising Revenue shall originate in the House of Representatives; but the Senate may propose or concur with Amendments as on other Bills.

Every Bill which shall have passed the House of Representatives and the Senate shall, before it become a Law, be presented to the President of the United States; If he approve he shall sign it, but if not he shall return it, with his Objections to that House in which it shall have originated, who shall enter the Objections at large on their Journal, and proceed to reconsider it. If after such Reconsideration two thirds of that House shall agree to pass the Bill, it shall be sent, together with the Objections, to the other House, by which it shall likewise be reconsidered, and if approved by two thirds of that House, it shall become a Law. But in all such Cases the Votes of both Houses shall be determined by Yeas and Nays, and the Names of the Persons voting for and against the Bill shall be entered on the Journal of each House respectively. If any Bill shall not be returned by the President within ten Days (Sundays excepted) after it shall have been presented to him, the Same shall be a Law, in like Manner as if he had signed it, unless the Congress by their Adjournment prevent its Return, in which Case it shall not be a Law.

Every Order, Resolution, or Vote to which the Concurrence of the Senate and House of Representatives may be necessary (except on a question of Adjournment) shall be presented to the President of the United States; and before the Same shall take Effect, shall be approved by him, or being disapproved by him, shall be repassed by two thirds of the Senate and House of Representatives, according to the Rules and Limitations prescribed in the Case of a Bill.

Section. 8. The Congress shall have Power To lay and collect Taxes, Duties, Imposts and Excises, to pay the Debts and provide for the common Defence and general Welfare of the United States; but all Duties, Imposts and Excises shall be uniform throughout the United States;

To borrow Money on the credit of the United States;

To regulate Commerce with foreign Nations, and among the several States, and with the Indian Tribes;

To establish an uniform Rule of Naturalization, and uniform Laws on the subject of Bankruptcies throughout the United States;

To coin Money, regulate the Value thereof, and of foreign Coin, and fix the Standard of Weights and Measures;

To provide for the Punishment of counterfeiting the Securities and current Coin of the United States;

To establish Post Offices and Post Roads;

To promote the Progress of Science and useful Arts, by securing for limited Times to Authors and Inventors the exclusive Right to their respective Writings and Discoveries;

To constitute Tribunals inferior to the supreme Court;

To define and punish Piracies and Felonies committed on the high Seas, and Offences against the Law of Nations;

To declare War, grant Letters of Marque and Reprisal, and make Rules concerning Captures on Land and Water;

To raise and support Armies, but no Appropriation of Money to that Use shall be for a longer Term than two Years;

To provide and maintain a Navy;

To make Rules for the Government and Regulation of the land and naval Forces;

To provide for calling forth the Militia to execute the Laws of the Union, suppress Insurrections and repel Invasions;

To provide for organizing, arming, and disciplining, the Militia, and for governing such Part of them as may be employed in the Service of the United States, reserving to the States respectively, the Appointment of the Officers, and the Authority of training the Militia according to the discipline prescribed by Congress;

To exercise exclusive Legislation in all Cases whatsoever, over such District (not exceeding ten Miles square) as may, by Cession of Particular States, and the Acceptance of Congress, become the Seat of the Government of the United States, and to exercise like Authority over all Places purchased by the Consent of the Legislature of the State in which the Same shall be, for the Erection of Forts, Magazines, Arsenals, dock-Yards, and other needful Buildings;—And

To make all Laws which shall be necessary and proper for carrying into Execution the foregoing Powers, and all other Powers vested by this Constitution in the Government of the United States, or in any Department or Officer thereof.

Section. 9. The Migration or Importation of such Persons as any of the States now existing shall think proper to admit, shall not be prohibited by the Congress prior to the Year one thousand eight hundred and eight, but a Tax or duty may be imposed on such Importation, not exceeding ten dollars for each Person.

The Privilege of the Writ of Habeas Corpus shall not be suspended, unless when in Cases of Rebellion or Invasion the public Safety may require it.

No Bill of Attainder or ex post facto Law shall be passed.

No Capitation, or other direct, Tax shall be laid, unless in Proportion to the Census or Enumeration herein before directed to be taken.

No Tax or Duty shall be laid on Articles exported from any State.

No Preference shall be given by any Regulation of Commerce or Revenue to the Ports of one State over those of another: nor shall Vessels bound to, or from, one State, be obliged to enter, clear, or pay Duties in another.

No Money shall be drawn from the Treasury, but in Consequence of Appropriations made by Law; and a regular Statement and Account of the Receipts and Expenditures of all public Money shall be published from time to time.

No Title of Nobility shall be granted by the United States: And no Person holding any Office of Profit or Trust under them, shall, without the Consent of the Congress, accept of any present, Emolument, Office, or Title, of any kind whatever, from any King, Prince, or foreign State.

Section. 10. No State shall enter into any Treaty, Alliance, or Confederation; grant Letters of Marque and Reprisal; coin Money; emit Bills of Credit; make any Thing but gold and silver Coin a Tender in Payment of Debts; pass any Bill of Attainder, ex post facto Law, or Law impairing the Obligation of Contracts, or grant any Title of Nobility.

No State shall, without the Consent of the Congress, lay any Imposts or Duties on Imports or Exports, except what may be absolutely necessary for executing its inspection Laws: and the net Produce of all Duties and Imposts, laid by any State on Imports or Exports, shall be for the Use of the Treasury of the United States; and all such Laws shall be subject to the Revision and Controul of the Congress.

No State shall, without the Consent of Congress, lay any Duty of Tonnage, keep Troops, or Ships of War in time of Peace, enter into any Agreement or Compact with another State, or with a foreign Power, or engage in War, unless actually invaded, or in such imminent Danger as will not admit of delay.

ARTICLE. II.

Section. 1. The executive Power shall be vested in a President of the United States of America. He shall hold his Office during the term of four Years, and,

together with the Vice President, chosen for the same Term, be elected, as follows:

Each State shall appoint, in such Manner as the Legislature thereof may direct, a Number of Electors, equal to the whole Number of Senators and Representatives to which the State may be entitled in the Congress: but no Senator or Representative, or Person holding an Office of Trust or Profit under the United States, shall be appointed an Elector.

The Electors shall meet in their respective States, and vote by Ballot for two Persons, of whom one at least shall not be an Inhabitant of the same State with themselves. And they shall make a List of all the Persons voted for, and of the Number of Votes for each; which List they shall sign and certify, and transmit sealed to the Seat of the Government of the United States, directed to the President of the Senate. The President of the Senate shall, in the Presence of the Senate and House of Representatives, open all the Certificates, and the Votes shall then be counted. The Person having the greatest Number of Votes shall be the President, if such Number be a Majority of the whole Number of Electors appointed; and if there be more than one who have such Majority, and have an equal Number of Votes, then the House of Representatives shall immediately chuse by Ballot one of them for President; and if no Person have a Majority, then from the five highest on the List the said House shall in like Manner chuse the President. But in chusing the President, the Votes shall be taken by States, the Representation from each State having one Vote; A quorum for this Purpose shall consist of a Member or Members from two thirds of the States, and a Majority of all the States shall be necessary to a Choice. In every Case, after the Choice of the President, the Person having the greatest Number of Votes of the Electors shall be the Vice President. But if there should remain two or more who have equal Votes, the Senate shall chuse from them by Ballot the Vice President.

The Congress may determine the Time of chusing the Electors, and the Day on which they shall give their Votes; which Day shall be the same throughout the United States.

No Person except a natural born Citizen, or a Citizen of the United States, at the time of the Adoption of this Constitution, shall be eligible to the Office of

President; neither shall any Person be eligible to that Office who shall not have attained to the Age of thirty five Years, and been fourteen Years a Resident within the United States.

In Case of the Removal of the President from Office, or of his Death, Resignation, or Inability to discharge the Powers and Duties of the said Office, the Same shall devolve on the Vice President, and the Congress may by Law provide for the Case of Removal, Death, Resignation or Inability, both of the President and Vice President, declaring what Officer shall then act as President, and such Officer shall act accordingly, until the Disability be removed, or a President shall be elected.

The President shall, at stated Times, receive for his Services, a Compensation, which shall neither be encreased or diminished during the Period for which he shall have been elected, and he shall not receive within that Period any other Emolument from the United States, or any of them.

Before he enters on the Execution of his Office, he shall take the following Oath or Affirmation:—"I do solemnly swear (or affirm) that I will faithfully execute the Office of President of the United States, and will to the best of my Ability, preserve, protect and defend the Constitution of the United States."

Section. 2. The President shall be Commander in Chief of the Army and Navy of the United States, and of the Militia of the several States, when called into the actual Service of the United States; he may require the Opinion, in writing, of the principal Officer in each of the executive Departments, upon any Subject relating to the Duties of their respective Offices, and he shall have Power to grant Reprieves and Pardons for Offences against the United States, except in Cases of Impeachment.

He shall have Power, by and with the Advice and Consent of the Senate, to make Treaties, provided two thirds of the Senators present concur; and he shall nominate, and by and with the Advice and Consent of the Senate, shall appoint Ambassadors, other public Ministers and Consuls, Judges of the supreme Court, and all other Officers of the United States, whose Appointments are not herein otherwise

provided for, and which shall be established by Law; but the Congress may by Law vest the Appointment of such inferior Officers, as they think proper, in the President alone, in the Courts of Law, or in the Heads of Departments.

The President shall have Power to fill up all Vacancies that may happen during the Recess of the Senate, by granting Commissions which shall expire at the End of their next Session.

Section. 3. He shall from time to time give to the Congress Information of the State of the Union, and recommend to their Consideration such Measures as he shall judge necessary and expedient; he may, on extraordinary Occasions, convene both Houses, or either of them, and in Case of Disagreement between them, with Respect to the Time of Adjournment, he may adjourn them to such Time as he shall think proper; he shall receive Ambassadors and other public Ministers; he shall take Care that the Laws be faithfully executed, and shall Commission all the Officers of the United States.

Section. 4. The President, Vice President and all civil Officers of the United States, shall be removed from Office on Impeachment for, and Conviction of, Treason, Bribery, or other high Crimes and Misdemeanors.

ARTICLE. III.

Section. 1. The judicial Power of the United States, shall be vested in one supreme Court, and in such inferior Courts as the Congress may from time to time ordain and establish. The Judges, both of the supreme and inferior Courts, shall hold their Offices during good Behavior, and shall, at stated Times, receive for their Services, a Compensation, which shall not be diminished during their Continuance in Office.

Section. 2. The judicial Power shall extend to all Cases, in Law and Equity, arising under this Constitution, the Laws of the United States, and Treaties made, or which shall be made, under their Authority;—to all Cases affecting Ambassadors, other public Ministers and Consuls;—to all Cases of admiralty and maritime Jurisdiction;—the Controversies to which the United States shall be a Party;—to Controversies between two or more States;—between a State and Citizens of another State;—between Citizens of different States;—between Citizens of the same State claiming Lands under Grants of different States, and between a State, or the Citizens thereof, and foreign States, Citizens or Subjects.

In all cases affecting Ambassadors, other public Ministers and Consuls, and those in which a State shall be Party, the supreme Court shall have original Jurisdiction. In all the other Cases before mentioned, the supreme Court shall have appellate Jurisdiction, both as to Law and Fact, with such Exceptions, and under such Regulations as the Congress shall make.

The Trial of all Crimes, except in Cases of Impeachment, shall be by Jury; and such Trial shall be held in the State where the said Crimes shall have been committed; but when not committed within any State, the Trial shall be at such Place or Places as the Congress may by Law have directed.

Section. 3. Treason against the United States, shall consist only in levying War against them, or in adhering to their Enemies, giving them Aid and Comfort. No Person shall be convicted of Treason unless on the Testimony of two Witnesses to the same overt Act, or on Confession in open Court.

The Congress shall have Power to declare the Punishment of Treason, but no Attainder of Treason shall work Corruption of Blood, or Forfeiture except during the Life of the Person attainted.

ARTICLE. IV.

Section. 1. Full Faith and Credit shall be given in each State to the public Acts, Records, and judicial Proceedings of every other State. And the Congress may by general Laws prescribe the Manner in which such Acts, Records and Proceedings shall be proved, and the Effect thereof.

Section. 2. The Citizens of each State shall be entitled to all Privileges and Immunities of Citizens in the several States.

A Person charged in any State with Treason, Felony, or other Crime, who shall flee from Justice, and be found in another State, shall on Demand of the executive Authority of the State from which he fled, be delivered up, to be removed to the State having Jurisdiction of the Crime.

No Person held to Service or Labour in one State, under the Laws thereof, escaping into another, shall, in Consequence of any Law or Regulation therein, be discharged from such Service or Labour, but shall be delivered up on Claim of the Party to whom such Service or Labour may be due.

Section. 3. New States may be admitted by the Congress into this Union; but no new State shall be formed or erected within the Jurisdiction of any other State; nor any State be formed by the Junction of two or more States, or Parts of States, without the consent of the Legislatures of the States concerned as well as of the Congress.

The Congress shall have Power to dispose of and make all needful Rules and Regulations respecting the Territory or other Property belonging to the United States; and nothing in this Constitution shall be so construed as to Prejudice any Claims of the United States, or of any particular States.

Section. 4. The United States shall guarantee to every State in this Union a Republican Form of Government, and shall protect each of them against Invasion; and on Application of the Legislature, or of the Executive (when the Legislature cannot be convened) against domestic Violence.

ARTICLE. V.

The Congress, whenever two thirds of both Houses shall deem it necessary, shall propose Amendments to this Constitution, or, on the Application of the Legislatures of two thirds of the several States, shall call a Convention for proposing Amendments, which, in either Case, shall be valid to all Intents and Purposes, as Part of this Constitution, when ratified by the Legislatures of three fourths of the several States, or by Conventions in three fourths thereof, as the one or the other Mode of Ratification may be proposed by the Congress; Provided that no Amendment which may be made prior to the Year One thousand eight hundred and eight shall in any Manner affect the first and fourth Clauses in the Ninth Section of the first Article; and that no State, without its Consent, shall be deprived of its equal Suffrage in the Senate.

ARTICLE. VI.

All Debts contracted and Engagements entered into, before the Adoption of this Constitution, shall be as valid against the United States under this Constitution, as under the Confederation.

This Constitution, and the Laws of the United States which shall be made in Pursuance thereof; and all Treaties made, or which shall be made, under the Authority of the United States, shall be the supreme Law of the Land; and the Judges in every State shall be bound thereby, any Thing in the Constitution or Laws of any State to the Contrary notwithstanding.

The Senators and Representatives before mentioned, and the Members of the several State Legislatures, and all executive and judicial Officers, both of the United States and of the several States, shall be bound by Oath or Affirmation, to support this Constitution; but no religious Test shall ever be required as a Qualification to any Office or public Trust under the United States.

ARTICLE. VII.

The Ratification of the Conventions of nine States, shall be sufficient for the Establishment of this Constitution between the States so ratifying the Same.

Done in Convention by the Unanimous Consent of the States present the Seventeenth Day of September in the Year of our Lord one thousand seven hundred and Eighty seven and of the Independence of the United States of America the Twelfth. In witness thereof We have hereunto subscribed our Names,

G°. WASHINGTON—Presd^t.
and deputy from Virginia

NEW HAMPSHIRE	NEW JERSEY	DELAWARE	NORTH CAROLINA
John Langdon	Wil: Livingston	Geo: Read	Wm Blount
Nicholas Gilman	David A. Brearley	Gunning Bedford jun	Richd Dobbs Spaight
	Wm Paterson	John Dickinson	Hu Williamson
MASSACHUSETTS	Jona: Dayton	Richard Bassett	
Nathaniel Gorham		Jaco: Broom	SOUTH CAROLINA
Rufus King	PENNSYLVANIA		J. Rutledge
	B Franklin	MARYLAND	Charles Cotesworth
CONNECTICUT	Thomas Mifflin	James McHenry	Pinckney
Wm Saml Johnson	Robt Morris	Dan of St Thos Jenifer	Charles Pinckney
Roger Sherman	Geo. Clymer	Danl Carroll	Pierce Butler
	Thos FitzSimons		
NEW YORK	Jared Ingersoll	VIRGINIA	GEORGIA
Alexander Hamilton	James Wilson	John Blair—	William Few
	Gouv Morris	James Madison Jr.	Abr Baldwin

AMENDMENTS TO THE CONSTITUTION

Articles in addition to, and Amendment of the Constitution of the United States of America, proposed by Congress, and ratified by the Legislatures of the several States, pursuant to the fifth Article of the original Constitution.

AMENDMENT I.

Congress shall make no law respecting an establishment of religion, or prohibiting the free exercise thereof; or abridging the freedom of speech, or of the press; or the right of the people peaceably to assemble, and to petition the Government for a redress of grievances.

AMENDMENT II.

A well regulated Militia, being necessary to the security of a free State, the right of the people to keep and bear Arms, shall not be infringed.

AMENDMENT III.

No Soldier shall, in time of peace be quartered in any house, without the consent of the Owner, nor in time of war, but in a manner to be prescribed by law.

AMENDMENT IV.

The right of the people to be secure in their persons, houses, papers, and effects, against unreasonable searches and seizures, shall not be violated, and no Warrants shall issue, but upon probable cause, supported by Oath or affirmation, and particularly describing the place to be searched, and the persons or things to be seized.

AMENDMENT V.

No person shall be held to answer for a capital, or otherwise infamous crime, unless on a presentment or indictment of a Grand Jury, except in cases arising in the land or naval forces, or in the Militia, when in actual service in time of War or public danger; nor shall any person be subject for the same offence to be twice put in jeopardy of life or limb; nor shall be compelled in any criminal case to be a witness against himself, nor be deprived of life, liberty, or property,

without due process of law; nor shall private property be taken for public use, without just compensation.

AMENDMENT VI.

In all criminal prosecutions, the accused shall enjoy the right to a speedy and public trial, by an impartial jury of the State and district wherein the crime shall have been committed, which district shall have been previously ascertained by law, and to be informed of the nature and cause of the accusation; to be confronted with the witnesses against him; to have compulsory process for obtaining witnesses in his favor, and to have the Assistance of Counsel for his defence.

AMENDMENT VII.

In Suits at common law, where the value in controversy shall exceed twenty dollars, the right of trial by jury shall be preserved, and no fact tried by a jury, shall be otherwise re-examined in any Court of the United States, than according to the rules of the common law.

AMENDMENT VIII.

Excessive bail shall not be required, nor excessive fines imposed, nor cruel and unusual punishments inflicted.

AMENDMENT IX.

The enumeration in the Constitution, of certain rights, shall not be construed to deny or disparage others retained by the people.

AMENDMENT X.

The powers not delegated to the United States by the Constitution, nor prohibited by it to the States, are reserved to the States respectively, or to the people.

AMENDMENT XI.

The Judicial power of the United States shall not be construed to extend to any suit in law or equity, commenced or prosecuted against one of the United States by Citizens of another State, or by Citizens or Subjects of any Foreign State. [January 8, 1798]

AMENDMENT XII.

The Electors shall meet in their respective states, and vote by ballot for President and Vice-President, one of whom, at least, shall not be an inhabitant of the same state with themselves; they shall name in their ballots the person voted for as President, and in distinct ballots the person voted for as Vice-President, and they shall make distinct lists of all persons voted for as President, and of all persons voted for as Vice President, and of the number of votes for each, which lists they shall sign and certify, and transmit sealed to the seat of the government of the United States, directed to the President of the Senate;—The President of the Senate shall, in the presence of the Senate and House of Representatives, open all the certificates and the votes shall then be counted;—The person having the greatest number of votes for President, shall be the President, if such number be a majority of the whole number of Electors appointed; and if no person have such majority, then from the persons having the highest numbers not exceeding three on the list of those voted for as President, the House of Representatives shall choose immediately, by ballot, the President. But in choosing the President, the votes shall be taken by states, the representation from each state having one vote; a quorum for this purpose shall consist of a member or members from two-thirds of the states, and a majority of all the states shall be necessary to a choice. And if the House of Representatives shall not choose a President whenever the right of choice shall devolve upon them, before the fourth day of March next following, then the Vice-President shall act as President, as in the case of the death or other constitutional disability of the President.—The person having the greatest number of votes as Vice-President, shall be the Vice-President, if such number be a majority of the whole number of Electors appointed, and if no person have a majority, then from the two highest numbers on the list, the Senate shall choose the Vice-President; a quorum for the purpose shall consist of two-thirds of the whole number of Senators, and a majority of the whole number shall be necessary to a choice. But no person constitutionally ineligible to the office of President shall be eligible to that of Vice-President of the United States. [September 25, 1804]

AMENDMENT XIII.

Section 1. Neither slavery nor involuntary servitude, except as a punishment for crime whereof the party shall have been duly convicted, shall exist within the United States, or any place subject to their jurisdiction.

Section 2. Congress shall have power to enforce this article by appropriate legislation. [December 18, 1865]

AMENDMENT XIV.

Section 1. All persons born or naturalized in the United States, and subject to the jurisdiction thereof, are citizens of the United States and of the State wherein they reside. No State shall make or enforce any law which shall abridge the privileges or immunities of citizens of the United States; nor shall any State deprive any person of life, liberty, or property, without due process of law; nor deny to any person within its jurisdiction the equal protection of the laws.

Section 2. Representatives shall be apportioned among the several States according to their respective numbers, counting the whole number of persons in each State, excluding Indians not taxed. But when the right to vote at any election for the choice of electors for President and Vice President of the United States, Representatives in Congress, the Executive and Judicial officers of a State, or the members of the Legislature thereof, is denied to any of the male inhabitants of such State, being twenty-one years of age, and citizens of the United States, or in any way abridged, except for participation in rebellion, or other crime, the basis of representation therein shall be reduced in the proportion which the number of such male citizens shall bear to the whole number of male citizens twenty-one years of age in such State.

Section 3. No person shall be a Senator or Representative in Congress, or elector of President and Vice President, or hold any office, civil or military, under the United States, or under any State, who, having previously taken an oath, as a member of Congress, or as an officer of the United States, or as a member of any State legislature, or as an executive or judicial officer of any State, to support the Constitution of the United States, shall have engaged in insurrection or rebellion against the same, or given aid or comfort to the enemies thereof. But Congress may by a vote of two-thirds of each House, remove such disability.

Section 4. The validity of the public debt of the United States, authorized by law, including debts incurred for payment of pensions and bounties for services in suppressing insurrection or rebellion, shall not be questioned. But neither the United States nor any State shall assume or pay any debt or obligation incurred in aid of insurrection or rebellion against the United States, or any claim for the loss or emancipation of any slave; but all such debts, obligations and claims shall be held illegal and void.

Section 5. The Congress shall have power to enforce, by appropriate legislation, the provisions of this article. [July 28, 1868]

AMENDMENT XV.

Section 1. The right of citizens of the United States to vote shall not be denied or abridged by the United States or by any State on account of race, color, or previous condition of servitude—

Section 2. The Congress shall have power to enforce this article by appropriate legislation. [March 30, 1870]

AMENDMENT XVI.

The Congress shall have power to lay and collect taxes on incomes, from whatever source derived, without apportionment among the several States, and without regard to any census or enumeration. [February 25, 1913]

AMENDMENT XVII.

The Senate of the United States shall be composed of two senators from each State, elected by the people thereof, for six years; and each Senator shall have one vote. The electors in each State shall have the qualifications requisite for electors of the most numerous branch of the State legislatures.

When vacancies happen in the representation of any State in the Senate, the executive authority of such State shall issue writs of election to fill such vacancies: *Provided,* That the legislature of any State may empower the executive thereof to make temporary appointments until the people fill the vacancies by election as the legislature may direct.

This amendment shall not be so construed as to affect the election or term of any senator chosen before it becomes valid as part of the Constitution. [May 31, 1913]

AMENDMENT XVIII.

After one year from the ratification of this article, the manufacture, sale, or transportation of intoxicating liquors within, the importation thereof into, or the exportation thereof from the United States and all territory subject to the jurisdiction thereof for beverage purposes is hereby prohibited.

The Congress and the several States shall have concurrent power to enforce this article by appropriate legislation.

This article shall be inoperative unless it shall have been ratified as an amendment to the Constitution by the legislatures of the several States, as provided in the Constitution, within seven years from the date of the submission thereof to the States by Congress. [January 29, 1919]

AMENDMENT XIX.

The right of citizens of the United States to vote shall not be denied or abridged by the United States or by any State on account of sex.

The Congress shall have power by appropriate legislation to enforce the provisions of this article. [August 26, 1920]

AMENDMENT XX.

Section 1. The terms of the President and Vice-President shall end at noon on the twentieth day of January, and the terms of Senators and Representatives at noon on the third day of January, of the years in which such terms would have ended if this article had not been ratified; and the terms of their successors shall then begin.

Section 2. The Congress shall assemble at least once in every year, and such meeting shall begin at noon on the third day of January, unless they shall by law appoint a different day.

Section 3. If, at the time fixed for the beginning of the term of the President, the President-elect shall have died, the Vice-President-elect shall become President. If a President shall not have been chosen before the time fixed for the beginning of his term, or if the President-elect shall have failed to qualify, then the Vice-President-elect shall act as President until a President shall have qualified; and the Congress may by law provide for the case wherein neither a President-elect nor a Vice-President-elect shall have qualified, declaring who shall then act as President, or the manner in which one who is to act shall be selected, and such person shall act accordingly until a President or Vice-President shall have qualified.

Section 4. The Congress may by law provide for the case of the death of any of the persons from whom the House of Representatives may choose a President whenever the right of choice shall have devolved upon them, and for the case of the death of any of the persons from whom the Senate may choose a Vice-President whenever the right of choice shall have devolved upon them.

Section 5. Sections 1 and 2 shall take effect on the 15th day of October following the ratification of this article.

Section 6. This article shall be inoperative unless it shall have been ratified as an amendment to the Constitution by the legislatures of three-fourths of the several States within seven years from the date of its submission. [February 6, 1933]

AMENDMENT XXI.

Section 1. The eighteenth article of amendment to the Constitution of the United States is hereby repealed.

Section 2. The transportation or importation into any State, Territory or possession of the United States for delivery or use therein of intoxicating liquors, in violation of the laws thereof, is hereby prohibited.

Section 3. This article shall be inoperative unless it shall have been ratified as an amendment to the Constitution by convention in the several States, as provided in the Constitution, within seven years from the date of the submission thereof to the States by the Congress. [December 5, 1933]

AMENDMENT XXII.

Section 1. No person shall be elected to the office of the President more than twice, and no person who has held the office of President, or acted as President, for more than two years of a term to which some other person was elected President shall be elected to the office of the President more than once. But this Article shall not apply to any person holding the office of President when this Article was proposed by the Congress, and shall not prevent any person who may be holding the office of President, or acting as President, during the term within which this Article becomes operative from holding the office of President or acting as President during the remainder of such term.

Section 2. This article shall be inoperative unless it shall have been ratified as an amendment to the Constitution by the legislatures of three-fourths of the several States within seven years from the date of its submission to the States by the Congress. [February 27, 1951]

AMENDMENT XXIII.

Section 1. The District constituting the seat of government of the United States shall appoint in such manner as the Congress may direct:

A number of electors of President and Vice-President equal to the whole number of Senators and Representatives in Congress to which the District would be entitled if it were a State, but in no event more than the least populous State; they shall be in addition to those appointed by the States, but they shall be considered, for the purposes of the election of President and Vice-President, to be electors appointed by a State; and they shall meet in the District and perform such duties as provided by the twelfth article of amendment.

Section 2. The Congress shall have the power to enforce this article by appropriate legislation. [March 29, 1961]

AMENDMENT XXIV.

Section 1. The right of citizens of the United States to vote in any primary or other election for President or Vice President, for electors for President or Vice President, or for Senator or Representative in Congress, shall not be denied or abridged by the United States or any State by reason of failure to pay any poll tax or other tax.

Section 2. The Congress shall have power to enforce this article by appropriate legislation. [January 23, 1964]

AMENDMENT XXV.

Section 1. In case of the removal of the President from office or of his death or resignation, the Vice President shall become President.

Section 2. Whenever there is a vacancy in the office of Vice President, the President shall nominate a Vice President who shall take office upon confirmation by a majority vote of both Houses of Congress.

Section 3. Whenever the President transmits to the President pro tempore of the Senate and the Speaker of the House of Representatives his written declaration that he is unable to discharge the powers and duties of his office, and until he transmits to them a written declaration to the contrary, such powers and duties shall be discharged by the Vice President as Acting President.

Section 4. Whenever the Vice President and a majority of either the principal officers of the executive departments or of such other body as Congress may by law provide, transmit to the President pro tempore of the Senate and the Speaker of the House of Representatives their written declaration that the President is unable to discharge the powers and duties of his office, the Vice President shall immediately assume the powers and duties of the office as Acting President.

Thereafter, when the President transmits to the President pro tempore of the Senate and the Speaker of the House of Representatives his written declaration that no inability exists, he shall resume the powers and duties of his office unless the Vice President and a majority of either the principal officers of the executive departments or of such other body as Congress may by law provide, transmit within four days to the President pro tempore of the Senate and the Speaker of the House of Representatives their written declaration that the President is unable to discharge the powers and duties of his office. Thereupon Congress shall decide the issue, assembling within forty-eight hours for that purpose if not in session. If the Congress, within twenty-one days after receipt of the latter written declaration, or, if Congress is not in session, within twenty-one days after Congress is required to assemble, determines by two-thirds vote of both Houses that the President is unable to discharge the powers and duties of his office, the Vice President shall continue to discharge the same as Acting President; otherwise, the President shall resume the powers and duties of his office. [February 10, 1967]

AMENDMENT XXVI.

Section 1. The right of citizens of the United States, who are eighteen years of age or older, to vote shall not be denied or abridged by the United States or by any State on account of age.

Section 2. The Congress shall have power to enforce this article by appropriate legislation. [June 30, 1971]

AMENDMENT XXVII.

No law, varying the compensation for the services of the Senators and Representatives shall take effect, until an election of Representatives shall have intervened. [May 8, 1992]

FROM GEORGE WASHINGTON'S FAREWELL ADDRESS (1796)

Friends and Citizens:

The period for a new election of a citizen to administer the executive government of the United States being not far distant, and the time actually arrived when your thoughts must be employed in designating the person who is to be clothed with that important trust, it appears to me proper, especially as it may conduce to a more distinct expression of the public voice, that I should now apprise you of the resolution I have formed, to decline being considered among the number of those out of whom a choice is to be made.

★ ★ ★

In looking forward to the moment which is intended to terminate the career of my public life, my feelings do not permit me to suspend the deep acknowledgment of that debt of gratitude which I owe to my beloved country for the many honors it has conferred upon me; still more for the steadfast confidence with which it has supported me; and for the opportunities I have thence enjoyed of manifesting my inviolable attachment, by services faithful and persevering, though in usefulness unequal to my zeal. If benefits have resulted to our country from these services, let it always be remembered to your praise, and as an instructive example in our annals, that under circumstances in which the passions, agitated in every direction, were liable to mislead, amidst appearances sometimes dubious, vicissitudes of fortune often discouraging, in situations in which not unfrequently want of success has countenanced the spirit of criticism, the constancy of your support was the essential prop of the efforts, and a guarantee of the plans by which they were effected. Profoundly penetrated with this idea, I shall carry it with me to my grave, as a strong incitement to unceasing vows that heaven may continue to you the choicest tokens of its beneficence; that your union and brotherly

affection may be perpetual; that the free Constitution, which is the work of your hands, may be sacredly maintained; that its administration in every department may be stamped with wisdom and virtue; that, in fine, the happiness of the people of these States, under the auspices of liberty, may be made complete by so careful a preservation and so prudent a use of this blessing as will acquire to them the glory of recommending it to the applause, the affection, and adoption of every nation which is yet a stranger to it.

Here, perhaps, I ought to stop. But a solicitude for your welfare, which cannot end but with my life, and the apprehension of danger, natural to that solicitude, urge me, on an occasion like the present, to offer to your solemn contemplation, and to recommend to your frequent review, some sentiments which are the result of much reflection, of no inconsiderable observation, and which appear to me all-important to the permanency of your felicity as a people. These will be offered to you with the more freedom, as you can only see in them the disinterested warnings of a parting friend, who can possibly have no personal motive to bias his counsel. Nor can I forget, as an encouragement to it, your indulgent reception of my sentiments on a former and not dissimilar occasion.

Interwoven as is the love of liberty with every ligament of your hearts, no recommendation of mine is necessary to fortify or confirm the attachment.

The unity of government which constitutes you one people is also now dear to you. It is justly so, for it is a main pillar in the edifice of your real independence, the support of your tranquility at home, your peace abroad; of your safety; of your prosperity; of that very liberty which you so highly prize. But as it is easy to foresee that, from different causes and from different quarters, much pains will be taken, many artifices employed to weaken in your minds the conviction of this truth; as this is the point in your political fortress against which the batteries of internal and external enemies will be most constantly and actively (though often covertly and insidiously) directed, it is of infinite moment that you should properly estimate the immense value of your national union to your collective and individual happiness; that you should cherish a cordial, habitual, and immovable attachment to it; accustoming yourselves to think and speak of it as of the palladium of your political safety and prosperity; watching for its preservation with jealous anxiety; discountenancing whatever may suggest even a suspicion that it can in any event be abandoned; and indignantly frowning upon the first dawning of every attempt to alienate any portion of our country from the rest, or to enfeeble the sacred ties which now link together the various parts.

For this you have every inducement of sympathy and interest. Citizens, by birth or choice, of a common country, that country has a right to concentrate your affections. The name of American, which belongs to you in your national capacity, must always exalt the just pride of patriotism more than any appellation derived from local discriminations. With slight shades of difference, you have the same religion, manners, habits, and political principles. You have in a common cause fought and triumphed together; the independence and liberty you possess are the work of joint counsels, and joint efforts of common dangers, sufferings, and successes.

But these considerations, however powerfully they address themselves to your sensibility, are greatly outweighed by those which apply more immediately to your interest. Here every portion of our country finds the most commanding motives for carefully guarding and preserving the union of the whole.

The North, in an unrestrained intercourse with the South, protected by the equal laws of a common government, finds in the productions of the latter great additional resources of maritime and commercial enterprise and precious materials of manufacturing industry. The South, in the same intercourse, benefiting by the agency of the North, sees its agriculture grow and its commerce expand. Turning partly into its own channels the seamen of the North, it finds its particular navigation invigorated; and, while it

contributes, in different ways, to nourish and increase the general mass of the national navigation, it looks forward to the protection of a maritime strength, to which itself is unequally adapted. The East, in a like intercourse with the West, already finds, and in the progressive improvement of interior communications by land and water, will more and more find a valuable vent for the commodities which it brings from abroad, or manufactures at home. The West derives from the East supplies requisite to its growth and comfort, and, what is perhaps of still greater consequence, it must of necessity owe the secure enjoyment of indispensable outlets for its own productions to the weight, influence, and the future maritime strength of the Atlantic side of the Union, directed by an indissoluble community of interest as one nation. Any other tenure by which the West can hold this essential advantage, whether derived from its own separate strength, or from an apostate and unnatural connection with any foreign power, must be intrinsically precarious.

While, then, every part of our country thus feels an immediate and particular interest in union, all the parts combined cannot fail to find in the united mass of means and efforts greater strength, greater resource, proportionably greater security from external danger, a less frequent interruption of their peace by foreign nations; and, what is of inestimable value, they must derive from union an exemption from those broils and wars between themselves, which so frequently afflict neighboring countries not tied together by the same governments, which their own rival ships alone would be sufficient to produce, but which opposite foreign alliances, attachments, and intrigues would stimulate and embitter. Hence, likewise, they will avoid the necessity of those overgrown military establishments which, under any form of government, are inauspicious to liberty, and which are to be regarded as particularly hostile to republican liberty. In this sense it is that your union ought to be considered as a main prop of your liberty, and that the love of the one ought to endear to you the preservation of the other.

These considerations speak a persuasive language to every reflecting and virtuous mind, and exhibit the continuance of the Union as a primary object of patriotic desire. Is there a doubt whether a common government can embrace so large a sphere? Let experience solve it. To listen to mere speculation in such a case were criminal. We are authorized to hope that a proper organization of the whole with the auxiliary agency of governments for the respective subdivisions, will afford a happy issue to the experiment. It is well worth a fair and full experiment. With such powerful and obvious motives to union, affecting all parts of our country, while experience shall not have demonstrated its impracticability, there will always be reason to distrust the patriotism of those who in any quarter may endeavor to weaken its bands.

★ ★ ★

To the efficacy and permanency of your Union, a government for the whole is indispensable. No alliance, however strict, between the parts can be an adequate substitute; they must inevitably experience the infractions and interruptions which all alliances in all times have experienced. Sensible of this momentous truth, you have improved upon your first essay, by the adoption of a constitution of government better calculated than your former for an intimate union, and for the efficacious management of your common concerns. This government, the offspring of our own choice, uninfluenced and unawed, adopted upon full investigation and mature deliberation, completely free in its principles, in the distribution of its powers, uniting security with energy, and containing within itself a provision for its own amendment, has a just claim to your confidence and your support. Respect for its authority, compliance with its laws, acquiescence in its measures, are duties enjoined by the fundamental maxims of true liberty. The basis of our political systems is the right of the people to make and to alter their constitutions of government. But the Constitution which at any time exists, till changed by an explicit and authentic act of the whole people, is sacredly obligatory upon all. The very idea of the power and the right of the people to establish government presupposes the duty of every individual to obey the established government.

★ ★ ★

I have already intimated to you the danger of parties in the State, with particular reference to the founding of them on geographical discriminations. Let me now take a more comprehensive view, and warn you in the most solemn manner against the baneful effects of the spirit of party generally.

This spirit, unfortunately, is inseparable from our nature, having its root in the strongest passions of the human mind. It exists under different shapes in all governments, more or less stifled, controlled, or repressed; but, in those of the popular form, it is seen in its greatest rankness, and is truly their worst enemy.

The alternate domination of one faction over another, sharpened by the spirit of revenge, natural to party dissension, which in different ages and countries has perpetrated the most horrid enormities, is itself a frightful despotism. But this leads at length to a more formal and permanent despotism. The disorders and miseries which result gradually incline the minds of men to seek security and repose in the absolute power of an individual; and sooner or later the chief of some prevailing faction, more able or more fortunate than his competitors, turns this disposition to the purposes of his own elevation, on the ruins of public liberty.

Without looking forward to an extremity of this kind (which nevertheless ought not to be entirely out of sight), the common and continual mischiefs of the spirit of party are sufficient to make it the interest and duty of a wise people to discourage and restrain it.

It serves always to distract the public councils and enfeeble the public administration. It agitates the community with ill-founded jealousies and false alarms, kindles the animosity of one part against another, foments occasionally riot and insurrection. It opens the door to foreign influence and corruption, which finds a facilitated access to the government itself through the channels of party passions. Thus the policy and the will of one country are subjected to the policy and will of another.

There is an opinion that parties in free countries are useful checks upon the administration of the government and serve to keep alive the spirit of liberty. This within certain limits is probably true; and in governments of a monarchical cast, patriotism may look with indulgence, if not with favor, upon the spirit of party. But in those of the popular character, in governments purely elective, it is a spirit not to be encouraged. From their natural tendency, it is certain there will always be enough of that spirit for every salutary purpose. And there being constant danger of excess, the effort ought to be by force of public opinion, to mitigate and assuage it. A fire not to be quenched, it demands a uniform vigilance to prevent its bursting into a flame, lest, instead of warming, it should consume.

It is important, likewise, that the habits of thinking in a free country should inspire caution in those entrusted with its administration, to confine themselves within their respective constitutional spheres, avoiding in the exercise of the powers of one department to encroach upon another. The spirit of encroachment tends to consolidate the powers of all the departments in one, and thus to create, whatever the form of government, a real despotism. A just estimate of that love of power, and proneness to abuse it, which predominates in the human heart, is sufficient to satisfy us of the truth of this position. The necessity of reciprocal checks in the exercise of political power, by dividing and distributing it into different depositaries, and constituting each the guardian of the public weal against invasions by the others, has been evinced by experiments ancient and modern; some of them in our country and under our own eyes. To preserve them must be as necessary as to institute them. If, in the opinion of the people, the distribution or modification of the constitutional powers be in any particular wrong, let it be corrected by an amendment in the way which the Constitution designates. But let there be no change by usurpation; for though this, in one instance, may be the instrument of good, it is the customary weapon by which free governments are destroyed. The precedent must always greatly overbalance in permanent evil any partial or transient benefit, which the use can at any time yield.

★ ★ ★

Observe good faith and justice towards all nations; cultivate peace and harmony with all. Religion and morality enjoin this conduct; and can it be, that good policy does not equally enjoin it? It will be worthy of

a free, enlightened, and at no distant period, a great nation, to give to mankind the magnanimous and too novel example of a people always guided by an exalted justice and benevolence. Who can doubt that, in the course of time and things, the fruits of such a plan would richly repay any temporary advantages which might be lost by a steady adherence to it? Can it be that Providence has not connected the permanent felicity of a nation with its virtue? The experiment, at least, is recommended by every sentiment which ennobles human nature. Alas! is it rendered impossible by its vices?

In the execution of such a plan, nothing is more essential than that permanent, inveterate antipathies against particular nations, and passionate attachments for others, should be excluded; and that, in place of them, just and amicable feelings towards all should be cultivated. The nation which indulges towards another a habitual hatred or a habitual fondness is in some degree a slave. It is a slave to its animosity or to its affection, either of which is sufficient to lead it astray from its duty and its interest. Antipathy in one nation against another disposes each more readily to offer insult and injury, to lay hold of slight causes of umbrage, and to be haughty and intractable, when accidental or trifling occasions of dispute occur. Hence, frequent collisions, obstinate, envenomed, and bloody contests. The nation, prompted by ill-will and resentment, sometimes impels to war the government, contrary to the best calculations of policy. The government sometimes participates in the national propensity, and adopts through passion what reason would reject; at other times it makes the animosity of the nation subservient to projects of hostility instigated by pride, ambition, and other sinister and pernicious motives. The peace often, sometimes perhaps the liberty, of nations, has been the victim.

★ ★ ★

The great rule of conduct for us in regard to foreign nations is in extending our commercial relations, to have with them as little political connection as possible. So far as we have already formed engagements, let them be fulfilled with perfect good faith. Here let us stop. Europe has a set of primary interests which to us have none; or a very remote relation. Hence she must be engaged in frequent controversies, the causes of which are essentially foreign to our concerns. Hence, therefore, it must be unwise in us to implicate ourselves by artificial ties in the ordinary vicissitudes of her politics, or the ordinary combinations and collisions of her friendships or enmities.

Our detached and distant situation invites and enables us to pursue a different course. If we remain one people under an efficient government, the period is not far off when we may defy material injury from external annoyance; when we may take such an attitude as will cause the neutrality we may at any time resolve upon to be scrupulously respected; when belligerent nations, under the impossibility of making acquisitions upon us, will not lightly hazard the giving us provocation; when we may choose peace or war, as our interest, guided by justice, shall counsel.

Why forego the advantages of so peculiar a situation? Why quit our own to stand upon foreign ground? Why, by interweaving our destiny with that of any part of Europe, entangle our peace and prosperity in the toils of European ambition, rivalship, interest, humor or caprice?

It is our true policy to steer clear of permanent alliances with any portion of the foreign world; so far, I mean, as we are now at liberty to do it; for let me not be understood as capable of patronizing infidelity to existing engagements. I hold the maxim no less applicable to public than to private affairs, that honesty is always the best policy. I repeat it, therefore, let those engagements be observed in their genuine sense. But, in my opinion, it is unnecessary and would be unwise to extend them.

Taking care always to keep ourselves by suitable establishments on a respectable defensive posture, we may safely trust to temporary alliances for extraordinary emergencies.

Harmony, liberal intercourse with all nations, are recommended by policy, humanity, and interest. But even our commercial policy should hold an equal and impartial hand; neither seeking nor granting exclusive favors or preferences; consulting the natural course of things; diffusing and diversifying by gentle means the streams of commerce, but forcing nothing; establishing (with powers so disposed, in order to give trade a stable course, to define the rights of our merchants, and to enable the government to support them) conventional rules of intercourse, the best that present circumstances and mutual opinion will permit, but temporary, and liable to be from time to time abandoned or varied, as experience and circumstances shall dictate; constantly keeping in view that it is folly in one nation to look for disinterested favors from another; that it must pay with a portion of its independence for whatever it may accept under that character; that, by such acceptance, it may place itself in the condition of having given equivalents for nominal favors, and yet of being reproached with ingratitude for not giving more.

★ ★ ★

Relying on its kindness in this as in other things, and actuated by that fervent love towards it, which is so natural to a man who views in it the native soil of himself and his progenitors for several generations, I anticipate with pleasing expectation that retreat in which I promise myself to realize, without alloy, the sweet enjoyment of partaking, in the midst of my fellow-citizens, the benign influence of good laws under a free government, the ever-favorite object of my heart, and the happy reward, as I trust, of our mutual cares, labors, and dangers.

Geo. Washington

THE SENECA FALLS DECLARATION OF SENTIMENTS AND RESOLUTIONS (1848)

1. DECLARATION OF SENTIMENTS

When, in the course of human events, it becomes necessary for one portion of the family of man to assume among the people of the earth a position different from that which they have hitherto occupied, but one to which the laws of nature and of nature's God entitle them, a decent respect to the opinions of mankind requires that they should declare the causes that impel them to such a course.

We hold these truths to be self-evident: that all men and women are created equal; that they are endowed by their Creator with certain inalienable rights; that among these are life, liberty, and the pursuit of happiness; that to secure these rights governments are instituted, deriving their just powers from the consent of the governed. Whenever any form of government becomes destructive of these ends, it is the right of those who suffer from it to refuse allegiance to it, and to insist upon the institution of a new government, laying its foundation on such principles, and organizing its powers in such form, as to them shall seem most likely to effect their safety and happiness. Prudence, indeed, will dictate that governments long established should not be changed for light and transient causes; and accordingly all experience hath shown that mankind are more disposed to suffer, while evils are sufferable, than to right themselves by abolishing the forms to which they are accustomed. But when a long train of abuses and usurpations, pursuing invariably the same object, evinces a design to reduce them under absolute despotism, it is their duty to throw off such government, and to provide new guards for their future security. Such has been the patient sufferance of the women under this government, and such is now the necessity which constrains them to demand the equal station to which they are entitled. The history of mankind is a history of repeated injuries and usurpations on the part of man toward woman, having in direct object the establishment of an absolute tyranny over her. To prove this, let facts be submitted to a candid world.

He has never permitted her to exercise her inalienable right to the elective franchise.

He has compelled her to submit to laws, in the formation of which she had no voice.

He has withheld from her rights which are given to the most ignorant and degraded men—both natives and foreigners.

Having deprived her of this first right of a citizen, the elective franchise, thereby leaving her without representation in the halls of legislation, he has oppressed her on all sides.

He has made her, if married, in the eye of the law, civilly dead. He has taken from her all right in property, even to the wages she earns.

He has made her, morally, an irresponsible being, as she can commit many crimes with impunity, provided they be done in the presence of her husband.

In the covenant of marriage, she is compelled to promise obedience to her husband, he becoming, to all intents and purposes, her master—the law giving him power to deprive her of her liberty, and to administer chastisement.

He has so framed the laws of divorce, as to what shall be the proper causes, and in case of separation, to whom the guardianship of the children shall be given, as to be wholly regardless of the happiness of women—the law, in all cases, going upon a false supposition of the supremacy of man, and giving all power into his hands.

After depriving her of all rights as a married woman, if single, and the owner of property, he has taxed her to support a government which recognizes her only when her property can be made profitable to it.

He has monopolized nearly all the profitable employments, and from those she is permitted to follow, she receives but a scanty remuneration. He closes against her all the avenues to wealth and distinction which he considers most honorable to himself. As a teacher of theology, medicine, or law, she is not known.

He has denied her the facilities for obtaining a thorough education, all colleges being closed against her.

He allows her in Church, as well as State, but a subordinate position, claiming Apostolic authority for her exclusion from the ministry, and, with some exceptions, from any public participation in the affairs of the Church.

He has created a false public sentiment by giving to the world a different code of morals for men and women, by which moral delinquencies which exclude women from society, are not only tolerated, but deemed of little account in man.

He has usurped the prerogative of Jehovah himself, claiming it as his right to assign for her a sphere of action, when that belongs to her conscience and to her God.

He has endeavored, in every way that he could, to destroy her confidence in her own powers, to lessen her self-respect and to make her willing to lead a dependent and abject life.

Now, in view of this entire disfranchisement of one-half the people of this country, their social and religious degradation—in view of the unjust laws above mentioned, and because women do feel themselves aggrieved, oppressed, and fraudulently deprived of their most sacred rights, we insist that they have immediate admission to all the rights and privileges which belong to them as citizens of the United States.

In entering upon the great work before us, we anticipate no small amount of misconception, misrepresentation, and ridicule; but we shall use every instrumentality within our power to effect our object. We shall employ agents, circulate tracts, petition the State and National legislatures, and endeavor to enlist the pulpit and the press in our behalf. We hope this Convention will be followed by a series of Conventions embracing every part of the country.

2. RESOLUTIONS

WHEREAS, The great precept of nature is conceded to be, that "man shall pursue his own true and substantial happiness." Blackstone in his Commentaries remarks, that this law of Nature being coeval with mankind, and dictated by God himself, is of course superior in obligation to any other. It is binding over all the globe, in all countries and at all times; no human laws are of any validity if contrary to this, and such of them as are valid, derive all their force, and all their validity, and all their authority, mediately and immediately, from this original; therefore,

Resolved, That such laws as conflict, in any way, with the true and substantial happiness of woman, are contrary to the great precept of nature and of no validity, for this is "superior in obligation to any other."

Resolved, That all laws which prevent woman from occupying such a station in society as her conscience shall dictate, or which place her in a position inferior to that of man, are contrary to the great precept of nature, and therefore of no force or authority.

Resolved, That woman is man's equal—was intended to be so by the Creator, and the highest good of the race demands that she should be recognized as such.

Resolved, That the women of this country ought to be enlightened in regard to the laws under which they live, that they may no longer publish their degradation by declaring themselves satisfied with their present position, nor their ignorance, by asserting that they have all the rights they want.

Resolved, That inasmuch as man, while claiming for himself intellectual superiority, does accord to woman moral superiority, it is pre-eminently his duty to encourage her to speak and teach, as she has an opportunity, in all religious assemblies.

Resolved, That the same amount of virtue, delicacy, and refinement of behavior that is required of woman in the social state, should also be required of man, and the same transgressions should be visited with equal severity on both man and woman.

Resolved, That the objection of indelicacy and impropriety, which is so often brought against woman when she addresses a public audience, comes with a very ill-grace from those who encourage, by their attendance, her appearance on the stage, in the concert. Or in feats of the circus.

Resolved, That woman has too long rested satisfied in the circumscribed limits which corrupt customs and a perverted application of the Scriptures have marked out for her, and that it is time she should move in the enlarged sphere which her great Creator has assigned her.

Resolved, That it is the duty of the women of this country to secure to themselves their sacred right to the elective franchise.

Resolved, That the equality of human rights results necessarily from the fact of the identity of the race in capabilities and responsibilities.

Resolved, therefore, That, being invested by the Creator with the same capabilities, and the same consciousness of responsibility for their exercise, it is demonstrably the right and duty of woman, equally with man, to promote every righteous cause by every righteous means; and especially in regard to the great subjects of morals and religion, it is self-evidently her right to participate with her brother in teaching them, both in private and in public, by writing and by speaking, by any instrumentalities proper to be used, and in any assemblies proper to be held; and this being a self-evident truth growing out of the divinely implanted principles of human nature, any custom or authority adverse to it, whether modern or wearing the hoary sanction of antiquity, is to be regarded as a self-evident falsehood, and at war with mankind.

Resolved, That the speedy success of our cause depends upon the zealous and untiring efforts of both men and women, for the overthrow of the monopoly of the pulpit, and for the securing to women an equal participation with men in the various trades, professions, and commerce.

FROM FREDERICK DOUGLASS'S "WHAT, TO THE SLAVE, IS THE FOURTH OF JULY?" SPEECH (1852)

* * *

This, for the purpose of this celebration, is the Fourth of July. It is the birthday of your National Independence, and of your political freedom. This, to you, is what the Passover was to the emancipated people of God. It carries your minds back to the day, and to the act of your great deliverance; and to the signs and to the wonders associated with that act and that day. This celebration also marks the beginning of another year of your national life; and reminds you that the Republic of America is now seventy-six years old. I am glad, fellow citizens, that your nation is so young. Seventy-six years, though a good old age for a man, is but a mere speck in the life of a nation. Three score years and ten is the allotted time for individual men; but nations number their years by thousands. According to this fact, you are, even now, only in the beginning of your national career, still lingering in the period of childhood. I repeat, I am glad this is so. There is hope in the thought, and hope is much needed, under the dark clouds which lower above the horizon. The eye of the reformer is met with angry flashes, portending disastrous times; but his heart may well beat lighter at the thought that America is young, and that she is still in the impressible stage of her existence. May he not hope that high lessons of wisdom, of justice and of truth, will yet give direction to her destiny? Were the nation older, the patriot's heart might be sadder and the reformer's brow heavier. Its future might be shrouded in gloom and the hope of its prophets go out in sorrow. There is consolation in the thought that America is young. Great streams are not easily turned from channels worn deep in the course of ages. They may sometimes rise in quiet and stately majesty, and inundate the land, refreshing and fertilizing the earth with their mysterious properties. They may also rise in wrath and fury, and bear away on their angry waves the accumulated wealth of years of toil and hardship. They, however, gradually flow back to the same old channel and flow on as serenely as ever. But, while the river may not be turned aside, it may dry up and leave nothing behind but the withered branch and the unsightly rock, to howl in the abyss-sweeping wind, the sad tale of departed glory. As with rivers, so with nations.

Fellow citizens, I shall not presume to dwell at length on the associations that cluster about this day. The simple story of it is, that seventy-six years ago the people of this country were British subjects. The style and title of your "sovereign people" (in which you now glory) was not then born. You were under the British Crown. Your fathers esteemed the English government as the home government, and England as the fatherland. This home government, you know, although a considerable distance from your home, did, in the exercise of its parental prerogatives, impose upon its colonial children such restraints, burdens and limitations as, in its mature judgment, it deemed wise, right and proper.

* * *

Feeling themselves harshly and unjustly treated by the home government, your fathers, like men of honesty and men of spirit, earnestly sought redress. They petitioned and remonstrated, they did so in a decorous, respectful and loyal manner. Their conduct was wholly unexceptionable. This, however, did not answer the purpose. They saw themselves treated with sovereign indifference, coldness and scorn. Yet they persevered. They were not the men to look back.

* * *

Citizens, your fathers . . . succeeded; and today you reap the fruits of their success. The freedom gained is yours; and you, therefore, may properly celebrate this anniversary. The Fourth of July is the first great fact in your nation's history—the very ringbolt in the chain of your yet undeveloped destiny.

Pride and patriotism, not less than gratitude, prompt you to celebrate and to hold it in perpetual remembrance. I have said that the Declaration of Independence is the ringbolt to the chain of your nation's destiny; so, indeed, I regard it. The principles contained in that instrument are saving principles. Stand by those principles, be true to them on all occasions, in all places, against all foes, and at whatever cost.

★ ★ ★

[The fathers of this republic] were peace men, but they preferred revolution to peaceful submission to bondage. They were quiet men; but they did not shrink from agitating against oppression. They showed forbearance, but that they knew its limits. They believed in order, but not in the order of tyranny. With them, nothing was "settled" that was not right. With them, justice, liberty and humanity were "final," not slavery and oppression. You may well cherish the memory of such men. They were great in their day and generation. Their solid manhood stands out the more as we contrast it with these degenerate times.

★ ★ ★

Fellow citizens, pardon me, allow me to ask, why am I called upon to speak here today? What have I, or those I represent, to do with your national independence? Are the great principles of political freedom and of natural justice, embodied in that Declaration of Independence, extended to us? and am I, therefore, called upon to bring our humble offering to the national altar and to confess the benefits and express devout gratitude for the blessings resulting from your independence to us?

★ ★ ★

But such is not the state of the case. I say it with a sad sense of the disparity between us. I am not included within the pale of this glorious anniversary! Your high independence only reveals the immeasurable distance between us. The blessings in which you, this day, rejoice, are not enjoyed in common. The rich inheritance of justice, liberty, prosperity and independence, bequeathed by your fathers, is shared by you, not by me. The sunlight that brought light and healing to you, has brought stripes and death to me. This Fourth of July is *yours*, not *mine*. *You* may rejoice, *I* must mourn.

★ ★ ★

Fellow citizens, above your national, tumultuous joy I hear the mournful wail of millions! whose chains, heavy and grievous yesterday, are today rendered more intolerable by the jubilee shouts that reach them. If I do forget, if I do not faithfully remember those bleeding children of sorrow this day, "may my right hand forget her cunning, and may my tongue cleave to the roof of my mouth!" To forget them, to pass lightly over their wrongs and to chime in with the popular theme would be treason most scandalous and shocking and would make me a reproach before God and the world. My subject, then, fellow citizens, is American slavery. I shall see this day and its popular characteristics from the slave's point of view. Standing there identified with the American bondman, making his wrongs mine, I do not hesitate to declare, with all my soul, that the character and conduct of this nation never looked blacker to me than on this Fourth of July. Whether we turn to the declarations of the past or to the professions of the present, the conduct of the nation seems equally hideous and revolting. America is false to the past, false to the present, and solemnly binds herself to be false to the future.

★ ★ ★

For the present, it is enough to affirm the equal manhood of the Negro race. It is not astonishing that, while we are plowing, planting and reaping, using all kinds of mechanical tools, erecting houses, constructing bridges, building ships, working in metals of brass, iron, copper, silver and gold; that, while we are reading, writing and ciphering, acting as clerks, merchants and secretaries, having among us lawyers, doctors, ministers, poets, authors, editors, orators and teachers; that, while we are engaged in all manner of enterprises common to other men, digging gold in California, capturing the whale in the Pacific, feeding sheep and cattle on the hillside, living, moving, acting, thinking, planning, living in families as husbands, wives and children, and, above all, confessing and worshiping the Christian's God and looking hopefully for life and immortality beyond the grave, we are called upon to prove that we are men!

Would you have me argue that man is entitled to liberty? that he is the rightful owner of his own body? You have already declared it. Must I argue the wrongfulness of slavery? Is that a question for republicans? Is it to be settled by the rules of logic and argumentation, as a matter beset with great difficulty, involving a doubtful application of the principle of justice, hard to be understood? How should I look today, in the presence of Americans, dividing and subdividing a discourse, to show that men have a natural right to freedom, speaking of it relatively and positively, negatively and affirmatively? To do so would be to make myself ridiculous and to offer an insult to your understanding. There is not a man beneath the canopy of heaven that does not know that slavery is wrong *for him*.

★ ★ ★

What, to the American slave, is your Fourth of July? I answer: a day that reveals to him, more than all other days in the year, the gross injustice and cruelty to which he is the constant victim. To him, your celebration is a sham; your boasted liberty an unholy license; your national greatness swelling vanity; your sounds of rejoicing are empty and heartless; your denunciation of tyrants brass-fronted impudence; your shouts of liberty and equality hollow mockery; your prayers and hymns, your sermons and thanksgivings, with all your religious parade and solemnity, are to Him mere bombast, fraud, deception, impiety and hypocrisy—a thin veil to cover up crimes which would disgrace a nation of savages. There is not a nation on the earth guilty of practices more shocking and bloody than are the people of the United States at this very hour.

Go where you may, search where you will, roam through all the monarchies and despotisms of the Old World, travel through South America, search out every abuse, and when you have found the last, lay your facts by the side of the everyday practices of this nation, and you will say with me, that, for revolting barbarity and shameless hypocrisy, America reigns without a rival.

★ ★ ★

Americans! your republican politics, not less than your republican religion, are flagrantly inconsistent. You boast of your love of liberty, your superior civilization and your pure Christianity, while the whole political power of the nation (as embodied in the two great political parties) is solemnly pledged to support and perpetuate the enslavement of three millions of your countrymen. You hurl your anathemas at the crowned-headed tyrants of Russia and Austria and pride yourselves on your democratic institutions, while you yourselves consent to be the mere *tools* and *bodyguards* of the tyrants of Virginia and Carolina. You invite to your shores fugitives of oppression from abroad, honor them with banquets, greet them with ovations, cheer them, toast them, salute them, protect them, and pour out your money to them like water; but the fugitives from your own land you advertise, hunt, arrest, shoot and kill. You glory in your refinement and your universal education; yet you maintain a system as barbarous and dreadful as ever stained the character of a nation—a system begun in avarice, supported in pride, and perpetuated in cruelty. You shed tears over fallen Hungary, and make the sad story of her wrongs the theme of your poets, statesmen and orators, till your gallant sons are ready to fly to arms to vindicate her cause against the oppressor; but, in regard to the ten thousand wrongs of the American slave, you would enforce the strictest silence and would hail him as an enemy of the nation who dares to make those wrongs the subject of public discourse! You are all on fire at the mention of liberty for France or for Ireland, but are as cold as an iceberg at the thought of liberty for the enslaved of America. You discourse eloquently on the dignity of labor; yet, you sustain a system which, in its very essence, casts a stigma upon labor. You can bare your bosom to the storm of British artillery to throw off a three-penny tax on tea, and yet wring the last hard-earned farthing from the grasp of the black laborers of your country. You profess to believe "that of one blood God made all nations of men to dwell on the face of all the earth"† and hath commanded all men, everywhere, to love one another; yet you notoriously hate (and glory in your hatred) all men whose skins are not colored like your own. You declare before the world, and are understood by the world to declare, that you *"hold these truths to be self-evident, that all men are created equal; and are endowed by their Creator with certain unalienable rights; and that among these are, life, liberty and the pursuit of happiness"; and yet, you hold securely, in a bondage which, according to your own Thomas Jefferson, "is worse than ages of that which your fathers rose in rebellion to oppose," a seventh part* of the inhabitants of your country.

Fellow citizens, I will not enlarge further on your national inconsistencies. The existence of slavery in this country brands your republicanism as a sham, your humanity as a base pretense, and your Christianity as a lie. It destroys your moral power abroad; it corrupts your politicians at home. It saps the foundation of religion; it makes your name a hissing and a byword to a mocking earth. It is the antagonistic force in your government, the only thing that seriously disturbs and endangers your union. It fetters your progress; it is the enemy of improvement; the deadly foe of education; it fosters pride; it breeds insolence; it promotes vice; it shelters crime; it is a curse to the earth that supports it; and yet you cling to it as if it were the sheet anchor of all your hopes.

★ ★ ★

Allow me to say, in conclusion, notwithstanding the dark picture I have this day presented, of the state of the nation, I do not despair of this country. There are forces in operation which must inevitably work the downfall of slavery.

---

*The fledgling Hungarian republic was invaded by Austria and Russia in 1849.

†Acts 17:26.

THE GETTYSBURG ADDRESS (1863)

Four score and seven years ago our fathers brought forth on this continent, a new nation, conceived in Liberty, and dedicated to the proposition that all men are created equal.

Now we are engaged in a great civil war, testing whether that nation, or any nation so conceived and so dedicated, can long endure. We are met on a great battle field of that war. We have come to dedicate a portion of that field, as a final resting place for those who here gave their lives that that nation might live. It is altogether fitting and proper that we should do this.

But, in a larger sense, we can not dedicate—we can not consecrate—we can not hallow—this ground. The brave men, living and dead, who struggled here, have consecrated it, far above our poor power to add or detract. The world will little note, nor long remember what we say here, but it can never forget what they did here. It is for us the living, rather, to be dedicated here to the unfinished work which they who fought here have thus far so nobly advanced. It is rather for us to be here dedicated to the great task remaining before us—that from these honored dead we take increased devotion to that cause for which they gave the last full measure of devotion—that we here highly resolve that these dead shall not have died in vain—that this nation, under God, shall have a new birth of freedom—and that government of the people, by the people, for the people, shall not perish from the earth.

Abraham Lincoln
November 19, 1863

ABRAHAM LINCOLN'S SECOND INAUGURAL ADDRESS (1865)

Fellow Countrymen:

At this second appearing to take the oath of the presidential office, there is less occasion for an extended address than there was at the first. Then a statement, somewhat in detail, of a course to be pursued, seemed fitting and proper. Now, at the expiration of four years, during which public declarations have been constantly called forth on every point and phase of the great contest which still absorbs the attention, and engrosses the energies of the nation, little that is new could be presented. The progress of our arms, upon which all else chiefly depends, is as well known to the public as to myself; and it is, I trust, reasonably satisfactory and encouraging to all. With high hope for the future, no prediction in regard to it is ventured.

On the occasion corresponding to this four years ago, all thoughts were anxiously directed to an impending civil war. All dreaded it—all sought to avert it. While the inaugural address was being delivered from this place, devoted altogether to *saving* the Union without war, insurgent agents were in the city seeking to *destroy* it without war—seeking to dissolve the Union, and divide effects, by negotiation. Both parties deprecated war; but one of them would *make* war rather than let the nation survive; and the other would *accept* war rather than let it perish. And the war came.

One eighth of the whole population were colored slaves, not distributed generally over the Union, but localized in the southern part of it. These slaves constituted a peculiar and powerful interest. All knew that this interest was, somehow, the cause of the war. To strengthen, perpetuate, and extend this interest was the object for which the insurgents would rend the Union, even by war; while the government claimed no right to do more than to restrict the territorial enlargement of it. Neither party expected for the war, the magnitude, or the duration, which it has already attained. Neither anticipated that the *cause* of the conflict might cease with, or even before, the conflict itself should cease. Each looked for an easier triumph, and a result less fundamental and astounding. Both read the same Bible, and pray to the same God; and each invokes His aid against the other. It may seem strange that any men should dare to ask a just God's assistance in wringing their bread from the sweat of other men's faces; but let us judge not that we be not judged. The prayers of both could not be answered; that of neither has been answered fully. The Almighty has His own purposes. "Woe unto the world because of offences! for it must needs be that offences come; but woe to that man by whom the offence cometh." If we shall suppose that American slavery is one of those offences which, in the providence of God, must needs come, but which, having continued through His appointed time, He now wills to remove, and that He gives to both North and South, this terrible war, as the woe due to those by whom the offence came, shall we discern therein any departure from those divine attributes which the believers in a living God always ascribe to Him? Fondly do we hope, fervently do we pray—that this mighty scourge of war may speedily pass away. Yet, if God wills that it continue until all the wealth piled by the bondsman's two hundred and fifty years of unrequited toil shall be sunk, and until every drop of blood drawn with the lash shall be paid by another drawn with the sword, as was said three thousand years ago, so still it must be said "the judgments of the Lord are true and righteous altogether."

With malice toward none; with charity for all; with firmness in the right as God gives us to see the right, let us strive on to finish the work we are in; to bind up the nation's wounds; to care for him who shall have borne the battle and for his widow and his orphan, to do all which may achieve and cherish a just and a lasting peace, among ourselves and with all nations.

THE POPULIST PLATFORM OF 1892

Assembled upon the 116th anniversary of the Declaration of Independence, the People's Party of America, in their first national convention, invoking upon their action the blessing of Almighty God, puts forth in the name and on behalf of the people of this country, the following preamble and declaration of principles:

PREAMBLE

The conditions which surround us best justify our co-operation; we meet in the midst of a nation brought to the verge of moral, political, and material ruin. Corruption dominates the ballot-box, the Legislatures, the Congress, and touches even the ermine of the bench. The people are demoralized; most of the States have been compelled to isolate the voters at the polling places to prevent universal intimidation and bribery. The newspapers are largely subsidized or muzzled, public opinion silenced, business prostrated, homes covered with mortgages, labor impoverished, and the land concentrating in the hands of the capitalists. The urban workmen are denied the right to organize for self-protection, imported pauperized labor beats down their wages, a hireling standing army, unrecognized by our laws, is established to shoot them down, and they are rapidly degenerating into European conditions. The fruits of the toil of millions are boldly stolen to build up the fortunes for a few, unprecedented in the history of mankind; and the possessors of these, in turn, despise the Republic and endanger liberty. From the same prolific womb of governmental injustice we breed the two great classes—tramps and millionaires.

The national power to create money is appropriated to enrich bondholders; a vast public debt, payable in legal tender currency, has been funded into gold-bearing bonds, thereby adding millions to the burdens of the people. Silver, which has been accepted as coin since the dawn of history, has been demonetized to add to the purchasing power of gold by decreasing the value of all forms of property as well as human labor, and the supply of currency is purposely abridged to fatten usurers, bankrupt enterprise, and enslave industry. A vast conspiracy against mankind has been organized on two continents, and it is rapidly taking possession of the world. If not met and overthrown at once it forebodes terrible social convulsions, the destruction of civilization, or the establishment of an absolute despotism.

We have witnessed for more than a quarter of a century the struggles of the two great political parties for power and plunder, while grievous wrongs have been inflicted upon the suffering people. We charge that the controlling influences dominating both these parties have permitted the existing dreadful conditions to develop without serious effort to prevent or restrain them. Neither do they now promise us any substantial reform. They have agreed together to ignore in the coming campaign every issue but one. They propose to drown the outcries of a plundered people with the uproar of a sham battle over the tariff, so that capitalists, corporations, national banks, rings, trusts, watered stock, the demonetization of silver, and the oppressions of the usurers may all be lost sight of. They propose to sacrifice our homes, lives, and children on the altar of mammon; to destroy the multitude in order to secure corruption funds from the millionaires.

Assembled on the anniversary of the birthday of the nation, and filled with the spirit of the grand general and chief who established our independence, we seek to restore the government of the Republic to the hands of "the plain people," with which class it originated. We assert our purpose to be identical with the purposes of the National Constitution, "to form a more perfect union and establish justice, insure domestic tranquility, provide for the common defense, promote the general welfare, and secure the blessings of liberty for ourselves and our posterity." We declare that this Republic can only endure as a free government while built upon the love of the whole people for each other and for the nation; that it cannot be pinned together by bayonets; that the civil war is over, and that every passion and resentment which grew out of it must die with it; and that we must be in fact, as we are in name, one united brotherhood of free men.

Our country finds itself confronted by conditions for which there is no precedent in the history of the world; our annual agricultural productions amount to billions of dollars in value, which must, within a few weeks or months, be exchanged for billions of dollars of commodities consumed in their production; the existing currency supply is wholly inadequate to make this exchange; the results are falling prices, the formation of combines and rings, the impoverishment of the producing class. We pledge ourselves, if given power, we will labor to correct these evils by wise and reasonable legislation, in accordance with the terms of our platform. We believe that the power of government—in other words, of the people—should be expanded (as in the case of the postal service) as rapidly and as far as the good sense of an intelligent people and the teaching of experience shall justify, to the end that oppression, injustice, and poverty shall eventually cease in the land.

While our sympathies as a party of reform are naturally upon the side of every proposition which will tend to make men intelligent, virtuous, and temperate, we nevertheless regard these questions—important as they are—as secondary to the great issues now pressing for solution, and upon which not only our individual prosperity but the very existence of free institutions depend; and we ask all men to first help us to determine whether we are to have a republic to administer before we differ as to the conditions upon which it is to be administered, believing that the forces of reform this day organized will never cease to move forward until every wrong is remedied, and equal rights and equal privileges securely established for all the men and women of this country.

PLATFORM

We declare, therefore—

First.—That the union of the labor forces of the United States this day consummated shall be permanent and perpetual; may its spirit enter into all hearts for the salvation of the Republic and the uplifting of mankind!

Second.—Wealth belongs to him who creates it, and every dollar taken from industry without an equivalent is robbery. "If any will not work, neither shall he eat." The interests of rural and civic labor are the same; their enemies are identical.

Third.—We believe that the time has come when the railroad corporations will either own the people or the people must own the railroads; and, should the government enter upon the work of owning and managing all railroads, we should favor an amendment to the Constitution by which all persons engaged in the government service shall be placed under a civil-service regulation of the most rigid character, so as to prevent the increase of the power of the national administration by the use of such additional government employees.

FINANCE.—We demand a national currency, safe, sound, and flexible, issued by the general government only, a full legal tender for all debts, public and private, and that without the use of banking corporations, a just, equitable, and efficient means of distribution direct to the people, at a tax not to exceed two per cent per annum, to be provided as set forth in the sub-treasury plan of the Farmers' Alliance, or a better system; also by payments in discharge of its obligations for public improvements.

1. We demand free and unlimited coinage of silver and gold at the present legal ratio of 16 to 1.

2. We demand that the amount of circulating medium be speedily increased to not less than $50 per capita.

3. We demand a graduated income tax.

4. We believe that the money of the country should be kept as much as possible in the hands of the people, and hence we demand that all State and national revenues shall be limited to the necessary expenses of the government, economically and honestly administered.

5. We demand that postal savings banks be established by the government for the safe deposit of the earnings of the people and to facilitate exchange.

TRANSPORTATION.—Transportation being a means of exchange and a public necessity, the government should own and operate the railroads in the interest of the people. The telegraph and telephone, like the post-office system, being a necessity for the transmission of news, should be owned and operated by the government in the interest of the people.

LAND.—The land, including all the natural sources of wealth, is the heritage of the people, and should not be monopolized for speculative purposes, and alien ownership of land should be prohibited. All land now held by railroads and other corporations in excess of their actual needs, and all lands now owned by aliens should be reclaimed by the government and held for actual settlers only.

EXPRESSION OF SENTIMENTS

Your committee on Platform and Resolutions beg leave unanimously to report the following:

Whereas, Other questions have been presented for our consideration, we hereby submit the following, not as a part of the Platform of the People's Party, but as resolutions expressive of the sentiment of this Convention:

1. *Resolved*, That we demand a free ballot and a fair count in all elections, and pledge ourselves to secure it to every legal voter without federal intervention, through the adoption by the States of the unperverted Australian or secret ballot system.

2. *Resolved*, That the revenue derived from a graduated income tax should be applied to the reduction of the burden of taxation now levied upon the domestic industries of this country.

3. *Resolved*, That we pledge our support to fair and liberal pensions to ex-Union soldiers and sailors.

4. *Resolved*, That we condemn the fallacy of protecting American labor under the present system, which opens our ports to the pauper and criminal classes of the world, and crowds out our wage-earners; and we denounce the present ineffective laws against contract labor, and demand the further restriction of undesirable emigration.

5. *Resolved*, that we cordially sympathize with the efforts of organized workingmen to shorten the hours of labor, and demand a rigid enforcement of the existing eight-hour law on Government work, and ask that a penalty clause be added to the said law.

6. *Resolved*, That we regard the maintenance of a large standing army of mercenaries, known as the Pinkerton system, as a menace to our liberties, and we demand its abolition; and we condemn the recent invasion of the Territory of Wyoming by the hired assassins of plutocracy, assisted by federal officers.

7. *Resolved*, That we commend to the favorable consideration of the people and the reform press the legislative system known as the initiative and referendum.

8. *Resolved*, That we favor a constitutional provision limiting the office of President and Vice-President to one term, and providing for the election of Senators of the United States by a direct vote of the people.

9. *Resolved*, That we oppose any subsidy or national aid to any private corporation for any purpose.

10. *Resolved*, That this convention sympathizes with the Knights of Labor and their righteous contest with the tyrannical combine of clothing manufacturers of Rochester, and declare it to be the duty of all who hate tyranny and oppression to refuse to purchase the goods made by the said manufacturers, or to patronize any merchants who sell such goods.

FRANKLIN D. ROOSEVELT'S FIRST INAUGURAL ADDRESS (1933)

I am certain that my fellow Americans expect that on my induction into the Presidency I will address them with a candor and a decision which the present situation of our Nation impels. This is preeminently the time to speak the truth, the whole truth, frankly and boldly. Nor need we shrink from honestly facing conditions in our country today. This great Nation will endure as it has endured, will revive and will prosper. So, first of all, let me assert my firm belief that the only thing we have to fear is fear itself—nameless, unreasoning, unjustified terror which paralyzes needed efforts to convert retreat into advance. In every dark hour of our national life a leadership of frankness and vigor has met with that understanding and support of the people themselves which is essential to victory. I am convinced that you will again give that support to leadership in these critical days.

In such a spirit on my part and on yours we face our common difficulties. They concern, thank God, only material things. Values have shrunken to fantastic levels; taxes have risen; our ability to pay has fallen; government of all kinds is faced by serious curtailment of income; the means of exchange are frozen in the currents of trade; the withered leaves of industrial enterprise lie on every side; farmers find no markets for their produce; the savings of many years in thousands of families are gone.

More important, a host of unemployed citizens face the grim problem of existence, and an equally great number toil with little return. Only a foolish optimist can deny the dark realities of the moment.

Yet our distress comes from no failure of substance. We are stricken by no plague of locusts. Compared with the perils which our forefathers conquered because they believed and were not afraid, we have still much to be thankful for. Nature still offers her bounty and human efforts have multiplied it. Plenty is at our doorstep, but a generous use of it languishes in the very sight of the supply. Primarily this is because the rulers of the exchange of mankind's goods have failed, through their own stubbornness and their own incompetence, have admitted their failure, and abdicated. Practices of the unscrupulous money changers stand indicted in the court of public opinion, rejected by the hearts and minds of men.

True they have tried, but their efforts have been cast in the pattern of an outworn tradition. Faced by failure of credit they have proposed only the lending of more money. Stripped of the lure of profit by which to induce our people to follow their false leadership, they have resorted to exhortations, pleading tearfully for restored confidence. They know only the rules of a generation of self-seekers. They have no vision, and when there is no vision the people perish.

The money changers have fled from their high seats in the temple of our civilization. We may now restore that temple to the ancient truths. The measure of the restoration lies in the extent to which we apply social values more noble than mere monetary profit.

Happiness lies not in the mere possession of money; it lies in the joy of achievement, in the thrill of creative effort. The joy and moral stimulation of work no longer must be forgotten in the mad chase of evanescent profits. These dark days will be worth all they cost us if they teach us that our true destiny is not to be ministered unto but to minister to ourselves and to our fellow men.

Recognition of the falsity of material wealth as the standard of success goes hand in hand with the abandonment of the false belief that public office and high political position are to be valued only by the standards of pride of place and personal profit; and there must be an end to a conduct in banking and in business which too often has given to a sacred trust the likeness of callous and selfish wrongdoing. Small wonder that confidence languishes, for it thrives only on honesty, on honor, on the sacredness of obligations, on faithful protection, on unselfish performance; without them it cannot live.

Restoration calls, however, not for changes in ethics alone. This Nation asks for action, and action now.

Our greatest primary task is to put people to work. This is no unsolvable problem if we face it wisely and courageously. It can be accomplished in part by direct recruiting by the Government itself, treating the task as we would treat the emergency of a war, but at the same time, through this employment, accomplishing greatly needed projects to stimulate and reorganize the use of our natural resources.

Hand in hand with this we must frankly recognize the overbalance of population in our industrial centers and, by engaging on a national scale in a redistribution, endeavor to provide a better use of the land for those best fitted for the land. The task can be helped by definite efforts to raise the values of agricultural products and with this the power to purchase the output of our cities. It can be helped by preventing realistically the tragedy of the growing loss through foreclosure of our small homes and our farms. It can be helped by insistence that the Federal, State, and local governments act forthwith on the demand that their cost be drastically reduced. It can be helped by the unifying of relief activities which today are often scattered, uneconomical, and unequal. It can be helped by national planning for and supervision of all forms of transportation and of communications and other utilities which have a definitely public character. There are many ways in which it can be helped, but it can never be helped merely by talking about it. We must act and act quickly.

Finally, in our progress toward a resumption of work we require two safeguards against a return of the evils of the old order; there must be a strict supervision of all banking and credits and investments; there must be an end to speculation with other people's money, and there must be provision for an adequate but sound currency.

There are the lines of attack. I shall presently urge upon a new Congress, in special session, detailed measures for their fulfillment, and I shall seek the immediate assistance of the several States.

Through this program of action we address ourselves to putting our own national house in order and making income balance outgo. Our international trade relations, though vastly important, are in point of time and necessity secondary to the establishment of a sound national economy. I favor as a practical policy the putting of first things first. I shall spare no effort to restore world trade by international economic readjustment, but the emergency at home cannot wait on that accomplishment.

The basic thought that guides these specific means of national recovery is not narrowly nationalistic. It is the insistence, as a first consideration, upon the interdependence of the various elements in all parts of the United States—a recognition of the old and permanently important manifestation of the American spirit of the pioneer. It is the way to recovery. It is the immediate way. It is the strongest assurance that the recovery will endure.

In the field of world policy I would dedicate this Nation to the policy of the good neighbor—the neighbor who resolutely respects himself and, because he does so, respects the rights of others—the neighbor who respects his obligations and respects the sanctity of his agreements in and with a world of neighbors.

If I read the temper of our people correctly, we now realize as we have never realized before our interdependence on each other; that we cannot merely take but we must give as well; that if we are to go forward, we must move as a trained and loyal army willing to sacrifice for the good of a common discipline, because without such discipline no progress is made, no leadership becomes effective. We are, I know, ready and willing to submit our lives and property to such discipline, because it makes possible a leadership which aims at a larger good. This I propose to offer, pledging that the larger purposes will bind upon us all as a sacred obligation with a unity of duty hitherto evoked only in time of armed strife.

With this pledge taken, I assume unhesitatingly the leadership of this great army of our people dedicated to a disciplined attack upon our common problems.

Action in this image and to this end is feasible under the form of government which we have inherited from our ancestors. Our Constitution is so simple and practical that it is possible always to meet extraordinary needs by changes in emphasis and arrangement without loss of essential form. That is why our constitutional system has proved itself the most superbly enduring political mechanism the modern world has produced. It has met every stress of vast expansion of territory, of foreign wars, of bitter internal strife, of world relations.

It is to be hoped that the normal balance of executive and legislative authority may be wholly adequate to meet the unprecedented task before us. But it may be that an unprecedented demand and need for undelayed action may call for temporary departure from that normal balance of public procedure.

I am prepared under my constitutional duty to recommend the measures that a stricken nation in the midst of a stricken world may require. These measures, or such other measures as the Congress may build out of its experience and wisdom, I shall seek, within my constitutional authority, to bring to speedy adoption.

But in the event that the Congress shall fail to take one of these two courses, and in the event that the national emergency is still critical, I shall not evade the clear course of duty that will then confront me. I shall ask the Congress for the one remaining instrument to meet the crisis—broad Executive power to wage a war against the emergency, as great as the power that would be given to me if we were in fact invaded by a foreign foe.

For the trust reposed in me I will return the courage and the devotion that befit the time. I can do no less.

We face the arduous days that lie before us in the warm courage of national unity; with the clear consciousness of seeking old and precious moral values; with the clean satisfaction that comes from the stern performance of duty by old and young alike. We aim at the assurance of a rounded and permanent national life.

We do not distrust the future of essential democracy. The people of the United States have not failed. In their need they have registered a mandate that they want direct, vigorous action. They have asked for discipline and direction under leadership. They have made me the present instrument of their wishes. In the spirit of the gift I take it.

In this dedication of a Nation we humbly ask the blessing of God. May He protect each and every one of us. May He guide me in the days to come.

FROM THE PROGRAM FOR THE MARCH ON WASHINGTON FOR JOBS AND FREEDOM (1963)

WHAT WE DEMAND*

1. Comprehensive and effective *civil rights legislation* from the present Congress—without compromise or filibuster—to guarantee all Americans

> access to all public accommodations
> decent housing
> adequate and integrated education
> the right to vote

2. Withholding of Federal funds from all programs in which discrimination exists.

3. *Desegregation of all school districts in 1963.*

4. Enforcement of the *Fourteenth Amendment*—reducing Congressional representation of states where citizens are disfranchised.

5. A new *Executive Order* banning discrimination in all housing supported by federal funds.

6. Authority for the Attorney General to institute *injunctive suits* when any constitutional right is violated.

7. A massive federal program to train and place all unemployed workers—Negro and white—on meaningful and dignified jobs at decent wages.

8. A national *minimum wage* act that will give all Americans a decent standard of living. (Government surveys show that anything less than $2.00 an hour fails to do this.)

9. A broadened *Fair Labor Standards Act* to include all areas of employment which are presently excluded.

10. A federal *Fair Employment Practices Act* barring discrimination by federal, state, and municipal governments, and by employers, contractors, employment agencies, and trade unions.

*Support of the March does not necessarily indicate endorsement of every demand listed. Some organizations have not had an opportunity to take an official position on all of the demands advocated here.

RONALD REAGAN'S FIRST INAUGURAL ADDRESS (1981)

WEST FRONT OF THE U.S. CAPITOL JANUARY 20, 1981

Senator Hatfield, Mr. Chief Justice, Mr. President, Vice President Bush, Vice President Mondale, Senator Baker, Speaker O'Neill, Reverend Moomaw, and my fellow citizens.

To a few of us here today this is a solemn and most momentous occasion, and yet in the history of our nation it is a commonplace occurrence. The orderly transfer of authority as called for in the Constitution routinely takes place, as it has for almost two centuries, and few of us stop to think how unique we really are. In the eyes of many in the world, this every-four-year ceremony we accept as normal is nothing less than a miracle.

Mr. President, I want our fellow citizens to know how much you did to carry on this tradition. By your gracious cooperation in the transition process, you have shown a watching world that we are a united people pledged to maintaining a political system which guarantees individual liberty to a greater degree than any other, and I thank you and your people for all your help in maintaining the continuity which is the bulwark of our republic. The business of our nation goes forward. These United States are confronted with an economic affliction of great proportions. We suffer from the longest and one of the worst sustained inflations in our national history. It distorts our economic decisions, penalizes thrift, and crushes the struggling young and the fixed-income elderly alike. It threatens to shatter the lives of millions of our people.

Idle industries have cast workers into unemployment, human misery, and personal indignity. Those who do work are denied a fair return for their labor by a tax system which penalizes successful achievement and keeps us from maintaining full productivity. But great as our tax burden is, it has not kept pace with public spending. For decades we have piled deficit upon deficit, mortgaging our future and our children's future for the temporary convenience of the present. To continue this long trend is to guarantee tremendous social, cultural, political, and economic upheavals.

You and I, as individuals, can, by borrowing, live beyond our means, but for only a limited period of time. Why, then, should we think that collectively, as a nation, we're not bound by that same limitation? We must act today in order to preserve tomorrow. And let there be no misunderstanding: We are going to begin to act, beginning today. The economic ills we suffer have come upon us over several decades. They will not go away in days, weeks, or months, but they will go away. They will go away because we as Americans have the capacity now, as we've had in the past, to do whatever needs to be done to preserve this last and greatest bastion of freedom.

In this present crisis, government is not the solution to our problem; government is the problem. From time to time we've been tempted to believe that society has become too complex to be managed by self-rule, that government by an elite group is superior to government for, by, and of the people. Well, if no one among us is capable of governing himself, then who among us has the capacity to govern someone else? All of us together, in and out of government, must bear the burden. The solutions we seek must be equitable, with no one group singled out to pay a higher price.

We hear much of special interest groups. Well, our concern must be for a special interest group that has been too long neglected. It knows no sectional boundaries or ethnic and racial divisions, and it crosses political party lines. It is made up of men and women who raise our food, patrol our streets, man our mines and factories, teach our children, keep our homes, and heal us when we're sick—professionals, industrialists, shopkeepers, clerks, cabbies, and truck drivers. They are, in short, "we the people," this breed called Americans.

Well, this administration's objective will be a healthy, vigorous, growing economy that provides equal opportunities for all Americans, with no barriers born of bigotry or discrimination. Putting America back to work means putting all Americans back to work. Ending inflation means freeing all Americans from the terror of runaway living costs. All must share in the productive work of this "new beginning," and all must share in the bounty of a revived economy. With the idealism and fair play which are the core of our system and our strength, we can have a strong and prosperous America, at peace with itself and the world.

So, as we begin, let us take inventory. We are a nation that has a government—not the other way around. And this makes us special among the nations of the Earth. Our government has no power except that granted it by the people. It is time to check and reverse the growth of government, which shows signs of having grown beyond the consent of the governed.

It is my intention to curb the size and influence of the federal establishment and to demand recognition of the distinction between the powers granted to the federal government and those reserved to the states or to the people. All of us need to be reminded that the federal government did not create the states; the states created the federal government.

Now, so there will be no misunderstanding, it's not my intention to do away with government. It is rather to make it work—work with us, not over us; to stand by our side, not ride on our back. Government can and must provide opportunity, not smother it; foster productivity, not stifle it.

If we look to the answer as to why for so many years we achieved so much, prospered as no other people on earth, it was because here in this land we unleashed the energy and individual genius of man to a greater extent than has ever been done before. Freedom and the dignity of the individual have been more available and assured here than in any other place on earth. The price for this freedom at times has been high, but we have never been unwilling to pay the price.

It is no coincidence that our present troubles parallel and are proportionate to the intervention and intrusion in our lives that result from unnecessary and excessive growth of government. It is time for us to realize that we're too great a nation to limit ourselves to small dreams. We're not, as some would have us believe, doomed to an inevitable decline. I do not believe in a fate that will fall on us no matter what we do. I do believe in a fate that will fall on us if we do nothing. So, with all the creative energy at our command, let us begin an era of national renewal. Let us renew our determination, our courage, and our strength. And let us renew our faith and our hope.

We have every right to dream heroic dreams. Those who say that we're in a time when there are no heroes, they just don't know where to look. You can see heroes every day going in and out of factory gates. Others, a handful in number, produce enough food to feed all of us and then the world beyond. You meet heroes across a counter, and they're on both sides of that counter. There are entrepreneurs with faith in themselves and faith in an idea who create new jobs, new wealth and opportunity. They're individuals and families whose taxes support the government and whose voluntary gifts support church, charity, culture, art, and education. Their patriotism is quiet, but deep. Their values sustain our national life.

Now, I have used the words "they" and "their" in speaking of these heroes. I could say "you" and "your," because I'm addressing the heroes of whom I speak—you, the citizens of this blessed land. Your dreams, your hopes, your goals are going to be the dreams, the hopes, and the goals of this administration, so help me God.

We shall reflect the compassion that is so much a part of your makeup. How can we love our country and not love our countrymen; and loving them, reach out a hand when they fall, heal them when they're sick, and provide opportunity to make them self-sufficient so they will be equal in fact and not just in theory?

Can we solve the problems confronting us? Well, the answer is an unequivocal and emphatic "yes." To paraphrase Winston Churchill, I did not take the oath I've just taken with the intention of presiding over the dissolution of the world's strongest economy.

In the days ahead I will propose removing the roadblocks that have slowed our economy and reduced productivity. Steps will be taken aimed at restoring the balance between the various levels of government. Progress may be slow, measured in inches and feet, not miles, but we will progress. It is time to reawaken this industrial giant, to get government back within its means, and to lighten our punitive tax burden. And these will be our first priorities, and on these principles there will be no compromise.

On the eve of our struggle for independence a man who might have been one of the greatest among the Founding Fathers, Dr. Joseph Warren, president of the Massachusetts Congress, said to his fellow Americans, "Our country is in danger, but not to be despaired of . . . On you depend the fortunes of America. You are to decide the important questions upon which rests the happiness and the liberty of millions yet unborn. Act worthy of yourselves." Well, I believe we, the Americans of today, are ready to act worthy of ourselves, ready to do what must be done to ensure happiness and liberty for ourselves, our children, and our children's children. And as we renew ourselves here in our own land, we will be seen as having greater strength throughout the world. We will again be the exemplar of freedom and a beacon of hope for those who do not now have freedom.

To those neighbors and allies who share our freedom, we will strengthen our historic ties and assure them of our support and firm commitment. We will match loyalty with loyalty. We will strive for mutually beneficial relations. We will not use our friendship to impose on their sovereignty, for our own sovereignty is not for sale. As for the enemies of freedom, those who are potential adversaries, they will be reminded that peace is the highest aspiration of the American people. We will negotiate for it, sacrifice for it; we will not surrender for it, now or ever.

Our forbearance should never be misunderstood. Our reluctance for conflict should not be misjudged as a failure of will. When action is required to preserve our national security, we will act. We will maintain sufficient strength to prevail if need be, knowing that if we do so we have the best chance of never having to use that strength. Above all, we must realize that no arsenal or no weapon in the arsenals of the world is so formidable as the will and moral courage of free men

and women. It is a weapon our adversaries in today's world do not have. It is a weapon that we as Americans do have. Let that be understood by those who practice terrorism and prey upon their neighbors. I'm told that tens of thousands of prayer meetings are being held on this day, and for that I'm deeply grateful. We are a nation under God, and I believe God intended for us to be free. It would be fitting and good, I think, if on each Inaugural Day in future years it should be declared a day of prayer.

This is the first time in our history that this ceremony has been held, as you've been told, on the West Front of the Capitol. Standing here, one faces a magnificent vista, opening up on the city's special beauty and history. At the end of this open mall are those shrines to the giants on whose shoulders we stand.

Directly in front of me, the monument to a monumental man, George Washington, father of our country. A man of humility who came to greatness reluctantly. He led Americans out of revolutionary victory into infant nationhood. Off to one side, the stately memorial to Thomas Jefferson. The Declaration of Independence flames with his eloquence. And then, beyond the Reflecting Pool, the dignified columns of the Lincoln Memorial. Whoever would understand in his heart the meaning of America will find it in the life of Abraham Lincoln.

Beyond those monuments to heroism is the Potomac River, and on the far shore the sloping hills of Arlington National Cemetery, with its row upon row of simple white markers bearing crosses and Stars of David. They add up to only a tiny fraction of the price that has been paid for our freedom. Each one of those markers is a monument to the kind of hero I spoke of earlier. Their lives ended in places called Belleau Wood, the Argonne, Omaha Beach, Salerno, and halfway around the world on Guadalcanal, Tarawa, Pork Chop Hill, the Chosin Reservoir, and in a hundred rice paddies and jungles of a place called Vietnam.

Under one such marker lies a young man, Martin Treptow, who left his job in a small town barbershop in 1917 to go to France with the famed Rainbow Division. There, on the western front, he was killed trying to carry a message between battalions under heavy artillery fire.

We're told that on his body was found a diary. On the flyleaf under the heading "My Pledge," he had written these words: "America must win this war. Therefore I will work, I will save, I will sacrifice, I will endure, I will fight cheerfully and do my utmost, as if the issue of the whole struggle depended on me alone."

The crisis we are facing today does not require of us the kind of sacrifice that Martin Treptow and so many thousands of others were called upon to make. It does require, however, our best effort and our willingness to believe in ourselves and to believe in our capacity to perform great deeds, to believe that together with God's help we can and will resolve the problems which now confront us.

And after all, why shouldn't we believe that? We are Americans.

God bless you, and thank you.

BARACK OBAMA'S FIRST INAUGURAL ADDRESS (2009)

My fellow citizens: I stand here today humbled by the task before us, grateful for the trust you've bestowed, mindful of the sacrifices borne by our ancestors.

I thank President Bush for his service to our nation—(*applause*)—as well as the generosity and cooperation he has shown throughout this transition.

Forty-four Americans have now taken the presidential oath. The words have been spoken during rising tides of prosperity and the still waters of peace. Yet, every so often, the oath is taken amidst gathering clouds and raging storms. At these moments, America has carried on not simply because of the skill or vision of those in high office, but because we, the people, have remained faithful to the ideals of our forebears and true to our founding documents.

So it has been: so it must be with this generation of Americans.

That we are in the midst of crisis is now well understood. Our nation is at war against a far-reaching network of violence and hatred. Our economy is badly weakened, a consequence of greed and irresponsibility on the part of some, but also our collective failure to make hard choices and prepare the nation for a new age. Homes have been lost, jobs shed, businesses shuttered. Our health care is too costly, our schools fail too many—and each day brings further evidence that the ways we use energy strengthen our adversaries and threaten our planet.

These are the indicators of crisis, subject to data and statistics. Less measurable, but no less profound, is a sapping of confidence across our land; a nagging fear that America's decline is inevilable, that the next generation must lower its sights.

Today I say to you that the challenges we face are real. They are serious and they are many. They will not be met easily or in a short span of time. But know this America: They will be met. (*Applause*)

On this day, we gather because we have chosen hope over fear, unity of purpose over conflict and discord. On this day, we come to proclaim an end to the petty grievances and false promises, the recriminations and worn-out dogmas that for far too long have strangled our politics. We remain a young nation. But in the words of Scripture, the time has come to set aside childish things. The time has come to reaffirm our enduring spirit; to choose our better history; to carry forward that precious gift, that noble idea passed on from generation to generation; the God-given promise that all are equal, all are free, and all deserve a chance to pursue their full measure of happiness. (*Applause*)

In reaffirming the greatness of our nation we understand that greatness is never a given. It must be earned. Our journey has never been one of short-cuts or settling for less. It has not been the path for the faint-hearted, for those that prefer leisure over work, or seek only the pleasures of riches and fame. Rather, it has been the risk-takers, the doers, the makers of things—some celebrated, but more often men and women obscure in their labor—who have carried us up the long rugged path towards prosperity and freedom.

For us, they packed up their few worldly possessions and traveled across oceans in search of a new life. For us, they toiled in sweatshops, and settled the West, endured the lash of the whip, and plowed the hard earth. For us, they fought and died in places like Concord and Gettysburg, Normandy and Khe Sahn.

Time and again these men and women struggled and sacrificed and worked till their hands were raw so that we might live a better life. They saw America as bigger than the sum of our individual ambitions, greater than all the differences of birth or wealth or faction.

This is the journey we continue today. We remain the most prosperous, powerful nation on Earth. Our workers are no less productive than when this crisis began. Our minds are no less inventive, our goods and services no less needed than they were last week, or last month, or last year. Our capacity remains undiminished. But our time of standing pat, of protecting narrow interests and putting off unpleasant decisions—that time has surely passed. Starting today, we must pick ourselves up, dust ourselves off, and begin again the work of remaking America. (*Applause*)

For everywhere we look, there is work to be done. The state of our economy calls for action, bold and swift. And we will act, not only to create new jobs, but to lay a new foundation for growth. We will build the roads and bridges, the electric grids and digital lines that feed our commerce and bind us together. We'll restore science to its rightful place, and wield technology's wonders to raise health care's quality and lower its cost. We will harness the sun and the winds and the soil to fuel our cars and run our factories. And we will transform our schools and colleges and universities to meet the demands of a new age. All this we can do. All this we will do.

Now, there are some who question the scale of our ambitions, who suggest that our system cannot tolerate too many big plans. Their memories are short, for they have forgotten what this country has already done, what free men and women can achieve when imagination is joined to common purpose, and necessity to courage. What the cynics fail to understand is that the ground has shifted beneath them, that the stale political arguments that have consumed us for so long no longer apply.

The question we ask today is not whether our government is too big or too small, but whether it works—whether it helps families find jobs at a decent wage, care they can afford, a retirement that is dignified. Where the answer is yes, we intend to move forward. Where the answer is no, programs will end. And those of us who manage the public's dollars will be held to account, to spend wisely, reform bad habits, and do our business in the light of day, because only then can we restore the vital trust between a people and their government.

Nor is the question before us whether the market is a force for good or ill. Its power to generate wealth and expand freedom is unmatched. But this crisis has reminded us that without a watchful eye, the market can spin out of control. The nation cannot prosper long when it favors only the prosperous. The success of our economy has always depended not just on the size of our gross domestic product, but on the reach of our prosperity, on the ability to extend opportunity to every willing heart—not out of charity, but because it is the surest route to our common good. (*Applause*)

As for our common defense, we reject as false the choice between our safety and our ideals. Our Founding Fathers—(*Applause*)—our Founding Fathers, faced with perils that we can scarcely imagine, drafted a charter to assure the rule of law and the rights of man—a charter expanded by the blood of generations. Those ideals still light the world, and we will not give them up for expedience sake. (*Applause*)

And so, to all the other peoples and governments who are watching today, from the grandest capitals to the small village where my father was born, know that America is a friend of each nation, and every man, woman and child who seeks a future of peace and dignity. And we are ready to lead once more. (*Applause*)

Recall that earlier generations faced down fascism and communism not just with missiles and tanks, but with the sturdy alliances and enduring convictions. They understood that our power alone cannot protect us, nor does it entitle us to do as we please. Instead they knew that our power grows through its prudent use; our security emanates from the justness of our cause, the force of our example, the tempering qualities of humility and restraint.

We are the keepers of this legacy. Guided by these principles once more we can meet those new threats that demand even greater effort, even greater cooperation and understanding between nations. We will begin to responsibly leave Iraq to its people and forge a hard-earned peace in Afghanistan. With old friends and former foes, we'll work tirelessly to lessen the nuclear threat, and roll back the specter of a warming planet.

We will not apologize for our way of life, nor will we waver in its defense. And for those who seek to advance their aims by inducing terror and slaughtering innocents, we say to you now that our spirit is stronger and cannot be broken—you cannot outlast us, and we will defeat you. (*Applause*)

For we know that our patchwork heritage is a strength, not a weakness. We are a nation of Christians and Muslims, Jews and Hindus, and non-believers. We are shaped by every language and culture, drawn from every end of this Earth; and because we have tasted the bitter swill of civil war and segregation, and emerged from that dark chapter stronger and more united, we cannot help but believe that the old hatreds shall someday pass; that the lines of tribe shall soon dissolve; that as the world grows smaller, our common humanity shall reveal itself; and that America must play its role in ushering in a new era of peace.

To the Muslim world, we seek a new way forward, based on mutual interest and mutual respect. To those leaders around the globe who seek to sow conflict, or blame their society's ills on the West, know that your people will judge you on what you can build, not what you destroy. (*Applause*)

To those who cling to power through corruption and deceit and the silencing of dissent, know that you are on the wrong side of history, but that we will extend a hand if you are willing to unclench your fist. (*Applause*)

To the people of poor nations, we pledge to work alongside you to make your farms flourish and let clean waters flow; to nourish starved bodies and feed hungry minds. And to those nations like ours that enjoy relative plenty, we say we can no longer afford indifference to the suffering outside our borders, nor can we consume the world's resources without regard to effect. For the world has changed, and we must change with it.

As we consider the role that unfolds before us, we remember with humble gratitude those brave Americans who at this very hour patrol far-off deserts and distant mountains. They have something to tell us, just as the fallen heroes who lie in Arlington whisper through the ages.

We honor them not only because they are the guardians of our liberty, but because they embody the spirit of service—a willingness to find meaning in something greater than themselves.

And yet at this moment, a moment that will define a generation, it is precisely this spirit that must inhabit us all. For as much as government can do, and must do, it is ultimately the faith and determination of the American people upon which this nation relies. It is the kindness to take in a stranger when the levees break, the selflessness of workers who would rather cut their hours than see a friend lose their job which sees us through our darkest hours. It is the firefighter's courage to storm a stairway filled with smoke, but also a parent's willingness to nurture a child that finally decides our fate.

Our challenges may be new. The instruments with which we meet them may be new. But those values upon which our success depends—honesty and hard work, courage and fair play, tolerance and curiosity, loyalty and patriotism—these things are old. These things are true. They have been the quiet force of progress throughout our history.

What is demanded, then, is a return to these truths. What is required of us now is a new era of responsibility—a recognition on the part of every American that we have duties to ourselves, our nation and the world; duties that we do not grudgingly accept, but rather seize gladly, firm in the knowledge that there is nothing so satisfying to the spirit, so defining of our character than giving our all to a difficult task.

This is the price and the promise of citizenship. This is the source of our confidence—the knowledge that God calls on us to shape an uncertain destiny. This is the meaning of our liberty and our creed, why men and women and children of every race and every faith can join in celebration across this magnificent mall; and why a man whose father less than 60 years ago might not have been served in a local restaurant can now stand before you to take a most sacred oath. (*Applause*)

So let us mark this day with remembrance of who we are and how far we have traveled. In the year of America's birth, in the coldest of months, a small band of patriots huddled by dying campfires on the shores of an icy river. The capital was abandoned. The enemy was advancing. The snow was stained with blood. At the moment when the outcome of our revolution was most in doubt, the father of our nation ordered these words to be read to the people:

"Let it be told to the future world . . . that in the depth of winter, when nothing but hope and virtue could survive . . . that the city and the country, alarmed at one common danger, came forth to meet [it]."

America: In the face of our common dangers, in this winter of our hardship, let us remember these timeless words. With hope and virtue, let us brave once more the icy currents, and endure what storms may come. Let it be said by our children's children that when we were tested we refused to let this journey end, that we did not turn back nor did we falter; and with eyes fixed on the horizon and God's grace upon us, we carried forth that great gift of freedom and delivered it safely to future generations.

Thank you. God bless you. And God bless the United States of America. (*Applause*)

PRESIDENTIAL ELECTIONS

Year	Number of States	Candidates	Parties	Popular Vote	% of Popular Vote	Electoral Vote	% Voter Participation
1789	11	**GEORGE WASHINGTON**	NO PARTY			69	
		John Adams	DESIGNATIONS			34	
		Other candidates				35	
1792	15	**GEORGE WASHINGTON**	NO PARTY			132	
		John Adams	DESIGNATIONS			77	
		George Clinton				50	
		Other candidates				5	
1796	16	**JOHN ADAMS**	FEDERALIST			71	
		Thomas Jefferson	Republican			68	
		Thomas Pinckney	Federalist			59	
		Aaron Burr	Republican			30	
		Other candidates				48	
1800	16	**THOMAS JEFFERSON**	REPUBLICAN			73	
		Aaron Burr	Republican			73	
		John Adams	Federalist			65	
		Charles C. Pinckney	Federalist			64	
		John Jay	Federalist			1	
1804	17	**THOMAS JEFFERSON**	REPUBLICAN			162	
		Charles C. Pinckney	Federalist			14	
1808	17	**JAMES MADISON**	REPUBLICAN			122	
		Charles C. Pinckney	Federalist			47	
		George Clinton	Republican			6	
1812	18	**JAMES MADISON**	REPUBLICAN			128	
		DeWitt Clinton	Federalist			89	

Year	Number of States	Candidates	Parties	Popular Vote	% of Popular Vote	Electoral Vote	% Voter Participation
1816	19	**JAMES MONROE**	REPUBLICAN			183	
		Rufus King	Federalist			34	
1820	24	**JAMES MONROE**	REPUBLICAN			231	
		John Quincy Adams	Independent			1	
1824	24	**JOHN QUINCY ADAMS**	NO PARTY	108,740	31.0	84	26.9
		Andrew Jackson	DESIGNATIONS	153,544	43.0	99	
		William H. Crawford		46,618	13.0	41	
		Henry Clay		47,136	13.0	37	
1828	24	**ANDREW JACKSON**	DEMOCRAT	647,286	56.0	178	57.6
		John Quincy Adams	National Republican	508,064	44.0	83	
1832	24	**ANDREW JACKSON**	DEMOCRAT	687,502	54.5	219	55.4
		Henry Clay	National Republican	530,189	37.5	49	
		William Wirt	Anti-Masonic	101,051	8.0	7	
		John Floyd	Democrat			11	
1836	26	**MARTIN VAN BUREN**	DEMOCRAT	765,483	51.0	170	57.8
		William H. Harrison	Whig			73	
		Hugh L. White	Whig	739,795	49.0	26	
		Daniel Webster	Whig			14	
		William P. Mangum	Whig			11	
1840	26	**WILLIAM H. HARRISON**	WHIG	1,274,624	53.0	234	80.2
		Martin Van Buren	Democrat	1,127,781	47.0	60	

Year	Number of States	Candidates	Parties	Popular Vote	% of Popular Vote	Electoral Vote	% Voter Participation
1844	26	**JAMES K. POLK**	DEMOCRAT	1,338,464	50.0	170	78.9
		Henry Clay	Whig	1,300,097	48.0	105	
		James G. Birney	Liberty	62,300	2.0		
1848	30	**ZACHARY TAYLOR**	WHIG	1,360,967	47.5	163	72.7
		Lewis Cass	Democrat	1,222,342	42.5	127	
		Martin Van Buren	Free Soil	291,263	10.0		
1852	31	**FRANKLIN PIERCE**	DEMOCRAT	1,601,117	51.0	254	69.6
		Winfield Scott	Whig	1,385,453	44.0	42	
		John P. Hale	Free Soil	155,825	5.0		
1856	31	**JAMES BUCHANAN**	DEMOCRAT	1,832,955	45.0	174	78.9
		John C. Frémont	Republican	1,339,932	33.0	114	
		Millard Fillmore	American	871,731	22.0	8	
1860	33	**ABRAHAM LINCOLN**	REPUBLICAN	1,865,593	40.0	180	81.2
		Stephen A. Douglas	Northern Democrat	1,382,713	29.0	12	
		John C. Breckinridge	Southern Democrat	848,356	18.0	72	
		John Bell	Constitutional Union	592,906	13.0	39	
1864	36	**ABRAHAM LINCOLN**	REPUBLICAN	2,206,938	55.0	212	73.8
		George B. McClellan	Democrat	1,803,787	45.0	21	
1868	37	**ULYSSES S. GRANT**	REPUBLICAN	3,013,421	53.0	214	78.1
		Horatio Seymour	Democrat	2,706,829	47.0	80	

Year	Number of States	Candidates	Parties	Popular Vote	% of Popular Vote	Electoral Vote	% Voter Participation
1872	37	**ULYSSES S. GRANT**	REPUBLICAN	3,596,745	55.6	286	71.3
		Horace Greeley	Democrat	2,843,446	43.9	66	
1876	38	**RUTHERFORD B. HAYES**	REPUBLICAN	4,036,572	48.0	185	81.8
		Samuel J. Tilden	Democrat	4,284,020	51.0	184	
1880	38	**JAMES A. GARFIELD**	REPUBLICAN	4,453,295	48.4	214	79.4
		Winfield S. Hancock	Democrat	4,414,082	48.3	155	
		James B. Weaver	Greenback-Labor	308,578	3.5		
1884	38	**GROVER CLEVELAND**	DEMOCRAT	4,879,507	48.5	219	77.5
		James G. Blaine	Republican	4,850,293	48.2	182	
		Benjamin F. Butler	Greenback-Labor	175,370	1.8		
		John P. St. John	Prohibition	150,369	1.5		
1888	38	**BENJAMIN HARRISON**	REPUBLICAN	5,447,129	47.9	233	79.3
		Grover Cleveland	Democrat	5,537,857	48.6	168	
		Clinton B. Fisk	Prohibition	249,506	2.2		
		Anson J. Streeter	Union Labor	146,935	1.3		
1892	44	**GROVER CLEVELAND**	DEMOCRAT	5,555,426	46.1	277	74.7
		Benjamin Harrison	Republican	5,182,690	43.0	145	
		James B. Weaver	People's	1,029,846	8.5	22	
		John Bidwell	Prohibition	264,133	2.2		
1896	45	**WILLIAM McKINLEY**	REPUBLICAN	7,102,246	51.0	271	79.3
		William J. Bryan	Democrat	6,492,559	47.0	176	

Year	Number of States	Candidates	Parties	Popular Vote	% of Popular Vote	Electoral Vote	% Voter Participation
1900	45	**WILLIAM McKINLEY**	REPUBLICAN	7,218,491	52.0	292	73.2
		William J. Bryan	Democrat; Populist	6,356,734	46.0	155	
		John C. Wooley	Prohibition	208,914	1.5		
1904	45	**THEODORE ROOSEVELT**	REPUBLICAN	7,628,461	56.4	336	65.2
		Alton B. Parker	Democrat	5,084,223	37.6	140	
		Eugene V. Debs	Socialist	402,283	3.0		
		Silas C. Swallow	Prohibition	258,536	1.9		
1908	46	**WILLIAM H. TAFT**	REPUBLICAN	7,675,320	52.0	321	65.4
		William J. Bryan	Democrat	6,412,294	43.4	162	
		Eugene V. Debs	Socialist	420,793	2.8		
		Eugene W. Chafin	Prohibition	253,840	1.7		
1912	48	**WOODROW WILSON**	DEMOCRAT	6,296,547	41.9	435	58.8
		Theodore Roosevelt	Progressive	4,118,571	27.4	88	
		William H. Taft	Republican	3,486,720	23.2	8	
		Eugene V. Debs	Socialist	900,672	6.0		
		Eugene W. Chafin	Prohibition	206,275	1.4		
1916	48	**WOODROW WILSON**	DEMOCRAT	9,127,695	49.4	277	61.6
		Charles E. Hughes	Republican	8,533,507	46.2	254	
		A. L. Benson	Socialist	585,113	3.2		
		J. Frank Hanly	Prohibition	220,506	1.2		
1920	48	**WARREN G. HARDING**	REPUBLICAN	16,153,115	60.6	404	49.2
		James M. Cox	Democrat	9,133,092	34.3	127	
		Eugene V. Debs	Socialist	915,490	3.4		
		P. P. Christensen	Farmer-Labor	265,229	1.0		
1924	48	**CALVIN COOLIDGE**	REPUBLICAN	15,719,921	54.0	382	48.9
		John W. Davis	Democrat	8,386,704	29.0	136	
		Robert M. La Follette	Progressive	4,832,532	16.5	13	

Year	Number of States	Candidates	Parties	Popular Vote	% of Popular Vote	Electoral Vote	% Voter Participation
1928	48	**HERBERT C. HOOVER**	REPUBLICAN	21,437,277	58.2	444	56.9
		Alfred E. Smith	Democrat	15,007,698	40.9	87	
1932	48	**FRANKLIN D. ROOSEVELT**	DEMOCRAT	22,829,501	57.7	472	56.9
		Herbert C. Hoover	Republican	15,760,684	39.8	59	
		Norman Thomas	Socialist	884,649	2.2		
1936	48	**FRANKLIN D. ROOSEVELT**	DEMOCRAT	27,757,333	60.8	523	61.0
		Alfred M. Landon	Republican	16,684,231	36.6	8	
		William Lemke	Union	892,267	2.0		
1940	48	**FRANKLIN D. ROOSEVELT**	DEMOCRAT	27,313,041	54.9	449	62.5
		Wendell L. Willkie	Republican	22,348,480	44.9	82	
1944	48	**FRANKLIN D. ROOSEVELT**	DEMOCRAT	25,612,610	53.5	432	55.9
		Thomas E. Dewey	Republican	22,017,617	46.0	99	
1948	48	**HARRY S. TRUMAN**	DEMOCRAT	24,179,345	49.7	303	53.0
		Thomas E. Dewey	Republican	21,991,291	45.3	189	
		J. Strom Thurmond	States' Rights	1,176,125	2.4	39	
		Henry A. Wallace	Progressive	1,157,326	2.4		
1952	48	**DWIGHT D. EISENHOWER**	REPUBLICAN	33,936,234	55.1	442	63.3
		Adlai E. Stevenson	Democrat	27,314,992	44.4	89	

Year	Number of States	Candidates	Parties	Popular Vote	% of Popular Vote	Electoral Vote	% Voter Participation
1956	48	**DWIGHT D. EISENHOWER**	REPUBLICAN	35,590,472	57.6	457	60.6
		Adlai E. Stevenson	Democrat	26,022,752	42.1	73	
1960	50	**JOHN F. KENNEDY**	DEMOCRAT	34,226,731	49.7	303	62.8
		Richard M. Nixon	Republican	34,108,157	49.6	219	
1964	50	**LYNDON B. JOHNSON**	DEMOCRAT	43,129,566	61.0	486	61.9
		Barry M. Goldwater	Republican	27,178,188	38.4	52	
1968	50	**RICHARD M. NIXON**	REPUBLICAN	31,785,480	43.2	301	60.9
		Hubert H. Humphrey	Democrat	31,275,166	42.6	191	
		George C. Wallace	American Independent	9,906,473	12.9	46	
1972	50	**RICHARD M. NIXON**	REPUBLICAN	47,169,911	60.7	520	55.2
		George S. McGovern	Democrat	29,170,383	37.5	17	
		John G. Schmitz	American	1,099,482	1.4		
1976	50	**JIMMY CARTER**	DEMOCRAT	40,830,763	50.0	297	53.5
		Gerald R. Ford	Republican	39,147,793	48.0	240	
1980	50	**RONALD REAGAN**	REPUBLICAN	43,904,153	50.9	489	52.6
		Jimmy Carter	Democrat	35,483,883	41.1	49	
		John B. Anderson	Independent	5,720,060	6.6		
		Ed Clark	Libertarian	921,299	1.1		

Year	Number of States	Candidates	Parties	Popular Vote	% of Popular Vote	Electoral Vote	% Voter Participation
1984	50	**RONALD REAGAN**	REPUBLICAN	54,455,075	58.8	525	53.1
		Walter F. Mondale	Democrat	37,577,185	40.5	13	
1988	50	**GEORGE H. BUSH**	REPUBLICAN	48,886,097	53.4	426	50.1
		Michael Dukakis	Democrat	41,809,074	45.6	111	
1992	50	**BILL CLINTON**	DEMOCRAT	44,909,326	42.9	370	55.0
		George H. Bush	Republican	39,103,882	37.4	168	
		H. Ross Perot	Independent	19,741,657	18.9		
1996	50	**BILL CLINTON**	DEMOCRAT	47,402,357	49.2	379	49.0
		Bob Dole	Republican	39,198,755	40.7	159	
		H. Ross Perot	Reform Party	8,085,402	8.4		
2000	50	**GEORGE W. BUSH**	REPUBLICAN	50,455,156	47.9	271	50.4
		Albert Gore	Democrat	50,992,335	48.4	266	
		Ralph Nader	Green Party	2,882,738	2.7		
2004	50	**GEORGE W. BUSH**	REPUBLICAN	62,040,610	50.7	286	56.2
		John F. Kerry	Democrat	59,028,111	48.3	251	
2008	50	**BARACK H. OBAMA**	DEMOCRAT	66,882,230	53	365	56.8
		John S. McCain	Republican	58,343,671	46	173	
2012	50	**BARACK H. OBAMA**	DEMOCRAT	62,611,250	51	332	53.6
		W. Mitt Romney	Republican	59,134,475	48	206	

ADMISSION OF STATES

Order of Admission	State	Date of Admission	Order of Admission	State	Date of Admission
1	Delaware	December 7, 1787	26	Michigan	January 26, 1837
2	Pennsylvania	December 12, 1787	27	Florida	March 3, 1845
3	New Jersey	December 18, 1787	28	Texas	December 29, 1845
4	Georgia	January 2, 1788	29	Iowa	December 28, 1846
5	Connecticut	January 9, 1788	30	Wisconsin	May 29, 1848
6	Massachusetts	February 7, 1788	31	California	September 9, 1850
7	Maryland	April 28, 1788	32	Minnesota	May 11, 1858
8	South Carolina	May 23, 1788	33	Oregon	February 14, 1859
9	New Hampshire	June 21, 1788	34	Kansas	January 29, 1861
10	Virginia	June 25, 1788	35	West Virginia	June 30, 1863
11	New York	July 26, 1788	36	Nevada	October 31, 1864
12	North Carolina	November 21, 1789	37	Nebraska	March 1, 1867
13	Rhode Island	May 29, 1790	38	Colorado	August 1, 1876
14	Vermont	March 4, 1791	39	North Dakota	November 2, 1889
15	Kentucky	June 1, 1792	40	South Dakota	November 2, 1889
16	Tennessee	June 1, 1796	41	Montana	November 8, 1889
17	Ohio	March 1, 1803	42	Washington	November 11, 1889
18	Louisiana	April 30, 1812	43	Idaho	July 3, 1890
19	Indiana	December 11, 1816	44	Wyoming	July 10, 1890
20	Mississippi	December 10, 1817	45	Utah	January 4, 1896
21	Illinois	December 3, 1818	46	Oklahoma	November 16, 1907
22	Alabama	December 14, 1819	47	New Mexico	January 6, 1912
23	Maine	March 15, 1820	48	Arizona	February 14, 1912
24	Missouri	August 10, 1821	49	Alaska	January 3, 1959
25	Arkansas	June 15, 1836	50	Hawaii	August 21, 1959

POPULATION OF THE UNITED STATES

Year	Number of States	Population	% Increase	Population per Square Mile
1790	13	3,929,214		4.5
1800	16	5,308,483	35.1	6.1
1810	17	7,239,881	36.4	4.3
1820	23	9,638,453	33.1	5.5
1830	24	12,866,020	33.5	7.4
1840	26	17,069,453	32.7	9.8
1850	31	23,191,876	35.9	7.9
1860	33	31,443,321	35.6	10.6
1870	37	39,818,449	26.6	13.4
1880	38	50,155,783	26.0	16.9
1890	44	62,947,714	25.5	21.1
1900	45	75,994,575	20.7	25.6
1910	46	91,972,266	21.0	31.0
1920	48	105,710,620	14.9	35.6
1930	48	122,775,046	16.1	41.2
1940	48	131,669,275	7.2	44.2
1950	48	150,697,361	14.5	50.7
1960	50	179,323,175	19.0	50.6
1970	50	203,235,298	13.3	57.5
1980	50	226,504,825	11.4	64.0
1985	50	237,839,000	5.0	67.2
1990	50	250,122,000	5.2	70.6
1995	50	263,411,707	5.3	74.4
2000	50	281,421,906	6.8	77.0
2005	50	296,410,404	5.3	81.7
2010	50	308,745,538	4.2	87.4

LABOR FORCE—SELECTED CHARACTERISTICS EXPRESSED AS A PERCENTAGE OF THE LABOR FORCE: 1800–2000

Year	Agriculture	Manufacturing	Domestic service	Clerical, sales, and service	Professions	Slave	Nonwhite	Foreign-born	Female
1800	74.4	—	2.4	—	—	30.2	32.6	—	21.4
1860	55.8	13.8	5.4	4.8[1]	3.0[1]	21.7	23.6	24.5[1]	19.6
1910	30.7	20.8	5.5	14.1	4.7	—	13.4	22.0	20.8
1950	12.0	26.4	2.5	27.3	8.9	—	10.0	8.7	27.9
2000	2.4	14.7	0.6	38.0[2]	15.6	—	16.5	10.3[2]	46.6
2010	1.6	10.1	1.6	40.2	22.2	—	18.7	15.8	46.7

[1]Values for 1870 are presented here because the available data for 1860 exclude slaves.
[2]1990.

IMMIGRATION, BY ORIGIN (in thousands)

Period	Europe	Americas	Asia
1820–30	106	12	—
1831–40	496	33	—
1841–50	1,597	62	—
1851–60	2,453	75	42
1861–70	2,065	167	65
1871–80	2,272	404	70
1881–90	4,735	427	70
1891–1900	3,555	39	75
1901–10	8,065	362	324
1911–20	4,322	1,144	247
1921–30	2,463	1,517	112
1931–40	348	160	16
1941–50	621	355	32
1951–60	1,326	997	150
1961–70	1,123	1,716	590
1971–80	800	1,983	1,588
1981–90	762	3,616	2,738
1991–2000	1,100	3,800	2,200

UNEMPLOYMENT RATE, 1890–2013

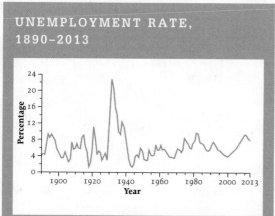

UNION MEMBERSHIP AS A PERCENTAGE OF NONAGRICULTURAL EMPLOYMENT, 1880–2012

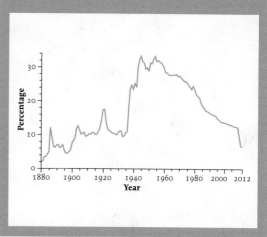

VOTER PARTICIPATION IN PRESIDENTIAL ELECTIONS, 1824–2012

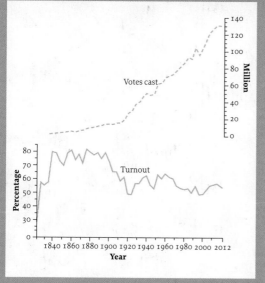

BIRTHRATE, 1820–2011

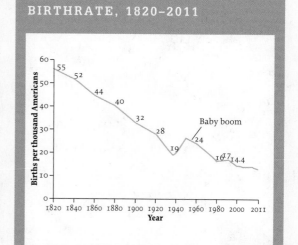

SUGGESTED READING

CHAPTER 1: A NEW WORLD

Books

Bender, Thomas. *A Nation among Nations: America's Place in World History* (2006). Attempts to place American history in an international context; the opening chapters offer a global portrait of the age of exploration and conquest.

Crosby, Alfred J. *The Columbian Exchange: Biological and Cultural Consequences of 1492* (1972). Examines the flow of goods and diseases across the Atlantic and their consequences.

Elliott, J. H. *Empires of the Atlantic World: Britain and Spain in America 1492–1830* (2006). A fascinating comparison of the development of two New World empires.

Fernández-Armesto, Felipe. *Pathfinders: A Global History of Exploration* (2006). A history of explorations throughout the centuries, including those of the fifteenth and sixteenth centuries.

Gutiérrez, Ramón A. *When Jesus Came, the Corn Mothers Went Away: Marriage, Sexuality, and Power in New Mexico, 1500–1846* (1991). Discusses the changes in Indian life in New Mexico as a result of Spanish colonization.

Mann, Charles C. *1491: New Revelations of the Americas before Columbus* (2005). A comprehensive portrait of life in the Western Hemisphere before the arrival of Europeans.

Richter, Daniel K. *Facing East from Indian Country* (2001). Examines the era of exploration and settlement as viewed through the experience of Native Americans.

Websites

Archive of Early American Images: www.brown.edu/Facilities/John_Carter_ Brown_ Library/pages/ea_hmpg.html

Exploring the Early Americas: www.loc.gov/exhibits/earlyamericas/

France in America: http://international.loc.gov/intldl/fiahtml/fiahome.html

Jamestown, Québec, Santa Fe: Three North American Beginnings: http://american history.si.edu/exhibitions/small _exhibition.cfm?key=1267&exkey=244

CHAPTER 2: BEGINNINGS OF ENGLISH AMERICA, 1607–1660

Books

Anderson, Victoria D. *New England's Generation: The Great Migration and the Formation of Society and Culture in the Seventeenth Century* (1991). A careful study of emigration from England to New England.

Brown, Kathleen. *Good Wives, Nasty Wenches, and Anxious Patriarchs: Gender, Race, and Power in Colonial Virginia* (1996). A pioneering study of gender relations and their impact on Virginia society.

Cronon, William. *Changes in the Land: Colonists and the Ecology of New England* (1983). A path-breaking examination of how English colonization affected the natural environment in New England.

Gleach, Frederic W. *Powhatan's World and Colonial Virginia: A Conflict of Cultures* (1997). A study of Indian culture and the impact of European colonization on it.

Pestana, Carla G. *The English Atlantic in an Age of Revolution, 1640–1661* (2001). Analyzes how the English Civil War reverberated in the American colonies.

Philbrick, Nathaniel. *Mayflower* (2006). An account of one of the most celebrated voyages of the colonial era, and the early history of the Plymouth colony.

Taylor, Alan. *American Colonies* (2001). A comprehensive survey of the history of North American colonies from their beginnings to 1763.

Websites

Plymouth Colony Archive Project: www.histarch.uiuc.edu/plymouth/index.html

Virtual Jamestown: www.virtualjamestown.org

CHAPTER 3: CREATING ANGLO-AMERICA, 1660–1750

Books

Bailyn, Bernard. *The Peopling of British North America* **(1986).** A brief survey of the movement of peoples across the Atlantic.

Berlin, Ira. *Many Thousands Gone: The First Two Centuries of Slavery in North America* (1998). The most extensive study of the origins and development of colonial slavery.

Lemon, James T. *The Best Poor Man's Country: A Geographical Study of Early Southeastern Pennsylvania* (1972). A study of agriculture and the environment in one of the most successful farming areas of colonial America.

Lepore, Jill. *The Name of War: King Philip's War and the Origin of American Identity* (1998). An examination not only of the war itself but also of its long-term consequences for Indian-white relations.

Mintz, Sidney. *Sweetness and Power: The Place of Sugar in Modern History* (1985). A global history of the significance of sugar in the making of the modern world.

Morgan, Edmund S. *American Slavery, American Freedom: The Ordeal of Colonial Virginia* (1975). An influential study of the slow development of slavery in seventeenth-century Virginia.

Norton, Mary Beth. *In the Devil's Snare: The Salem Witchcraft Crisis of 1692* (2002). A study of the witch trials that places them in the context of anxieties over Indian warfare on the Massachusetts frontier.

Saxton, Martha. *Being Good: Women's Moral Values in Early America* (2003). Examines social standards for women's behavior and how women tried to live up to them.

Websites

The Atlantic Slave Trade and Slave Life in the Americas: http://hitchcock.itc.virginia.edu/Slavery/index.php

Afro-Louisiana History and Genealogy: www.ibiblio.org/laslave/

CHAPTER 4: SLAVERY, FREEDOM, AND THE STRUGGLE FOR EMPIRE TO 1763

Books

Anderson, Fred. *Crucible of War: The Seven Years' War and the Fate of Empire in British North America, 1754–1766* (2000). A general history of the Seven Years' War and its consequences.

Clark, Charles E. *The Public Prints: The Newspaper in Anglo-American Culture, 1665–1740* (1994). Presents the early history of newspapers in colonial America.

Gomez, Michael A. *Exchanging Our Country Marks: The Transformation of African Identities in the Colonial and Antebellum South* (1998). The most detailed study of the process by which Africans became African-Americans.

Greene, Jack P. *The Quest for Power: The Lower Houses of Assembly in the Southern Royal Colonies, 1689–1776* (1963). A careful examination of how elected assemblies expanded their authority in the eighteenth-century South.

Noll, Mark. *The Rise of Evangelicalism: The Age of Edwards, Whitefield, and the Wesleys* (2004). Explores the Great Awakening on both sides of the Atlantic and its impact on religious life.

Rediker, Marcus. *The Slave Ship: A Human History* (2007). A fascinating and disturbing account of the Atlantic slave trade that focuses on the captains, sailors, and slaves aboard the slave ships.

White, Richard. *The Middle Ground: Indians, Empires, and Republics in the Great Lakes Region, 1650–1815* (1991). The book that developed the idea of a middle ground where Europeans and Indians both exercised authority.

Websites

Africans in America: www.pbs.org/wgbh/aia/

Web de Anza: http://anza.uoregon.edu

CHAPTER 5: THE AMERICAN REVOLUTION, 1763–1783

Books

Armitage, David. *The Declaration of Independence: A Global History* (2007). Traces the international impact of the Declaration of Independence in the years since it was written.

Bailyn, Bernard. *The Ideological Origins of the American Revolution* (1967). A classic study of the ideas that shaped the movement for independence.

Breen, T. H. *Marketplace of Revolution: How Consumer Politics Shaped American Independence* (2004). An examination of how the colonists' very dependence on British consumer goods led them to resent interference with trade.

Countryman, Edward. *The American Revolution* (rev. ed., 2002). A brief summary of the Revolution's causes, conduct, and consequences.

Foner, Eric. *Tom Paine and Revolutionary America* (1976). Examines the ideas of the era's greatest pamphleteer of revolution and how they contributed to the struggle for independence.

Nash, Gary. *The Urban Crucible: Social Change, Political Consciousness, and the Origins of the American Revolution* (1979). Explores how the social history of American cities contributed to the coming of the Revolution.

Royster, Charles. *A Revolutionary People at War: The Continental Army and American Character* (1979). A social history of the army and the impact of military service on American soldiers.

Websites

Declaring Independence: www.loc.gov/exhibits/declara/declara1.html

The American Revolution and Its Era: Maps and Charts of North America and the West Indies: http://memory.loc.gov/ammem/gmdhtml/armhtml/armhome.html

The Coming of the American Revolution: www.masshist.org/revolution/

CHAPTER 6: THE REVOLUTION WITHIN

Books

Berkin, Carol. *Revolutionary Mothers: Women in the Struggle for American Independence* (2005). Presents profiles of women who took part in the movement for independence.

Calloway, Colin. *The American Revolution in Indian Country* (1995). Examines how the Revolution affected Indians in each region of the United States.

Frey, Sylvia R. *Water from the Rock: Black Resistance in a Revolutionary Age* (1991). A study of the many ways blacks sought to gain freedom for themselves during the Revolution.

Hatch, Nathan O. *The Democratization of American Christianity* (1989). A comprehensive account of the Revolution's impact on religion, and its aftermath.

Kruman, Marc. *Between Authority and Liberty: State Constitution Making in Revolutionary America* (1997). The most detailed account of how state constitutions were changed during the era.

Schama, Simon. *Rough Crossing: Britain, the Slaves and the American Revolution* (2006). A detailed look at the experience of the thousands of slaves who escaped to British lines and their fate after the end of the War of Independence.

Taylor, Alan. *The Divided Ground: Indians, Settlers, and the Northern Borderland of the American Revolution* (2006). Examines the Revolution and its consequence in the Iroquois region of upstate New York.

Wood, Gordon. *The Radicalism of the American Revolution* (1992). An influential work that sees the Revolution as transforming a hierarchical society into a democratic one.

Websites

Creating the United States: http://myloc.gov/exhibitions/creatingtheus/Pages/ default.aspx

Religion and the Founding of the American Republic: www.loc.gov/exhibits/ religion/religion.html

The Geography of Slavery in Virginia: www2.vcdh.virginia.edu/gos/

CHAPTER 7: FOUNDING A NATION, 1783–1789

Books

Amar, Akhil Reed. *Bill of Rights: Creation and Reconstruction* (1998). Presents the history of the Bill of Rights from its ratification through the Reconstruction era.

Berkin, Carol. *A Brilliant Solution: Inventing the American Constitution* (2002). A lively account of the proceedings of the Constitutional Convention.

Cornell, Saul. *The Other Founders: Anti-Federalism and the Dissenting Tradition in America, 1788–1828* (1999). A careful examination of the ideas of those who opposed ratification of the Constitution.

MacLeod, Duncan J. *Slavery, Race, and the American Revolution* (1974). A British scholar's interpretation of the role of race and slavery in the revolutionary era.

Nedelsky, Jennifer. *Private Property and the Limits of American Constitutionalism* (1990). Analyzes how the protection of private property shaped the writing of the Constitution.

Rakove, Jack. *Original Meanings: Politics and Ideas in the Making of the Constitution* (1996). An influential interpretation of the ideas that went into the drafting of the Constitution.

Wood, Gordon S. *The Creation of the American Republic, 1776–1789* (1969). Presents the evolution of American political ideas and institutions from the Declaration of Independence to the ratification of the Constitution.

Websites

Creating the United States: http://myloc.gov/exhibitions/creatingtheus/Pages/ default.aspx

National Constitution Center www.constitutioncenter.org

CHAPTER 8: SECURING THE REPUBLIC, 1790–1815

Books

Appleby, Joyce. *Capitalism and a New Social Order: The Republican Vision of the 1790s* (1984). Explores how the Jeffersonians sought simultaneously to expand economic enterprise and equality of opportunity.

Hofstadter, Richard. *The Idea of a Party System: The Rise of Legitimate Opposition in the United States, 1780–1840* (1969). Considers how Americans began by rejecting the idea of organized political parties and ended up accepting their legitimacy.

Kerber, Linda K. *Women of the Republic: Intellect and Ideology in Revolutionary America* (1980). A study of prevailing ideas about women's place in the new republic.

McCoy, Drew. *The Elusive Republic: Political Economy in Jeffersonian America* (1980). An influential study of the economic and political outlooks and policies of Federalists and Jeffersonians.

Miller, John C. *Crisis in Freedom: The Alien and Sedition Acts* (1952). Examines how the Adams administration sought to use the power of the federal government to stifle dissent and the free press.

Rothman, Adam. *Slave Country: American Expansion and the Origins of the Deep South* (2005). A pioneering study of how the United States secured control of what are now the Gulf states, opening the door for the expansion of slavery.

Waldstreicher, David. *In the Midst of Perpetual Fetes: The Making of American Nationalism, 1776–1820* (1997). Explores how Americans celebrated and thought about their nation's independence in the years of the early republic.

Websites

Rivers, Edens, Empires: Lewis and Clark and the Revealing of America: www.loc.gov/exhibits/lewisandclark /lewisandclark.html

CHAPTER 9: THE MARKET REVOLUTION, 1800–1840

Books

Butler, Jon. *Awash in a Sea of Faith: Christianizing the American People* (1990). A history of American religion with emphasis on evangelical movements, including the Second Great Awakening.

Clark, Christopher. *The Roots of Rural Capitalism: Western Massachusetts, 1780–1860* (1990). Considers how the market revolution transformed economic and social life in one region of the North.

Dublin, Thomas. *Women at Work: The Transformation of Work in Lowell, Massachusetts, 1826–1860* (1975). A pioneering study of the working and nonworking lives of Lowell "factory girls."

Faragher, John M. *Sugar Creek: Life on the Illinois Prairie* (1986). Traces the growth of a frontier community from early settlement to market society.

Harris, Leslie. *In the Shadow of Slavery: African-Americans in New York City, 1626–1863* (2003). A study that emphasizes the exclusion of African-Americans from the economic opportunities offered by the market revolution.

Ryan, Mary P. *Cradle of the Middle Class: The Family in Oneida County, New York, 1790–1865* (1981). Examines how economic change helped to produce a new kind of middle-class family structure centered on women's dominance of the household.

Wilentz, Sean. *Chants Democratic: New York City and the Rise of the American Working Class, 1788–1850* (1984). A study of the early labor movement in one of its key centers in antebellum America.

Websites

American Transcendentalism Web: www.vcu.edu/engweb/transcendentalism/index.html

Erie Canal Time Machine: www.archives.nysed.gov/projects/eriecanal/

Women in America, 1820–1842: http://xroads.virginia.edu/~HYPER/ DETOC/fem/home.htm

CHAPTER 10: DEMOCRACY IN AMERICA, 1815–1840

Books

Ashworth, John. *"Agrarians" and "Aristocrats": Party Ideology in the United States, 1837–1846* (1983). A careful study of political ideas in the last years of Jacksonian politics, stressing increasing class divisions between the parties.

Freehling, William G. *Prelude to Civil War: The Nullification Controversy in South Carolina, 1816–1836* (1966). Still the standard account of the nullification crisis during Jackson's presidency.

Howe, Daniel W. *The Political Culture of the American Whigs* (1979). Illuminates the key ideas that held the Whig Party together.

Keyssar, Alexander. *The Right to Vote: The Contested History of Democracy in the United States* (2000). The most up-to-date history of the right to vote in America from the colonial era to the present.

Wallace, Anthony. *The Long, Bitter Trail: Andrew Jackson and the Indians* (1993). A brief history of Jackson's Indian policies, especially Indian Removal in the southern states.

Watson, Harry. *Liberty and Power: The Politics of Jacksonian America* (1990). A valuable brief account of the politics of the 1820s and 1830s.

Wilentz, Sean. *The Rise of American Democracy: Jefferson to Lincoln* (2005). A comprehensive history of democratic ideas and politics from the American Revolution to the Civil War.

Websites

Democracy in America, Alexis de Tocqueville: http://xroads.virginia.edu/~HYPER/DETOC/home.html

George Catlin and His Indian Gallery: http://americanart.si.edu/exhibitions/online/catlin/index.html

Legacy: Spain and the United States in the Age of Independence, 1763–1848: http://latino.si.edu/SpainLegacy/Archive/index.html

CHAPTER 11: THE PECULIAR INSTITUTION

Books

Berlin, Ira. *Slaves without Masters: The Free Negro in the Antebellum South* (1974). A careful study of the status of free blacks, stressing differences between the Upper and Lower South.

Davis, David Brion. *Inhuman Bondage: The Rise and Fall of Slavery in the New World* (2006). Places the history of slavery in the United States firmly in a hemispheric context.

Genovese, Eugene D. *Roll, Jordan, Roll: The World the Slaves Made* (1974). A classic study of the paternalist ethos and the culture that developed under slavery.

Gutman, Herbert G. *The Black Family in Slavery and Freedom* (1976). A pioneering examination of how slaves created and sustained families under the harsh conditions of slavery.

Johnson, Walter. *Soul by Soul: Life inside the Antebellum Slave Market* (1999). Considers the operations of the New Orleans slave market as a window into slavery as a whole.

Joyner, Charles D. *Down by the Riverside: A South Carolina Slave Community* (1984). Studies slave communities in coastal South Carolina, emphasizing the blend of African and American influences.

McCurry, Stephanie. *Masters of Small Worlds: Yeoman Households, Gender Relations, and the Political Culture of Antebellum South Carolina* (1995). Studies the lives of men and women in non-slaveholding families, to explore their links with the planter class.

Websites

Born in Slavery: Slave Narratives from the Federal Writers' Project: http://lcweb2.loc. gov/ammem/snhtml/snhome.html

Documenting the American South: http://docsouth.unc.edu

Gilder Lehrman Center for the Study of Slavery, Resistance, and Abolition: www.yale.edu/glc/index.htm

Slaves and the Courts, 1740–1860: http://memory.loc.gov/ammem/sthtml/sthome.html

CHAPTER 12: AN AGE OF REFORM, 1820–1840

Books

Boylan, Anne M. *The Origins of Women's Activism: New York and Boston, 1797–1840* (2002). Considers how middle-class urban women organized numerous associations for social improvement and thereby gained a place in the public sphere.

Bushman, Claudia L. and Richard L. Bushman. *Building the Kingdom: A History of Mormons in America* (2001). A survey of the history of American Mormons.

Goodman, Paul. *Of One Blood: Abolitionists and the Origins of Racial Equality* (1998). Explores the origins of racial egalitarianism in the movement against slavery.

Harding, Vincent. *There Is a River: The Black Struggle for Freedom in America* (1981). A study that links slave resistance and black abolitionism as phases of a common struggle for freedom.

Nye, Russell B. *Fettered Freedom: Civil Liberties and the Slavery Controversy, 1830–1860* (1949). Examines the impact of mob activities and other violations of civil liberties on the growth of abolitionism.

Rothman, David J. *The Discovery of the Asylum: Social Order and Disorder in the New Republic* (1971). Relates the rise of prisons, orphanages, and asylums and their common characteristics.

Tyrrell, Ian. *Sobering Up: From Temperance to Prohibition in Antebellum America, 1800–1860* (1979). Traces the movement against the sale and use of liquor and how it changed in the first part of the nineteenth century.

Websites

Samuel J. May Anti-Slavery Collection: http://ebooks.library.cornell.edu/m/mayantislavery//

Women and Social Movements in the United States, 1600–2000: http://asp6new.alexanderstreet.com/wam2/wam2 .index.map.aspx

CHAPTER 13: A HOUSE DIVIDED, 1840–1861

Books

Anbinder, Tyler. *Nativism and Slavery: The Northern Know-Nothings and the Politics of the 1850s* (1992). A detailed study of the relationship between nativism and antislavery politics in the North.

Cronon, William. *Nature's Metropolis: Chicago and the Great West* (1992). An influential account of the rise of Chicago and the city's relationship to its agricultural hinterland.

Foner, Eric. *Free Soil, Free Labor, Free Men: The Ideology of the Republican Party before the Civil War* (1970). A discussion of the basic ideas that united Republicans in the 1850s, especially their "free labor ideology."

Potter, David M. *The Impending Crisis, 1848–1861* (1976). Still the standard account of the nation's history in the years before the Civil War.

Sinha, Manisha. *The Counterrevolution of Slavery: Politics and Ideology in Antebellum South Carolina* (2002). A detailed study of how a vigorous defense of slavery developed in South Carolina, which justified the decision for secession.

Stampp, Kenneth. *And the War Came: The North and the Secession Crisis, 1860–61* (1950). An examination of Northern actions and attitudes during the secession crisis.

Stephanson, Anders. *Manifest Destiny: American Expansionism and the Empire of Right* (1995). Considers how the idea of an American mission to spread freedom and democracy has affected American foreign policy throughout the country's history.

Websites

Getting the Message Out: National Campaign Materials, 1840–1860: http://dig.lib.niu.edu/message/

Gold Rush!: http://museumca.org/goldrush/

The Mexican-American War and the Media: www.history.vt.edu/MxAmWar/INDEX.HTM#

The Oregon Trail: www.isu.edu/~trinmich/Oregontrail.html

Uncle Tom's Cabin and American Culture: http://jefferson.village.virginia.edu/utc/

CHAPTER 14: A NEW BIRTH OF FREEDOM: THE CIVIL WAR, 1861–1865

Books

Berlin, Ira, ed. *Slaves No More: Three Essays on Emancipation and the Civil War* (1992). A careful account of the causes and consequences of emancipation during the war.

Faust, Drew G. *This Republic of Suffering* (2008). A powerful account of how the experience of mass death affected American culture, religion, and politics.

Lawson, Melinda. *Patriot Fires: Forging a New Nationalism in the Civil War North* (2002). Considers how both public and private groups, in order to mobilize support for the war effort, promoted a new idea of American nationalism.

McPherson, James M. *Battle Cry of Freedom: The Civil War Era* (1988). The standard account of the coming of the war, its conduct, and its consequences.

Neely, Mark E. *The Fate of Liberty: Abraham Lincoln and Civil Liberties* (1991). Explores how the Lincoln administration did and did not meet the challenge of preserving civil liberties while fighting the war.

Quarles, Benjamin. *Lincoln and the Negro* (1962). A judicious account of the evolution of Lincoln's policies regarding slavery, emancipation, and the rights of African-Americans.

Richardson, Heather C. *Greatest Nation of the Earth: Republican Economic Policies during the Civil War* (1997). Considers the far-reaching impact of the economic measures adopted by the Union during the war.

Rubin, Anne S. *Shattered Nation: The Rise and Fall of the Confederacy, 1861–1868* (2005). An up-to-date account of the Confederate experience.

Websites

A House Divided: America in the Age of Lincoln: www.digitalhistory.uh.edu/ahd/index.html

Civil War Women: http://library.duke.edu/specialcollections/collections/digitized/civil-war-women/

The American Civil War Homepage: http://sunsite.utk.edu/civil-war/

The Valley of the Shadow: Two Communities in the American Civil War: http://valley.vcdh.virginia.edu

CHAPTER 15: "WHAT IS FREEDOM?": RECONSTRUCTION, 1865–1877

Books

Butchart, Ronald E. *Schooling the Freed People: Teaching, Learning, and the Struggle for Black Freedom* (2010). Relates the efforts of black and white teachers to educate the former slaves and some of the conflicts that arose over the purposes of such education.

DuBois, Ellen C. *Feminism and Suffrage: The Emergence of an Independent Women's Movement in America, 1848–1869* (1978). Explores how the split over the exclusion of women from the Fourteenth and Fifteenth Amendments gave rise to a movement for woman suffrage no longer tied to the abolitionist tradition.

Foner, Eric. *Nothing but Freedom: Emancipation and Its Legacy* (1983). Includes a comparison of the emancipation experience in different parts of the Western Hemisphere.

Foner, Eric. *Reconstruction: America's Unfinished Revolution, 1863–1877* (1988). A comprehensive account of the Reconstruction era.

Hahn, Steven. *A Nation under Our Feet: Black Political Struggles in the Rural South from Slavery to the Great Migration* (2003). A detailed study of black political activism, stressing nationalist consciousness and emigration movements.

Hyman, Harold M. *A More Perfect Union: The Impact of the Civil War and Reconstruction on the Constitution* (1973). Analyzes how the laws and constitutional amendments of Reconstruction changed the Constitution and the rights of all Americans.

Litwack, Leon F. *Been in the Storm So Long: The Aftermath of Slavery* (1979). A detailed look at the immediate aftermath of the end of slavery and the variety of black and white responses to emancipation.

Rable, George C. *But There Was No Peace: The Role of Violence in the Politics of Reconstruction* (1984). The only full-scale study of violence in the Reconstruction South.

Websites

After Slavery: Race, Labor, and Politics in the Post-Emancipation Carolinas: www.afterslavery.com

America's Reconstruction: People and Politics after the Civil War: www.digitalhistory.uh.edu/reconstruction/index.html

Freedmen and Southern Society Project: www.history.umd.edu/Freedmen/

The Andrew Johnson Impeachment Trial: www.law.umkc.edu/faculty/projects/ftrials/impeach/impeachmt.htm

GLOSSARY

Abolitionism Social movement of the pre–Civil War era that advocated the immediate emancipation of the slaves and their incorporation into American society as equal citizens.

Affirmative action Policy efforts to promote greater employment opportunities for minorities.

Agricultural Adjustment Act (1933) New Deal legislation that established the Agricultural Adjustment Administration (AAA) to improve agricultural prices by limiting market supplies; declared unconstitutional in United States v. Butler (1936).

Aid to Families with Dependent Children Federal program, also known as "welfare," of financial assistance to needy American families; created in 1935 as part of the Social Security Act; abolished in 1996.

Alamo, Battle of the Siege in the Texas War for Independence, 1836, in which the San Antonio mission fell to the Mexicans.

Alien and Sedition Acts (1798) Four measures passed during the undeclared war with France that limited the freedoms of speech and press and restricted the liberty of noncitizens.

America First Committee Largely midwestern isolationist organization supported by many prominent citizens, 1940–1941.

American Civil Liberties Union Organization founded during World War I to protest the suppression of freedom of expression in wartime; played a major role in court cases that achieved judicial recognition of Americans' civil liberties.

American Colonization Society Organized in 1816 to encourage colonization of free blacks to Africa; West African nation of Liberia founded in 1822 to serve as a homeland for them.

"American exceptionalism" The belief that the United States has a special mission to serve as a refuge from tyranny, a symbol of freedom, and a model for the rest of the world.

American Federation of Labor Founded in 1881 as a federation of trade unions composed mostly of skilled, white, native-born workers; its long-term president was Samuel Gompers.

American System Program of internal improvements and protective tariffs promoted by Speaker of the House Henry Clay in his presidential campaign of 1824; his proposals formed the core of Whig ideology in the 1830s and 1840s.

Amistad Ship that transported slaves from one port in Cuba to another, seized by the slaves in 1839. They made their way northward to the United States, where the status of the slaves became the subject of a celebrated court case; eventually most were able to return to Africa.

Anarchism Belief that all institutions that exercise power over individuals, especially government, are illegitimate; it flourished among certain native-born individualists in the nineteenth century and radical immigrants in the early twentieth century.

Antietam, Battle of One of the bloodiest battles of the Civil War, fought to a standoff on September 17, 1862, in western Maryland.

Antifederalists Opponents of the Constitution who saw it as a limitation on individual and states' rights; their demands led to the addition of a Bill of Rights to the document.

Appomattox Courthouse, Virginia Site of the surrender of Confederate general Robert E. Lee to Union general Ulysses S. Grant on April 9, 1865, marking the end of the Civil War.

Arab Spring Revolutionary demonstrations and protests that swept the Middle East in 2011.

Army-McCarthy hearings Televised U.S. Senate hearings in 1954 on Senator Joseph McCarthy's charges of disloyalty in the army; his tactics contributed to his censure by the Senate.

Articles of Confederation First frame of government for the United States; in effect from 1781 to 1788, it provided for a weak central authority and was soon replaced by the Constitution.

Atlanta Compromise Speech to the Cotton States and International Exposition in 1895 by educator Booker T. Washington, the leading black spokesman of the day; black scholar W. E. B. Du Bois gave the speech its derisive name and criticized Washington for encouraging blacks to accommodate segregation and disenfranchisement.

Atlantic Charter Issued August 12, 1941, following meetings in Newfoundland between President Franklin D. Roosevelt and British prime minister Winston Churchill, the charter signaled the Allies' cooperation and stated their war aims.

Atlantic slave trade The systematic importation of African slaves from their native continent across the Atlantic Ocean to the New World, largely fuelled by rising demand for sugar, rice, coffee, and tobacco.

Atomic Energy Commission Created in 1946 to supervise peacetime uses of atomic energy.

Axis powers In World War II, the nations of Germany, Italy, and Japan.

Aztec Mesoamerican people who were conquered by the Spanish under Hernán Cortés, 1519–1528.

Baby boom Markedly higher birthrate in the years following World War II; led to the biggest demographic "bubble" in American history.

Bacon's Rebellion Unsuccessful 1676 revolt led by planter Nathaniel Bacon against Virginia governor William Berkeley's administration because of governmental corruption and because Berkeley had failed to protect settlers from Indian raids and did not allow them to occupy Indian lands.

Baker v. Carr (1962) U.S. Supreme Court decision that established the principle of "one man, one vote," that is, that legislative districts must be equal in population.

Bakke v. Regents of the University of California (1978) Case in which the U.S. Supreme Court ruled against the California university system's use of racial quotas in admissions but allowed the use of race as one factor in admissions decisions.

Balance of trade Ratio of imports to exports.

Bank of the United States Proposed by the first secretary of the treasury, Alexander Hamilton, the bank opened in 1791 and operated until 1811 to issue a uniform currency, make business loans, and collect tax monies. The Second Bank of the United States was chartered in 1816 but President Andrew Jackson vetoed the recharter bill in 1832.

Barbary pirates Plundering pirates off the Mediterranean coast of Africa; President Thomas Jefferson's refusal to pay them tribute to protect American ships sparked an undeclared naval war with North African nations, 1801–1805.

Barbed wire First practical fencing material for the Great Plains was invented in 1873 and rapidly spelled the end of the open range.

Bay of Pigs invasion Hoping to inspire a revolt against Fidel Castro, the CIA sent 1,500 Cuban exiles to invade their homeland on April 17, 1961, but the mission was a spectacular failure.

The Beats A term coined by Jack Kerouac for a small group of poets and writers who railed against 1950s mainstream culture.

Bill of Rights First ten amendments to the U.S. Constitution, adopted in 1791 to guarantee individual rights against infringement by the federal government.

Black Codes (1865–1866) Laws passed in southern states to restrict the rights of former slaves; to nullify the codes, Congress passed the Civil Rights Act of 1866 and the Fourteenth Amendment.

Black Legend Idea that the Spanish New World empire was more oppressive toward the Indians than other European empires; was used as a justification for English imperial expansion.

Black Power Post-1966 rallying cry of a more militant civil rights movement.

Bland-Allison Act (1878) Passed over President Rutherford B. Hayes's veto, the inflationary measure authorized the purchase each month of 2 to 4 million dollars' worth of silver for coinage.

"Bleeding Kansas" Violence between pro- and antislavery settlers in the Kansas Territory, 1856.

Boston Massacre Clash between British soldiers and a Boston mob, March 5, 1770, in which five colonists were killed.

Boston Tea Party On December 16, 1773, the Sons of Liberty, dressed as Indians, dumped hundreds of chests of tea into Boston Harbor to protest the Tea Act of 1773, under which the British exported to the colonies millions of pounds of cheap—but still taxed—tea, thereby undercutting the price of smuggled tea and forcing payment of the tea duty.

Boxer Rebellion Chinese nationalist protest against Western commercial domination and cultural influence, 1900; a coalition of American, European, and Japanese forces put down the rebellion and reclaimed captured embassies in Peking (Beijing) within the year.

***Bracero* program** System agreed to by Mexican and American governments in 1942 under which tens of thousands of Mexicans entered the United States to work temporarily in agricultural jobs in the Southwest; lasted until 1964 and inhibited labor organization among farm workers since braceros could be deported at any time.

Brains trust Group of advisers—many of them academics—assembled by Franklin D. Roosevelt to recommend New Deal policies during the early months of his presidency.

Bretton Woods Town in New Hampshire and site of international agreement in 1944 by which the American dollar replaced the British pound as the most important international currency, and the World Bank and International Monetary Fund were created to promote rebuilding after World War II and to ensure that countries did not devalue their currencies.

Brook Farm Transcendentalist commune in West Roxbury, Massachusetts, populated from 1841 to 1847 principally by writers (Nathaniel Hawthorne, for one) and other intellectuals.

***Brown v. Board of Education of Topeka* (1954)** U.S. Supreme Court decision that struck down racial segregation in public education and declared "separate but equal" unconstitutional.

Bull Run, Battles of (First and Second Manassas) First land engagement of the Civil War took place on July 21, 1861, at Manassas Junction, Virginia, at which Union troops quickly retreated; one year later, on August 29–30, Confederates captured the federal supply depot and forced Union troops back to Washington.

Bunker Hill, Battle of First major battle of the Revolutionary War; it actually took place at nearby Breed's Hill, Massachusetts, on June 17, 1775.

"Burned-over district" Area of western New York strongly influenced by the revivalist fervor of the Second Great Awakening; Disciples of Christ and Mormons are among the many sects that trace their roots to the phenomenon.

Bush Doctrine President George W. Bush's foreign policy principle wherein the United States would launch a war on terrorism.

***Bush v. Gore* (2000)** U.S. Supreme Court case that determined the winner of the disputed 2000 presidential election.

Busing The means of transporting students via buses to achieve school integration in the 1970s.

Calvinism Doctrine of predestination expounded by Swiss theologian John Calvin in 1536; influenced the Puritan, Presbyterian, German and Dutch Reformed, and Huguenot churches in the colonies.

Camp David accords Peace agreement between the leaders of Israel and Egypt, brokered by President Jimmy Carter in 1978.

Caravel A fifteenth-century European ship capable of long-distance travel.

Carpetbaggers Derisive term for northern emigrants who participated in the Republican governments of the Reconstruction South.

Chancellorsville, Battle of Confederate general Robert E. Lee won his last major victory and General "Stonewall" Jackson died in this Civil War battle in northern Virginia on May 1–4, 1863.

Checks and balances A systematic balance to prevent any one branch of the national government from dominating the other two.

Chinese Exclusion Act (1882) Halted Chinese immigration to the United States.

Civil Rights Act of 1866 Along with the Fourteenth Amendment, guaranteed the rights of citizenship to former slaves.

Civil Rights Act of 1957 First federal civil rights law since Reconstruction; established the Civil Rights Commission and the Civil Rights Division of the Department of Justice.

Civil Rights Act of 1964 Outlawed discrimination in public accommodations and employment.

Civil Service Act of 1883 Established the Civil Service Commission and marked the end of the spoils system.

Closed shop Hiring requirement that all workers in a business must be union members.

Coercive Acts/Intolerable Acts (1774) Four parliamentary measures in reaction to the Boston Tea Party that forced payment for the tea, disallowed colonial trials of British soldiers, forced their quartering in private homes, and reduced the number of elected officials in Massachusetts.

Cold War Term for tensions, 1945–1989, between the Soviet Union and the United States, the two major world powers after World War II.

Collective bargaining The process of negotiations between an employer and a group of employees to regulate working conditions.

Columbian exchange The transatlantic flow of goods and people that began with Columbus's voyages in 1492.

Common school Tax-supported state schools of the early nineteenth century open to all children.

Common Sense A pamphlet anonymously written by Thomas Paine in January 1776 that attacked the English principles of hereditary rule and monarchical government.

Commonwealth v. Hunt (1842) Landmark ruling of the Massachusetts Supreme Court establishing the legality of labor unions.

Communitarianism Social reform movement of the nineteenth century driven by the belief that by establishing small communities based on common ownership of property, a less competitive and individualistic society could be developed.

Compromise of 1850 Complex compromise devised by Senator Henry Clay that admitted California as a free state, included a stronger fugitive slave law, and delayed determination of the slave status of the New Mexico and Utah territories.

Compromise of 1877 Deal made by a Republican and Democratic special congressional commission to resolve the disputed presidential election of 1876; Republican Rutherford B. Hayes, who had lost the popular vote, was declared the winner in exchange for the withdrawal of federal troops from involvement in politics in the South, marking the end of Reconstruction.

Congress of Industrial Organizations (CIO) Umbrella organization of semiskilled industrial unions, formed in 1935 as the Committee for Industrial Organization and renamed in 1938.

Congress of Racial Equality (CORE) Civil rights organization started in 1942 and best known for its Freedom Rides, bus journeys challenging racial segregation in the South in 1961.

Conspicuous consumption Phrase referring to extravagant spending to raise social standing, coined by Thorstein Veblen in The Theory of the Leisure Class (1899).

Constitutional Convention Meeting in Philadelphia, May 25–September 17, 1787, of representatives from twelve colonies—excepting Rhode Island—to revise the existing Articles of Confederation; convention soon resolved to produce an entirely new constitution.

Containment General U.S. strategy in the Cold War that called for containing Soviet expansion; originally devised by U.S. diplomat George F. Kennan.

Continental army Army authorized by the Continental Congress in 1775 to fight the British; commanded by General George Washington.

Continental Congress Representatives of the colonies met first in Philadelphia in 1774 to formulate actions against British policies; the Second Continental Congress (1775–1789) conducted the war and adopted the Declaration of Independence and the Articles of Confederation.

Convict leasing System developed in the post–Civil War South that generated income for the states and satisfied planters' need for cheap labor by renting prisoners out; the convicts were often treated poorly.

Copperheads Republican term for northerners opposed to the Civil War; it derived from the name of a poisonous snake.

Coral Sea, Battle of the Fought on May 7–8, 1942, near the eastern coast of Australia, it was the first U.S. naval victory over Japan in World War II.

Cotton gin Invented by Eli Whitney in 1793, the machine separated cotton seed from cotton fiber, speeding cotton processing and making profitable the cultivation of the more hardy, but difficult to clean, short-staple cotton; led directly to the dramatic nineteenth-century expansion of slavery in the South.

Counterculture "Hippie" youth culture of the 1960s, which rejected the values of the dominant culture in favor of illicit drugs, communes, free sex, and rock music.

Court-packing plan President Franklin D. Roosevelt's failed 1937 attempt to increase the number of U.S. Supreme Court justices from nine to fifteen in order to save his Second New Deal programs from constitutional challenges.

Coverture Principle in English and American law that a married woman lost her legal identity, which became "covered" by that of her husband, who therefore controlled her person and the family's economic resources.

Crédit Mobilier scandal Millions of dollars in overcharges for building the Union Pacific Railroad were exposed; high officials of the Ulysses S. Grant administration were implicated but never charged.

Creoles (*Criollos* in Spanish) Persons born in the New World of European ancestry.

Cuban missile crisis Caused when the United States discovered Soviet offensive missile sites in Cuba in October 1962; the U.S.-Soviet confrontation was the Cold War's closest brush with nuclear war.

Cult of domesticity The nineteenth-century ideology of "virtue" and "modesty" as the qualities that were essential to proper womanhood.

Crop-lien system Merchants extended credit to tenants based on their future crops, but high interest rates and the uncertainties of farming often led to inescapable debts.

D-Day June 6, 1944, when an Allied amphibious assault landed on the Normandy coast and established a foothold in Europe, leading to the liberation of France from German occupation.

Dartmouth College v. Woodward (1819) U.S. Supreme Court upheld the original charter of the college against New Hampshire's attempt to alter the board of trustees; set precedent of support of contracts against state interference.

Dawes Act Law passed in 1887 meant to encourage adoption of white norms among Indians; broke up tribal holdings into small farms for Indian families, with the remainder sold to white purchasers.

Declaration of Independence Document adopted on July 4, 1776, that made the break with Britain official; drafted by a committee of the Second Continental Congress, including principal writer Thomas Jefferson.

Deindustrialization Term describing decline of manufacturing in old industrial areas in the late twentieth century as companies shifted production to low-wage centers in the South and West or in other countries.

Deism Enlightenment thought applied to religion; emphasized reason, morality, and natural law.

Democratic Party Established in 1828 and led by Andrew Jackson and Martin Van Buren, the party was a major opponent of the Whig Party until the Civil War; unlike the Whigs, Democrats believed government should adopt a hands-off approach toward the economy.

Democratic-Republican Societies Organizations created in the mid-1790s by opponents of the policies of the Washington administration and supporters of the French Revolution.

Department of Homeland Security Created to coordinate federal antiterrorist activity following the 2001 terrorist attacks on the World Trade Center and Pentagon.

Depression Period in which economic output declines sharply and unemployment rises; it applied especially to the Great Depression of the 1930s.

Depression of 1893 Worst depression of the nineteenth century, set off by a railroad failure, too much speculation on Wall Street, and low agricultural prices.

Disenfranchise To deprive of the right to vote; in the United States, exclusionary policies were used to deny groups, especially African-Americans and women, their voting rights.

Division of Powers The division of political power between the state and federal governments under the U.S. Constitution (also known as federalism).

Dixiecrats Deep South delegates who walked out of the 1948 Democratic National Convention in protest of the party's support for civil rights legislation and later formed the States' Rights Democratic (Dixiecrat) Party, which nominated Strom Thurmond of South Carolina for president.

Dollar Diplomacy A foreign policy initiative under President William Howard Taft that promoted the spread of American influence through loans and economic investments from American banks.

Dominion of New England Consolidation into a single colony of the New England colonies—and later New York and New Jersey—by royal governor Edmund Andros in 1686; dominion reverted to individual colonial governments three years later.

Dred Scott v. Sandford (1857) U.S. Supreme Court decision in which Chief Justice Roger B. Taney ruled that Congress could not prohibit slavery in the territories, on the grounds that such a prohibition would violate the Fifth Amendment rights of slaveholders, and that no black person could be a citizen of the United States.

Due-process clause Clause in the Fifth and the Fourteenth Amendments to the U.S. Constitution guaranteeing that states could not "deprive any person of life, liberty, or property, without due process of law."

Dust Bowl Great Plains counties where millions of tons of topsoil were blown away from parched farmland in the 1930s; massive migration of farm families followed.

Eighteenth Amendment (1919) Prohibition amendment that made illegal the manufacture, sale, or transportation of alcoholic beverages; repealed in 1933.

Ellis Island Reception center in New York Harbor through which most European immigrants to America were processed from 1892 to 1954.

Emancipation Proclamation (1863) President Abraham Lincoln issued a preliminary proclamation on September 22, 1862, freeing the slaves in areas under Confederate control as of January 1, 1863, the date of the final proclamation, which also authorized the enrollment of black soldiers into the Union army.

Embargo Act of 1807 Attempt to exert economic pressure by prohibiting all exports from the United States, instead of waging war in reaction to continued British impressment of American sailors; smugglers easily circumvented the embargo, and it was repealed two years later.

Emergency Banking Relief Act (1933) First New Deal measure that provided for reopening the banks under strict conditions and took the United States off the gold standard.

Emergency Immigration Act of 1921 Limited U.S. immigration to 3 percent of each foreign-born nationality in the 1910 census; three years later, Congress restricted immigration even further.

Encomienda System under which officers of the Spanish conquistadores gained ownership of Indian land.

Enlightenment Revolution in thought in the eighteenth century that emphasized reason and science over the authority of traditional religion.

Environmental Protection Agency (EPA) Created in 1970 during the first administration of President Richard M. Nixon to oversee federal pollution control efforts.

Equal Rights Amendment Amendment to guarantee equal rights for women, introduced in 1923 but not passed by Congress until 1972; it failed to be ratified by the states.

Era of Good Feelings Contemporary characterization of the administration of popular Republican president James Monroe, 1817–1825.

Erie Canal Most important and profitable of the canals of the 1820s and 1830s; stretched from Buffalo to Albany, New York, connecting the Great Lakes to the East Coast and making New York City the nation's largest port.

Espionage and Sedition Acts (1917–1918) Limited criticism of government leaders and policies by imposing fines and prison terms on those who opposed American participation in the First World War.

Eugenics "Science" of improving the human race by regulating who can bear children; flourished in early twentieth century and led to laws for involuntary sterilization of the "feeble-minded."

Fair Deal Domestic reform proposals of the Truman administration; included civil rights legislation, national health insurance, and repeal of the Taft-Hartley Act, but only extensions of some New Deal programs were enacted.

Fair Employment Practices Commission Created in 1941 by executive order, the FEPC sought to eliminate racial discrimination in jobs; it possessed little power but represented a step toward civil rights for African-Americans.

Family wage Idea that male workers should earn a wage sufficient to enable them to support their entire family without their wives having to work outside the home.

Federalism A system of government in which power is divided between the central government and the states.

Federal Trade Commission Act (1914) Established the Federal Trade Commission to enforce existing antitrust laws that prohibited business combinations in restraint of trade.

The Federalist Collection of eighty-five essays that appeared in the New York press in 1787–1788 in support of the Constitution; written by Alexander Hamilton, James Madison, and John Jay and published under the pseudonym "Publius."

Federalist Party One of the two first national political parties; led by George Washington, John Adams, and Alexander Hamilton, it favored a strong central government.

Feminism Term that entered the lexicon in the early twentieth century to describe the movement for full equality for women, in political, social, and personal life.

Fifteenth Amendment Constitutional Amendment ratified in 1870, which prohibited states from discriminating in voting privileges on the basis of race.

"Fifty-four forty or fight" Democratic campaign slogan in the presidential election of 1844, urging that the northern border of Oregon be fixed at 54°409 north latitude.

Filibuster In the nineteenth century, invasions of Central American countries launched privately by groups of Americans seeking to establish personal rule and spread slavery; in the twentieth century, term for the practice of members of the U.S. Senate delivering interminable speeches in order to prevent voting on legislation.

***Fletcher v. Peck* (1810)** U.S. Supreme Court decision in which Chief Justice John Marshall upheld the initial fraudulent sale contracts in the Yazoo Fraud cases; it upheld the principle of sanctity of a contract.

Fordism Early twentieth-century term describing the economic system pioneered by Ford Motor Company based on high wages and mass consumption.

Fort McHenry Fort in Baltimore Harbor unsuccessfully bombarded by the British in September 1814; Francis Scott Key, a witness to the battle, was moved to write the words to "The Star-Spangled Banner."

Fort Sumter First battle of the Civil War, in which the federal fort in Charleston (South Carolina) Harbor was captured by the Confederates on April 14, 1861, after two days of shelling.

Four Freedoms Freedom of speech, freedom of worship, freedom from want, and freedom from fear.

Fourteen Points President Woodrow Wilson's 1918 plan for peace after World War I; at the Versailles peace conference, however, he failed to incorporate all of the points into the treaty.

Fourteenth Amendment (1868) Guaranteed rights of citizenship to former slaves, in words similar to those of the Civil Rights Act of 1866.

Franchise The right to vote.

"Free person of color" Negro or mulatto person not held in slavery; immediately before the Civil War, there were nearly a half million in the United States, split almost evenly between North and South.

Free Soil Party Formed in 1848 to oppose slavery in the territory acquired in the Mexican War; nominated Martin Van Buren for president in 1848. By 1854 most of the party's members had joined the Republican Party.

Free Speech Movement Founded in 1964 at the University of California at Berkeley by student radicals protesting restrictions on their right to distribute political publications.

Freedmen's Bureau Reconstruction agency established in 1865 to protect the legal rights of former slaves and to assist with their education, jobs, health care, and landowning.

Freedom Rides Bus journeys challenging racial segregation in the South in 1961.

French and Indian War Known in Europe as the Seven Years' War, the last (1755–1763) of four colonial wars fought between England and France for control of North America east of the Mississippi River.

Fugitive Slave Act of 1850 Gave federal government authority in cases involving runaway slaves; aroused considerable opposition in the North.

Fundamentalism Anti-modernist Protestant movement started in the early twentieth century that proclaimed the literal truth of the Bible; the name came from The Fundamentals, published by conservative leaders.

Gadsden Purchase (1853) Thirty thousand square miles in present-day Arizona and New Mexico bought by Congress from Mexico primarily for the Southern Pacific Railroad's transcontinental route.

Gag Rule Rule adopted by House of Representatives in 1836 prohibiting consideration of abolitionist petitions; opposition, led by former president John Quincy Adams, succeeded in having it repealed in 1844.

Geneva Accords (1954) A document that had promised elections to unify Vietnam and established the 17th Parallel demarcation line which divided North and South Vietnam.

Gentlemen's Agreement (1907) The United States would not exclude Japanese immigrants if Japan would voluntarily limit the number of immigrants coming to the United States.

Gettysburg, Battle of Fought in southern Pennsylvania, July 1–3, 1863; the Confederate defeat and the simultaneous loss at Vicksburg marked the military turning point of the Civil War.

Gibbons v. Ogden **(1824)** U.S. Supreme Court decision reinforcing the "commerce clause" (the federal government's right to regulate interstate commerce) of the Constitution; Chief Justice John Marshall ruled against the State of New York's granting of steamboat monopolies.

GI Bill of Rights (1944) The legislation that provided money for education and other benefits to military personnel returning from World War II.

Gideon v. Wainwright **(1963)** U.S. Supreme Court decision guaranteeing legal counsel for indigent felony defendants.

The Gilded Age Mark Twain and Charles Dudley Warner's 1873 novel, the title of which became the popular name for the period from the end of the Civil War to the turn of the century.

Glass-Steagall Act (Banking Act of 1933) Established the Federal Deposit Insurance Corporation and included banking reforms, some designed to control speculation. Repealed in 1999, opening the door to scandals involving banks and stock investment companies.

Globalization Term that became prominent in the 1990s to describe the rapid acceleration of international flows of commerce, financial resources, labor, and cultural products.

Glorious Revolution A coup in 1688 engineered by a small group of aristocrats that led to William of Orange taking the British throne in place of James II.

Gold standard Policy at various points in American history by which the value of a dollar is set at a fixed price in terms of gold (in the post–World War II era, for example, $35 per ounce of gold).

Good Neighbor Policy Proclaimed by President Franklin D. Roosevelt in his first inaugural address in 1933, it sought improved diplomatic relations between the United States and its Latin American neighbors.

Gospel of Wealth The idea proposed by Andrew Carnegie in 1889 that those who are wealthy have an obligation to use their resources to improve society.

Grandfather clause Loophole created by southern disfranchising legislatures of the 1890s for illiterate white males whose grandfathers had been eligible to vote in 1867.

Granger movement Political movement that grew out of the Patrons of Husbandry, an educational and social organization for farmers founded in 1867; the Grange had its greatest success in the Midwest of the 1870s, lobbying for government control of railroad and grain elevator rates and establishing farmers' cooperatives.

Great Awakening Fervent religious revival movement in the 1720s through the 1740s that was spread throughout the colonies by ministers like New England Congregationalist Jonathan Edwards and English revivalist George Whitefield.

Great Compromise (Connecticut Compromise) Settled the differences between the New Jersey and Virginia delegations to the Constitutional Convention by providing for a bicameral legislature, the upper house of which would have equal representation for each state and the lower house of which would be apportioned by population.

Great Depression Worst economic depression in American history; it was spurred by the stock market crash of 1929 and lasted until World War II.

Great Migration Large-scale migration of southern blacks during and after World War I to the North, where jobs had become available during the labor shortage of the war years.

Great Society Term coined by President Lyndon B. Johnson in his 1965 State of the Union address, in which he proposed legislation to address problems of voting rights, poverty, diseases, education, immigration, and the environment.

Greenback-Labor Party Formed in 1876 in reaction to economic depression, the party favored issuance of unsecured paper money to help farmers repay debts; the movement for free coinage of silver took the place of the greenback movement by the 1880s.

***Griswold v. Connecticut* (1965)** Supreme Court decision that, in overturning Connecticut law prohibiting the use of contraceptives, established a constitutional right to privacy.

Gulf of Tonkin resolution (1964) A resolution passed by Congress authorizing the president to take "all necessary measures to repel armed attack" in Vietnam.

Gulf War Military action in 1991 in which an international coalition led by the United States drove Iraq from Kuwait, which it had occupied the previous year.

Habeas corpus, Writ of An essential component of English common law and of the U.S. Constitution that guarantees that citizens may not be imprisoned without due process of law; literally means, "you may have the body"; suspended by President Lincoln during the Civil War and limited by President Bush after the attacks of September 11, 2001.

Hacienda Large-scale farm in the Spanish New World empire worked by Indian laborers.

Harlem Renaissance African-American literary and artistic movement of the 1920s centered in New York City's Harlem neighborhood; writers Langston Hughes, Jean Toomer, Zora Neale Hurston, and Countee Cullen were among those active in the movement.

Harpers Ferry, Virginia Site of abolitionist John Brown's failed raid on the federal arsenal, October 16–17, 1859; Brown became a martyr to his cause after his capture and execution.

Hart-Celler Act (1965) Eliminated the national origins quota system for immigration established by laws in 1921 and 1924; led to radical change in the origins of immigrants to the United States, with Asians and Latin Americans outnumbering Europeans.

Hartford Convention Meeting of New England Federalists on December 15, 1814, to protest the War of 1812; proposed seven constitutional amendments (limiting embargoes and changing requirements for officeholding, declaration of war, and admission of new states), but the war ended before Congress could respond.

Hawley-Smoot Tariff Act (1930) Raised tariffs to an unprecedented level and worsened the Great Depression by raising prices and discouraging foreign trade.

Haymarket affair Violence during an anarchist protest at Haymarket Square in Chicago on May 4, 1886; the deaths of eight, including seven policemen, led to the trial of eight anarchist leaders for conspiracy to commit murder.

Hessians German soldiers, most from Hesse-Cassel principality (hence, the name), paid to fight for the British in the Revolutionary War.

Holding company Investment company that holds controlling interest in the securities of other companies.

Homestead Act (1862) Authorized Congress to grant 160 acres of public land to a western settler, who had to live on the land for five years to establish title.

Homestead Strike Violent strike at the Carnegie Steel Company near Pittsburgh in 1892 that culminated in the defeat of the Amalgamated Association of Iron and Steel Workers, the first steelworkers' union.

House Un-American Activities Committee (HUAC) Formed in 1938 to investigate subversives in the government and holders of radical ideas more generally; best-known investigations were of Hollywood notables and of former State Department official Alger Hiss, who was accused in 1948 of espionage and Communist Party membership. Abolished in 1975.

Hundred Days Extraordinarily productive first three months of President Franklin D. Roosevelt's administration in which a special session of Congress enacted fifteen of his New Deal proposals.

Impeachment Bringing charges against a public official; for example, the House of Representatives can impeach a president for "treason, bribery, or other high crimes and misdemeanors" by majority vote, and after the trial the Senate can remove the president by a vote of two-thirds. Two presidents, Andrew Johnson and Bill Clinton, have been impeached and tried before the Senate; neither was convicted.

Implied powers Federal powers beyond those specifically enumerated in the U.S. Constitution; based on the "elastic clause" of Article I, Section 8, of the Constitution that allows Congress to enact laws that promote the "general welfare."

"In God We Trust" Phrase placed on all new U.S. currency as of 1954.

Indentured servant Settler who signed on for a temporary period of servitude to a master in exchange for passage to the New World; Virginia and Pennsylvania were largely peopled in the seventeenth and eighteenth centuries by English and German indentured servants.

Indian Removal Act (1830) Signed by President Andrew Jackson, the law permitted the negotiation of treaties to obtain the Indians' lands in exchange for their relocation to what would become Oklahoma.

Individualism Term that entered the language in the 1820s to describe the increasing emphasis on the pursuit of personal advancement and private fulfillment free of outside interference.

Industrial Workers of the World Radical union organized in Chicago in 1905 and nicknamed the Wobblies; its opposition to World War I led to its destruction by the federal government under the Espionage Act.

Inflation An economic condition in which prices rise continuously.

Insular Cases Series of cases between 1901 and 1904 in which the Supreme Court ruled that constitutional protection of individual rights did not fully apply to residents of "insular" territories acquired by the United States in the Spanish-American War, such as Puerto Rico and the Philippines.

Interstate Commerce Commission Reacting to the U.S. Supreme Court's ruling in Wabash Railroad v. Illinois (1886), Congress established the ICC to curb abuses in the railroad industry by regulating rates.

Iran-Contra affair Scandal of the second Reagan administration involving sales of arms to Iran in partial exchange for release of hostages in Lebanon and use of the arms money to aid the Contras in Nicaragua, which had been expressly forbidden by Congress.

Iraq War Military campaign in 2003 in which the United States, unable to gain approval by the United Nations, unilaterally occupied Iraq and removed dictator Saddam Hussein from power.

Iron Curtain Term coined by Winston Churchill to describe the Cold War divide between western Europe and the Soviet Union's eastern European satellites.

Isolationism The desire to avoid foreign entanglements that dominated the United States Congress in the 1930s;

beginning in 1935, lawmakers passed a series of Neutrality Acts that banned travel on belligerents' ships and the sale of arms to countries at war.

Jamestown, Virginia Site in 1607 of the first permanent English settlement in the New World.

Japanese-American internment Policy adopted by the Roosevelt administration in 1942 under which 110,000 persons of Japanese descent, most of them American citizens, were removed from the West Coast and forced to spend most of World War II in internment camps; it was the largest violation of American civil liberties in the twentieth century.

Jay's Treaty Treaty with Britain negotiated in 1794 by Chief Justice John Jay; Britain agreed to vacate forts in the Northwest Territories, and festering disagreements (border with Canada, prewar debts, shipping claims) would be settled by commission.

Jim Crow Minstrel show character whose name became synonymous with racial segregation.

Kansas Exodus A migration in 1879 and 1880 by some 40,000–60,000 blacks to Kansas to escape the oppressive environment of the New South.

Kansas-Nebraska Act (1854) Law sponsored by Illinois senator Stephen A. Douglas to allow settlers in newly organized territories north of the Missouri border to decide the slavery issue for themselves; fury over the resulting repeal of the Missouri Compromise of 1820 led to violence in Kansas and to the formation of the Republican Party.

Kellogg-Briand Pact Representatives of sixty-two nations in 1928 signed the pact (also called the Pact of Paris) to outlaw war.

Keynesianism Economic theory derived from the writings of British economist John Maynard Keynes, which rejected the laissez-faire approach in favor of public spending to stimulate economic growth, even at the cost of federal deficits; dominated economic policies of administrations from the 1940s to the mid-1970s.

"King Cotton diplomacy" An attempt during the Civil War by the South to encourage British intervention by banning cotton exports.

King Philip's War Began in 1675 with an Indian uprising against white colonists. A multi-year conflict, the end result was broadened freedoms for white New Englanders and the dispossession of the region's Indians.

Knights of Labor Founded in 1869, the first national union lasted, under the leadership of Terence V. Powderly, only into the 1890s; supplanted by the American Federation of Labor.

Know-Nothing (American) Party Nativist, anti-Catholic third party organized in 1854 in reaction to large-scale German and Irish immigration; the party's only presidential candidate was Millard Fillmore in 1856.

Korean War Conflict touched off in 1950 when Communist North Korea invaded South Korea; fighting, largely by U.S. forces, continued until 1953.

Ku Klux Klan Organized in Pulaski, Tennessee, in 1866 to terrorize former slaves who voted and held political offices during Reconstruction; a revived organization in the 1910s and 1920s stressed white, Anglo-Saxon, fundamentalist Protestant supremacy; the Klan revived a third time to fight the civil rights movement of the 1950s and 1960s in the South.

Kyoto Protocol (1997) An international agreement that sought to combat global warming. To great controversy, the Bush administration announced in 2001 that it would not abide by the Kyoto Protocol.

Laissez-faire Term adopted from French, meaning "let people do as they choose," describing opposition to government action to regulate economic or personal behavior.

Land Ordinance of 1785 Directed surveying of the Northwest Territory into townships of thirty-six sections (square miles) each, the sale of the sixteenth section of which was to be used to finance public education.

League of Nations Organization of nations to mediate disputes and avoid war established after World War I as part of the Treaty of Versailles; President Woodrow Wilson's "Fourteen Points" speech to Congress in 1918 proposed the formation of the league, which the United States never joined.

Lend-Lease Act (1941) Permitted the United States to lend or lease arms and other supplies to the Allies, signifying increasing likelihood of American involvement in World War II.

Levittown Low-cost, mass-produced developments of suburban tract housing built by William Levitt after World War II on Long Island and elsewhere.

Lexington and Concord, Battle of The first shots fired in the Revolutionary War, on April 19, 1775, near Boston; approximately 100 minutemen and 250 British soldiers were killed.

Leyte Gulf, Battle of Largest sea battle in history, fought on October 25, 1944, and won by the United States off the Philippine island of Leyte; Japanese losses were so great that they could not rebound.

Liberalism Originally, political philosophy that emphasized the protection of liberty by limiting the power of government to interfere with the natural rights of citizens; in the twentieth century, belief in an activist government promoting greater social and economic equality.

Liberty Party Abolitionist political party that nominated James G. Birney for president in 1840 and 1844; merged with the Free Soil Party in 1848.

Lincoln-Douglas debates Series of senatorial campaign debates in 1858 focusing on the issue of slavery in the territories; held in Illinois between Republican Abraham Lincoln, who made a national reputation for himself, and incumbent Democratic senator Stephen A. Douglas, who managed to hold onto his seat.

Little Bighorn, Battle of Most famous battle of the Great Sioux War took place in 1876 in the Montana

Territory; combined Sioux and Cheyenne warriors massacred a vastly outnumbered U.S. Cavalry commanded by Lieutenant Colonel George Armstrong Custer.

Lochner v. New York **(1905)** Decision by Supreme Court overturning a New York law establishing a limit on the number of hours per week bakers could be compelled to work; "Lochnerism" became a way of describing the liberty of contract jurisprudence, which opposed all governmental intervention in the economy.

Long Telegram A telegram by American diplomat George Kennan in 1946 outlining his views of the Soviet Union that eventually inspired the policy of containment.

Louisiana Purchase President Thomas Jefferson's 1803 purchase from France of the important port of New Orleans and 828,000 square miles west of the Mississippi River to the Rocky Mountains; it more than doubled the territory of the United States at a cost of only $15 million.

Loyalists Colonists who remained loyal to Great Britain during the War of Independence.

Lusitania British passenger liner sunk by a German U-boat, May 7, 1915, creating a diplomatic crisis and public outrage at the loss of 128 Americans (roughly 10 percent of the total aboard); Germany agreed to pay reparations, and the United States waited two more years to enter World War I.

Lyceum movement Founded in 1826, the movement promoted adult public education through lectures and performances.

Lynching Practice, particularly widespread in the South between 1890 and 1940, in which persons (usually black) accused of a crime were murdered by mobs before standing trial. Lynchings often took place before large crowds, with law enforcement authorities not intervening.

Manhattan Project Secret American program during World War II to develop an atomic bomb; J. Robert Oppenheimer led the team of physicists at Los Alamos, New Mexico.

Manifest Destiny Phrase first used in 1845 to urge annexation of Texas; used thereafter to encourage American settlement of European colonial and Indian lands in the Great Plains and the West and, more generally, as a justification for American empire.

Marbury v. Madison **(1803)** First U.S. Supreme Court decision to declare a federal law—the Judiciary Act of 1801—unconstitutional.

March on Washington Civil rights demonstration on August 28, 1963, where the Reverend Martin Luther King Jr., gave his "I Have a Dream" speech on the steps of the Lincoln Memorial.

Marshall Plan U.S. program for the reconstruction of post–World War II Europe through massive aid to former enemy nations as well as allies; proposed by General George C. Marshall in 1947.

Massive resistance In reaction to the Brown decision of 1954, effort by southern states to defy federally mandated school integration.

Maya Pre-Columbian society in Mesoamerica before about A.D. 900.

Mayflower Compact Signed in 1620 aboard the Mayflower before the Pilgrims landed at Plymouth, the document committed the group to majority-rule government.

McCarran Internal Security Act (1950) Passed over President Harry S. Truman's veto, the law required registration of American Communist Party members, denied them passports, and allowed them to be detained as suspected subversives.

McCarthyism Post–World War II Red Scare focused on the fear of Communists in U.S. government positions; peaked during the Korean War; most closely associated with Joseph McCarthy, a major instigator of the hysteria.

McCulloch v. Maryland (1819) U.S. Supreme Court decision in which Chief Justice John Marshall, holding that Maryland could not tax the Second Bank of the United States, supported the authority of the federal government versus the states.

McNary-Haugen bill Vetoed by President Calvin Coolidge in 1927 and 1928, the bill to aid farmers would have artificially raised agricultural prices by selling surpluses overseas for low prices and selling the reduced supply in the United States for higher prices.

Meat Inspection Act (1906) Passed largely in reaction to Upton Sinclair's The Jungle, the law set strict standards of cleanliness in the meatpacking industry.

Medicaid Great Society program established in 1965 that provided free medical care to the poor.

Medicare Key component of Great Society of Lyndon B. Johnson; government program created in 1965 to pay medical costs of elderly and disabled Americans.

Mercantilism Policy of Great Britain and other imperial powers of regulating the economies of colonies to benefit the mother country.

Mestizo Spanish word for person of mixed Native American and European ancestry.

Mexican War Controversial war with Mexico for control of California and New Mexico, 1846–1848; the Treaty of Guadalupe Hidalgo fixed the border at the Rio Grande and extended the United States to the Pacific coast, annexing more than a half-million square miles of Mexican territory.

Midway, Battle of Decisive American victory near Midway Island in the South Pacific on June 4, 1942; the Japanese navy never recovered its superiority over the U.S. navy.

Military-industrial complex The concept of "an immense military establishment" combined with a "permanent arms industry," which President Eisenhower warned against in his 1961 Farewell Address.

Mill girls Women who worked at textile mills during the Industrial Revolution who enjoyed new freedoms and independence not seen before.

Minstrel show Blackface vaudeville entertainment popular in the decades surrounding the Civil War.

Miranda v. Arizona (1966) U.S. Supreme Court decision required police to advise persons in custody of their rights to legal counsel and against self-incrimination.

Missouri Compromise Deal proposed by Kentucky senator Henry Clay in 1820 to resolve the slave/free imbalance in Congress that would result from Missouri's admission as a slave state; Maine's admission as a free state offset Missouri, and slavery was prohibited in the remainder of the Louisiana Territory north of the southern border of Missouri.

Molly Maguires Secret organization of Irish coal miners that used violence to intimidate mine officials in the 1870s.

Monitor and Merrimac, Battle of the First engagement between ironclad ships; fought at Hampton Roads, Virginia, on March 9, 1862.

Monroe Doctrine President James Monroe's declaration to Congress on December 2, 1823, that the American continents would be thenceforth closed to European colonization, and that the United States would not interfere in European affairs.

Montgomery bus boycott Sparked by Rosa Parks's arrest on December 1, 1955, for refusing to surrender her seat to a white passenger, a successful year-long boycott protesting segregation on city buses; led by the Reverend Martin Luther King Jr.

Moral Majority Televangelist Jerry Falwell's political lobbying organization, the name of which became synonymous with the Religious Right—conservative evangelical Protestants who helped ensure President Ronald Reagan's 1980 victory.

Mormons Founded in 1830 by Joseph Smith, the sect (officially, the Church of Jesus Christ of Latter-day

Saints) was a product of the intense revivalism of the "burned-over district" of New York; Smith's successor Brigham Young led 15,000 followers to Utah in 1847 to escape persecution.

Muckrakers Writers who exposed corruption and abuses in politics, business, meatpacking, child labor, and more, primarily in the first decade of the twentieth century; their popular books and magazine articles spurred public interest in reform.

Mugwumps Reform wing of the Republican Party that supported Democrat Grover Cleveland for president in 1884 over Republican James G. Blaine, whose influence peddling had been revealed in the Mulligan letters of 1876.

Multiculturalism Term that became prominent in the 1990s to describe a growing emphasis on group racial and ethnic identity and demands that jobs, education, and politics reflect the increasingly diverse nature of American society.

***Munn v. Illinois* (1877)** U.S. Supreme Court ruling that upheld a Granger law allowing the state to regulate grain elevators.

NAFTA Approved in 1993, the North American Free Trade Agreement with Canada and Mexico allowed goods to travel across their borders free of tariffs; critics argued that American workers would lose their jobs to cheaper Mexican labor.

Nat Turner Rebellion Most important slave uprising in nineteenth-century America, led by a slave preacher who, with his followers, killed about sixty white persons in Southampton County, Virginia, in 1831.

National Association for the Advancement of Colored People (NAACP) Founded in 1910, this civil rights organization brought lawsuits against discriminatory practices and published The Crisis, a journal edited by African-American scholar W. E. B. Du Bois.

National Defense Education Act (1958) Passed in reaction to America's perceived inferiority in the space race; encouraged education in science and modern languages through student loans, university research grants, and aid to public schools.

National Industrial Recovery Act (1933) Passed on the last of the Hundred Days, it created public-works jobs through the Federal Emergency Relief Administration and established a system of self-regulation for industry through the National Recovery Administration, which was ruled unconstitutional in 1935.

National Organization for Women Founded in 1966 by writer Betty Friedan and other feminists, NOW pushed for abortion rights, nondiscrimination in the workplace, and other forms of equality for women.

National Road First federal interstate road, built between 1811 and 1838 and stretching from Cumberland, Maryland, to Vandalia, Illinois.

National Security Act (1947) Authorized the reorganization of government to coordinate military branches and security agencies; created the National Security Council, the Central Intelligence Agency, and the National Military Establishment (later renamed the Department of Defense).

National Youth Administration Created in 1935 as part of the Works Progress Administration, it employed millions of youths who had left school.

Nativism Anti-immigrant and anti-Catholic feeling especially prominent in the 1830s through the 1850s; the largest group was New York's Order of the Star-Spangled Banner, which expanded into the American (Know-Nothing) Party in 1854.

Naval stores Tar, pitch, and turpentine made from pine resin and used in shipbuilding; an important industry in the southern colonies, especially North Carolina.

Navigation Acts Passed by the English Parliament to control colonial trade and bolster the mercantile system, 1650–1775; enforcement of the acts led to growing resentment by colonists.

Neutrality Acts Series of laws passed between 1935 and 1939 to keep the United States from becoming involved in war by prohibiting American trade and travel to warring nations.

New Deal Franklin D. Roosevelt's campaign promise, in his speech to the Democratic National Convention of 1932, to combat the Great Depression with a "new deal for the American people"; the phrase became a catchword for his ambitious plan of economic programs.

New Freedom Democrat Woodrow Wilson's political slogan in the presidential campaign of 1912; Wilson wanted to improve the banking system, lower tariffs, and, by breaking up monopolies, give small businesses freedom to compete.

New Frontier John F. Kennedy's program, stymied by a Republican Congress and his abbreviated term; his successor Lyndon B. Johnson had greater success with many of the same concepts.

New Harmony Founded in Indiana by British industrialist Robert Owen in 1825, the short-lived New Harmony Community of Equality was one of the few nineteenth-century communal experiments not based on religious ideology.

New Left Radical youth protest movement of the 1960s, named by leader Tom Hayden to distinguish it from the Old (Marxist-Leninist) Left of the 1930s.

New Nationalism Platform of the Progressive Party and slogan of former president Theodore Roosevelt in the presidential campaign of 1912; stressed government activism, including regulation of trusts, conservation, and recall of state court decisions that had nullified progressive programs.

New Orleans, Battle of Last battle of the War of 1812, fought on January 8, 1815, weeks after the peace treaty was signed but prior to the news reaching America; General Andrew Jackson led the victorious American troops.

New South Atlanta Constitution editor Henry W. Grady's 1886 term for the prosperous post–Civil War South he envisioned: democratic, industrial, urban, and free of nostalgia for the defeated plantation South.

Nineteenth Amendment (1920) Granted women the right to vote.

Ninety-Five Theses The list of moral grievances against the Catholic Church by Martin Luther, a German priest, in 1517.

Nisei Japanese-Americans; literally, "second generation."

Normalcy Word coined by future president Warren G. Harding as part of a 1920 campaign speech—"not nostrums, but normalcy"—signifying public weariness with Woodrow Wilson's internationalism and domestic reforms.

North Atlantic Treaty Organization (NATO) Alliance founded in 1949 by ten western European nations, the United States, and Canada to deter Soviet expansion in Europe.

Northwest Ordinance of 1787 Created the Northwest Territory (area north of the Ohio River and west of Pennsylvania), established conditions for self-government and statehood, included a Bill of Rights, and permanently prohibited slavery.

Nullification Concept of invalidation of a federal law within the borders of a state; first expounded in Thomas Jefferson's draft of Kentucky resolution against Alien and Sedition Acts (1798); cited by South Carolina in its Ordinance of Nullification (1832) of the Tariff of Abominations, used by southern states to explain their secession from the Union (1861), and cited again by southern states to oppose the Brown v. Board of Education decision (1954).

Occupy Wall Street A grassroots movement in 2011 against growing economic inequality, declining opportunity, and the depredations of Wall Street banks.

Office of Price Administration Created in 1941 to control wartime inflation and price fixing resulting from shortages of many consumer goods, the OPA imposed wage and price freezes and administered a rationing system.

Okies Displaced farm families from the Oklahoma dust bowl who migrated to California during the 1930s in search of jobs.

Oneida Community Utopian community founded in 1848; the Perfectionist religious group practiced "complex marriage" under leader John Humphrey Noyes.

OPEC Organization of Petroleum Exporting Countries.

Open Door Policy In hopes of protecting the Chinese market for U.S. exports, Secretary of State John Hay demanded in 1899 that Chinese trade be open to all nations.

Open shop Situation in which union membership is not a condition of employment in a factory or other business.

Operation Dixie CIO's largely ineffective post–World War II campaign to unionize southern workers.

Oregon Trail Route of wagon trains bearing settlers from Independence, Missouri, to the Oregon Country in the 1840s through the 1860s.

Ostend Manifesto Memorandum written in 1854 from Ostend, Belgium, by the U.S. ministers to England, France, and Spain recommending purchase or seizure of Cuba in order to increase the United States' slaveholding territory.

Panic of 1819 Financial collapse brought on by sharply falling cotton prices, declining demand for American exports, and reckless western land speculation.

Panic of 1837 Beginning of major economic depression lasting about six years; touched off by a British financial crisis and made worse by falling cotton prices, credit and currency problems, and speculation in land, canals, and railroads.

Panic of 1857 Beginning of economic depression lasting about two years and brought on by falling grain prices and a weak financial system; the South was largely protected by international demand for its cotton.

Panic of 1873 Onset of severe six-year depression marked by bank failures and railroad and insurance bankruptcies.

Peace of Paris Signed on September 3, 1783, the treaty ending the Revolutionary War and recognizing American independence from Britain also established the border between Canada and the United States, fixed the western border at the Mississippi River, and ceded Florida to Spain.

Pendleton Civil Service Act (1883) Established the Civil Service Commission and marked the end of the spoils system.

Pentagon Papers Informal name for the Defense Department's secret history of the Vietnam conflict; leaked to the press by former official Daniel Ellsberg and published in the New York Times in 1971.

Pequot War An armed conflict in 1637 that led to the destruction of one of New England's most powerful Indian groups.

"Perfectionism" The idea that social ills once considered incurable could in fact be eliminated, popularized by the religious revivalism of the nineteenth century.

"Pet banks" Local banks that received deposits while the charter of the Bank of the United States was about to expire in 1836. The choice of these banks was influenced by political and personal connections.

Philippine War American military campaign that suppressed the movement for Philippine independence after the Spanish-American War; America's death toll was over 4,000 and the Philippines' was far higher.

Pilgrims Puritan Separatists who broke completely with the Church of England and sailed to the New World aboard the Mayflower, founding Plymouth Colony on Cape Cod in 1620.

Pinckney's Treaty Treaty with Spain negotiated by Thomas Pinckney in 1795; established United States boundaries at the Mississippi River and the thirty-first parallel and allowed open transportation on the Mississippi.

Plantation An early word for a colony, a settlement "planted" from abroad among an alien population in Ireland or the New World. Later, a large agricultural enterprise that used unfree labor to produce a crop for the world market.

Planter In the antebellum South, the owner of a large farm worked by twenty or more slaves.

Platt Amendment (1901) Amendment to Cuban constitution that reserved the United States' right to intervene in Cuban affairs and forced newly independent Cuba to host American naval bases on the island.

***Plessy v. Ferguson* (1896)** U.S. Supreme Court decision supporting the legality of Jim Crow laws that permitted or required "separate but equal" facilities for blacks and whites.

Poll tax Tax that must be paid in order to be eligible to vote; used as an effective means of disenfranchising black citizens after Reconstruction, since they often could not afford even a modest fee.

Popular Front A period during the mid-1930s when the Communist Party sought to ally itself with socialists and New Dealers in movements for social change, urging reform of the capitalist system rather than revolution.

Popular sovereignty Allowed settlers in a disputed territory to decide the slavery issue for themselves; program most closely associated with Senator Stephen A. Douglas of Illinois.

Populist Party Founded in 1892, it advocated a variety of reform issues, including free coinage of silver, income tax, postal savings, regulation of railroads, and direct election of U.S. senators.

Port Huron Statement (1962) A manifesto by Students for a Democratic Society that criticized institutions ranging from political parties to corporations, unions, and the military-industrial complex, while offering a new vision of social change.

Potsdam Conference Last meeting of the major Allied powers, the conference took place outside Berlin from July 17 to August 2, 1945; United States president Harry Truman, Soviet dictator Joseph Stalin, and British prime minister Clement Attlee finalized plans begun at Yalta.

Proclamation of Amnesty and Reconstruction President Lincoln's proposal for reconstruction, issued in 1863, allowed southern states to rejoin the Union if 10 percent of the 1860 electorate signed loyalty pledges, accepted emancipation, and had received presidential pardons.

Proclamation of 1763 Royal directive issued after the French and Indian War prohibiting settlement, surveys, and land grants west of the Appalachian Mountains; caused considerable resentment among colonists hoping to move west.

Progressive Party Created when former president Theodore Roosevelt broke away from the Republican Party to run for president again in 1912; the party supported progressive reforms similar to the Democrats but stopped short of seeking to eliminate trusts. Also the name of party backing Robert La Follette for president in 1924.

Progressivism Broad-based reform movement, 1900–1917, that sought governmental action in solving problems in many areas of American life, including education, public health, the economy, the environment, labor, transportation, and politics.

Proposition 13 Measure approved by California voters in 1978 prohibiting future increases in property taxes; marked beginning of "tax revolt" as major political impulse.

Public sphere The world of political organization and debate in private associations and publications outside the control of government.

Pueblo Revolt Uprising in 1680 in which Pueblo Indians temporarily drove Spanish colonists out of modern-day New Mexico.

Pullman Strike Strike against the Pullman Palace Car Company in the company town of Pullman, Illinois, on May 11, 1894, by the American Railway Union under Eugene V. Debs; the strike was crushed by court injunctions and federal troops two months later.

Pure Food and Drug Act (1906) First law to regulate manufacturing of food and medicines; prohibited dangerous additives and inaccurate labeling.

Puritans English religious group that sought to purify the Church of England; founded the Massachusetts Bay Colony under John Winthrop in 1630.

Quakers (Society of Friends) Religious group in England and America whose members believed all persons possessed the "inner light" or spirit of God; they were early proponents of abolition of slavery and equal rights for women.

Radical Republicans Group within the Republican Party in the 1850s and 1860s that advocated strong resistance to the expansion of slavery, opposition to compromise with the South in the secession crisis of 1860–1861, emancipation and arming of black soldiers during the Civil War, and equal civil and political rights for blacks during Reconstruction.

Railroad Strike of 1877 Interstate strike, crushed by federal troops, which resulted in extensive property damage and many deaths.

Reaganomics Popular name for President Ronald Reagan's philosophy of "supply side" economics, which combined tax cuts with an unregulated marketplace.

Reconquista The "reconquest" of Spain from the Moors completed by King Ferdinand and Queen Isabella in 1492.

Reconstruction Act (1867) Established temporary military governments in ten Confederate states—excepting Tennessee—and required that the states ratify the Fourteenth Amendment and permit freedmen to vote.

Reconstruction Finance Corporation Federal program established in 1932 under President Herbert Hoover to loan money to banks and other institutions to help them avert bankruptcy.

Red Scare Fear among many Americans after World War I of Communists in particular and noncitizens in general, a reaction to the Russian Revolution, mail bombs, strikes, and riots.

Redeemers Conservative white Democrats, many of them planters or businessmen, who reclaimed control of the South following the end of Reconstruction.

Regulators Groups of backcountry Carolina settlers who protested colonial policies.

Republican motherhood The ideology that emerged as a result of American independence where women played an indispensible role by training future citizens.

Republican Party Organized in 1854 by antislavery Whigs, Democrats, and Free Soilers in response to the passage of the Kansas-Nebraska Act; nominated John C. Frémont for president in 1856 and Abraham Lincoln in 1860; also the name of the party formed by Thomas Jefferson and James Madison in the 1790s.

Republicanism Political theory in eighteenth-century England and America that celebrated active participation in public life by economically independent citizens as central to freedom.

Revolution of 1800 First time that an American political party surrendered power to the opposition party; Jefferson, a Republican, had defeated incumbent Adams, a Federalist, for president.

Right-to-work State laws enacted to prevent imposition of the closed shop; any worker, whether or not a union member, could be hired.

Roe v. Wade (1973) U.S. Supreme Court decision requiring states to permit first-trimester abortions.

Roosevelt Corollary (1904) President Theodore Roosevelt announced in what was essentially a corollary to the Monroe Doctrine that the United States could intervene militarily to prevent interference from European powers in the Western Hemisphere.

Rough Riders The first U.S. Volunteer Cavalry, led in battle in the Spanish-American War by Theodore Roosevelt; they were victorious in their only battle near Santiago, Cuba, and Roosevelt used the notoriety to aid his political career.

Sacco-Vanzetti case A case held during the 1920s in which two Italian-American anarchists were found guilty and executed for a crime in which there was very little evidence linking them to the particular crime.

Salem witch trials A crisis of trials and executions in Salem, Massachusetts, in 1692 that resulted from anxiety over witchcraft.

Santa Fe Trail Beginning in the 1820s, a major trade route from St. Louis, Missouri, to Santa Fe, New Mexico Territory.

Saratoga, Battle of Major defeat of British general John Burgoyne and more than 5,000 British troops at Saratoga, New York, on October 17, 1777.

Scalawags Southern white Republicans—some former Unionists—who supported Reconstruction governments.

Schenck v. U.S. (1919) U.S. Supreme Court decision upholding the wartime Espionage and Sedition Acts; in the opinion he wrote for the case, Justice Oliver Wendell Holmes set the now-familiar "clear and present danger" standard.

Scientific management Management campaign to improve worker efficiency using measurements like "time and motion" studies to achieve greater productivity; introduced by Frederick Winslow Taylor in 1911.

Scopes trial (1925) Trial of John Scopes, Tennessee teacher accused of violating state law prohibiting teaching of the theory of evolution; it became a nationally celebrated confrontation between religious fundamentalism and civil liberties.

Scottsboro case (1931) In overturning verdicts against nine black youths accused of raping two white women, the U.S. Supreme Court established precedents in Powell v. Alabama (1932), that adequate counsel must be appointed in capital cases, and in Norris v. Alabama (1935), that African-Americans cannot be excluded from juries.

Second American Revolution The transformation of American government and society brought about by the Civil War.

Second Great Awakening Religious revival movement of the early decades of the nineteenth century, in reaction to the growth of secularism and rationalist religion; began the predominance of the Baptist and Methodist churches.

Second Great Migration The movement of black migrants from the rural South to the cities of the North and West, which occurred from 1941 through World War II, that dwarfed the Great Migration of World War I.

Segregation Policy of separating persons on the basis of race in schools, transportation, and other public facilities; de facto segregation refers to social customs that accomplish this, de jure segregation to laws requiring it.

Seneca Falls Convention First women's rights meeting and the genesis of the women's suffrage movement; held in July 1848 in a church in Seneca Falls, New York, organized by Elizabeth Cady Stanton and Lucretia Coffin Mott.

"Separate but equal" Principle underlying legal racial segregation, upheld in Plessy v. Ferguson (1896) and struck down in Brown v. Board of Education (1954).

Separation of Powers Feature of the U.S. Constitution, sometimes called "checks and balances," in which power is divided between executive, legislative, and judicial branches of the national government so that no one can dominate the other two and endanger citizens' liberties.

Servicemen's Readjustment Act (1944) The "GI Bill of Rights" provided money for education and other benefits to military personnel returning from World War II.

Settlement houses Late-nineteenth-century movement to offer a broad array of social services in urban immigrant neighborhoods; Chicago's Hull House was one of hundreds of settlement houses that operated by the early twentieth century.

Seventeenth Amendment (1913) Progressive reform that required U.S. senators to be elected directly by voters; previously, senators were chosen by state legislatures.

Shakers Founded by Mother Ann Lee in England, the United Society of Believers in Christ's Second Appearing settled in Watervliet, New York, in 1774 and subsequently established eighteen additional communes in the Northeast, Indiana, and Kentucky.

Sharecropping Type of farm tenancy that developed after the Civil War in which landless workers—often former slaves—farmed land in exchange for farm supplies and a share of the crop.

Shays's Rebellion (1787) Massachusetts farmer Daniel Shays and 1,200 compatriots, seeking debt relief through issuance of paper currency and lower taxes, attempted to prevent courts from seizing property from indebted farmers.

Sherman Antitrust Act (1890) First law to restrict monopolistic trusts and business combinations; extended by the Clayton Antitrust Act of 1914.

Sherman Silver Purchase Act (1890) In replacing and extending the provisions of the Bland-Allison Act of 1878, it increased the amount of silver periodically bought for coinage.

Single tax Concept of taxing only landowners as a remedy for poverty, promulgated by Henry George in Progress and Poverty (1879).

Sit-down strikes Tactic adopted by labor unions in the mid- and late 1930s, whereby striking workers refused to leave factories, making production impossible; proved highly effective in the organizing drive of the Congress of Industrial Organizations.

Sit-ins Tactic adopted by young civil rights activists, beginning in 1960, of demanding service at lunch counters or public accommodations and refusing to leave if denied access; marked the beginning of the most militant phase of the civil rights struggle.

Sixteenth Amendment (1913) Legalized the federal income tax.

***Smith v. Allwright* (1944)** U.S. Supreme Court decision that outlawed all-white Democratic Party primaries in Texas.

"Social contract" In leading industries, labor and management hammered out what has been called a new "social contract." Unions signed long-term agreements that left decisions regarding capital investment, plant location, and output in management's hands, and they agreed to try to prevent unauthorized "wildcat" strikes.

Social Darwinism Application of Charles Darwin's theory of natural selection to society; used the concept of the "survival of the fittest" to justify class distinctions and to explain poverty.

Social Gospel Preached by liberal Protestant clergymen in the late nineteenth and early twentieth centuries; advocated the application of Christian principles to social problems generated by industrialization.

Social Security Act (1935) Created the Social Security system with provisions for a retirement pension, unemployment insurance, disability insurance, and public assistance (welfare).

Socialist Party Political party demanding public ownership of major economic enterprises in the United States as well as reforms like recognition of labor unions and women's suffrage; reached peak of influence in 1912 when presidential candidate Eugene V. Debs received over 900,000 votes.

Sons of Liberty Organizations formed by Samuel Adams, John Hancock, and other radicals in response to the Stamp Act.

South Carolina Exposition and Protest Written in 1828 by Vice-President John C. Calhoun of South Carolina to protest the so-called Tariff of Abominations, which seemed to favor northern industry; introduced the concept of state interposition and became the basis for South Carolina's Nullification Doctrine of 1833.

Southeast Asia Treaty Organization (SEATO) Pact among mostly Western nations signed in 1954; designed to deter Communist expansion and cited as a justification for U.S. involvement in Vietnam.

Southern Christian Leadership Conference (SCLC) Civil rights organization founded in 1957 by the Reverend Martin Luther King Jr., and other civil rights leaders.

"Southern Manifesto" (1956) A document that repudiated the Supreme Court decision in *Brown v. Board of Education* and supported the campaign against racial integration in public places.

Spoils system The term—meaning the filling of federal government jobs with persons loyal to the party of the president—originated in Andrew Jackson's first term.

Sputnik First artificial satellite to orbit the earth; launched October 4, 1957, by the Soviet Union.

Stagflation A combination of stagnant economic growth and high inflation present during the 1970s.

Stalwarts Conservative Republican Party faction during the presidency of Rutherford B. Hayes, 1877–1881; led by Senator Roscoe B. Conkling of New York, Stalwarts opposed civil service reform and favored a third term for President Ulysses S. Grant.

Stamp Act (1765) Parliament required that revenue stamps be affixed to all colonial printed matter, documents, and playing cards; the Stamp Act Congress met to formulate a response, and the act was repealed the following year.

Standard Oil Company Founded in 1870 by John D. Rockefeller in Cleveland, Ohio, it soon grew into the nation's first industry-dominating trust; the Sherman Antitrust Act (1890) was enacted in part to combat abuses by Standard Oil.

Staple crop Important cash crop, for example, cotton or tobacco.

Steamboats Paddlewheelers that could travel both up- and down-river in deep or shallow waters; they became commercially viable early in the nineteenth century and soon developed into America's first inland freight and passenger service network.

Stono Rebellion A slave uprising in 1739 in South Carolina that led to a severe tightening of the slave code and the temporary imposition of a prohibitive tax on imported slaves.

Strategic Defense Initiative ("Star Wars") Defense Department's plan during the Reagan administration to build a system to destroy incoming missiles in space.

Student Nonviolent Coordinating Committee (SNCC) Founded in 1960 to coordinate civil rights sit-ins and other forms of grassroots protest.

Students for a Democratic Society (SDS) Major organization of the New Left, founded at the University of Michigan in 1960 by Tom Hayden and Al Haber.

Sugar Act (Revenue Act of 1764) Parliament's tax on refined sugar and many other colonial products.

Taft-Hartley Act (1947) Passed over President Harry Truman's veto, the law contained a number of provisions to weaken labor unions, including the banning of closed shops.

Tariff Federal tax on imported goods.

Tariff of Abominations (Tariff of 1828) Taxed imported goods at a very high rate; aroused strong opposition in the South.

Tariff of 1816 First true protective tariff, intended to protect certain American goods against foreign competition.

Tax Reform Act (1986) Lowered federal income tax rates to 1920s levels and eliminated many loopholes.

Tea Party A grassroots Republican movement, named for the Boston Tea Party of the 1770s and developed in 2009, that opposed the Obama administration's sweeping legislative enactments and advocated for a more stringent immigration policy.

Teapot Dome Harding administration scandal in which Secretary of the Interior Albert B. Fall profited from secret leasing to private oil companies of government oil reserves at Teapot Dome, Wyoming, and Elk Hills, California.

Tennessee Valley Authority Created in 1933 to control flooding in the Tennessee River valley, provide work for the region's unemployed, and produce inexpensive electric power for the region.

Tenure of Office Act (1867) Required the president to obtain Senate approval to remove any official whose appointment had also required Senate approval; President Andrew Johnson's violation of the law by firing Secretary of War Edwin Stanton led to Johnson's impeachment.

Tet Offensive Surprise attack by the Viet Cong and North Vietnamese during the Vietnamese New Year of 1968; turned American public opinion strongly against the war in Vietnam.

Thirteenth Amendment Constitutional amendment adopted in 1865 that irrevocably abolished slavery throughout the United States.

Three-fifths clause A provision signed into the Constitution in 1787 that three-fifths of the slave population would be counted in determining each state's representation in the House of Representatives and its electoral votes for president.

Three Mile Island Nuclear power plant near Harrisburg, Pennsylvania, site of 1979 accident that released radioactive steam into the air; public reaction ended the nuclear power industry's expansion.

Title IX Part of the Educational Amendments Act of 1972 that banned gender discrimination in higher education.

Tonkin Gulf Resolution (1964) Passed by Congress in reaction to supposedly unprovoked attacks on American warships off the coast of North Vietnam; it gave the president unlimited authority to defend U.S. forces and members of SEATO.

Totalitarianism The term which described aggressive, ideologically driven states that sought to subdue all of civil society to their control, thus leaving no room for individual rights or alternative values.

Townshend Acts (1767) Parliamentary measures (named for the chancellor of the Exchequer) that taxed tea and other commodities, and established a Board of Customs Commissioners and colonial vice-admiralty courts.

Trail of Tears Cherokees' own term for their forced removal, 1838–1839, from the Southeast to Indian lands (later Oklahoma); of 15,000 forced to march, 4,000 died on the way.

Transcendentalism Philosophy of a small group of mid-nineteenth-century New England writers and thinkers, including Ralph Waldo Emerson, Henry David Thoreau, and Margaret Fuller; they stressed personal and intellectual self-reliance.

Transcontinental railroad First line across the continent from Omaha, Nebraska, to Sacramento, California, established in 1869 with the linkage of the Union Pacific and Central Pacific railroads at Promontory, Utah.

Truman Doctrine President Harry S. Truman's program announced in 1947 of aid to European countries—particularly Greece and Turkey—threatened by communism.

Trust Companies combined to limit competition.

Twenty-first Amendment (1933) Repealed the prohibition of the manufacture, sale, and transportation of alcoholic beverages, effectively nullifying the Eighteenth Amendment.

Twenty-second Amendment (1951) Limited presidents to two full terms of office or two terms plus two years of an assumed term; passed in reaction to President Franklin D. Roosevelt's unprecedented four elected terms.

Twenty-sixth Amendment (1971) Lowered the voting age from twenty-one to eighteen.

U.S.S. Maine Battleship that exploded in Havana Harbor on February 15, 1898, resulting in 266 deaths; the American public, assuming that the Spanish had mined the ship, clamored for war, and the Spanish-American War was declared two months later.

Uncle Tom's Cabin Harriet Beecher Stowe's 1852 antislavery novel popularized the abolitionist position.

Underground Railroad Operating in the decades before the Civil War, the "railroad" was a clandestine system of routes and safehouses through which slaves were led to freedom in the North.

Understanding clause Added to southern state constitutions in the late nineteenth century, it allowed illiterate whites to circumvent literacy tests for voting by demonstrating that they understood a passage in the Constitution; black citizens would be judged by white registrars to have failed.

Unitarianism Late-eighteenth-century liberal offshoot of the New England Congregationalist Church; rejecting the Trinity, Unitarianism professed the oneness of God and the goodness of rational man.

United Farm Workers Union for the predominantly Mexican-American migrant laborers of the Southwest, organized by César Chavez in 1962.

United Nations Organization of nations to maintain world peace, established in 1945 and headquartered in New York.

Universal Negro Improvement Association Black nationalist movement active in the United States from 1916 to 1923, led by Marcus Garvey.

USA Patriot Act (2001) A mammoth bill that conferred unprecedented powers on law-enforcement agencies charged with preventing domestic terrorism, including the power to wiretap, read private messages, and spy on citizens.

V-E Day May 8, 1945, the day World War II officially ended in Europe.

Versailles Treaty The treaty signed at the Versailles peace conference after World War I which established President Woodrow Wilson's vision of an international regulating body, redrew parts of Europe and the Middle East, and assigned economically-crippling war reparations to Germany, but failed to incorporate all of Wilson's fourteen points.

Vertical integration Company's avoidance of middlemen by producing its own supplies and providing for distribution of its product.

Veto President's constitutional power to reject legislation passed by Congress; a two-thirds vote in both houses of Congress can override a veto.

Vicksburg, Battle of The fall of Vicksburg, Mississippi, to General Ulysses S. Grant's army on July 4, 1863, after two months of siege was a turning point in the war because it gave the Union control of the Mississippi River.

Vietnam War Longest war in which the United States has been involved; began with giving American financial assistance to France, who sought to maintain control over Vietnam colony; moved to dispatching advisers to bolster the government of South Vietnam; and finally sent over 500,000 American soldiers by the mid-1960s; resulted in massive antiwar movement, eventual American withdrawal, and communist victory in 1975; only war the United States has lost.

Virginia and Kentucky Resolutions (1798–1799) Passed by the Virginia and the Kentucky legislatures; written by James Madison and Thomas Jefferson in response to the Alien and Sedition Acts, the resolutions advanced the state-compact theory of the Constitution. Virginia's resolution called on the federal courts to protect free speech. Jefferson's draft for Kentucky stated that a state could nullify federal law, but this was deleted.

Virginia and New Jersey Plans Differing opinions of delegations to the Constitutional Convention: New Jersey wanted one legislative body with equal representation for each state; Virginia's plan called for a strong central government and a two-house legislature apportioned by population.

Volstead Act (1919) Enforced the Prohibition amendment, beginning January 1920.

Voting Rights Act of 1965 Passed in the wake of Martin Luther King Jr.'s, Selma to Montgomery March, it authorized federal protection of the right to vote and permitted federal enforcement of minority voting rights in individual counties, mostly in the South.

Wabash Railroad v. Illinois (1886) Reversing the U.S. Supreme Court's ruling in Munn v. Illinois, the decision disallowed state regulation of interstate commerce.

Wade-Davis bill (1864) Radical Republicans' plan for reconstruction that required loyalty oaths, abolition of slavery, repudiation of war debts, and denial of political rights to high-ranking Confederate officials; President Lincoln refused to sign the bill.

Wagner Act (National Labor Relations Act of 1935) Established the National Labor Relations Board and facilitated unionization by regulating employment and bargaining practices.

War Industries Board Run by financier Bernard Baruch, the board planned production and allocation of war materiel, supervised purchasing, and fixed prices, 1917–1919.

War of 1812 Fought with Britain, 1812–1814, over issues that included impressment of American sailors, interference with shipping, and collusion with Northwest Territory Indians; settled by the Treaty of Ghent in 1814.

War on Poverty Announced by President Lyndon B. Johnson in his 1964 State of the Union address; under the Economic Opportunity Bill signed later that year, Head Start, VISTA, and the Jobs Corps were created, and programs were created for students, farmers, and businesses in efforts to eliminate poverty.

War Powers Act Law passed in 1973, reflecting growing opposition to American involvement in Vietnam War; required congressional approval before president sent troops abroad.

War Production Board Created in 1942 to coordinate industrial efforts in World War II; similar to the War Industries Board in World War I.

Warren Court The U.S. Supreme Court under Chief Justice Earl Warren, 1953–1969, decided such landmark cases as Brown v. Board of Education (school desegregation), Baker v. Carr (legislative redistricting), and Gideon v. Wainwright and Miranda v. Arizona (rights of criminal defendants).

Washington Armaments Conference Leaders of nine world powers met in 1921–1922 to discuss the naval race; resulting treaties limited to a specific ratio the carrier and battleship tonnage of each nation (Five-Power Naval Treaty), formally ratified the Open Door to China (Nine-Power Treaty), and agreed to respect each other's Pacific territories (Four-Power Treaty).

Watergate Washington office and apartment complex that lent its name to the 1972–1974 scandal of the Nixon administration; when his knowledge of the break-in at the Watergate and subsequent coverup was revealed, Nixon resigned the presidency under threat of impeachment.

Webster-Hayne debate U.S. Senate debate of January 1830 between Daniel Webster of Massachusetts and Robert Hayne of South Carolina over nullification and states' rights.

Welfare state A term that originated in Britain during World War II to refer to a system of income assistance, health coverage, and social services for all citizens.

Whig Party Founded in 1834 to unite factions opposed to President Andrew Jackson, the party favored federal responsibility for internal improvements; the party ceased to exist by the late 1850s, when party members divided over the slavery issue.

Whiskey Rebellion Violent protest by western Pennsylvania farmers against the federal excise tax on whiskey, 1794.

Wilmot Proviso Proposal to prohibit slavery in any land acquired in the Mexican War, but southern senators, led by John C. Calhoun of South Carolina, defeated the measure in 1846 and 1847.

Women's Christian Temperance Union Largest female reform society of the late nineteenth century; it moved from opposing sale of liquor to demanding the right to vote for women.

Works Progress Administration (WPA) Part of the Second New Deal, it provided jobs for millions of the unemployed on construction and arts projects.

Wounded Knee, Battle of Last incident of the Indian Wars took place in 1890 in the Dakota Territory, where the U.S. Cavalry killed over 200 Sioux men, women, and children.

Writs of assistance One of the colonies' main complaints against Britain, the writs allowed unlimited search warrants without cause to look for evidence of smuggling.

XYZ affair French foreign minister Tallyrand's three anonymous agents demanded payments to stop French plundering of American ships in 1797; refusal to pay the bribe was followed by two years of undeclared sea war with France (1798–1800).

Yalta conference Meeting of Franklin D. Roosevelt, Winston Churchill, and Joseph Stalin at a Crimean resort to discuss the postwar world on February 4–11, 1945; Joseph Stalin claimed large areas in eastern Europe for Soviet domination.

Yellow journalism Sensationalism in newspaper publishing that reached a peak in the circulation war between Joseph Pulitzer's New York World and William Randolph Hearst's New York Journal in the 1890s; the papers' accounts of events in Havana Harbor in 1898 led directly to the Spanish-American War.

Yeoman farmers Small landowners (the majority of white families in the Old South) who farmed their own land and usually did not own slaves.

Yick Wo v. Hopkins Supreme Court decision in 1886 overturning San Francisco law that, as enforced, discriminated against Chinese-owned laundries; established principle that equal protection of the law embodied in Fourteenth Amendment applied to all Americans, not just former slaves.

Yorktown, Battle of Last battle of the Revolutionary War; General Lord Charles Cornwallis along with over 7,000 British troops surrendered at Yorktown, Virginia, on October 17, 1781.

Young Americans for Freedom Organization of conservative students founded in 1960; played major role in 1964 presidential campaign of Barry Goldwater and in rebirth of conservatism in the 1960s.

Zimmermann Telegram From the German foreign secretary to the German minister in Mexico, February 1917, instructing him to offer to recover Texas, New Mexico, and Arizona for Mexico if it would fight the United States to divert attention from Germany in the event that the United States joined the war.

CREDITS

PHOTOS

1 Collection du monastère des Ursulines de Québec, Musée des Ursulines de Québec (1997.1017); **5** Photo Courtesy of Edward E. Ayer Collection, The Newberry Library, Chicago; **7** National Park Service, Chaco Culture National Historic Park, Chaco Archive neg. no. 25462; **9** Bridgeman Art Library; **10** Library of Congress; **11** Courtesy Lilly Library, Indiana University, Bloomington, IN; **16** Granger Collection; **19** Granger Collection; **20** The Art Archive at Art Resource, NY; **22** Museo de la Basilica de Guadalupe, Mexico City; **23** Library of Congress; **30** National Museum of American History, Smithsonian Institution, Behring Center; **33** Bettmann/Corbis; **35** GLC03582 Novi Belgi Novaeque Angliae (New Netherland and New England) by Nicholas Visscher, 1682/ Courtesy of The Gilder Lehrman Institute of American History; **36** Museum of the City of New York; **38** Woburn Abbey, Bedfordshire, UK/The Bridgeman Art Library; **42** The John Carter Brown Library at Brown University; **43** Granger Collection; **46** The London Art Archive/Alamy; **47** Museum of Art, Rhode Island School of Design. Gift of Robert Winthrop. Photography by Erik Gould; **49 (top)** Granger Collection; **(bottom)** National Portrait Gallery, Smithsonian Institution/Art Resource, NY; **50** George Arents Collection, New York Public Library. Art Resource, NY; **51** Corbis; **54** American Antiquarian Society; **55** Courtesy of the Massachusetts Archives; **56** Worcester Art Museum, Worcester, Massachusetts, Gift of William A. Savage; **57** Massachusetts Historical Society; **60** The New York Public Library/Art Resource, NY; **64** Annenberg Rare Book and Manuscript Library, Van Pelt-Dietrich Library Center, U Penn; **65** Library of Congress; **66** Mrs. Elizabeth Freake and Baby Mary, unknown artist, 1963.134, Worcester Art Museum, Worcester, Massachusetts; **68** Private Collection/Bridgeman Art Library; **69** By permission of the British Library/Art Resource; **72**

Art Resource; **86** The John Carter Brown Library at Brown University; **77** Library of Congress; **79** Unidentified artist, British, 18th century or first quarter 19th century; *Quaker Meeting*; Oil on canvas; 64.1 x 76.2cm (25 1/4 x 30in.); Museum of Fine Arts, Boston; Bequest of Maxim Karolik; 64.456. Photograph (c) 2013 Museum of Fine Arts, Boston; **82** © British Library Board. All Rights Reserved/ The Bridgeman Art Library; **84** National Maritime Museum, London; **89** Rare Books Dividsion, The New York Public Library, Astor, Lenox and Tilden Foundations. Art Resource, NY; **95** Benjamin West, Pennsylvania Academy of the Fine Arts; Joseph and Sarah Harrison Collection; **97** Winterthur Museum; **99** Photograph (c) 2013 Museum of Fine Arts, Boston; **101** Gift of Edgar William and Bernice Chrysler Garbisch, Image © 2006 Board of Trustees, National Gallery of Art, Washington; **111** Granger Collection; **106** Library of Congress; **109** © Musée d'histoire de Nantes – Château des ducs de Bretagne/ Alain Guillard; **104** Abby Aldrich Rockefeller Folk Art Museum, Colonial Williamsburg Foundation, Williamsburg, VA; **114** Charleston Library Society; **117** Chicago Historical Society; **118** Library of Congress; **120** The Library Company of Philadelphia; **123** Library of Congress; **124** Portrait of Benjamin Franklin, Mason Chamberlin, Oil on canvas, 1762, Philadelphia Museum of Art: Gift of Mr. and Mrs Wharton Sinkler, 1956; **126** National Portrait Gallery, London; **129** Benard de la Harpe, "Carte Nouvelle de la Partie de l'Ouest de la Province de la Louisiane" [map], 1720, Louisiana Research Collection, Tulane University; **131** Library of Congress; **139** *George Washington's War in Caricature and Print.* Kenneth Baker, Grub Street Publishing; **141** Library of Congress; **143** The Colonial Williamsburg Foundation; **144** Kunhardt/Picture History; **147** Library of Congress; **148** Michael Nicholson/Corbis; **149** Library of Congress; **151** Chicago Historical Society; **153** American Philosophical Society; **154** American Antiquarian Society; **155**

Sid Lapidus Collection. Rare Books Division. Department of Rare Books and Special Collections. Princeton University Library; **165** Library of Congress; **159** Anne S.K. Brown Military Collection, Brown University; **167** Library Company of Philadelphia. Gift of the artist, 1792; **169** National Gallery of Art, Washington, Gift of Mrs. Robert Homans; **170** Historical Society of Pennsylvania; **172** Courtesy of the New-York Historical Society; **173** York County Historical Society, America, USA/The Bridgeman Art Library; **175** American Antiquarian Society; **177** Bettmann/ Corbis; **178** Reproduced by permission of the Huntington Library, San Marino, California; **179** Library of Congress; **182** Corbis; **185** Library of Congress; **188** Collection of The New-York Historical Society; **184** Bequest of Miss Lucy T. Aldrich 39.002 Museum of Art, Rhode Island School of Design, Providence; **189** Southern Historical Collection, Wilson Library, The University of North Carolina at Chapel Hill; **190** Charles Wilson Peale, Portrait of John and Elizabeth Lloyd Cadwalader, and their daughter Anne, Philadelphia Museum of Art: Purchased from the Cadwalader Collection with funds contributed by the Myrin Trust and the gift of an anonymous donor; **191** Library of Congress; **193** Collection of the New-York Historical Society/Bridgeman Art Library; **200** Print Collection, Miriam and Ira D. Wallach Division of Art, Prints, and Photographs, The New York Public Library; Astor, Lenox, and Tilden Foundations. Art Resource, NY; **201 (top)** Library of Congress; **(bottom)** Independence National Historical Park; **202** Library of Congress; **205** The Library of Virginia; **206** MPI/Getty Images; **207** Library of Congress; **209** Granger Collection; **214** Library of Congress; **216** Chicago Historical Society; **218** Granger Collection; **219**; Virginia Historical Society, Richmond/Bridgeman Art Library; **221** Photography by Erik Arneson (c) Nicholas S. West; **223** Fenimore Art Museum, Cooperstown, New York. Photo by Richard Walker; **224** Library of Congress;

(both) Library of Congress; **434** Library of Congress; **435** Friends Freedmen's Association teachers in a school in Norfolk, 1863. Collection Number 950, Haverford College Special Collections; **436** National Archives; **438** provided courtesy (c) HarpWeek LLC; **439** © The Metropolitan Museum of Art/Art Resource, NY; **441** Chicago Historical Society; **443** Library of Congress; **444 (top)** Library of Congress; **(bottom)** Photographic History Collection, Division of Information Technology and Communications, National Museum of American History, Smithsonian Institution; **445** Granger Collection; **447** Smithsonian American Art Museum, Washington, DC/Art Resource, NY; **448** Library of Congress; **449** Cook Collection, Valentine Richmond History Center; **453 (top)** Library of Congress; **(bottom)** Kemper Leila Williams Foundation /The Historic New Orleans Collection; **455** Library of Congress; **456** Library of Congress; **457** Ed Sullivan Collection, Special Collections, University of Hartford; **459** Library of Congress; **460** Library of Congress; **462** Library of Congress; **463** (both) Library of Congress; **464** Granger Collection; **466** Clements Library Collection, University of Michigan; **467** Granger Collection; **469** (both) Library of Congress; **473** Library of Congress.

TEXT, TABLES, AND FIGURES

28 Bartolomé de las Casas: *History of the Indies*, translated and edited by Andrée Collard (New York: Harper & Row, 1971), pp. 82, 112–115. Copyright © 1971 by Andrée M. Collard, renewed © 1999 by Joyce J. Con-

trucci. Reprinted by permission of Joyce J. Contrucci; **62** Thomas Hutchinson: "The Examination of Mrs. Anne Hutchinson at the Court of Newtown." Reprinted by permission of the publisher from *The History of the Colony and Province of Massachusetts Bay, Vol. II* by Thomas Hutchinson, edited by Lawrence Shaw Mayo, pp. 366–391, Cambridge, Mass.: Harvard University Press, Copyright © 1963 by the President and Fellows of Harvard College. Copyright © renewed 1964 by Lawrence Shaw Mayo; **91** (Table 3.1) Aaron S. Fogleman, "From Slaves, Convicts, and Servants to Free Passengers: The Transformation of Immigration in the Era of the American Revolution," Journal of American History 85 (June 1998) 43–76; **93** Johannes Hanner: Letter by an Immigrant to Pennsylvania, 1769, *Unpublished Documents on Emigration from the Archives of Switzerland*, Albert B. Faust, *Deutsch-Amerikanische Geschichtsblätter*, Vol. 18–19, pp. 37–39. Translation by Volker Berghahn. Reprinted by permission of Volker Berghahn; **112** (Table 4.1) Ira Berlin, *Many Thousands Gone: The First Two Centuries of Slavery in North America* (Cambridge, Mass.: Harvard University Press, 1998) 369–70; **186** Abigail Adams: "Abigail Adams to John Adams, 31 March 1776." Reprinted by permission of the publisher from *The Adams Papers: Adams Family Correspondence, Volume I: December 1761–May 1776*, edited by L.H. Butterfield, Cambridge, Mass.: The Belknap Press of Harvard University Press, Copyright © 1963 by the Massachusetts Historical Society; **217** (Table 7.1) U.S. Bureau of the Census, *A Century of Population Growth* (Washington, D.C., 1900), 47, 57; **228** Democratic-Republican Society of Pennsylvania: Excerpt from minutes of The Democratic Society of Pennsylvania, December 18, 1794. The Historical

Society of Pennsylvania (HSP), Collection # Am. 315/3150. Reprinted with permission; **257** (Table 9.1) U.S. Bureau of the Census, *Historical Statistics of the United States* (Washington, D.C.,1975), 24–36; **314** (Table 11.1) U.S. Bureau of the Census, *A Century of Population Growth* (Washington, D.C., 1900) 133; **318** (Table 11.2) Census of 1850; **332** Joseph Taper: Excerpts from "Letter from Joseph Taper to Joseph Long, November 11, 1840" in the Joseph Long Papers located in the Rare Book, Manuscript, and Special Collections Library, Duke University. Reprinted by permission; **477** (Table 16.1) U.S. Bureau of the Census, *Historical Statistics of the United States* (Washington D.C., 1975), 134; **523** (Table 17.1) Arwin D. Smallwood, *The Atlas of African-American History and Politics* (New York, 1998), 106; **546** (Table 18.1) U.S. Bureau of the Census, *Historical Statistics of the United States* (Washington D.C., 1975), 11–12; **547** (Table 18.2) Census of 1920; **549** (Table 18.3) U.S. Bureau of the Census, *Historical Statistics of the United States* (Washington D.C., 1975), 131; **550** (Table 18.4) U.S. Bureau of the Census, *Historical Statistics of the United States* (Washington, D.C., 1975), 139; **551** (Table 18.5) U.S. Bureau of the Census, *Historical Statistics of the United States* (Washington D.C., 1975), 716; **A-56** U.S. National Archives and Records Administration; **A-57** Historical Statistics of the United States (1975); Statistical Abstract of the United States (1991, 1996); Population Estimates Program, Population Division, U.S. Census Bureau. Every effort has been made to contact the copyright holder of each of the selections. Rights holders of any selections not credited should contact Permissions Department, W. W. Norton & Company, Inc., 500 Fifth Avenue, New York, NY 10110, in order for a correction to be made in the next reprint.

INDEX

Page numbers in *italics* refer to illustrations.

Abe Lincoln's Last Card, 413
abolition movement, 109, 170, 183–89, 274,
    312, 320, *339*, 348–56, *349*, *350*, *351*, *355*,
    363–64, 381, 415
  Abby Kelley and, 340
  Abraham Lincoln and, 390, 413–14
  African-Americans and, 312, *313*, 330–37,
    349, 353–54
  British, 185
  in Civil War, 413, 435
  colonization and, 348–49
  in early U.S., 188, 234
  Frederick Douglass and, 312, *313*
  John Brown and, 391–92
  The Liberator newspaper for, 284, *363*
  obstacles to, in early U.S., 183
  pacifism and, 352
  rise in militant form of, 349–50
  after Turner's rebellion, 337
  in Virginia, 336–37
  women's rights linked to, 356, 363–64
Acadians, 131
Acoma pueblo, 27
Act Concerning Religion (1649), 70
Act of Union (1707), 105
Adams, Abigail (1744–1818), 168, *169*, 178, 190
  letters to John Adams by, 168, 186, 190
Adams, Charles Francis (1807–1886), 379
Adams, Henry (b. 1843), 443
Adams, John (1735–1826), 141, 183, 194, *233*,
    234, 294
  Abigail Adams's letters to, 168, 186, 190
  Boston Massacre and, 147
  Constitutional Convention and, 202
  education and, 175
  in election of 1796, 231
  in First Continental Congress, 149
  Fries's Rebellion and, 231
  presidency of, 231–36
  religion and, 173
  on the right to vote, 171
  on the Stamp Act, 144
  Thomas Paine and, 152
  Treaty of Paris and, 165
  on women's rights, 189
  XYZ affair and, 232, *232*
Adams, John Quincy (1767–1848), 290, 294,
    355, 379
  in *Amistad* case, 334–35
  in election of 1824, 291, *294*

  in election of 1828, 295
  views on federal power, 294
Adams, Samuel (1722–1803), 149, 175, 209
Adams-Onís Treaty (1819), 256
Address at Sanitary Fair, Baltimore
    (Lincoln), 421
Africa, 2, 13–15, *15*, 74, 105, 135
  religion from, 113–14
African-Americans, 284–85
  in abolition movement, 312, *313*, 330–37,
    349, 353–54
  in American Revolution, 158–59, *159*
  barred from public land, 275
  and Black Codes, 455–56, 457
  citizenship and, 352–53, 462–63
  in Civil War, 416–17, *417*, 434–35
  Constitution and, 217–18
  decline in economic status of, 275
  early emancipation struggles of, 184–85,
    190–91
  as Ethiopian Regiment, 159
  as First Rhode Island Regiment, *159*
  free blacks, 82, 110, 188–89, 322–23, 349
  freedom petitions and, 184
  Freedom's Journal newspaper for, 284, 354
  Jefferson on, 218–19, *219*
  and jobs in New York City, 275
  and Ku Klux Klan, *see* Ku Klux Klan
  labor and, 274–75
  in Louisiana, 240–41
  market revolution and, 274–75, 278
  in Maryland colony, 83
  as part of society, 349–50, 352–53
  in politics, 464
  population of, *217*
  in Quaker society, 79
  in Reconstruction, 453, 456–58, 459–62,
    459, 463–65
  religion of, *330*
  and segregation, *see* segregation
  in Seminole War, 303
  as soldiers for Confederacy, 431
  as viewed by Jackson, 296
  voting rights of, 119, 281, 282, 285
  wages and, 274, 435
  westward expansion and, 259, 260
  see also Great Migration; slavery; slaves
African Methodist Episcopal Church, 274
Age of Jackson, 283, 296–303, 308, 348
Agreement of the People, 69

agriculture, 2, 6, 14, 21, *72*, 101, 216, 223, *224*,
    226, 251, 318
  American Revolution and, 177
  in Civil War, 423
  Democratic Party and, 297
  and immigration, 95
  Indian, 46–47
  industrial revolution and, 385
  invention of, 3
  Jamestown and, 47, 48
  Jefferson's views on, 238–39
  market revolution and, 251, 260
  promotion by J. Q. Adams of, 294
  Pueblo Indians and, 6
  tobacco and, 50
  women and, 10, 11, 101
"Agrippa," 211
Alabama, 255, 301
Alamance, Battle of, 145
Alamo, 370
Alaska, Russian fur traders in, 127
Albany, N.Y., 252
Albany Plan of Union (1754), 137
Albuquerque, N.Mex., 127
Alcorn, James L. (1816–1894), 465
Alexander II, czar of Russia (1818–1881), 410
Alexander VI, Pope (1431?–1503), 22
Alien Act (1798), 232–33, 265
Allen, Ethan (1738–1789), 145, 151
Allen, Joseph, 150
Amazon, 22
America as a Symbol of Liberty, 154
American Anti-Slavery Society, 351, *351*, 363
American Bible Society, 347
American colonies, 39, 43
  Anglicization of, 100
  artisans of, 97–98
  assemblies in, 121
  backcountry of, 96
  cities of, 97
  diversity of, 3, 90–95, 102
  election campaigns in, 170
  elite class in, 99–100
  and English Civil War, 69–70
  expansion of, 105
  expansion of England's, 74–80
  Glorious Revolution in, 87–89
  government in, 119–22
  hierarchical structure in, 100
  liberties in, 44–45

American colonies (*continued*)
  literacy in, 122–23
  maps of, *94*
  middle class in, 102
  politics in, 119–22
  population of, 50, 90–91, 109
  poverty in, 100–101
  Protestantism in, 52, 69–70, 87–89, 91, 94, 95
  reduced death rate in, 102
  as refuge, 42–43
  relationship with Indians in, 78
  society of, 96–97, 99–102
  voting rights in, 119, 170
  western frontier of, 130
  women's role in, 101–2, *101*
  see also American Revolution
American Colonization Society, 348
American Crisis, The (Paine), 159, 161
American Flag, The, 417
American Foot Soldiers, Yorktown Campaign, 159
American National Red Cross, 426
American Party, *see* Know-Nothing Party
American Philosophical Society, 122
American Revolution, 139–66, *157*, 182–83, *189*, 226, 236, 250, 312, 350, 352
  American advantages in, 158
  American mutinies in, 162
  Andrew Jackson in, 281
  Articles of Confederation and, 195
  background of, 140–49
  battles of, 159–64
  black soldiers in, 158–59, *159*
  British advantages in, 158
  casualties in, 158, 406
  creation of national identity and, 215
  debt created by, 223
  democracy and, 169–72, 231
  early battles of, 151, 159–62
  economic effect of, 177–78, 200
  equality and, 168
  family life and, 190
  force strength in, 158
  indentured servitude and, 168, 176
  Indians and, 168, 169, 181–82, 191
  low point of, 162
  Loyalists in, 178–81, *180*
  map of battles in, *160*
  Paine's view of, 152–53, 156
  religious freedom and, 172–75
  slavery and, 169, 182–89, 190–91, 330
  in South, 161–62, *163*
  Spanish help in, 161
  views of elite on, 170
  voting rights and, 172
  women and, 146, 189–90, *189*
"American Scholar, The" (Emerson), 270
American Standard, 363

American System, 285–87, *286*, 291, 294, 297, 309
"American system of manufactures," 262
American Temperance Society, 345
American Tract Society, 347
America Triumphant and Britannia in Distress, 191
Am I Not a Man and a Brother?, 355
Amistad, 334–35
Amity and Commerce, Treaty of (1778), 161
Amsterdam, 34
Anabaptists, 95
Anaconda Plan, 407
Andersonville, Ga., Confederate prison at, 406, 456
Andes Mountains, 3, 20
And Not This Man (Nast), *469*
Andrews, Sidney (1837–1880), 446
Andros, Edmund (1637–1714), 75–77, 88
Anglican Church, 60, 69, 87, 88, 95, 148
  American Revolution and, 175, 179
  creation of, 40
  Dissenters and, 87
  Puritans and, 53–54
Anglo-Dutch war, 75
Anthony, Saint, 30
Anthony, Susan B. (1820–1906), 462, *462*
Antietam, Battle of, 410, 414
Anti-Federalists, 209–12, 214
Antigua, *82*
Antinomianism, 61
Antrobus, John, *330*
Apaches, 30
Appalachian Mountains, 196, 251
  crossing of, 256
  population west of, 256
Appeal in Favor of That Class of Americans Called Africans, An (Child), 352
Appeal of the Independent Democrats, 382
Appeal to the Coloured Citizens of the World, An (Walker), 349
Appomattox Courthouse, 438, 454
Aragon, 16
Aristotle (384–322 B.C.E.), 170
Arizona, 6, 373
Arkansas, 256
Armada Portrait (Gower), *38*
Arminianism, 124
Armour, Philip D. (1832–1901), 425
Army, U.S., African-Americans in, 416–17
Army of Northern Virginia, Confederate, 409
Army of the Potomac, Union, 408, 410, 431, 433
Arnold, Benedict (1741–1801), 151, 162, *191*
Articles of Confederation (1781), 195–202, *197*, 203, 204, 207, 208, 223
  weaknesses of, 200
artisans, 261, 274
  African-Americans as, 274
  see also craftsmen

Ashanti people, 113
Asia, 13–14, *15*
  and Native Americans, 3
assemblies, colonial, 121
  governor vs., 122
  Parliament vs., 142
  rise of, 121
asylum of liberty, U.S. as, 153, 154–55, 174, 218
asylums, 347
Atlanta, Ga.:
  Sherman's capture of, 433
  slave trade in, *317*
Atlantic trade, of New England colonies, 106–7, *107*
Attucks, Crispus (ca. 1723–1770), 147
Augusta County, Va., 100
Austin, Moses (1761–1821), 370
Austin, Stephen (1793–1836), 370
Avilés, Pedro Menéndez de, *see* Menéndez de Avilés, Pedro
Azores, 14
Aztecs, 3, *5*, 17, 19, *19*, 20
  smallpox epidemic and, 19

backcountry, colonial, 96, *213*
Bacon, Nathaniel (1647–1676), 84–85
Bacon's Rebellion, 83–85, *84*, 86
Bahamas, 16
Balboa, Vasco Núñez de (1475–1519), 17, *18*
balloons, hot air, 405
Baltimore and Ohio (B&O), 254, *254*
Bank of England, 306
Bank of the United States, 223, 285–88, 297, *305*
  battle with Jackson of, 304–5
  Congress and, 304–5
  Second, 287–88, *305*
bankruptcy, 277
Bankruptcy Scene, A, 200
banks, 297, 452
  national, 223–24, 285–88, 423, 425; *see also* Bank of the United States
Banneker, Benjamin (1731–1806), 218–19, 225
Banner of the Society of Pewterers, 193
Baptists, 126, 269, 378
  African-American, 328
  Free-Will, 175
  in Gabriel's Rebellion, 235
  in Great Awakening, 126
  in Massachusetts colony, 173
  in Second Great Awakening, 328
  Seventh Day, 95
Barbados, 82, 105
  as founder of Carolina colony, 78
  population of, 82
Barbary Coast, 81, 241
Barbary Wars, 241
Bargain of 1877, 471–72
Barlow, Joel (1754–1812), 219

Barrow plantation, maps of, *446*
Barton, Clara (1821–1912), 426
Baton Rouge, La., 255
Beecher, Lyman (1775–1863), 265
Bell, John (1797–1869), 396
Benin, 14
Benito Cereno (Melville), 285
Bentham, Jeremy, 191
Bering Strait, 3
Berkeley, John (1602–1678), 79
Berkeley, William (1606–1677), 83–84, *84*, 87
Bernard, Francis (1712–1779), 143
Bible, 22–23, 53, *55*, 56, 57, 60, 61, *64*, *106*, 127, 328–29, 333, 336, 347
    King James version, 265
    slavery in, 319, 333, 378
Bible Commonwealth, 58, 60, 89
Biddle, Nicholas (1786–1844), 304–5, *305*
Bill for Establishing Religious Freedom (Jefferson), 174
Bill of Rights (American), 212, 214, *300*, 458, 461
Bill of Rights (English), 87, 214, 215
Birney, James G. (1825–1864), 364, 372
birthrate, decline in U.S., 276
Bismarck, Otto von (1815–1898), 418
black Americans, *see* African-Americans
Black Codes, 455–56, *455*, 457
Black Legend, 23, 24–25, 28, 30, 36
Blackwell, Henry (1825?–1909), 359
Blair, Francis P., Jr. (1821–1875), 459
"Bleeding Kansas," 387–88
Bloomer, Amelia (1818–1894), 359
Body of Liberties (1641), 58
Bombardment of Fort Sumter (Currier and Ives), *400*
Book of Mormon, The (Smith), 272, 273
Booth, John Wilkes (1838–1865), 438
border states:
    in Civil War, 412, 413
    Emancipation Proclamation and, 415
Boston, Mass., 97, 122, 141, 265
    population of, 97
    poverty in, 100
    Puritans in, 66
    religious tolerance in, 173
    Townshend boycott in, 146
    Washington's army abandons, 159
Boston Associates, 262
Boston Gazette, 117
Boston Massacre, 146–47, *147*
Boston News-Letter, 122
Boston Tea Party, 148
Boucher, Jonathan (1738–1804), 157
Bowdoin, James (1726–1790), 200
Bowser, David B., *419*
Braddock, Edward (1695–1755), 131
Bradford, William (1590–1657), 65
Bradwell, Myra (1831–1894), 462
Brady, Mathew (1822–1896), *419*

Brazil, 17, 22, 35, 81, 82, *108*, 109, 416
    Dutch control of, 34
    slavery in, 320, 322, 330
Breckinridge, John C. (1821–1875), 395, 396
Breed's Hill, Battle of, 151
Brent, Margaret (1601–1670?), 51–52
Brer Rabbit stories, 329
Bristol, England, 106
British-Americans:
    British colonies, *see* American colonies
    pride in, 151
British Empire, 82, 152, 255
    abolishment of slavery in, 320, *320*, 337
    American vs. British view of, 143
    expansion of, 74–80
British liberty, *see* English liberty
British navy, 241
bronze, 14
Brooks, Preston (1819–1857), 388, *388*
Brown, John (1800–1859), 391–92, *394*, 395, 420, *460*
Brown, Joseph E. (1821–1894), 317
Brown, Matt, 449
Brown, Olympia, 461
Brownson, Orestes (1803–1876), 278
Brown v. Board of Education, 461
Bruce, Blanche K. (1841–1898), 464
Bryan, George (1731–1791), 212
Buchanan, James (1791–1868), 388, 389, 398
Buchanan administration, 389
Buena Vista, Battle of, 373
Buffalo, N.Y., 252
Buffalo Chase over Prairie Bluffs (Catlin), *303*
Bulger, Andrew (1789–1858), *247*
Bull Run, First Battle of, 408
Bull Run, Second Battle of, 410
Bunker Hill, Battle of, 151, 294
Burgoyne, John (1722–1792), 161
Burke, Edmund (1729–1797), 182
Burns, Anthony (1829–1862), 381
Burnside, Ambrose E. (1824–1881), 431
Burr, Aaron (1756–1836), 231, 233, *234*
Bute, Lord, 149
Butler, Andrew P. (1796–1857), *388*
Butler, Benjamin F. (1818–1893), 412

Cabeza de Vaca, Alvar Núñez (ca. 1490–1557?), 25
Cabot, John (ca. 1450–ca. 1499), 17, *18*
Cabral, Pedro (1467–1520), 17, *18*
Cabrillo, Juan Rodriguez (d. 1543), 25
Caesar (former slave), *188*
Cahokia, 5
Caitlin, George, *303*
Cajuns, 131
Calhoun, Floride (1792–1866), 300
Calhoun, John C. (1782–1850), 293, 381
    American System and, 286
    annexation of Texas and, 371

compact theory of, 300
concurrent majority theory of, 300
Declaration of Independence as viewed by, 320
Democratic Party and, 308
nationalism and, 299
nullification crisis and, 299–300
sectionalism and, 299
slavery as viewed by, 320
states' rights and, 300
as vice president, 299
as War Hawk, 242
California, 369, 372, 373
    enters Union, 380
    gold rush in, 376–77
    migration to, 368
    population of, 128–29, 369, 376, 377
    Spanish settlements in, 127–28
Californios, 368
Calvert, Cecilius, Lord Baltimore (1605–1675), 52
Calvert, Charles, Lord Baltimore (1637–1715), 86, 88
Calvin, John (1509–1564), 53
Calvinists, 89
Cambridge, Mass., 57
    first American printing press in, 57
Canada, 6, 129, 143, 179, 244, 294
    border with United States, 294
    ceded to Great Britain, 131
    French, 32–33, 92
    as slave refuge, 330, 334, 381
    U.S. invasion of, 244, 303
    War Hawks' plan for annexation of, 242
    see also French Canada
canals, *249*, 252–54, *253*, 286
Canary Islands, 14, 16
Cape Cod, 54–55
Cape of Good Hope, 15
Cape Verde Islands, 14
capitalism:
    development of, 34
    as threat to freedom, 224
    women and, 276
"captains of industry," 425
caravels, 14
Caribbean, 20, 22, 24, 35, 40, 105, 106–7
    French, 131
    as part of slave empire, 394
    see also West Indies
Caribbean Islands, 34
Carnegie, Andrew (1835–1919), 425
Carolina colony, 87
    founding of, 77–78
    fur trade in, 110–11
    hierarchical society of, 78
    Indians in, 78
Caroline, Fort, 25–27
carpetbaggers, 464–65

Carroll, James, 173
Carter, Landon (1710–1778), 110
Carter, Robert, III (1728–1804), 188
Carter family, 130
Cartwright, John (1740–1824), *157*
Cass, Lewis (1782–1866), 379
Castile, 16
Catawba Indians, *9*, 96
Catherine of Aragon (1485–1536), 40
Catholics, Catholicism, 17, 32, 41, 53–54, 86,
    87, 137, 149, *149*, 173, 346, 375, 376,
    385–86
  in American colonies, 95, 173
  banned in Ireland, 70
  Church of England and, 40, 53, 68, 86
  in Civil War, *419*
  French and, 137
  Germans as, 94
  Know-Nothing Party vs., 385–86
  liberties of, 174
  in Maryland colony, 52, 69–70, 88
  Native Americans and, 22–24, 27, 30, 33
  as Papists, 92
  in Pennsylvania colony, 95
  Protestants vs., 265
  riots against, 265–66
  Spanish colonies and, 21, 22–24, 27, 30, 36
Catlin, George (1796–1872), *387*
Cayugas, 7
Celia (slave; d. 1855), 321–22
censorship, in Colonial America, 123
Central America, 3, *4*, 24, *26*
Central Pacific, 423
Chaco Canyon, 6, *6*
Chamberlain, Mason, *124*
Champlain, Samuel de (1567–1635), 32–33, *33*
Chancellorsville, Battle of, 431
Chariot of Liberty, A, 150
Charles I, king of England (1600–1649), 52,
    54, 68, *68*, 69
Charles II, king of England (1630–1685), 68,
    69, 74–75, 77, 87
Charleston, S.C., 97, 100, 115, 162, 188
  black community in, 323, 334
  slave trade in, 78
Charter of Liberties and Privileges (1683), 77
Charter of Liberty (1682), 79
Chartist movement, 380
checks and balances, 204–5, 208, 209
Cheney family, *101*
Cherokee Nation v. Georgia, 302–3
Cherokee Phoenix, 284
Cherokees, 7, 96, 181, 196, 243, 246, 301–3,
    303, 424
  Constitution of, 301–2, *303*, 424
Chesapeake Bay, 39, 165
Chesapeake region, 43–44, *48*, 55, 66, 82,
    91, 105–6
  boycott in, 146

indentured servants in, 110
  as runaway slave refuge, 115
  settlement of, 47–52
  slavery in, 109–10, 115
  society in, 110
  tenant farmers in, 110
  tobacco in, *48*, 50, *50*, *51*, 80, 83, 91, 98, 99,
    102, 109–10
Chicago, Ill., 260, 262
  as manufacturing center, 385
Chicago Sanitary Fair, *426*
Chickasaws, 7, 196, 301
Child, Lydia Maria (1802–1880), 352, 357
China, 13–14, 15, 20
Chinese, Chinese immigrants, 376–77, 423, 453
Choctaws, 7, 181, 196, 301
Christ, Jesus, *see* Jesus
Christianity, 9, 12, 13, 17, 22, 24, *49*, 60, 64,
    174–75, 241
  and free exercise of religion, 69–70, 78–79
  growth of, in U.S., 269
  liberty and, 346
  Native Americans and, *1*, *9*, *22*, 28, 29,
    41, 128
  in New World, 36
  republicanism and, 175
  Second Great Awakening, 269, 272
  sects of, 95
  slavery and, 83, 113–14, 127, 328–29, 356
  see also specific denominations
"Christian liberty," 12
Christian Republicanism, 175
Christian Sparta, U.S. as, 175
church and state:
  Puritans and, 58
  separation of, 173, 174–75
churches, tax support of, 95, 174
Church of England, *see* Anglican Church
Church of Jesus Christ of Latter-day Saints,
    see Mormons
Cincinnati, Ohio, 260, *261*
  race riots in, 274
cities, growth of, 260–61
citizenry, virtuous, 117, 175–76
citizenship, 457–58, 461, 462–63
  of African-Americans, 352–53, 462–63
  Fourteenth Amendment and, 352, 462
  Native Americans and, 215–17
  second-class, *see* segregation
Civil Rights Act (1875), *441*, 470
civil rights and liberties:
  abuses of, 214
  Alien and Sedition Acts and, 232–33, 265
  in American colonies, 39, 44–45, 118–19,
    169, 170
  American Revolution and, 171–72, 174
  Civil War and, 418, 422
  in England, 67–70
  legislation on, 465

see also Bill of Rights (American);
    constitutional amendments, U.S.;
    freedom; McCarthy era; women's
    rights
Civil Rights Bill (1866), 456–57
Civil War, U.S., 317, 367, *400*, 402–40, *402*,
    442, *443*
  agriculture in, 423
  beginning of, 399–400
  black soldiers in, 416–17, *417*
  blockade in, 407
  campaigns of, *409*, *411*, *432*
  casualties in, 403, 406, 407, 410, 416,
    422, 446
  Catholics in, *419*
  civil liberties and, 418, 422
  Confederate advantages in, 404
  draft in, 405, 425, 427, 428–29
  emancipation and, 403, 410–17, *414*, 416,
    417, *419*, 435, 439
  end of, 436–38
  financing of, 425
  as first modern war, 403–10
  industry in, 422–23
  photography in, 407
  propaganda in, 406–7
  resources for warfare in, 407
  as Second American Revolution, 417–27
  Sherman's March to the Sea in, 436, *437*
  songs of, *418*, 423
  technology of, 405–6, *406*
  transportation in, *408*
  Union advantages in, 404
  West in, 410, *411*, 433
  women in, 425–26, *425*
Clark, William (1770–1838), 239–40, *240*
class:
  in American Society, 274, 276, 298
  development of, 276
  education and, 348
  see also middle class
Clay, Henry (1777–1852), 256, *305*, 307
  American Colonization Society and, 348
  American System and, 285, 286
  annexation of Texas and, 371, 372
  Compromise of 1850 and, 380–81
  election of 1824 and, 291
  in election of 1832, 305
  nickname of, 296
  nullification crisis and, 301
  as War Hawk, 242
Clermont, 252
Clinton, De Witt (1769–1828), 247, 252
Clinton, Henry (1738–1795), 161, 185
Cloud, N. B. (1809–1875), *468*
coal, 423
Cobb, Howell (1815–1868), 431
Coercive Acts, *see* Intolerable Acts
coffee, 97, 106

Coles, Edward (1786–1868), 219
Colfax, La., massacre in, 468, 470
Colfax, Schuyler (1823–1885), *460*
colonization, of slaves, 348–49, 350, 413
Colored Rule in a Reconstructed (?) State
    (Nast), *469*
Columbian Exchange, 19
Columbian Magazine, 177
Columbus, Christopher (1451–1506), 2, 13
    voyages of, 16–17, *16*, *18*, 19
Columbus's Landfall, *16*
Committee of Correspondence, 144
Committee of Safety, 88, 150, 178
common law, development of English, 67
common schools, 347–48
Common Sense (Paine), 152–53, 156, 157, 191
"Commonwealth and Free State", England
    as, 68
communication, 194, 251
communism, *342*
communitarians, 344
compass, 14
Compromise of 1850, 380–81, *381*, 382
Concord, Battle of, 151, *151*, *160*
Confederate States of America, 398–400,
    420, 428–31, *437*
    black soldiers and, 431
    currency of, *429*
    division among, 428–29
    economic problems of, 429–30
    government of, 428
    Senate of, 431
    Union sympathizers in, 430
    women and, 430–31
Congregationalists, 53, 57, 95, 125, 173, 356
    American Revolution and, 175
    Half-Way Covenant and, 67
    in Massachusetts, 174
Congress, U.S., 301
    under Articles of Confederation, 195, 196
    authority of, 288, 300
    Bank of the United States and, 305–6
    under Constitution, 203–5
    and currency, 177, 425
    Deborah Sampson pensioned by, 189
    Independent Treasury policy and, 307
    National Road authorized by, 252, 286
    oaths of allegiance and, 179
    petitioned for emancipation, 234
    political parties in, 222
    presidential veto and, 305, 457
    Reconstruction policies of, 454
    slavery and, 234, 378
    and wage and price controls, 178
    see also House of Representatives, U.S.;
        Senate, U.S.
Connecticut, 196, *207*
    militia of, *151*
    slavery in, 188

Connecticut colony:
    militia of, 151
    in Pequot War, 64–65
    women in, 102
conquistadores, 5, 17, 19, 20, 23, *23*
constitution:
    Cherokee, 301–2, 303, 424
    English, 117
    of Texas, 376
Constitution, U.S., 202–8, *214*, 229, 291
    African-Americans and, 442, 461–62
    American System and, 286–87
    Andrew Jackson and, *282*
    Calhoun's view of, 300
    celebration pageants for, 194
    checks and balances in, 204–5, 208, 209
    compact theory of, 300
    Confederate constitution and, 398
    free blacks and, 217
    Garrison's suggested abrogation of, 350
    J. Q. Adams and, 294
    Louisiana Purchase and, 238
    Marbury v. Madison in, 237
    national bank and, 288
    Native Americans and, 214, 215–17
    political parties and, 222
    powers granted under, 204–5
    preamble to, 207
    ratification of, 194, 207–15, *207*, *213*
    signing of, *209*
    slavery and, 205–7, *205*, 214, 352, 381,
        389, 390
    state vs. federal powers in, 215
    strict constructionism and, 225, 286,
        288, 294
    three-fifths clause of, 205, 234, 247
    Webster's view of, 300
    women's rights and, 461, 462
    see also Constitutional Convention
Constitution, USS, 244
constitutional amendments, U.S.:
    First, 215, 233
    Second, 215
    Eighth, 215
    Ninth, 215
    Tenth, 215
    Twelfth, 234
    Thirteenth, 436
    Fourteenth, 352, 457–58, 461, 462, 470
    Fifteenth, 460, *460*, 462
    Seventeenth, 391
Constitutional Convention (1787), 202–8,
    202, *206*
Constitutional Union Party, 396
constitutions, state, 170
Continental Army, 153, 158, *159*
    demoralization of, 161
    strength of, 158
Continental Association, 150

Continental Congress, *see* First Continental
    Congress; Second Continental
    Congress
"coolies," 423
Copely, John Singleton (1738–1815), *218*
Copperheads, 426
Cornish, Samuel (ca. 1795–1858), 354
Cornwallis, Lord Charles (1738–1805),
    162–65
Coronado, Francisco Vásquez de
    (1510–1554), 25
Cortés, Hernán (1485–1547), *5*, 17, *18*, 19, *19*
Cosby, William (1690–1736), 123
cotton, *258*, 262, 287, 306, 313, *325*, 428,
    449, 453
    exporting of, 314
    market revolution and, *258*, 259
    in New Orleans, *316*
    and North, 314
    plantations, *see* planters, plantations,
        cotton
    and wealth in South, 385
    see also Cotton Kingdom
Cotton Belt, 324, 449
cotton gin, *258*, 259
Cotton Kingdom, 257–59, *258*, 259, 281, 287,
    315–16, 327, 397, 428
Council of the Indies, 21
Country Party, 117–18, 121
"cousinocracy," 99
Covenant Chain, 75
coverture, 12–13, 189
Cowpens, S.C., American victory at, 162
craftsmen, 261, 264, 266, 277
    African-Americans as, 274, 323
    see also artisans
Crawford, Thomas (1813?–1857), 367, *367*
Crawford, William H. (1732–1782), 291
Creek Indians, 78, 96, 181, 243, 246, 291,
    301, 303
Creole, 335
Creoles, 113
Crèvecoeur, Hector St. John de (1735–1813),
    217–18
cricket, 116
criollos, 21
Crisis, The, *344*
Crittenden, John J. (1786–1863), 398, 412
Cromwell, Oliver (1599–1658), 68, 70
crop lien system, 449–52
crop rotation, 42
Crowe, Eyre (1824–1910), *311*
Cruikshank, U.S. v., 470
Cuba, 16, 27, 28, 289, 294, 394
"cult of domesticity," 275–76, *275*, 362
currency, 177, 200, 204, 223, 287, 297,
    304, 425
    Confederate, *429*, 430
Currency Act (1764), 142, 144

Currier, Nathaniel (1813–1888), *252*, *400*, *457*
Cutting Sugar Cane, *82*
Cuzco, *23*

"Dandy Jim," *285*
Daniels, John Daniel, *323*
Dartmouth College v. Woodward, 266
Daughters of Liberty, 146
David (Indian), *47*
Davis, David (1815–1886), 422
Davis, Jefferson (1808–1889), 367, *367*, 398,
    400, 428, 435
    Abraham Lincoln compared to, 428
Davis, Joseph (1784–1870), 435
D-Day, 410
De Bow's Review, 333
de Bry, Theodor (1528–1598), *10*, *23*, *42*
debt, imprisonment for, 277
Declaration of Independence (1776), 153–54,
    174, 191, 194, 215, 320
    ideas of equality in, 169
    Lincoln's views on, 391
    Native Americans and, 181
    slavery and, 153, 219, 336, 352, 353, 354
"Declaration of Josephe" (Josephe), 29
Declaration of Sentiments, 357
Declaration of the Immediate Causes of Secession,
    397–98
Declaratory Act (1766), 144
Deep South, 257, 281, 313, 314, 315, 318, 334,
    394, 397
Deere, John (1804–1886), 260
deficit, federal, *see* national debt
deism, 124
    separation of church and state and, 173
Delany, Martin R. (1812–1885), *460*
Delaware Indians, 132
Delegation of Advocates of Women's Suffrage
    Addressing the House Judiciary Committee,
    A, *462*
Democracy in America (Tocqueville), 250,
    282–83
Democratic Party, 297–98, 307–8, *308*, 371,
    373, 378, 382–83, 386, 388, 390, 391,
    394, 403, 414, 422
    and Bank of the United States, 304–5, *305*
    in the Civil War, 427
    creation of, 291
    1860 convention of, 395–96
    Fifteenth amendment and, 460
    John C. Calhoun and, *308*
    nomination of Buchanan and, 388
    press of, 298, *308*, 422
    in Reconstruction, *459*, 466–67, 469,
    470–72
    views on freedom of, 297–98
    see also specific elections and campaigns
Democratic-Republican societies, 229, 231
Democratic Review, 376

Denmark, in the West Indies, 82
Departure of the 7th Regiment, *402*
depression, economic:
    of 1819, 277, 287–88
    of 1837, 254, 277, 306
    of 1873, 470
    of 1929, *see* Great Depression
de Soto, Hernando (1496–1542), 25
Destruction by Fire of Pennsylvania Hall, *355*
Detroit, Mich., 132
Dial, 358
Dias, Bartholomeu (1450–1500), 15
Dickinson, John (1731–1808), *170*
Diggers, 69
Dinwiddie, Robert (1693–1770), 130
Discourse Concerning Western Planting, A
    (Hakluyt), 41
diseases:
    Africans and, 80, 109
    in Civil War, 406
    Indians and, 2, 19–20, 25, 33, 43, 46, 61,
    81, 90
    in Jamestown, 47
    Pilgrims and, 55
"Disquisition on Government, A"
    (Calhoun), 293
Dissenters, 60, 87, 95, 119, 126, 148
diversity, *172*
division of powers, in U.S. Constitution,
    204–5, 208, 209
Dix, Dorothea (1802–1887), 356
Dominican Republic, 16
Dominion of New England, 88
Donelson, Fort, 410
Doolittle, Amos B., *232*, *246*
Dorr, Thomas (1805–1854), 282
Dorr War, 282
Douglas, Stephen A. (1813–1861), 382, 388,
    389–91, *391*, 395–96
Douglass, Frederick (1817–1895), 312, *313*,
    334, *341*, 356, 413, *460*
    on abolition, 439, 444
    autobiography of, 353
    biography of, 312
    on the Constitution, 352
    Independence Day speech of, 354
    on plantations, 317
    on slavery, 356, 359
"dower rights," 51
Downfall of Mother Bank, The, *305*
draft:
    in Civil War, 404, 425, 427, 428–29
    "twenty-negro" provision and, 429
Drayton, Thomas F. (1809–1891), 420
Dred Scott case, 389–90, *390*, 391, 396
Dudley, Thomas (1576–1653), 62
Dunkers, 94, 95
Dunmore, John Murray, earl of (1732–1809),
    152, 158, 159, 185

Duquesne, Fort, 131
Dutch East India Company, 34
Dutch Empire, 34–36, 75
    see also Netherlands
Dutch Reformed Church, 35
Dutch West India Company, 34, 36, *36*

East, 260
Eastern Bank of Alabama, *429*
East India Company, 148
East Indies, 13, 17
Eaton, Peggy (1799?–1879), 300
economic freedom:
    American Revolution and, 175–78
    free labor and, 176
    hoarding and, 177
    price controls and, 178
economy:
    of Confederate States of America, 429–30
    early U.S., 175–78, 194, 196, 200
    1819 downturn of, 277, 287–88
    of New England colonies, 65–67
    see also depression, economic; market
    revolution; recessions
Ecuador, 289
Edict of Nantes (1598), 32
Edisto Island, S.C., 450
education:
    common school and, 347–48
    of freed slaves, 434, 444, *444*, *446*,
    447, 448
    public, 170, 175, 277, 347–48, 465, *466*, *467*
    reform, 341
    slaves barred from, 321
    social classes and, 347–48
    women and, 228, 230
Edwards, Jonathan (1703–1758), 125
Eickemeyer, Rudolph (1831–1895), *444*
Eighth Amendment, 215
Electioneering in the South, *463*
elections and campaigns:
    of 1789, 222
    of 1792, 231
    of 1796, 231
    of 1800, 233–34, *234*
    of 1804, 242
    of 1808, 242
    of 1816, 288
    of 1820, 288
    of 1824, 291, *291*
    of 1828, 294–96, *296*
    of 1836, 307
    of 1840, 307–9, *308*
    of 1844, 370–72
    of 1848, 379
    of 1852, 382
    of 1856, 387–88, *389*
    of 1858, 389, 390–91, 392–93
    of 1860, *366*, 395–96, *396*

of 1862, 414
of 1864, 434
of 1868, 459–60, *460*
of 1872, 469
of 1876, 471–72, *472*
in Middle Colonies, 120, *120*
in New England colonies, 120
Electoral College, 204, 205, 206, 231, 233, 242, *296*
Twelfth Amendment and voting by, 234
as undemocratic, 283
Electoral Commission (1877), 472
Eliot, John (1604–1690), *64*
Elizabeth I, queen of England (1533–1603), *38*, 39, 40, 41
Elliott, Robert B. (1842–1884), *441*
Emancipation Proclamation (1862), 403, 414–16, *414*, 417, 423, 450
Emancipation Proclamation, Preliminary (1862), *413*, 414
Embargo (1807), 241–42, 262
Emerson, John (d. 1843), 389
Emerson, Ralph Waldo (1803–1882), 151, 267–68, *268*, 270, 278, 340, 364
enclosure movement, 42
encomienda system, 24
Enforcement Acts (1870–71), 468, 470
England, 39, 105
Civil War of, 68, *68*, 69–70, 86–87
and colonization of America, 38–71
as "Commonwealth and Free State," 68
debate over freedom in, 68–69
emigration from, 43–44
empire expansion by, 74–80
Glorious Revolution of, 86–87
as haven for former slaves, 185
Ireland conquered by, 40
justification for colonization by, 11, 41–43
political upheavals of, 67–70
poor economic conditions in, 42–43
population of, 42, 43
prejudice in, 80–81
Protestantism in, 40, 69, 70, 116
Reformation in, 40
War of Jenkins' Ear and, 115–16
in West Indies, 82
see also British Empire; Great Britain
England, Church of, *see* Anglican Church
England's Grievance Discovered (Gardiner), *89*
English colonies, *see* American Colonies
English common law, development of, 67
English Country Party, 121
English liberty, 67, 69, 77, 85, 112, 117, 140, 141, 143, 151
English Toleration Act (1690), 89
Enlightenment, 124–25
entail, 177
Equiano, Olaudah (1745–1797), 105–6, *106*, 109, 114, 135

"Era of Good Feelings," 288
Erie Canal, *249*, 250, 252–54
Ethiopian Regiment, of Lord Dunmore, 159
Europe, European powers, 2, *15*
Enlightenment in, 124
expansion of, 3, 5, 13–16
hierarchical society of, 12–13
negative views of Indians in, 10–11
New World rivalry of, 127–30, *128*
social status in, 12–13
speed of American exploration by, 16–20
Western, 2
see also specific countries
Evans, George Henry (1805–1856), 379
executive branch, U.S. government, 237
Exodus, book of, 329
Ex parte Milligan, 422
Exposition and Protest, 299
extraterritoriality, 206

factories, system, 261–62, *261*
"Factory Life as It Is, by an Operative," 271
Fallen Timbers, Battle of, 216
Falmouth, Maine, 153
Family Record, *443*
farms, *see* agriculture
Farragut, David G. (1801–1870), 410
Federal Hall, 222
federalism, 204, *207*
Federalist, The (Hamilton, Madison, and Jay), 208
Federalist Party, 227, 231, 244, 288
in election of 1800, 233, *234*
in election of 1804, 242
elimination of, 247
platform of, 226
Female Anti-Slavery Society, 340
feminism, 356–64
see also gender relations; women; women's rights
femme sole (unmarried woman), 51
Ferdinand, king of Spain (1452–1516), 16, *16*
feudalism, 78
field labor, 50
Fifteenth Amendment, 460, *460*, 462
Fifty-fourth Massachusetts Volunteers, 416
Filling Cartridges at the U.S. Arsenal of Watertown, Massachusetts, *425*
Fillmore, Millard (1800–1874), 381, 388
Finney, Charles Grandison (1792–1875), 268, 272, 351
"fire-eaters," 395
First African Church, The, *445*
First Amendment, 215, 233
First Continental Congress (1775), 149
First Rhode Island Regiment, *159*
First Seminole War, 303
fish, 106
Fisher, Sidney George, 461

Fisk University, 444
Fitzhugh, George (1806–1881), 320, 390
Five Civilized Tribes, 301, *302*
Five Generations of a Black Family, 444
Five Iroquois Nations, 75–77, *77*
Five Points (Catlin), *387*
Fletcher v. Peck, 237
Florentine Codex, *19*
Florida, *10*, 20, 22, 25, 78, 122, 161, 255, 301, 303
ceded to Great Britain, 132
colonization of, 25, 27
as haven for fleeing slaves, 115
population of, 127
Seminoles in, 303
U.S. acquisition of, 259, 294
War Hawks' plan for conquest of, 242
Force Bill, 301
Foreign Anti-Slavery Society, 363
Forrest, Nathan B. (1821–1877), 417
Fort Caroline, 25–27
Fort Donelson, 410
Forten, Charlotte (1837–1914), 434
Fort Henry, 410
Fort Louisbourg, 131
Fort McHenry, 244
Fort McIntosh, 196
Fort Pillow, 417
Fort Stanwix, 196
Fort Sumter, 400, *400*, 407, 420
Fort Ticonderoga, 131, 151
Fort Wagner, 416
Fort Washington, 161
Foster, Stephen S. (1809–1881), 340
Founding Fathers, as slaveholders, 183, 184, 205, 219
Fourteenth Amendment, 352, 457–58, 461, 462, 470
Fragment on Government (Bentham), 191
Frame of Government, 79
France, 17, 42, 89, 96, 115, 116, 130–32, 194, 394
American Revolution and, 158, 161
Catholicism and, 137
change of government in, 380
justification for colonization by, 11
Louisiana Purchase and, 237–39, *239*
New World exploration of, 30–33
population compared to England, 43
seizure of American ships by, 231–32
trade with, 231
in wars with Great Britain, 225, 241–42
in West Indies, 82
see also French Empire
France Bringing the Faith to the Indians of New France, *1*
Franciscans, 30, *30*
Frank Leslie's Illustrated Newspaper, 277, *455*, 462

Franklin, Benjamin (1706–1790), 122, 124, *124*, 137
  at Constitutional Convention, 202, 207
  as deist, 125
  as head of Pennsylvania Abolition Society, 234
  Stamp Act and, 146
  Treaty of Amity and Commerce and, 161
  Treaty of Paris and, 165
  writings of, 124
Frazier, Garrison (b. 1797), 442
Freake, Elizabeth (1642–1713), *66*
Freake, John (1635–1675), *66*
Fredericksburg, Va., *111*
free blacks, 188–89, 217, 322–23
  as laborers, 323
  in New Orleans, 323
  see also African-Americans; slaves, emancipated
"freeborn Englishman," 67, 68
Freedmen's Bureau, 444, 447–48, 457, *459*
Freedmen's Bureau, The, 448
Freedmen's Bureau Bill (1866), 457
freedom, 104–38
  in Age of Jackson, 298–99
  American Revolution and, 140, 169, 170, 190–91
  Civil War and, 418, 423, *438*
  Democratic vs. Whig view of, 297–98
  desire of slaves for, 85, *114*, 115–16, 184–85, 187, 329–30
  economic, 43
  European idea of, 11, 12–13
  expansion of, 105
  of expression, 122–23, 171, 214, 215, 229, 233, 314, 355
  feminism and, 358
  Indians and, 11–12, 181–82, 217
  individualism and, 267–68, 272
  as inducement to English colonization, 43
  industrialization and, 264
  Lincoln's views of, 418, 421
  Locke on, 218
  market revolution and, 272
  in New Netherland, 34–35
  political power vs., 121
  of the press, 122–23, 176, 214, 215, 314, 355
  Ralph Waldo Emerson and, 270
  in Reconstruction, 442, 443–54
  reform and, 346
  of religion, 214, 215
  religious, *see* religious freedom
  of speech, *see* freedom, of expression
  Stamp Act and, 140, 142
  in utopian societies, 344
  after War of 1812, 250–51
  Whig views of, 298
  white vs. Indian, 181–82
  see also religious freedom

freedom dues, 44, 52
freedom petitions, African-Americans and, 184
Freedom's Journal, 284, 354
Freed Slaves Celebrating President Lincoln's Decree of Emancipation, 415
free labor, 176, 386–87, 447
freemen, in Pennsylvania, 79
Free Soil Party, 379–80, 386
free trade, 178
Free Woman, 358
Frelinghuysen, Theodore (1817–1885), 125
Frémont, John C. (1813–1890), 373, 388, 413, 434
French and Indian War, *see* Seven Years' War
French Canada, 32–33
French Empire, 20, 30–33, 82, 129–30
French Revolution, 132, 191, 225–26, 227
Fries, John (1750–1818), 232
Fries's Rebellion, 232
Fugitive Slave Act (1850), 381–82, *381*
fugitive slaves, 234, 303, 380, 381–82, 412, *412*, 413
  Abraham Lincoln and, 398
  as contraband in Civil War, 412, 415
  in U.S. Constitution, 234
  see also slaves, runaway
Fuller, Margaret (1810–1850), 358, *358*
Fulton, Robert (1765–1815), 252
Fundamental Constitutions of Carolina (1669), 78
fur trade, 32, 45, 46–47, 98, 102
  animal populations and, 47
  Five Iroquois Nations and, 77
  in New France, 32
  of Pequots, 64
  Russian, 127
  Treaty of Paris and, 136

Gabriel (slave; 1776–1800), 235–36, 335
Gabriel's Rebellion, 235–36
Gadsden Purchase, *375*
Gaffney, Mary (b. 1846), 449
gag rule, regarding abolition, 355
Galloway, Joseph (1731–1803), 152
Gama, Vasco da (1460–1524), 15
Gardiner, Ralph, *89*
Garfield, James A. (1831–1881), 443
Garnet, Henry Highland (1815–1882), 354
Garrison, William Lloyd (1805–1879), 337, 349–50, *349*, 351–52, 363, *363*, 460
gender relations:
  European, 11
  Native American, 10
  see also women; women's rights
General Court (Conn.), 64
General Court (Mass.), 57–58, 63, 66, 88, 89
General History of Virginia (Smith), *49*
Genoa, 16, 17

George III, king of England (1738–1820), 140, 153, 157
Georgia, 255, 301, 302, 303, 450
  government in, 171
  population of slaves in, 112
  slavery in, 206
  Trail of Tears in, 303
  voting rights in, 285
Georgia colony, 27, 119
  in American Revolution, 159, 162
  creation of, 111
  Declaration of Independence and, 153
  Loyalists in, 179
  slavery in, 115, 184
German-Americans, 130, *265*
Germans, German immigrants, 91–95, 96, 130, *265*, 346
"German triangle," 264
Gettysburg, Battle of, 432, *432*
Gettysburg Address, The, 418, 419
Ghent, Treaty of (1814), 246
Gibbons v. Ogden, 266
Gideon's Band, 434
Gifford, Abigail, 59
Gilbert, Humphrey (1539–1583), 41
Glorious Revolution, 86–87
Goddess of Liberty, 250
Godkin, E. L. (1831–1902), 469
"God Save the King," 116
gold, 19, 20, 21, 23, 26, 39, 43, 47, 48, 74, 82, 306
  in California gold rush, 376–77
  coinage, 121
  currency and, 287
  as inducement to exploration, 25, 27, 42
  tobacco as substitute for, 50
gold rush, California, 376–77
Gould, Jay (1836–1892), 425
government, U.S.:
  Constitutional debate over, 202, 211
  debt of, *see* national debt
  society and, 212
  structure of, 202–3
  see also specific branches
Gower, George (ca. 1540–1596), *38*
grain, 106, 224
Grand Council of the Five Iroquois Nations, 77
"grandees," 84
Grand Federal Procession, *193*
Grant, Ulysses S. (1822–1885), 410, 433, *433*, *437*, *460*, 468, 469
  background of, 410
  in election of 1868, 459–60
  Ku Klux Klan and, 468
  Lee's surrender to, 438
  at Petersburg, 436
  scandals under, 467
  Southern violence and, 470

Great Awakening, 114, 125–27, *126*
    impact of, 126–27
Great Awakening, Second, 268–73, *272*,
    345, 350
    individualism and, 272
    Mormons and, 273
Great Awakening, slavery and, 328
Great Britain, 17, *18*, 97, 181, 194, 291, 294, 394
    American boycott of, 150
    Chartist movement in, 380
    creation of, 105
    empire of, 20, 21, 131
    Oregon Territory and, 368, *369*, 372
    patriotism of, 116–17
    regulation of American trade with, 98
    seizure of American ships by, 231–32
    trade with, 231
    war debt of, 141
    in war with France, 225, 241–42
    see also British Empire; England
Great Depression:
    homelessness and, *368*
    see also New Deal
Great Famine, as cause of Irish
    immigration, 264
Great Lakes, 33, 250
Great Lakes region, 77, 129, 132
Great League of Peace, 7
Great Migration, 55, 67
Great Society, 447
Greeley, Horace (1811–1872), 469
Green, James K. (1823–1891), 463
Greene, Nathanael (1742–1786), 162
Greenland, 16
Green Mountain Boys, 146, 151
Greenville, Treaty of (1795), 216, *216*, 243
Grenville, George (1712–1770), 142
Grimké, Angelina (1805–1879), 352,
    356–57, 358
Grimké, Sarah (1792–1873), 356–57
Guadalupe Hidalgo, Treaty of (1848),
    373, 375
Guadeloupe, 131
Guilford Courthouse, N.C., American victory
    at, 162
Gulf Coast, 25
Gulf of Mexico, *5*, 6, 32
Gullah Jack, 336
Gullah language, 115
Gutenberg, Johannes (1390–1468), 17
Guthrie, Tex., *453*

habeas corpus, 67
haciendas, 21
Haiti, 16, 82, 235, *235*, 336, 413, 415
    creation of, 235
Haitian Revolution, 235, *235*
Hakluyt, Richard (1552?–1616), 41–42
Half-Way Covenant (1662), 67

Hamilton, Alexander (1757?–1804), 201, *201*,
    202, 209, 219, 233–34, 236
    French Revolution as viewed by, 225
    religion and, 173
    selected as head of Treasury
        Department, 222
    social hierarchy as viewed by, 226
    Treasury program of, 222, 226
    war with France desired by, 232
Hamilton, Andrew (1676–1741), 124
Hammond, James Henry (1807–1864),
    316, 330
Hampton, Wade (1818–1902), 471
Hampton University, 444
Hancock, John (1737–1793), 147, 157, 208
Hänner, Johannes, 93
Harmony community, 344–45
Harpers Ferry, 391–94, *395*
Harper's Magazine, 343
Harper's Monthly, 359
Harper's Weekly, *425*, 445, 448, *463*,
    469, 473
Harrison, William Henry (1773–1841), 244,
    307–9, *308*
Hartford, Conn., 60
Hartford Convention, 247
Harvard College, 57, *57*, 270
Hat Act (1732), 140
Havana, Cuba, 25
Hawley, Joseph (1723–1788), 153
Hayes, Rutherford B. (1822–1893), 471–72
Hayne, Robert Y. (1791–1839), 300
Haynes, Lemuel (1753–1833), 184, *184*
Henry, Fort, 410
Henry, Patrick (1736–1799), 143, 149, 206–7,
    209, 214
Henry VIII, king of England (1491–1547), 40
Henson, Josiah (1789–1883), 353
Herald Of Freedom, 363
Heroes of America, 430
Herrnhuters, 95
Hessians, 159, 161
Hicks, Edward (1780–1849), *72*
Higginson, Martha, 356
Highland Scots, 179
Hispaniola, 16–17, 24, 28
History of the American Revolution, The
    (Ramsay), 210
History of the Indies (Las Casas), 28
hoarding, to fix prices, 177
Hodges, Willis A. (1815–1890), 323
Hogarth, William (1697–1764), *147*
Holland, *see* Netherlands
Holy Experiment, Pennsylvania colony's, 136
Holyoke, Mass., *261*
Homer, Winslow (1836–1910), *447*
Homestead Act (1862), 423
Hooker, "Fighting Joe" (1814–1879), 431
Hooker, Thomas (1586–1647), 60

Hopis, 6
Hornet (American warship), *246*
Hornet and the Peacock, Or, John Bull in Distress,
    The (Doolittle), *246*
Horseshoe Bend, Battle of, 246
House of Burgesses, Va., 48, 83, 85, 99, 120,
    143, 174
House of Commons, British, 68, 121, *141*, 143
House of Lords, British, 68, 69
House of Representatives, U.S., 203–4, 206,
    233, *280*, *456*, 470
    abolition and, 355
    African-Americans in, 464
    creation of, 203
    in election of 1824, 291
    Johnson's impeachment and, 458–60
Houston, Sam (1793–1863), 370
Howard, O. O. (1830–1909), 447, 450
Howard University, 444
Howe, Samuel Gridley (1801–1876), 363
Howe, William (1729–1814), 151, 159, 161
Hudson, Henry (d. 1611), 34
Hudson River, 250, 252
Hudson Valley, 36
Hughes, John, 265
Huguenots, *10*, 25–27, 32
    see also Christianity
hunting, 46–47
Hurons, 132
Hutchinson, Anne (1591–1643), 61, 62, 69
Hutchinson, Thomas (1711–1780), 140

Iberian Peninsula, 16
Ibo people, 113
Illinois, 255
    blacks barred from, 275
    Lincoln-Douglas campaign in, 390–91,
        392–93
    38th Infantry of, *405*
Illustrated London News, *427*
immigrants, immigration, 2, 90, *91*, *264*,
    265–66, *265*, 386
    from England, 39, 43–44, 50–51,
        54–55, 90
    from France, 32
    from Germany, 130, *265*, 346
    growth of, 265–66
    from Ireland, *265*, 266, 346
    Know-Nothings and, 386
    numbers of, *264*, *265*, 266
    population of, 263–64
    riots against, 266
    of Scotch-Irish, *91*, 130
    from Spain, 21–22
    see also specific nationalities
impeachment, of Andrew Johnson, 458–60
impressment, 117, 225, 241, 246
Inauguration of Mr. Lincoln, 399
Incas, 3, 19, *26*

income taxes, *see* taxes, income
indentured servitude, 3, 44–45, 50–51, *51*, 52, 81, 82, 188
  American Revolution and, 168, 176
  in Carolina, 78
  decline of, 176
  in New England, 65, 66
  in Pennsylvania, 113
  slavery compared with, 80
  in Virginia, 82, 83, 85, 110
Independence Day Celebration in Centre Square (Krimmel), *283*
Independence Hall, *202*
Independent Monitor, 468
Independent Treasury, 307
India, 13, 15, 131, 143, 148
Indiana, 255
  blacks barred from, 275
Indian removal, 301–3, *302*
  see also Native Americans
Indian Removal Act (1830), 301
indigo, 106, 110
individualism, 267–68
  freedom and, 267–68, 272
  market revolution and, 267–73
  reform and, 346
  Second Great Awakening and, 272
Indonesia, 15
industrial revolution, 257, 261–62, *263*, 313, 385, 403
industry, 425, *425*
  in Civil War, 422–23, *425*
  factory system and, 261–62
  law and, 266
  workers' life and, 264
  see also manufacturing; market revolution; *specific industries*
inflation, 177–78
influenza, 19
information revolution, 283–84
In Side of the Old Lutheran Church in 1800, York, Pa., 173
Interesting Narrative of the Life of Olaudah Equiano, or Gustavus Vassa, the African, The (Equiano), 105, *106*, 135
Intolerable Acts (1774), 148–49
Iowa, blacks barred from, 275
Iraq War, 406
Ireland, 80, 91
  conquered by England, 40
  English control over, 70
  English immigration to, 43
Irish, Irish immigrants, *265*, 266, 346
Irish-Americans, 266, 386
ironclads, 405
Iroquois, 7, *11*, *33*, 130, 132, 181
  relations with New York colony, 73
Iroquois Confederacy, 36, 75, 181
Isabella, queen of Spain (1451–1504), 16

Is This a Republican Form of Government? (Nast), *473*
Ives, James (1824–1895), *400*, *457*

Jackson, Andrew (1767–1845), 250, 294, 296–303, *296*, 355, 371, 381
  American Colonization Society and, 348
  annexation of Texas and, 370
  in battle with Bank of the United States, 304–5, *305*
  defies Supreme Court, 303
  dubbed "King Andrew," 281, *282*
  in election of 1824, 291
  in election of 1828, 295–96, *296*
  inauguration of, 281
  Indians and, 281, 296, 301–2
  Indian wars of, 255
  Kitchen Cabinet of, 297
  nickname of, 297
  in nullification crisis, 301
  "pet banks" and, 306
  rise of democracy and, 281, 284
  as slaveholder (1767–1845), 246
  state banks and, 306
  veto power and, 305
  views of blacks of, 296
  in War of 1812, 246
Jackson, Rachel (1767–1828), 295
Jackson, Thomas "Stonewall" (1824–1863), 432
Jacksonville, Fla., 27
Jacobin clubs, 227
Jamaica, 22, 28, 115
  Maroon War in, *335*
  seizure by England of, 70
James, duke of York (1633–1701), *see* James II, king of England
James I, king of England (1566–1625), 39, 50, 68
James II, king of England (1633–1701), 75, 77, 87, 88, *97*
James River, 39
Jamestown, Va., 47–49, *48*, 85
  death rate at, 47
  difficult beginnings of, 47–48
  founding of, 39
  Indian conflicts in, 50–51
  Indian relations with, 49–51
  Indian uprising of 1622, 50–51
Japan, trade with, 377–78
Japanese immigrants, Japanese-Americans, World War II internment of, 214
Jay, John (1745–1829), 165, 188, 209, 222, 225
Jay, William (1792–1837), 355
Jay's Treaty (1795), 225–26
Jefferson, Thomas (1743–1826), 99, 120, 202, 226, 295, 357
  on African-Americans, 218–19, *219*
  agriculture and, *224*
  on Alien and Sedition Acts, 233

  campaign portrait of, *233*
  Declaration of Independence and, 153, 154, 169, 174, 181, 191, 215
  in election of 1796, 231
  in election of 1800, 233–34, *234*
  in election of 1804, 242
  and elimination of Federalist Party, 247
  "empire of liberty" and, 194
  foreign policy of, 241
  freedom and, 177
  French Revolution and, 225
  Haiti and, 235
  inauguration of, 236
  Indian policies of, 243
  Louisiana Purchase and, 237–40
  on Missouri Compromise, 289
  national bank opposed by, 223–24
  on Native Americans, 216
  Ordinance of 1784 and, 198
  public schools and, 175–76
  religion and, 125, 173
  selected secretary of state, 223
  on Shays's rebellion, 200
  as slaveholder, *219*
  strong local self-government sought by, 236–37
  trade as viewed by, 241
  western land speculation of, 181
  writings of, 150
Jemison, Edwin Francis (d. 1862), *405*
Jennings, Samuel (1755?–1834?), *167*
jeremiads, 67
Jerry (slave), 381
Jesuits, *11*, 33, 77
Jesus, 29, *30*, 79, 175, 329, 336, 349
  Mormons and, 272–73
Jews, 34
  in American colonies, 95
  in colonial Pennsylvania, 79, 95
  in colonial Rhode Island, 60
  enslavement of, 329
  in New Amsterdam, 35
  in Spain, 22
  U.S. population of, 403
  voting rights and, 174
John, king of England (1166–1216), 67
"John Brown's Body," *418*
John Quincy Adams, 286
Johnson, Andrew (1808–1875), 317, 450
  background of, 454
  emancipation and, 454
  impeachment of, 458–60
  Reconstruction policies of, 448, 450, 454–57, *457*, *458*
  veto power and, 457
Johnson, Samuel (1709–1784), 183
Johnson v. M'Intosh, 302
Johnston, Joseph E. (1807–1891), 409
Joliet, Louis (1645–1700), 32

Josephe, 29
Journal of Commerce, 298
Jubilee of Liberty, 250
judicial review, 237
Judiciary Act of 1789, 237
Julius Caesar (Shakespeare), 168

Kansas, 382, 389
    violence in, 388
Kansas-Nebraska Act (1854), 382–83, *383*,
    386, 388
Kaufmann, Theodore (1814–1896), *464*
Kearney, Stephen W. (1794–1848), 373
Kelley, Abby (1810–1887), 340, *341*, 363
Kemmelmayer, Frederick (ca. 1760–
    ca. 1821), *227*
Kendall, Amos (1789–1869), 355
Kentucky, 196
    in Panic of 1819, 287
    resolution in legislature of, 233
    voting rights in, 285
Key, Francis Scott (1779–1843), 244
King, Charles Bird (1785–1862), *243*
King, Martin Luther, Jr. (1929–1968), 372
King, Rufus (1755–1827), 288
"King Andrew," 281, *282*
King James Bible, 265
King Philip's War, 73, 86, *86*
Kitchen Ball at White Sulphur Springs, Virginia
    (Mayr), *329*
Kitchen Cabinet, 297
Know-Nothing (American) Party, 385–86, 388
Knox, Henry (1750–1806), 151, 216
Kongo, 115
Krimmel, John Lewis (1786–1821), *283*
Ku Klux Klan, 467–68, *468*

La Bahia, N.Mex., 127
labor:
    African-Americans and, 274–75
    agricultural, 264
    costs, 261
    demand for, 266
    gang, 323–24
    Philadelphia Mechanic's Advocate newspaper
        for, 284
    radicals, 85
    Republican Party (modern) and free,
        386–87
    rise of free, 176
    unemployment and, 306
    as wage earners, 176, 264
    in West, 267
    women and, 275–76, 358–59
    and work hours, 264, 277
    see also unions
"Laboring Classes, The" (Brownson), 278
labor movement, 277–78, 348
    early nineteenth century, 277

in Panic of 1837, 306
    see also unions
*Lady's Magazine and Repository of Entertaining
    Knowledge*, 231
Lafayette, Marquis de (1757–1834), 165, 250
La Isabella, 17
Lakin, A. S. (1810–1890), *468*
Lancaster, Pa., massacre of Indians at, 136
Land Commission, 465
Land Grant College Act (1862), 423
land grants, 121
La Salle, René-Robert Cavelier, Sieur de
    (1643–1687), 32
Las Casas, Bartolomé de (1474–1566), 24,
    28, 41
Latrobe, Benjamin (1764–1820), *142*
Laurens, Henry (1724–1792), 188
Laurens, John (1754–1782), 188
law, corporate, 266
Lecompton Constitution, 389–90
Lee, Richard Henry (1732–1794), 149
Lee, Robert E. (1807–1870), 394, 407, 410,
    431–33, *433*, 436–38, *437*
Lee family, 130
Leisler, Jacob (ca. 1640–1691), 88
Lely, Peter (1618–1680), *84*
Le Monde Illustré, *415*
L'Enfant, Pierre Charles (1754–1825), 225, 236
Lenni Lanapes, 96
Leopard, 242
Letter of Thomas F. Drayton, 420
Letters from an American Farmer
    (Crèvecoeur), 217
Letters on the Equality of the Sexes (Sarah
    Grimké), 357
Levellers, 69, *69*
Lewis, Meriwether (1774–1809), 239–40, *240*
Lewis and Clark expedition, 239–40, *240*
    Native-Americans and, 240
Lexington, Battle of, 151, *151*, 160
liberalism, 118–19
Liberal Republican Party, 468–69
Liberator, 284, 337, 349, *349*, 351, 358, *363*
Liberia, 348–49
Liberty and Washington, 223
Liberty Bell, *339*, 353
Liberty Displaying the Arts and Sciences
    (Jennings), *167*
Liberty Party, *363*, 364, 372
Liberty Tree, 145, 151, *151*
libraries, public, 122, 124
Library Company of Philadelphia, 122
Lieber, Francis (ca. 1798–1872), 298
Life in California (Robinson), 369
Lima, Peru, 21
Lincoln, Abraham (1809–1865), 207, *366*, *391*,
    409, 411–12, *419*, 436–38, 454, *460*
    Address at Sanitary Fair of, 421
    assassination of, 438

and black suffrage, 418
    in 1858 Senate campaign, 389, 390–91
    elected president, 396, 397, *397*
    in election of 1860, 395–96
    emergence of, 388–96
    inaugural address of, 399
    and Jefferson Davis compared, 428
    and Mexican War, 373
    plans for reconstruction of, 435–36
    second inaugural address, 436
    slavery as viewed by, 390–91, 413
    Southern secession and, 399
    and suspension of habeas corpus, 422
    war planning and, 407–8
    see also Emancipation Proclamation
Lincoln, Benjamin (1733–1810), 200
Lincoln administration, 397, 412, 416, 422,
    426, 428
Lincoln and the Female Slave (Bowser), *419*
Little Turtle (1752–1812), 216
Liverpool, 106
livestock, 47, 106, 216, 260
Locke, John (1632–1704), 118, *118*, 150, 154, 218
Logan, James (1674–1751), 96
Long, Joseph, 332
Long Island, N.Y., 78
Lords of Trade, 88
Los Adaes, N.Mex., 127
Los Angeles, Calif., 128
Lossing, Benson, *343*
Louisiana, *238*, 256, 435
    obtained by Spanish, 127
    2nd Regiment of, *405*
Louisiana Purchase (1803), 237–41, *239*, *240*,
    288, *289*, 294, 378, 382
    Texas and, 371
Louisiana Territory, 131, 240–41
    population of, 129
    slave uprising in, 115
Louis XVI, king of France (1754–1793), 225
Lovejoy, Elijah P. (1802–1837), 355
Lowell, Mass., 262, 264, 271, 277
Lowell Offering, 264
Loyalists, 162, 165, 178–81, *179*, *180*
Loyal Nine, 140
loyalty, oaths, 179
Luther, Martin (1483–1546), 22–23
Lutherans, 94, 95
Lyon, Matthew (1749–1822), 232
Lyon, Pat, *274*

Mackintosh, Ebenezer (1737–1816), 140
Macon's Bill No. 2, 242
Madeira, 14
Madison, James (1751–1836), 154, 201, *201*,
    244, 295
    agriculture and, *224*
    Alien and Sedition Acts as viewed by, 233

Madison (*continued*)
American System plan of, 285
Bank of the United States opposed by, 223–24
Bill of Rights and, 212, 214, 216
church-state separation and, 174
at Constitutional Convention, 202–5
elected president, 242
elimination of Federalist Party and, 247
Federalist and, 208–9
in *Marbury v. Madison*, 237
religion and, 173, 174
as slaveholder, 205
trade policy of, 242
Virginia Plan and, 203
on war, 244
Magellan, Ferdinand (1480–1521), 17, *18*
Magna Carta (1215), 67
Maine, 256
entrance into union of, 288
voting rights in, 285
malaria, 110
Malvern Hill, Battle of, *405*
Manchester, N.H., *264*
Manhattan Island, 34
manifest destiny, 267, 368–78
Manigault, Louis, *412*
Manila, 20
Mann, Horace (1796–1859), 347
Mansfield, Lord, *149*
manufacturing:
in early nineteenth century, 261–62
J. Q. Adams's promotion of, 294
see also industry
Marbury, William, 237
Marbury v. Madison, 237
March to the Sea, *437*
Marie-Séraphique (slave ship), *109*
Marine Corps, U.S., 241
Marion, Francis (1732?–1795), 162
market revolution, 249–79, *253*, 281–82
African-Americans and, 274–75
agriculture and, 251, 260
"American system of manufactures" and, 262
canals and, 252–54, *253*, 286
cotton and, 256, *258*
freedom and, 272, 277
individual and, 267–73
manufacturing and, *260*, 261–64
middle class created by, 274, 276
prosperity and, 273–78, *274*
railroads and, 254, 260
Republicans and, 385
rise of banks in, 285–88
roads and, 251, *253*
rural areas and, 260
Second Great Awakening and, 272
society and, 259–66

technology and, 257–59, 260–62, *263*
textile mills and, 261–63, *263*, *264*
transportation and, 251, 260, 266
urban areas and, 260–61
water power and, 262, *263*
women and, 275–76
Maroon War (1795), *335*
Marquette, Jacques (1637–1675), 32
Married, 275
Marshall, John (1755–1835), 201, 266
American Colonization Society and, 348
death of, 306
French Revolution as viewed by, 225
nationalism and, 288
Native Americans and, 302–3
strong Supreme Court favored by, 237
see also Supreme Court, U.S.
Marshall Court, 237
Martin (slave), 235
Martinique, 131
Mary I, queen of England (1516–1568), 40
Mary II, queen of England (1662–1694), 87
Maryland, 225
constitution of, 172
settlement of, *48*
slave trade in, 259
uprising in, 88
voting rights in, 172, 285
Maryland colony, 43–44, 52, 77, 87–88, 99
close ties to Britain of, 109
free blacks in, 83
government of, 52, 120
indentured servitude in, 52
"plundering time" in, 69
as proprietorship, 52
religion in, 52, 69–70
tobacco in, 52
Mason, George (1725–1792), 203
Mason-Dixon Line, 312
Massachusett language, *64*
Massachusetts, 294
constitution of, 174
government in, 171
Shays's rebellion in, 200–201
U.S. Constitution and, 212
war debt and, 225
Massachusetts Bay Company, 55, 57
Massachusetts Charter (1629), 69, *149*
Massachusetts colony, *54*, 55–63, 66–67, 89, 142, 173
General Court of, 57–58, 66, 88
government of, 56–58
and King Philips War, 73
militia of, *151*
in Pequot War, 64–65
population of, 55
Quakers in, 69
repeals economic regulations, 66
seal of, *55*

self-governing towns in, 56–57
slave trade in, 106
uprising in, 140
Massachusetts Magazine, 230
"masterless men," 43
Matteson, Tompkins Harrison (1813–1884), *280*
Mayflower, 54
Mayflower Compact (1620), 54
Mayr, Christian (ca. 1805–1851), *329*
Mazzini, Giuseppe (1805–1872), 418
McCarthy era, 214
McClellan, George B. (1826–1885), 408–10, 414, 434
McCormick, Cyrus (1809–1884), 260
McCulloch v. Maryland, 288
McHenry, Fort, 244
McIntosh, Fort, 196
Meade, George G. (1815–1872), 432
measles, 19, 109
medicine men, 9
Mediterranean Sea, 16
Meeting of the General Council of the Army at Putney, 69
"melting pot", U.S. as, 95, 217
Melville, Herman (1819–1891), 285
Memorial against Non-English Immigration (1727), 92
Memphis, Tenn., Reconstruction riot in, 458
Menéndez de Avilés, Pedro (1519–1574), 25–27
Mennonites, 92, 94, 95, 179
mercantilism, 66, 74
Merrimac, 405
Merrimack River, 262
message to Congress, 292, 294
see also State of the Union Address
mestizos, 22
Metacom (King Philip; d. 1676), 73
Methodism, 125
Methodists, 95, 328, 378, *418*
African-American, 328, 444
in Great Awakening, 126
in Second Great Awakening, 269, 328
métis (French-Indian children), 33
Mexican Cession, 375
Mexican War, 371, 372–76, *374*, 378, 379
Mexico, 3, 6, 19, 24, 25, *26*, 27, 255, 294, 374–76, 394
abolition of slavery in, 370, 376
conquering of, 19
Cortés's exploration of, *19*
frontier of, 368–69
independence of, 129, 289, 368, 370
invention of agriculture in, 3
population decline of, 19
Texas revolt and, 370
Mexico City, Mexico, 20, *20*, 21, 29, 122, 373
population of, 97

Miami Confederacy, 216

Michigan, 256

Middle Ages, 13

middle class:
    created by market revolution, 274, 276
    market revolution and, 276

Middle Colonies, 44, 96–97, 99, 106
    in election of 1800, 233
    slavery in, 115

middle ground, 130

Middle Passage, 109, *109*

Middle States, 225
    construction of roads in, 252

militias:
    Connecticut colony and, 151
    New York and, *402*

Miller, Lewis (1796–1882), *259*

Milton, John (1608–1674), 68

missionaries, 27, 30, 130, 216, 369
    Jesuit, 33
    Spanish, 22–24, 27, 122, 128–29

Mississippi, 237, 256, 301

Mississippi River, 32, 129, 181, 182, 250, 252, 255, *273*

Mississippi Valley, 5, 6, 127, 129, 243, 254, 435

Missouri, 255
    entrance into union of, 288

Missouri Compromise (1820), 288–89, *289*, 336, 378, 382, *383*, 389, 398

Mitred Minuet, The, 149

Mobile, Ala., 129, 259, *430*

Moby Dick (Melville), 285

Mohawks, 7, 217

monarchy, U.S. rejection of, 169, 171

Monitor, 405

Monroe, James (1758–1831), 235, 288, 292
    Era of Good Feelings under, 288
    Monrovia named for, 348

Monroe Doctrine, 290, 292, 294
    American foreign policy and, 289
    nationalism and, 290, 292
    neutrality and, 290

Monrovia, Liberia, 348

Monterey, Calif., 128

Moors, 16

Moravian Brethren, 94, 95, 179

Moravian Indians, 136

More, Thomas (1478–1535), 341

Morgan, Daniel (1736–1802), 162

Morgan, J. P. (1837–1913), 425

Morgues, Jacques Le Moyne de (d. 1588), *10*

Mormons, 272–73, *273*, *369*
    Brigham Young and, 273
    in Nauvoo, Ill., 273
    in New York, 272
    polygamy and, 273
    in Salt Lake City, 273
    and Second Great Awakening, 273
    see also Christianity

Morris, Gouverneur (1752–1816), 205, 207

Morse, Samuel F. B. (1791–1872), 254

Moses, 329

Mother and Daughter Reading, Mt. Meigs, Alabama (Eickemeyer), *444*

Mott, Lucretia (1793–1880), 357

"mound builders," 5–6

mulattos, 115

Murray, Judith Sargent (1751–1820), 228, 230

music, *418*, *423*

Muslims, 16, 22, 125, 241
    in Pennsylvania colony, 95

"mustee" (mixed race), *114*

My Bondage and My Freedom (Douglass), 359

Mystic, Conn., 64–65

Mystic River, *65*

Nantes, France, *109*

Napoleon I, emperor of France (1769–1821), 238, 242, 244, 247

Napoleon III, emperor of France, 380

Narragansett Indians, *47*, 64

Nast, Thomas (1840–1902), 469, *473*

Natchez, Miss., 259

Natchez Indians, 115

Nation, The, 469

national debt, 223, 297

nationalists, nationalism, 201–2, 242, *283*, 285–89, 294, 296
    Civil War and, 418–19
    John C. Calhoun and, 299
    Monroe Doctrine and, 290
    South and rise of, 394–95

Native Americans, 16, 46, 95–96, *95*, 101, 115, 214–15, 216, 255
    in alliance with French, 32
    American Revolution and, 168, 169, 181–82
    in attempted conversion to Catholicism, 22–24, 27, 33
    in battles with Spanish, 25, 27–30
    California gold rush and, 377
    in Carolina, 78
    Cherokee Phoenix newspaper for, 284
    Christianity and, *1*, 9, 22, 28, 29, 41, 128
    Civil War and, 423–24, *424*
    coastal tribes of, 61, 64–65
    colonial assemblies and, 121
    conflicts with colonists, 45
    conflict with Jamestown of, 50–51
    Declaration of Independence and, 181
    displacing of, 45
    diverse societies of, 7
    of eastern North America, 6–7
    economy of, 9–10
    English relations with, 45–47, 244
    epidemics and, 2, 19–20, 25, 33, 43, 46, 61, 81, 90
    Europeans' negative views of, 10–11, 32
    European trade with, 46–47, 55, 78, 130

    forced labor of, 3, 21, 23–24, 27, 41–42, 78, 129
    freedom and, 11–12, 181, 217
    gender relations of, 10
    George Washington and, 181, 216
    government of, 6–7, 11
    intermixing with Europeans by, 22, 45
    Irish compared with, 40
    Jackson and, 255, 281, 296, 301–3
    Jamestown and, 49–51
    Jefferson's policies on, 243
    land as viewed by, 9, *9*
    loss of Southern land of, 259
    maps of tribes of, *8*
    matrilineal societies of, 10
    in Mexican Cession, 375
    of New England, 10
    New England and, *47*
    New France and, 32–33
    New York colony and, 75–77
    as "noble savages," 10
    origins of, 3
    pan-Indian identity of, 132
    and Pennsylvania colony, 136
    Pilgrims and, 55
    Puritans and, 61–65
    railroads and, 423
    religions of, 7–9, *7*, *9*, *11*
    removal of, 301–3, *302*
    Seven Years' War and, 131
    sexual division of labor of, 10, 11
    slavery and, 21, 24, 73, 81, 377
    societies of, 3
    trade among, 5, 6, *9*, 10
    uprisings of, 27–30, 73, 78, 136, 181
    U.S. treaties with, 196, 215, 216
    in Virginia, 84, 96
    voting rights and, 119
    war atrocities against, 181
    War of 1812 and, 244
    in West, *303*
    of western North America, 6
    westward expansion of U.S. and, 196, 243, 368
    women's roles among, 10
    see also Indian removal

Native Americans, population of, 3, 196, 301
    in California, 128, 377
    decline of, 6, 19–20, 21, 23, 27
    in Florida, 127
    in New England, 61–64

nativism, 265–66, 386

Nat Turner's Rebellion, 336–37, 351

Naturalization Act (1790), 218

Naturalization Act (1798), 232

Nauvoo, Ill., Mormons in, 273, *273*

Navajos, 30, 424
    Long Walk of, 424, *424*

Navigation Acts, 74, 88, 98, 142, 178

Navy, U.S.:
    African-Americans in, 416
    in Mexican War, 373
    at Tripoli, 241
Nebraska, 382
Neolin, 132, 134
Netherlands, 32, 34, 74, 92, 97, 294
    in Anglo-Dutch war, 75
    colonization and, 11, 30, 54
    freedom in, 34
    in West Indies, 81
    see also Dutch Empire
Neue Jerusalem, Das, 272
Nevada, 373
New Amsterdam, 34, 35, *35*, 75
    role of women in, 75
New Deal, 447
New Display of the United States,
    A (Doolittle), 232
New England, *263*
    building of roads in, 252
    Dominion of, 88
    in election of 1796, 231
    in election of 1800, 233
    in election of 1804, 242
    in election of 1824, 291
    Indian of, 47
    inducement to settle, 43–44
    industrialization of, 262, 264
    Puritan emigration to, 54
    shipbuilding in, 75
    trade with West Indies, 66
New England colonies, 44, 53–67, 87, 88, 95,
    97, 130, 137, 158, 184
    Atlantic trade of, 106, *107*
    division in, 59–67
    economy of, 65–67
    hierarchical society of, 58
    map of, *59*, *86*
    Native Americans in, 10
    population growth of, 100
    slavery in, 112
    social equality in, 66
    triangular trade of, 109
Newfoundland, 16, 17, 41
New France, 30–33, *31*, 122
    Indians and, 32–33
    population of, 32
New Hampshire colony, *144*, 146
    chartering of, 66
New Harmony, Ind., 344
New Jersey:
    constitution of, 172, 188
    election of 1796 and, 231
    slaves in, 188
New Jersey colony, 44, 79, 95, 96
    Washington's army in, *160*, 161
New Jersey Dutch Reformed, 125
New Jersey Plan, 203

New Lanark, Scotland, 344
New Laws, 24
New Lights, 126
New Mexico, 6, *6*, 27–30, *30*, 33, 122, 127,
    373, 376
    population of, 369
New Netherland, 30, *31*, 32, 74–75
    freedom in, 34–35
    population of, 35
    religious freedom in, 35
    seal of, *36*
    slavery in, 34
    uprisings in, 36
New Orleans, La., *129*, *239*, 240, 315–16,
    316, 465
    battle of, 246, *283*, 291
    black community in, 323, 335–36, 436
    in Civil War, 410, *411*
    cotton trade in, 315–16, *316*
    population of, 240, 315
    Reconstruction riot in, 458
    slave auctions in, 314
    slave rebellion in, 335–36
    slave trade in, 259
    sugar trade in, 315
News from America, 65
New Spain, *26*
newspapers, *see* press
New Sweden, 36
New World, 1–37, *4*, 41
    commerce in, 70, 74
    conquering of, 16–20
    dangers of, 43
    peoples of, 3–11, 17, 19–20
    settling of, *4*
    slavery in, 2–3, 21, 81–82, 109
    women and, 22
New York, 7, 196, *341*
    constitution of, 174
    election of 1796 and, 231
    legislature, 267
    militia, *402*
    Mormons in, 272
    religious liberty in, 174
    U.S. Constitution and, 212, *214*
    voting rights in, 172
New York, N.Y., 6, 34, 97, 116, *172*, 252–54,
    252, *256*, 260, 314
    African-Americans in, 275
    anti-immigration riots in, 266
    as capital of U.S., 222
    population of, 97
    population of slaves in, 112, 188
    religious diversity in, *172*
    slavery ended in, *188*
    slave uprising in, 115
New York colony, 44, 75–77, 87, 88, 95, 130
    African-Americans lose jobs in, 75
    anti-British rebellion in, 88

    British boycott in, 150
    growth of, 96
    Loyalists in, 179, *180*
    Native Americans and, 73, 75–77
    population of, 75
    slavery in, 112, 115
    slave trade in, 106
    Stamp Act Congress and, 143, 145
    Vermont split from, 146
    Washington's army in, *160*, 161
New York Evening Post, 356
New York Harbor, 34
New York Herald, 283
New York Illustrated, *430*
New York Sun, 283
New York Times, 422
New York Tribune, 358, 469
New York Weekly Journal, 123, *123*
New Zealand, 281
Ninety-Five Theses (Luther), 22
Ninigret II, *47*
Ninth Amendment, 215
Non-Intercourse Act (1809), 242
North:
    in election of 1824, 291
    industrial revolution in, 257
North, Frederick (1732–1792), 148, *149*
North America, 3, *4*, 5, 40–41, *76*, *164*
    Dutch in, 34–36
    early population of, 19, 24
    English colonization of, 38–71
    exploration of, 25
    Indians of, 5–7, *8*
    map of east coast of, *94*
North Briton, 148
North Carolina, 41, 119, 196, 301
    Outer Banks, *7*
    U.S. Constitution and, 212, *214*
North Carolina colony, 96
    in American Revolution, 162
    Loyalists in, 179, *180*
    Regulators in, 145
Northwest Ordinance (1787), 198, 389
Northwest Passage, 34
Notes on the State of Virginia (Jefferson), 218
Nova Scotia, 131
    as haven for former slaves, 185
Noyes, John Humphrey (1811–1886),
    343–44
Nueces River, 372
nullification crisis, 299–301
nurses, in Civil war, 425

Oglethorpe, James (1696–1785), 111
Ohio, 196, 256
    population of, 256
Ohio Company (1750s), 130, 131
Ohio Company (1780s), 198
Ohio River, 32, 130, 250

Ohio River Valley, 5, 77, 130, 181, 198, 216, 239, 254
    Indians of, 132
Oklahoma, Trail of Tears in, 303
Old Lights, 126
Old Northwest, 255
Old Plantation, The, 104
Old Southwest, 255
Old State House Bell, *339*
Oliver, Andrew (1706–1774), 140, 144
Oliver family, *99*
Oñate, Juan de (ca. 1551–ca. 1626), 27
"On Civil Disobedience" (Thoreau), 372
Oneida community, 343–44
Oneidas, 7, 181
Onondagas, 7
"On the Equality of the Sexes" (Murray), 230
Opechancanough, 50
Oration on the Beauties of Liberty (Allen), 150
Ordinance of 1784, 198
Oregon Territory, 240, 255
    blacks barred from, 275
    Great Britain and, 368, *369*
    migration to, 368, *369*
    U.S.-British dispute over, 372
Ostend Manifesto, 394
O'Sullivan, John L. (1813–1895), 267, 376
Otis, Harrison James (1725–1783), 142, 190, 233
Ottawa Indians, 132
"outwork" system, 262
Ovando, Nicolás de (ca. 1451–ca. 1511), 17
Overseer Doing His Duty, An, 111
Owen, Robert (1771–1858), 344–45, *344*
Owen, Robert Dale (1801–1877), *344*

Pacific Ocean, 17, 20, 240
pacifism:
    abolitionists and, 352
    Quaker, 79
Paine, Thomas (1737–1809), *154*, 161, 169, 171, 183
    Common Sense and, 152–53, 156
Pale, 40
Panama, 17
Panic of 1819, 287–88
Panic of 1837, 306
Papacy, 40
Papists, 92
Paris, Treaty of (1763), 131, 136
Paris, Treaty of (1783), 165
Parliament, British, 39, 68, 88, 92, *157*
    army of, 68, 69
    Bill of Rights and, 87
    Charles I's conflict with, 68
    colonists' desire for representation in, 141
    forces in Maryland colony, 69
    taxation on America by, 140, 141–45, *141*, 153

parties, political, 296–98, 383–88
    newspapers and, 297, 298
    origins of U.S., 222, 226–27
    patronage and, 296–97
    views of Van Buren of, 295
    see also specific parties
Paterson, N.J., Thomas Rodgers and, 274
Pat Lyon at the Forge, 274
patronage, political parties and, 296–97
Paul III, Pope (1468–1549), 24
Peacock (British warship), *246*
Peale, Charles Willson (1741–1827), *190, 201*
Pearl Harbor, 410
Pemberton, John C. (1814–1881), 433
Penn, William (1644–1718), 78–79, 95, 96, 136
Penn family, *95*
Pennsylvania, 7, 188
    constitution of, 170, *170*, 171–72
    and election of 1796, 231
    religious laws in, 299
    Whiskey Rebellion and, 226
Pennsylvania Abolition Society, 234
Pennsylvania colony, 72, 78, 92, 93, 95, 96, 99, 130, 136
    American Revolution and, 170, 179
    freemen in, 79
    government in, 78–79, 120, *120*
    Holy Experiment of, 136
    immigration to, 44, 92, 95
    Loyalists in, 179
    Native Americans and, 136
    population of, 96
    religious freedom in, 87, 95, 172
    slaves in, *72*
    social order in, 78–79
    standard of living in, 97–98
Pennsylvania Gazette, 122
Pennsylvania Magazine, *154*
"penny press," 283
People's Convention, 282
People the Best Governors, The (anon.), 170
Pequot Indians, 64–65, *65*
Pequot War, 64–65
perfectionism, and religion and reform, 345
Perry, Oliver H. (1785–1819), 244
Peru, 3, 19, 20, *23*, 25, 26, 289
"pet banks," 306
Petersburg, Battle of, 433, 436
Petitions of Slaves to the Massachusetts Legislature, 187
Philadelphia, Pa., 6, 97–98, 100, 131, 178, 262
    in American Revolution, 161
    anti-immigration riots in, 266
    boycott of Britain in, 150
    Constitutional celebrations in, 194
    Constitution ratified in, 194

population of, 97
shipbuilding in, 194
skilled workers of, 97
slaves in, 113
trade with West Indies, 98
Philadelphia Mechanic's Advocate, 284
Philadelphia Society for the Promotion of Agriculture, *224*
Philip, King (Wampanoag chief; d. 1676), 73, *86*
Philip II, king of Spain (1556–1598), 25
Philippines, 20
Phillips, Wendell (1811–1884), 439
Phillipsburgh Proclamation, 185
photography, in Civil War, 407
Pickett, George E. (1825–1875), 432–33
Piedmont, 110
Pierce, Franklin (1804–1869), 382, 388
Pietists, 95
Pike, James (1913–1969), *151*
Pike, James S. (1811–1882), 469
Pilgrims, 54–55
Pillow, Fort, 417
Pinckney, Charles C. (1746–1825), 242
Pinckney, Thomas (1750–1825), 231
Pinckney's Treaty (Treaty of San Lorenzo) (1795), 238
pirates, 25
    Barbary Coast, 81
Pitt, William (1708–1778), 131
Pizarro, Francisco (ca. 1475–1541), 19
Plains of Abraham, 131
Plantation Burial, 330
planter class, 317–18
planters, plantations, 70, 98, 99, *238*, 259–60, 281, 317–18, *322*, 323–24, 379, 435, 465
    cotton, 259–60, *324*, 370, 435
    as dominating South, 315, 317
    emancipated slaves and, *446*
    post-Civil War, 446–47, 448, 449
    Protestants and, 70
    rice, 104–11, 324
    slavery on, 3, 14, 81, 98, 99, 110–11
    sugar, 81–82, *82*, 109, 324, 335, 379
    tobacco, 98, 99, 109–10
Playa Mayor, Mexico City, 20
"Plea for the West, A" (Beecher), 265
"plundering time", in Maryland colony, 69
Plymouth Colony, 53–55, 89
Pocahontas (ca. 1596–1617), 49, *49*
Polk, James K. (1795–1849), 307, 371–72, 373, 389
polygamy, 273
Ponce de León, Juan (1460–1521), 25
Pontiac (ca. 1720–1769), 134, 136
Pontiac's Rebellion, 132, 136
Poor Richard's Almanack, 124
Pope, John (1822–1892), 410
Popé (d. 1688), 27–30

"popery," *see* Catholics, Catholicism
popular sovereignty, 379, 382, 389–90, 395
population:
  of African-Americans, 188–89, *217*
  in American colonies, 50, 90–91, 109
  of Barbados, 82
  black, of English Caribbean, 82
  of Boston, 97
  of California, 128–29, 369, 376, 377
  of Civil War border states, 412
  of Confederacy, 405
  of early South America, 19, 24
  of England, 42, 43
  of Florida, 127
  of France compared with England, 43
  of immigrants, *265*, 266
  of Indians, 19, 21, 96
  of Indians, decline in, 6, 19–20, 23
  of Jews in America, 403
  of Los Angeles, 128
  of Louisiana, 129
  of Massachusetts, 55
  of Mexican Cession, 375
  of Mexico, 19, 24
  of Mexico City, Mexico, 97
  of Native Americans, *see* Native
      Americans, population of
  of New England Indians, 61–64
  of New France, 32
  of New Mexico, 27, 127, 369
  of New Netherland, 36
  of New Orleans, 240, 315
  of New York, 75
  of New York City, 97
  of Pennsylvania, 96
  of Philadelphia, 97
  of slaves, 85, 109, 112–13, 188–89, 194, 240,
      312–13, *314*, *315*, 415
  of Southern Indians, 301
  of Spanish America, 21
  of Texas, 370
  of Union, 405
  of United States, 194, 250, *255*
  of urban centers, 262
  of West, 243
  in Western states, *255*
  west of Appalachian Mountains, 256
  world, *25*
Portia (Abigail Adams), 168
*Portrait of John and Elizabeth Lloyd Cadwalader
    and Their Daughter Anne* (Peale), *190*
Port Royal, in South Carolina Sea Islands, *114*
Portsmouth, N.H., 66
Portugal, *18*, 22, 39, 81, 82
  loses Brazil to Dutch, 34
  navigation of, 14–15, *15*
  and West Africa, 14–15
Poverty Point, 5
Powhatan (ca. 1550–1618), 48–49, *49*

Presbyterians, 91, 95
  American Revolution and, 175
  in Great Awakening, 125, 126
Presidential Reconstruction, 454–55
presidents, presidency, U.S., 203, 204
  veto power of, 305, 457
  see also specific presidents
presidios, 128
press, *230*, *372*, 376
  "alternative," 284
  attack on Washington by, 227
  circulation of, 284
  in Civil War, *406*, 407, 409, 422
  Democratic, 298, 308, 422
  in election of 1830, 297
  growth of, 227, 284
  politics and, 297, 298
  during Reconstruction, 469, 470
  Republican (Jeffersonian), 233
  Republican (modern), 409, 422
  rise of, 284
  sensationalism in, 283–84
  slavery and antislavery, 321, 336, 354,
      355, 379
  women's rights and, 358
  see also freedom, of the press
prices, control of, 178
primogeniture, 177
printing press, 57
prisons, 347
  debt and, 277
private property, *342*
  shunned by Shakers, 343
  in Utopian societies, 345
Proclamation of 1763, 132–36, 141, 181
Prophetstown, 243
proprietorship, 57, 77–78, 79, 87, 88, 99
  Maryland as, 52
Prospective Scene in the City of Oaks, A, *468*
Prostrate State, The (Pike), 470
Protestant Association, 88
Protestant Reformation, 35
Protestants, 23, 137, 298, 346, 356, 376
  in American colonies, 87–89, 91, 94, 95
  in Amsterdam, 34
  Catholics vs., 265
  Dissenters, and, 60, 87
  in England, 40, 69, 70
  French, 25, 32
  Indians and, 23
  in Maryland colony, 52, 69–70, 88
  in New York colony, 77
  planter class, 70
  and spread of Protestantism, 41
  tax support of, 174
  voting rights and, 173
  see also Christianity; *specific denominations*
Prussia, 294
public goods, 178

*Public Whipping of Slaves in Lexington, Missouri,
    in 1856, A*, *326*
"Publius," 208
Pueblo Bonita, 6, *6*
Pueblo Indians, 6, 27, 30, 102, 127
Pueblo Revolt, 27–30, *30*, 86
pueblos, 6
Puerto Rico, 25, 289
Punch, *413*
Puritans, Puritanism, 54–55, 89, 346
  beliefs of, 53, 57–60, *61*, 63
  church and state and, 59
  emigration to New England, 54
  families of, 55–56, *56*, 63
  Indians and, 61–65
  intolerance in, 58–60, 61, 63, 69
  liberties of, 58
  rise of, 53–54
  sermons of, 53
  slavery and, 58
  women's role in, 55–56, 63, 66
  worldly success as viewed by, 54, 67
pyramids, Egyptian, 5

quadrant, 14
Quaker Meeting, A, *79*
Quakers, 69, 78–79, *79*, 95, 107, 136, 179, 183
  Gabriel's Rebellion and, 235–36
  liberty of, 78–79
  as pacifists, 79
  slavery repudiated by, 79, 348, 356
Quebec, 32, *141*
Quebec Act (1774), 149, *149*, 173
Quito, Ecuador, 21

race, racism:
  Andrew Johnson and, 454
  and class, 284
  lack of opportunities and, 274–75
  as pillar of slavery, 319
  Reconstruction and, 467, 470
  riots and, 274
  theories of, 375–76
  see also segregation
Radical Reconstruction, 454–57
Radical Republicans, 412, 434, 436, 456, *456*,
    458–59
railroads, 254, *254*, 260, 264, *384*, 449
  in Civil War, 405, 407, 423, 428
  in Northwest, 385
  in Reconstruction, 466
  Southern, 317
  transcontinental, 382, 396, 423
"Railsplitter, The," *366*
Raleigh, Walter (1554–1618), *7*, 41, 42
Ramsay, David (1749–1815), 210
Randolph, Richard, 185–88
Rapidan River, *408*
Rapp, George (1757–1847), 344

"re-Africanization," 113
reaper, 260
reconquista, 16
Reconstruction, 312, 416, 434–35, 441–74, *471*
  African-Americans in, *441*, 453, 456–58, 459–62, *459*
  battle over, 454–55
  black officeholders during, 464
  Chinese laborers during, 453
  Johnson's policies in, 448, 454–57, *457*, 458
  overthrow of, 466–74, *473*
  public schools in, 465, *466*, *467*
  radical, 454–57
  railroads built in, 466
  violence in, 467–68
  white farmers in, 449–52
  women's rights and, 461–62
  see also Presidential Reconstruction; Radical Reconstruction; Second Reconstruction
Reconstruction Act (1867), 458, 462
Redeemers, 470
redemptioners, 95
  see also indentured servitude
Red Scare, 214
Red Sticks (Creeks), 246
Reed, Esther (1746–1780), 190
Reed, Joseph (1741–1785), 190
reform, 339–65
  freedom and, 346
  religion and, 345
  temperance and, 345
  utopian communities and, 341–45
Reformation, 22–23, 40, 41, 53
Regulators, 145, 200
religion:
  from Africa, 113–14
  of African-Americans, rise in, 444, *446*
  and attempted conversions of Indians, 9, 22–24, 27, 33
  Bible and, 22–23, 53, 56, 57, 60
  Bible Commonwealth and, 58, 60, 89
  Enlightenment and, 124–25
  and founding of Connecticut, 60
  in Maryland, 52, 69–70
  missionaries and, 22–24, 27, 33, 122, 128–29, 216
  Native American, 7–9, *7*, *9*, *11*
  reform and, 345
  Salem witch trials and, 89–90
  and separation of church and state, 58, 95, 173–75
  slaves and, 113–14
  Thomas Jefferson and, 125, 173, 174
  witchcraft and, 89–90
  see also Great Awakening, Great Awakening, Second; *specific denominations*
Religious Camp Meeting, 269

religious freedom:
  in American colonies, 2, 88–89, 95
  in Carolina, 78
  in early U.S., 125, 172–75
  in England, 69
  First Amendment and, 214, 215
  in Maryland colony, 52, 88
  in New England colonies, 88–89
  in New Netherland, 35
  in New York City, *172*
  in New York colony, 75, 77
  in Pennsylvania, 171
  in Pennsylvania colony, 78–79
  in Rhode Island, 60
  voting rights and, 174
  see also diversity
repartimiento system, 24
Report on Manufactures (Hamilton), 223
republicanism, 115, 117, 119
  Christian, 175
"republican motherhood," 275
Republican Party (Jeffersonian), 226, 230, 231, 233, *234*
  in election of 1824, 291
  platform of, 227
  press of, 233
Republican Party (modern), 390, 391, 414, 426
  as antislavery, 386–87
  black voters and, 463
  Johnson's impeachment and, 458–60
  Liberal, 468–69
  and Lincoln's nomination, 396
  press of, 409, 422
  radicals in, 413
  in Reconstruction, 447, 454–60, 463, 465, 467, 468–69, 470, 471–72
  rise of, 383–88
  see also Radical Republicans; *specific elections and campaigns*
Residence of David Twining, The (Hicks), 72
Revels, Hiram (1827–1901), *460*, 464, *464*
Revenue Act (1767), 142
Revere, Paul (1735–1818), *117*, 147, *147*, 151
"Revolution of 1800," 233–34
Rhine River, 92
Rhode Island, 201
  Dorr War in, 282
  Narragansetts of, *47*
  U.S. Constitution and, 212, *214*
  voting rights in, 282
Rhode Island colony, 60, 88, 95, 158–59, 172
  religious freedom in, 60
  slave trade in, 106
rice, 106, 324, *325*
  slavery and, 110–11
  in Southern colonies, 78, 99, 109, 110–11
Richmond, Va., 235, 408, 410, 430, *437*, 438
  population of slaves in, 235
Richmond *Enquirer*, 321

Richmond's Slave Market Auction (Crowe), *311*
Ridge, Major (ca. 1771–1839), 243
rifles, in Civil War, 405
"rights of Englishmen," 67
Rindisbacher, Peter (1806–1834), *247*
Rio Grande, 372
riots:
  draft, *427*
  race, 274
  Reconstruction, 458
Riots in New York, The: The Mob Lynching a Negro in Clarkson Street, *427*
roads, 252, *253*, 286
Roanoke Island, Va., 41
Robinson, Alfred (1806–1895), 369
Rochester, N.Y., 252
Rockefeller, John D. (1839–1937), 425
Rodgers, Thomas (1792–1856), 273
Rolfe, John (1585–1622), 49–50
Rome, ancient, 20, 77
  slavery in, 81, 367, *367*
rosemary, 14
Ross, John (1790–1866), 243, 303
Ross, Thomas J., 451
Rossiter, Thomas Pritchard (1818–1871), *206*
Rowlandson, Mary (1637?–1711), 64
Royal Africa Company, 74, 85
Royal Army, 158–59
Royal Navy, 98, 105, 117
Royal University of Mexico, 57
"Rule Britannia," 116
runaway slaves, *see* fugitive slaves; slaves, runaway
Rush, Benjamin (1745–1813), 152, 184, 194
  public schools and, 175
Russia, 294
  Alaskan fur traders from, 127
Russwurm, John B. (1799–1851), 354
Ryan, Martha, *189*

Sacajawea (ca. 1786–ca. 1812), 240
Sahara Desert, 14
St. Augustine, Fla., 27, 127
St. Clair, Arthur (1736–1818), 216
Saint Domingue, 82, 188, 235, *235*
St. Lawrence River, 32
St. Lawrence valley, 129
St. Louis, Mo., 5, 181
St. Simons Island, 27
Salem, Mass., 89–90
Salt Lake City, Utah, *369*
  Mormons in, 273
Sampson, Deborah (1760–1827), 189
San Antonio, N.Mex., 127
San Diego, Calif., 128
Sandy (runaway slave), *219*
San Francisco, Calif., 128
Sanitary Fairs, 421, 426, *426*
San Jacinto, Battle of, 370

San Juan, P.R., 28

San Lorenzo, Treaty of (Pinckney's Treaty) (1795), 238

Santa Anna, Antonio López de, 370, 373

Santa Barbara, Calif., 128

Santa Fe, N.Mex., 27, 127

Saratoga, Battle of, *160*, 161

Savage, Edward (1761–1817), *56*

Savage Family, The (Savage), *56*

Savannah, Ga., 115, 162, 188, *397*

scalawags, 464–65

Scandinavian immigrants, 264

Schurz, Carl (1829–1906), 461

Scotch-Irish, 91, 96, 130, 136

    as immigrants to America, 91, 96, 130, 136

Scotland, 91, 105

Scott, Dred (ca. 1800–1858), 389–90, *390*, 391, 396

Scott, Winfield (1786–1866), 373, 382

Scourge of Aristocracy, The (Lyon), 232

Sea Islands, South Carolina, *114*, 434–35, 448

    Special Field Order 15 and, 442

secession, 398, *404*

    see also South

Second Amendment, 214

"Second American Revolution," 417–27

Second Confiscation Act, 413

Second Continental Congress, 151, 152, 153, 162, 168, 173, 186

Second Great Awakening, *see* Great Awakening, Second

Second Reconstruction, civil rights movement as, 473

Second Seminole War, 303

sectionalism:

    Calhoun and, 299

    fear of political, 295

Sedition Act (1798), 231–32, 236

segregation, 465

    see also race, racism

"self-made" man, 273–74, *274*, 312

    Andrew Jackson as, 281

    Frederick Douglass as, 312

Selling a Freeman to Pay His Fine at Monticello, Florida, 455

Selling of Joseph, The, (Sewall), 183

Seminoles, 255, 291, 301

    fugitive slaves and, 303, 334

Seminole War:

    First, 303

    Second, 303

Senate, U.S., 203–4, 281

    African-Americans in, 464

    creation of, 203

    and Johnson's impeachment, 458–60

Seneca Falls Convention, 357–58, 359

Seneca Falls Declaration of Sentiments, 357

Seneca Indians, 7

separation of powers, in U.S. Constitution, 204–5

separatists, 53

September 11, 2001, terrorist attacks of, 410

Sequoia, *303*

serfs, 78

Serra, Junípero (1713–1784), 128–29

Seven Days' Campaign, 410

Seventeenth Amendment, 391

Seventh Day Baptists, 95

Seven Years' War, 105, 130–31, *133*, 134, 162

    effects of, 131–32, 136, 137, 141

Sewall, Samuel (1652–1730), 183

Seward, William H. (1801–1872), 381, 387, 413–14

sex, women's rights and, 359–62

Seymour, Horatio (1810–1886), 459

Shackle Broken—by the Genius of Freedom, The (Elliott), *441*

Shakers, 343, *343*, 344

shamans, 9

sharecropping, 449, 451, *452*, 466

Shaw, Robert Gould (1837–1863), 416

Shays, Daniel (1747?–1825), 200

Shays's Rebellion, 200–201, 207

Shenandoah Valley, 96, 101

Sherman, William T. (1820–1891), 433, 442, 447–48

    March to the Sea of, 436, *437*

Shiloh, Battle of, 410, *411*

shipbuilding:

    in New England, 75

    in Philadelphia, 194

Shoemakers' Strike in Lynn-Procession in the Midst of a Snow-Storm, of Eight Hundred Women Operatives, The, 277

Shoshones, 240

Sierra Leone, as haven for former slaves, 185

Signing of the Constitution, The (Rossiter), *206*

silver, 19, 20, 21, 23, 25, 43, 74, 82, 306

    coinage, 121

    currency and, 287

Sinners in the Hands of an Angry God (Edwards), 125

Sioux, 424, *424*

Slater, Samuel (1768–1835), 261–62

Slaughterhouse Cases (1873), 470

Slave Market of America, 351

slavery, 80–85, 104–16, 311–38, 344, 345

    abolished in Mexico, 370, 376

    American, origins of, 80–85

    American Revolution and, 169, 182–89, *182*, 191, 330

    in ancient Rome, 81, 367, *367*

    arguments in favor of, 318–19

    Biblical passages as justification for, 319, 333, 378

    British Empire's abolishment of, 320, *320*, 337

    in Chesapeake region, 109–10, 115

    Christianity and, 83, 328–29, 356

    in cities, 324

    Civil War and, 410–17

    Congress and, 378

    Constitution and, 205–7, *205*, 214

    cotton gin and, 259

    Democratic Party and, 297–98

    divisiveness of, 235

    Dred Scott decision and, 389–90

    in Europe, 15, 81

    expansion of, 106

    federal government and, 299

    Free Soil position and, 379

    gender roles in, 327–28

    in Georgia, 206

    in Georgia colony, 114–15

    history of, 81–82

    indentured servitude vs., 80

    Indian, abolition of, 24

    Indians and, 21, 24, 73, 81, 377

    law and, 337

    in Lincoln-Douglas campaign, 390–91, 392–93

    Lincoln's views of, 390

    Locke and, 118

    in Louisiana, 240–41

    in Mediterranean, 81

    in Middle Colonies, 109–10, 112

    in Missouri Territory, *289*

    in New England, 66, 109, 112

    in New Netherland, 34

    newspapers and, 321, 336, 354, 355, 379

    in New World, 2–3, 21, 24, 81–82, *107*, 109

    in Northern colonies, 112

    Northern vs. Southern, 112

    party politics and, 383

    paternalist ethos and, 318

    as "peculiar institution," 312, 318

    perceived advantages of, 81

    planter class and, 317–18

    Puritanism and, 58

    Quaker repudiation of, 79

    racism as justification for, 319

    Republican Party (modern) opposed to, 386–87

    on rice plantations, 98, 99, 110–11

    Seward's views on, 387

    slave resistance to, *114*, 115–16, 330–37, *331*

    South as affected by, 313–16

    in Southern colonies, 109, 176

    strengthening of, 394

    in Texas, 371

    on tobacco plantations, 98, 109–11

    United States as center of, 313

    in Virginia colony, 48, 83, 85, 109, 110–11

    after War of 1812, 250–51

    in West Indies, 21, 73, 78, 81, *108*, 109

westward expansion and, 198, 259–60, 312–13, 377, 378–80, 387–88

Wilmot proviso and, 378–79

see also abolition movement

"Slavery and the Bible," 333

slaves, 25, 44, 48, *51*, 72, *82*, 100, 118, *324*, 325, *326*

in Antigua, *82*

barred from education, 321

in Carolina colony, 78

and Christianity, 328–29

Christianity and, 113–14

Civil War and, 431

colonization of, 348–49, 350, 413

culture of, 113–16, 326–30, *330*

death rate of, 85, 109

diet and health of, 322

disciplining of, 325–26

emancipated, 188, *188*, 410–17, 439

family life of, 326–27, *329*

folk tales of, 329

freedom desired by, 85, *114*, 115–16, 184–85, 187, 329–30, 348

fugitive, 235, 303, 332, 334, *334*, *335*, 380, 381–82, 398, 412, *412*, 413, 415

gang labor and, 323–24

harbored by Seminoles, 303

holdings, *318*, *319*

importation from Africa of, 81–82, 206

labor of, 323–24

law and, 321–22

Native Americans as, 73, 377

New York uprising of, 115

population of, *112*, 235, 415

prohibition on importation of, 313

religion and, 113–14, 319, *319*, 333, 378

revolts, 235–36, 335–36, 351

rights of, 82–83

runaway, *114*, *219*

runaway, advertisement for, 334, *334*

witchcraft and, 114

slaves, emancipated, 443, *444*

Andrew Johnson and, 454

suffrage and, 442, 444, 459–60

slaves, population of:

in British colonies, 111

in colonies, 183

in New York City, 188

in U.S., 194, 312–13, *314*, *315*

slave ships, *109*

slave trade, 34, 75, 80, 105–13, *107*, 135, *311*, 314, *317*, 394

abolished in Washington, D.C., 380

advertisement for, 327

and Africa, 2, 14–15

Atlantic, 106

auctions in, 314

in Charleston, S.C., 78

Congressional prohibition on, 314

Constitution and, 205–7, *205*

cotton plantations and, 259

in draft of Declaration of Independence, 153

families and, 326–27

Middle Passage of, 109, *109*

in New Orleans, 259, 314

prohibition of, 206, 259

reopening of, 259

within U.S., 259

Slave Trader, Sold to Tennessee (Miller), *259*

"slavocracy", Southern planters as, 317

smallpox, 19, 55

Smith, Adam (1723–1790), 2, 13, 178, 191

Smith, John (1580–1631), 39, 43, 47–48, *49*

Smith, Joseph, 272–73

Smith, Melancton (1744–1798), 212

social contract, 118

socialism, *342*

Society of Friends, *see* Quakers

Society of Pennsylvania, 229

Sonoma, Calif., 128

Sons of Liberty, 144, *144*, 147

Soulé, Pierre (1801–1870), 394

South, 225

cotton crop in, 259

economy of, 314–16, *323*

election of 1796 and, 231

in election of 1824, 291

factory production in, 264

family life in antebellum, *316*

political influence of, 291

secession of, 398

slavery and, 313–16, *323*

slave trade in, 259

urban areas of, 452

see also Confederate States of America

South America, 3, *4*, 20, *26*

early population of, 19, 24

South Carolina, 179, 196, 281, *441*, 450

at Constitutional Convention, 205

constitution of, 171

in nullification crisis, 299–301

Reconstruction in, 465, 470

Sea Islands of, *114*

secession of, 397

slavery in, 206, 299

slave trade in, 259

upcountry of, 259

South Carolina colony, 96, *104*, 119, 120, 149

in American Revolution, 159, 162

Declaration of Independence and, 153

elite class in, 99

Indians in, 96

Loyalists in, 179, *180*

population of slaves in, 110

Regulators in, 145

slavery in, 114–15, *114*, 115–16, 153, 183, 185, 206

task system, 110

South Carolina Gazette, 114

Sovereignty and Goodness of God, The (Rowlandson), 64

Spain, *10*, 17, *18*, 19, *19*, 22–24, 39, 42, 43, 96, 131–32, 194, 294, 394

American Revolution and, 161

and Catholicism, 41

Columbus sponsored by, 16

loses Jamaica to England, 70

slavery in, 15

in War of Jenkins' Ear, 116

in West Indies, 81

Spanish America, 17, 19–30, 40, 45, 255

beginnings of, 17, 19

boundaries of, 127

in Florida, 20, 25, 27, 78, 122, 127

government of, 21

immigrants to, 21–22

independence of, 289–90

Indians and, 21–30, 78

interracial mixing in, 22

justification for conquest of, 11, 22–24, 25

in Louisiana, 241

in New Mexico, 27–30, 127

in North America, 127

population of, 21

Pueblo Indians and, 6, 27, 30

size of, 20

in Texas, 127

women in, 22

Spanish Armada, *38*, 41

Spanish Empire, 20–30

Spanish Inquisition, 27

Special Field Order 15, 442

specie, 287

Specie Circular, 306

Spencer, Lilly M. (1822–1902), *406*

Spiegel, Marcus M. (1829–1864), 403

spoils system, 297

see also parties, political; patronage

Spotswood, Alexander (1676–1740), 85

squatters, 255, *255*

Stamp Act (1765), 140, *144*

repeal of, 144

resistance to, 142–45

Stamp Act Congress (1765), 143

Stanton, Edwin M. (1814–1869), 442, 459

Stanton, Elizabeth Cady (1815–1902), 357, 462, *462*

Stanwix, Fort, 196

"Star-Spangled Banner, The" (Key), 244

"starving time," 47

state-church separation, 173, 174–75

State of the Union Address (1815), 292

State of the Union Address (1825), 294

states' rights, 300

Andrew Johnson's views of, 455

Calhoun and, 300

states' rights (continued)
in Constitution, 214
nullification and, 299–301
Statue of Freedom, 367, *367*
steamboats, 250, 252, *252*, 261
Stegner, Wallace (1913–1993), 267
Stephens, Alexander (1812–1883), 398, 408
Stevens, Thaddeus (1792–1868), 456, *456*
Stockbridge Indians, 182
Stone, Lucy (1818–1893), 340, 359
Stono, S.C., 116
Stono Rebellion, 116
Story, Joseph (1779–1845), 281
Stowe, Harriet Beecher (1811–1896), 353, *353*
strict constructionism, 224, 286, 288, 294
strikes, 277, *277*
women and, *277*
Stuart, Gilbert (1755–1828), *169*
Stuart kings, 68
Stuyvesant, Petrus (1610?–1672), 35
Suffolk Resolves (1775), 149–50
suffrage, *see* voting rights
sugar, 66, 70, 81, *82*, 98, 106, 324, *325*
as most profitable crop, 82
plantations, *see* planters, plantations,
sugar
trade in New Orleans, 315
Sugar Act (1764), 142, *144*
Sullivan, John (1741–1795), 181
Summary View of the Rights of British America, A
(Jefferson), 150
Sumner, Charles (1811–1874), 388, *388*, 456, 461
Sumter, Fort, 400, *400*, 407, 420
supply and demand, law of, 178
Suppressed Book about Slavery, The, *326*
Supreme Court, U.S., 203, 223, 237, 281, 288,
302–3, 461, 462, 470, 472
Amistad and, 334–35
in Civil War, 422
Dred Scott decision of, 389–90
Jackson's defiance of, 303
and judicial review power, 237
as undemocratic, 283
see also Marshall Court
Susquehanna Indians, 96
Susquehanna River, 92
Sutter, Johann A. (1803–1880), 376
Syracuse, N.Y., 252

Tallmadge, James (1778–1853), 288
Taney, Roger B. (1777–1864), 266, 306, 389
Taper, Joseph, 330, 332
Tappan, Arthur (1786–1865), 351
Tappan, Lewis (1788–1873), 351
"tariff of abominations," 299
tariffs, 200, 201, 224, 286, 287, 298, 309,
396, 425
of 1828, 299
of 1832, 301

J. Q. Adams and, 294
lowered by Democrats, 298
Polk and, 372
Tarleton, Banastre (1754–1833), 162
taxes, 50, 145–46, 207, 287
under Articles of Confederation, 195
in Civil War, 425, 430
dispute over, 168
in Great Britain, 68
on imported slaves, 116
imposed by British Parliament, 140,
141–45, *141*, 153
income, 425
Jefferson's abolition of, 236
John Adams and, 168
in Massachusetts colony, 58
poll, 83
and representation, 142–43
right to consent to, 77
to support churches, 95, 174
on tea, 148
in Virginia colony, 84, 85
on whiskey, 223, 224
on women, 83
Taylor, Zachary (1784–1850), 379, 381
as Mexican War general, 372, 373
tea, 97, 148
Tea Act (1773), 148
*Teachers in the Freedmen's School in Norfolk,
1863*, *435*
technology, 46
agriculture and, 259, 260
in Civil War, 405–6, *406*
effects of, on exploration, 14
manufacturing and, 261–62
market revolution and, 257–59, 260,
261–62, *263*
Tecumseh (1768–1813), 243–44
Tejanos, 370
telegraph, 254
in Civil War, 405
temperance, 298, 341, 345, *345*
see also Prohibition
Tennent, Gilbert (1703–1764), 125
Tennent, William (1673–1746), 125
Tennessee, 196
Ku Klux Klan founded in, 467–68
Tenochtitlán, 3, *5*, 17, 19, *19*, 20
Ten-Percent Plan of Reconstruction,
435–36
Tenskwatawa (1775–1836), 243, *243*
Tenth Amendment, 214
Tenure of Office Act (1867), 458
Ten Views in Antigua, *82*
Texas, 127, 255, 369
annexation of, 373, 376
independence from Mexico of, 370
population of, 370
revolt in, 370

slavery in, 371
U.S. annexation of, *371*
textile industry:
during Civil War, 422–23
and immigration, 264
and market revolution, 261–63, *263*, *264*
Thames, Battle of, 244
Thanksgiving, 55
Thirteenth Amendment, 436
Thomas, Jesse (1777–1853), 288
Thomas, Lorenzo (1804–1875), 416
Thoreau, Henry David (1817–1862),
268, 372
Thoughts on African Colonization, 350
Thoughts on Government (J. Adams), 171
three-fifths clause of U.S. Constitution, 205,
206, 234, 247
Ticonderoga, Fort, 131, 151
Tidewater, 110
Tilden, Samuel J. (1814–1886), 471
Times, The, 307
Tippecanoe, Battle of, 244
Tituba, 90
tobacco, 66, 106, 224, 259, *325*, 449
in Chesapeake region, 43–44, *48*, 50, *50*,
51, 52, 80, 83, 98, 102
health effects of, 50
plantations, 98
as substitute for gold, 50
and workers' death rate, 82
Tobacco Belt, 449
Tocqueville, Alexis de (1805–1859), 250, 267,
282–84
Toleration Act (1689), 87
Toussaint L'Ouverture, François Dominique
(1744–1803), 235, *235*
Towne, Laura M. (1825–1901), 434
Townshend, Charles (1725–1767), 145–46
Townshend Acts, repeal of, 146
Townshend crisis, 145–46
trade, 16, 30, 32, 97
in British-French war, 241–42
of Dutch Empire, 30, 32
in early U.S., 251
English mercantilism and, 74
European, with Africa, 14, 15
European, with Asia, 13–14, *15*
European, with Indians, 46–47, 55, 78
expansion of, *97*
free, 178
fur, 32, *36*, 46–47, 64, 77, 98, 102,
127, 136
among Indians, 5, 6, *9*, 10
as inducement to exploration, 42
in Jefferson's inaugural address, 236
Navigation Acts and, 74
New England and, 66
of Rhode Island, 201
routes of, 13–14, *15*

transatlantic, 2, 98–99, 105
  see also free trade; slave trade
Trail of Tears, 303
transcendentalism, 267–68, 358
transportation, 194, 251, *252, 256,* 266, 286
  market revolution and, 251, *252, 256,*
    260, 266
  in Northwest, 260
  see also canals; railroads
*Transportation of Cargo by Westerners at the Port
  of Yokohama* (Utagawa), 377
Travis, James W., *405*
Treasury Department, U.S., 307
Treaty of Ghent (1814), 247
Treaty of Greenville (1795), 216, *216,* 243
Treaty of Guadalupe Hidalgo (1848),
    373, 375
Treaty of Paris (1763), 131, 136
Treaty of Paris (1783), 165, 179, 182
Treaty of San Lorenzo (Pinckney's Treaty)
    (1795), 238
treaty system, 216
Trelawny, Edward (1792–1881), 115
Trenton, Battle of, 161
Tripoli, 241
Trumbull, Lyman (1813–1896), 457, 468
Truth, Sojourner (1799–1883), 358–59
Tubman, Harriet (1820–1913), 334
Turner, Nat (1800–1831), 336, *337,* 351
Tweed Ring, 467
Twelfth Amendment, 234
"twenty-negro" provision, 429
Two Treatises on Government (Locke), 118, *118*
Tyler, John (1790–1862), 282, 308, 335,
    370–71
Tyler administration, 335, 370–71

Uncle Tom's Cabin (Stowe), 353, *353*
Underground Railroad, 334
Underhill, John (1609–1672), *65*
unemployment, 306
Union League, 463, 464
Union Pacific Railroad, 423
unions, 341
  see also labor; labor movement; *specific
    unions*
*United States Magazine and Democratic
  Review,* 284
United States Sanitary Commission, 426
  see also nurses
United States v. Cruikshank, 470
Universalists, 175
Utagawa Sadahide (1807–1873), *377*
Utah, 373
Utopia (More), 341
utopian communities, 341–45, *342*

vagrants, 42
Valley Forge, Pa., 161

Van Buren, Martin (1782–1862), 303, 370, 371
  Amistad and, 334
  and annexation of Texas, 370
  background of, 294–95
  and depression of 1837, 307
  and election of 1828, 295
  Free Soil Party and, 379
  as Jackson's Secretary of State, 300
  nickname of, 296
  sectionalism and, 295
Vassa, Gustavus, *see* Equiano, Olaudah
Venerate the Plough, 224
Venezuela, 289–90
Vera Cruz, Mexico, 373
Vermont:
  colony of, 145–46
  constitution of, 172, 188
  government in, 171
*Very Brief Account of the Destruction of the Indies,
  A* (Las Casas), 24
Vesey, Denmark (1767?–1822), 336
Vespucci, Amerigo (1454–1512), 17, *18*
veto, presidential, 305, 457
vice presidency, U.S., 204
Vicksburg, Battle of, *406,* 432, 433, 435
View from Bushongo Tavern, 177
*View of the Causes and Consequences of the
  American Revolution, A* (Boucher), 157
Vikings, 16
Village of Secoton, The (White), 7
Vindication of the Rights of Woman, A
    (Wollstonecraft), 230
Vinland, 16
Virginia, 177, 183, 196, 225
  domination of federal government by, 247
  Gabriel's Rebellion in, 235–36
  government of, 171
  resolution in legislature of, 233
  slavery in, *328,* 336–37
  slave trade in, 259
  U.S. Constitution ratified by, 212
  voting rights in, 172
Virginia, University of, 174
Virginia colony, *9,* 39, 42, 43–44, *43,* 48, 49–50,
    52, 54, 87, 96, 99, 105, 119, 130, 146, 157
  Bacon's rebellion and, 83–85
  black population in, 85
  elite class in, 99
  as first royal colony, 49–50
  free blacks in, 83, 110, 119
  Indians in, 84, 96
  poverty in, 84, 100–101
  settlement of, *48*
  slavery in, 83, 85, 109–11, *205*
  Stamp Act and, 143
  status of children in, 83
  tobacco wharf in, *111*
  white society of, 50
  women's role in, 50–51

Virginia Company, 39, 48, 49
Virginia Luxuries, 328
Virginia Plan, 203
Virgin Islands, slave uprising in, 116
Virgin Mary, 29
Virgin of Guadalupe, *22*
"virtual representation", in British
    Parliament, 141, *141*
virtuous citizenry, 117, 175–76
Visit from the Old Mistress, A (Homer), *447*
voting rights, 174, 283, 284, 386
  for African-Americans, 323, 418, 459–60,
    461–62
  in American colonies, 119, 170
  emancipated slaves and, 442, 444,
    459–60
  Loyalists and, 179
  property qualifications and, 170, 171, 282
  religious freedom and, 174
  in U.S., 170
  for women, 119, 284, 357, 460, 461–62, *462*

Wade-Davis Bill, 436
wages, 176, 178, 261, 264, 277–78
  African-Americans and, 274, 435
  decline in real, 306
  equal pay for equal work and, 357
  hourly, 264
  and right to vote, 282
  slavery compared with working for, 277
  strike for higher, 277
  women and, 276, 358, 359
Wagner, Fort, 416
Wahabbism, 125
Wahunsonacock, *see* Powhatan
    (c. 1596–1617)
Walden (Thoreau), 268
Walker, David (1796?–1830), 349
Walker, William (1824–1860), 394
Walking Purchase (1737), 96
"wall of separation", Jefferson's, 173
  see also church and state, separation of
Waltham, Mass., 262
Wampanoags, 73
wampum, *77*
War Hawks, 242
War News from Mexico (Woodville), *372*
War of 1812, *221,* 244–46, *245,* 262, 285,
    287, 408
  causes of, 242, 244
War of Independence, *see* American
    Revolution
War of Jenkins' Ear, 115–16
War Party at Fort Douglas (Rindisbacher), *247*
Warren, James (1726–1808), 190
Warren, Mercy Otis (1728–1814), 190
War Spirit at Home (Spencer), *406*
Washington, D.C., 236
  British invasion of, *245*

Washington, Fort, 161
Washington, George (1732–1799), 99, 130,
        136, *139*, 151, 250, *283*, 388
    in battle against French and Indians, 131
    cabinet of, 222
    Constitutional Convention and, 202
    at Constitution signing, *206*
    in Continental Congress, 149
    death of, 219, 223
    Delaware crossing of, 159, 161
    and exclusion of blacks from military,
        158, 159
    Farewell Address of, 231
    inauguration of, 222
    Native Americans and, 181, 216
    re-election of, 231
    Republican press abuse of, 227
    as slaveholder, 219
    war strategy of, 159, 161
    Whiskey Rebellion and, 226, *227*
    at Yorktown, 162–65
Washington, Madison, 335
Washington, Martha (1732–1802), 219
water power, *263*
Wayne, Anthony (1745–1796), 216, *216*
Wealth of Nations, The (Smith), 2, 178, 191
Webster, Daniel (1782–1852), *305*
    American Colonization Society and, 348
    Compromise of 1850 and, 380–81, *381*
    nullification crisis and, 300, 301
Webster, Noah (1758–1843), 176
Weld, Theodore (1803–1895), 351
Welles, Gideon (1802–1878), 416
West:
    in election of 1824, 291
    manifest destiny and, 267
    Native Americans in, *303*
    population growth in, 243
    rise of, 255–56
West, Benjamin (1730–1813), *95*
Western Ordinances, *199*
West India Company, 34, 36, *36*
West Indies, 2, 25, 34, 98, 116, 142, 143, 200,
        201, 394
    American embargo of, 150
    in American Revolution, 161
    economy of, 81–82
    European owners of, 81
    immigration to, 43, 179, 185
    New England trade with, 66
    Philadelphia's trade with, 98
    slavery in, 21, 73, 78, 81–82, *108*, 318, 322,
        326, 330, 354
    tobacco in, 50
West Jersey Concessions (1677), 79
West Point, N.Y., 162
westward expansion of U.S., 196–98, *197*,
        287, *375*
    African-Americans and, 259, 260

Civil War and, 410, *411*
    Confederation government and, 196
    Douglas's views on, 382
    Jefferson's views on, 223–24
    Madison's views on, 209, 223–24
    market revolution and, 251, 255–56, 267
    Native Americans and, 196, 215–17, 243
    of the North, 260
    numbers of people in, 368
    Ordinance of 1784 and, 198
    slavery and, 198, 259–60, 312–13, 377,
        378–80, 387–88
    of the South, 259–60
wheat, 260
Wheatley, Phillis (1753?–1784), 185, *185*
Whig Party, 297–98, 305, 307–9, *308*, 347,
        371, 372, 373, 469
    Abraham Lincoln as member of, 390
    beliefs of, 297–98
    collapse of, 382–83
    creation of, 291
    division between Democrats and, 297–98
    in election of 1836, 307
    in election of 1840, 307
    in election of 1848, 378
    freedom as viewed by, 298
Whiskey Rebellion, 226, *227*, 230, 231
Whiskey Ring, 467
White, John (1585–1593), *7, 46*
Whitefield, Edwin, *255*
Whitefield, George (1714–1770), 126, *126*
White Hall Plantation, 238
Whitman, Walt (1819–1892), 250
Whitney, Eli (1765–1825), 259, 264
Whittier, John Greenleaf (1807–1892), 363
Wilkes, John (1727–1797), 147, *148*
William III, king of England (1650–1702),
        87, 88
William Penn's Treaty with the Indians, 95
Williams, Roger (1820–1910), 10, 60, *60*, 61
Wilmington, Del., 36
Wilmot, David (1814–1868), 378
Wilmot Proviso, 378–79, 381
Wilson, James (1742–1798), *206*
Winstanley, Gerard (1609?–1660), 69
Winthrop, James (1752–1821), 211
Winthrop, John (1588–1649), 42, *54*, 61, 63,
        64, 346
    Anne Hutchinson and, 61, 62
    liberty as viewed by, 54, 63
    Speech to Massachusetts General Court
        of, 63
Winthrop, John, II (1606–1676), *47*
Wirz, Henry (1823–1865), 456
Wisconsin, 256
Wisconsin Territory, 389
Wise, Henry A. (1806–1876), 394
witchcraft:
    in England, *89*

    in New England, 89–90
    slaves and, 114
Wolfe, James (1727–1759), 105
Wollaston, John (ca. 1642–1749), *126*
Wollstonecraft, Mary (1759–1797), 230
Woman in the Nineteenth Century, 358
Woman's Emancipation, 359
women:
    agriculture and, 10, 11, 101
    and American Revolution, 146, 189–90
    capitalism and, 276
    and Civil War, 425–26, *425*
    colonial roles of, 101–2, *101*
    Confederacy and, 430–31
    and "cult of domesticity," 275, *275*, 362
    Daughters of Liberty, 146, 189–90
    and decline in birthrate, 275–76
    education and, 228, 230
    free speech and, 356–57
    in gold rush, 376
    industrialization and, 262–63, 264,
        264
    labor and, 276
    market revolution and, 275–76
    Native American, 10
    in New Amsterdam, 75
    in New Netherland, 34–35
    in New World, 22
    in New York colony, 75
    of planter class, 317
    politics and, 190
    poll tax on, 83
    and "republican motherhood," 275
    subservience of European, 12–13
    in Virginia colony, 50–51
    and wages, 358, 359
    in the work force, 275–76, 358–59
    see also gender relations
women's rights, 12–13, 230, *231*, 276, 340,
        341, 356–64
    Abigail Adams and, 168
    American Revolution and, 168, 189–90
    Declaration of Sentiments and, 357
    and education, 228, 230
    equal pay for equal work and, 357
    families and, 362
    Frederick Douglass and, 312
    John Locke and, 118
    in Louisiana, 240
    newspapers and, 358
    in Quaker society, 79, *79*
    Reconstruction and, 460, 461–62
    Seneca Falls Convention and,
        357–58, 359
    sex and, 359–62
    and suffrage, 119, 284, 357, 426, 460,
        461–62, *462*
    in Utopian societies, 342, 344
    see also gender relations; women

Woodside, Archibald (1720–1806), *221*

Woodville, Richard D. (1825–1855), *372*

Woolman, John (1720–1772), 107

Worcester v. Georgia, 303

Workingmen's Parties, 277

World Anti-Slavery Convention, 357

Wright, Jonathan (1840–1887), 464

Wyatt, Francis (c. 1575–1644), 49

XYZ affair, 232, *232*

Yamasee Indians, 78

York, Pa., *173*, *177*

Yorktown, Battle of, 162, *163*

Yoruba people, 113

Young, Brigham (1801–1877), 273

Young Lady's Book, 275

Zenger, John Peter (1697–1746), 124–25, *124*

Zheng, Admiral, 14

Zuni Indians, 6